Psychological Anthropology

World Anthropology

General Editor

SOL TAX

Patrons

CLAUDE LÉVI-STRAUSS
MARGARET MEAD
LAILA SHUKRY EL HAMAMSY
M. N. SRINIVAS

MOUTON PUBLISHERS · THE HAGUE · PARIS
DISTRIBUTED IN THE USA AND CANADA BY ALDINE, CHICAGO

Psychological Anthropology

Editor

THOMAS R. WILLIAMS

MOUTON PUBLISHERS · THE HAGUE · PARIS

DISTRIBUTED IN THE USA AND CANADA BY ALDINE, CHICAGO

General Editor's Preface

Although many of its problems have been studied by anthropologists for a half century or more, psychological anthropology crystallized as a new field of study barely in time to be recognized as such by the IXth ICAES in 1973. It first became recognized here by the international community, and a new field is therefore to some degree defined by the selections in the present book, by its Introduction and by its concluding essay. Begun thus in an international context, psychological anthropology is in some ways ahead of its time.

Like most contemporary sciences, anthropology is a product of the European tradition. Some argue that it is a product of colonialism, with one small and self-interested part of the species dominating the study of the whole. If we are to understand the species, our science needs substantial input from scholars who represent a variety of the world's cultures. It was a deliberate purpose of the IXth International Congress of Anthropological and Ethnological Sciences to provide impetus in this direction. The *World Anthropology* volumes, therefore, offer a first glimpse of a human science in which members from all societies have played an active role. Each of the books is designed to be self-contained, each is an attempt to update its particular sector of scientific knowledge and is written by specialists from all parts of the world. Each volume should be read and reviewed individually as a separate volume on its own given subject. The set as a whole will indicate what changes are in store for anthropology as scholars from the developing countries join in studying the species of which we are all a part.

The IXth Congress was planned from the beginning not only to include as many of the scholars from every part of the world as possible, but also with a view toward the eventual publication of the papers in high-quality volumes. At previous Congresses scholars were invited to bring papers which were then read out loud. They were necessarily limited in length; many were only summarized; there was little time for discussion; and the sparse discussion could only be in one language. The IXth Congress was an experiment aimed at changing this. Papers were written with the intention of exchanging them before the Congress, particularly in extensive pre-Congress sessions; they were not intended to be read at the Congress, that time being devoted to discussions — discussions which were simultaneously and professionally translated into five languages. The method for eliciting the papers was structured to make as representative a sample as was allowable when scholarly creativity — hence self-selection — was critically important. Scholars were asked both to propose papers of their own and to suggest topics for sessions of the Congress which they might edit into volumes. All were then informed of the suggestions and encouraged to re-think their own papers and the topics. The process, therefore, was a continuous one of feedback and exchange and it has continued to be so even after the Congress. The some two thousand papers comprising *World Anthropology* certainly then offer a substantial sample of world anthropology. It has been said that anthropology is at a turning point; if this is so, these volumes will be the historical direction-markers.

As might have been foreseen in the first post-colonial generation, the large majority of the Congress papers (82 percent) are the work of scholars identified with the industrialized world which fathered our traditional discipline and the institution of the Congress itself: Eastern Europe (15 percent); Western Europe (16 percent); North America (47 percent); Japan, South Africa, Australia, and New Zealand (4 percent). Only 18 percent of the papers are from developing areas: Africa (4 percent); Asia-Oceania (9 percent); Latin America (5 percent). Aside from the substantial representation from the U.S.S.R. and the nations of Eastern Europe, a significant difference between this corpus of written material and that of other Congresses is the addition of the large proportion of contributions from Africa, Asia, and Latin America. "Only 18 percent" is two to four times as great a proportion as that of other Congresses; moreover, 18 percent of 2,000 papers is 360 papers, 10 times the number of "Third World" papers presented at previous Congresses. In fact, these 360 papers are more than the total of ALL papers published after the last International Congress of Anthropological and Ethnological Sciences which was held in the United States (Philadelphia, 1956).

The significance of the increase is not simply quantitative. The input of scholars from areas which have until recently been no more than subject matter for anthropology represents both feedback and also long-awaited theoretical contributions from the perspectives of very different cultural, social, and historical traditions. Many who attended the IXth Congress were convinced that anthropology would not be the same in the future. The fact that the next Congress (India, 1978) will be our first in the "Third World" may be symbolic of the change. Meanwhile, sober consideration of the present set of books will show how much, and just where and how, our discipline is being revolutionized.

Readers of *Psychological anthropology* are likely to be interested in other books in this series on ritual, medicine, mental health, language, life styles, education, and the like; and in those on how human differences relate to regional environments and cultures, ethnicity and population changes, and to sex, class, and degrees of urbanization.

Chicago, Illinois   SOL TAX
September 3, 1975

Table of Contents

PART SIX

Introduction

THOMAS R. WILLIAMS

In July, 1972, Dr. Sol Tax requested that I assume responsibility for organizing a IXth ICAES session and editing papers concerned with the topic of psychological anthropology. In the next month, as I considered Dr. Tax's request, I had occassion to think at length concerning a field that recently has undergone a change in its designation (from "culture and personality" to "psychological anthropology"), has been an area of special concern for some widely known and quite articulate anthropologists, and was said by some (Siegel 1970: v) to be moribund. I concluded that assuming the tasks of organizing a Congress session and editing papers written especially for an international conference of anthropologists meant that I would have to carefully review the widely scattered and often contradictory literature of psychological anthropology.

And so, after accepting Dr. Tax's invitation, I began to prepare myself through reading once again in the literature of psychological anthropology. It may be helpful to readers of this IXth ICAES Volume, and particularly students and colleagues with recent interests in psychological anthropology, for me to share with them in a summary fashion some of the understandings I have of this area of anthropology. This brief summary is presented in five parts. The first part describes the development of the field of psychological anthropology. The next two parts of the summary are concerned with a brief account of the central focus of concern in psychological anthropology, and a short review of the possible meaning of the recent change in the designation for this area of research. The fourth part of the summary outlines the major conceptual orientations of research in psychological anthropology. Then, in the fifth part of this summary discussion, principal methods of research in psychological anthropology are discussed briefly. It is important to note that I have not discussed the latest, "new ideas" or current practical applications of psychological anthropology knowledge, since these kinds of discussions are more appropriate for a handbook or "review" article. It should be clear too, that I do not intend this summary discussion to be used as "the" definitive account of the field of psychological anthropology. Rather, these summary comments are intended to provide readers unfamiliar with the area of psychological anthropology with a discussion that sets a context for the IXth ICAES papers included in this volume.

DEVELOPMENT OF PSYCHOLOGICAL ANTHROPOLOGY

I relearned from my review of the literature of the field of psychological anthropology that beginning a half century ago, the efforts of a few anthropologists, and particularly Franz Boas, Ruth Benedict, Edward Sapir, and Margaret Mead, had led to an abiding interest among anthropologists concerning the development and behavior of the individual in culture. Mead (1972: x) has noted that Boas had said in 1922 that he realized the study of diffusion of culture was finished, for it had been clearly demonstrated that cultures could borrow from each other and that each culture did not have to go through a specific evolutionary process. Now, Boas said, anthropologists had to tackle the questions of which aspects of individual human behavior and personality were biologically given, and which were due to having been born into one culture rather than another, in a technologically more advanced or simpler culture, or on one continent rather than another. Enduring formulations of basic ideas concerning these specific questions soon were offered by Benedict (1934a, 1934b, 1938), Sapir (1924, 1929, 1932, 1934a, 1934b), and Mead (1928a, 1928b, 1930a, 1930b, 1932, 1933, 1935, 1937).[1]

These new ideas, which often were greeted by other anthropologists

---

[1]   This brief summary of historical developments in psychological anthropology is not intended to be a definitive one. For detailed discussions of the history of this field see, Sapir (1934a), Kluckhohn (1944), Hallowell (1953, 1954), Singer (1961), Herskovits (1951), Kroeber (1948, 1955), Lowie (1937), Kluckhohn and Murray (1948), Kluckhohn, Murray and Schneider (1956), Meggers (1946), Volkart (1951), *International Social Science Bulletin* (1955), Inkeles and Levinson (1954), Kaplan (1957), Piddington (1957), Spindler (1957), Heuse (1953), Spiro (1968), Bateson (1944), Mead (1953a, 1961, 1963), Devereux (1945), and Bruner (1964). I also recognize that the ideas and writings of Malinowski, Kroeber, Radcliff-Brown, White and others had great influence on the basic thinking and the research of Boas, Benedict, Sapir, and Mead, and that later, there were other anthropologists whose works also contributed materially to the refinement of basic ideas in the field of psychological anthropology.

(cf. Lowie 1937; Nadel 1951) and some scholars in related fields (cf. Orlansky 1949; Lindesmith and Strauss 1950) with skepticism or even open hostility, were subsequently refined, in a period of about two decades, through a series of innovative conceptual advances in the research of Malinowski (1923, 1927a, 1927b, 1929, 1939), Kluckhohn (1939, 1941, 1946, 1947, 1954), Linton (1936, 1938, 1939, 1945, 1949, 1956),Herskovits (1934, 1948, 1951, 1952), Hallowell (1934, 1936, 1937, 1938, 1939, 1941, 1945, 1955), Gillin (1939, 1944, 1946, 1948, 1956), M.E. Opler (1935, 1936a, 1936b, 1938a, 1938b, 1938c, 1948), La Barre (1938, 1945, 1946a, 1946b, 1947a, 1947b, 1954), Henry (1936, 1940, 1941a, 1941b, 1948, 1951a, 1951b, 1955), Mandelbaum (1943, 1949, 1953), Landes (1937, 1938a, 1938b, 1940), Devereux (1939, 1940, 1945), and Du Bois (1937a, 1937b, 1941, 1944).[2] In addition, a few scholars in some closely allied disciplines, and particularly in psychiatry and psychology, notably Bateson (1935, 1936, 1941, 1942a, 1942b, 1944), Erikson (1939, 1943, 1950), Frank (1938, 1949, 1951), Fromm (1944, 1949), Kardiner (1939, 1945a, 1945b), Murphy (1947), Róheim (1922, 1971 [1925], 1932, 1934a, 1934b, 1943) and Sullivan (1937, 1939, 1940, 1953b [1946], 1948, 1953a) were at the same time contributing new theoretical insights, as well as some critiques of anthropological studies by Boas, Benedict, Sapir, Mead, and others.

Then, in the next two decades, a growing number of anthropologists began making substantial contributions to the field of psychological anthropology, mainly directed at clearly defining basic concepts and research orientations, in order to promote more accurate and replicable conclusions. Among others, the research and publications of Aberle, Barnouw, Bennett, Bruner, Caudill, Cohen, DeVos, Dorothy Eggan, John and Anne Fischer, Gladwin, Geertz, Goodman, John and Irma Honigmann, Hsu, Kaplan, Langess, LeVine, Lewis, Rhoda Metraux,

---

[2] The question of whether Malinowski was, or was not, one of the first anthropologists, along with Boas, Benedict, Sapir, and Mead, to contribute to the beginning of the field of psychological anthropology can be argued both ways. It is clear that Malinowski had an early and long-lasting interest in the relationships between psychoanalysis and anthropology (Malinowski 1923) and in the ways that differing social organizations affected individual psychology and behavior (Malinowski 1927a, 1927b). Barnouw (1973:113–128) places his discussion of Malinowski's writings concerning the effects of childhood experiences on adult personality on a par with those of Benedict and Mead and prior to the influences on psychological anthropology of Linton, Kardiner, and DuBois. On the basis of my own reading, I am inclined to believe that Malinowski was an important contributor to the beginnings of the field of psychological anthropology. However, others see Malinowski's challenges to Freud's ideas concerning sexuality and its development (Jones 1925) as narrow polemics. Similarly, Kroeber's ideas (1948) concerning the relation of the individual to culture, can be viewed as seminal, or only as stimuli, to Boas, Benedict, Sapir, and Mead to proceed in theoretical directions already being developed.

Naroll, Norbeck, Marvin Opler, Schneider, Slotkin, George and Louise Spindler, Spiro, Wallace, and John and Bernice Whiting advanced the basic ideas first articulated by Boas, Benedict, Sapir, and Mead, and subsequently refined by Malinowski, Kluckhohn, Linton, and others, to the contemporary form and style of expression that now is termed as either, "culture-and-personality," or "psychological anthropology."[3]

It is my conclusion, based on a review of the literature of the field of psychological anthropology, that a consensus has developed among anthropologists over the past half century concerning the central focus, major conceptual orientations, and some principal methods of research in this area of anthropology.

A CENTRAL FOCUS OF CONCERN

Most anthropologists now concentrating on research in the field of psychological anthropology appear to understand their central focus of concern to be an overt and intense interest in the fate of individuals in specific cultural settings. This focus of concern has been most clearly identified by Honigmann (1954: 18), who also pointed out, following Mead's (1953b: 643) earlier comment on the matter, that among anthropologists, an interest in the fate of individuals in specific cultures also is marked by the use of some type of psychological theory in an effort to make manifest the phenomenon of culture as it is reflected in the thoughts, feelings and acts of individuals. I noted only a few statements as I re-read the literature of psychological anthropology, and particularly the works published subsequent to 1954, that seemed to basically disagree with Honigmann's statement of the central focus of concern in the field of

---

[3]   References to the research and publications of Aberle, Barnouw, et al. can be found in the bibliographies in Haring (1956), Heinicke (1953), B. Whiting (1953), Honigmann (1954, 1967), Barnouw (1963, 1973), Hsu (1961, 1972), Kaplan (1961), Hunt (1967), Middleton (1970), Wallace (1961, 1968, 1970), LeVine (1963, 1973), Fischer (1965), and Pelto (1967). Discussions of the nature of research and conclusions reached by Aberle, Barnouw, et al. also are found in summary and review articles by Honigmann (1959, 1973), Wallace and Fogelson (1961), Wallace (1962), LeVine (1963), Fischer (1965), Pelto (1967), DeVos and Hippler (1969), Triandis, Malpass, and Davidson(1971) and Barkow (1973). In addition, there are a number of other texts which describe and discuss such research. See, for instance, Aronoff (1967), Bateson (1972), Hsu (1954), Kluckhohn, Murray, and Schneider (1956), Kluckhohn and Murray (1948), Goodman (1967), Hunt (1967), Sargent and Smith (1949), Cohen (1961), and Opler (1959). Interested readers will find that the *Decennial index (1949–1958)*, and the *Cumulative index (1959–1969)* of the *American Anthropologist (1961, 1971)* contain a large number of citations to works by specialists in psychological anthropology, under a variety of headings.

psychological anthropology.[4] However, I did note that there has been, and continues to be a considerable amount of disagreement among psychological anthropologists (cf. Barkow 1973) about the relative emphasis to be placed upon use of particular concepts, such as "culture" or "personality," and thus concerning the types of research problems that ought to be properly included as part of the field of psychological anthropology.

For example, although Barnouw (1963, 1973) seems generally to accept Honigmann's statement of the central focus of concern in psychological anthropology, his textbook discussion of this field seems essentially directed toward providing a clear understanding of the formation, and the operation of individual personality, by considering its "cultural and social determinants" (Barnouw 1963: 26). And, while Wallace (1961, 1970) apparently also accepts Honigmann's formulation of the central focus of concern in psychological anthropology, he notes that he prefers to make two basic assumptions in his research in this field: (1) that it is the primary business of anthropology, and anthropologists, to develop a scientific theory of culture and (2) that any theory seeking to explain culture must also include "noncultural phenomena" in its concerns. Wallace notes (1961: 1, 1970: 3) that, "many of these noncultural phenomena can be subsumed under the general rubric of personality." Wallace (1970: 243) then argues that the "true function" of a culture-and-personality approach in anthropology is not to describe the "psychological correlates" of culture as these are manifested in individual personality, as for instance through individual motivation and emotion, but rather to take the "documented facts" of "cultural evolution," "culture change," and "cultural diversity" as basic cultural phenomena to be explained as these are reflected in the behavior of individuals. Thus, Wallace (1970: 243) sees the primary task of the specialists in psychological anthropology to be the description of individual behavior that reflects, "... the classes of micro-phenomena that are the parameters of the classes of macro-phenomena," which other anthropologists, when

---

[4] A notable example is Hunt's (1967; ix–x) definition of the central focus of concern in the field of psychological anthropology as being a primary interest in the study of individual personality through cross-cultural testing of specific hypotheses derived from psychology (or "a cross-cultural empirical psychology") and in evolving more efficient theories about human behavior through the integration (or "interdigitation") of social and psychological theory. Hunt notes that anthropologists concerned with this type of approach in psychological anthropology thus have the option of three research strategies: (1) testing psychological hypotheses cross-culturally; (2) adding psychological theory to the social theory already being used to "make sense" of data and (3) to build a more effective theory of human behavior to make data of individual personality understandable and useful in the solution of contemporary human social and psychological problems.

studying culture, describe for groups of individuals (e.g. villages, tribes, societies). In other words, Wallace and Barnouw appear to have placed themselves at, or near, the opposite ends of a conceptual continuum when they contemplate the relative emphasis to be placed on use of the concepts of "culture" or "personality," in research in psychological anthropology.[5]

In another text discussion of the field of psychological anthropology, Hsu (1961, 1972) has described the "core of culture and personality" study as consisting of data produced through a unique "angle of approach" (Hsu 1972: 5) to individual psychological and social behavior. Hsu (1972: 6) describes this unique approach as producing data of widely shared "social ideas" which he believes to form the basis of all enduring interrelationships between the individual and his society. Although Hsu appears to generally agree with Honigmann's definition of the central focus of concern in psychological anthropology, he also rejects any dependence on the psychological concept of personality in analysis of widely shared social ideas, noting (Hsu 1972: 6) that some anthropologists working in the field of psychological anthropology tend to treat the concept of personality as indistinguishable from, or to be subsumed under the concept of culture, or treat the concept of personality in ways that are much "deeper" than most other anthropologists can cope with or understand. And, Hsu (1972: 8) notes that the concept of personality, as it is usually employed by psychological anthropologists differs greatly from the way this concept is used by psychologists.

Thus, Hsu observes (1972: 8) that while psychologists concentrate on the idiosyncratic, or unique, personality of the individual, most anthropologists working in the field of psychological anthropology tend to deal with only those specific characteristics of the individual's "mind" that are shared as part of a wider fabric of human minds, whether in one community, tribe, or society, or in all of human society. Hsu goes on (1961, 1972) to indicate that he believes that the most essential characteristics of an individual's "mind" are in fact the widely shared social ideas held by most persons in a culture. He indicates (1972: 10) that he believes these widely shared social ideas, which he notes may be either "conscious" or "unconscious" in their form, are the essential and primary "psychic materials" which specialists in psychological anthropology should be concerned with, whether or not widely shared social ideas are manifested by

---

[5]   Wallace (1968) has also made some other comments concerning the central focus of study in psychological anthropology. It should be noted too that both Wallace and Barnouw (1973) continue to find varieties of psychoanalytic theory useful in interpreting individual behavior.

individuals, or by groups of individuals (e.g. families, kin groups, villages, tribes, etc.,) and whether or not such individuals or groups of individuals are categorized as "primitive," "civilized," "non-literate," "literate," "urban," "industrial," and so on.

In another text concerned with describing the origin, development and the nature of individual "personal autonomy" or freedom, Goodman (1967) indicates that she considers her work to be essentially a study in psychological anthropology. However, Goodman goes on to say, "in this book the frame of reference is largely nonpsychological" (1967: 13). Thus, although Goodman seems to share with Honigmann, and others, the belief that the central focus of concern in psychological anthropology should be upon the fate of individuals in specific cultural settings, she shares with Hsu a basic rejection of the use of any type of psychological theory in interpreting individual behavior, thoughts or feelings. Instead, Goodman chooses to view psychological anthropology as a field that ought to be concerned essentially with the study of specific relationships between the individual and his culture, or as she states it (Goodman 1967: 3) the "drama of individual thrust and cultural press."

In his 1954 text, which was the first written for use in courses in the field of psychological anthropology, Honigmann placed special emphasis upon discussions of the "development, satisfactions, and perplexities of an individual in a given cultural milieu" (1954: 345–346). Honigmann adopted the general theoretical position (1954: 18, 29) that through paying considerable attention to the process of growing up in particular communities, a specialist in psychological anthropology research could form a basic account of the formation and patterning of individual personality (1954: 170). But Honigmann also made it clear that he regards as being of "primary significance" in research in psychological anthropology only the specific features of an individual personality that can be linked to "group or community factors." He specifically discarded consideration of the purely idiosyncratic elements of individual personality by anthropologists engaged in research in psychological anthropology (1954: 171). Thus, in his 1954 consideration of research in the field of psychological anthropology, Honigmann gives relatively equal weight to the concepts of "culture" and "personality" by defining each concept (1954: 171) in ways that focus research upon the links, or points of conjunction and interplay between personality and culture.[6]

---

[6] Honigmann (1954: 171) has defined the concepts of CULTURE and PERSONALITY as, "personality refers to an individual's socially standardized patterns of action, thought and feeling," while "culture denotes the socially standardized patterns of activity, thought, and feeling of some enduring social group."

It should be noted, however, that in a revision of his 1954 work, Honigmann (1967: xi, 3) adopts a different theoretical position concerning the relative emphasis to be placed on the concepts of culture and personality that more nearly approximates the one expressed by Wallace (1961, 1970). In his 1967 text, Honigmann notes that "culture and personality, the subject of this book is another approach to cultural understanding," and "psychological anthropology, as this viewpoint has come to be known, studies culture as it is embodied in its carriers' personalities." Thus, while Honigmann (1967: 3) continues to view the "interplay" (or links) between culture and personality as an essential point of concern in basic research in psychological anthropology, he has come to expression of a theoretical position (1967: 352), where he has acknowledged his adoption of Sapir's advice to concentrate the study and description of culture in the locus of the person, that is, to consider culture, and the study of culture, as the concept and activity of primary importance in psychological anthropology.

A 1956 text of articles edited by Kluckhohn, Murray, and Schneider (see also Kluckhohn and Murray 1948) includes some introductory remarks by Kluckhohn and Murray (1956: xv–xviii, 3–49, 53–67) in which they take a "field approach" to psychological anthropology, that is, where they reject any notion that there is, or ought to be, any conceptual separation between the concepts of "personality" and "culture" (see Spiro 1951). Rather, Kluckhohn and Murray note (1956: xv) that knowledge of culture must ultimately rest upon knowledge of the personalities of the individuals sharing that culture, while knowledge of individual personalities must be derived from understanding the cultural context in which individuals live. Thus, for Kluckhohn and Murray, the basic facts concerning culture and personality are "inextricably interwoven" in such a way that one concept really defines the other. For Kluckhohn and Murray (see also Kluckhohn: 1954) the central concern in the field of psychological anthropology is to make inquiry into the nature of the relationships of interdependence between the personality characteristics of a people and their culture. But, while Kluckhohn and Murray have adopted a "field approach" to definition and use of the concepts of culture and personality, they also appear to generally agree with Honigmann (1954: 18) that the central focus of concern in psychological anthropology ought to be an intense interest in the fate of individuals in specific cultural contexts, as interpreted through some type of psychological theory.

It is important to note that recently, Spiro (1961a, 1968, 1972) has proposed a major departure from this central focus of concern in psychological anthropology. Beginning from a theoretical position first articulated in an innovative 1951 discussion, where he developed the essence of the Kluckhohn and Murray "field approach" and argued strongly against treating the concepts of culture and personality as distinct entities, Spiro has advanced the idea that since the acquisition of culture by individuals is "often" marked (Spiro 1968: 558) by personal conflict, struggle, frustration, and tension, it therefore is necessary for research in psychological anthropology to focus on the capacity of culture for gratifying and frustrating basic human needs. In defining this theoretical position over the past ten years, Spiro has proposed that these two facets of culture (i.e. a capacity for frustrating and for gratifying individual needs) constitute the "two major axes" (Spiro 1968: 558) of all social science inquiry, that is, research on culture stability and culture change, and that together these constitute "the generic problems of culture and personality research; what are the psychological conditions that promote persistence and innovation in human social and cultural systems?"

Thus, Spiro proposes that the central focus of concern in psychological anthropology be shifted from an overt and intense interest in the fate of individuals in specific cultural contexts, as interpreted through some type of psychological theory, to a specific effort to understand the role that human personality dynamics ("psychological conditions" or human "needs") plays in the maintenance of and changes in whole cultural and social systems.

Hsu (1972: 570) notes that Spiro's "principal thesis" in his proposed revision of the central focus of concern in the field of psychological anthropology really seems to differ "only in emphasis" from the one that Hsu has developed (Hsu 1954, 1961, 1972). Hsu points out that he believes research in psychological anthropology must be concerned primarily with the origin of individual psychological characteristics as these are formed by the patterns of child rearing, social institutions, and ideologies of a culture, as well as trying to account also for changes in such child-rearing patterns, social institutions, and ideologies. Hsu notes too that he believes that Spiro only is insisting that in ranking these two primary tasks for specialists in psychological anthropology, the second, or basic research on change (in child-rearing patterns, social institutions, and ideologies) is the more important work for psychological anthropologists.

However, a careful study of Spiro's recent discussions in the field of psychological anthropology (1961a, 1961b, 1965, 1967, 1968, 1971, 1972) indicates that he has proposed a major theoretical change in the central focus of concern in psychological anthropology. Spiro does not appear to be at all interested, as are most of his colleagues in this field, in seeking to balance out the concept of culture with the concept of personality, or in subsuming the concept of personality under the concept of culture, or *vice versa*. Rather, as Spiro (1972: 604) notes in concluding an "overview" of research in psychological anthropology, "I have suggested that, rather than persist as a distinctive subdiscipline within the total range of the anthropological sciences, culture-and-personality conceive of itself as part of that subdiscipline — social anthropology — which is concerned with the analysis of social and cultural systems." Spiro (1972: 582–583) makes it clear that he is not saying that his suggested reorientation of the central focus of concern in psychological anthropology means that other, and past, research efforts have been wasted, misguided, or unwarranted. He notes that he believes that the essential points, and answers, to the questions that concerned Boas, Benedict, Sapir, and Mead, and other pioneers in culture-and-personality studies now have been clearly demonstrated. Spiro (1972: 583) observes that since the hypothesis that sociocultural variables are vital in the process of individual personality development and operation has now been demonstrated to be true, then it is time for psychological anthropologists to move on to try to discover the basic ways that the operation and maintenance of whole cultures and social systems are dependent on the internalization of these systems within the personalities of individual members of cultures. Spiro points out too that he believes his suggested reorientation of the central focus of concern in psychological anthropology is not really a "new or original suggestion." He cites his belief, although he does not document it, that much of culture-and-personality research contains within it a "trend" which he feels he is only strengthening and broadening by his theoretical proposals. Whether or not the claim by Spiro to only be adding to an existing trend in psychological anthropology is valid, the fact remains that he has proposed a substantive and major change in the central focus of concern in this field. It is important to note that while there seems to have been no real interest to date among his colleagues in psychological anthropology in Spiro's suggested reorientation for the field, his own recent research and writing is providing a body of literature (1965, 1967, 1971) that may be sufficient for him to provide effective empirical bases for his theoretical arguments and for his colleagues to use as the basis of their judgments of his suggestions for their abandonment of their subspeciality in anthropology.

In summary, then, what do we find to be the current central focus of concern in the field of psychological anthropology? It appears that at present, most specialists in this field of anthropology generally accept Honigmann's definition (1954: 18) that psychological anthropologists have as their central professional concern an overt and intense concern with the fate of individuals in specific cultural settings, with this interest, both in its application in research and in descriptions of data, being expressed through the use of some type of psychological theory. However, it is important to recall that a widespread acceptance among psychological anthropologists, except for Spiro and Hsu and some others, of this central focus of concern also is accompanied at present by a substantial amount of disagreement concerning the proper theoretical place of, and emphasis to be given to, the concepts of culture and personality and of ways these concepts may be said to be related.[7] This conceptual disagreement has sometimes been mistaken as meaning there is no central focus of research concern in psychological anthropology (see Orlansky 1949; Lindesmith and Strauss 1950; Nadel 1951; Piddington 1957). Instead, it really reflects the healthy state of the field of psychological anthropology, since as Kuhn (1966) has observed, divergent conceptual emphases are not at all unusual in a developing scientific field, and may be taken as a sign a discipline is actively seeking greater clarity and precision in its approach to research on phenomena. It borders on the

[7]   Four publications appearing during the time this work was in preparation contain marked contrasts in discussions of the central theoretical focus and conceptual problems in psychological anthropology. Bourguignon (1973) has written a "review" that purports to examine research in psychological anthropology. This work is notable for an insistence on presentation of discussion of possible relationships among what Spiro (1968: 559) has characterized as the more "exotic" phenomena studied by psychological anthropologists. Thus, the discussion makes little contribution to understanding the nature, focus of concern, or major directions of research in psychological anthropology, since Bourguignon regularly crosses from one theoretical position to another, while also shifting levels of abstraction. This makes the "review" opaque, confused, and of little value to readers unfamiliar with the field of psychological anthropology or Bourguignon's narrowly drawn concerns with topics such as "spirit possession." In marked contrast, LeVine (1973) has written a readable, articulate, and very knowledgeable review of the nature of and central focus of concern in psychological anthropology. LeVine's comments will be helpful to readers concerned with extending the discussion in this introduction. Barnouw (1973), in a revision of his 1963 text, has written a lucid and helpful account of the ways the concept of personality can be emphasized in research in psychological anthropology. Barkow's account (1973) of the central focus of concern and conceptual emphases in psychological anthropology is tightly reasoned, readable, and offers the conclusion that the subdiscipline needs a "biosocial" reorientation. Barkow notes that human social relationships, interactions, and social structures must always be viewed as having been organized through natural selection and as being generated ontogenetically by feedback processes based on certain environmentally stable *hominid* characteristics. Barkow's reasoning and arguments follow those advanced by others and suggest an option to the reorientation for the field of psychological anthropology advanced by Spiro (1968, 1972), for those dissatisfied with current directions and theoretical orientations in this field of anthropology. Also Honigmann's discussion (1973) further clarifies the theoretical position described in the text above.

absurd, and reflects badly on an understanding of the literature of psychological anthropology to suggest, as some have recently (Siegel 1970: v), that the field is not developing and contains no new departures. Quite the opposite is the case; psychological anthropology is very much "alive" and in a sound, healthy condition, with a large number of very able, and highly articulate specialists, active in basic research in a number of important areas of concern.

A CHANGE IN TITLE

Hsu (1961: 6) notes that for over twenty years research on the relationships between the individual and his culture had labored under the cumbersome title of "culture and personality." Following particular theoretical orientations and arguments, which have been summarized in the third part of this discussion, Hsu (1961: 8) concluded it would be useful to eliminate the word "personality" entirely from the designation of this subdiscipline of anthropology, through the substitution of a new designation, PSYCHOLOGICAL ANTHROPOLOGY. Hsu (1961: 8–9) noted that although some anthropologists would probably object to the new title, he could see no "insurmountable obstacles against it." Hsu observed that some anthropologists might object to the new designation on the grounds that it could lead to a proliferation of new anthropological subdisciplines. He countered this possible objection (1961: 9) by pointing out that giving an anthropological subdiscipline "a more logical name" should not lead to such a problem, any more than the long term use of the title "culture and personality" had done to that point. Hsu (1961: 9) also noted that some anthropologists might object to the new designation on the grounds that the subdiscipline would turn out to be neither psychology nor anthropology, but some kind of intellectual "no man's land." He countered this possible objection by noting several recent precedents for combining areas of research in other disciplines (e.g. biochemistry, astrophysics, etc.,) and pointed out that there was not the slightest indication that recent alliances of conceptual schemes in other fields of study had caused any lessening of intellectual quality or effort. Hsu concluded his suggestion for a change in the designation of the field with a series of comments intended to "clarify" his proposal. The essence of these comments was that Hsu really intended, and hoped, to open a discussion of the issues involved, rather than to close off further consideration of the point.

However, Hsu's suggestion for a continuing discussion and debate of the merits of his proposal seems to have been largely ignored by his colleagues in psychological anthropology. There has been no extended debate in journal or text publications of Hsu's reasoning in suggesting a change in the designation of this subdiscipline of anthropology. Instead, some anthropologists appear to have read Hsu's comments, agreed with them, and to have subsequently adopted the title of "psychological anthropology" for their research and writing in this area.

The 1949–1958 subject index of the *Decennial index* of the *American Anthropologist* (1961) contains no heading for "psychological anthropology," although there are a wide variety of subjects listed under the headings of "psychological," "psychiatry," "psychoanalytic," "psycho-cultural," and "psycholinguistics." This index also contains a number of references under the heading of "personality." In contrast, the succeeding *Cumulative index* of the *American Anthropologist* (1971), covering the years 1959–1969, or approximately eight years following publication of Hsu's 1961 proposal for a change in the designation of the field of culture-and-personality, contains approximately 75 citations under the heading of "psychological anthropology," as well as approximately 184 other citations under this same heading in the "book review index" section.

It can be argued that a major shift in the subject heads between the two most recent indexes of the *American Anthropologist* in fact reflects a general acceptance of Hsu's proposal for a new designation for the field of culture and personality. And a review of the titles of papers and of meeting sessions and symposia listed in the programs for the Annual Meetings of the American Anthropological Association between 1961 and 1972 also seems to provide support for this conclusion; the use of the designation "psychological anthropology" can be seen to increase markedly over this eleven-year period, while at the same time the title "culture-and-personality" becomes very much less used.

However, such "evidence" for a widespread acceptance of Hsu's proposal for a new designation for the field of culture-and-personality may be misleading and a reflection only of the ways that an editor of the *Cumlulative index* chose to "key word" articles under one topic heading that, in the preceding *Decennial index* had been listed under a wide variety of other subject headings. Certainly, decisions of an editor, or a program chairman, to classify works in particular fields, or subdisciplines, reflect personal preference and intellectual style, as well as an informed judgment based on substantive knowledge of recent developments in a field of study. But, such choices may not at all reflect a widespread and general acceptance by scholars in "psychological anthropology" of Hsu's suggestions.

In the 1972 revision of the text in which he first proposed a change in the designation for culture-and-personality studies, Hsu (1972: 9) points out that his proposal, "... has gained considerable acceptance in the profession." It must be assumed that Hsu is basing his claim on the kind of evidence cited above. However, it is possible to draw an opposite conclusion. For example, two of three culture-and-personality texts, published in revised editions after Hsu's 1961 proposal, have retained the title of "culture-and-personality," while a third text has a title that has been altered from its original title to more strongly emphasize a particular conceptual approach.

Thus, although Honigmann chose in 1967 to alter the title of the revision of his 1954 text from *Culture and personality* to *Personality in culture*, apparently to more accurately reflect his acceptance of the importance of the concept of culture in research in this area of anthropology, he appears to have generally ignored Hsu's suggestions for a change in the designation of the field.[8] And, in a second edition of a 1961 text, Wallace (1970) chose to retain the title *Culture and personality* for his work and made no mention in his revised text concerning Hsu's 1961 proposal. Barnouw (1973) in a revision of a 1963 text, chose to retain the title of *Culture and personality* for his work, after noting (1973: 3) that Kluckhohn and Murray (1948: 44) had suggested "culture in personality," and "personality in culture," as better designations for the field, while Hsu, with his suggestion of "psychological anthropology" had also expressed strong dissatifcation with the title of culture-and-personality. However, Barnouw (1973: 3) observed, in contrast to Hsu's claim (1972: 9) "... the most usual designation continues to be 'culture and personality'" and that he [Barnouw] prefers to hyphenate the phrase to "... emphasize its unity."

It should be noted, in support of Hsu's claim for the widespread acceptance and use of his suggested designation, that at least one text, compiled and edited by Hunt (1967) some six years after Hsu's proposal, carries the subtitle of "Readings in Psychological Anthropology." But Hunt does not discuss Hsu's 1961 proposal. It is also useful to know that some articles appearing in recent handbooks and collections of articles have carried the main title of *Psychological anthropology* (see Pelto 1967).

It seems, then, that one could take the apparent resistance of some of Hsu's peers, who have recently published texts in the field of "culture-and-personality" as some evidence that at least some anthropologists have

---

[8]   Honigmann (1967: 32) only refers in passing to Hsu's proposal (1961) with the comment, "Francis L. K. Hsu gives his conception of culture and personality in 'Psychological Anthropology in the Behavioral Sciences'."

not accepted his proposal for a change in the general designation of such research. In the absence of any extended discussion by Honigmann, Wallace, Barnouw, and others, it is only possible to speculate concerning the reasons for some authors choosing to ignore Hsu's proposal. It is not clear whether other scholars have basic theoretical objections to Hsu's proposal, or have acted only from more practical considerations in retaining the title of "culture-and-personality" for their texts; publishers are not inclined to change titles of successful texts.

What can be said of the current status of agreement or disagreement on a general designation for the subdiscipline of anthropology that is focused on the fate of individuals in specific cultural contexts? I think it can be said that this issue may be resolved simply by common use, that is, by the way most anthropologists specializing in the field come to style their research to others. This does not mean that there are no important theoretical and conceptual issues involved in the matter of a title for this field of anthropology. It should be recalled that Hsu has seriously advocated total elimination of the concept of personality from theoretical use and the substitution of some entirely new types of concepts and theory (Hsu 1961, 1963, 1965, 1971a, 1971b, 1972). Therefore, it would seem that Hsu's proposal deserves general adoption only after extended and thorough debate and discussion of its basic theoretical and conceptual merits, rather than because it provides a less awkward phrase to utter when lecturing, or a more convienent index heading, or subject matter classification. For the present, and perhaps for some time in the future, anthropologists interested in the fate of individuals in given cultural contexts, and making an effort to use some type of psychological theory to understand these life careers, will have a choice of designations for describing their research and activities. They also have the responsibility for carefully examining the theory and concepts implied in their choice of designation.[9]

---

[9] It should be noted that the use of Hsu's proposed designation as a title for the IXth ICAES Congress session and volume should not be taken to imply that I agree with Hsu's theoretical position or his use of particular concepts in defining this field of research. To the contrary, I have basic reservations concerning Hsu's proposal. I have used this title (i.e. psychological anthropology) because Dr. Tax's request to me to act as a session organizer and editor was put in these specific terms. I have not felt it proper to change the nature of his request to fit my own conceptions of this field of anthropology. Readers should also be aware that the use of the designation, PSYCHOLOGICAL ANTHROPOLOGY, did in fact "put off" some Congress participants and contributors who did not wish to have their work or presentations styled as having to do with "psychology" or "psychological" concepts, despite the obvious use of such theory and concepts in their work.

CONCEPTUAL ORIENTATIONS

In a review of research and theory in the field of "culture and personality" Spiro (1968) noted that for a long period, until well into the 1930's, the disciplines of anthropology and psychology were separated by a considerable intellectual gap created through use of different conceptual orientations. As a discipline, anthropology had been theoretically oriented toward the study and solution of "macroproblems" and focussed primarily on understanding and solution of the twin macroproblems of historical development and evolutionary trends in culture. Spiro observes that in contrast, psychology had been theoretically oriented toward solution of "microproblems," or problems limited in time and space, and focused on understanding essentially a-historical and non-cultural phenomena that could be studied and experimentally controlled in laboratory settings. Spiro believes that psychoanalytic theory and methods of research first were used by anthropologists interested in individual development and behavior in different cultural settings as a principal means of bridging the broad conceptual gap between anthropology and psychology. As a body of scientific theory, psychoanalytic ideas, and concepts tended to be more closely related to the new interests developed by Boas, Benedict, Sapir, Mead, and others, because psychoanalytic theories tended to be largely MOLAR, rather than MOLECULAR, in their general orientation, that is, concerned with the whole of an individual's life career and behavior and not with singular or special events limited in time and space. Too, as both Mead (1953a, 1961, 1963) and Kluckhohn (1944) have noted in their accounts of the growth of relations between psychoanalysis and anthropology, psychoanalytic theory attracted anthropologists interested in the development and behavior in invividuals in different cultural settings because this body of theory essentially is NON-EXPERIMENTAL, NON-QUANTITATIVE, heavily DESCRIPTIVE, and largely EMPIRICALLY oriented in its approaches to research on the origin, development, and functioning of individual personality and behavior. Each one of these conceptual orientations (NON-EXPERIMENTAL, NON-QUANTITATIVE, DESCRIPTIVE, EMPIRICAL) were firmly established as part of the "intellectual set" of most anthropologists at the time Boas suggested that attention be given to the fate of individuals in specific cultural settings. And, while they were much less easily discerned in psychoanalytic theory and writings, general orientations were present in this discipline toward concern with both CAUSATION in and PREDICTION of individual acts and an effort to understanding PATTERNS and PROCESSES at work in individual life careers and experiences. Each one of these orientations came to be shared to a greater, or lesser extent, by anthropologists as they turned toward study of the fate of individuals in specific cultures.

Thus, anthropologists seeking a workable psychological theory for understanding individual development and behavior in different cultural settings turned to psychoanalysis for ideas and concepts that seemed to be derived from conceptual orientations that were already being widely used in anthropology.[10] Anthropologists did not turn initially to academic, or experimental, psychology for theory and concepts to use in research on individual development and behavior in different cultures because most such work was conducted with orientations that were heavily experimental and quantitative and focused on specific events limited in time and space. Few anthropologists could then see the utility, or meaning, of the behavioristic psychology of Thorndike, Hull, and other experimental psychologists.[11]

These nine conceptual orientations (i.e. MOLAR, NON-QUANTITATIVE, etc.,) were continuing interests on the part of anthropologists in conducting CROSS-CULTURAL (or TRANSCULTURAL) research. At the time of the beginning of culture-and-personality studies, anthropologists were heavily committed to field studies in other, and particularly "non-Western" cultures. This particular, and special, conceptual orientation meant that while early culture-and-personality specialists focused their research at local community levels, such as the development of individuals in families, villages, or tribes, their basic orientation toward cross-cultural research meant that they had an over-riding concern directed toward the understanding of the fate of individuals in a HUMAN, or a species-wide, setting rather than being limited to a strictly local level of one family, village, or tribe. In turn, this special conceptual orientation in anthropology re-enforced another, and somewhat latent, orientation in research that seems to have been widely shared among anthropologists at the time of the beginning of culture-and-personality studies. This orientation, which may be termed, HOLISM, continually focuses attention on the abstraction level of an entire, or whole, culture, whether or not an anthropologist is working on a limited problem or at a local (i.e. family, village, etc.) level of research. A HOLISTIC conceptual orientation means that although the

---

[10] It should be noted that anthropology also has some conceptual orientations that are shared with other scientific disciplines; anthropology is concerned with SYSTEMATIC use of scientifically LOGICAL THOUGHT and EMPIRICAL TECHNIQUES in conducting studies of particular events, objects or the relations between events and objects. Anthropology also is a CONCEPTUALIZING discipline, that is, concerned with developing abstract statements of empirical reference that are precise and predictive in nature.

[11] For a discussion of Thorndike-Hull behavior theory and its use in anthropology, see Williams (1972: 42–66).

anthropologist might be recording specific data of individual behavior and life careers in a particular cultural setting, these data are recorded as part of the TOTAL cultural context, on the assumption that complete understanding of individual behavior, or careers, was to be gained ONLY through comprehension of the ways such discrete data formed part of and fitted with knowledge of a total culture. A transcultural conceptual orientation re-enforced a holistic orientation in anthropology through making anthropologists constantly wary of conclusions that did not specify cultural qualifiers, that is, clearly note that a statement was valid only for this individual, or that village in a particular region, or this "part" of such-and-such a culture, and so on. The pioneers in culture-and-personality research were well aware of the practice, both among psychoanalysts and academic psychologists, of generalizing to the whole human species, or to human society, on the basis of very limited information concerning one feature, part or aspect of behavior at a restricted, or local level.

And, as the field of culture-and-personality studies developed, these general conceptual orientations were joined to yet another long-standing orientation in anthropology. This conceptual orientation, which has been called TRANSTEMPORAL, can be defined as a basic concern among anthropologists that cultural events or behavior forms must be understood in their essential historical perspective, that is, in the context of time, however lengthy a span of events may be in terms of years, centuries, or millennia. This conceptual orientation, which was derived from a long standing interest in anthropology in the historical development of and evolutionary trends in culture, had a direct counterpart in the assumptions made by Freud and other early psychoanalytic theorists that to deal effectively with and to finally understand individual behavior it was ultimately necessary to look to the origin in the history of "cultures," "societies," and "races" for some particular features of individual behavior and psychodynamics that were durable, continuing, and lasting through long spans of time. Thus, psychoanalytic theory, with its heavily transtemporal orientation, was seen by early specialists in culture-and-personality studies as a useful theory with a parallel conceptual orientation.

Psychoanalytic theory and concepts became used by anthropologists interested in the fate of individuals in specific cultural settings because it offered a seemingly effective way to bridge the yawning intellectual chasm between a traditional microproblem oriented, experimental, quantitative and a-historical psychology and an anthropological tradition characterized by some quite different conceptual orientations. While most of the severe anthropological criticisms of culture-and-personality research conducted during the 1920's and 1930's were levelled at such studies for their strong emphases on analysis of the relationships between individual adult behavior and specific events in early infancy and childhood (i.e. feeding, weaning, toilet training, etc.,) the central point such critics usually missed, or chose to ignore, was the fact of the basic similarities of the conceptual orientations of anthropology and psychoanalysis that made it possible, really for the first time, for anthropologists to use any type of psychological theory for explanation of the fate of individuals in specific cultural settings.

Today, research in psychological anthropology retains, as a set of quite distinctive conceptual orientations, basically a CROSS-CULTURAL, HOLISTIC and TRANSTEMPORAL outlook, and is marked as well by essentially DESCRIPTIVE, EMPIRICAL, MOLAR, PATTERN, and PROCESS orientations. Insistent demands made upon psychological anthropologists as the result of severe criticisms of their research by other anthropologists has led recently to a growing use of a "field experimental" orientation and a seeking of more rigor in statements that imply or claim causation in events or offer predictions of individual behavior in specific cultural contexts. The movement in psychological anthropology away from a determinedly non-experimental orientation toward a systematic and more sophisticated effort to use controls and "controlled experiments" in research, parallels a similar movement in other anthropological subdisciplines (see Lewis 1953) that has been growing over the past two decades. Recent efforts to introduce symbolic and formal logic, advanced mathematics and quantitative techniques into statements of causation and prediction of individual life careers and behavior in specific cultural contexts mark an effort by at least some psychological anthropologists to be more, rather than less, rigorous and scientific in their research (Wallace 1970). For many anthropologists, much of contemporary research in psychological anthropology seems "soft" in its logical structure and slipshod in its methods (Wallace 1970: 4). But the present movement in psychological anthropology away from a non-experimental and non-quantitative conceptual orientation towards the type of experimental and quantitative orientation long used in disciplines such as physiology, biochemistry, and experimental psychology indicates that research in this area of anthropology now is more likely than not to become accepted as "hard" or "scientific" in nature (see Whiting and Child 1953). It is not uncommon today to find comments in reviews of research in the field of psychological anthropology that note — often with ill-disguised satisfaction on the part of the author — the diminishing influence of psychoanalytic ideas and concepts on contemporary research in this field of anthropology. It is clear that anthropology and psychoanalytic psychology are no longer as closely allied as they were in the 1920's and 1930's, during the early period of development of culture-and-personality studies. This is partly the consequence of intellectual maturation and growth by the anthropologists specializing in psychological anthropology and partly because of the growing incorporation into anthropology generally of new conceptual orientations that provide experimental, quantitative, and formal symbolic techniques and means for investigation of the fate of individuals in specific cultural settings. It would be helpful, however, for those now taking up an interest in research and teaching in psychological anthropology to recall that this field literally got its initial impetus because the conceptual orientations of psychoanalytic psychology provided a way to bridge the chasm that existed between anthropology and psychology as disciplines. It was in psychoanalysis that early specialists in culture-and-personality research found a workable psychological theory to help explain the fate of individuals in specific cultural contexts. The fact that some concepts used in psychoanalytic psychology, then, and now, demonstrably are not valid, pretentious, vague, or patently distort known facts of human evolution and cultural development should not be taken as the basis for ignoring the common, and lasting, intellectual heritage of psychological anthropology and psychoanalysis, in their common and continuing concern with the fate and life careers of individuals.

METHODS OF RESEARCH

Spiro (1968) has noted that during the initial period of culture-and-personality research, that is from the mid-1920's until the early 1940's, anthropological field methods of direct observation of individual behavior and interviewing of selected (or "key") informants were judged to be generally inadequate for use in detailed studies of the fate of individuals in given cultural contexts, and for understanding the relationships that exist between the concepts of culture and personality. As a consequence of this belief on the part of the early specialists in culture-and-personality studies, new research methods were borrowed, largely intact, from other disciplines, and particularly from psychiatry, clinical psychology, and psychoanalysis. The new methods included: (1) depth interviewing of key informants; (2) use of projective test and devices (including the Rorschach Test, drawing analysis, doll play, and the Thematic Apperception Test); (3) the collection and analysis of dreams; (4) careful recording of individual life histories; and (5) intensive, long-term observation of interpersonal interaction within families that had been selected to represent different segments of a society. In the initial period of culture-and-personality research, these new methods were applied in a wide variety of studies by a number of anthropologists concerned with research in this area of anthropology. Barnouw (1973) has provided detailed discussions of the introduction and initial use of these particular research methods in culture-and-personality studies.

It is important to note, however, that the "borrowed" methods used in the initial period of culture-and-personality research were considered to be quite esoteric by the more discipline-bound anthropologists. When such methods were used in conjunction with what were viewed by more traditionally oriented anthropologists as even more esoteric theories of personality and learning borrowed from psychoanalysis, the more discipline-bound anthropologists often declared culture-and-personality research to be inconclusive, imprecise and to contribute little to an understanding of the nature of culture. The condemnations of culture-and-personality research methods were vigorous and not infrequently highly polemical. Charges of methodological vagueness and the use of techniques characteristic of "art" rather than "science" continued to be leveled at all culture-and-personality research through most of the 1940's and 1950's that employed projective, dream, or life history methods.

On the other hand, while suffering the severe opposition of many colleagues, culture-and-personality specialists began to depend increasingly upon the use of depth interviews and intensive observations of selected persons, since these particular "borrowed" research methods seemed to have largely escaped criticism, despite the fact that they were also borrowed from psychological research and study. This may have been the consequence of a slowly growing acceptance by anthropologists, over a period of some 30 years, of the sophistication needed in making observations and in securing information from key subjects concerning culture. Thus, one long-term consequence of the introduction of new research methods in culture-and-personality studies has been the gradual abandonment of use of projective tests, dream analysis, and life history collection by most psychological anthropologists, while at the same time specialists in other subdisciplines of cultural and social anthropology have taken over and regularly use some form of the "borrowed" psychoanalytic methods of depth interviewing and intensive observation of key subjects. Another way to put this important point would be to note that today, anthropologists in a wide variety of subdisciplines (e.g. ecological studies, cognitive studies, sociolinguistics, ideology studies, kinship studies, etc.,) accept as normal procedures of field research some methods of study borrowed by early culture-and-personality specialists from psychoanalytic research.

Psychological anthropologists tend to recognize now that there are a number of difficult problems in the use of depth interviews and intensive observations that remain to be solved. Among these problems are: (1) finding a way to make useful quantifications of data of observation and interview; (2) finding ways of conducting depth interviews through use of questionaires, administered in either written (in a literate society) or oral form, and as appropriate for local conditions, that will demonstrate the ways responses "interlock" or re-inforce one another; (3) dealing systematically with existing contrasts between cultural ideals and reality, and between "manifest" and "latent" functions of cultural forms; (4) developing techniques for gathering data of observation and interview that will cope with the problems raised by the fact that the anthropologist carries constructs of reality with him, and learns things about a culture that are unknown to members of that culture (Harris 1968: 568–604); and (5) finding ways of sampling and validating for an entire culture and society data gathered by depth interviews and intensive observations in a restricted area (i.e. family, neighborhood, village, etc.) or part of a culture or society.

Barnouw (1973: 239–270) has reviewed contemporary use of the methods of intensive observation and depth interview in psychological anthropology. He has aptly illustrated the point that while specialists in this area of research tend to be much more sophisticated than their other colleagues concerning knowledge of limits of these methods of study, they also have devoted little attention to solving the kinds of methodological problems noted above, or in paying attention to the whole area of what has been termed as "unobtrusive" methods of observation of behavior (see Webb, Campbell, Schwartz, and Sechrest 1966) that holds distinct possibilities for increasing methodological accuracy and rigor in psychological anthropology. Perhaps the most important point to be made concerning research methods in contemporary psychological anthropology is that specialists in this field no longer have to be specially trained or supervised by mentors from other disciplines, such as psychiatry, clinical psychology, or psychoanalysis, in the research procedures of depth interviewing and intensive observation of behavior of selected persons. Today, such typical methodological skills are possessed by all trained psychological anthropologists and regularly are taught to their advanced students. It would seem that in the near future, specialists in psychological anthropology will want to turn once again to those methods, including projective devices, dream analysis, and collection of life history materials, that largely were abandoned during the decade of the mid-1950's to the mid-1960's under the harsh criticisms of colleagues scornful of the special nature and apparent inappropriateness of such procedures, to determine if these methods really can be employed to gather and analyze data concerning the fate of individuals in specific culture settings. At present, primary dependence upon use of depth interviews and intensive observations seems to severely limit the scope and the theoretical precision of research in psychological anthropology. New methods of research appear to be warranted, if those methods (i.e. projective tests, dream analysis, life history collection, and analysis) formerly used and then later abandoned, turn out on close examination to be insufficient for studies in psychological anthropology. And, the substantive questions that have been raised concerning depth interviewing and intensive observation methods must be answered if psychological anthropology is to move on to the production of generalizations of a high level of validity, authority, and scope.

EDITORIAL PROCEDURES

The process of selecting papers for publication in this IXth ICAES volume on psychological anthropology has been determined to a large extent by the general procedures established by the President and Organizing Committee for the conduct of Congress sessions. By the opening day of the IXth ICAES, on September 1, 1973, approximately 3,226 registrants had submitted some 2,200 completed manuscripts to the Congress office in Chicago, Ill. My task as one of the organizers of the 104 different Congress sessions was to select from among more than 2,000 papers the works specifically concerned with topics in the field of psychological anthropology.[12]

I began my editorial work in early September, 1972 by reading through all of the titles and abstracts of Congress papers submitted to that time. I continued to read titles and abstracts of Congress papers, as these were sent to me in the next year from the Congress office, up to a point two weeks before the Congress convened. In October, 1972, and at various other times in the year between September, 1972 and September, 1973, on the basis of title and abstract content, I requested that the Congress office send me particular papers. Some papers that I requested were not available, since authors had failed to complete their work after submitting

---

[12]   As a member of the IXth Congress Organizing Committee I did participate in the decision-making process that led to a few of my problems as a session organizer and editor.

titles and abstracts to the Congress office. Thus, I was unable to read some papers at all, and was finally reduced to dealing with approximately three hundred different papers that arrived from the Congress office. A substantial portion of this number of papers did not reach me until June and July, 1973, or in the months just prior to the Congress. By August 1, 1973 I had selected a limited number of papers from among all of those I had received and had read. During the week of the Congress I also received a large number of papers from authors attending the Congress; on the day that the Congress closed I had some seventy-five additional papers for consideration.

In effect, these delays in receiving completed Congress papers for editorial review meant that when the IXth ICAES meetings closed on September 8, 1973 I still had not read carefully or considered a number of papers I had thought on the basis of their titles and abstract content possibly might be included as part of the Congress session and publications concerned with psychological anthropology. As a consequence, I spent much of my time during the fall of 1973, in the months following the close of the Congress, reading and selecting papers for publication. This raised serious problems, since the publisher's deadline for submission of completed manuscripts was September 30, 1973. The failure to include some specific Congress papers in these volumes that may have been concerned with topics in psychological anthropology primarily is a matter of the logistics of dealing with so large a number of papers. But, the failure of some authors to complete papers, or to hand in papers that were fully complete for publication, and so required extensive revision, also complicated and confounded my editorial tasks. My editorial frustrations, such as they were, were considerably lightened during the Congress when a colleague, trying to rewrite and revise his paper for publication in this volume noted, "well, the situation is absolutely impossible, but not really very serious!"

Now, it should be noted that after careful consideration, I have selected for publication only a limited number of the more than 300 papers submitted to me as a session organizer and editor for the IXth ICAES volume on psychological anthropology. Essentially this choice for publication was based upon the charge given by Dr. Tax, as President of the Congress, to the editors of ICAES volumes when he noted that to be published, papers must be professionally competent, readable, and complete for publication. I found, as I noted above, that some of the papers I might have selected for publication could not be included in this volume simply because they had not been prepared in a form, or written in a style, that could be used in a Congress volume concerned with psychological anthropology that was to be used by students and colleagues in anthropology and other disciplines. A few very good papers simply were too lengthy, more than 200 pages in several instances, to be published in this volume. Some authors did not feel that there was sufficient time to make the changes in their papers that they wished to make before publication of their work. Of course, I exercised my "editorial judgment" in selection of papers to appear in the Congress volume on psychological anthropology. This means that I eventually reached the point in the editorial process where I felt that some papers merited publication, while others did not seem to me complete for publication, or concerned directly with topics in the field of psychological anthropology. My editorial decisions should not reflect upon the ability or the future contributions of anyone whose paper was submitted to the IXth ICAES Congress, and reviewed by me for inclusion in the Congress session and publication concerned with psychological anthropology. It should be noted too, that without editorial assistance, and with limited time, I simply had to choose Congress papers that were, in my considered opinion, ready for presentation and publication under Dr. Tax's charge to session organizers and editors.

I also made another editorial decision at the outset of my work with Congress papers concerned with psychological anthropology. I felt that because of the limited time available for my work, and because of the logistic problems in handling a large number of papers that I would not seek to require a common writing format for Congress papers selected for publication. Thus, papers in this volume vary in their format and style of presentations of data and conclusions. If I had been given another year or so after the close of the Congress, it might have been possible to ask authors to revise their papers to follow a common format for publication. But that time was not available to me. Yet, there may be some virtue in publishing papers from a World Congress of anthropologists in the several formats that reflect the diversity and plural nature of the discipline of anthropology. Anyone attending the IXth ICAES sessions could have easily seen, as William T. Farrell (a *New York Times* correspondent) did as he observed the Congress activities (1973), "like the people they study (anthropologists) are short, tall, light, dark, fat, skinny, loud, quiet, bored, alert." While the papers included in this volume do not cover all the possible formats of presentation, they still represent different approaches by anthropologists to presentation of data and conclusions. The contrast in formats will be noticeable to readers since papers have been grouped together for publication without regard to their format; hence, there will be some marked contrasts between succeeding papers in the ways data and conclusions are presented. Such contrasts do not, in my opinion, detract at all from the content and merit of the papers.

I also made another crucial editorial decision at the beginning of my work with the IXth ICAES papers. I decided that I would proceed in my tasks through emphasizing the general doctrine of the UNITY OF SCIENCE. This doctrine notes that all the separate activities of scientists, however disparate their immediate purposes and aims may be, eventually do mutually support and sustain each other. Thus, I concluded that as a Congress session organizer and editor I would not attempt to become a sole and final judge of what does and does not constitute the contemporary field, and "acceptable" research in psychological anthropology. Rather, I chose to proceed from a general philosophical position that, given some widely acceptable minimal criteria for selecting papers, my choices would in fact finally support and sustain each other. I believe the usefulness of adopting this position was borne out in the ways that a number of anthropologists participating in the IXth ICAES session on psychological anthropology found — to their apparent and openly expressed surprise — that they had basic research interests and intellectual concerns in common with other anthropologists whose academic and institutional "labels" and designations were quite different from their own. It has often been said (Spiro 1968: 558) that culture-and-personality research hardly exists outside of the United States. By emphasizing the doctrine of the unity of science during the time of my work as a session organizer and editor for the IXth ICAES, I found a large number of anthropologists concerned with the fate of individuals in specific cultural contexts, interpreting data gathered in such studies with some variety of psychological theory and using the methods of intensive observation, depth interview, etc., to conduct their research. To put the point another way, I found in my work that outside the U.S. there are a large number of anthropologists — who for economic, social, political, or other social institutional reasons — do not style themselves as "psychological anthropologists," but who nonetheless regularly conduct research and write papers, monographs, and texts that clearly are within the field of psychological anthropology. It is not true to say that psychological anthropology is largely confined to the United States and to the work of American specialists. It is possible to reach a conclusion that psychological anthropology is essentially an American concern if one fails to talk with and to read the works of anthropological colleagues from other world areas where it may be uncommon, or unwise, to style oneself and his research as having to do with "culture" or "personality" or "psychology." This same problem, on a much larger scale, confronted the ICAES organizing committee and Dr. Tax when they set out to identify the world community of anthropologists. In many countries and areas of the world, anthropologists call themselves by other names and work in very different kinds of institutional settings from those familiar to their American and West European colleagues. The total number of anthropologists in the world rose sharply in a frequency count when the classification label used for identification was changed from a "name" (i.e. anthropologist) to an activity (i.e. performing essentially "anthropological" tasks). And so, I believe, it is with the world community of anthropologists concerned with the fate of individuals in given cultural settings and using some type of psychological theory to gather and interpret data of individual life careers and behavior.

Prior to the beginning of the IXth ICAES meetings I prepared and mailed a statement to be used in discussion of the field of psychological anthropology and the papers included in the Congress session concerned with this field of anthropology. In essence, this document was a *précis* of the discussion included in the first portions of this "Introduction." Hence, it will not be reproduced here because of limitations of space. This document was mailed to all those Congress members whose papers I had selected by title and abstract, and reading, up to August 1, 1973. Additional copies were mailed to a number of other Congress participants whose interests in psychological anthropology were known to me from personal contact or familiarity with their published works (i.e. Francis L. K. Hsu, Robert LeVine, etc.). An invitation was included in the document mailed to the Congress members whose papers I had been working with, or with known interests in the field of psychological anthropology, to attend a two hour pre-Congress planning session to be held in Chicago on August 31, 1973. The purpose of the pre-Congress session was to provide organization for the formal Congress session on psychological anthropology. Approximately 65 persons attended the pre-Congress planning session. This meeting involved discussion of the definition of the field, ways to arrange or classify Congress papers according to the definitions of psychological anthropology offered in both the discussion and the document mailed to pre-Congress planning session participants, and alternative procedures for physically organizing the formal Congress session.

On the basis of these discussions in the pre-Congress planning meeting, I organized a series of informal meetings between various Congress members to try to provide for a systematic way to conduct the formal Congress session on psychological anthropology and to carry out my editorial responsibilities. In the five-day period between the pre-Congress session, and the formal session, I held or organized a half dozen informal discussion meetings with Congress members, talked to approximately 45 colleagues in individual conferences concerning their papers and the Congress session on psychological anthropology, and discussed these matters with at least one hundred other anthropologists. The informal discussion meetings, attended by varying numbers of individuals, ranging from a half dozen to twenty, were very productive of ideas about ways to organize a formal Congress session, and most informative with regard to my editorial responsibility.

Approximately 400 persons attended the formal Congress session on psychological anthropology, chaired by Margaret Mead. The session began with brief oral presentations of their research in psychological anthropology by a panel of 11 scholars, then proceeded to presentation from the floor of brief research reports by 18 other scholars, and closed with a lengthy question-and-answer period during which members of the audience directed questions to the scholars making reports on their research, offered comments and suggestions or raised questions concerning a variety of topics in psychological anthropology.[13] The session concluded with summary remarks and observations by Dr. Mead.[14]

At the close of the IXth ICAES Congress, I was left with some difficult decisions concerning ways to effectively group papers for their publication in a Congress volume concerned with psychological anthropology. Some colleagues had suggested that the best way to group papers would

---

[13]   The panel of scholars consisted of: Margaret Mead, American Museum of Natural History, Chairman; Starkey Duncan Jr., University of Chicago; Walburga von Raffler-Engel, Vanderbilt University; Jay B. Crain, Sacramento State University and University of California, Davis; Gerald Erchak, State University of New York, Geneseo; John Bushnell, Brooklyn College; Vittorio Lanternari, University of Rome; Lourdes Quisumbing, University of San Carlos, Philippines; Afredo Mendez-Dominguez, University del Valle de Guatemala; Lorna McDougall, The Claremont Colleges; Alexander Lopasic, University of Reading; Jerome Barkow, Dalhousie University. Reports from the floor were presented by Solange Petit-Skinner, San Francisco; Anees Haddad, Loma Linda University; Hassan El-Shamy, Indiana University; Roy Simmons, Auckland Museum; Michael Everett, University of Kentucky; Cara Richards, Transylvania College; M. Estellie Smith, State University of New York, Brockport; Charles Bishop, State University of New York, Oswego; Sory Camara, University of Bordeaux; Clifton Amesbury, Richmond, California; Edward Haskell, New York; Michael Salovesh, Northern Illinois University; Bela Maday, National Institutes of Health; Lorand Szalay, American Institutes for Research; E. Richard Sorenson, National Institutes of Health; Jack A. Lucas, Central Connecticut College; S. Aronoff, Israel; S. Gupta, University of Illinois-Champaign-Urbana.
[14]   The IXth ICAES session on *Psychological anthropology* (Session Number 644) was tape recorded in its entirety in four languages and was visually documented by means of a videotape system recording the speakers' presentations. Space limitations preclude the inclusion of a transcript of all questions and answers during the session.

be by specific topics or areas of research activities in the field of psychological anthropology. However, other colleagues had advised me to group Congress papers by following a set of clearly defined criteria for choosing to recognize certain kinds of anthropological research as being in the field of psychological anthropology and then defining sub-groups of papers though their "natural" affinities, or similarities of research concern. The first approach seemed to be quite easy, since there had been a number of "reviews" of research in psychological anthropology that listed the major topics and areas of research in this field. Thus, Wallace and Fogelson (1961: 42–78) had listed fifteen areas of research activities in psychological anthropology: (1) National Character Studies; (2) Child Development and the Family; (3) Social Psychiatry; (4) Sociocultural Theories and Studies of Mental Illness; (5) Cross-cultural and Culturally-specific Studies of Mental Disorders; (6) Hospital Studies; (7) Cross-cultural and Culturally-specific Studies of Therapeutic Systems; (8) Culture Change Studies; (9) Acculturation and the Anthropology of Development; (10) Rapid Culture Change; (11) Processes of Culture Change; (12) Communication and Cognition; (13) The Biology of Behavior; (14) Mental Evolution; and (15) Physiological Variables in Culture-relevant Behavior.

Readers familar with the basic literature in the field of psychological anthropology since 1961 will recognize that research has proceeded to expand rapidly in some of these topic areas, as for instance in communication and cognition, the biology of behavior, mental evolution, and physiological variables in culture-relevant behavior, while in other areas literally whole new subdisciplines have emerged to formally incorporate a number of the topics listed by Wallace and Fogelson; for instance the subdiscipline of the "anthropology of mental health" now tends to incorporate research on topics (3) through (7) on the list of topics above. Thus, the Congress session "Anthropology and Mental Health" was concerned with the discussion of papers and research in these areas (i.e. social psychiatry, etc.). Readers familiar with the literature of psychological anthropology since 1961 will also recognize that some topics of research listed by Wallace and Fogelson have had very little attention (e.g. national character studies).

In my initial "sorting out" of IXth ICAES papers, after I had chosen each paper for publication, I used a listing similar to the one proposed by Wallace and Fogelson (1961). I soon found this way of grouping papers to be insufficient for my purpose of trying to illustrate through groups of papers the major topics of research in contemporary psychological anthropology. Congress participants either did not prepare any papers in some areas of psychological anthropology, or there were large numbers of papers in some topic areas. Since there was to be a IXth ICAES session concerned with "anthropology and mental health," a certain number of Congress papers that might have been included as part of the session and the publication in psychological anthropology were not available to me for editorial review and use; an agreement was reached by the IXth ICAES organizing committee that papers would not be duplicated in different Congress volumes, although they could be "cross-listed" for purposes of identification.

Thus, I abandoned use of a "topic heading" approach to grouping Congress papers concerned with psychological anthropology, and turned instead to defining subgroups of papers through use of what I perceived to be their similarities of research concern or expression. I recognize that this approach to organizing papers for publication is not the most felicitous one.

It is important to note that I do not intend these groupings to be inclusive, that is, summaries of the research conducted in particular areas of psychological anthropology. And these sections do not contain extensive citations to other works that are related to a particular grouping of Congress papers. Students and colleagues with newly developed interests in particular topics in psychological anthropology will find that the citations contained in most Congress papers will provide a sufficient basis for beginning reading on selected topics of research. In other words, it should be possible to follow out many specialized research interests through building a bibliography from the bibliographies included in papers that have been grouped together in this volume on psychological anthropology. Recent texts by Honigmann (1967), Wallace (1970), Barnouw (1973), and LeVine (1973) can be used to gather added citations for further reading on particular topics of research and to provide additional background concerning a type or tradition of research that is represented in a specific grouping of Congress papers. I am aware that each grouping used in this volume could have been expanded to incorporate comment on the tradition of psychological anthropology research represented in a particular group of papers. But space limitations in publication preclude inclusion of more than brief editorial comments.

CONCLUSION

It is my belief that there is a valid reason for publication of these Congress papers. It seems to me that a basic concern with the fate of individuals in specific cultural settings, as interpreted through some type of psychological theory, is directly relevant to understanding at least some of the problems that continue to plague our world and threaten the survival of the human species. I believe that the conceptual orientations, ideas, methods, and generalizations — however tentative or "low level" such generalizations may be at present — produced by anthropologists and their colleagues in other disciplines concerned with the fate of individuals in different cultural contexts are very important intellectual resources, if we are ever to cope successfully with continuing forms of human aggression, poverty, famine, disease, racism, discrimination, prejudice, and so on. I am not really very concerned with how we may name, or style, our research activities and interests. But I am quite interested in using the ideas we have available to us to try to deal with our basic human problems. In this sense, then, I believe these papers in psychological anthropology deserve publication, for somewhere, at sometime, hopefully sooner rather than later, a reader may be stimulated by the content of a paper, or a series of papers, to move on to the next steps in our basic understanding of the fate of individuals in different cultural settings. Perhaps that could be the "one giant step" that could benefit us all by giving us totally new ways to solve our old human problems. I have been told by my more cynical and tired colleagues that such optimism is entirely misplaced and very much out of fashion in today's world, where man possesses the power to destroy all life on the earth in minutes, and following the grim demonstrations of Nazi genocide, and the many examples of attempted systematic destruction of whole peoples and cultures for narrow political ends.

Perhaps my dispirited colleagues will be proven right ultimately; man may not be able to survive the social and cultural forces he has invented, and cannot seem to understand or effectively control. But, I think we must at least try, for not to do so would be an admission that all the lonely struggles to learn about man ... as those engaged in by Boas, Benedict, Sapir, Mead and others ... were after all only meaningless and futile gestures of defiance by a species fated to have the power to be self-conscious and to discover its past, yet powerless to determine its own way and future. So, however incomplete these IXth ICAES papers may be, and whatever faults they may demonstrate concerning research in the anthropological subdiscipline of psychological anthropology, the real test of their meaning will lie eventually in whether this collection of ideas in the year 1973 can stimulate new research toward the next efforts in trying to cope with basic human problems, particularly as these concern the fate of specific individuals in different cultural settings. I am content to allow these papers from the IXth ICAES to speak for themselves, on their own merits. I hope that somehow, in some way, these papers may also speak, however indirectly or muted, to the issues of the future survival and well-being of man. This may be too much of a burden to place upon brief and limited papers written for one international congress of anthropologists. But at least we can try, for failure would seem more than man can bear.

REFERENCES

American Anthropologist
   1961   *Decennial index (1949–1958)*. American Anthropologist 63(2): Part 2.
   1971   *Cumulative index (1959–1969)*. American Anthropologist 73(1): Part 2.
ARONOFF, J.
   1967   *Psychological needs and cultural systems: a case study*. Princeton: Van Nostrand.
BARKOW, J.
   1973   Darwinian psychological anthropology: a biosocial approach. *Current Anthropology* 14:373–387.
BARNOUW, V.
   1963   *Culture and personality*. Homewood, Illinois: Dorsey.
   1973   *Culture and personality* (first revised edition). Homewood, Illinois: Dorsey.
BATESON, G.
   1935   Culture contact and schismogenesis. *Man* 35:178–183.
   1936   *Naven*. Cambridge: Cambridge University Press.
   1941   The frustration-aggression hypothesis and culture. *Psychological Review* 48:350–355.
  1942a Some systematic approaches to the study of culture and personality. *Character and Personality* 11:76–84.
  1942b "Social planning and the concept of 'deutero-learning'," in *Symposia, Conference on Science, Philosophy and Religion in Their Relation to the Democratic Way of Life*, volume two, 81–97. Garden City, New York.
   1944   "Cultural determinants of personality," in *Personality and the behavior disorders*, volume two. Edited by J. McV. Hunt, 714–735. New York: Ronald.
   1972   *Steps to an ecology of mind*, New York: Ballantine.
BENEDICT, R.
  1934a Anthropology and the abnormal. *Journal of General Psychology* 10: 59–80.
  1934b *Patterns of culture*. Boston: Houghton-Mifflin.
   1938   Continuities and discontinuities in cultural conditioning. *Psychiatry* 1:161–167.
BOURGUIGNON, E.
   1973   "Psychological anthropology," in *Handbook of social and cultural anthropology*. Edited by J. Honigmann. Chicago: Rand-McNally.

BRUNER, E.
1964 "The psychological approach in anthropology," in *Horizons of anthropology*. Edited by Sol Tax. Chicago: Aldine.

COHEN, Y.
1961 *Social structure and personality: a casebook*. New York: Holt, Rinehart and Winston.

DEVEREUX, G.
1939 Mohave culture and personality, *Character and Personality* 8:91–109.
1940 Primitive psychiatry, part one. *Bulletin of the History of Medicine* 8: 1194–1213.
1945 "The logical foundations of culture and personality studies," in *New York Academy of Sciences, transactions* II, 7(5):110–130.

DE VOS, G., A. HIPPLER
1969 "Cultural psychology: comparative studies of human behavior," in *Handbook of social psychology*, volume four. Edited by G. Lindzey and E. Aronson, 323–417. Reading, Massachusetts: Addison-Wesley.

DU BOIS, C.
1937a Some anthropological perspectives on psychoanalysis. *Psychoanalytic Review* 24:246–263.
1937b Some psychological objectives and techniques in ethnography. *Journal of Social Psychology* 8:285–300.
1941 "Attitudes toward food and hunger in Alor," in *Language, culture and personality: essays in memory of Edward Sapir*. Edited by L. Spier, A. I. Hallowell, and S. Newman, 272–281. Menasha, Wisconsin: The Sapir Memorial Fund.
1944 *The people of Alor*. Minneapolis: University of Minnesota Press.

ERIKSON, E. H.
1939 Observations on Sioux education. *Journal of Psychology* 7:101–156.
1943 Observations on the Yurok: childhood and world image. *University of California Publications in American Archaeology and Ethnology* 35 (10).
1950 *Childhood and society*. New York: Norton.

FARRELL, W. T.
1973 "Convening anthropologists reflect diversity of the races they study." *New York Times*. Saturday, September 8, page M 33.

FISCHER, J. L.
1965 "Psychology and anthropology," in *Biennial review of anthropology, 1965*. Edited by B. Siegel and A. Beals, 211–261. Stanford: Stanford University Press.

FRANK, L. K.
1938 Cultural control and physiological autonomy. *American Journal of Orthopsychiatry* 8:622–626.
1949 *Society as the patient: essays on culture and personality*. New Brunswick, New Jersey: Rutgers University Press.
1951 *Nature and human nature*. New Brunswick, New Jersey: Rutgers University Press.

FROMM, E.
1944 Individual and social origins of neurosis. *American Sociological Review* 9:380–384.

1949   "Psychoanalytic characterology and its application to the understanding of culture," in *Culture and personality*. Edited by S. S. Sargent and M. W. Smith. New York: The Viking Fund.

GILLIN, J.

1939   Personality in preliterate societies. *American Sociological Review* 4: 681–702.

1944   Custom and the range of human response. *Character and Personality* 13:101–134.

1946   "Personality formation from the comparative cultural point of view," in *Sociological foundations of the psychiatric disorders of childhood*. Woods Schools, Child Research Clinic and Conferences. (Reprinted in Kluckhohn and Murray [1948]).

1948   Magical fright. *Psychiatry* 11:387–400.

1956   The making of a witch doctor. *Psychiatry* 19:131–136.

GOODMAN, M. E.

1967   *The individual and culture*. Homewood, Illinois: Dorsey.

HALLOWELL, A. I.

1934   Culture and mental disorder. *Journal of Abnormal and Social Psychology* 29:1–9.

1936   Psychic stresses and cultural patterns. *American Journal of Psychiatry* 92:1291–1310.

1937   Temporal orientation in western civilization and in a preliterate society. *American Anthropologist* 39:647–670.

1938   Fear and anxiety as cultural and individual variables in a primitive society. *Journal of Social Psychology* 9:25–47.

1939   "The child, the savage and human experience," in *Woods Schools, Child Research Clinic and Conferences: proceedings* 6:8–34.

1941   The social function of anxiety in a primitive society. *American Sociological Review* 6:869–881.

1945   The Rorschach technique in the study of personality and culture. *American Anthropologist* 47:195–210.

1953   "Culture, personality and society," in *Anthropology today*. Edited by A. L. Kroeber, 597–620. Chicago: University of Chicago Press.

1954   "Psychology and anthropology," in *For a science of social man*. Edited by J. Gillin, 160–226. New York: Macmillan.

1955   *Culture and experience*. Philadelphia: University of Pennsylvania Press.

HARING, D. G.

1956   *Personal character and the cultural milieu* (third revised edition). Syracuse: Syracuse University Press.

HARRIS, M.

1968   *The rise of anthropological theory*. New York: Crowell.

HEINICKE, C.

1953   *Bibliography on personality and social development of the child*. Social Science Research Council, Pamphlet 10, New York.

HENRY, J.

1936   The personality of the Kaingang Indians. *Character and Personality* 5: 113–123.

1940   Some cultural determinants of hostility in Pilaga Indian children. *American Journal of Orthopsychiatry* 10:111–120.

1941a *The jungle people*. New York: Random House.
1941b Rorschach technique in primitive cultures. *American Journal of Orthopsychiatry* 11:230–234.
1948 Cultural discontinuity and the shadow of the past. *Scientific Monthly* 66:248–254.
1951a The inner experience of culture. *Psychiatry* 14:87–103.
1951b Family structure and psychic development. *American Journal of Orthopsychiatry* 21:59–73.
1955 Projective testing in ethnography. *American Anthropologist* 57:245–255, 264–270.

HERSKOVITS, M. J.
1934 "Freudian mechanisms in primitive Negro psychology," in *Essays presented to C. G. Seligman*. Edited by E. E. Evans Pritchard, 75–84. London: K. Paul, Trench, Trubner.
1948 *Man and his works. The science of cultural anthropology*, chapter 4. New York: Knopf.
1951 "On cultural and psychological reality," in *Conference on Social Psychology at the Crossroads*. Edited by J. H. Rohrer and M. Sherif. New York: Harper.
1952 "Some psychological implications of Afro-American studies," in *Acculturation in the Americas*. Selected Papers of the XXIX International Congress of Americanists, volume two. Edited by Sol Tax, 152–160. Chicago.

HEUSE, G. A.
1953 *La Psychologie Ethnique*. Paris: Librairie Philosophique, J. Vrin.

HONIGMANN, J.
1954 *Culture and personality*. New York: Harper.
1959 "Psychocultural Studies," in *Biennial review of anthropology, 1959* Edited by B. Siegel and A. Beals, 67–106. Stanford: Stanford University Press.
1967 *Personality in culture*. New York: Harper and Row.
1973 "Personality in Culture," in *Main currents in cultural anthropology*. Edited by R. Naroll, chapter seven. Englewood Cliffs, N.J.: Prentice-Hall.

HSU, F. L. H.
1952 Anthropology or psychiatry: a definition of objectives and their implications. *Southwestern Journal of Anthropology* 8:227–250.
1963 *Caste, clan and club*. New York: Van Nostrand.
1965 The effect of dominant kinship relationships on kin and non-kin behavior: a hypothesis. *American Anthropologist* 67:638–661.
1971a *Kinship and culture*. Chicago: Aldine.
1971b Psychosocial homeostasis and Jen: new concepts for advancing psychological anthropology. *American Anthropologist* 73:23–44.

HSU, F. L. H., *editor*
1954 *Aspects of culture and personality*. New York: Abelard-Schuman.
1961 *Psychological anthropology*. Homewood, Illinois: Dorsey.
1972 *Psychological anthropology*. Cambridge, Massachusetts: Schenkman.

HUNT, R., *editor*
1967 *Personalities and Culture*. New York: Natural History Press.

INKELES, A., D. LEVINSON
1954 "National character," in *Handbook of social psychology*, volume two. Edited by G. Lindzey, 977–1020. Cambrdige, Massachusetts: Addison-Wesley.

INTERNATIONAL SOCIAL SCIENCE BULLETIN
1955 Social factors in personality. *International Social Science Bulletin* 7(1).

JONES, E.
1925 Mother right and the sexual ignorance of savages. *International Journal of Psycho-Analysis* 6:109–130.

KAPLAN, B.
1957 "Personality and social structure," in *Review of sociology*. Edited by J. B. Gittler. New York: Wiley.

KAPLAN, B., editor
1961 *Studying personality cross-culturally*. Evanston: Row, Peterson.

KARDINER, A.
1939 *The individual and his society*. New York: Columbia University Press.
1945a *The psychological frontiers of society* (with R. Linton, C. Du Bois, and J. West). New York: Columbia University Press.
1945b "The concept of basic personality structure as an operational tool in the social sciences," in *The science of man in the world crises*. Edited by R. Linton. New York: Columbia University Press.

KLUCKHOHN, C.
1939 Theoretical bases for an empirical method of studying the acquisition of culture by individuals. *Man* 39:98:103.
1941 "Patterning as exemplified in Navaho culture," in *Language, culture and personality: essays in memory of Edward Sapir*. Edited by L. Spier, A. I. Hallowell, and S. Newman. Menasha, Wisconsin: The Sapir Memorial Fund.
1944 "The influence of psychiatry on anthropology in America during the past 100 years," in *One hundred years of American psychiatry*. Edited by J. K. Hall, G. Zilboorg, and H. A. Bunker, 589–617. New York: Columbia University Press.
1946 Personality formation among the Navaho Indians. *Sociometry* 9: 128–132.
1947 Some aspects of Navaho infancy and early childhood. *Psychoanalysis and the Social Sciences* 1:37–86.
1954 "Culture and behavior," in *Handbook of social psychology*, volume two. Edited by G. Lindzey, 921–976. Cambridge, Massachusetts: Addison-Wesley Press.

KLUCKHOHN, C., H. A. MURRAY, editors
1948 *Personality in nature, society and culture*. New York: Knopf.

KLUCKHOHN, C., H. A. MURRAY, D. SCHNEIDER, editors
1956 *Personality in nature, society and culture*. New York: Knopf.

KROEBER, A. L.
1948 *Anthropology*. New York: Harcourt, Brace.
1955 "History of anthropological thought," in *Yearbook of anthropology*, 293–311. New York: Wenner-Gren Foundation for Anthropological Research.

KUHN, T.
  1966   *The structure of scientific revolutions.* Chicago: University of Chicago Press.
LA BARRE, W.
  1938   *The peyote cult.* Yale University Publications in Anthropology 19.
  1945   Some observations on character structure in the Orient: the Japanese. *Psychiatry* 8(3).
  1946a Social cynosure and social structure. *Journal of Personality* 14:169–183.
  1946b Some observations on character structure in the Orient: the Chinese. *Psychiatry* 9(3, 4).
  1947a Primitive psychotherapy in native American cultures: peyotism and confession. *Journal of Abnormal and Social Psychology* 42:294–309.
  1947b The cultural basis of emotions and gestures. *Journal of Personality* 16: 49–68.
  1954   *The human animal.* Chicago: University of Chicago Press.
LANDES, R.
  1937   "The personality of the Ojibwa." *Character and Personality* 6:51–60.
  1938a *The Ojibwa woman.* Columbia University Contributions to Anthropology 31.
  1938b The abnormal among the Ojibwa Indians. *Journal of Abnormal and Social Psychology* 33:14–33.
  1940   A cult matriarchiate and male homosexuality. *Journal of Abnormal and Social Psychology* 35:386–397.
LE VINE, R. A.
  1963   "Culture and personality," in *Biennial review of anthropology, 1963.* Edited by B. Siegel and A. Beals, 107–145. Stanford, California: Stanford University Press.
  1973   *Culture, behavior and personality.* Chicago: Aldine.
LEWIS, O.
  1953   Controls and experiments in field work," in *Anthropology today.* Edited by A. L. Kroeber, 452–472. Chicago: University of Chicago Press.
LINDESMITH, A. R., A. L. STRAUSS
  1950   A critique of culture-personality writings. *American Sociological Review* 15:587–600.
LINTON. R.
  1936   *The study of man.* New York: D. Appelton-Century.
  1938   Culture, society and the individual. *Journal of Abnormal and Social Psychology* 33:425–436.
  1939   The effects of culture on mental and emotional processes. *Association for Research in Nervous and Mental Diseases* 19:293–304.
  1945   *The cultural background of personality.* New York: D. Appelton-Century.
  1949   The personality of peoples. *Scientific American* 181:11–15.
  1956   *Culture and mental disorders.* Springfield, Illinois: Thomas.
LOWIE, R.
  1937   *The history of ethnological theory.* New York: Farrar and Rinehart.
MALINOWSKI, B.
  1923   Psycho-analysis and anthropology. *Psyche* 4:293–322.

1927a *The father in primitive psychology.* New York: W. W. Norton.
1927b *Sex and repression in savage society.* London: Routledge and Kegan Paul.
1929   *The sexual life of savages in Northwestern Melanesia.* London: George Routledge.
1939   The group and the individual in functional analysis. *American Journal of Sociology* 44:938–964.

MANDELBAUM, D.
1943   Wolf-child histories from India. *Journal of Social Psychology* 17: 25–44.
1953   On the study of national character. *American Anthropologist* 55:174–187.

MANDELBAUM, D., *editor*
1949   *Selected writings of Edward Sapir in language, culture and personality.* Berkeley: University of California Press.

MEAD, M.
1928a *Coming of age in Samoa.* New York: Morrow.
1928b The role of the individual in Samoan culture. *Journal of the Royal Anthropological Institute of Great Britain and Ireland* 58: 481–495.
1930a An ethnologist's footnote to totem and taboo. *Psychoanalytic Review* 17:297–304.
1930b *Growing up in New Guinea.* New York: Morrow.
1932   An investigation of the thought of primitive children with special reference to animism. *Journal of the Royal Anthropological Institute of Great Britain and Ireland* 62:173–190.
1933   More comprehensive field methods. *American Anthropologist* 35:1–15.
1935   *Sex and temperament in three primitive societies.* New York: Morrow.
1953a "Some relationships between social anthropology and psychiatry," in *Dynamic psychiatry.* Edited by Franz Alexander and H. Ross. Chicago: University of Chicago Press.
1953b "National character," in *Anthropology today.* Edited by A. L. Kroeber, 642–667. Chicago: University of Chicago Press.
1961   "Psychiatry and ethnology," in *Psychiatrie der Gegenwart*, volume three: *Soziale und Angewandte Psychiatrie.* Edited by H. W. Gruhle and W. Mayer-Gross. Berlin.
1963   "Culture and personality," in *The encyclopedia of mental health*, volume two. Edited by A. Deutsch and H. Fishman. New York: Encyclopedia of Mental Health.
1972   "Introduction," in T. R. Williams, *Introduction to socialization: hu'an culture transmitted*, ix–xi. St. Louis: C. V. Mosby.

MEAD, M., *editor*
1937   *Cooperation and competition among primitive peoples.* New York: McGraw-Hill.

MEGGERS, B. J.
1946   Recent trends in American ethnology. *American Anthropologist* 48: 176–214.

MIDDLETON, JOHN, *editor*
1970   *From child to adult.* Garden City, New York: Natural History Press.

MURPHY, G.
1947   *Personality.* New York: Harper.

NADEL, S. F.
1951   *The foundations of social anthropology.* New York: Free Press.
OPLER, M. E.
1935   The psychoanalytic treatment of culture. *Psychoanalytic Review* 22: 138–157.
1936a An interpretation of ambivalence of two American Indian tribes. *Journal of Social Psychology* 7:82–116.
1936b Some points of comparison and contrast between the treatment of functional disorders by Apache shamans and modern psychiatric practice. *American Journal of Psychiatry* 92:1371–1387.
1938a Personality and culture: a methodological suggestion. *Psychiatry* 1: 217–220.
1938b The use of peyote by the Carrizo and Lipan Apache tribes. *American Anthropologist* 40: 217–221.
1938c Further comparative anthropological data bearing on the solution of a psychological problem. *Journal of Social Psychology* 9:477–481.
1948   Some implications of culture theory for anthropology and psychology. *American Journal of Orthopsychiatry* 18:611–621.
OPLER, M. K., *editor*
1959   *Culture and mental health: cross-cultural studies.* New York: Macmillan.
ORLANSKY, H.
1949   Infant care and personality. *Psychological Bulletin* 46:1–48.
PELTO, P.
1967   "Psychological anthropology," in *Biennial review of anthropology, 1967.* Edited by B. J. Siegel and A. R. Beals, 140–208. Stanford, California: Stanford University Press.
PIDDINGTON, R.
1957   *An introduction to social anthropology,* volume two. Edinburgh: Oliver and Boyd.
RÓHEIM, G.
1922   Ethnology and folk-psychology. *International Journal of Psychoanalysis* 31:189–222.
1932   Psycho-analysis of primitive types: Doketa. *International Journal of Psycho-Analysis* 13:1–224.
1934a *The riddle of the sphinx.* London: Hogarth.
1934b "The study of character development and the ontogenetic theory of culture," in *Essays in honor of C. G. Seligman.* Edited by E. E. Evans-Pritchard. London: K. Paul, Trench, Trubner.
1943   *The origin and function of culture.* Nervous and Mental Disease Monograph Series 63.
1971 [1925] *Australian totemism.* New York: Humanities Press.
SAPIR, E.
1924   Culture, genuine and spurious. *American Journal of Sociology* 29: 401–429.
1929   "The unconscious patterning of behavior in society," in *The unconscious.* Edited by E. S. Drummer. New York: Harper.
1932   Cultural anthropology and psychiatry. *Journal of Abnormal and Social Psychology* 27: 229–242.

1934a The emergence of the concept of personality in a study of cultures. *Journal of Social Psychology* 5: 408–415.

1934b "Personality," in *Encyclopaedia of the social sciences*, volume twelve. Edited by F. Seligman and A. Johnson. New York: Macmillan.

SARGENT, S. S., M. W. SMITH, *editors*

1949   *Culture and personality*. New York: The Viking Fund.

SIEGEL, B. J.

1970   "Foreword," in *Biennial review of anthropology*. Edited by B. J. Siegel and A. R. Beals. Stanford, California: Stanford University Press.

SINGER, M.

1961   "A survey of culture and personality theory and research," in *Studying personality cross-culturally*. Edited by B. Kaplan, 9–90. Evanston, Illinois: Row-Peterson.

SPINDLER, G.

1957   "New trends and applications in anthropology," in *National Council for Social Studies yearbook, 1957*. Washington, D.C.: National Council for Social Studies.

SPIRO, M.

1951   Culture and personality: the natural history of a false dichotomy. *Psychiatry* 14:19–46.

1959   "Culture heritage, personal tension and mental illness in a South Seas culture," in *Culture and mental health*. Edited by M. K. Opler. New York: Macmillan.

1961a "An overview and suggested reorientation," in *Psychological anthropology*. Edited by F. L. K. Hsu, 459–492. Homewood, Illinois: Dorsey Press.

1961b "Social systems, personality and functional analysis," in *Studying personality cross-culturally*. Edited by B. Kaplan, 93–127. Evanston, Illinois: Row-Peterson.

1965   "Religious systems as culturally constituted defense mechanisms," in *Context and meaning in cultural anthropology*. Edited by M. E. Spiro. Glencoe, Illinois: Free Press.

1967   *Burmese supernaturalism: a study in the explanation and resolution of suffering*. Englewood Cliffs, New Jersey: Prentice Hall.

1968   "Culture and personality," in *International encyclopaedia of the social sciences*, volume three. Edited by D. S. Sills, 558–563. New York: Macmillan and The Free Press.

1971   *Buddhism and society*. New York: Harper and Row.

1972   "An overview and suggested reorientation," in *Psychological anthropology*. Edited by F. L. K. Hsu, 573–607. Cambridge, Massachusetts: Schenkman.

SULLIVAN, H. S.

1937   A note on the implications of psychiatry, the study of interpersonal relations, for investigation in the social sciences. *American Journal of Sociology* 42:848–861.

1939   A note on formulating the relationship of the individual and the group. *American Journal of Sociology* 44:932–937.

1940   The human organism and its necessary environment. *Psychiatry* 3:14–27.

1948   Towards a psychiatry of peoples. *Psychiatry* 11:105–116.
1953a   *The interpersonal theory of psychiatry.* New York: Norton.
1953b   [1946]   *Conceptions of modern psychiatry.* New York: Norton.
TRIANDIS, H., R. S. MALPASS, A. R. DAVIDSON
1971   "Cross cultural psychology," in *Biennial review of anthropology.* Edited by B. J. Siegel. Stanford, California: Stanford University Press.
VOLKART, E. H.
1951   *Social behaviour and personality: Contributions of W. I. Thomas to theory and social research.* New York: Social Science Research Council.
WALLACE, A. F. C.
1961   *Culture and personality.* New York: Random House.
1962   "The new culture-and-personality," in *Anthropology and human behavior.* Edited by T. Gladwin and W. Sturtevant, 1–12. Washington, D.C.: Anthropological Society of Washington.
1965   The problem of the psychological validity of componential analyses. *American Anthropologist* 67:229.
1968   "Anthropological contributions to the theory of personality," in *The study of personality.* Edited by E. Norbeck, D. Price Williams, and W. McCord, 41–53. New York: Holt, Rinehart and Winston.
1970   *Culture and personality* (first revised edition). New York: Random House.
WALLACE, A. F. C., R. D. FOGELSON
1961   "Culture and personality," in *Biennial review of anthropology, 1961.* Edited by B. Siegel and A. Beals, 42–78. Stanford, California: Stanford University Press.
WEBB, E., D. CAMPBELL, R. SCHWARTZ, L. SECHREST
1966   *Unobtrusive measures: nonreactive research in the social sciences.* Chicago: Rand-McNally.
WHITING, B. B.
1953   *Selected ethnographic sources on child training.* New York: Social Science Research Council, Pamphlet 10.
WHITING, J. W. M., I. L. CHILD
1953   *Child training and personality.* New Haven: Yale University Press.
WILLIAMS, T. R.
1972   *Introduction to socialization: human culture transmitted.* St. Louis: Mosby.

PART ONE

Variations on a Theme by Ruth Benedict

DAVID G. MANDELBAUM

Ruth Benedict wrote a prelude for prospective readers of her book *Patterns of culture* in the summary paragraphs that appeared on the jacket. She said that the manners and morals of the tribes she discusses "and our own as well, are not piecemeal items of behavior, but consistent ways of life" (Mead 1959: 212). She sketched two kinds of life consistency. One she labelled Apollonian and was illustrated in the lives of the several tribes of the American Southwest classed together as Pueblo Indians. The other she termed Dionysian and showed how it was used by the Kwakiutl tribe of the Northwest Coast of North America. Each is a dominant motif applied by the people throughout their respective societies and cultures. These two motifs involve quite opposite values but together they are linked, Ruth Benedict implies rather than states, as a theme for the anthropological study of man (1946 [1934]: 41, 168). It is the thematic question as to where any people fit, if they do at all, in the scale between the Apollonian and Dionysian poles.

The theme is introduced with references to intimations of it in the works of William Dilthey and Oswald Spengler and is developed in the subsequent discussion of the Pueblo tribes. Cultural configurations are, according to Benedict, as compelling and significant in complex societies as they are in tribal societies, but the material in our own civilization "is too intricate and too close to our eyes for us to cope with it successfully" (1946 [1934]: 51).

DUAL MOTIFS AS THEMATIC QUESTION

The two motifs are stated in contrastive perspective.

The desire of the Dionysian, in personal experience as in ritual, is to press through it toward a certain psychological state, to achieve excess. The closest analogy to the emotions he seeks is drunkenness and he values the illumination of frenzy. [By contrast] the Apollonian distrusts all this, and often has little idea of the nature of such experience. He keeps to the middle of the road, stays within the known map, does not meddle with disruptive psychological states. In Nietzsche's fine phrase even in the exaltation of the dance he "remains what he is and retains his civic name" (Benedict 1946 [1934]: 72).

Ruth Benedict says that she took the two terms and the idea of their contrast from Nietzsche's essay on Greek tragedy. The idea has been advanced by other students of ancient Greece. Bertrand Russell not only identified the opposed patterns, but also placed them in a more general context. He noted that a distinguishing characteristic of civilized, as contrasted with noncivilized societies, is the more systematic application of prudence or forethought through established law, custom, and religion. In Greek civilization, Russell observed: "The worshipper of Dionysius reacts against prudence. In intoxication, physical or spiritual, he recovers an intensity of feeling which prudence had destroyed; he finds the world full of delight and beauty ..." Much of what is greatest in human achievement, he continued, involves some sweeping away of prudence by passion. Without the Dionysian element, life would be uninteresting; with it, it is dangerous. And Russell concluded this passage with the observation that "prudence versus passion is a conflict that runs through history. It is not a conflict in which we ought to side wholly with either party" (Russell 1946: 34).

Patterns of culture tells how some peoples have elevated one of the dual motifs to such dominance that it becomes an integrating principle of the whole culture. The anthropological maxim that Ruth Benedict eloquently conveyed is that a way of life cannot be understood as a mere inventory of traits, that there are strong, salient principles in some cultures which the people use to guide their actions, to build their lives, to help make sense of their existence. She did caution that "Like certain individuals, certain social orders do not subordinate activities to a ruling motivation." Among some groups there is no pervasive cultural motif unless, we may add here, the dissonance itself is considered to be the characteristic note. Ruth Benedict speculated that if we knew the histories of such groups over a sufficiently long period, we might discover that in time the "disharmonious borrowings tend to achieve harmony" (Benedict 1946 [1934]: 206–208). Her own dominant concern in *Patterns of culture* was with those peoples whose cultures are closely integrated around characteristic motifs. The two kinds of integration are described not as absolute categories for a taxonomy of cultures, but rather as differing emphases in a people's values and actions.

THE MOTIFS AS TONIC PRESENTATIONS OF SELF

The book interested and stimulated many; it has become one of the most widely read in the whole of anthropological literature. But the case examples were overstated. Several critiques have pointed out that the depiction of Pueblo peoples as leading a smoothly harmonious social life and as being averse to displays of excess of any kind, omits the continual and bitter factional quarrels, passes over the problems of drunkenness and covert violence, and gives a glossier interpretation of child beating, vicious gossip, and driving personal ambitions than other observers have made (Barnouw 1973: 96–102). Moreover, Ruth Benedict's description plays down the considerable differences among the various Pueblo groups and generalizes too broadly about the Dionysian character of all other American Indian cultures.

So also is the depiction of the Kwakiutl overdrawn. (A third case example from Dobu was based on slighter field evidence and is omitted from our present consideration.) Although such terms as "paranoid" and "megalomanic" occur in Benedict's description of the Kwakiutl, there was an amiable side to their life (Codere 1950: 18–19, 115). Most of their lives were spent in fishing, cooking, carving, and other soberly regular and regulated activities. Even their frenzied public displays appear to have been methodically staged. Thus at the initiation ritual into the Cannibal Society, the dancer, according to Benedict's description, "fell upon the onlookers with his teeth and bit a mouthful of flesh from their arms. His dance was that of a frenzied addict enamored of the 'food' that was held before him, a prepared corpse carried in the outstretched arms of a woman" (1946 [1934]: 162, 164, 166). As it turns out from other testimony, the corpse may have been the costumed carcass of a small black bear and those whom the dancer seized in his frenzy had been persuaded beforehand to allow themselves to be bitten and were rewarded with special gifts (Drucker 1955: 151–152).

The sketches of Pueblos and Kwakiutl thus tell more about how people in each group commonly liked to see themselves and present themselves to others than about the nuances of actual behavior and the many real exceptions to the professed self-image. Yet despite the overstatements, Ruth Benedict's presentation of the motifs, and the idea of their thematic relation, may be useful for understanding various societies through a broad range of circumstances. The theme seems to involve a common element of the human condition; the motifs are transposable to differing modes of conduct.

THEME AND MOTIFS RESTATED

To restate the theme, we begin with some simple truisms, possibly banal but certainly basic. In the course of his life, a person learns to conduct himself according to the regularities appropriate to his culture and the requirements enforced by members of his society. These regularities and requirements periodically thwart the impulses and desires he has for himself as an individual. Each culture provides for both the regular, restrained conduct needed for social action and for the freer, more impulsive behavior necessary for personal satisfaction. This is not to say that there is a permanent undeclared war between individual and society; one's kin and companions are the source of personal reward and development as well as of restriction and deprivation. It is rather that an individual tends to feel himself unduly constrained by his society's regularities from time to time; the occasions and the intensity of such feelings differ according to culture, circumstance, and personality. As we know from the anthropological literature, and notably from *Patterns of culture*, societies differ greatly in how their members fulfill each need, in what life experiences and aspects of culture are deemed appropriate for either emphasis, in what degree each is expressed, and in what light each is viewed.

Alcohol, for example, is taken in some societies as the sovereign means to individual ecstasy; among other peoples, it is enjoyed regularly, ritually, moderately — as it were, soberly. Suicide may be a last desperate act of personal expression or it may be wrapped in ritual and culturally prescribed at a certain juncture of social and personal circumstance. Almost any phase of experience may be given either emphasis. Similarly, one people may make many occasions for lavish personal gratification; others narrowly restrict the frequency and scope of such occasions. Certain groups and roles WITHIN a society may bear special assignment for one or the other emphasis. Some groups cherish an image of themselves that loudly amplifies one or the other tendency, as the Pueblo Indians strove for the outward impression of the one and the Kwakiutl of the other.

Bertrand Russell wrote that the Greeks of the classic period "had a maxim 'nothing too much,' but they were excessive in everything — in pure thought, in poetry, in religion, and in sin." He goes on to modify this by saying that there were in fact two tendencies in Greece and that: "It was the combination of passion and intellect that made them great, while they were great" (Russell 1946: 39). How any people combine the two and how they separate these emphases is an anthropological question worth the asking.

MODULATION, SHIFT, SWING

Pursuit of that question leads to a corollary inquiry, which involves the study of how people change such emphases through time, why they come to shift their value emphases and to use different means of expressing them. Ruth Benedict made note of such a shift when she mentioned in passing (1946 [1934]: 209) that the Kwakiutl "have not always boasted the consistent civilization we have described." They apparently had a more atomistic social apparatus before the group moved from inland territories to the coast.

In numerous historical instances, military success has been a prime factor in value realignment. The Moghuls in India and the Manchus in China conquered and then settled into a more complex and tightly disciplined society than their own. The raiding brotherhoods took on the role of rulers, took over the state bureaucracy, geared themselves toward preserving the vast order of their government rather than toward maintaining their former concerns with raids, plunder, and moving on. In other instances, military defeat has led to value shifts. Whatever the combination of values was that made the Greeks great in the fifth century B.C., it was much altered in the succeeding generations after the devastating wars of subsequent centuries.

The development of technology and economy may set off modulations in dominant motifs. Some of the tribal peoples who have changed from swidden to plough agriculture have consequently revised their emphases, particularly in political organization and. religion, toward greater preoccupation with prudence, order, regularity, and restraint. To be sure, some shift in values may have to precede such technological change; this is suggested by the fact that there are tribal peoples who have known for centuries about the productive potential of plow agriculture and have still preferred to retain the use of swidden cultivation and the kind of life that is compatible with that technology.

Devotees of new religious sects have often testified to the changes in their own life values and in those of their fellow adherents after their conversion to the fresh revelation. These witnesses usually tell of their joyous personal liberation from the restraining shackles of their former state of belief and belonging. The subsequent history of such sects, as we shall note again, often shows a swing back to the kind of set ritual and collective order from which they or their forerunners had earlier freed themselves.

Such swings in dominant emphases have been amply demonstrated in the history of Western art, music, and literature. The terms "classical" and "romantic" are justifiably suspect because of so much woolly use that has been made of them, because of the multiple, even contradictory, meanings that have been attached to each label, and because of the over-zealous cramming into the overly simple categories that has been forced by pedantic taxonomists. Nonetheless there has been in these fields a recurrent change from a prevailing emphasis on the beauties of order, convention, and restraint to a greater appreciation of individual expression, spontaneity, and free movement. To be sure, the greatest artists, whose work has had appeal over successive generations, have always managed to combine the two, no matter where the prevailing emphasis happened to be during their own productive times. Their skill in this has proved to be all the greater because so much of what is perceived as either individually innovative or interestingly symmetrical depends on the conventions of the time. So, for example, some of Mozart's deliberately discordant effects, abrupt departures from eighteenth century musical expectations, now have little impact on present-day listeners, accustomed as they are to far more violent musical departures.

Current movements in the literature and fine arts of Western nations are generally away from standards for orderly symmetry and restrained development. The arguments for a "counterculture" in politics and life-styles, as well as in art, articulately advocate a shift to the Dionysian side of the scale. So vividly do these movements fill the current scene that we may tend to underrate the persistence with which some peoples have maintained a particular set of value emphases through a variety of fortunes and environments over centuries. In long perspective, the durability of a people's integrating principles may be as impressive as their change-ability.

IN LIFE PASSAGE AND PERSONALITY

Do these motifs resound only in the full orchestration of collective and culture or can they be detected also in the playing out of the individual's performance? Apparently they can be so recognized in individual conduct,

and a good many societies make special social provision for those personalities who prefer to march to the beat of different drummers. In some
the culturally projected life plan allows for different emphases at different
periods of the life passage. Frequently a young man's urge to be freed
from the restraints of his earlier years is acknowledged; his desire to strike
out for himself and to use his new strength to establish his personhood is
accommodated. The role of warrior in some tribal societies provided for
such personal needs and also met group requirements for defense or
attack. In more complex societies, the role of soldier might fulfill both
purposes, even though that role was swathed in the especially rigid regulations of the military.

Other cultures mark quite a different tempo in the distribution of value
emphases over the life-span. Thus among the traditional Brahmin and
Vaishya classes of India (respectively priests-scholars and merchants by
traditional occupation) young men were not supposed to have such lee-
way. They might surreptitiously test caste restraints, but their proper time
for any personal expression was when they themselves became elders and
heads of families. For a woman of these groups the most constrictive
time of life came precisely during young womanhood, when she was newly
married and not yet the mother of flourishing children. As an unmarried
girl she could be relatively freer in her conduct than she could be as a
young wife, and the most liberated period of her career occurred when she
became a matron, mother of grown sons and daughters, wife of the head
of the family, and ruler of the women's world in her compound.

There is another kind of social provision for personal preference along
the range marked by the dual motifs. It lies in the choice among available
roles. Under the aegis of religion in India, there were, and are, honored
roles for the playing out (*sforzando*) of either life motif. A man of the
higher caste groups could devote himself to full days and years of ritual,
either as a priest or simply as a devout believer, if his personal desire was
for regular, regulated, methodical conduct. But if he were strongly inclined
toward the unbounded life of the free spirit, he might become a holy man,
a *sadhu* or *sanyassin*. Hindu scripture enjoins a man to take up the state of
sanyassin toward the end of his life cycle, but he could, in fact, do so at
any stage of his adult career. Once a man became a *sanyassin*, he could
wander about the countryside as his personal whim propelled him, practically and sometimes quite formally cut off from all his previous social
obligations and restraints; he would be a person without caste membership, shorn of most of his former caste practices, and dressed differently
than he had been in his former roles—hair now long and matted, clothing
scanty or even absent—his state of undress proclaiming his state of spir-

itual liberation, although the undress is in fact a kind of required uniform for incumbents of that holy role.

Another possible role for Indian villagers of independent spirit is that of shaman. It is a role open to men of the lower caste ranks in most parts of village India; to become a successful shaman a man must usually have considerable practical intelligence as well as the capacity to be convincingly possessed by a spirit. This role is occasionally assumed by women of similar social strata, rarely by members of the higher caste groups.

A shaman is a kind of apotheosis of the Dionysian motif, a mortal who, by his singular luck or ability, is able to communicate directly with supernatural powers and to use this personal ability to affect the lives of others. The behavior proper during shamanistic possession differs considerably among cultures. I have seen South Indian shamans who have gone into a quivering frenzy of movement when the spirit enters them and have heard the voice of the spirit coming forth, as if squeezed out, in hoarse cries; the shaman may demonstrate his state of possession by such feats as standing, skin unbroken, on the sharp edge of an upheld sword. By contrast, shamans among the Todas of the Nilgiri Hills in South India only walk briskly back and forth during the times of their possession; they may gesture more broadly than is normal, but they engage in colloquy with fellow tribesmen, who ask questions of the spirit, and are not averse to arguing with the spirit on occasion.

This may be the place to recall that the oracle at Delphi was consecrated to Apollo. The motto, "nothing in excess," was carved on the shrine to Apollo there. But in the shrine the Pythia, the woman shaman, would regularly become possessed and the voice of Apollo would speak through her (Dodds 1956: 70–72). So the actual cult of Apollo was not itself an unmixed representation of the Apollonian ideal type.

All individuals do not replicate, blindly and automatically, the value definitions stressed in their culture. Ruth Benedict's (1946 [1934]) concluding chapter, "The individual and the pattern of culture," develops this idea. In it she notes that most people in a society conform to the value emphases set by their culture, to the general expectations commonly shared by their fellows. Nonetheless, she continues, it is the individual who makes his life out of the "raw material" of his culture. Individuals are not automatons and not all persons find the values of their time and social setting to be personally congenial. True, those whose personal preference and public behavior best coincide with the dominant emphases tend to be socially favored. But a particular normality does not last forever. Normality and abnormality are culturally defined and the standards for both vary among cultures and, over time, within a culture. Ruth

Benedict ended the book on the note that if these ideas are embraced as customary belief in our society:

we shall arrive then at a more realistic social faith, accepting as grounds of hope and as new bases for tolerance the coexisting and equally valid patterns of life which mankind has created for itself from the raw materials of existence (1946 [1934]: 257).

Whether all patterns of life should be taken as "equally valid" has been vigorously challenged and, indeed, Benedict did not in her subsequent work stand on any extreme interpretation of cultural relativity. Her main thesis about the relation of individual and culture has not been disputed; it had been stated by other anthropologists before and has since become part of the textbook canon. But there has been very little further exploration of the dual motifs either in studies of personality or of culture. There are suggestions in *Patterns of culture* (1946 [1934]: 42) that the idea is applicable to both, that the two motifs delineate a range of behavior that can be studied usefully whether the observer's focus is on culture or on personality. If they can be applied in either perspective and in both, they should provide a bridge concept of considerable potential. To be sure, the two can only furnish one part of a set of dimensions; that part is certainly not, by itself, a kind of double helix of culture or a universal octave any more than such pairs as introvert-extrovert or guilt-shame have proved to be. But that part may be one element in the composition of a better mode of analysis than we now have.

CYCLE AND REFRAIN

Changes in value configurations, whether of culture or of personality, have yet to be extensively studied by anthropologists although some valuable work in the subject was done by the Harvard Value Study (see Vogt and Albert 1966). Psychologists and psychoanalysts have generally tended to be more interested in the regular unfolding and constancy of a personality configuration than in major alterations of it. Freud and succeeding psychoanalysts have shown us how each person builds up his own melodic plot out of primordial chords, how he tends to seek the same kind of environmental accompaniment wherever he may be, how he develops a characteristic rhythm of life, how he seeks similar harmonic progressions through his life, and how, in some case histories, he repeatedly winds up in jarring disharmonic din.

The configuration of a culture can be examined for comparable constancy and, against the background of constancy, changes can be studied. Thus in Indian civilization there seems to have been a constant differentiation between the transcendental and the pragmatic aspects of religion (cf. Mandelbaum 1966, 1970: 223–224, 410–413). The transcendental functions have to do with the long-term welfare of society, with the preservation of the received social and sacred systems, and with the proper progression of events through the year and of persons through their life cycle. The transcendental deities are conceived as being universal, the rites for these transcendental functions are staged in a regular round, the practitioners of this aspect of religion are priests who use the Sanskrit scriptures. The pragmatic aspects, in contrast, are for personal benefits and local exigencies, particularly for the cure of illness and for success in personal ventures. The rites for these functions are performed ad hoc; the relevant deities are usually local spirits; and the practitioners are shamans, usually from the lower caste groups, who use the vernacular tradition. While there is overlap between the two complexes, they have generally been kept distinct by the people, being utilized without mutual conflict for their respective purposes.

The same kind of differentiation has been noted in other parts of the world and has been discussed in anthropological literature as the differences between priest and shaman. In terms of the dual motifs, the priest is the functionary of the Apollonian needs and emphases, the shaman of the Dionysian.

Religious change in India, and this has included much of the social change as well, has followed a consistent course. For some two and a half millennia, since at least the time of the Buddha, holy men have arisen to teach a new doctrine that promises liberation from the established ritual and priesthood, from the inadequate services of shamans, and from the dominant order of society. If such a holy man gathers a large number of devotees, they tend to develop regular ways of worship and teaching. They develop a cult which combines transcendental and pragmatic functions. As the cult attracts more and more adherents, they find it necessary to devise their own social organization and they form a sect. Historically, successful sects have in time come to function as caste groups, and their adherents have rejoined the established caste order which the original devotees had spurned in order to follow their inspired guru.

This process still goes on in India. A major reason why men and women are attracted to the vision of a great guru and bind themselves to his service is that they feel that the established scripture, ritual, priesthood, and shamans do not fulfill their personal needs. These all become too impersonal; the individual feels himself lost, neglected, and overlooked as a person. He turns to a figure who, like the shaman, gives witness to his direct, personal contact with supernal power; but unlike the ordinary shaman whose scope is local and abilities limited, the founding guru tells of eternal solutions and overarching psychic reward. Elsewhere I have tried to examine why and how these movements for liberation from the established order have regularly come to be reabsorbed in it (1970: 523–544). A related question is why the established order of religion and society in India has periodically come to be so dissonant to so many. Perhaps when Apollonian functionaries become increasingly powerful and specialized, they tend increasingly to concentrate on the separate bureaucratic world of their specialty and neglect some fundamental needs of the people.

Some process of this kind may underlie the contemporary trend in a number of societies toward more Dionysian, even Dionysiac, expressions than were formerly prevalent (see Adler 1972). Insofar as such movements are most vigorously carried on by young men and women, they may be current versions of the familiar urge of young people to define themselves by counter-definition. But these movements seem to have broader appeal than just to the surge of youth, and the swing may be part of a long-term counterpoint in a civilization between Apollonian and Dionysian refrains.

IN THE STUDY OF MAN

Anthropologists are not generally indifferent to the prevailing refrains of their culture; historians of anthropology may discover similar swings in the development of the discipline. But, as a survey of studies of Pueblo Indians made by Bennett (1946) shows, anthropologists with broadly similar training, who have done their fieldwork in about the same period, do nonetheless make quite differing interpretations of the same societies and the same social motifs. Bennett says that certain of them, including Ruth Benedict, have emphasized the benignly "organic" aspect of Pueblo culture while others have stressed the "repressive" aspects, the covert tension, anxiety, and suspicion. The disparity is about what phases of Pueblo life to accent in the observer's account rather than about what face the Pueblos themselves liked to present. From the tone of her comments in *Patterns of culture*, Ruth Benedict does seem to favor the "organic" view of the Apollonian Pueblos, but she was inclined to mark the "repressive" emphases when alluding to apparently Apollonian characteristics of American culture (1946 [1934]: 238, 252–253). But the book, we should note, did not attempt to work out a meticulous methodology for identification of Apollonian and Dionysian emphases, with all facts impeccably related and all analytical details clearly stated. That task remains to be done. The wide, continuing popularity of the book and its considerable importance derive from its other qualities, especially from the way in which Ruth Benedict combined the dual motifs in her work. Thus Mead has characterized the book as one "which for a generation has stood as a bridge between those who cherish the uniqueness of individual achievement and those who labor to order the regularities in all human achievement" (1959: xv–xvi).

The study of society and culture, like all physical and social sciences, must give primary emphasis to the Apollonian mode. But, like the other sciences, it also requires Dionysian passages and interludes in order to achieve the aims that anthropologists set for themselves. In science, as in social life generally, the participant commonly tries to combine the two motifs in some satisfactory way. As he makes these attempts toward harmonious combination of the dual motifs and of other motifs, his life takes on the quality of a performing art.

Ruth Benedict wrote that a culture is like a work of art. A people's playing out of their culture can surely be so considered. It seems, also, that the composed account of a culture by at least some anthropologists can be appreciated in that sense.

REFERENCES

ADLER, NATHAN
    1972   *The underground stream, new life styles and the antinomian personality.*
        New York: Harper and Row.
BARNOUW, VICTOR
    1973   *Culture and personality.* (Revised edition). Homewood, Illinois: The
        Dorsey Press.
BENEDICT, RUTH
    1946 [1934]   *Patterns of culture.* New York: Penguin Books.
BENNETT, JOHN W.
    1946   The interpretation of Pueblo culture. *Southwestern Journal of Anthro-*
        pology 24:361–374.
CODERE, HELEN
    1950   *Fighting with property: a study of Kwakiutl potlatching and warfare*
        1752–1930. Monograph of the American Ethnological Society 18.
        New York: American Ethnological Society.
DODDS, E. R.
    1956   *The Greeks and the irrational.* Berkeley and Los Angeles: University
        of California Press.

DRUCKER, PHILIP
  1955   *Indians of the northwest coast.* New York: McGraw Hill.
MANDELBAUM, DAVID G.
  1966   Transcendental and pragmatic aspects of religion. *American Anthropologist* 68:1174–1191.
  1970   *Society in India.* Berkeley and Los Angeles: University of California Press.
MEAD, MARGARET
  1959   *An anthropologist at work; writings of Ruth Benedict.* Boston: Houghton Mifflin.
RUSSELL, BERTRAND
  1946   *A history of Western philosophy.* London: George Allen and Unwin.
VOGT, E. Z., ETHEL M. ALBERT
  1966   *People of Rimrock; a study of values in five cultures.* Cambridge, Massachusetts: Harvard University Press.

The Quest of the Argonauts

LORNA McDOUGALL

All over the world, the journey or the voyage is an important ritual motif (Van Gennep 1960: 153 ff.). Since the publication of Van Gennep's *Rites of passage*, at least, anthropologists have been aware of the importance attached to place by practitioners of ritual and, more specifically, of the frequent importance of moving the ritual events outside the arena of everyday affairs.

Less extreme and exotic instances of changing location and removing the participants from the scene of everyday events occur in many rites which do not explicitly concern themselves with anything as grand as a full-fledged voyage. Recently, many studies, including those by Victor Turner (among the Ndembu), have shown the importance of "the bush" in a number of different rites (Turner 1967, 1969). The natives' stress on the "wild" setting suggests the interpretation of place as an index of social position: the person without social position or without an established cultural role belongs outside the social or domestic setting and finds his rightful symbolic and literal place in the chaos of the natural environs. He may re-enter the human sphere only after he has regained, by ritual means, an appropriate rank and role in society.

Van Gennep, Turner, and even Lévi-Strauss concur more or less in attributing a sociological importance to the location of ritual. The contrast village/bush, so prevalent in Ndembu symbolism, is perfectly in keeping with Lévi-Strauss' interpretation of ritual as expression of the basic nature/culture distinction which motivates social thinking and human actions. While it is valuable to recognize the value of place as a social indicator in ritual interpretation, I should like to suggest that this by no means exhausts the possibilities. What the motif of voyage and the motif of nature have in common is the idea of displacement, of removing ritual actors from the theatre of the commonplace, from their usual venue. It is to the concept of displacement itself that I should now like to call attention, since it will take us beyond consideration of the "social" significance of distance and into the concept of man's psycho-biological unity.

The ritual under examination here is drawn from the literature on the Trobriands, including Malinowski's classic *Argonauts of the Western Pacific*, first published in 1922. Kula is one of the more striking instances of ritual dislocation since it involves a voyage of several hundred miles for some natives. The available documents are detailed and relatively complete.

I shall summarize the outline of events briefly: detailed description by Malinowski tends to mask the thrust of the plot so that simplification and skeletalization are necessary to lay bare the shape of the ritual itself.

Kula is a form of intertribal commerce or exchange practised in the islands of the Melanesian archipelago, including the Trobriands, part of the d'Entrecasteaux group, and part of the Amphletts. Mauss describes Kula as a "grand potlatch" (Mauss 1967: 27). Kula has in common with the potlatch the fact that it is an elaborate form of exchange and is highly competitive.

The articles of exchange in Kula (red shell necklaces and white armshells) are called *soulava* and *mwali*. Articles of two kinds, and two kinds only, are constantly traveling in opposite directions along the "ring" of the Kula exchange circuit.

In the direction of the hands of a clock, moves constantly one of these kinds — long necklaces of red shell, called *soulava*. ... In the opposite direction moves the other kind — bracelets of white shell called *mwali*. ... Each of these articles, as it travels in its own direction on the closed circuit, meets on its way articles of the other class, and is constantly being exchanged for them. Every movement of the Kula articles, every detail of the transactions is fixed and regulated by a set of traditional rules and conventions, and some acts of the Kula are accompanied by an elaborate magical ritual and public ceremonies (Malinowski 1922: 81).

The overseas Kula voyage (*uvalaku*) is led and financed by the chiefs of certain maritime subclans who own canoes (1922: 116–120). It is essentially an aristocratic pursuit. An inland Kula serves to amass valuables to give to visitors who will reciprocate the *uvalaku* expedition in the future (1922: 188). The inland Kula includes exchanges of fish and vegetables (always *gimwali*) and the ceremonial exchange of fish and yams (always *wasi*) between coastal and inland villages as well as the Kula valuables (*vaygu'a*) which are exchanged for food in the villages where the valuables are manufactured (1922: 190). Thus the production of food may indirectly affect Kula through its exchange for a valuable which can then enter the Kula ring proper. Malinowski maintains that the exchange of food commodities (*wasi*) is entirely distinct from Kula except in this respect (1922).

Kula voyagers travel empty-handed outward bound. They go seeking the necklaces and shells. Each man has a Kula partner whom he will retain (barring quarrels) for life. The direction of exchange will always remain the same; if on the first occasion the itinerant Trobriander received a necklace from a particular man then he will continue to receive necklaces from him. Thus necklaces and shells are never received from the same man (Malinowski 1922: 93). There is no confusion of roles. The number of Kula partners a man has will vary with his rank. He must have a minimum of two — one for arm-shells, the other for necklaces (1922: 91).

Kula exchange is sharply distinguished from barter (*gimwali*). Trade is never carried on with a Kula partner (1922: 363, 390). The Kula partner is wooed, cajoled, and even courted, until he finally yields the desired object. The exchange is strictly ceremonial.

The itinerant Trobriander sails in the hope that he will be able to persuade his distant Kula partner to part with a particularly important Kula object. The traveler spends much of the time immediately after landing in beautifying himself in order to appear attractive to his Kula host (Malinowski 1922: 355). Appearance is very important because in native psychophysical theories "the EYES are ... the seat of admiration, wish and appetite in matters of sex, of greed for food and for material possessions" (1922: 339; emphasis added). Beauty of appearance will therefore arouse all kinds of desirable reactions, and indeed reactions of desire, in the partner who will wish to please in return. He will desire to show his generosity. The soliciting of the Kula valuable is similar to courtship of a woman — in Dobu at least (Fortune 1932: 215). In Kula, as in love, beauty is thus an asset.

A native spell expresses the feelings of the seeking sailor thus: "My head is made bright with ritual paint, my face flashes. I have acquired a beautiful shape, like that of a chief; I have acquired a shape that is good. I am the only one; my renown stands alone" (Malinowski 1922: 339). He expresses his self-esteem. If he is of high rank he knows he can expect important objects when his magic has been effective; if he is a commoner he must expect less, although his fortunes too will be affected by his skill as a magician.

Malinowski comments on magic:

Although actual beauty cannot be imparted by spells, yet the feeling of being beautiful through magic may give assurance, and influence people in their behaviour and deportment, and as in the transaction it is the manner of the soliciting party which matters, this magic, no doubt, achieves its aim by psychological means (1922: 336).

In the spell we see beauty equated with nobility — beauty pertains to the chief in the nature of things — beauty of appearance will help the seeker to acquire specially fine Kula objects which will reflect his own prestige and status. The giver in his turn also acquires moral superiority:

The giver is quite as keen as the receiver that the gift should be generous, though for different reasons. Then, of course, there is the important consideration that a man who is fair and generous in the Kula will attract a larger stream [of partners] to himself than a mean one (1922: 98).

The visitor has performed all his safety rites and beauty rites, but is still feeling apprehension as he approaches his partner (Malinowski 1922: 345); he cannot feel certain of his partner's goodwill, and it seems as though the reason for this is that the partner, willing to take part in the Kula for his own benefit, really does not feel this good will. "It is the customary rule that the Trobrianders should be received first with a show of hostility and fierceness; treated almost as intruders" (1922: 346). The fierceness subsides after a small drama — the scaling of the palm trees and the removal of the fruit by the visitors to Dobu (1922). Nonetheless, the exchange will be carried out with feigned indifference if not outright hostility.

However much he may want to appear attractive the visitor must show no interest in the gift; he must never seem eager. "In the ceremonial distributions as well as in the Kula, the present is thrown down by the giver, sometimes actually, and often it is not even picked up by the receiver, but by some insignificant person in his following" (1922: 190). Malinowski even describes the emotion of the donor as one of "histrionic anger" (1922: 353).

The valuables can neither be demanded nor complained about directly, but only solicited through important intermediary gifts (1922: 356) or received as returns for equal transactions.

If I have given a *vaga* (opening gift of valuable) to a partner of mine let us say a year ago, and now, when on a visit, I find that he has an equivalent *vaygu'a*, I shall consider it his duty to give it to me. If he does not do so, I am angry with him and justified in being so (1922: 353).

Not only would he have the right to be angry but in this case a man would also have the right to steal the object, despite the fact that histrionic anger would result. In general, however, the protocol of exchange demands less pronounced reactions; the gift should be given in an offhand, abrupt, ALMOST angry manner, and received with nonchalance and disdain (1922: 352).

The actual relationship with the partner contrasts with what is desired. Magic expresses this relationship in terms of hugging, befriending, and "taking to the bosom" as with a little child (Malinowski 1922: 338), not in the anger of reality. Sexual overtones surround the transaction; the meeting of the valuables is a marriage. The spell of the *Ta'uya* begs them to "come together" and describes the state of excitement of the partner (1922: 340). The excitement is likened to a dog, which explains why

"they invoke the dog in the *mwasila*, because when master of dog comes, the dog stands up and licks; in the same way, the inclinations of the Dobu people." Another explanation is more sophisticated: "the reason is that dogs play about nose to nose. Supposing we mentioned the word, as it was of old arranged, the valuables do the same. Supposing we had given away armshells, the necklaces will come, they will meet" (1922: 348).

The exchanges of valuables are accomplished on major expeditions in the following order: *vaga*, an opening gift; *yotile*, a return gift; *basi*, an intermediate gift, given when an appropriate object, equalling in value what has been received, is not available, i.e. a pledge that such is forthcoming; and finally *kudu*, a clinching gift.

Kudu deserves notice because it means to bite and thus the *Kudu* gift is "the one that bites" (1922: 357); this terminology follows out the sexual metaphor. Biting, more particularly biting off the eyelashes, plays an important part in lovemaking (Malinowski 1932: 250). The ethnographer comments, "This, I was told, is done in orgasm as well as in the less passionate preliminary stages [of lovemaking]" (1932: 281). If the receiver is not satisfied with his *yotile* he will complain that the return gift is not a proper "'tooth' for his gift, that it is not a real 'marriage' that it is not properly 'bitten'" (Malinowski 1922: 356–357).

Each partner relies basically on the fairness of the other to exchange equivalent objects. Each is, however, ambitious. Vanity and desire to be renowned are characteristics of the native feelings in the Kula (1922: 110) and ownership of a particularly fine arm-shell or necklace confers a prestige upon the individual who receives it, as well as upon his community.

... it must be remembered that each one of the first-class arm-shells and necklaces has a personal name and history of its own, and as they circulate around the big ring of Kula, they are all well known, and their appearance in a given district always creates a sensation. Now, all my partners — whether from overseas or from within the district — compete for the favour of receiving this particular article of mine, and those who are specially keen try to obtain it by giving me *pokala* (offerings) and *kaributu* (solicitary gifts) (1922: 99).

The regard for the other's fairness in the transaction is an act of bravery in the face of danger. Partners are equated with clansmen (*kakaveyogu*) who are potentially enemies in contrast to kinsmen (*veyogu*) who are "of the same navel string" (1922: 276) and who are by definition friendly.

The trust in fairness must be maintained over time. The principle of Kula, that a ceremonial gift must be repaid by an equivalent gift AFTER A LAPSE OF TIME (from a few hours or even minutes to a year or more), is inviolable. A valuable can never be exchanged from hand to hand as are objects in barter, nor may its value ever be quibbled about: you must wait and trust (1922: 96; Fortune 1932: 233). "Sharp practice, promising a valuable you do not possess, is not unknown" (Fortune 1932: 217–218) and trust is not always validated. Kula means danger.

The Kula objects themselves are, in the eyes of the natives, if not Malinowski, very beautiful and highly prized. They are personified objects — they are named after their makers (Seligman 1910: 514) and people may even be named after them. They have a history (Seligman 1910: 89) whose recital resembles that of a genealogy; they accompany a man to his grave where they are piled over the body so that they may carry his life force into the world to come (Malinowski 1922: 512–513, 1932: 362). They constitute a part of bride price (Malinowski 1932: 77; Fortune 1932: 189).

The red necklaces are received into the right hand; they travel round the Kula ring in a clockwise or west-to-east direction. They are thought to be male. The white armbands are received into the left hand and travel in the opposing east-to-west direction. They are thought to be female (Malinowski 1922: 93). Following up on the image of courtship mentioned by Fortune, we find that the natives speak of the "marriage of Kula objects" (1922: 356). There are one or two other objects which in the past accompanied the arm-shells and necklaces: *doga* or circular boar's tusks (that were almost as important as the bands themselves) and *bosu*, whale bone lime spatulae (that were decorated with spondylus shells). *Bosu* were a relatively unimportant adjunct to the necklaces and, like the *doga*, were almost unknown by the time of Malinowski's study (1922: 358). *Vaygu'a* are worn by women to display their husband's importance (1922: Plate XIX).

Brief reference to the magic surrounding the Kula voyage gives some indication of the native conceptions of the dangers endured to secure possession of the ritual valuables. According to Malinowski, all magic is intended to offset dangers. The magic is performed over the canoe as it is being constructed in order to make it swift, steady, safe, and lucky in Kula. Further magical rites are done to avert the dangers of sailing and finally there is the *mwasila*, magic of Kula itself (1922: 102). The magic is summarized by Malinowski himself in tabular form (1922: 415; see Table

1), the information in the last column indicating the course of magical events.

One or two interesting points about magic which do not show up in Malinowski's tabulation are raised by the ethnographer, i.e. the connections between magic and sex, particularly the female sex. There is a fairly constant set of associations: Kula magic, love magic, danger, witches, women. The mention of any one of these is likely to lead to discussion of the others.

Kula means magic. A man successful in Kula has good magic. Kula is a form of male courtship and Kula magic is said to resemble love magic (Malinowski 1922: 310; Fortune 1932: 229). Kula magic also derives from the same source as do the dreaded witches (female) who are the primary threat to the success of the expedition: Iwa, an island where the spirits of the dead killed in sorcery pass on their way to Tuma, the native heaven (Malinowski 1922: 77). Women are both the source of danger and the means to counteract that danger. As we shall see, they are to be both feared and emulated. Interestingly, the pandanus streamers used both to decorate the canoes (1922: 216) and to make them speedy resemble the streamers used by witches when they fly through the air. The ability to fly is what is chiefly desired of a canoe, and there are myths about the canoe, *Kudayuri*, which once could accomplish the feat, an ability now lost to man (1922: 320). In contrast, witches, who are women, are still able to levitate, and are to be feared. The natives on the voyage are heard to use the "deprecating euphemism" *vivila* (woman), to describe the flying witches (1922: 236).

Witches are most likely to threaten the expedition through causing shipwreck (1922: 247–248), although they have connection with all forms of death at sea: sharks; the "gaping depth;" small sea animals; crabs (1922: 245); and also the remarkable jumping stones (*vineylida*) which spring to the surface and hold fast to the canoe much as would a large octopus, which is also feared (1922: 235–236) and which is to be appeased by sacrificing a small boy (1922: 234). The fear of witches expressed here is merely a specific form of a much more general fear of woman, often found in myth.

Women who live on the island of Kaytalugi, to the north of the Trobriands, epitomize Trobriand men's fear of the destructive female. The women who live there are beautiful, big, and strong, and they walk about unshaven (contrary to Trobriand custom); boy children cannot survive their mercies. They exhibit unbounded passion and the natives discuss at length the fate of a shipwrecked sailor in their hands. The behaviour of these women, so much feared, resembles that of their own women at the

Table 1. Kula magic and the corresponding activities
First stage of canoe building

Season and approximate duration	Place	Activity		Magic
Beginning: June–August	*Raybwag*	Felling of tree (done by the builder and helpers)	inaugurated by	the *Vabusi Tokway* (offering and spell) aiming at the expulsion of the wood sprite from the tree (performed by owner or builder)
Immediately afterwards	Same place	Trimming of the log canoe (done by builder with helpers)		No magic
A few days later	Road	Pulling the log (done by all villagers)	helped out by	double rite of lightness (*Kaymomwa'u* and *Kaygagabile*)
On morning after arrival at village	Main place in the village	The log is left as it is	until	the magical act (*Kapitunena Duku*) ceremonially inaugurating the work over the canoe
Evening of the same day	Main place in the village	Working out of the outside of the log		No magic accompanying it
Several days or weeks following	Main place	Scooping out of the inside of the canoe	inaugurated by	*Ligogu* spell, over the *kavilali*, the adze with the movable handle
Towards the end of foregoing period	In the village before builder's house	Other parts of canoe made ready by builder and helpers		No magic
After all work is over				Concluding rite: *Kapitunena Nanola Waga*

Table 1 (continued)
Second stage of canoe building

Time	Place	Activity		Magic
First day of work	On sea-front of a Lagoon village, or on a beach of one of Eastern villages	Fixing the prowboards	inaugurated by	*Katuliliva Tabuyo* rite, performed over ornamental prowboards by the *toliwaga*. It belongs to the *mwasila* (Kula magic)
		The following activities are	inaugurated by	*Vakakaya* rite. A magical ceremonial cleansing of the canoe, performed by the owner or builder to remove all evil influence and thus to make the canoe fast
		Lashing of the canoe	associated with	the *Wayugo* spell (lashing creeper) rite; the most important of the magical performances in the second stage. Done by builder or owner to make canoe swifter and stronger
(At times, the lashing cannot be done in one day and has to be continued into another session)		Caulking of the canoe	associated with	*Kaybasi* (caulking) magic; spell uttered over caulking by builder or owner to make canoe safe
Second sitting: during this the caulking is done and the three exorcisms performed afterwards	On the sea front of a Lagoon village or on a beach of one of Eastern villages			*Vakasulu*, an exorcism
				Vaguri, an exorcism
				Kaytapena waga, an exorcism
		Painting of the canoe	associated with	magic of: *Kaykoulo* (black paint); *Malakava* (red paint); *Pwaka* (white paint)

Table 1 (continued)
The ceremonial launching of a canoe

Activity	Magic
The launching and trial run inaugurated by	*Kaytalula wadola waga* rite, belonging to the *mwasila* cycle of magic

After this, there comes the interval, filled out by the *Kabigidoya* (ceremonial visiting), by the preliminary trade and other preparations for the expedition overseas.

The magic during, and preparations before the departure
Time: some three to seven days before setting sail

Activity	Magic
Preparing the canoe for sailing (placing of the mats on the platform, and of the frames in the body): inaugurated by	*Yawarapu* rite over the coco-palm leaves, done by the *toliwaga* to ensure success in the Kula *Kayikuna sulumwoya* rite over the aromatic mint *Kaymwaloyo* rite over the mint boiled in coco-nut oil, performed by the *toliwaga*
Packing of the trade goods: associated with	*Gebobo* rite (called also: *Kipwo'i sikwabu*), made over four coconuts by a friend or relative-in-law of the *toliwaga*, to make all the food last (the spell expresses only the desire for a good Kula)

All this magic belongs to the *mwasila*, and it has to be performed by the *toliwaga*, with the exception of the last spell.

Canoe magic, performed at the final start on overseas voyage

The series of rites starts at the moment when the canoes are ready to set sail on the long voyage on Pilolu. They are not associated with a progressive series of acts; they all refer to one aim: canoe speed and reliability. They are all performed by the *toliwaga*.

Activity: overseas sailing, inaugurated by a series of magical rites Time: morning of the second day of the expedition Place: the beach of Muwa Aim of magic: imparting of speed to canoe Performer of the rites: the *toliwaga*	*Kadumiyala*, ritual rubbing or cleansing of the canoe with leaves charmed over *Bisila* magic; pandanus streamers, previously chanted over, are tied to the mast and rigging *Kayikuna veva;* swaying the sheet rope uttering an incantation *Vabusi momwa'u;* "expelling the heaviness" out of a canoe by means of a stale potato *Bisiboda patile;* a rite of evil magic to make other canoes slow and thus achieve relative speed

Table 1 (continued)

The Mwasila, *performed on arrival at the final destination*

A. Beauty magic	Magic
Activity: washing, anointing, and painting Place: the beach, on or near which the party rest before starting on the last stage (on the way to Dobu, Sarubwoyna beach; on the way to Sinaketa, Kaykuyawa) Performers: The spells are uttered usually by the *toliwaga*, sometimes by an elder member of the crew	*Kaykakaya* – ritual washing and rubbing with charmed leaves *Luya* (coco-nut) spell – over the scraped coco-nut used for anointing *Sinata* (comb) spell – over the comb *Sayyaku* – aromatic black paint *Bowa* – ordinary charcoal blacking *Talo* – red paint of crushed arecanut
B. Magic of the final approach	Magic
Activity: The fleet are paddling (on the approach to Dobu) or punting (to Sinaketa) in a body Performers: In each canoe, simultaneously, the *toliwaga* and two members of the crew Aim: to "shake to mountain" to produce an impression on the partners awaiting on the beach	*Ta'uya* – the ritual blowing of the conch shell, which has been charmed over before *Kayikuna-tabuyo* – the swaying of the front prow-board while the spell is being uttered *Kavalikuliku* – the spell by the *toliwaga* *Kaytavilena mwoynawaga* – the incantation uttered at the stern towards the *Koya*
C. Magic of safety	Magic
Activity: entering the Dobuan village (this magic is performed only when Boyowans come to the *Koya*)	*Ka'ubana'i,* charm uttered over ginger, which is then ritually spat over the Dobuan village and the partners, and makes their hearts soft
D. Magic of persuasion	Magic
Activity: the wooing in Kula (*wawoyla*) of the overseas partner by the visitor	*Kwoygapani* – a spell uttered over a piece of arecanut, given subsequently to the partner

A canoe spell, uttered on the departure home

Activity: loading of the canoe with the gifts received from overseas partners, with the trade gain, and with the provisions for the home journey	*Kaylupa* – a spell to make the canoe lighter, to "lift" it out of the water

Source: Malinowski (1922: 415–418). Used by permission of Routledge and Kegan Paul Ltd.

Also: "From the book *Argonauts of the Western Pacific* by Bronislaw Malinowski, Preface by Sir James G. Fraser. Published by E. P. Dutton and Co., Inc. in a paperback edition and used with their permission."

yousa (1922: 53–54; 223). Witches of the female sex are also thought to eat men and a small girl learning to be a witch will demonstrate her crude tastes by eating the raw flesh of pigs or fish (1922: 240). Truly the female is deadlier than the male.

Women and, more especially, wives are invariably held responsible for the death of a man (Malinowski 1932: 137; Fortune 1932: 150). In Trobriand philosophy, there is no concept of "accident" any more than Evans-Pritchard described for the Azande (Evans-Pritchard 1937).

Taboos attempt to control the behavior of women with regard to the Kula, but in the final analysis, it seems to be women who control Kula success, just as they contribute to male success in enhancing or maintaining men's positions within the social system. A wife is directly responsible for the social position of her husband through the wealth she acquires in the form of *urigubu* (tribute) from her brothers (Malinowski 1932: 353). Kula relations differ from everyday commerce with women, however, in that the women are always left out. Indeed the purpose of the first halt on the expedition is to "separate the Kula adventurers from dogs, women and children" (Fortune 1932: 214). The control by women of Kula remains extremely important if indirect; they are supposed to maintain sexual continence during the time their husbands are absent, and failure to observe this taboo makes the canoes slow. Women are often blamed for blighting the expedition when the men return to the homeland (Malinowski 1922: 206). Also, efforts are made to keep women away from the canoes before sailing (the Trobriand sailors are as superstitious about women aboard as are sailors of almost every other land) and no woman is permitted to enter a new canoe before it sails (1922: 229); on an *uvalaku* all the canoes are either new or relashed (1922: 206). Women are JEALOUS of Kula (Fortune 1932: 214).

Besides the taboos, of course, active magic is to be performed to control women and the other dangers to the expedition. Dangers at sea, which as we have seen have female connections, are counteracted by *kaygu'a* or 'magic of mist' (1922: 245). Magic of mist is, curiously enough, acquired from a man's mother (1922: 262–264). Remarkable too, is the fact that while much magic is intended to control female activity, it frequently imitates female functions. Malinowski refers to a number of rites as "rites of impregnation" (1922: 405); a man's sister keeps her magic "in her belly" (1922: 315), and, like magic of mist, rain magic is acquired from female sources (Fortune 1932: 214). Male imitation of the female function is indicated by Malinowski most clearly when he locates magic within the male body: "the force of magic, crystallized in the magical formulae, is carried by men of the present generation IN THEIR BODIES;" specifically, men keep their magic "in their bellies," whence it escapes through the medium of the voice (Malinowski 1922: 409; emphasis added).

The efficacy of male magic or rather sorcery, is tested first against the women closest to a man — his mother and sister (1922: 74) indicating that if he can commit matricide successfully a man should also be successful in bewitching his male peers or rivals on the Kula expedition. Male sorcerers never have to take the responsibility for killing, however; a death is by convention attributed only to the female magical agency. Although the men are aware that some among them possess powers of sorcery, such men may excuse themselves from their deathly activities by attributing killing only to the *werebana*, the dreaded female witches (Fortune 1932: 151).

Magic represents an attempt by man to control the course of events, and the kind of magic practised generally indicates what is considered a desirable outcome, as well as the nature of the principal dangers. The preliminary magical rites of Kula are principally intended: to thrust away evil and superimpose good; to purify the men, who may not eat or relieve themselves during the day for the duration of the sea voyage (Malinowski 1922: 229); "decontaminate" them, and make them fit for their great and exciting mission, the acquisition of the prized valuables. Rites cleanse the canoe, make it sail faster (fly), put down competition, and make each canoe better than all the others. The rivalry of Kula surfaces here — each canoe seeks to lead, each man seeks to excell all others in his canoe. A further rite, not tabulated by Malinowski in his accounting of the magic, is performed over the *lilava* bundle and is important: the *lilava* bundle, a ritual bundle made up of a few trade goods, a plaited armlet, a comb, a lime pot, and a bundle of betel nut, all folded up in several layers of new matting, contains the magical virtue of the *lilava* spell. It is placed in the centre of the canoe, and is not opened until the expedition arrives (Malinowski 1922: 202). *Lilava* magic is supposed to produce rain when the bundle is opened. Rain magic is, like other weather magic, controlled by men although it is derived from a female (1922: 398).

It is possible to interpret Kula rites in the terms offered by Van Gennep. There is a tripartite structure to the rites (rites of separation, rites of transition, and rites of incorporation), representing a passage between two social situations (Van Gennep 1960: 11).

The rites of preparation would include the building of the canoes (from which women are excluded), during which social ties between the builders are expressed and during which the crew of the canoe is effectively chosen (Malinowski 1922: 119). Separation is represented by the symbolic death of the husband-wife relationship, expressed by lack of sexual contact prior to the voyage, and would include also the rite performed by a man's wife, who immediately before sailing goes into the forest to pluck the root of a certain plant, to be laid in a gourd alongside a betel nut and placed in the canoe for consumption by her husband before meeting his Kula partner (Fortune 1932: 224). Transition would include all events both outward and homeward bound, as well as the Kula exchange itself, whilst incorporation would include the final counting of the valuables on the beach (Malinowski 1922: 375), the celebration of the entire community upon the return of the seafarers, and the resumption of normal husband-wife relations.

The status achieved by the men as a result of the voyage represents a state of personal and district honor and respect, expressed in jubilation; but chieftainships do not change hands, the men behave upon their return as they did before they left. The change is one of spirit, and of self-regard, and of wealth. In order to understand this it is necessary to pay some attention to the central myths of Kula, especially the stories of Tokosikuna (1922: 308–309), Kasabwaybwayreta, and Gumakarakedake (1922: 322–324), which are variants of the same tale. From these it becomes clear that in part the purpose of the Kula voyage in the native mind is rejuvenation, as well as prestige.

Malinowski comments:

In both [myths] the heroes start as old, decrepit and very ugly men. By their magical powers, they rejuvenate in the course of the story, the one permanently, the other just sloughing off his skin for the purpose of a Kula transaction. In both cases, the hero is definitely superior in the Kula, and by this arouses the envy and hate of his companions (1922: 326).

Tokosikuna is an old, crippled, ugly man — so ugly that no one will marry him. Through a mixture of cunning and daring he succeeds in gaining possession of the magic flute of Digumenu. The magic which he has acquired on his dangerous mission now makes him young and beautiful, able to cast off his rough, pitted, old skin. The man is now so attractive that all the women want to marry him and do so. Enraged, the other men try to kill him, and send him off to get a giant clam shell, hoping the clam will kill him, but he manages to break open the clam shell instead of losing his own head inside it. The men then send him to catch a shark; again he saves his own life by superhuman strength in strangling the giant fish. Later he tears a boar's mouth asunder, making the others despair of ever being rid of him. Finally his companions try to kill him at sea, and send him out in an unseaworthy canoe, lashed only with soft, brittle pandanus. And here, Malinowski submits, begins the real part of the

Kula myth. The men in the canoes leave their vessels in Gawa and go to the village to Kula. They collect all the smaller armshells, but none of the large important ones. Tokosikuna leaves his canoe to conduct Kula after they have all returned. He receives all the most important necklaces. The same takes place in Iwa and Kitava. They pass through Kitava, Vakuta, Gumasila. Finally, near Gabuka, his canoe lashings fail and he sinks. He calls out to the other canoes to take his valuables. "You married all our women," they answer, "and now the sharks will eat you...." However, Tokosikuna swims away to safety, cursing his companions, and preventing the success of their Kula transaction in Dobu (1922: 308–309).

The overwhelming success of Tokosikuna is attributable to two factors: his control of very powerful magic and his great beauty. These two factors remain critical in the Kula. A man may be ugly, but if he has great magic he will succeed in the quest for valuables. "Kula is a miracle of magic" (Fortune 1932: 215). "Look, I am not good looking, yet so many girls want me. The reason of that is that I have good magic" (Malinowski 1922: 421). In this, Kula resembles sex. The Dobuans go so far as to believe that men and women mate only because men are constantly exerting magical power over women as women are over men (Fortune 1932: 235). What Kula proves above all, above even the political potency of the greatest chief, is that man possesses the "personal beauty" which is the prime requisite for success; and it is magic alone which is responsible for this beauty, just as magic alone accounts for sex (Fortune 1932: 235). Thus Kuva magic is intended to achieve precisely what Tokosikuna achieved; beauty, attractiveness to women, power. He was able to rid himself of his own ugly skin and to rejuvenate — a capacity whose significance only becomes clear when it is understood that Kula valuables continue to allow a man to re-enter the life cycle, by admitting him to Tuma, where the spirit of new life is created (Malinowski 1922: 28). As we shall see, Kula is a bid for immortality of a rather unusual kind.

The story of Tokosikuna is important because it demonstrates that the "mythological" background to Kula continually represents conditions, both sociological and cultural, similar to those obtaining at the time of Malinowski's field work. Myth is seen to take place in a timeless medium or, more simply, to reflect values which still remain influential in the present. Malinowski stresses this fact (Malinowski 1922: 336), but the timelessly present quality of myths still seems to puzzle him since he accepts, at some level, the western notion that somehow myth is just history too old or ill-recorded to be dated. But, as far as everyday-life details are concerned, the myths describe accurately what is still the case. Each man is still fighting to be the Tokosikuna of his area — the most successful with women, the most successful in Kula — and each man seeks magic to that end.

Malinowski also tells us that the myths form the basis for the system of magic (1922: 303) and "if the magic could be recovered, men would again fly in their canoes, they could rejuvenate, defy ogres and perform the many heroic deeds which they did in ancient times" (1922: 303). In other words, men perform magic in order to bring about a repetition of mythical events. Kula is concerned with the control of present events.

The Kula ritual is an attempt to live out the central mythical stories: to assert virility, beauty, and immortality. The landscapes of the voyage are literally legendary places, the settings of action in eternal dramas and recognized as such.

A stone hurled by one of the heroes into the sea after an escaping canoe; a sea passage broken between two rocks by a magical canoe; here two people turned into a rock; there a petrified *waga* [canoe] — all this makes the landscape represent a continuous story or else the culminating dramatic incident of a familiar legend (1922: 298).

The voyaging natives relive the dramas of mythical personages, who continue to be associated with special districts. Mythical heroes are conceived of as "clansmen." Movement between the islands is a theatrical representation in which the bravest, most beautiful men get the best parts.

Perhaps it is participation in this ritual drama itself which is the cause of the Kula voyage. This is what the natives seem to be saying. Yet we have Malinowski's word that no one knows the totality of the drama; no one person knows the entire outline (1922: 83). They know that their own motive, Malinowski continues, is the desire to possess the valuables. Can we go any further than this? Van Gennep's tripartite structure would indicate a passage from symbolic death to rebirth — but whose? and why? Attempting to answer this, let us look at some available explanations of Kula.

Malinowski offers a total functional explanation of Kula. He sees in it the institution which links all other aspects of Trobriand social life. After the maintenance of life itself and the satisfaction of basic needs, the most important index of social success is success in Kula. Accordingly, Malinowski sees Kula primarily as "the ceremonial exchange of the two articles" (1922: 83). However, we also find him expressing the opinion that "voyaging to far-off countries, endowed with natural resources unknown in their own homes, the Kula sailors return each time richly laden with these, the spoils of their enterprise" (1922: 100).

Malinowski is careful to stress that the acquisition of mere trade items is not the most important aspect of the Kula, and also goes to some pains to refute the image current at the time of his writing of "Primitive Economic Man":

He [the Trobriander] works prompted by motives of a highly complex, social and traditional nature, and toward aims which are certainly not directed towards the satisfaction of present wants, or to the direct achievement of utilitarian purposes (1922: 60).

The ceremonial exchange IS carried on side by side with ordinary barter and trade, and the voyage takes men to places where goods are available which are not obtainable on their own island (1922: 83), but gaining goods through trade is merely a by-product of the Kula expedition. Kula "is carried out for its own sake, in fulfilment of a deep desire to possess" (1922: 510), and represents "an exchange of an entirely novel type" (1922: 511), half-ceremonial and half-commercial.

Malinowski takes this occasion to draw direct attention to the functional interaction between "the influence on one another of the various aspects of an institution, the study of the social and PSYCHOLOGICAL mechanism on which the institution is based" (1922: 517; emphasis added). I should like to draw attention to the reference to the psychological mechanism made by Malinowski here. Malinowski has for so long been the father of functionalism in a sociological sense that it is often forgotten that he ever mentioned psychology. However, only because he provides information about Trobriand psychology is it possible to attempt an analysis of the present kind. Malinowski stands alone among ethnographers in providing information, not merely about social institutions, but about attitudes towards them and feelings generated by their existence.

The thrust of Malinowski's criticism of contemporary views of primitive economic man runs hard against the "conception of the primitive as a rational being, who wants nothing but to satisfy his simplest needs, and does it according to the economic principle of least effort" (1922: 516). Despite his functional approach, Malinowski is the last to confuse social values with practicality, or the economic with the utilitarian. He recognizes the practical aspects of Kula, but refuses to interpret them outside the native philosophy, which subordinates means to ends:

I do not, by subordinating the two things [canoe building and trade] in importance to the Kula, mean to express a philosophical reflection or a personal opinion as to the relative value of these pursuits from the point of view of some social teleology. ...

By ranging the Kula as the primary and chief activity, and the rest as secondary ones, I mean that this precedence is implied in the institutions themselves (1922: 100–101).

I would like to point out, in addition, that despite the great detail in which Malinowski reports on Kula, while demonstrating quite convincingly that it is a total social institution, he fails to account for its necessity. The natives carry out Kula — but why? Why should Kula, with all the attendant tasks and difficulties, be such a COMPELLING activity?

Marcell Mauss attempts to explain Kula as an instance of prestation, as an exaggerated case in a general system of social exchange, which serves to take "the whole tribe out of the narrow circle of its own frontiers" and which, in addition, forces contact between different villages and settlements within the tribes (Mauss 1967: 26). This opinion is impeccable, and offers us the further insight that since Kula is an instance of prestation, the objects exchanged are primarily symbols of a relationship rather than goods of an economic nature (1967: 71). Mauss sees the interrelation of the mystical and practical (trade?) aspects of Kula as an example of the forces which bind clans together and keep them separate, which divide their labor and constrain them to exchange (1967: 71). In other words Kula is the essence of society and its motto might be, "exchange or die."

The constraining nature of the gift, the demand each gift makes that it be returned, expresses for Mauss the most primitive mechanism of social intercourse. As a matter of fact, the Kula objects, with their histories and connections with individuals, are perfect examples of Mauss' "pledge," which is "imbued with the personality of the partner who gave it" (1967: 61). And it is certainly clear that part of the function of Kula is to foster precisely this feeling in the native mind. But still the nagging question remains, since the islands of the Kula ring do not have to depend on each other's resources for subsistence as a necessity, why should they be linked at all?

Uberoi, in *The politics of the Kula ring*, like Malinowski himself, stresses the importance of Kula as a social mechanism of give and take (Uberoi 1962), facilitating "interrelations of interest." He argues that the alliances abroad are vital, whilst Malinowski emphasizes that they are not necessary to the maintenance of life itself. For Uberoi, the Kula symbolizes the reciprocity which sustains a society at home as well as that which sustains its vital alliances abroad. Kula is a POLITICAL necessity.

Kula is a political necessity because

it provides socially sanctioned occasions for the assertion of individual self-interest; and it provides the idiom in terms of which the corporate units of Trobriand society can work out their political relations. ... It makes the constituent units of each society, and even members of each unitary group compete with one another for prizes held by their *kula* partners on a neighbouring island. In this way the inevitable dissensions within a group, and rivalries between groups, are turned outwards, and serve to keep alive and active the overseas alliances which link together the separate islands to form the Kula Ring (Uberoi 1962: 97–98).

Uberoi recognizes here the displacement of hostility which the Kula voyage represents. Intervillage hostility is chronic in the islands of the Kula ring (1962: 209) and there are in addition many sources of conflict experienced by the individual male within his own village, not to mention among his kinsmen. All of the males in a single village are of the same lineage (1962: 85) and this local lineage constitutes the watershed of vengeance-seeking groups: within it blood money is not paid, and in cases of provocation to the point of acute anger between members, there exists only recourse to individual direct action: every man for himself. Such vengeance may go as far as fratricide, for which the only appropriate punishment is suicide (1962: 75). Malinowski indicates that strong hatreds and consequently, acts of violence, exist between brothers both in legend and in everyday life, even if sometimes fraternal relations may also be warm (1962: 75). Uberoi argues that since violence is not sanctioned within the lineage group and since intervillage warring is dysfunctional, hostility is, as a result, transformed into the symbolic competition of Kula, less harmful to all concerned.

Uberoi also argues that foreign alliances are essential to the maintenance of the political structure within the islands. Chiefs retain their importance and renown only by participation in the Kula exchange.

Kula relations... provide an external point of reference for the definition of relative ranks within one district, and also between the different districts. On this view, it would be expected that the 'top people' of each *kula*-making district would claim the same rank, regardless of inequalities in the comparative power; and that of two villages or districts of otherwise comparable standing, the higher rank would belong to the one which was more proficient in the *kula*, and had the more advantageous external affiliations (1962: 124).

The symbolic exchange of valuables appears to contribute to status and wealth more importantly than trading does. Production of food surplus and domestic utensils support the Kula only indirectly. The ceremonial exchange provides the cover for exchange of utilities, even though essentials such as stone, clay, rattan, bamboo, and sago are among the items traded (1962: 149, quoting Malinowski 1935: 8). Western conceptions of the acquisitive, materialistic nature of mankind will not serve to explain Kula by dubbing it utilitarian: it is not the marketplace which occasions Kula exchange, but Kula which "establishes the peace of the marketplace" (1962: 140).

Each of the available accounts of Kula adds to our understanding: Malinowski's because he throws into high relief the all-pervasive character of Kula; Mauss because he gives perspective on the social obligation which underlies the institution and relates it to exchanges of a comparable kind in other parts of the world; Uberoi because he suggests multiple motives for participation in the voyage by the individual, and stresses functional aspects of the exchange in terms of the political system, and also because he alone recognizes the component of displacement which characterizes Kula ritual: quarrels at home become rivalries abroad (1962: 108). Taken together these explanations give a considerable depth of understanding of behavior surrounding Kula; yet the reason for the voyage has not become clear. Presumably, on Uberoi's view, the voyage is necessary because it is the actual mechanism by which hostility is externalized; but hostility could be externalized without such elaborate exchange, as indeed it is among many African tribes, including the Nuer (Evans-Pritchard 1940). In the past, war has indeed occurred with some regularity in the islands (Seligman 1910: 663); but what remains is veiled, ritualized hostility, not open aggression. The ritual voyage is still unexplained.

What, then, is the great value of maintaining a special relationship with a fictive clansman of sorts, at such personal cost? And why should a tribe require to be taken out of its own narrow circle? Can we assume that wanderlust constitutes an undeniable urge? or may we find a more satisfactory solution through seeking what Mauss calls "la vertu qui force les dons à circuler"; that is to say, the life force of the objects? The question was clearly in Malinowski's own mind. He describes "the net result" of Kula as "the acquisition of a few dirty, greasy, and insignificant native trinkets, each of them a string of flat, partly discoloured, partly raspberry-pink or brick-red discs, threaded one behind the other into a long, cylindrical roll" (Malinowski 1922: 351).

I believe the reason why the ritual is carried out is expressed in the ritual itself. It is in the CARRYING OUT itself that the importance of the Kula lies. Kula is not so much an expression of what does not happen in Trobriand life, as an expression of what does happen, but which people cannot feel. It is to be interpreted literally. Its meaning is what it does.

Men cannot live with the idea that they are ugly, that, unpleasant, harsh though it may, the life they have is all they have. Nor can they accept the "uselessness" of the male as opposed to the productive nature of the female. Yet each of these feelings is part of everyday life for the Trobriander. You do not perform beauty magic if you regard yourself as beautiful; you do not seek rejuvenation if you feel yourself young, nor a return to childhood if you have fully experienced the joys of infancy; you do not need to assert virility if you are fully in touch with the needs and functions of your body. In Kula ritual, each of these themes receives expression. Magic spells assert that men need beauty to participate successfully in the social system; at the same time they reveal how ugly the practitioners feel themselves to be. Individuals suppress this lack of self-esteem in everyday life — we have assurance that they even compensate, in addition, and instead of behaving modestly, act bombastically (Seligman 1910: 38–39); they also suppress or, rather, repress recognition of the male procreative role, as well as realization that life is "nasty, brutish and short." Kula ritual permits the expression of all of these feelings in symbolic form — which is by definition a form which renders them inaccessible to consciousness, and thus prevents them from imposing a tragic burden of grief and pain on the individual.

Ugliness and death are perhaps difficult enough to bear but it seems, from Kula symbolism, that denial of paternity is at least as hard to bear, more particularly because participation in the procreative act is socially enjoined, even while its significance is denied. Biological necessity demands that a father take part in the creation of a child; the total organism cannot withstand denial of this fact, and so it is expressed, recognized, obliquely and unconsciously, in ritual form. The implication here is that it is impossible to deny biological events, events whose performance is coded into body behaviour, a point which will be taken up below.

Ritual provides the opportunity to act out feelings which are too devastating in their impact for the organism to bear. What is acted out need not be felt. Yet, what is acted out are the feelings which cannot be borne. Any situation which gives rise to excruciating pain, particularly after infancy and early childhood, runs the risk of being symbolized rather than felt and of preventing the child from realizing the truth of the pain he is feeling: pain of hunger, of loneliness, of thrashing, and so on. Symbolization is an adaptive human mechanism, preventing destruction of the organism through overload. The apotheosis of the ability to shut off pain is exemplified by mystics who walk through fire or sleep on beds of nails, but these are merely more exotic instances of an ability common to all mankind.

Fear, for example, is a reaction which in large enough doses will prove maladaptive for the individual. Lévi-Strauss describes death as a result of fear of sorcery, remarking that "physical integrity cannot withstand the dissolution of the social personality" (Lévi-Strauss 1963: 168) and Malinowski confirms that in his experience in the Trobriands, such deaths do indeed come to pass (Malinowski 1932: 305, Note). Ritual serves to give expression to emotions which would have serious, possibly fatal, consequences were they experienced directly. In other words, ritual is an example of DISPLACEMENT in the psychological sense; it is not so much a "wish fulfillment" resembling dreams in the Freudian interpretation, as an index of feeling actually occurring but repressed or feeling not permitted to reach the conscious level. Thus the ritual itself releases the tension of the repressed feeling, to the extent that it is bearable at least. The action of ritual is cathartic, temporarily at least, since it is in the nature of ritual to require repetition at intervals. Displacement, through the voyage, becomes literal rather than metaphoric.

The hypothesis offered here is directly opposed to the explanation of death by magic according to Lévi-Strauss. Lévi-Strauss claims that we must see magical behavior as the response to a situation which is revealed to the mind through emotional manifestations, but whose essence is intellectual (Lévi-Strauss 1963: 168). I hope to show that magic is rational in its expression but emotional in its origin.

The displacement of the Kula voyage is not just an arbitrary symbol but the precisely correct symbol for the feeling analogs involved. The degree of displacement of the voyage is proportional to the degree of displacement of feeling. The symbols precisely express and exteriorize feelings which cannot be admitted to consciousness. Accordingly, we would not expect the natives to be able to articulate the reasons for their actions in Kula. According to Malinowski the natives do NOT know what they are doing, yet their actions speak as loudly as any words would, and these are the ultimate authority in the understanding of Kula.

Understanding of Kula can only proceed through connecting the ritual actions with the repressed feelings of everyday life in the Trobriands. Let us see how this hypothesis works out. What do the actions of Kula ritual tell us? They say that Trobriand men spend much time and energy constructing canoes and take pains with their seamanship. They leave their homelands, breaking off day-to-day contacts, especially contact with their wives; sail off over dangerous shark-infested waters, subject to the vagaries of tropical storms and terrorized by witches and the depths, to distant islands of their archipelago; then make themselves as attractive as they know how, with facepaint and magic; woo their Kula partners, whom they characterize as "clansmen" or potential enemies, even though as partners they are pledged to do them no harm; and cajole them into parting with objects of specifically male or female sex, possession of which will bring each possessor a part in an on-going history of the circulation of that object, by association with a special name. In each exchange, one man takes the role of male, the other that of female, but the same men will reverse roles with other partners. And the exchange will produce temporary association with a named object — the only infant that the Trobriand father will ever be able to procreate, according to native philosophy. This child results from the "marriage" of Kula objects. The Kula voyage is a bringing of fertilizing rain in the *lilava*, by the eagerly anticipated guest.

The objects exchanged, indissoluble as they are from the individuals exchanging them, begin to make sense. They are "children" of either male or female sex "begat" by men, in a society which theoretically does not recognize the role of the male in procreation. The Kula ACTS OUT the biological male role in a situation in which it is openly denied; this explains the importance of the names of the objects and their attachment to individuals. The names are the means by which a man and an object are linked, a connection with his "offspring." They are the male history, a means of being recognized after a man is dead, or of carving out a place in time, parallelling the matrilineal system of inheritance of Trobriand society.

Understanding the Kula valuables to be offspring helps to connect a number of events which are otherwise beyond our grasp; Kula valuables are the essential part of bride price, on the eye for an eye reckoning you have to give a child to get one, and you do not marry, in this social context, to legitimize sex but to legitimize children. The symbolically procreative nature of Kula also accounts for the waiting time between gifts. Gestation takes time. The different kinds of gift mark different stages of the sexual relations. Kula is confined to sexually potent males, young and old men do not participate. Fortune describes another incident in which this reading of the Kula symbolism is helpful: a widow is, by reason of distance, unable to pay *kunututu*, the customary armshell, to her husband's gravediggers, "SO INSTEAD OF THE ARMSHELL the widow parted with her FEMALE CHILD who went with her dead father's sister to her far away place there to stay until she bore a child to replace her father" (Fortune 1932: 194; emphasis added).

The small number of named valuables gains in significance. The Kula ritual mimics sexual encounter, but every sexual encounter will not culminate in pregnancy, hence every man cannot be successful in each attempt. This has the effect of enhancing masculine competition and strengthening the use of magic; it lends potency to the successful.

Finally the hostility of the Kula exchange denotes in Trobrianders aggression towards women, whilst in Dobuans it denotes hostility to the child. Trobrianders seek infants, Dobuans detest them but find them necessary. Differences in Trobriand and Dobuan Kula will be taken up later.

Interpretation of Kula events as expression of what actually happens also sheds light on several other aspects of the exchange; in Dobu Kula partnerships break up with the same regularity as do marriages (Malinowski 1932: 214). In magic the result is verbally anticipated and does not act as an appeal (Malinowski 1922: 451); it is actually pure DESCRIPTION.

Kula objects themselves are gifted with procreative power. They are important in the life cycle. They will gain entry to Paradise for their possessor, and Paradise, the island of Tuma, is where babies come from. The necessity of carrying valuables to enter Tuma connects men directly with the procreation of children. The *vaygu'a* of a community are displayed to the spirits annually so that they will be pleased (Malinowski 1922: 512). As a result the dead of the spirit world will impregnate women "*per vaginam*" as Malinowski says (Malinowski 1932: 150). The biological necessity of the father is accounted for by this indirect mechanism.

Kula objects will gain entry to a beautiful place for a man. Paradise is where there is a perpetual scented bacchanal of dancing and chanting on spacious village places or on beaches of soft sand. Above all, women there are attractive and tractable, for it is freedom of sex that is to be found in this ideal land (1932: 361–362). Sex is "... set about with its appropriate trappings of personal vanity, display, luxury, good food, and beautiful surroundings" (1932: 361–362). Thus Kula is not only the exchange between men of named male or female objects: the possession of these objects is what will enable a man to rejuvenate himself after death like the old legendary heroes. He will, if admitted to Tuma, be the source of life for a new baby; he will become young again. Thus the idea of continuity of life through the male receives expression in Kula. The Kula "ring" is completed, a "ring" which represents a life cycle. But this procreative exchange is just the beginning of an understanding. What follows is a connecting up of the events of the Kula voyage and some beliefs about it with the social expression of "what is."

The first theme that comes to mind is the fear of women expressed in the "dangers" of the voyage. Malinowski is at pains to emphasize that Trobrianders have an easy and relaxed attitude to sexuality. How is it then that women are feared so greatly? Fear of women is expressed in the symbols of the voyage, precisely because it cannot be felt at home; men must act out their fears if they may not be felt directly.

Trobriand men perform the sex act keenly, and would be incapacitated by feeling directly the fear of women which they experience as fear of dangers of the ocean and witches. That the greatest fear experienced by the sailors is a displaced fear is evidenced by the fact that the greatest fear, of shipwreck, has not materialized within living memory (Seligman 1910: 537). Further, the times of sailing, November-December and March-April ensure that the danger of shipwreck is minimized, since winds "come from definite directions" (Malinowski 1922: 225).

Aggression and hostility seem to form the basis of the sexual relationship despite the apparent sexual freedom — a freedom which Malinowski stresses over and over — in reality women are symbolized as dangerous and to be feared. Women are also symbolized as essential even to the success of Kula, since they have the power to make it unsuccessful. Kula is not expressing the need to avoid women, but the need to "detoxify" them as sources of hostility and fear.

Women are directly experienced as agents of sexual aggression. Sexual contact is poeticized by the Trobriander into metaphors of biting and scratching, "drinking my blood," and "pulling my hair" (1922: 280). Erotic contact is in reality initiated through scratching. Further, "In the rough stage of passion the woman is the more active, ONLY WOMEN MAY ACTUALLY LACERATE THEIR LOVERS" (1922: 281; emphasis added). A man may derive social prestige from "having good magic," i.e. being a good lover, but the scars on his back indicate the price he has paid for his reputation. It is the object of erotic scratching to HURT and draw blood (1922: 280; emphasis added).

A close reading of Malinowski tends to refute his constantly reiterated characterization of the Trobriands as a paradise of love-making. The act of love is accomplished with a "minimum amount of body contact" (1922: 280) and its free expression is limited. Sex like excretory functions and nudity is not felt or regarded as "natural," but rather as naturally to be avoided in public and open conversation and always to be concealed from others in behavior (1922: 335). Children, it is true, are exposed to their parents' sexual activities from the beginning and only told to "cover their head with a mat" — an act of exclusion which bears the seed of trauma, but even their activities, on which Malinowski expatiates at length, are activities of the "bush" (1922: 48). In adolescence also, sex in the bachelor's house should be "as unobtrusive as possible" (1922: 63).

Several festivals and rituals seem to allow women more freedom in expression of aggression than is allowed to men. In theory, the *yausa* is the occasion of male abuse and rape (1922: 231–236). In previous times youths could conduct *ulatile* or love-making expeditions to villages other than their own. Again such expeditions were customary, but secret, involving possible retribution by the ordinary sweethearts of the *ulatile* group or the youths of the other village. The girls were permitted to strike blows to express their aggression (1922: 224) and were in addition allowed to make similar sorties after sexual prey on their own account.

Actual events are again reflected in myth:

Here [myth of source of love magic] as in most mythological and legendary incidents, the man remains passive and the woman is the aggressor. We find analogies to this in the stories about *Kaytalugi* and in the behaviour of the women during the *Yausa*, and in the reception given by the female spirits to newcomers in the next world (1922: 460).

Malinowski wryly remarks that it was Eve who gave the apple to Adam, and Isolde who held out her drink to Tristan.

The Kula exchange acts out all the mixed feelings a man has toward sex, since Kula is sexual in nature. This is why the objects are exchanged with indifference, anger, nonchalance, and disdain (1922: 6). These feelings are responses to aggressive behavior. It should be borne in mind that although the seekers in Kula treat their partners as women, the partners are still men, a point which seems to favor the "hostility" to women.

What in reality a man seeks from a woman, he seeks in Kula from a man. And what the man seeks from the woman is, in this case, offspring and acceptance of his role in impregnation. Consequently, the symbolism of the wind, whose great good graces are invoked upon the voyage, becomes clear: Yarata, the northwest wind is a PREGNANT WOMAN, who gives birth to a daughter (Fortune 1932: 212–213). The homosexual element is played down by Malinowski (Malinowski 1922: 338), but nonetheless is readily recognizable.

Aggression by the female in the sex act is only a small part of the hostility which a Trobriand man experiences. The aggression of the Kula act symbolizes male-male hostility which has some but, as we have seen, inadequate direct expression in social life. The position of the Trobriand man, whatever his rank, is one in which he experiences conflict of many different kinds. The systems of descent and inheritance are sources of repeated conflict. Father love runs up against mother right.

Malinowski deals in some detail with the nature of mother right. Basically, "we find in the Trobriands a matrilineal society in which descent, kinship, and every social relationship are legally reckoned through the mother only" (Malinowski 1932: 2). Thus,

Social position is handed on in the mother-line from a man to his sister's children, and this exclusively matrilineal conception of kinship is of paramount importance in the restrictions and regulations of marriage, and in the taboos on sexual intercourse. The working of these ideas of kinship can be observed, breaking out with a dramatic intensity, at death. For the social rules underlying burial, lamentation, and mourning, together with certain very elaborate ceremonies of food distribution, are based on the principle that people joined by the tie of maternal kinship form a closely knit group, bound by an identity of feelings, of interests, and of flesh. And from this group, even those united to it by marriage and by the father-to-child relation are sharply excluded, as having no natural share in the bereavement (1932: 4).

Kula valuables permit a certain attenuation of the mother-right principle and constitute personal property for a man in a very important way: they are the only property which a man can give to his offspring. Canoes and land are inalienable for the father's lineage, cannot be given to his son who is, by definition, of a different clan. Only a man's Kula valuables are his to dispose of as the wishes (Uberoi 1962: 102). Thus Kula objects represent a direct link between a man and his son, where little or no other recognition of the biological nature of the father-son relationship is permitted. It should be noted that a man's sister's sons, who also have claim to his property, including land and canoes, since they are of his clan, do not willingly watch the valuables slip from their grasp. However valuables disappear only for the duration of the father's lifespan; upon his death they must be returned to the estate by the son, at least in part, so that they can be redistributed to affinal relatives (1962: 102, Note 2 quoting Malinowski 1932: 177). At this time the system reaffirms what it has maintained all along: a man's real heirs are his sister's sons; they are his blood and navel-string kin.

According to Uberoi the gift by father to son is to be interpreted only politically, hence a man will give his valuables not to his own favorite son, but to sons born to "politically important rather than arbitrarily favourite mothers" (1962: 105). The gesture has no personal affective significance at all and serves only as an act of structural import: "every 'man of rank, wealth, and power' owes his position to his in-laws: the 'promptings of paternal love' are simply irrelevant" (1962: 106). This "political" interpretation of the father-son relationship negates the existence of conflicting feeling aroused by the mother right and father love. Yet Malinowski's repeated emphasis on the emotional problem resulting from the conflict cannot be so easily dismissed, even though the objection may have some substance; Uberoi may account for why a particular son is favored over another, what he does not account for is the effort on the part of the father to give to the son at all, when he could be contributing directly to his politically more important sister's sons.

A man finds himself in a difficult position: he feels great affection for his children by his wife, to whom he is not related; but he is legally responsible for his sister's children. On the one hand, he is denied legal power over the children whom he loves and on the other he can scarcely love the children of his sister, in early infancy at least, for the rule of residence (virilocal) ensures that he will rarely see them. Hence, in the concrete example which Malinowski reports, "the chief is always much more attached to his children than to his maternal kinsmen" (Malinowski 1932: 10).

The question of exercise of authority by both husband and wife's brother is even more vexed, however. In practice, a man loves his own (actually biological) children, with whom he lives in their early years, and is legally responsible for his sister's offspring, but in fact the WOMAN in each household exercises a counterbalancing power. "The man is considered to be the master, for he is in his own village, the house belongs to him, but the woman has, in other respects, a considerable influence: she and her family have a great deal to do with the food supply of the household; she is the owner of separate possessions in the house; and she is — next to her brother — the legal head of the family." The wife "does her work independently" and "will order the husband about if she needs his help" (1932: 15).

The male position is thus always difficult. It may be more clear-cut in the matter of distribution of goods and food production than it is in any psychological sense, but, even here, it has its problems. A father will always favor his own over his sister's children, and will demand tribute from the latter, despite the law.

Like every typical Trobriand father [the chief] takes, sentimentally, at least, their [his children's] side in any dispute; and he invariably tries to grant them as many privileges and benefits as possible. This state of affairs is naturally not altogether appreciated by the chief's legal successors, his maternal kinsmen, the children of his sister (1932: 10).

The ambivalence of play between respect and affection expressed here is one source of male-male interactional difficulty and competition. Not only is the chief referred to here at odds with his lawful blood relations, but his son and his maternal nephew, who are both in pursuit of his material possessions, one by law, the other by sentiment, are predestined enemies (1932: 13). Thus the split between law and sentiment effected by the residence rules and rules of inheritance sets up the fundamentally competitive relationship among men.

Competition is expressed in many areas of Trobriand life besides the Kula. Even gardening involves competition (Malinowski 1922: 60–61). But the special nature of the problem, set up by the opposition of structure and sentiment in the rules of descent and inheritance, sets up a conflict within the individual which cannot be legally sanctioned by society and which implies constant tension and decision making for the Trobriand man, since each man is likely to be both a husband and a brother. BY LAW, from a man's point of view, it is your wife's brother to whom your children belong. Your children will not inherit your possessions, but his. Kula permits open expression of the competition, aggression, and especially jealousy, which are forbidden, but felt nevertheless, in the normal run of things.

We have seen that Kula is an opportunity to act out the feelings which cannot be directly experienced: fear, anger, jealousy. These are all negative feelings, whilst the overall thrust of Kula is positive. The home-coming of the Kula voyagers is accompanied by great celebration and joy. The reason for this is that Kula is multi-functional; it is a male-male transaction, but its benefits are felt by the whole community. Why? Because procreation is a community interest *par excellence*.

So far, the hypothesis that Kula enables men to act out the procreative role which is sociologically denied them and to act out the fears directly related to their sexual and social situations seems to hold good.

The Kula exchange is not merely a sexual exchange, a "marriage"; it is as powerful as an incestuous sexual exchange — "the lure of forbidden fruit ... has forever associated love and the magic of love with the myth of incest" (1922: 332). Indeed Kula magic and love magic are closely related, a connection which makes sense in view of the fact that the Kula partner, like a spouse, must be wooed. Interestingly, the productive magic of Kula is not the only magic associated with a man's close female relatives — black magic is connected with both mother and sister, and its efficacy must first be tested upon these two figures before a man may be certain of his success in the sorcerer's art (Malinowski 1922: 74). Antagonism to the mother and the sister are thus revealed and can be further connected with specific aspects of the Kula proceedings.

A man's sister occupies an ambivalent position in his feelings, and in the case of Kula magic it is she who is the object of his affections. Love magic is a magic originating in sister incest. The story of the origin of love magic establishes a valid precedent for the efficiency of love magic. It proves the spells and rites of *Iwa* and of *Kumilbwaga* are so powerful that they can even break down the terrible barriers which separate brother and sister and persuade them to commit incest (Malinowski 1932: 459).

All magic overcomes dangers, if it is successful. But Kula magic, akin to love magic, not only overcomes and wards off dangers of the ocean associated with the female sex, it persuades the female in the relationship to yield up her valuables — literally. Successful magic overcomes female slyness, persuades the female to give her treasures to you, not to someone else, although treachery may be involved if the magic is not successful, and you may be promised a necklace or arm-shell which you will never receive. The exchange is not carried out with "females in general" such as are involved in the ocean hazards, but with a "woman" in particular, who will be the "acting" mother of your valuables, hence the reference to "mother" in the spells of *Kaykakaya* and *Ka' ubana'i* (1932: 337, 347–348). Now, Malinowski finds the natives extremely unwilling to discuss the sister, but he reports that dreams of the sister, though talked about only with extreme reticence, are very frequent (1932: 332). This dream is indeed one of the few which disturbs the native mind to a significant extent, and is a source of anxiety. "A man is sometimes sad, ashamed and ill-tempered. Why? Because he has dreamed that he had connection with his sister. ... Such dreams are a well known nuisance" (1932: 332). The anxiety is aroused by the figure of the sister reflected in the great use of magic, but more importantly, it must be remembered that a man is biologically related to his sister's children and not to his wife's. He is related to his sister's children "by the navelstring" — that is, by true kinship. True kinship is expressed by this phrase habitually, but the phrase is more cryptic than it appears (1932: 276).

The significance of Kula magic seems to suggest that the sister is the symbolic personage with whom Kula is carried out. Given that Kula valuables engender new life, the logic of the symbolism would seem to suggest that the spirits of the dead enter not the man's wife's (children's) children, but his sister's (children's) children, merely by the logic of the matrilineal principle.

Men do not care to acknowledge matriliny however. A man attempts to favor his own children as much as possible; he does not like passing on his goods to his sister's offspring. The Kula actions, carried on as they are with dislike, coldness, anger, and disdain, give opportunity to express feelings regarding this state of affairs. I submit that although the sister is the desired woman, she creates nothing but difficulties as a mate for her brother, and that Kula ritual is expressing the conflict a man feels between desiring her and hating her. Of course neither of these feelings is permitted expression in everyday life. The relationship with the sister is characterized by strict neutrality and no emotional reaction. The sister of a man bends down when he approaches, if she is adult, and during adolescence a boy is conscious that he is her guardian.

Brother and sister thus grow up in a strange sort of domestic proximity: in close contact, and yet without any personal or intimate communication; near to each other in space, near by rules of kinship and common interest; and yet, as regards personality, always hidden and mysterious. They must not even look at each other and they must never exchange any light remarks, never share their feelings and ideas (Malinowski 1932: 440).

"Rigidity of behaviour and a sobriety in conversation" (1932: 439) are all they share together. Yet the supreme taboo is the sister incest taboo (1932:

437) and "the sister remains for her brother the centre of all that is sexually forbidden — its very symbol" (1932: 440).

In the life history of a man, his sister plays a decisive part. Her presence is responsible for the little boy's removal from the parental home. Because he has a sister, and because intimacy with her is taboo, the little boy is taken away from his natal shelter, as soon as the "incest taboo" takes effect. The exact age when this takes place is not given, but a drastic change in social relations accompanies it.

The child, accustomed to little or no interference with most of its whims or wishes, receives a real shock when suddenly it is roughly handled, seriously reprimanded and punished whenever it makes any friendly, affectionate, or even playful advances to the other small being [a sister, to whom the term *luguta*, indicating sexual prohibition, refers] constantly about in the household. Above all the child experiences an emotional shock when it becomes aware of the expression of horror and anguish on the faces of its elders when they correct it (1932: 438).

Malinowski suggests that prior to separation, and "the incest taboo," the children are largely indulged. As a result, a little boy's sister is both his first affectionate companion as well as the means of separating him from his parents. When she grows up, her children are the legal charge of her brother, but he neither knows these children early, nor does he care about them. On the contrary, he feels they extract from him that which rightfully belongs to his wife's children. Small wonder that feelings toward the sister are violently desirous and angry at the same time.

The sober relations of everyday intercourse between brother and sister are controlled by role behaviour, by a code which does not permit expression of the confused emotions which are actually felt. Role behavior by definition limits the responses of the individual and prevents him from acting spontaneously, that is to say, according to how he feels. Feelings however are organic and cannot be rationalized out of existence indefinitely, particularly when they are so powerful. Kula allows a man to treat another man as though he were his sister, towards whom he feels both desire and anger, but Kula permits this in a context in which the man does not become fully conscious of his conflict as a permanent reaction. Kula releases tension.

"Sister" symbolism in Kula by no means exhausts the "meaning" of the symbolic acting out, although it accounts, I think, for the reluctance of the Trobriander to admit to biological paternity. Fortune tells us of an experiment he carried out, discussing with the Trobrianders the possibility of procreation involving the biological father: "My Dobuan friends warned me not to mention the matter in the Trobriands before I went there. Once I was there I deliberately made the experiment. The Trobrianders asserted the spiritual belief, just as Dr. Malinowski has published it" (Fortune 1932: 239).

Fortune's evidence not only supports Malinowski's, but provides us with conclusive proof that the Trobrianders do not consider a man and his son to be of the same bodily substance for reasons of a psychological kind, and not because of ignorance of paternity. The so-called ignorance is actually a block to the conscious realization that a man may not be the father of his sister's children — even though the collective representations decree that he shall be considered related to them through blood, or the navel-string, whilst he is related to his own offspring only by propinquity. The Trobrianders do not WANT to recognize paternity. In Kula they are expressing a conflict which is the inevitable result of the belief system: social custom accepts that a man IS indeed closely related to his sister's offspring, but denies him sexual access to his sister; in contrast, a man has biological access to his wife, but denies that he is father to her children.

Fortune claims that the Dobuans are well aware of the existence of physiological paternity. If we examine their beliefs closely it turns out that while they deny the spiritual explanation of pregnancy given by the Trobrianders, they themselves only see man as the vehicle through which procreative juices flow and not as creator of these substances. Semen is thought to be coco-nut milk which has passed through the body of the male (1932: 239); it is not a "natural" body substance however, just as sex is not a "natural" act.

Dobuans recognize that pregnancy does not necessarily follow from intercourse. "The spells used to create pregnancy are the one isolated instance of magic directed towards an effect which it is recognized may occur also naturally" (1932: 241). Intercourse may need a little magical aid to result in pregnancy. It may be possible to quibble a little with the theory that Dobuans consider paternity and pregnancy NATURAL, but their beliefs on the subject are less displaced than those of the Trobrianders.

Differences in social conditions account for why Dobuans do not experience the need to deny paternity. Fortune also comments upon this: "it will be clear that the Trobriand theory might have arisen with facility from a state of society such as exists in Dobu, particularly if rank were introduced in Dobu to make a legal conflict between *susu* and marital grouping more spectacular and its decision more widely known and accepted" (1932: 241). Fortune connects the political distinctions between Dobu and the Trobriands with theories of pregnancy here, but he does not offer any elaboration. Dobuan social organization is acephalous and the system of aristocracy among the Trobrianders is atypical of Melanesia (Uberoi 1962: 124). It should be observed that the existence of rank has little bearing on the actual Kula ritual. From the penultimate halt where the beautifying spells are uttered, the rites are strictly INDIVIDUAL (Fortune 1932: 228); Kula is tied in with rank in the Trobriands, where it is harnessed to the political organization, but even there the indications are that it retains an importance for the individual rather than for the clan. Differences in hierarchy distinguish Dobuan and Trobriand systems, but there are similar forms of social organization and as a result there is an overlap in the regulations of sexual activity and marriage.

Dobuan society sets up the same structural opposition between the brother-sister constellation, the *susu*, and the husband-wife constellation as does Trobriand society, but there are behavioral differences, including specifically much less stringent regulation of brother-sister relations: "it will be clear from the Dobuan situation how a brother-sister *tabu* would strengthen the family by marriage. There is no hint of any such *tabu*, however, in Dobu, except that young unmarried men do not sleep in the same house with their young unmarried sisters. ... It is not a brother-sister *tabu*, for a youth with no sister is excluded from his parents house..." (1932: 10).

Given that the rule of alternate residence in Dobu divides influence much more equally between the kin of husband and wife (1932: 9) and that socialization practices differ, the brother-sister relations need not carry the same total burden in Dobu as they do in the Trobriands, although the differences might on the whole be of degree rather than of kind. Fortune remarks that Kula in Dobu is substantially different from the same institution in the Trobriands, a difference indicated by differences in ritual (1932: 209). Although previously treated as interchangeable, Dobuan and Trobriand Kulas are not to be explained identically though displacement through ritual is common to both. A closer examination of social institutions in Dobu would have to precede a precise appraisal of the need for displacement.

Some similarities between Dobuan and Trobriand beliefs do deserve notice. We have seen that Fortune claims Dobuans do not deny paternity — whether they go as far as recognizing the natural biological function of relations between the sexes seems dubious however. Whilst Dobuans do not deny altogether the natural relation of father to son, they do seem to have trouble with the natural quality of relations between the sexes, and this they share with their Trobriand neighbours. Sex for both is a highly unnatural act, in which the body is by no means an unconstrained agent. In Dobu, sex is attributed ENTIRELY to magical motivations: there would be no attraction between the sexes but for the operation of magic (1932: 235), a view of sex shared in the Trobriands, though perhaps not in such an extreme form. A Trobriand boy will, it appears, perform love magic only after he has failed to arouse any response from his beloved without it (Malinowski 1932: 307). In the grossest terms, if the Trobrianders deny paternity as a natural function, the Dobuans deny sexual drive. Yet each society surrounds success in the sexual sphere with acute competition and much fear, along with social injunctions to perform frequently.

Fortune characterizes the Dobuan attitude toward sex as similar "in essentials" to "that which in the present day and generation is termed Mid-Victorianism. ... In Dobu adultery is considered pretty, and a very fine achievement. Virtue in marriage is the dullness of a fool" (Fortune 1932: 241–242). "Shame... is felt at direct reference to sex life (1932: 246) ...but there is a lascivious delight in cut and run adulteries and seductions" (1932: 247).

Marriage in Dobu proves to be a rather unreliable affair; it provides for legal procreation, but offers little to the individual by way of a stable relationship. In Dobu, every man supervises his wife's conduct closely, since he fears her infidelity. This supervision may extend to her performance of her natural functions in the bush (1932: 247). Yet sooner or later, infidelity is bound to occur. Jealousy is a constant factor in all human adult relations. Fear is a constant companion. Dobuans are brought up as children to fear the villages into which they will later marry: it is marriage which pits private passion against an unreceptive village *susu* alliance (1932: 278). The position is quite extreme: "typically marriage dissolves, reforms, dissolves and reforms, and might reform again after dissolution less WERE THE MEANS OF SUICIDE MORE EFFECTIVE" (1932: 278; emphasis added). Even though the sister taboo is less pronounced, conflict still arises between the marital and natal groupings to which a man belongs; the husband-wife relationship is pitted against the brother-sister (Fortune 1932: 8).

Marriage in Dobu calls a halt to the unbridled sexual activity of adolescence when, indeed, housing depends upon it: a young man is thrust out of his parental home and must needs find a young woman who will accept his favors and provide somewhere for him to sleep (her parent's house) (1932: 21). Sexual activity continues to be highly valued after marriage, as is fidelity, in theory, but pregnancy is a different matter. The child represents a barrier to intimacy between spouses, to the extent that a man may try to get rid of the child by holding it over a fire, so that it will die from shock (1932: 246). This practice is obviously not sanctioned but it is an index of father-child hatred and jealousy. The poverty of father-child relations is greatly promoted by the frequency of divorce also. Hostility to the child is related to hostility to the Kula object here.

All in all, social conditions place the Dobuan man, like the Trobriander, in many situations of stress, including frenetic sex and sorcery, living with a hostile affinal group, interruption of marital relations through birth of a child. Very simply, as Benedict points out, Dobuans are victims of rampant paranoia (Benedict 1934).

One point of ritual in Dobu seems to indicate a slightly different thrust: the role of the wife. The wifely task of gathering a certain root, asserted to be *sibukaka*, takes place on the morning before departure of the Kula fleet. A man consumes the *sibukaka* root immediately before meeting his Kula partner, because it has been charmed by his wife in such a way that it will prove persuasive to his partner. The charm "dwells on the thunder that his voyage will awaken in the heavens, the privy whisperings of the charmer to the owners of *mwali* or *bagi*, the shaking effect that he will produce in the eager bodies of his partner, his partner's wife and child, and finally how they will dream in the night of him and rise from the dream" (Fortune 1932: 224).

The participation in this sanctioning rite by the wife indicates that it is fertility for the couple which is sought. Dobuan Kula magic remains somewhat similar to Trobriand magic, however, and we must assume that there is some similarity of intent between the spells. Each is concerned with control of women as well as with the pursuit of male vanity and perfection. Hostility to women is no less pronounced in Dobu than elsewhere in the Ring. In Dobu, females supernaturally vest their destructive power in *kaiana*-flaming pubes (1932:99). And marriage for the Dobuan man forces alliance with a "member of a group that may only modify its underlying hostility at best" (1932:8).

Despite some differences, the overall aim of Kula seems to remain similar in important respects: the practitioner of Kula is in each place concerned with desires to seek beauty, and this is an index of success in love; he desires also the allied ability to rejuvenate (remain beautiful) and to become immortal, in some sense. The acquisition of valuables, symbolic of these capacities, is no less important in Dobu than it is in the Trobriands, or indeed elsewhere along the Kula Ring.

Much less information is available as to the social fate of Kula valuables in Dobu, although they are reportedly used in burial ceremonies in the Southern Massim area as in the Northern area, where the Trobriands lie (Seligman 1910:612; Fortune 1932:194). Whether they are connected with spiritual life and after life in the Trobriand sense is not at all clear, especially in light of the fact that Dobuans specifically deny the Trobriand "spiritual" conception theory. The actual theories of conception in the Trobriands and Dobu seem closer than any of the ethnographers are disposed to believe, and social conflicts are also largely of the same kind, despite differences in social regulations and in political structure.

The aim of the Kula is precisely expressed in the magic which is to bring it to fruition: magic literally controls "everything that vitally affects man" (Malinowski 1922: 398). Magic was born of woman (1922: 398) and Kula represents an attempt on the part of men to usurp the procreative role of woman. Kula acts out the sexual relations of marriage, expresses the antagonism of the male to the marital role assigned him by society and conditioning, and permits expression of the lack of self-esteem felt by the male in everyday life, where it cannot be recognized by the conscious mind lest the individual become dysfunctional.

Kula asserts a man's procreative ability and, in the case of the Trobriands particularly, gives expression to the sister taboo, the supreme taboo, which again has no natural expression.

The message of brother-sister relations expressed in Kula might even be profitably analyzed in terms of exchange in Lévi-Straussian style: in order to acquire a wife and children, a man must give away his sister. He exchanges a woman who is not marriageable for one who is. In everyday life both the affections between a man and his children and a man and his sister are denied, even while a man seeks expression for each. In the Trobriand system, it is as though the exchange were only half completed. A man gives his sister away, but remains responsible for her children, her well-being, and her nourishment; he receives a wife, whose brothers are responsible for her as he is for his sister, but denies his part in the procreation of her children, even though he recognizes her as mother of those children. A man gives his sister away, but not her children; he receives a wife, but not her children; in each case it is the sexual component of the relationship which is skewed and which necessitates the mental gymnastics and dramatic release of the Kula expedition, where, among other things, all of the women are left behind for a time, in brief physical respite. Exchange is only partial, as the burden of Kula throughout the Kula Ring islands remains one of marriage and exchange, and procreation.

The incontrovertible biological fact that a man is father to his children is the truth which must be denied for such a social arrangement to function. Upon its denial rests the legal obligation undertaken by the maternal uncle to support his sister's children, an obligation which runs counter to the normal conditioned direction of affection. If paternity were to be recognized for what it is, a direct and unambiguous relationship between father and child, it would be difficult to reconcile a man to the support of children who are not his, as in this social system.

Denial is a means employed by the organism to avoid the tragic consequences of recognition of each relationship. Recognition would be tragic for the individual because he would have to admit that the social structure which he labors to maintain (by supporting his sister's children) runs precisely contrary to the course of his own desires (to be father to his own offspring). In addition, the social structure involves him in hostile relations with his sister, who becomes the guardian of her children's rights and moral guardian of the rights of the lineage, hence who exacts tribute from her brother and takes it away from his children.

The facts of Trobriand life are always threatening to surface; hostilities tend to appear everywhere, though they are nowhere sanctioned: between brother and brother, between brother and sister, between husband and wife (from different lineages as well as sexes) between man and man, between child and child, between siblings, between parents and children. The fundamental link which connects all of these relationships is the denial of paternity and Kula is merely an attempt to act out the frustrations which result from this denial, an acting out which involves the exchange of symbolic sexual objects at a great remove from the scene of sexual intercourse.

Detailed analysis of Kula ritual and symbolism, rather than this crude outline of the major events could, I think, take the point further, but I believe that the point of ritual displacement and the meaning of the voyage are now clear. Displacement in the ritual indicates displacement of feeling. That is why the motif of voyaging is always one of QUESTING, whether the traveller be an original Argonaut or a modern one. Just as an object given away is always synonymous with the self, the aim of the quest is always self-discovery, for Ulysses as for the Trobriand Islanders. The sailor travels empty handed, and returns fulfilled.

The theoretical interest of this illustration is mainly that it tries to see symbols in relation to feelings rather than as elements in a perceptual or conceptual scheme. Symbols are a way of making unacceptable feelings bearable, by providing some release of the tension of holding the feelings inside or repressing them.

Usually symbols are thought of as "standing for something else." Thus every symbol must have a referent. This creates the further problem of distinguishing the symbol from the referent: "There must be a motive for choosing, as between two entities or two systems, one to be the symbol of the other" (Langer 1953: 27.) Usually, Langer continues, "the decisive reason for choosing is that one system is easier to perceive and handle than the other." Symbol and referent are thus often almost arbitrarily distinguished.

Conceptual meaning for Langer is somehow separate from its symbol. "Symbols are not proxy for their objects, but are VEHICLES FOR THE CONCEPTION OF OBJECTS." (Langer 1957: 60–61.) This view is similar to that which underlies the structuralist justification of separation of form and content (Lévi-Strauss 1969: 9–11). By definition symbolic thought is abstractive thought, according to this approach. Langer continues: to conceive a thing or a situation is not the same thing as to "react toward it" overtly or to be aware of its presence; behavior toward CONCEPTIONS is what words normally evoke (emphasis added). Feeling is clearly distinguished from symbolizing here. Often in studies of symbols and symbolic or "primitive" thought, lip service is all that is paid to feeling, whilst, as we have seen in Kula, symbols are not something other than what they mean but essentially the ONLY expression that meaning can receive. Kula symbols give expression to reactions and feelings which cannot be faced when they are experienced.

Now inherent in this contention is the notion that symbolic thinking is not an end in itself, but rather an adaptive mechanism in a situation where feeling is not experienced by the human organism: feelings which are not processed into bodily reaction at the time they are experienced are stored within the mind and body to surface later in a precise symbolic form, which is often outwardly unrecognizable — except in fragmented form. Literal displacement is a symbolic expression of displacement of feeling from its source and occasion. The symbolism of ritual is neither arbitrary nor imprecise; the events, even though they follow the structural abstraction separation-transition-aggregation laid down by Van Gennep, cannot be understood in terms of abstractions only; and finally this structure cannot be abstracted from its own content as Lévi-Strauss would have us believe. The discovery of the "hidden logical structure" of myth (Lévi-Strauss 1969: 339) is an obstacle to understanding the savage mentality. There is no "image of the world which is already inherent in the structure of the mind" (1969: 341). Our uniquely human ability, witnessed by the unique laterality of our brain, is to be both self-conscious and conscious of the existential interaction between ourselves and the world around us.

My purpose here is not to explain in detail the relation between structural analysis and brain laterality, a task which I have attempted elsewhere (McDougall 1972), but merely to call attention to its implications. Under certain conditions, the laterality of the human brain and the differing functions of the right and left sides permit the sides to function independently. In the grossest terms, the different functions are associated with thinking and feeling in the left and right sides respectively (Janov 1973: 24), or more precisely, thinking and feeling are processed differently in different areas of the brain. Lateral splitting is subsequent to vertical splitting, however. Vertical splitting represents a control by the limbic system, through the hippocampus and amygdala and their direct connections to the frontal cortex, of human reactions to pain and painful situations. Limbic activity is what is responsible for the human ability to repress certain feelings rather than registering them as pain. The limbic system acts as a monitor of consciousness and rechannels blocked pain, diffusing its energy and routing it to a variety of other cortical pathways. The stored of unfelt pain activates the reticular activating system which eventually, through action (either inhibitory or stimulating) on the hypothalamus, affects the entire physical system (1973: 28–30).

Thus, under certain conditions, thought can be divorced from action, and feeling from thought.

I believe this possibility is exemplified everywhere in anthropological literature; it would be impossible to cite all the references to the discrepancy between native thought and action. Indeed this discrepancy is one which every trainee field worker is instructed to watch out for. Malinowski comments on the lack of connection: information about Kula from an individual who practises it has to be

... dragged out of the informant, or to put it more correctly, he has to be made to enlarge on points, to roam over all the subjects covered by the myth, and from his statements then, one has to pick out and piece together the other bits of the puzzle (Malinowski 1922: 264).

Fortune also remarks upon divorce of thought and action:

... complete pre-nuptial freedom is accompanied with the utmost prudishness and shame in speech and in social convention, a most interesting divorce of action and theory, and one striking case to be placed beside other such divorces of action and theory as we have already seen in Dobu (Fortune 1932: 248–249).

As Western anthropologists, our attitudes are confused on the availability of native explanations. On the one hand there is a romantic longing in us to believe that ritually active societies are those in which men are closest to their feeling and being, that where native exegesis is lacking in these societies it is because the facts have simply been "forgotten." But we cannot have it both ways, either the human brain is acting as it feels — integrating thought and action — in which case there ought to be an explanation of events, or it is not functioning integrally, and this is the reason for the lack of synthesis observed. Of course there are many degrees of "explanation", corresponding to the differing degrees of dysfunction. Sometimes, symbols can be recognized as symbols, can be distinguished from the feeling which motivates their production, sometimes acting out can be appreciated for what it is. The Dogon, for example seem to recognize their symbolic system as developing from symbol built on symbol, abstraction upon abstraction; at this point the system seems to become self generating and a wise old man like Ogotemmeli can figure out the connections between symbols for himself (Gejaule 1965). However, if the hypothesis, that feelings of a painful nature are rendered UNCONSCIOUS by being expressed in symbolic form rather than receiving direct bodily processing, is in fact correct, then we would not expect the symbols to be consciously applicable. Otherwise we would have a contradiction on our hands.

It is perfectly understandable that Malinowski's subjects of study should know the symbols of Kula and recognize their compelling power but that they should be ignorant of the total outline of the dramatic action. They must have the symbols to motivate the action, but knowing the action would again make conscious what must be denied — the fact that fathers are indeed biologically related to their children. Since social facts denies this, and denies a man much part in the raising of his son after infancy, a man experiences pain at the conflict in which he finds himself. The culture seems to be deliberately perverse: you can love what you do not father, but you don't; and you may not love what you do father, even though you want to. In each case, a man acts one way and feels another; the social system is destined to bring about a split in consciousness. As a result, feelings which cause pain and deny what the BODY KNOWS, that men are necessary to human reproduction, are rerouted in the brain itself (1965: 54). Much remains to be discovered about the precise nature of this repressive mechanism, but its availability to the human being as the consequence of the differential workload between the hemispheres is soundly established.

What I am trying to say here is that denial of bodily functions and their biological consequences is impossible. What is possible is that conscious knowledge of such processes, and I would be inclined to include "virgin birth" along with ignorance of paternity, may be repressed, where the social circumstances are sufficiently powerful to make the knowledge painful. By keeping the knowledge repressed, the body can continue to function. After all, if the Trobriand Islanders really were convinced that men were dispensable, they would not continue to endure the strains and stresses of sexual intercourse. But they cannot be convinced of this, since the body at some level inaccessible to consciousness "knows" how to act and needs to act that way.

Kula asserts, in a symbolic form, a fact necessary to the continuation of life in society itself: that men are indeed biological fathers. Instead of receiving open and conscious recognition, the paternal procreative role receives indirect ritual acting out. Kula is a dramatization of the encounter between the sexes, a "marriage," including all the ambivalent feelings involved in that encounter. It is the crux of social life, the most important event because the life process itself, including birth, is absolutely the most important to a human being and cannot be denied. If this importance cannot be consciously recognized for what it is, the adaptive ability of the brain will allow this fact expression in unconscious symbolic form, in order to safeguard the life process itself.

The notion that there are societies in which physiological processes are not known about is a function of the identical repressive mechanism in the person passing that judgment and is based on the assumption that it is from the outside that we learn about our bodily functioning. On the contrary, if we had to learn "how to" digest, for example, the human race would not have survived more than a couple of days, and certainly not long enough to teach a subsequent generation.

We know "how to" perform the basic life functions at birth, or we would die. And we feel our bodily processes most acutely when we are youngest. What we learn socially is to ignore them. A small infant will react to pain or hunger by crying; an adult will THINK "I am hungry" and probably take appropriate action. The conscious course of action is open only to the adult; the child is all feeling and unable to act on his own behalf. But in the child CONSCIOUSNESS AND FEELING ARE ONE. If the child were to grow up with the two brain hemispheres working harmoniously both horizontally and vertically, he would experience the pain of hunger at the same time as consciously recognizing this and, soon after, acting upon it.

Although no reliable estimate is available for the total number of people in the Western world who are unable to respond to their bodies in terms of what is necessary, and who therefore eat as a response to stress and not to hunger, their number is a substantial testimony to the disharmonious relations between their brain hemispheres. They are "out of touch" with their bodies; or, to use another term, they are alienated from natural processes.

The underlying but rarely articulated credo of anthropology is, of necessity, that there are similar organic processes at work in men everywhere, at least until we can show otherwise. If this were not the case, comparison at a sociological level would lose its legitimacy. Accordingly, we have to assume that the symbolizing mind is everywhere the same; but we must beware of projecting our own cultural thinking uncritically. "When an exotic custom fascinates us, it is generally because it presents us with a distorted reflection of a familiar image, which we confusedly recognize as such without managing to identify it" (Lévi-Strauss 1969: 239). The reason we fail to identify the foreign image is because we fail to identify our own. Our understanding would be greatly enhanced by self-knowledge. Perhaps the only way we can progress is by learning to identify the image; by allowing knowledge and self-knowledge to flow together.

REFERENCES

BENEDICT, RUTH
  1934 *Patterns of culture.* Boston: Houghton Mifflin.
EVANS-PRITCHARD, E. E
  1937 *Witchcraft, oracles and magic among the Azande.* Oxford: Clarendon Press.
  1940 *The Nuer: a description of the modes of livelihood and political institutions of a Nilotic people.* Oxford: Clarendon Press.
FORTUNE, R. F.
  1932 *Sorcerers of Dobu: the social anthropology of the Dobu islanders of the Western Pacific.* London: Routledge.
GEJAULE, MARCEL
  1965 *Conversations with Ogotemmeli: an introduction to Dogon religious ideas.* Oxford: The University Press.
JANOV, ARTHUR
  1973 The nature of consciousness. *Journal of Primal Therapy* I(1):7–63.
LANGER, SUSANNE K.
  1953 *Feeling and form: a theory of art developed from philosophy in a new key.* London: Routledge and Kegan Paul.
  1957 [1942] *Philosophy in a new key: a study in the symbolism of reason, rite and custom.* Cambridge: Harvard University Press.
LÉVI-STRAUSS, CLAUDE
  1963 *Structural anthropology.* Translated by Claire Jacobson and Brooke A. Schoepf. New York: Basic Books.
  1969 *The raw and the cooked: introduction to a science of mythology.* Translated by John and Doreen Weightman. New York: Harper and Row.
MALINOWSKI, BRONISLAV
  1922 *Argonauts of the Western Pacific.* London: Routledge and Kegan Paul. (Also in paperback edition. Preface by Sir James G. Fraser. New York: E. P. Dutton.)
  1932 *The sexual life of savages in Northwestern Melanesia: an ethnographic*

account of courtship, marriage, and family life among the natives of the Trobriand Islands, British New Guinea. London: Routledge and Kegan Paul.

MAUSS, MARCEL
1967   *The gift: forms and functions of exchange in archaic societies.* Translated by Ian Gunnison. New York: W. W. Norton.

MC DOUGALL, LORNA
1972   "The split brain and the savage mind." Paper presented to the Southern California Anthropological Association. Long Beach.

SELIGMAN, C. G.
1910   *The Melanesians of British New Guinea.* Cambridge: The University Press.

TURNER, VICTOR W.
1967   *The forest of symbols: aspects of Ndemu ritual.* Ithaca and London: Cornell University Press.
1969   *The ritual process.* Chicago: Aldine.

UBEROI, J. P.
1962   *The politics of the Kula ring: an analysis of the findings of Malinowski.* Manchester: The University Press.

VAN GENNEP, ARNOLD
1960   *The rites of passage.* Translated by Monica B. Vizadom and Gabrielle L. Coffee. London: Routledge and Kegan Paul.

The Archaic Illusion: A Re-examination of Lévi-Strauss' View of the Developing Child

JUDITH K. BROWN

To the anthropologist concerned with *The elementary structures of kinship*, Lévi-Strauss' chapter, "The archaic illusion," may seem to be a digression. The chapter presents Lévi-Strauss' views concerning the developing child. Although his ideas are provocative and bear on important educational issues, the literature of child development, so far as I am aware, contains no reference to this particular work by Lévi-Strauss. The neglect is undeserved.

To be sure, Lévi-Strauss' brief chapter does not attempt to present a complete and coherent theory of child development. He is disturbingly vague about the specific periods of childhood to which he refers. He speaks of "infant thought" (1969: 85), but draws his illustrations from Susan Isaac's observational studies of preschool children. Too little distinction is made among various aspects of development, particularly the cognitive and the social.[1] Terms, such as "mental structures" and "schemes of sociability" (1969: 85), are introduced which cry for definition. In spite of these serious shortcomings, the basic ideas presented are worthy of examination.

For Lévi-Strauss the archaic illusion from which the chapter derives its title suggests that the mind of the "civilized" child resembles that of the "primitive" adult. The illusion arises because we must put ourselves in a childlike frame of mind to comprehend the unfamiliar (indeed, the anthro-

---

[1] Murphy, in his comments on "The archaic illusion," notes the following: "Within the vast architecture of the *Structures*, however, was a theme that waited to be developed. This is the congruence of the structures of society, language, and thought" (1971:178). "Lévi-Strauss' later writings clearly indicate that social structures and the structure of thought must be homologous" (1971:180).

pologist in the field often appears childlike to the people he is studying) and, as observers of the unfamiliar, we project our own childlike attitudes onto the subject of our observation. Lévi-Strauss regards this as an illusion and a fallacy. He insists, however, that the mind of the child offers invaluable insights for the anthropologist, not because of its similarity to the mind of the "primitive" adult, but because it "provides a common basis of mental structures and schemes of sociability for all cultures, each of which draws on certain elements for its own particular model" (1969: 85). A variety of contradictory structures and schemes are discernible in the mind of the child. This is not because he is at a simpler stage of development, but because the child has not yet had the extensive experience of one particular culture and has not yet been subjected to the pressures of socialization. As experience and socialization proceed, certain structures are rejected as inappropriate, while those customary in the child's culture are retained and elaborated. This view contrasts with the more widely held developmental theories of Piaget and Kohlberg, who both view development as a process of accretion. Indeed, Piaget comes in for sharp criticism from Lévi-Strauss in the chapter under consideration.

The evidence which Lévi-Strauss marshals for his position, aside from the citations of the observational materials of Susan Isaacs, is perhaps somewhat unconventional for developmental psychology. It consists of two analogies. The first, and the more convincing, draws on evidence from language development. Lévi-Strauss likens the extinction of those vocalizations which are inappropriate to the language the child will learn and the simultaneous gradual acquisition of meaningful speech to the reduction of available structures and the gradual social learning of the developing child. Lévi-Strauss writes: "Learning a language presents the same problems as the infant's first steps into social life .... The variety of sounds that the speech organs can articulate is almost unlimited. However, each language retains only a very small number of all possible sounds .... Every language makes a selection and from one viewpoint this selection is regressive. Once this selection is made, the unlimited possibilities available on the phonetic plane are irremediably lost. On the other hand, prattling is meaningless, while language allows people to communicate with one another, and so utterance is inversely proportional to significance" (1969: 93–94).

The second analogy likens social development to sexual development. Lévi-Strauss describes the Freudian view of childhood sexuality as manifesting "in a rudimentary form, and co-existently, all the types of eroticism among which the adult will seek his specialization" (1969: 94). Similarly, childhood thought should be viewed as polymorphous and the child as a "polymorphous socialite," until experience and socialization compel the child to make a choice among a variety of rudimentary and conflicting structures.

I would like to suggest two additional analogies drawn from the developmental literature. Emotional development appears to proceed from the general to the specific. The neonate can express only distress and non-distress, and he communicates these experiences only in a general way which involves the whole being. More differentiated emotional states appear gradually, and their expression is channeled into culturally specified patterns. In maturity an emotion may be communicated by a brief gesture or merely by a facial expression (Thompson 1962).

A second analogy is suggested by motor development. Although the pattern is not established unequivocally, the literature of developmental psychology frequently refers to the mass-specific trend. This is based on the observation that the fetus and the neonate will respond to stimulation with generalized movements of the entire body. As development proceeds, the infant responds with more parsimonious and appropriate movement (Thompson 1962).

Although Lévi-Strauss' view is at variance with that of most developmental psychologists, similar suggestions have found their way into the literature. Ainsworth's (1967) observational study of a small group of Ganda infants offers an example, although she acknowledges the influence of Piaget, among others, on her work. According to Ainsworth, it is through attachment to the mother that the infant begins his relationship with the world outside himself. A variety of patterns are available for experiencing and expressing this attachment, and a choice is made among these patterns. Ainsworth writes:

The human infant is equipped with the potential for a number of patterns of attachment behavior, in which it is likely that no one is essential and crucial (1967: 434).

The view to which I adhere is that the child is born with a behavioral repertoire which includes responses already biased toward mediating social interaction — and that this is part of his built-in, species-specific equipment. In addition to actions which have a primarily social function, his repertoire includes some which have a potential multiple function [*sic*] and can be turned to social ends (1967: 438).

The second example is drawn from Bruner's "On cognitive growth II" (1967). Here Bruner writes:

In one sense it is a loss for the growing human being to "lose" his older, more innocent conceptions and skills, but at the same time it appears to be a necessary condition for acculturation (and indeed, for cultural control of the individual) that there be this "childhood amnesia" as Schachtel... has called it (1967: 64). Growth has a way of minimizing the conflicted ways of knowing (1967: 66).

Lévi-Strauss' view of the developing child has relevance for two current, major educational endeavors: the provision of meaningful education for the culturally disadvantaged child in our own society, and the establishment of schools in westernizing tribal and peasant societies.

The terms "culturally disadvantaged" or "culturally deprived" appear to imply that children so labeled lack something which can be provided by adding a compensating "enrichment" to their education.[2] The "disadvantaged" child's difficulty in acquiring certain competences can be countered by adding something to the curriculum or to the life experience. A different strategy is suggested by Lévi-Strauss' view of the developing child. The "disadvantaged" child should not be seen as lacking something which can be added by the educator. Rather the child through experience and socialization has chosen a different organizing structure in the context of which learning takes place. In order for the child to gain certain competences, it is necessary to intercede at an early age, when his thinking is still "polymorphous." On the other hand, the older child must be forced back to the polymorphous stage and compelled to make an alternative choice of structures. The method implies the use of coercion on the part of the educator, and a rejection of the choices that the "disadvantaged" child would make on the basis of his own experience and as a member of his own group.[3] This approach is perhaps more honest, but it is also less acceptable to the educator of the "disadvantaged" than the additive one.

Similarly the introduction of Western schooling in other parts of the world appears in a new light. In *The new mathematics and an old culture: a study of learning among the Kpelle of Liberia*, Gay and Cole (1967) insist

[2]   Howard expresses the same view: "I can think of no more unfortunate label for children who do not respond to our middle-class model for education than 'culturally disadvantaged'. ... It is misleading because it implies an absence of cultural experience rather than a different set of cultural experiences. This leads many teachers to presume that their task with these youngsters is to fill a void. ... The phrase 'culturally disadvantaged' is irritating because it is so ethnocentric" (1970:159).

[3]   Bernstein has made a similar observation in comparing the educational experiences of working-class and middle-class children. Bernstein writes: "The working-class child is concerned mainly with the present, and his social structure, unlike that of the middle-class child, provides little incentive or purposeful support to make the methods and ends of the school personally meaningful. The problems of discipline and classroom control result not from isolated points of resistance or conflict but from the attempt to reorient a whole pattern of perception with its emotional counterpart. ... The school provides an important means by which the middle-class child enhances his self-respect and that ... is not so for the working-class child. His self-respect is in fact more often damaged" (1958:172).

that the Kpelle child must not lose his identity through schooling and that his cultural heritage must be preserved (1967: 96). Yet they write:

> The Kpelle schoolchild does not... organize his universe of school experience in a meaningful way. He does not look analytically at the structure or shape of visual stimuli. He does not pattern the words he hears, nor does he think of mathematics in terms of laws and regularities. Instead, he accepts each item of knowledge as an isolated gem, connected in some mysterious way to the wisdom of accepted authority. We see this lack of analysis, this unquestioning acceptance of authority, as the primary stumbling block to the Kpelle child's progress in school (1967: 93–94).

I suggest that it is not possible for the Kpelle child to retain his heritage (which includes the unskeptical acceptance of authority) AND to approach the world with a questioning, scientific attitude. Only one can prevail, because the two are contradictory. In "The archaic illusion," Lévi-Strauss (1969) suggests that such choices are the very essence of enculturation.

Years ago, in reading George Bernard Shaw's *Major Barbara*, I was puzzled by Undershaft's statement to his daughter, Barbara: "You have learned something. That always feels at first as if you had lost something." Lévi-Strauss' "The archaic illusion" indicates the extent and the significance of that loss.

REFERENCES

AINSWORTH, MARY D. SALTER
1967   *Infancy in Uganda: infant care and the growth of love*. Baltimore: Johns Hopkins University Press.
BERNSTEIN, BASIL
1958   Some sociological determinants of perception. *British Journal of Sociology* 9:159–174.
BRUNER, JEROME S.
1967   "On cognitive growth II," in *Studies in cognitive growth: a collaboration at the center for cognitive studies*. Edited by Bruner, Olver, and Greenfield, 30–67. New York: John Wiley.
GAY, JOHN, MICHAEL COLE
1967   *The new mathematics and an old culture: a study of learning among the Kpelle of Liberia*. New York: Holt, Rinehart and Winston.
HOWARD, ALAN
1970   *Learning to be Rotuman: enculturation in the South Pacific*. New York: Teachers College Press.
LÉVI-STRAUSS, CLAUDE
1969   *The elementary structures of kinship*. Translated and edited by Rodney Needham. Boston: Beacon Press.

MURPHY, ROBERT
1971   *The dialectics of social life.* New York: Basic Books.
THOMPSON, GEORGE G.
1962   *Child psychology: growth trends in psychological adjustment* (second edition). Boston: Houghton Mifflin.

The Species-Specific Framework of Man and Its Evolution

DANIEL KRAKAUER

The confusion regarding the evolution of man's psyche is due at least partly to an apparent lack of understanding of its "structure" and functioning. The problem is akin to the riddle of the origin of species a century ago. Darwin could not have solved it without knowing the physical structures and functions of animals and plants. Similarly, we cannot solve the problem of how human behavior evolved until we can describe human mentality in ways pertinent to the question. A comprehensible succinct species-specific description or "framework" of man's psychological organization would be most useful. (Holloway 1968: 37).

It seems surprising that such a description is not available. Man has been assiduously studied by psychologists and psychoanalysts for a long time. Or is it that the information is there, obscured by different points of view, by complicated and often unclear concepts, by semantics, by sheer volume of literature, and by a shortage of people familiar with the essentials of the several disciplines involved?

An affirmative answer to the question is offered here. It makes use of knowledge that by and large has been avoided or neglected by zoologists and anthropologists, i.e., some of the basic discoveries and insights of Sigmund Freud (Lorenz 1966: Introduction). However psychoanalysis may be criticized as a therapeutic tool, its value as a research method into human mental functioning is unequalled (La Barre 1954: xii, xiii; Arlow 1959; Waelder 1962). The concepts outlined herein have been studied, developed, tested and confirmed for fifty to seventy years. They are basic to much present-day psychological theory. And, as I shall attempt to demonstrate, they match with and contribute to a straightforward Darwinian explanation of the evolution of human behavior.

Maslow's "Theory of Human Motivation" is integrated herein with Freudian theory. Maslow's theory is about thirty years old, and has been increasingly tested and applied (Maslow 1943, 1970). A recent partial bibliography lists some 200 references to fieldwork and studies based on Maslow's "need" hierarchy (Roberts 1972).

Clearly, a full expression of this integrative approach to the evolution of human behavior would require a volume. Nevertheless, it is my hope and belief that this condensation provides a conceptual framework of human nature broad enough, concise enough, and realistic enough to throw further light on man and his evolution.

Not all aspects of the evolution of behavior are puzzling. The development of man's intellectual capacities, such as for thinking, remembering, and self-awareness, is clear enough in Darwinian terms. They were naturally selected; i.e., they improved man's survival and reproductive capacities. In fact, man's intelligence, imperfect as it is, is beyond a doubt the principal reason for his dominant status (Hallowell 1960: 350; Huxley 1964: xxxii). But the bewildering and conflicting variety of feelings and desires that evolved along with intelligence, and the apparent maladaptation and excessive aggression of many of his activities have seemed difficult to explain as resulting from natural selection (Holloway 1968: 41).

The enigma of man's behavior is easy enough to illustrate. Survival, for example, is as essential to man as to any other species; yet there are thousands of suicides annually by young as well as old; daredevil racers, explorers, and circus performers tempt death constantly; history books and newspapers tell endlessly of people who sacrifice themselves for love, for spite, for principle, for pride, for religion, or for country.

Human sexuality encompasses not only copulation, which is essential to survival of the species, but also a wide range of noncopulative practices, as well as frigidity and impotence, abstinence, masturbation, and homosexuality.

Human appetite for food ranges from omnivorous to very limited. All sorts of nonadaptive variations exist: obese gluttony, intense inhibition to perfectly good foods, hunger strikes, and even fatal disinterest. (Mead 1958: 489; Spitz 1965).

Man's social relationships range from reclusion to consuming deathpact love; from parochial self-interest to world citizenship.

He frequently exhibits aggression of an order almost unknown to the rest of the animal kingdom. It seems to be aroused for little cause and almost at the crook of a finger. Human aggression occurs either on an individual or mass scale. Frequently, it has resulted in war, with the slaughter of vast numbers of males in their prime — hardly a contribution to the survival of the species.

THE RELATIONSHIP OF INTELLIGENCE, INSTINCTS, AND BEHAVIOR

Man's wide and conflicting range of behavior and affect is, in fact, a collateral, necessary, and inescapable concomitant of intelligence, because *intelligence must be accompanied by strong motivation and weak behavioral constraints.*

In order for any intelligent species to operate effectively, the following related conditions must exist:

1. The species must be capable of much flexibility of behavior. The successful application of intelligence requires adaptability both mental and physical. When an intelligent animal finds a new way to cope, or formulates a new idea, it must be able to put it into practice. No matter how brilliant a monkey might be, if it could not bear to leave its tree or change its diet, it would simply not have enough behaviorial flexibility for its intellect to exploit, not to mention its anatomical limitations (Fletcher 1957: 60).

2. The species must have inner direction and strong motivation. No matter how intelligent, a species cannot survive for intellectual reasons; there are no intellectual reasons for surviving. Not only must its members have the physical capacity to survive; they must very much WANT to survive: to eat, to copulate, to associate, to fight back, etc. Their intellects must be chiefly engrossed with concerns that enhance survival and reproduction (Hallowell 1961: 253). The wellsprings of all behavior are emotional.

3. Yet despite the strong inner direction, the species must be capable of some emotional detachment or objectivity. It is not possible to think clearly when channelled by prejudices or wishful thinking, paralyzed by fear, or straight-jacketed by preconceptions. Objectivity, imagination, and the capacity to keep "cool" are essential adjuncts to good judgment.

It is clear from the first requirement that an intellectual species could not evolve if its behavior and motivation were patterned chiefly by instincts. ("Instincts" in this paper refers to patterns of behavior more or less genetically determined.) Instincts have limited flexibility, at best. Requirement 2 dictates that an inherited guiding and motivating mechanism is absolutely necessary, but somehow, unlike instincts, not tied to a limited range of behavior. And requirement 3 calls for a delicate balance between intellect and affect that promises a considerable degree of internal conflict (Hebb 1954; Freedman 1958: 461).

The necessary lack of instincts creates two additional requirements that must be satisfied in an intelligent species in the course of natural selection.
4.   The species must be able to learn viable patterns of behavior during infancy and early childhood to replace missing instincts. The complicated task of consolidating the psyche and developing maturity must begin as quickly as possible.
5.   The species must be able to learn self-control. Instincts prescribe a portion of aggression roughly suitable to the situation, and proscribe unsuitable amounts (Roe 1963: 324). But with the loss of instincts comes a loss of the boundaries of emotion. Boundaries too have to be learned and, like attitudes and behavior, mostly during infancy and childhood.

THE HOMO SAPIENS-SPECIFIC PSYCHOLOGICAL FRAMEWORK

The *Homo sapiens*-specific psychological framework described by Freud and clarified and extended by many later workers clearly matches the requirements proposed above for an intelligent species. Maslow's concise theory of motivation provides further clarification for our purposes. The highly simplified outline offered here attempts to present the picture without resorting to difficult psychoanalytic language.
1.   The Structural Theory (Freud 1923; Magoun 1960; Arlow and Brenner 1967).   The human psyche has three centers of function, designated id, ego, and superego.
A.   The id includes man's inherited and unlearned urges, appetites and needs, and the instinctual drives which motivate him to try to satisfy his needs. The id is mostly unconscious, outside of awareness. It is intense and powerful enough to exert a constant directing influence on all human activities. It channels the ego, but is divorced enough to permit the ego some objectivity.
B.   The ego is the thinking and adapting center of function. It includes the conscious capacities: perception, memory, thinking, imagination, emotion, and control of the voluntary muscles. It also has some unconscious components.
C.   The superego is the learned "program," mostly unconscious, replacing in *Homo sapiens* the inherited attitudes and controls of species with instincts. The superego becomes an important part of the individual's unconscious directing mechanism (Fletcher 1957: 225).

2. The Instinctual Drive Theory (Freud 1957 [1915]; Brenner 1957; Cameron 1963). The motivation supplied by the id consists of two major "instinctual drives," the libidinal instinctual drive and the aggressive instinctual drive. (Due to an unfortunate translator's choice, most psychoanalytic literature employs the word "instincts" instead of "instinctual drives.") (Moore and Fine 1968).

The libidinal instinctual drive urges the individual towards pleasure, affection, and dependency. The aggressive instinctual drive motivates the individual towards achievement, domination, and independence. Man is constantly motivated by both instinctual drives acting jointly, although some acts may contain much of one drive and little of the other.

3. A Dynamic Theory of Human Motivation (Maslow 1943, 1970: 35–38). Human motivations group into about five categories of hierarchic, dynamic, survival-serving "needs." As in all other species, they are inherited. Unlike all other species, human motivations are inhibitable. Needs are not instincts; they are goals, the objectives of the instinctual drives.

The need categories (and examples) are:

A. Physiological: food and drink, sex, sleep, etc.

B. Safety: survival, self-defense, security, etc.

C. Belongingness: human contact, sociability, friendship, love, etc.

D. Esteem: praise, recognition, importance, self-esteem, etc.

E. Cognitive and Esthetic: curiosity, play, thinking, imagining, self-expression, etc.

4. The Oedipus Complex (Freud 1953 [1900]; Róheim 1950; Waelder 1964). The human infant goes through a series of psychological stages, the most striking of which is the Oedipus complex (see subparagraph D).

A. The newborn infant slowly develops an awareness of its mother and feelings of total dependence. At this stage, the goals of its instinctual drives are the most elementary physiological, safety, and belongingness satisfactions (Schiller 1952; Romer 1958: 72; Spitz 1965).

B. At about one year, the infant develops an awareness that there are rivals for the attention of the mother, principally the father figure. With its congenital anxious need for survival and safety, the infant inevitably perceives the father figure as a great threat, about which it feels almost helpless.

C. Towards age two, the infant begins to perceive that the father figure is powerful, and important to its safety. It then reaches out to attract him also into its orbit. Elementary esteem needs, such as getting attention, become prominent. The ego starts to develop. Unconscious learning from parents and others ensues as superego character formation begins.

D. By age three, sexuality appears at the id level (and remains until

death). The unconscious attachment of male children to the mother gets stronger as does their earlier begun rivalry with the father. Girls turn towards the father and develop rivalry towards the mother. At the same time, in their seductive reach toward the opposite parent, they identify with and tend to imitate the parent of their own sex (Waelder 1964: 113).
E.   In the ensuing two or three years, superego learning of attitudes and values approaches completion. The ego, mediating among the id, the superego, and its own limited perception of reality, arbitrates the many, often conflicting, interior and exterior pressures as best it can.
F.   The arrival of puberty, with conscious sexuality and strong drives toward independence, complicates further the task of the ego.
G.   In the teen years and on, further consolidation and integration of ego functioning occurs, with large variation in pattern and degree of maturity in each individual.

PSYCHOANALYTIC THEORY AND EVOLUTION

The outline of observed and well-validated human mental functioning presented above fits well with the theoretical requirements for a species with conscious intelligence.

The id functional center is the inherited guiding mechanism, the built-in program of appetites and goals that motivates each individual from the day he is born. Without the id layer or its equivalent, *H. sapiens,* or for that matter any intellectual species that evolved, could not exist.

The Instinctual Drive Theory, together with the Theory of Motivation, describe the nature of the motivational system that evolved. In lieu of instincts are the two goal-directed drives, the libidinal instinctual drive towards comfort and dependency, and the aggressive instinctual drive toward survival and dominance. The goals of both drives are the same; the unconscious, inherited needs. Needs are dynamic and hierarchic, are expressed in many varied ways, and are partly inhibitable or deflectable by the ego. The needs were selected because they guide man towards successful behavior. The similarity of human need-oriented behavior to behavior resulting from the instincts of the social mammals, is striking.

Instead of instincts specifying what to fear, when to fight back, where to seek shelter, man has safety needs. He approaches life with caution; he seeks all-knowing leaders; he makes self-protective laws and establishes police and armies; he consults medical doctors, or "witch" doctors; he develops beguiling personality traits.

Instead of specific social patterns, man has belongingness needs which cause him to live and work together. This fosters individual and sexual specialization, family development and protection, better communication, and cooperative action (Etkin 1964).

Instead of dominance-oriented instincts, man has esteem needs urging him to become worthy and important, to overcome obstacles, to take the lead, to succeed.

The instinctual drives are on call for mobilizing the individual in response to his unconscious needs. The intensity of their activity is frequently very high, being more related to individual fears, perceptions, and wishes than to reality.

The ego, the thinking and adapting center, begins to develop in the first year of life, and improves rapidly in consciousness and capacity for several years. In psychologically mature individuals its growth continues indefinitely (Hartmann 1958).

The list of ego functions shows its central importance for enhancing adaptation to the environment. The conscious manipulation of ideas, conscious recall, the capacity for critical perception, imagination, the ability to inhibit (or at least, deflect) instinctual drives — all are aspects of the improved cognitive control which distinguishes our own species (Ford and Beach 1951).

The evolution of the ego is clearly a key development in the evolution of man. The separation of motivation and thinking into rather distinct functional centers probably led to an "explosive" change. It is interesting to note that it was the developing ego that gave rise to the id. The id was not first (Waelder 1964: 102).

Selection for the superego could not have been far behind selection for the id. As instincts weakened in the course of natural selection, they had to be replaced by an inherited mechanism that facilitated quick learning of successful behavior patterns (Schiller 1952; Mead 1958: 489; Schneirla 1964: 555). In order to survive, the human infant could not wait long to consolidate its psyche and get started on the complicated job of growing up.

The superego and ego mechanisms for early learning of attitudes, values, and self-control was the naturally selected solution. The child reaches for, absorbs, or sometimes reactively reverses the values, attitudes, and controls of its significant adults — usually its parents. It develops concepts of "good" and "bad," "right" and "wrong," and "safe" and "dangerous."

For better or worse, it develops an evaluation of and attitude about itself, and unconsciously decides what it must demand of itself. It learns about familial bonds and tensions and projects them to include the whole world. It develops its patterns of selfishness or generosity, aggressiveness or meekness, impetuousness or self-control, sexuality or chastity.

It is not surprising that under such circumstances the superego is frequently unrealistic, that conscience, guilt, emotionality and self-control often develop with excessive strength or weakness, and are frequently directed against the self.

The emotional set established in the young *Homo sapiens* is not totally rigid. There is simultaneous ego development, marked by a growing adaptability and maturity. The success of the species is in part because some individuals do grow greatly in wisdom or cunning. Due to the ego's capacity for communication, this wisdom is made available to fellow humans, orally and in writing (Huxley 1958).

EMOTION AND AGGRESSION

The infant's instinctual needs for survival, safety, and belongingness are imperious. Its libidinal and aggressive instinctual drives are poised and ready to respond in almost any degree. Its immature and inexperienced mind is naturally fearful and anxious. During early ego and superego formation, therefore, panic responses are more the rule than the exception.

Under the influence of the intense unstructured needs and powerful instinctual drives, maladaptive or disproportionate patterns of response are frequently set that stay on for life. Many humans focus on and exaggerate specific sub-needs, and pursue them with excessive libidinal or aggressive drive. On the other hand, many humans develop over-control, repressing their needs and their drives; being better behaved, such people are less noticed.

Man's overt aggression is a part of this very picture — as the Instinctual Drive Theory makes clear. (Brenner 1971). Overt aggression is not a thing apart, as so many writers have assumed. It is one manifestation of the aggressive instinctual drive, the most extreme expression of a continuum that includes the impulsion to act (Nissen 1958: 195), aggressivity (Freedman and Roe 1958: 470–471; Lorenz and Newman 1971), and dominance.

Disproportionate aggression, like disproportionate motivation, occurs so commonly because instinctual drives are necessarily intense unconscious motivators, the control of which is not by instincts, but by learning which is often weak or erratic.

Overt aggression therefore will occur in individuals who have excessively strong aggressive instinctual drives, who have weakly developed superego and ego controls, whose needs are seriously threatened, or who are driven by the moralistic demands of their own harsh superego to force their standards, or even death, on others. It will also occur, and on a large scale, when approval by father figures or peers leads individuals to bypass some of their own inner controls. In such event, war or massacre may result. The ease with which many people can be threatened and the enormity of the aggression triggered, are pervasive problems in human relations.

Disproportionate libidinal instinctual drive reactions are also common, such as overeating, alcoholism, drug addiction, and excessive self-sacrifice.

Disproportionate drives plus superego over-control lead to another common phenomenon of our intelligent species, the civilization diseases; ulcers, high blood pressure, and depression are common examples. These and other physiological or psychological disturbances occur when the drives have no other adequate outlet.

HOMO SAPIENS, THE CONFLICTED SPECIES

An intelligent species is also necessarily a conflicted species. Without instincts, which for the most part limit available choices, man must be constantly making up his mind. The choices are many and difficult. To begin with, man's deepest needs are in conflict, even though each is making a contribution to the success of the species. The need for safety, to look out for himself, conflicts with the belongingness need that disposes man to be self-sacrificing. The need to climb the human "pecking order" conflicts with needs to play it safe or to help others.

On top of the instinctual conflicts, come the superego conflicts, the guilts, the intensified fears, the very necessary mechanisms of self control. These are often directly opposed to the strivings of the id. The ego is forced to compromise as best it can.

In most cultures, man must make daily decisions and choices small and large. Here too the ego must carry a continuous burden.

Thus each member of our species grows up constantly coping with and attempting to integrate and coordinate a panoply of intense and often conflicting feelings, emotions, and needs. In the process most people are "successful," but rarely happy. This is to be expected. Constant striving has survival value; happiness does not.

In spite of the fact that under these circumstances overt aggression sometimes breaks out in epidemic proportions and is present always in endemic proportions, our species is highly successful, biologically speaking.

SUMMARY

High intelligence is a powerful survival mechanism, but requires strong motivation, intellectual detachment, and capacity for a wide range of behavior, including the virtual absence of instincts. To replace the missing instincts, there must be an efficient mechanism for learning successful ways of behavior and self-control.

Three centers of mental function evolved interdependently, naturally selected because they resulted in intelligent, adaptable and motivated individuals. As first described by Sigmund Freud, they are the ego (the detached intellect), the id (the motivator) and the superego (the behavior-learning mechanism). The kind of id drives and the psychological stages that were selected (such as the Oedipus complex) explain the nature of human behavior, including aggression. The goal direction of the id drives is described in Maslow's theory of motivation.

Uncircumscribed by instincts, and with controls and values that are partly and often erratically learned, man exhibits great range, variation and confliction in behavior, motivation, emotion, and self-control. Overt aggression is one manifestation.

REFERENCES

ARLOW, J. A.
  1959   "Psychoanalysis as scientific method," in *Psychoanalysis, scientific method, and philosophy*. Edited by S. Hook, 201–211. New York: New York University Press.
ARLOW, J. A., C. BRENNER
  1967   *Psychoanalytic concepts and the structural theory*. New York: International Universities Press.
BRENNER, C.
  1957   *An elementary textbook of psychoanalysis*. New York: Doubleday Anchor.
  1971   The psychoanalytic concept of aggression. *International Journal of Psychoanalysis* 52:137–144.
CAMERON, N.
  1963   *Personality development and psychopathology*. Boston: Houghton Mifflin.
CARPENTER, C. R.
  1968   "The contribution of primate studies to the understanding of war," in *War*. Edited by M. Fried, M. Harris, and R. Murphy, 49–58. Garden City, New York: The Natural History Press.
DARWIN, C.
  1955   [1872]   *The expression of emotions in man and animals*. New York: Philosophical Library.

ETKIN, W.
1964 *Social behavior and organization among vertebrates.* Chicago: University of Chicago Press.

FLETCHER, R.
1957 *Instinct in man.* New York: International Universities Press.

FORD, C. S., F. A. BEACH
1951 *Patterns of sexual behavior.* New York: Harper and Bros.

FREEDMAN, L. Z., A. ROE
1958 "Evolution and human behavior," in *Behavior and evolution.* Edited by A. Roe and G. G. Simpson, 455–479. New Haven: Yale University Press.

FREUD, S.
1953 [1900] "The interpretation of dreams," in *The standard edition of the complete psychological works of Sigmund Freud,* volumes four and five. Edited by J. Strachey. London: Hogarth.
1957 [1915] "Instincts and their vicissitudes," in *The standard edition of the complete psychological works of Sigmund Freud,* volume fourteen. Edited by J. Strachey. London: Hogarth.
1923 *The ego and the id.* London: Hogarth.

HALLOWELL, A. I.
1960 "Self, society and culture in phylogenetic perspective," in *The evolution of man.* Edited by S. Tax, 309–371. Chicago: University of Chicago Press.
1961 "The protocultural foundations of human adaptation," in *Social life of early man.* Edited by S. L. Washburn, 236–255. Chicago: Aldine.

HARTMANN, H.
1958 *Ego psychology and the problem of adaptation.* New York: International Universities Press.

HEBB, D. O., W. R. THOMPSON
1954 "Social significance of animal studies," in *Handbook of Social Psychology,* volume one. Edited by G. Lindzey, 532–561. Reading, Massachusetts: Addison, Wesley.

HOLLOWAY, R. L., JR.
1968 "Human aggression: the need for a species-specific framework," in *War.* Edited by M. Fried, M. Harris, and R. Murphy, 29–48. Garden City, New York: The Natural History Press.

HUXLEY, J. S.
1957 *New bottles for new wine.* New York: Harper.
1958 "Cultural process and evolution," in *Behavior and evolution.* Edited by A. Roe, and G. G. Simpson, 437–454. New Haven: Yale University Press.
1964 *Evolution the modern synthesis* (with new introduction). New York: Wiley.

LA BARRE, W.
1954 *The human animal.* Chicago: University of Chicago Press.

LORENZ, K.
1966 *On aggression.* New York: Harcourt, Brace and World.

LORENZ, K., E. NEWMAN
1971 Transcript of interview on *Speaking Freely*. New York: WNBC-TV Community Affairs Department.

MAGOUN, H. W.
1960 "Evolutionary concepts of brain function following Darwin and Spencer," in *The evolution of man*. Edited by S. Tax, 187–209. Chicago: University of Chicago Press.

MASLOW, A. H.
1943 A dynamic theory of human motivation. *Psychological Review* 50: 370–396.
1970 *Motivation and personality* (second edition). New York: Harper and Row.

MAYR, E.
1963 *Animal species and evolution*. Cambridge: Harvard University Press.

MEAD, M.
1958 "Cultural determinants of behavior," in *Behavior and evolution*. Edited by A. Roe, G. G. Simpson, 480–503. New Haven: Yale University Press.

MOORE, B. E., B. D. FINE, *editors*
1968 *A glossary of psychoanalytic terms and concepts* (second edition). New York: The American Psychoanalytic Association.

NISSEN, H. W.
1958 "Axes of behavioral comparison," in *Behavior and evolution*. Edited by A. Roe, and G. G. Simpson, 183–205. New Haven: Yale University Press.

ROBERTS, T. B.
1972 "Maslow's human motivation needs hierarchy: a bibliography." Leaflet. De Kalb: Northern Illinois University.

ROE, A.
1963 "Psychological definitions of man," in *Classification and human evolution*. Edited by S. L. Washburn, 320–331. Chicago: Aldine.

RÓHEIM, G.
1950 *Psychoanalysis and anthropology*. New York: International Universities Press.

ROMER, A. S.
1958 "Phylogeny and behavior with special reference to vertebrate evolution," in *Behavior and evolution*. Edited by A. Roe and G. G. Simpson, 48–75. New Haven: Yale University Press.

SAUER, C. O.
1961 "Sedentary and mobile bents in early societies," in *Social life of early man*. Edited by S. L. Washburn, 256–266. Chicago: Aldine.

SCHILLER, P. H.
1952 Innate constituents of complex responses in primates. *Psychological Review* 59:177–191.

SCHNEIRLA, T. C.
1964 "Instinctive behavior, maturation-experience and development," in *Principles of animal psychology*. Enlarged edition by N.R.F. Maier and T. C. Schneirla, 555–579. New York: Dover.

SCHUR, M., L. B. RITVO
1970 A principle of evolutionary biology for psychoanalysis. *Journal of the American Psychoanalytic Association* 18:422–439.
SIMPSON, G. G.
1964 *This view of life.* New York: Harcourt, Brace and World.
SPERRY, R. W.
1958 "Developmental basis of behavior," in *Behavior and evolution.* Edited by A. Roe and G. G. Simpson, 128–139. New Haven: Yale University Press.
SPITZ, R. A.
1965 *The first year of life.* New York: International Universities Press.
SPUHLER, J. N.
1959 "Somatic paths to culture," in *The evolution of man's capacity for culture.* Arranged by J. N. Spuhler. Detroit: Wayne State University Press.
WADDINGTON, C. H.
1967 *The ethical animal.* Chicago: The University of Chicago Press.
WAELDER, R.
1962 Psychoanalysis, scientific method, and philosophy. *Journal of the American Psychoanalytic Association* 10:617–637.
1964 *Basic theory of psychoanalysis.* SB 80. New York: Schocken.
WASHBURN, S. L.
1959 "Speculations on the interrelations of the history of tools and biological evolution," in *The evolution of man's capacity for culture.* Arranged by J. N. Spuhler. Detroit: Wayne State University Press.

The Oedipus Complex and the Bengali Family in India (A Study of Father-Daughter Relations in Bengal)

MANISHA ROY

Notwithstanding the risk of dealing with a passé subject, I intend to examine the utility of the Oedipus complex theory[1] in the context of a culture that neither Freud nor any Freudian studied. My justifications relate to the general subject matter of personality and culture, and they are as follows: (1) if psychoanalysis rejects the Oedipus complex theory as being useless in analyzing cross-cultural data,[2] one must see exactly where the problem lies, (2) in understanding adult personality within the sociocultural dynamics of any culture, the theory may at least help to formulate meaningfully whatever existing information we have, and (3) in this process of understanding, it is possible to come out with a modified version of the theory for fruitful use in wider comparative contexts than is commonly believed.[3]

I was led to attempt such an examination by my observations of family

I wish to thank Professors A. K. Ramanujan of the University of Chicago and Melford E. Spiro of the University of California, San Diego, for their helpful comments on the first draft of this paper.

[1] The term Oedipus complex will be used here as a general term to mean Oedipal tendencies in both male and female. The implications of the myth of Oedipus Rex that underlie Freud's coining of the term are therefore irrelevant here.

[2] Sinha mentions one of the early psychoanalysts in Calcutta, Dr. Girindrasekhar Bose, whose correspondence with Freud says, "... my Indian patients do not exhibit castration symptoms to such a marked degree as my European cases .... The Oedipus mother is very often a combined parental image and this is a fact of great importance." (Letter dated April 11, 1929.)

I had personal communication with four psychoanalysts and psychiatrists on this matter. All of them were trained in the West and practiced in both Western countries and India. They categorically reject the utility of the Oedipus complex theory in the analysis of their Indian patients.

[3] See for example Parsons (1969) and Stephens (1962).

dynamics among upper and upper-middle class Bengali families in urban India. I discovered that crucial aspects of adult personality must be explained by early child-rearing as well as later enculturation practices within the given framework of the culture — which in its turn is couched in a very distinctive cultural milieu influenced by a unique religious ideology. My study of Bengali childhood indicates strong Oedipal tendencies that have definite and discernible outcomes in later life. Though strong Oedipal tendencies are generated within Bengali families, specific socio-cultural factors make the individual handling and coping with the complex uniquely interesting. Whether one can use the theory as postulated by Freud is another question.

This brings me to the theory itself. According to Freud, in the Western nuclear family a child gives up the sexual fantasies centered on the parent of the opposite sex in his latency period and then identifies with the parent of the same sex whom he or she takes over as ego-ideal. The object-cathexes are given up and replaced by identifications because of the castration fears (Freud 1923).

From my formulation of Freud's theory it is immediately clear that I am selecting only that part of the theory which emphasizes the "passing" of the complex rather than its genesis. The problem of acquiring data on "instinct" and "fantasy" in very early childhood (which Freud believed were connected with the genesis of the complex) is obvious, whether one is working in non-Western or Western contexts.[4] The dearth of any kind of clinical data from Bengal on this problem compels me to restrict myself to the second part of the theory, concentrating on aspects of the process of object choice, identification, and the mechanism of the resolution of the complex. This aspect also relates to the social structure (availability of the choice of object) and to the cultural norm (supporting the choice), and renders a non-Western case more focused in its variability and distinctiveness.

With regard to the feasibility of treating the part of the theory in the context of societies Freud did not study, I must mention two papers (Parsons 1969; Ramanujan 1972) written on the Oedipus complex in two different cultures. Ramanujan traces the presence of Oedipus-like episodes in Indian mythology with a reversal in the direction of aggression and desire (father suppressing sons and desiring daughters and mother desiring

---

[4]   My search for psychoanalytic data on the fantasy structure of Indian patients failed. In a personal communication (January 1973) Dr. H. B. M. Murphy of the Section of Transcultural Psychiatric Studies, McGill University, Montreal, Canada, suggested that, unlike his European patients, the Indian female patients rarely fantasized early pseudomemories of being seduced by their fathers.

sons and exiling daughters). Parsons examines the development of the
Oedipus complex within the context of the southern Italian family system, and finds a similar reversal in the direction of aggression and the
expression of attraction within the general pattern of unlike sexes attracting and like sexes repelling. The answer to the pertinent question of why
the direction of the Oedipus complex is reversed (as illustrated by Indian
mythology and southern Italian sociology) seems to lie in some similarity
of social and cultural factors. However, I shall not address myself to the
aspect of direction, which may well be connected with the authority
structure in the family system.

A HYPOTHESIS

In a Bengali upper- or middle-class family the father and daughter are
highly cathected libidinal objects. The girl is treated as a substitute sexual
object by her father and father-figures during her later childhood and in
adolescence, even after puberty. This results in a strong emphasis on
romantic cross-sex ties within the family rather than on same-sex identifications; incestuous fantasies are repressed, preserved, and delayed in
such a way that they may never be fully replaced by actual sexual relationships within a marriage. The resolution waits until an extrafamilial object
choice is available, at least in some cases.

Though I have chosen to concentrate on the Oedipus complex in a girl
within the Bengali family system, I should point out that the Oedipus
complex of the young boy is not quite a mirror reflection of the girl's. The
difference between the two cases does not just originate from the sex difference of the "egos." One significant variable is the length of time the
individuals remain as highly cathected libidinal objects; for a mother and
son this is a lifetime, whereas the daughter is removed in her late adolescence from the family by the practice of patrilocal marriage. As this time
factor is a crucial one, it is appropriate to treat the two cases separately.
However, by concentrating on the woman and the father-daughter dyad,
I am not claiming that the problem of the Oedipus complex in a woman's
life can be fully understood without referring to its counterpart, the
Oedipus complex in a male.

ESSENTIAL STRUCTURAL CONCEPTS

In this society a familial role always embodies what I would call a "composite image." The role is composite not in terms of kinship categories (as is never the case in a descriptive kinship system like the Bengali system) but in terms of various affective components that may overlap with the affective components of other roles. Though a person occupying a role is clearly distinguished as a "father," a "mother," or even a "second older brother," in both address and reference terms, in the context of the interpersonal relationship, any given role may not only overlap but replace other roles. For example, a father may offer protection, nurturance, affection, and companionship to the daughter, thus combining in one person a father, mother, brother, and uncle. This is especially true during very early childhood and later adolescence in this section of Indian society. This aspect of composite role-overlap seems to be a necessary condition for a joint family to operate. The fact that the father embodies the affective components of various father-figures vis-à-vis his daughter (an uncle, a male teacher, a grandfather, a husband to her mother, and even a god like Śiva) is crucial for our concern. How that comes about will be clear only in a discussion of the developmental process in the early part of a woman's life cycle (for details see Roy 1972). As I am concerned only with the problems and resolution of the Oedipus complex in a woman's life, the discussion need not take the reverse direction, i.e. the father as the ego vis-à-vis his daughter. However, it may be mentioned in passing that this "composite image" of a role may also be true for a daughter-figure, especially when she is an adolescent. At any rate, it is important to remember that the "father" I shall refer to is actually a father-figure in terms of affective components, although he is also the father, a parent of the opposite sex, to his daughter. I believe that the latter aspect of the father's role in relation to his daughter is an important factor in accentuating her Oedipal tendencies.

TWO ESSENTIAL RELIGIOUS AND MYTHOLOGICAL IDEOLOGIES

Religious ideology in this culture acts not only as a reflection of sociological and cultural reality but also as a major sanctioning agent for behavioral norms. The sociocultural concepts often find expression in the mythology supported by a strong religious ideology. The most important of the Bengali mythological and religious concerns are the goddess and her worship. The roles of the goddess as perceived by her worshipers show a certain "compositeness." On one level, the goddess the Bengalis worship during ten days in autumn every year is Durgā. Durgā (according to the story told in the *Chandi* portion of *Mārkandeya Purāna* scripture) is mighty in power and beauty; she is also the personification of *shakti*, "the creative energy of nature". She is, at her moment of triumph, ten-armed, riding a living lion, killing the buffalo-demon, the gods' enemy. The worship of Durgā every year offers a cultural ritual to acknowledge the power of a goddess whom her supplicants adore, love, and fear. The aspect of feat, however, is more expressed in an effort to appease Kāli, the destructive version of the same goddess who resides in almost every town, city, and village of Bengal, demanding sacrifices, because her benediction is death. A Bengali man rises from his bed in the morning uttering and repeating the words "mother Durgā" and "mother Kāli," remembering her for her protective power in his everyday life. Finally, there is the third aspect of the goddess, named Jagaddhātri, who is worshiped for her affectionate, tender, motherly qualities. Though all three of these roles of the goddess are worshiped at different times of the year, the mythology offers the identity of the goddess on a very human level. In the mind of a supplicant, she presents the several developmental roles of a woman, beginning with a little girl Umā, who is the daughter of the powerful king Daksha, and later the wife of Śiva. She is a daughter,[5] a wife, and also a mother who brings her four children with her during her ten-day visit in autumn to her father's home, which in the ritual is the home of every Bengali man and woman.

Thus, a religion based on popular mythology brings the most powerful goddess down into a familial relationship — in the role of a daughter — for her worshipers. She is superordinate in one context and subordinate in another. The supplicant is the child as he addresses Durgā and Kāli as "mother;" he is also father to Durgā as she visits her father's home. This dual identification on the part of the worshiper makes the goddess-complex in Bengal expressive of love, affection, fear, and tenderness, rather than devotion and fear alone.

The combination of various affective components that make up the Bengali father's feelings toward his daughter — whom he also often calls

[5] In Bengal numerous folk songs were composed by Ramprasad, a well-known devotee of goddess Kāli, on the theme of the child-goddess Umā's leaving her father's household for her husband's. The simple and direct appeal in these lyrics depicting the sorrow of separation between the married daughter and her parents is very great indeed. The sentiment is very close to the reality, where, according to the Hindu custom, many girls are still married off at an early age, especially in rural Bengal. A free translation of one such song runs as follows: (Umā's mother is addressing her husband Giri, Umā's father) "Giri, I am not going to send her back, when Umā comes this time; I shall not pay any heed to anyone, even if they gossip. If Mrityunjay (Umā's husband) wants her back / I shall argue with my daughter and / I shall not listen to him just because he is my son-in-law."

"mother," as he does his own mother and the goddess — is not only reflected in the religious mythology but continues to be supported by it through the cognitive acceptance of the concept of goddess-worship. One may even suggest that this cognitive acceptance is based on a collective consciousness in a Durkheimian sense and is passed on from generation to generation on the social level, while a process of internalization takes place within the individuals.[6] Or perhaps cultural symbols such as the goddess-complex arise in the area where the culture both exploits (by actual effective closeness) and inhibits (by imposing taboos) primary drives. Thus, goddess-worship in Bengal may be viewed as an outcome of the sublimated libidinal wishes of father toward daughter and son toward mother. Following the same line of interpretation, the tabooed object (the daughter) becomes internalized in such a way that the goddess comes to play the role of the superego, the conscience of the whole Bengali society.

The second religious factor in this culture, a growing girl's worship of Śiva and Kṛṣṇa encourages her fantasies about a husband/lover object. Unlike the goddess, in whose worship the whole community becomes the worshiper, Śiva and Kṛṣṇa are worshiped by individuals on a very personal level. Śiva is the god all girls are encouraged to worship in order to be blessed by a Śiva-like husband. Śiva is an ideal husband to Umā. While Śiva remains the distant god residing in the mountains as Umā's future husband (as her father is to the girl's mother), a girl's emotional satisfaction is reaped from identifying herself with Rādhā, the consort-lover of Kṛṣṇa. Kṛṣṇa, the charming cowherd, loved passionately by all the milkmaids, occupies a very important place among the Bengali household deities. A girl in this culture is exposed to an array of religious, pseudo-religious, and popular literature, as well as other mass media revolving around and highlighting the theme of the exalting but adulterous love between Kṛṣṇa and Rādhā, the ultimate divine love. The girl is told to aspire for a husband like Śiva, but her attraction for Kṛṣṇa as a lover, charmer, and often mischievous tease is insurmountable although Kṛṣṇa never takes on the image of an ideal husband on either the mythological or the folk level. This split of the two male gods representing almost dichotomous male personalities in the personal world of a growing girl's adolescence has a strong impact on her ideas and concepts regarding the men with whom she interacts.

[6]   See Parson's analysis of the Madonna complex in southern Italy (1969). However, unlike her, I only suggest that the Bengali goddess-worship is in part an interpretative apparatus, as well as a more discernible ideological sanction and a reflection of the social reality.

(It is possible to argue that the splitting of the goddess into the powerful Durgā and fearful Kālī does not have quite similar implications in the personality formation of a man. In the first place, both aspects refer to the same goddess, who also has a human social image, namely, a woman and a mother. The dichotomy that the two personality types Durgā and Kālī produce is not self-contradictory but only two sides of one goddess, highlighted according to the contexts. Besides, both aspects are worshiped by men and women alike. She is a national goddess, a protector-mother for all. No Bengali man is found to worship either form of the goddess as a personal deity. As for a woman, not only are Śiva and Kṛṣṇa two separate gods but they also are introduced by separate mythologies and life histories. Further, according to the interpretation of the Vaishnava cult, Kṛṣṇa lived on this earth as a human being and loved a common woman of flesh and blood — which increases his appeal to a woman.)

Thus, the influence of the dichotomous images of Śiva and Kṛṣṇa as ideal husband and ideal lover is very significant in the formative years of a Bengali girl; she remains very close to the father-figure of her joint family, who embodies at times both images. For example, she may sometimes view her father as a distant figure like Śiva (vis-à-vis her mother), because her parents do not demonstrate any affectionate interaction within the family; she may even occasionally identify with the mother and idealize the father as a desirable husband for herself. The culture tells her it is good to have a husband who, like Śiva, is honorable, distant, and respectable. However, her very warm and close interaction with her father-figures — some of whom, such as a young uncle or a cousin, may take the role of a teasing, loving Kṛṣṇa and become subsumed in the father in her adolescence — also makes the father with his composite roles appear like both Śiva and Kṛṣṇa. But for a man, the goddess is always a desexualized mother who acts as a cultural superego as well as a protector. How such a goddess reflects and symbolizes the Oedipal tendencies of a man in this culture can be discussed on another occasion. It may suffice to note at this point that despite the different quality of the Durgā/Kālī and Śiva/Kṛṣṇa mythic images, the influences they exert upon the male-female interactions and relationships turn out to be equally problematic.

FAMILY DYNAMICS

I will now turn to the joint-family dynamics where the Oedipus complex itself is generated and, I argue, perpetuated and delayed, offering a woman a major emotional content throughout her life.

Two points must be mentioned at the very beginning of this section. First, as in most northern Indian families, a daughter is physically removed from the scene of her father's family after her marriage. Second, in this part of Bengali society the length of time a daughter spends in her father's home before marriage is about twenty years, i.e. until her early adulthood. Besides, her whole adolescence is spent in close emotional contact with her father. This closeness becomes more intense because of the knowledge of the inevitable separation after marriage. During her early childhood she spends the first two or three years entirely with the mother-figures; her introduction to the world of the father-figures begins at an age when she can distinguish, differentiate, and learn to use her emotions. She discovers that the father-figures pay more attention to her than do her mother and aunts, who continue to give her food and care but no overt affection and love. The men, on the other hand, play with her, bring gifts to her, and let her exploit their feelings for her. The foundation of her various feelings — love, affection, tenderness, anger, teasing, domination, subordination, dependence — is laid by this world of father-figures, which also becomes the escape-world for her from the world of women who discipline her and tell her about her future duties as a woman. Thus, from her father-figures she learns, in a pleasant way, to nurture the emotions. By the time she becomes an adolescent, a girl learns to concentrate on one father-figure, usually her own father, who is a composite of all other father-figures. The social and cultural restrictions against any relationship with a person of the opposite sex outside her joint family during her adolescence pushes her toward the men in her own family — notably her father — and she is given considerable scope to exploit the situation, although a strong incest/taboo operates for both father and daughter.

The repressive mechanism to ignore sex appears to be quite effective, at least in the case of a growing girl.[7] The sexual information that an adolescent girl receives from her peers and such extrafamilial sources as movies, novels, etc., is also pushed aside to be realized later, for the society does not allow any actual sexual outlets at this stage. She waits eagerly

---

[7]   The word "sex" (as it is used in Western parlance) does not exist in Bengali. Even among their peers, girls talk about it as related to matters of romance, marriage, and so on. Within the family the subject is taboo. However, there are various indirect verbal and nonverbal communications possible to indicate sex-related matters, such as undesirable, unrespectable lust among OTHER people such as the neighbors and characters in novels and movies. It is a forbidden world that a girl only enters without the knowledge of her family. She feels slight guilt about indulging in such talks and readings as her peers may provide. Therefore, it is also extremely difficult to elicit information on such feelings and behavior from the members of these households.

for the marriage — the only sanctioned situation where she can relate to a man emotionally as well as sexually.

The Hindu wedding ceremony itself is noteworthy in this context. The elaborate ritual enacts the actual severance between the daughter and the father. The father ritually "gives away" the daughter to her husband, the man who is to replace her father. For the bride the personal excitement is at its peak because of the anticipation of a full life of emotional and physical union with her husband — a replacement of her father, whose composite role vis-à-vis herself only planted the seeds of libidinal expectations, never gratified them. A girl's incestuous tensions approach a release at last. I suspect that the strength of these incestuous wishes may even account for the very dramatic and explosive quality of the Hindu wedding ritual. However, the wedding, which not only symbolizes the aspect of separation between daughter and father but also physically removes her from the father's household, does not succeed in emancipating her from her Oepipal tendencies. Because of the composite nature of her father's role, which has been satisfying as well as inspiring a host of affective responses in her, nothing after marriage takes its place. In her husband's joint family none of her affinal male relatives, such as her father-in-law, older brother-in-law, and husband, offers the replacement, either individually or collectively. Because of the social customs of subtle avoidance and distance that underlie the relationship between a young married woman and her older male affines, these relationships remain only peripheral, founded on duty rather than on emotions. Her disappointments, particularly in her husband, fail to offer her the conditions for an intimate emotional interdependence. Unlike her father, who was a father-figure to her in her natal joint family, her husband does not embody a composite role. He is only one figure who offers her sexual access, some protection, and often unexpressed affection. He represents the distant figure of Śiva, the cultural ideal of a husband. She craves the warm, open, and emotionally charged intimacy that she experienced with her father. Despite her sexual relations with her husband, her erotic expectations remain unfulfilled because of the lack of associative romance that she hoped her husband would bring. Physical union becomes a practice that must be justified by procreation, not by the pleasure and exaltation that Rādhā and Kṛṣṇa were supposed to have had. I cannot discuss here the development factors in the husband's life to show that he learns to nurture quite different expectations from his marriage, thus adding to the total frustration of the wife.

Immediately after the marriage, therefore, a young woman reaps whatever pleasure she can from her relationship with her husband's younger brother (or brother-figure), with whom she has more freedom to establish a warm friendship tinted with romantic overtones. The unmarried young brother-in-law, who occupies a marginal position in his own joint family, bound by cultural restrictions against keeping company with the opposite sex outside the family, is only too eager to respond to his young sister-in-law. This relationship offers her partial satisfaction for the unfulfilled romantic expectations in her marriage. However, this is only partially so. Bengali familial customs usually sanction only a platonic friendship and only for a period of time — until the brother-in-law enters his own marriage.

A woman's next possibility is to transfer her affective needs to her first-born son, who offers a more engrossing physical involvement at least for the first three or four years and the more satisfying prospect of a lifelong attachment and emotional interdependence. However, despite all the familial and cultural emphasis on the "glory of motherhood," sooner or later a woman discovers that her son too does not offer a true emotional replacement for her father. A son depends on his mother emotionally, but he gets more than he offers. She becomes emotionally weary and lonely by the time the son begins his own married life. However, the lifelong proximity of the son and the mother (unlike the father-daughter dyad) in a joint family does act as the central axis in the perpetuation of the joint family, despite the emotional dissatisfaction on the part of at least one of the participants. The incestuous tension of this relationship is never very close to the surface, and the culture provides innumerable symbols and customs to repress such emotion. All other social relations in a joint family appear to function only to allow this mother-son relationship to remain a viable structure. In fact, one may even argue that the father-daughter dyad offers a countervailing aspect to the permanency of the mother-son dyad. But this is a structural explanation viewed from the angle of the viability of the joint family.

To return to the woman, even her involvement with her son cannot totally satisfy her. She goes back to the fantasy of her own father. Her age at this stage is also a very important factor, and the person she next turns to is a man from outside her family — not a father, a husband, or even a son, but a religious guide, a guru, who comes close to the original father-figure.

The guru at last represents the COMPOSITE ROLE of her own father in her natal joint family, primarily because the relationship, being extrafamilial, is not founded on strict familial norms and ideals. The normative aspect of the relationship is founded on broad religious and cultural ideals. A disciple should address a guru as *bābā* 'father' and treat him respectfully and with utter obedience. A guru, on the other hand, treats a disciple with affection, guidance, understanding, and nurturance. He must be strong enough to accept the demand of the disciple for total nurturance. He is supposed to guide the disciple to find his or her way to be united with God and attain ultimate salvation. This ideal perfectly suits the emotional needs of a Bengali woman. In her declining years (often near menopause) she craves to become a helpless infant as well as a woman, as she was in her late adolescence with her own father. She attempts to recapture this fantasy by becoming a child-woman to her guru, whom she calls *bābā* and to whom she emphasizes her utter helplessness as well as her love and devotion, as Rādhā offered Kṛṣṇa, her god/lover.[8]

A structural and cultural norm creates conditions that almost predetermine a successful relationship from the woman's point of view. In this culture it is considered extremely commendable for a woman of middle age to become a disciple of a guru and to devote all her time to religious activities. The joint family endorses this because a middle-aged woman should not be too involved with her family and "get in everybody's way." Also, a religious woman brings prestige to her family. The vital psychological factor is, of course, the need of the woman to have a total emotional relationship with her guru, who is completely acceptable in terms of familial, cultural, and social standards. The guru's association with the Vaishnava cult, the literature in which he is particularly well-versed, and his frequent use of the love theme of Rādhā-Kṛṣṇa in his talks and sermons to his diciples make it easier for the woman to identify him with god Kṛṣṇa, who is also a god of love. She can relate to her guru, at least in her fantasy, as Rādhā related to Kṛṣṇa.

Thus, her relationship with the guru comes close to the fulfillment of her craving for a father-figure who is also a combination of Śiva and Kṛṣṇa images. The Oedipus complex that was generated in her early childhood, maintained and perpetuated in her adolescence, and prolonged in her youth at last is resolved by the fulfillment in her relationship with a guru — a figure who combines the roles of father, son, brother, and god. Whereas the biological family is the place of origin and perpetuation of the Oedipus complex, the resolution must come from outside the natal or affinal family.

---

[8]　See Roy (1972), for details on confessions by women in which it is quite clear that their satisfaction and gratification with their gurus may include strong sexual fantasies, if not the actual act.

CONCLUSION

In summary, we found: (1) the father becomes a father-figure encompassing a number of roles represented by the other male relatives of the growing girl, and this composite element of the father's role becomes the crucial factor in the prolongation of the Oedipus complex, (2) the resolution of the complex may take place only outside the joint family structure in a dyadic relationship with a religious man who successfully replaces the originally cathected libidinal object, the father, with strong support from the cultural and religious ideology, and (3) Bengali religious and cultural ideology may be supportive of the Oedipus complex within an individual by offering the person a cultural superego figure from within the religion; therefore, in this culture it is a goddess, not one of the parents, who comes to take on the role of the cultural superego.

REFERENCES

FREUD, S.
  1923   The passing of the Oedipus complex. *International Journal of Psychoanalysis* 4:419–424.
  1933   *New introductory lectures on psychoanalysis.* New York: W. W. Norton.
  1955   *The interpretation of dreams.* New York: Basic Books.
  1958   "A special type of choice of object made by men," in *On creativity and unconscious.* New York: Harper and Brothers.
PARSONS, ANN
  1969   "Is Oedipus complex universal?" in *Belief, magic and anomie: essays in psychosocial anthropology*, 1–66. New York: Free Press.
RAMANUJAN, A. K.
  1972   "The Indian Oedipus," in *Indian literature: a symposium.* Edited by A. Poddar, 127–137. Simla: Indian Institute of Advanced study.
ROY, M.
  1972   "Ideal and compensatory roles in the life-cycle of an upper-class Bengali woman in India." Unpublished Ph. D. dissertation, University of California, San Diego.
SINHA, T. C.
  1966   Development of psychoanalysis in India. *International Journal of Psychoanalysis* 47(2–3):430–439.
STEPHENS, WILLIAM N.
  1962   *The Oedipus complex: cross-cultural evidence.* Glencoe: Free Press.

PART TWO

Researching the Psychology
of Culture Change

LOUISE S. SPINDLER

Anthropologists have largely discarded the nomenclature "culture and personality," sometimes equated with a "school," and more recently have referred to the area which subsumes many of the interests of the earlier workers in culture and personality, as well as other more recent concerns, as "psychological anthropology." This term seems to be the only one general enough to cover the many kinds of psychologically oriented studies being carried on today by anthropologists, mainly in North America (see Pelto 1967). With this designation, researchers can escape the legacy of strong criticisms levelled at culture and personality research, such as the claim that they took a "uniformitarian" view of shared personality characteristics, which failed to take account of intra-society diversity and the role of culture in organizing that diversity, along with the criticism that culture and personality researchers were singularly preoccupied with psychoanalytic explanations and neglected cognitive and physiological factors (Wallace 1970).

During the last decade, stemming mainly from ethnoscience and ethnosemantics, componential analyses, and psycho-linguistic techniques and models has come a strong, and to some extent resurgent, interest on the part of psychological anthropologists in cognition, i.e. the thought processes and especially their structuring. There have been forerunners in this area. Malinowski was interested in these kinds of data and many configurationalists made attempts to describe the ways in which people impose meaning upon the world around them: R. Benedict (patterns), Kluckhohn (key principles), Opler (themes), Hoebel (postulates), Sapir (covert patterns), and L. Thompson, Redfield, and Hallowell (world view). Some anthropologists were more explicit than others about the importance of cognition *per se*. As early as 1936, Gregory Bateson (1958: 220) realized the importance of recognizing the cognitive aspects of personality, complementing and offsetting the focus on the emotional and biological concepts (mainly Freudian) in wide usage at the time. His concept of EIDOS did just that. It may be defined as an expression in culturally defined behavior of the cognitive aspects of the personality of individuals (Bateson 1958: 118).

The concept of "world view," effectively developed first by R. Redfield (1952) and represented in Hallowell's well-known studies of the Ojibwa, is predominantly of cognitive genre. Hallowell generalizes from the Ojibwa data:

All cultures provide cognitive orientation toward a world in which man is compelled to act. A culturally constituted world view... by means of beliefs, available knowledge and language, mediates personal adjustment to the world through such psychological processes as perceiving, recognizing, conceiving, judging, and reasoning. It is a blueprint for a meaningful interpretation of objects and events... (1963: 106).

The ethnoscientist's aim is to elicit replicable data from the informant's point of view. The approach represents a systematic attempt to discover the knowledge a group of people are using to organize their behaviors. The relationship between cognitive structure and taxonomies elicited by ethnoscientific methods is controversial. The taxonomies, however, do represent the way people categorize, code, and define their own experience. They are a significant dimension of the materials with which men perceive and think. The approach itself may be static and may be applicable in its most rigorous form to only certain cultural domains (see Romney and D'Andrade 1964; Burling 1964). Nevertheless, the taxonomies elicited may well be one of the best indices to cognitive convergence and divergence in psychocultural systems.

The culture concept has been redefined to fit the emphases on the ideational, mentalistic aspects of culture, Ward Goodenough, for example, has offered a definition that relates to the development of ethnoscience and cognitive anthropology and, in turn, to research in psychocultural anthropology.

... it [culture] does not consist of things, people, behavior, or emotions. It is rather an organization of these. ... It is the forms of things that people have in mind, their models for perceiving, relating, and otherwise interpreting them (Goodenough 1961).

At an earlier date other anthropologists, such as Kluckhohn and Kelley (1945), had offered related definitions. They identified culture as "designs for living," "patterns" of ideas, and symbolic-meaningful systems, but the trends of the times were not congruent with these attempts.

Goodenough's definition links cognition and culture. The new focus offers a common meeting ground for linguists, ethnoscientists, and psychological anthropologists interested in cognition. With this new orientation a few anthropologists are taking a new look at the Rorschach and other projective techniques, more of them are enthusiastic about symbolic analyses (including Freudian, Lévi-Straussian, and Jungian analyses), and others are re-examining concepts such as world view (see recent use of this concept in Kearney 1972) and are making better-informed appraisals of many of these earlier constructs and approaches.

THE PSYCHOLOGY OF CULTURE CHANGE

The introductory comments above are intended to set the stage, in contemporary terms, for a more specialized focus on the psychological approach to culture change, a field of inquiry which has appeared only recently in anthropological research. Worldwide urbanization and industrialization is bringing hundreds of small, technologically and politically emergent societies under the pressures of heretofore unfelt new and upsetting problems of adaptation. The era of urbanization and industrialization was preceded by and still intermingles with the era of culture change and acculturation brought about by the dramatic expansion of Western culture during the nineteenth century. Anthropologists have become more and more interested in these processes. The conditions leading to demoralization and disintegration, versus those associated with successful adaptation, are underlying foci of attention, though not always explicitly stated. At some undefined point the study of acculturation and culture change grades off into the study of urbanization. Psychological processes have always been included, but with varying degrees of emphasis and adequacy of formulation.

The earlier attempts to deal with these kinds of processes focused on the specific cultural traits that were selected or excluded during the cultural contact situation, rather than on the psychological mechanisms involved. The major part of the "Memorandum for the study of acculturation," sponsored by the Social Science Research Council in 1936, was devoted to a scheme for the analysis of cultural traits. In the section on "psychological mechanisms," the individual is discussed as the unit of analysis, with emphasis on his personality and social status. The equation of the individual with psychological process leaves the problem at an idiosyncratic level. This equation was one reason for the rejection of psychologizing by some anthropologists; they saw such a focus as a form of reductionism from the cultural level that is likely to lead nowhere (G. and L. Spindler 1963: 521). The 1936 memo does, however, include a form of psychology as a major dimension and indicates that anthropologists interested in culture change felt the need to move toward a more adequate formulation of the psychological process even at that early date.

In 1954 anthropologists, under the auspices of the Social Science Research Council, again tried to devise an orderly approach to the study of acculturation. In this memorandum individuals, as such, were not included, but "intercultural roles" were. The memorandum seems more advanced in its use of psychological concepts, as it includes ideological, motivational, and perceptual sets as factors in role-playing. The frame of reference is, however, still cultural. As the process of acculturation is conceived, a coherent, organized system (culture) responds, through people, to the impact of another system.

This orientation has contemporary overtones. A major criticism to be leveled against it, however, is that when the cultural system begins to disintegrate and individuation takes place, the formulation is no longer adequate. This frame of reference cannot explain why or how the system disintegrates unless neopsychological formulations, such as "perception of new alternatives," "anxiety about the efficacy of traditional solutions," or "striving for prestige in emergent status systems" are utilized. Both the 1936 and 1954 memos explicitly acknowledge the existence of a psychological dimension, but both appear to place a great burden upon the culture concept (G. and L. Spindler 1963: 520–524). And the concept in 1954 was implicitly couched in terms of what a person does, rather than in terms of how and what he thinks.

A. Irving Hallowell was one of the first anthropologists to design his research on acculturative processes with the focus on psychological adaptation. In his research with the Ojibwa (1952), he utilized psychological tools and concepts to relate psychological processes to changes in culture as people adapted to changes wrought in the conditions of their existence by the impact of Euro-American culture, economics, and political power.

Since the problems George Spindler and I have encountered over the past twenty-five years in our research are shared by many workers interested in the psychology of culture change, from this point on the discussion will draw heavily upon strategies used by us, with a critique of each in turn. A variety of strategies used in combination with a variety of data will be covered. Each model and strategy was built with knowledge acquired about the shortcomings of earlier models and strategies. The following analyses can be thought of as a case study of trials and errors. We feel that after building models and devising new techniques the anthropologist should return to the field to retest and revise his creations. The publications referred to begin with "An experimental design in the study of the psychology of culture change" (G. Spindler and Goldschmidt 1952) and end with *Dreamers without power: the Menomini Indians* (G. and L. Spindler 1971) and *Burgbach: urbanization and identity in a German village* (G. Spindler 1973).

AN EXPERIMENTAL DESIGN

The specific aim during the first periods of research, starting in 1948 with our first study of the Menomini Indians of Wisconsin, has been to find a way to relate the manifest aspects of socioeconomic and cultural life to the manner in which people in change perceive and respond to the world about them. Our interest, however, was never in the individual as such, but rather in the shared processes of psychocultural adaptation. The Rorschach projective technique was used in the first phases of the Menomini study as an expression of perceptual structure. A sociocultural schedule with 23 indexes and 180 coded items ranging from mode of living (house type, income) to items on the belief system (G. Spindler 1955) represented the manifest sociocultural dimension. In a sense, both the Rorschach responses and sociocultural indices could be considered products of an individual's perceptual organization. It was necessary, however, to keep them rigorously separated for analytic purposes. With our aims in mind and with these particular techniques decided upon, George Spindler and Walter Goldschmidt devised a model that was an approximation of an experimental design (G. Spindler and Goldschmidt 1952). The focus was on the covariance between processes. The four statistically validated (G. Spindler 1955) levels of acculturation constituted what may be regarded as the independent variable and the patterns of perceptual structure derived from statistical treatment of Rorschach indices the dependent variable.

We now regard the concept of "levels" of acculturation as too passive. In our most recent publication on the Menomini (G. and L. Spindler 1971) we regard our acculturative "levels" as various forms of coping, adaptive strategies that deal actively with the situation created by the confrontation between two highly divergent, in fact incongruent, psycho-cultural systems — the Menomini and the North American-European. "Acculturative levels" infers a kind of passive assimilation into the latter by the former. While assimilation did occur and will continue to occur, it is not all that did or will happen. Each of our "levels" of acculturation were represented by groups that we term sociocultural categories. Each of these resisted, adopted, or adopted only partially the dominant culture. The shift in interpretation can be seen clearly in the difference between any of our publications in the fifties and our most recent (1971) on the Menomini. Other workers who have been in this field for twenty years or more seem to have the same problem, though not all have developed a new interpretive approach. It is interesting that the change in stance is not alone, or even primarily a result of new scientific knowledge or accumulated theory. It is an adaptation on the part of the anthropologist to a change in the tenor of the times. Our terminology in this paper must fall short of a full expression of these trends, for if it were reformulated, it would not be an accurate representation of what we actually did. This is a part of the case study we are presenting of our work.

In the initial stages of designing our research, we were heavily influenced by Hallowell's study of the Ojibwa (1952). In this pioneer study, Hallowell isolated three Ojibwa groups representing different levels of acculturation (terms as used then). Through analyses of Rorschach protocols utilizing composite group profiles comprised of averages of special Rorschach determinants, he found continuity of the same basic psychological pattern through three stages of acculturation — with a persistent core of generic traits which could be identified as Ojibwa (Hallowell 1951: 38).

In our research with the Menomini we were able to isolate four sociocultural groups on the basis of religious identification (G. Spindler 1955). Statistical tests were applied to socioeconomic and cultural indexes, such as house type, education, use of medical facilities, etc., which validated the existence of a continuum of acculturative adaptation running from a native-oriented to two acculturated groups. The Rorschach technique was then applied to a sample of 68 adult males drawn from the four sociocultural categories in the continuum. The females were dealt with later (L. Spindler 1962) and compared to the males (L. and G. Spindler 1958). The differences between the categories, on the basis of Rorschach as well as sociocultural indices, proved to be statistically significant, numerous, and consistent. The two ends of the adaptive continuum, most unlike in the sociocultural dimension, were most unlike in the psychological dimension. The highly socioculturally deviant Peyote group was differentiated more frequently in Rorschach scores from every other Menomini group than was any acculturative category. An intensive study was made of the Peyotists, with collections of visions, autobiographical interviews, and extensive observations of both ritual and everyday behavior (G. Spindler 1952). It was clear that the cult represented a systematic deviation, a term developed by E. M. Lemert (1951). The psychological deviation, as revealed by Rorschach responses, is expressed in ways that are strikingly parallel to the unique directives and behaviors that distinguish the Peyote Cult in its sociocultural dimensions. It is the only Menomini category in which human movement responses exceed the animal movement responses, where introspective responses are numerous and where overt, relatively uncontrolled emotions are displayed in Rorschach responses. The Rorschach responses, the peyote ritual, and peyote belief system are highly integrated — virtually expressions, of each other. The fantasy expressed in their responses revolves about the relation of the individual to the supernatural. These fantasies also express deep anxiety and self-doubt, attitudes which were revealed in the autobiographical interviews and in behaviors and beliefs in the ritual content. This analysis is given complete expression in *Dreamers without power* (G. and L. Spindler 1971). These kinds of relationships between perceptual-cognitive organization and behavior patterns, we felt, were not only qualitatively but quantitatively interesting and offered important clues for further research.

Methodologically speaking, *even without interpretation of the presumed psychological meaning of Rorschach scores*, this pattern of deviation and differentiation among all the categories tells us much about the covariance of psychological and sociocultural processes in acculturative adaptation. We could posit that changes in external behaviors and symbols representing behavior during the acculturative process are paralleled by changes in the perceptual structure representative of each group.

We could have stopped here. However, after making explicit the questionable validity of many standard interpretive hypotheses applied to Rorschach scores, we proceeded to apply them consistently to the already demonstrated differences between sociocultural groups as these seemed to at least offer clues to the meaning of these complex relationships (G. and L. Spindler 1963: 527–528). In general we could say that application of these interpretive hypotheses produced results highly congruent with ethnographic observation and led us to new hypotheses that we could, and did, investigate in the field.

Comments on the Rorschach

Anthropologists using concepts such as world view or dealing with the basic premises of a culture must adduce these from what informants do and say in cultural context. Since the researcher has no data derived by techniques external to the particular cultural system, he is culture bound, almost wholly "emic" (for elaboration see the section below on the instrumental activities inventory), in his approach. He has no way of generalizing. Likewise, using the approach of the ethnoscientist, the epitome of the emic approach, the fieldworker can only collect responses to culturally phrased questions. The ethnoscientist's aim is to get to the point where he can predict what the informant's response will be in reference to a specific domain being investigated. In all of these kinds of strategies, a circularity trap becomes a problem, insofar as cognitive structure and process is of interest, as it was in a different way for the early workers in the field of culture and personality. All of these approaches are teleological in that the researcher derives cognitive products from cultural products. Culture and cognitive structure all become expressions of each other.

We decided in the early phases of our research that, in order to elicit relevant forms of perceptual structure, we must use an instrument that is external to the culture being studied; one that would allow the respondent to make a novel response not anticipated by a cultural pattern. Thus, our approach at that point was "etic." The Rorschach furnishes stimuli from outside the culture. We may not know what the responses to these stimuli mean. But when consistent changes in Rorschach patterning occur in different sociocultural categories, we surmise that differential psychological adaptations are being expressed. We can then try to figure out what these differential adaptations are, using categories meaningful across cultural domains. At the same time, the Rorschach approach is emic (Lindzey 1961) to the extent that it elicits the subjective reality of the informants in a way impossible with objective-type scheduled questionnaires.

In our own research, we used the Rorschach because we could elicit responses from which cognitive as well as affective and motivational processes may be inferred. Our use is tangential or even irrelevant to the conventional applications of the Rorschach as an instrument for personality assessment of individuals in our own society. We used standardized but culturally ambiguous stimuli to elicit culturally variant responses. The results are cryptic and often difficult to assess, but seem to furnish data that are sufficiently abstracted from the highly unique, emic, cultural-relevant responses (as those in life histories) to permit controlled comparisons of culture cases.

The Rorschach activates a set of complex processes which are little understood. Responses to the Rorschach are products of a person's cognitive-perceptual process, formed within a cultural milieu. They can be used to detect whether the psychological organization of persons or groups is changing in correspondence with change in the social, cultural, or biological (age, sex) milieu, even though their specific meaning can only be inferred.

Since the Rorschach interpretations were formulated with implicit assumptions about the universe held by members of Western culture, the field worker should be extremely cautious about using standard qualitative interpretations. There are many levels of interpretation possible. It is possible, for example, to emphasize perceptual processes, examining the parts of the inkblots used by the informant in his percept formation. Some, for example, create integrated wholes; others dwell on minute, isolated details.

Extensive criticisms have been levelled at studies dependent upon Rorschach results. In some cases, the criticisms stem from a misuse of the Rorschach. The fieldworker should have sufficient, reliable training in its use and some clinical experience. The technique, in the hands of amateurs, can be potentially dangerous for the subject and may produce results less than reliable for the researcher. Certain criticisms are unwarranted, however, as an implicit assumption is made that Rorschach data can be regarded as the basic, primary data of an anthropological study. Viewed in this light, demands are made of the Rorschach or other projective tests that are unrealistic. As Honigmann states:

Projective tests were not originally designed for such stringent use. They best provide auxiliary sources of information for a clinical psychologist or anthropologist to utilize along with an abundance of other knowledge... about the people he is studying (Honigmann 1967).

Our work, as mentioned, made use of Rorschach data in conjunction with sociocultural indices, interview materials, data from participant observation, and the expressive autobiographic interview technique. As this latter technique afforded us elaborate materials on the life adjustments of a reasonably large, selected sample of informants who represented both typical and deviant adaptations within each acculturative category, it needs a few words of explanation. The expressive autobiographic interview (EAI) is a cross between a structured interview and a chronological autobiography. The respondent is asked to tell the story of his or her life, but intervention by the anthropologist at critical points relevant to special foci (i.e. value conflicts, experiences in white society, witchcraft, sex), turns the autobiography to relevant considerations and permits an economy of time that is not possible with the full autobiography. This technique furnishes a useful complement to Rorschach data. In cases where an individual's Rorschach pattern is radically deviant, the fieldworker can elicit data on the special kinds of environmental stimuli to which the individual has had to adapt. The technique is most successful after the anthropologist knows enough about a people and their culture to be able to identify the key points around which to center inquiries. We selected our EAI sample on the basis of Rorschach data, in part, for this data identified psychologically deviant as well as modal individuals. (For more complete details see G. Spindler 1952 and G. and L. Spindler 1970).

Both the Spindlers and Hallowell, in their use of the Rorschach, committed two fallacies. One is the "global fallacy" and the other the "jumping fallacy." They are both typical anthropological fallacies insofar as studies of the psychology of acculturation are concerned and so merit some discussion. The "global fallacy" may be defined as the attempt to deal with a complex holistic construct like "personality" or "perceptual structure" as a variable. This is apparent in nearly everything that has been said about the Menomini and Ojibwa. It is a logical strategy in the light of the nature of anthropology as a discipline. It does raise rich, complex issues with respect to the covariance of psychological and sociocultural processes. It also raises serious methodological problems that cannot be lightly dismissed.

The "jumping fallacy" may be defined, following Leonard Doob (1960), as the application of unvalidated interpretive hypotheses concerning the meaning of Rorschach scores and profiles. The strategy is doubly complicated by the fact that we were doing cross-cultural research. We do not excuse ourselves on the basis of having to take what the psychologists give us in the way of tools and theories. If we know psychological theory and methodology, we can invent our own — at considerable cost of time and ingenuity. But to us the jumping strategy has value. We asked: "What will happen if we set up the most parsimonious standard interpretations available in the literature on projective techniques and apply them to a sample of persons whose characteristic overt behaviors are intimately known to us?" The results seemed to us to justify the decision. The interpretations based directly on Rorschach scores seem too functionally congruent with our other observations to be discarded.

It is apparent that we were applying a clinical, phenomenological, interpretive approach. We were aware of the dangers of ad hoc reasoning and the closure tendencies we all exhibit in the search for plausibility. The consistent relationships between Rorschach data and sociocultural observations led us to the inference that the Rorschach was tapping significant psychological processes in depth with sufficient reliability to allow us to use it as a complex index of psychological processes.

A STATISTICAL MODEL FOR RORSCHACH DATA

In 1958, being acutely aware of the disrepute into which the Rorschach had fallen, we attempted a new strategy in our efforts to reduce distortion of data. We used it in an attempt to describe differences between adult Menomini men and women in psychological adaptations to the exigencies of sociocultural change (L. and G. Spindler 1958: 217–233). At that time these differences were a little-studied area.

We discarded all conventional interpretations of the meaning of scores in analyzing the covariance of psychological process with manifest sociocultural adaptation and dealt exclusively with the concentration and dispersion of Rorschach scores in the various acculturative categories and in comparisons of males and females. By means of this approach we were able to say at what point in the acculturative continuum significant changes in psychological structure occurred, whether sociocultural deviation is accompanied by psychological deviation, and how relatively homogeneous a group is psychologically. The Rorschach used in this special manner provided information on modalities and distribution of psychological adaptations in culture change that would be difficult to gather or treat without a similar tool that provided quantitative data.

The strategy may be described as follows: the four acculturative categories for males and females had been validated statistically. Statistically significant differences were found in the distribution of Rorschach indices between categories for the men, but NOT for the women. However, significant differences were found between males and females without respect to acculturative categories (L. and G. Spindler 1958: 220). With the knowledge that gross overall psychological differences did exist between males and females in the sample, the problem became one of finding a technique that would make it possible to refine and exploit the meaning of these differences.

A modal technique applied to Tuscarora Indian Rorschachs by Anthony Wallace (1952) seemed to be a useful first step. In contrast to the application of the technique by Wallace, however, we used a modal perceptual structure for each sex as a measuring stick against which the Rorschach responses of males and females for each sociocultural category could be compared. The criticisms often levelled at the use of a concept such as "modal personality" used to represent an entire culture were automatically obviated.

With one modal perceptual structure established for the women and another for the men, it became possible to answer certain questions, i.e. which of the modal characteristics of each acculturative group account for the overall differences in psychological adaptation between the sexes? What is the distribution of the modal perceptual type throughout the continuum of acculturation for the two sexes? What is the location of what we chose to call the "psychocultural center of gravity" (PCG) for the men and women in the acculturative continuum and how is it different for the two sexes? That is, with which acculturative category does the perceptual structure for each sex sample as a whole converge? We were able to answer these questions with this strategy.

All of the differences uncovered by the gross test of male-female difference, mentioned earlier, were represented by the differences between the group perceptual structures, showing that there was not a fortuitous convergence of fractionated psychological factors drawn from diverse psychological types that could be held responsible for the differences. We could also say that the modal male perceptual structure for the entire sample was most like the modal structure of the transitional acculturative category and that the one for the females was most like that of the native-oriented group.

There are important implications to this discovery (L. and G. Spindler 1958: 226). For example, the prototypical perceptual structure for the women is native-oriented and it exhibits continuity throughout the acculturative continuum up to the elite acculturated position. At this point there is a "cutoff." It was also revealed that the psychocultural position for males is practically the reverse of that for the females (L. and G. Spindler 1958: 225). The central tendency of psychological adaptation for Menomini males in the sample is far toward full acculturation. These findings, based on statistical manipulations, were confirmed and amplified when the social and cultural materials for each person in the modal group were examined (L. and G. Spindler 1958: 226–231; G. Spindler 1955; L. Spindler 1956).

ROLES, VALUES, AND PERCEPTUAL STRUCTURE INTERRELATED

Two new variables were introduced in "The study of Menomini women and culture change" (L. Spindler 1962); they were role playing behaviors and values. The previous studies had utilized relationships between sociocultural and psychological variables, but social interaction, in contrast to cultural patterning, had been de-emphasized. Symbols representing behaviors and value orientations (i.e. house type, use of native medicines, etc.)

had been included in the sociocultural index schedule. At this point it seemed important to include social interaction, in terms of role playing, as an important variable with a high potential for tying together social, cultural, and psychological data. The main focus of this study was to find the relationships existing between the social (represented in interaction patterns via role playing), the cultural (represented by values), and the psychological (represented by Rorschach materials) variables during the process of culture change.

After the basic changes in these variables were determined for the representative women in each category on the acculturative continuum, the problem involved the tracing of interrelationships (1) between the three dimensions in each of the sociocultural categories, established by means of the same statistical procedures as those used for the males, and (2) between categories, describing HOW the shared values and value orientations of a group were implemented in role-taking and social interaction and how the perceptual structuring is or is not related to the other two dimensions. Although these dimensions in any individual are all related aspects of social behavior and/or products of cognitive process, by treating them as separate entities it is possible to define with greater rigor which kinds of values and value orientations and what manner of role-taking is associated most directly with the patterning of perceptual structuring.

The materials for value orientations and specific values were derived from expressive autobiographic interview materials (described earlier), observations of overt behaviors, and specific value preferences expressed in the sociocultural indices collected. It was found, for example, that a continuum of values (i.e. display of native objects, use of Indian medicines) was concomitant with the continuum of acculturative categories and that a sharp break occurred between groups whose members have been identified with Menomini religious groups and those that have not (L. Spindler 1962: 92). Data for role-taking as mother, wife, and social participant as reference groups were drawn from autobiographical materials supplemented by direct observation. The range was from the model for the conservative Menomini woman, who was a recipient of social action, interacting in a "latescent" manner (L. Spindler 1962) to the model of the elite acculturated woman who was an originator of social action.

The construction of a modal class from Rorschach indices (Wallace 1952) allowed for a comparison of the group profile for each category to the modal profile for the women from all categories, as it did in our male-female comparisons. The conservative group profile, which was convergent with the modal pattern, was sharply divergent from the profile of the elite acculturated group, which converged with that of middle-class white women included in a control sample.

With the data in the social, cultural, and psychological dimensions, it was possible to draw conclusions and formulate hypotheses about their interrelationships. Some correlations were statistically demonstrable. For example, "the modal perceptual structure is associated with the expression of specific Menomini values" and "the two extremes of the acculturative continuum are distinguished by a distinct set of interrelated social, cultural and psychological attributes" (L. Spindler 1962: 94–95). Other relationships were drawn mainly from autobiographical materials and were somewhat more inferential. For example, "basic attitudes towards the supernatural are crucial factors in effecting changes in the perceptual structure" (L. Spindler 1962: 96). And, on the basis of the results from our attempts to this point, we remained convinced that, as Fred Voget once wrote:

> The extent to which the different variables [in a socio-cultural system] continue to form (or may need to form) an interrelated system through change phases is crucial to the understanding of structuring processes (Voget 1971).

CONTROLLED COMPARISONS AND THE INSTRUMENTAL ACTIVITIES INVENTORY

In 1954 Fred Eggan wrote on the method of controlled comparison which offered good leads for introducing further checks and controls for fieldworkers (Eggan 1954). Hallowell's studies of the Ojibwa and ours of the Menomini used a type of research design that might be called "comparative" in that the several sociocultural categories are compared with each other. However, neither study attempted to compare beyond the boundary of a single culture.

After completing the first phases of the Menomini study, we hypothesized that the same reformulation of perceptual structure found among the most acculturated Menomini would occur in other situations where the conditions of acculturation were approximately the same and Western culture was dominant. After a reconnaissance of North American Indian communities, we chose the Blood Indian Reserve in Alberta, Canada. Here we could attempt to control some of the major variables in the psychocultural adaptations of the two groups. In both cases there existed the relatively isolated reservation community, the prejudicial attitudes of surrounding whites, and the unique feature of a highly productive industry using rich natural resources within the boundaries of the reservation: in the Menomini case, the lumber industry, in the Blood Indian case, cattle ranching and wheat growing. It was hypothesized that the elite Menomini represented a psychological as well as socioeconomic transformation because success, recognizable in the terms of the dominant culture, was available to them, with the possibility of identifying with the goals of this culture. Thus we expected a similar type of adjustment process.

We knew that many aspects of the old Blood Indian culture were still alive, so we posited a sizeable native-oriented or traditional group, comparable to that of the Menomini. The fact that the Blood were also Algonkian speakers was of some relevance in searching for controls and independent variables.

In studying these two communities we used the same techniques, including the Rorschach, autobiographies, interviews, a sociocultural index schedule, extensive participant observation, relevant ethnohistorical data, and a new kind of eliciting technique which we devised for use in the Blood Indian research called the Instrumental Activities Inventory (IAI) (G. and L. Spindler 1965). Again, our aim was to compare the relationship between manifest cultural change, including changes in material culture, group membership, religious practice, subsistence, etc., and psychological adaptation, in both its perceptual-cognitive and affective dimensions. Through the use of this controlled comparative approach, some important and unanticipated kinds of data were made available.

The Blood Indian sample like the Menomini could, it appeared, be divided into categories on the basis of overt sociocultural indices. We were able to distinguish two extremes in overt acculturation — old timers (and some middle-aged and even younger people), who spoke little English and identified with the traditional culture, and the young Blood who had attended school, spoke English more comfortably than their own language, and knew little of the old culture. The bulk of the population was, however, culturally between these two extremes at the time of our study (1958–1964).[1] Most of the Blood still speak their own language and many belong to traditional organizations, evidencing considerable cultural homogeneity. The research revealed that acculturative adaptation and socioeconomic status were not necessarily concomitant among the Blood Indians. Some men and women who were highly successful ranchers, for example, spoke their native language well and belonged to traditional societies. Rorschach data clearly indicated less difference between sociocultural categories than was found among the Menomini. Even the apparently most acculturated persons were not differentiated, on the basis

---

[1]   We have done fieldwork with the Blood intermittently since 1964, but with somewhat different objectives that are tangential to the focus of this paper.

of Rorschach scores, as a group apart from others. We surmised that the Blood, unlike the Menomini, were able to cope with the demands of the surrounding cultural system without a corresponding psychological reformulation. And the socioeconomic elite and culturally conservative alike were able to keep a strong cultural identity. To present hypothesized reasons for this type of adaption would go beyond the focus of this paper (see G. Spindler 1968; L. Spindler 1973), but the causes lay in part in the differences in conditions to which the two groups had to adapt and in the fact that psychological reformulation was not necessary for a Blood Indian in order to cope successfully with the dominant white culture, as they already had many of the required psychological features which were lacking among the Menomini.

It might seem that researchers using a type of controlled comparison as just described might be taking a first step in resolving the conflict in orientation existing today between those using an "emic" approach and those using an "etic" approach, since the two approaches are combined here. For example, the two cultures were first thoroughly studied separately (emically), with emphases on the social and psychological structures, seeking the antecedent and consequent variables but also eliciting interpretations and perceptions from the people themselves. The two cultures were then compared in an attempt to generalize about relationships between sociocultural and psychological variables in an effort to factor out more universal relationships between antecedents and consequences (etic).

The Instrumental Activities Inventory as a Technique

Notwithstanding the collection of comparable data for the Menomini and the Blood, we did not feel that we really understood how the Blood perceived themselves or those of the dominant culture. In an effort to remedy this lack, we developed the IAI for use with the Blood. This development is evidence of our dissatisfaction with the Rorschach. It consists of twenty-four line drawings, drawn by a professional Blood Indian artist, representing Indians engaged in activities — activities that are instrumental to achievement and maintenance of life styles and socioeconomic statuses which are recognized and valued in the Blood community. There are three major classes of instrumental activities within the Blood community representing the range of degree of adaptation to the outside world. These include activities within the framework of the most traditional aspects of the culture, such as being a medicine man; those in the community in its more contemporary and less traditional aspects, such as participating in rodeos; and those within the terms imposed by the Western economy and social system, such as being a store keeper or accountant (G. and L. Spindler 1965).

Projective Techniques Antecedent to the IAI

Like most tools, the IAI is a lineal descendant of others. It is in part a projective technique in the tradition of Henry Murray's Thematic Apperception Test (TAT), though we prefer the term "eliciting technique." The IAI is broadly related to all projective techniques in that the user must make the assumption that what people say in response to visual stimuli bears some significant relationship to their psychic organization as well as to their behavior. We designed the test to elicit responses more directly related to actual behavior on the one hand and to the cognitive organization of those behaviors on the other, than those generated by the Rorschach or TAT.

Beginning with William E. Henry's development of a modified TAT for use with Hopi and Navajo Indians (Henry 1947), other modifications have been made for particular cultures. The assumptions and purposes of the researchers using these modifications are basically the same as those using the original TAT. These modifications, however, approach the IAI in that they are attempts to make the stimuli operationally meaningful in the context of the respondent. They suffer methodologically, however, from the fact that it is difficult to chart the original Murray TAT interpersonal situations in variable cultural contexts. Thus the value that might be claimed for standardization of stimuli is destroyed. The Rorschach technique has a better claim for standardized stimuli, since the inkblots themselves contain no specific cultural content.

Of the various inventions of picture techniques by anthropologists, we owe the most to the experiment developed by Walter Goldschmidt and Robert Edgerton (1961) for the study of values applied to the Spindler sample of Menomini sociocultural categories. The authors claim as the most important difference between their technique and the TAT that they are attempting to measure culturally established patterns of behavior rather than individual personality dynamics. Edgerton administered a set of eleven cards, each presenting two alternatives in value choices on a single card. Significant variations in responses of Menomini individuals for the various acculturative categories were obtained, also providing additional confirmation of their meaningfulness as categories. While the IAI and this picture technique exhibit certain features in common, the rationale for each differs in certain important respects. We believe that the focus in the IAI upon instrumental activities leads to a more total conception of the individual's relationship to his social environment. In the IAI each picture represents only one instrumental activity. In this manner we felt that we could avoid imposing dichotomous choices upon the respondent in the stimulus frame of a single picture. It is possible that dichotomies which are real in Western culture are false within the framework of the conservative groups in other cultures. We wanted to elicit the native perception of instrumental relationships. The Blood IAI presents twenty-four specific alternatives from which the respondent can choose — in any order and with any emphasis he wishes. Only after the respondent has made free choices do we "force" some choices between pairs and trios of drawings and on the basis of the respondent's first choice. Respondents are also asked to explain why they made the choices they did.

Sets of instrumental activities drawings were later designed and used by us for a study of Mistassini Cree teenagers and for a study of German schoolchildren and their schools. Adaptations have been made by other researchers for various projects that are now in progress.

We found the IAI extremely useful in eliciting data relevant to our several objectives. One objective was to discover how evaluative choices of instrumental alternatives are related to antecedent experience as indicated by sex, schooling, socioeconomic status, religious affiliation, etc. Another objective in using the IAI was to be able to describe the specific values projected into the rationales given for choices by our respondents. Data relevant to this area is in accord with the general hypothesis that the Blood community is relatively homogeneous in its basic cultural substrata and also provided us with highly specific information about Blood values and their dynamic interrelationships. The most important objective in using the IAI was to isolate persistent cognitive orientations that pervade the specific perceptions and evaluations of instrumental activities. We were able to isolate integrating principles and types of thinking operative in the Blood Indian management of perceived social reality and the manner in which they were able to maintain cognitive control (see G. and L. Spindler 1965; G. Spindler 1968). The data showed, for example, that the Blood exhibited a low tendency towards stereotypic thinking and that they did not think conditionally (in retrospect or into the future). Things are as they are or were as they were and one cannot make them different in fantasy. A number of other cognitive orientations were drawn from the IAI data.

A Special Theoretical Model for Use with the IAI

The instrumental model first developed in the Blood Indian study was further refined in a study of urbanization processes occurring in two villages in southern Germany. The IAI was, of course, redrawn with a series of pictures specially designed for the area. The sample was drawn from several classrooms of children at educational levels ranging from the third to the ninth grade and from their parents and teachers. We emphasize here the theoretical model rather than the results of the research (see G. Spindler [1973, 1974] for the complete analysis).

The broad premises and concepts included in the theoretical model can be stated as follows: we assume that a cultural system operates so long as acceptable behaviors usually produce anticipatable and desired results and unacceptable behaviors usually produce anticipatable and undesired results. These behaviors are instrumental to goals, such as states of being or possessions, etc., associated with desired life styles. The relationship between activities and goals can be termed an INSTRUMENTAL LINKAGE. Instrumental linkages are systematized, inter-related, and constitute the core of any cultural system (as rationalized within this model). Belief systems are ritualized statements that support key instrumental linkages. They help maintain the credibility of these linkages. In schools, churches, and initiation ceremonies children are taught what these and others are, how they work, and why some are better than others. The result of this teaching in the individual is a cognitive structure that is a working model of the cultural system. This working model permits the individual to maintain control of his life space in a cultural system, so long as the established instrumental relationships continue to function. Cognitive control as socially relevant is therefore the ability of the individual to maintain a working model, in his mind, of potentially productive instrumental linkages and their organization. This model, as we have said, is formed in the mind by cultural transmission. During rapid culture change established instrumental linkages are challenged by new information and behavior models and their credibility is weakened. Alternative linkages are recognized, acquire credibility, and become operable. This process may be studied and for us constitutes a key focus in the study of the psychology of cultural change and urbanization. In using this model one may be concerned with either the culture system processes (such as technological or economic) that result in new instrumental linkages, or with the perception, selection, and cognitive ordering of alternative linkages by individuals (G. Spindler 1973: 118).

The purpose in administering the IAI with this theoretical model in mind was to discover how the children cognitively managed instrumental choices and ranking when the cultural system was transforming during rapid urbanization. Line drawings were modified to include activities instrumental to the attainment of goals considered appropriate in the Remstal valley of southern Germany, in traditional as well as urbanizing sectors.

With the data from the IAI analyzed in terms of the relevant theoretical assumptions, we were able to isolate and identify the cognitive organizations of the children as well as parents and teachers in the sample. The cognitive organizations pivoted around three potentially conflicting dimensions. The analysis permitted us to see how the children managed to maintain cognitive control in a changing milieu and what role the school played as a culture transmitting agency (G. Spindler 1973: 131).

RORSCHACH-IAI COMPARISONS

We found that the data produced by the IAI and the Rorschach techniques intergrade. The Blood, for example, usually perceive real objects, people, or animals in the Rorschach ink-blots in an action context; they usually encompass relatively small, sharp details in the ink-blots; and they ascribe a concrete and specific meaning to them. These features of Blood Rorschach responses are congruent with what the IAI revealed about the thinking processes of the Blood Indians, particularly with respect to cognitive orientations concerning activity, stereotypic thinking, immediacy and practicality, and literality.

The Rorschach moves the fieldworker further into the personality structure of a group than does the IAI — into the psychic control areas, the management of anxiety and of emotions as well as the intellectual organization, and into the respondent's fantasy life. These are admittedly problematic areas and yet we, at least, are reluctant to lay them aside entirely in favor of a wholly cognitive approach. The IAI is less concerned with "personality" and more concerned with what people do or think they can do in the real world. The respondent selects from a number of different instrumental relationships and supports his decision by explaining why he or she made those choices. The focus is more on the concerns of the anthropologist than upon those of the psychologist. The IAI moves us directly into the area of the respondent's cognitive management of perceived social realities. And when we are researching cognitive management and perceptual organization, we are dealing with some of the same phenomena as the ethnoscientist, but in a different way. Both are essentially emic approaches. However, we feel that given a clear and operational theoretical model of instrumental linkages in cultural systems, we are in a position to utilize our elicited data etically, regarding instrumental relationships in given cultural domains as conceptually equivalent across cultures. The road to this development is not entirely clear at this moment and much work remains to be done.

If we had to choose between one or the other of the two techniques, we would be reluctant to forego the depth and understanding that the Rorschach data provide, despite their problematic character. However, we would choose the IAI because it moved us into an area of perception and coding of alternative cognitive modes which are more directly relevant to the study of culture change.

THE PAST AND THE FUTURE: CONCLUDING REMARKS

In reviewing the attempts of researchers (including ourselves) in the field of psychological anthropology in general and psychocultural change in particular, we are convinced of the importance of using eclectic, experimental approaches. Models and techniques must be flexible and adaptable to new knowledge gained from many fields (i.e. physiology, psychology, anthropology, psychoanalysis, ethnology, and ecology). And it is incumbent upon the anthropologist, with a limitless number of testing grounds, to test his models, return to the field, collect data, and change the techniques again. We have attempted to do this. Although there is continuity in our work, especially in its orientation towards a perceptual-cognitive approach, we are at a very different place now than we were when we began using the Rorschach. Our purposes have remained essentially the same, but our theoretical models and instrumentation have changed.

Whatever techniques are utilized, the vast majority of anthropological research is dependent upon data from language. The ethnoscientist assumes that the events and things in a people's conceptual world are mirrored in the semantic categories of their language (Tyler 1969). Yet the psychological validity of a componential analysis inferring a covert taxonomy is not high. Further, the structures used, which may not be as free of Western cultural bias as they seem, are static and do not refer to process — to changes in time.

Anthropologists have offered leads from time to time which might aid in releasing the worker from his singular involvement with language as data or warn us of the traps inherent in relying too completely on language data. For example, Thomas Gladwin, in his study of navigation processes among the Trukese (1964: 174), writes:

... The simultaneous integration of several discrete thought processes defies verbalization. The navigator can probably inventory all of the factors to which he must be alert, but the process whereby these are weighted and combined is both complex and fluid.

Gladwin concludes that the cognitive strategy of the Trukese is inductive, in contrast to the strategy of the European which is deductive. And there have been similar kinds of data reported from other field workers.

Gregory Bateson suggests that we seek means other than language for delineating deep, underlying cognitive patterns. He contends that the human mind is a deep structure, its conscious aspect dealing only with bits and pieces. On the other hand, the deep values of unconscious thought deal with relationships and patterns rather than with things. And these kinds of relationships defy coding and linguistic description. He argues that man projects these whole patterns in art, which should offer many clues to the psychocultural anthropologist. At present we are observing and coding only a distorted picture of how the mind is coding knowledge, Bateson writes. This situation may continue until we have new breakthroughs in the field of neurophysiology, which will allow for the mapping of the cognitive processes involved in ingesting the desiderata of a culture (Bateson 1972).

Jack Fischer has worked with these kinds of leads (1961) using psychoanalytic and linguistic approaches to study art styles as cultural cognitive maps. Rubinfine's research in psychoanalysis is also related to these leads (1961). He suggests that symbolic thinking must be thought of as a continuum extending from full consciousness to bare consciousness and characterized by a movement from verbal to pictorial symbolism.

In attempting to assess what has been accomplished in psychocultural anthropology, we would agree with our colleagues who surveyed facets of the field in 1971 when they commented:

... there are not enough studies that take the emic-etic dilemma seriously and attempt to design data collection so as to obtain some of the advantages of each approach (Triandis, Malpass, and Davidson 1971).

The two approaches to data have been viewed as conflicting approaches. The emic approach is represented in its most extreme form by the ethnoscientists and is related to claims by Malinowski and Boas that cultures must be understood in their own terms. This view studies behavior from within the culture, as seen from the informant's view, in order to discover what structure his or her views may have; both the antecedents and consequences of this behavior are found in the particular cultural system. The etic view, on the other hand, aims at a search for universal laws of human behavior. This view requires concepts that are culture-free, conceptually equivalent, or universal. The researcher creates his own structures in gathering and interpreting data, but they must be related to a theoretical model. Here the antecedents and consequences of thought and behavior are variables that represent potentially universal aspects of the world.

The advantages of combining both approaches in a study of psychocultural change seem self-evident. Cornelius Osgood in 1965 offers one solution (see Triandis, Malpass, and Davidson 1971). He starts with an etic construct that appears to have universal status, such as "human beings share a common framework for differentiating the affective meanings of signs," and develops emic ways of measuring it in his development of multinational semantic differentials. If a fieldworker uses only the emic approach, he cannot do cross-cultural work. On the other hand, the anthropologist who uses only the etic approach could bypass the most important aspects of the larger phenomena he is studying. Both approaches seem essential to an understanding of the psychology of culture and cultural change.

At present we are far from being able to put thinking processes and cultural forms together with anything more than metaphors. Nevertheless, one of the central processes in the study of culture change must be cognition, particularly in its management or control dimensions.

Given the uniqueness of the cognitive structure in each psychocultural system, and the central role of cognition in instrumental choices leading to action, then one of the central processes in culture change is released when a "native" thinker is confronted with an alien and dominant cognitive system (G. Spindler 1968: 339).

REFERENCES

BATESON, GREGORY
    1958   *Naven*. Stanford: Stanford University Press.
    1972   "Grace and information in primitive art," in *The study of primitive art*. Edited by R. Firth. New York: Oxford University Press.
BURLING, ROBBINS
    1964   Cognition and componential analysis: God's truth or hocus pocus. *American Anthropologist* 66:20–28.
DOOB, L. W.
    1960   *Becoming more civilized, a psychological exploration*. New Haven, Connecticut: Yale University Press.

EGGAN, FRED
  1954   Social anthropology and the method of controlled comparison.
         American Anthropologist 56:743–763.
FISCHER, JOHN
  1961   Art styles as cultural cognitive maps. *American Anthropologist* 63:79–
         83.
GLADWIN, THOMAS
  1964   "Culture and logical process," in *Explorations in cultural anthropology.*
         Edited by Ward Goodenough. New York: McGraw-Hill.
GOLDSCHMIDT, WALTER, ROBERT EDGERTON
  1961   A picture technique for the study of values. *American Anthropologist*
         63:26–45.
GOODENOUGH, W. H.
  1961   Comment on cultural evolution. *Daedalus* 90: 521–528.
HALLOWELL, A. I.
  1951   The use of projective techniques in the study of sociopsychological
         aspects of acculturation. *Journal of Projective Techniques* 15(1):27–44.
  1952   "Ojibwa personality and acculturation," in *Acculturation in the
         Americas: proceedings and selected papers on the Twenty-ninth Inter-
         national Congress of Americanists.* Edited by Sol Tax. Chicago:
         University of Chicago Press.
  1963   "The Ojibwa world view and disease," in *The image of man in medicine
         and anthropology.* Edited by I. Galston. New York: International
         Universities Press.
HENRY, WILLIAM E.
  1947   The thematic apperception technique in the study of culture-personal-
         ity relations. *Genetic Psychology Monographs* 35:3–135.
HONIGMANN, JOHN
  1967   *Personality and culture.* New York: John Wiley and Sons.
KEARNEY, MICHAEL
  1972   *The winds of Ixtepiji.* New York: Holt, Rinehart and Winston.
KLUCKHOHN, CLYDE, W. H. KELLEY
  1945   "The concept of culture," in *The science of man in the world crisis.*
         Edited by R. Lanton. New York: Columbia Univers'ty Press.
LEMERT, EDWIN M.
  1951   *Social pathology.* New York: McGraw-Hill.
LINDZEY, GARDNER
  1961   *Projective techniques and cross-cultural research.* New York: Appleton-
         Century-Crofts.
PELTO, PERTTI
  1967   "Psychological anthropology," in *Biennial review of anthropology.*
         Edited by B. J. Siegel. Stanford: Stanford University Press.
REDFIELD, ROBERT
  1952   The primitive world view. *Proceedings of the American Philosophical
         Society* 96:30–36.
ROMNEY, KIMBALL A., ROY G. D'ANDRADE, *editors*
  1964   *Transcultural studies in cognition.* American Anthropological Associa-
         tion special publication. *American Anthropologist* 66(3). Part 2.

RUBINFINE, D. L.
1961 "Perception, reality testing and symbolism," in *The psychoanalytic study of the child*, volume sixteen. Edited by H. Hartmann, M. Kris, Anna Freud, R. Eissler, 73–89. New York: International Universities Press.
SPINDLER, GEORGE D.
1952 Personality and peyotism in Menomini Indian acculturation. *Psychiatry* 15:151–159.
1955 *Sociocultural and psychological processes in Menomini acculturation*, volume five. Culture and Society Series. Univ. of California Press.
1968 "Psychocultural adaptation," in *The study of personality: an interdisciplinary appraisal*. Edited by E. Norbeck. New York: Holt, Rinehart and Winston.
1973 *Burgbach: urbanization and identity in a German village*. New York: Holt, Rinehart and Winston.
1974 "Schooling in Schönhausen: a study of cultural transmission and instrumental adaptation in an urbanizing German village," in *Education and cultural process: toward an anthropology of education*. Edited by G. Spindler. New York: Holt, Rinehart and Winston.
SPINDLER, GEORGE, LOUISE SPINDLER
1963 "Psychology in anthropology: applications to culture change," in *Psychology: a study of a science*. Edited by Sigmund Koch. New York: McGraw-Hill.
1965 Instrumental activities inventory: a technique for the study of the psychology of acculturation. *Southwestern Journal of Anthropology* 21:1–23.
1970 "Fieldwork among the Menomini," in *Being an anthropologist*. Edited by George D. Spindler. New York: Holt, Rinehart and Winston.
1971 *Dreamers without power: the Menomini Indians*. New York: Holt, Rinehart and Winston.
SPINDLER, GEORGE D., WALTER GOLDSCHMIDT
1952 Experimental design in the study of culture change. *Southwestern Journal of Anthropology* 8:68–83.
SPINDLER, LOUISE
1956 "Women and culture change: a case study of the Menomini Indians." Unpublished doctoral dissertation, Stanford University.
1962 *Menomini women and culture change*. American Anthropological Association Memoir 91.
1973 "Culture change," in *Culture in process* (second edition). Edited by A. Beals, G. Spindler, and L. Spindler. New York: Holt, Rinehart and Winston.
SPINDLER, LOUISE, GEORGE SPINDLER
1958 Male and female adaptations in culture change. *American Anthropologist* 60:217–233.
TRIANDIS, H., R. S. MALPASS, A. R. DAVIDSON
1971 "Cross-cultural psychology," in *Biennial review of anthropology*. Edited by B. J. Siegel. Stanford: Stanford University Press.
TYLER, S.
1969 *Cognitive anthropology*. New York: Holt, Rinehart and Winston.

VOGET, FRED
1971   "Cultural change," in *Biennial review of anthropology*. Edited by B. J. Siegel. Stanford: Stanford University Press.

WALLACE, A. F. C.
1952   *The modal personality structure of the Tuscarora Indians as revealed by the Rorschach Test*. Bureau of American Ethnology Bulletin 150. Washington: U.S. Government Printing Office.
1970   *Culture and personality*. New York: Random House.

Projective Doll Play Reconsidered: The Use of a Group Technique with Rural Mexican Children

JOHN BUSHNELL, DONNA BUSHNELL

BACKGROUND

The use of doll play as an investigative technique in the field of psychological anthropology has attracted little attention and perhaps even less enthusiasm. The number of studies of this kind that one is likely to encounter in the literature can literally be counted on the fingers of one hand. Best known is the Henrys' research (1944) on sibling rivalry among the Pilagá using the Levy dolls (although the prescribed Levy technique was abandoned in favor of a freer format). Earlier Róheim (1941, 1962) had experimented with the use of toys while working with children in central Australia and Melanesia. Ritchie (1957) employed an extended doll family with one to five year olds as part of a comprehensive investigation of Maori personality development. In a study of Puerto Rican children Landy (1959) employed pipe-cleaner people and simple furniture for what he termed free doll play.

The student in search of a summary or overview of findings, methodology or rationale — never mind a comprehensive appraisal of the technique! — will surely be disappointed. Honigmann in his pioneering textbook (1954) notes that Jules and Zunia Henry obtained confirming data via doll play regarding hostility toward parents and children but the approach is not further elaborated as a resource tool. In the revised edition (1967), the entry "doll play" has disappeared from the index and the topic from the book. Barnouw includes a subsection on doll play in

The restudy of San Juan Atzingo was supported by a grant from the Wenner-Gren Foundation for Anthropological Research for which the authors wish to express their deep appreciation.

his *Culture and personality* (1963, revised 1973) but the static state of affairs is underscored by the fact that when the revised edition was published after a ten-year interval, his treatment of the topic remained unaltered. *Psychological anthropology* (Hsu 1972) contains no discussion of this matter notwithstanding a chapter on the use of projective tests although there are relevant entries included in a supplementary bibliography.

Lindzey in *Projective techniques and cross-cultural research* (1961) merely notes in passing that among doll play studies of nonliterate peoples there is the Henrys' work and an analysis of Guatemalan (Chekchi) data by D. Levy, devoting most of his review to a consideration of the development of the non-cross-cultural application of the toy technique (a detailed and updated summation along these same lines can be found in Haworth 1968). Influences from the areas of child development, clinical diagnosis and treatment, and normal personality assessment can be traced in the work of Levy, Erikson, L. K. Frank, Lowenfeld, Beuhler, Sears, L. B. Murphy, and others in similarly related disciplines. The play materials range from Levy's triad of dolls (mother, child, and nursing baby) to extensive assortments such as Lowenfeld's World Test with its array of 150-plus toys. Levy's design confronts the subject with a structured situation while the toys of the World Test are not organized in any prescribed manner. Similar to the latter are the Miniature Life Toys of Lois Murphy (1956) which include a variety of human and animal figures, furniture, vehicles, and building materials. Again, the playthings are typically presented as a random collection and the subject's initial approach to this conglomeration constitutes part of the record.

Treatment of the data has veered widely between quantitative and qualitative approaches. For example, Erikson's early observations on pre-adolescents were interpreted from a psychoanalytic viewpoint. Sears's extensive doll play studies, focused on aggression and dependency, stressed standardization and quantification. Murphy and her collaborators, feeling that too little attention had been devoted to the study of defenses, conflicts, and anxieties, placed a heavy emphasis on the qualitative and dynamic rather than the psychometric. In the anthropological arena, Landy's Puerto Rican experiment followed Sears's methodology and rationale. In our Mexican work, we are perhaps closest to Murphy in our manner of both structuring and analyzing the test.

The lack of interest over the past decade or so regarding doll play in psychocultural research may be attributed, in some measure at least, to a paper by Landy (1960) read before the international anthropological Congress in 1956. Referring to his Valle Caña experience, he detailed a number of obstacles and procedural difficulties. Children in the sampled families were reluctant to come to the tester's house, were uncomfortable when left alone with Landy and his assistant, and played minimally, repetitiously, or sometimes not at all. There were specific cultural values that also proved to be deterrents, i.e. dolls were more to be admired than played with; it was considered unmanly for boys to handle dolls. Notwithstanding the minimal data yielded by the method, Landy was able to code, process, and analyze the protocols as an adjunct to his larger study. However, he was explicit in his statement that while the technique may work well in a setting such as the Harvard child study laboratory, his Puerto Rican results were far too meager for the time invested and he therefore would not attempt doll play again in the field.

Landy also reported one datum that points to a potential resolution of a number of the hazards that were encountered. In an attempt to "warm up" subjects who refused to play by themselves, he tried group play, combining the nonproductive children with successful ones. Although the nonparticipators never reached the subsequent point of engaging in solitary play, "*they did participate to some extent in group play*" (Landy 1960: 165, original emphasis). In the Henrys' Pilagá study, the dolls were intended for use with one subject at a time but it was found to be impossible to limit the sessions to one participant as other children in the family or neighboring playmates almost invariably injected themselves into the play. Thus, in effect, the Henrys' project came to involve group dynamics. It seems probable that Róheim in planning to use play as a field technique had initially anticipated working with individual children inasmuch as he acknowledged his indebtedness to Melanie Klein who interpreted the play sessions of very young patients in the same manner as the verbalizations of adult analysands. However, for reasons not explained, all of his play sequences involved groups. Using a makeshift collection of miscellaneous toys and objects (i.e. ape, goat, paper trumpet, mirror, water globe with snow scene, native in canoe), he held a series of twenty-four sessions with a group of four central Australian children. After an initial period or two marked by anxiety and doubts as to what was expected, these young subjects are reported to have produced play sequences replete with sexuality and aggression (Róheim 1962). Similar, though less extreme responses were encountered with the children of Normanby Island (Róheim 1941). However one may evaluate Róheim's orthodox psychoanalytic view of his data, the fact remains that the published protocols reveal a picture of childhood concerns, anxieties, and defenses that would be exceedingly difficult to discern by observation alone. Nevertheless, his work has been little noted and appears not to have stimulated similar applications or refinements of the technique.

This, then, was the rather dismal state of affairs regarding doll play as an ethnographic adjunct at the time we were planning a twenty-year cross-disciplinary restudy of a Mexican indigenous folk community. Given our interest in both the psychodynamic and developmental aspects of village character and cognitive orientation, it seemed to us that this projective technique designed especially for children might be well-suited for inclusion in our psychocultural armamentarium notwithstanding the general disinterest, if not negativism, with which it was viewed.

RATIONALE

Our decision to employ doll play as a research technique must be viewed in the context of our overall purpose, namely, to conduct a follow-up study of both personality and culture in the highland village of San Juan Atzingo. Thus, our work included a variety of traditional participant-observational techniques, census-taking, and open-ended interviews plus a battery of psychological tests. The latter consisted of the Thematic Apperception Test, the Rorschach, figure drawing, and group doll play. Correctly anticipating that the more formal testing techniques would meet with considerable resistance, we felt that play sessions would be perceived as relatively nonthreatening and might even be a pleasurable experience for the participants. Such did, in fact, prove to be the case with minor exceptions.

Based upon our prior knowledge of the community, our familiarity with the literature on doll play, and some previous experience with the technique at Vassar College, we decided that in order to encourage participation and thereby obtain as much data as possible, we should provide an optimally permissive, free play situation. We were quite certain that if we were to attempt to observe the children of Atzingo individually in a structured play setting, we would have to contend both with the reluctance and suspicion of parents and with potentially paralyzing anxiety, embarrassment and constriction on the part of the subjects. Therefore we elected to permit natural play groups of children to participate when and as they pleased, limited of course by considerations of time, space, the nature of the play materials, and the tolerance of the observers! Thus, we opted in favor of eliciting a quantity of hopefully rich material from a potentially skewed sample of children as against the likelihood of obtaining more dubious results à la Landy with a rigorous sampling based on age, sex, family, socioeconomic, and similar criteria. We were aware, of course, that we would compound the problems of handling the data. There could be both within- and between-session contamination *vis à vis* themes, modes of interacting, and the like. The behavior of first-time players might well be different from that of experienced participants. A hypothetical "unit," i.e. an act or sequence involving aggression, for example, could be expected to have a different significance when carried out by several children than when expressed by a single individual. However, even if it had been possible to partial out effects of this order, we would have inclined toward the opinion that a formal scoring method employing arbitrary response units, assigned weights, or inferred needs would tend to bypass our primary concern with the molar rather than the molecular, the qualitative rather than the quantitative aspects of behavior. Given our choice of a group technique, it seemed appropriate to focus our attention chiefly (though not exclusively) on group phenomena, group processes, and group trends rather than upon individual behavior, dynamics or personality profiles.

We were interested in children's play *qua* play as well as in whatever projective or reflective data might be derived from the "test." During our original field work in Atzingo children were seldom observed to play[1] except for occasional relatively passive games, sporadic horse play, and random solitary or parallel activities such as chasing turkeys, jumping into a fodder pile, or throwing stones. There were virtually no toys, a fact which has changed but little over the past two decades. However, the interest which both adults and children paid in 1950 to those few playthings which our own small children brought to the village strongly suggested that we would get a positive response to toys of whatever sort we might include in our test repertoire.

TOYS AND TECHNIQUES

Our set of play materials (see Table 1, Appendix A) was based in broad outline on Lois Murphy's concept of "miniature life toys," that is, people and objects resembling those represented in the world or "life

---

[1] Murphy (1956: 10–11) noted a similar paucity of play in rural India and concluded that because of involvement in the adult world, the children's fantasy-reality balance is weighted more heavily toward reality. Our data indicate that, notwithstanding early and continued participation in virtually all aspects of Mexican village life, children, when given the opportunity, can enter into the world of fantasy.

space" of the child (Murphy 1956).[2] To a basic assortment of dolls, furniture, vehicles, animals, etc., we introduced certain modifications which we hoped would enhance the attractiveness of the materials and perhaps encourage the elicitation of culture-specific themes. To this end we added an assortment of Mexican pottery ware, a wooden chocolate stirrer, a piece of *petate*, a palm broom, firewood, and several baskets. The family dolls were converted to rural Mexican folk by using darkened hair (with braids for mother and daughter) and adding such items of attire as aprons, *sombreros*, *ponchos*, *huaraches*, or *calzones* (traditional white pants). Non-Mexicanized dolls included naked babies, plastic cowboys and hunter, and an Amish doll in typical costume.

It should be noted that the original kit of toys was gradually eroded as the play project progressed. There was some inevitable breakage and considerable petty pilferage. An early casualty was the toilet which disappeared inexplicably prior to the first session and therefore does not appear on the inventory. Parenthetically, although there are no toilets or latrines in or even near Atzingo, the toy wash basin was often employed for toileting babies and small children. An improvised "one-seater" made by cutting a hole in a small wooden table was described only once as a toilet.

In a few instances we were able to replace missing items from a reserve supply, i.e. candles, nursing bottle, pistol, babies, which may account for the reappearance of previously missing items in relatively late sessions. As a consequence, the stimuli were probably seldom, if ever wholly identical (in contrast to the TAT or Rorschach) for the twenty-three sessions. In any case, the stimulus configuration inevitably shifts somewhat as a function of choice, order, arrangement, and similar operant variables.

Children were invited informally to our one-room living quarters to play with the toys. Whenever two or more arrived, they were encouraged to participate for an unspecified period of time. Individuals came and left as they chose except in cases of peer pressure or occasional suggestions from us that they drop out so that others might have an opportunity to play. Our floor served as the play area where the children usually sat, knelt, or squatted. Two large blocks of wood (*bancos*) and a small chair could be used as seats if desired. Playthings were generally presented in a random collection although now and then overlapping groups of children simply took over semi-organized clusters of toys.

---

[2]   Murphy (1956: 11, 26) has stressed the need to gear the toys to the cultural or subcultural background of the subject population, her testing programs having included children from urban, suburban, and rural United States as well as India.

As a matter of policy we seldom asked questions and virtually never intervened in the activities of the players nor interacted at the level of play. A written record was made of each session in its entirety (insofar as it was possible) with attention not only to play activity *per se* but also to the selection and rejection of toys and the patterns of interaction among the participants. It was rare for anyone to ask us for directions or approval; the more general procedure was for the children themselves to instruct, demonstrate, encourage, or set limits as, for example, when an adventuresome boy would be called back by his playmates as he attempted to drive the truck out the door, or when one girl would show another that the clothes would not come off the dolls.

Initially we offered children who had completed a play session a small object (i.e. whistle, "cricket," or plastic figure unrelated to those in the set) as a reward and as a potential inducement to others. Although it became clear that this would not have been necessary, they did accept their gifts eagerly. As our supply of trinkets began to dwindle, we gave out small pieces of candy, gum, crackers, or dried fruits, particularly to repeat players. The time inevitably arrived when there were no longer any presents or tidbits to give, so we made cocoa or *cafe con leche* to share with our subjects.

CHARACTERISTICS OF SUBJECTS

By and large, the composition of the play sessions reflected the day-to-day associations occurring among village children (excluding, obviously, the solitary state of the young child who frequently must occupy himself or herself while tending the house, the flock, or an infant carried on the back). Most commonly (twenty of twenty-three sessions) siblings came to play in twos, threes, or fours. Sometimes two sibling groups arrived together and frequently, though not always, these children were cousins to each other. If the children in a given group were not all actually kin, they were usually very close neighbors and almost invariably interrelated through a variety of *compadrazgo* (godparent) ties. Only rarely did an unattached child participate in a session. When such was the case, he or she was usually a left-over, so to speak, from a previous session or present because of involvement in other aspects of the testing program, i.e. figure drawing.

Group size varied from two to eight children, the average being four per session. By chance, the sex distribution ratio was evenly balanced with half of the sixty-four participants girls and half boys (see Table 2).

Forty-five (70 percent) of the children played only once and of the remainder most took part in only two sessions (see Table 3). A small group of enthusiasts were present for three or more sessions and would have played even more often if we had given them any encouragement!

Subjects ranged in age from toddlers to teenagers (two to sixteen years), the ages of girls being somewhat more evenly distributed than those of the boys. The median age for girls and for boys differed by only one year, lying between eight and nine for the former and between nine and ten for the latter.

Sex and age bore no particular relationship to group size, the composition of groups being determined primarily by the nature of the children's familial and social bonds. While some sessions were composed chiefly of approximate age mates, others were characterized by considerable spread (see the Appendix to this article).

Any attempt to describe our subject population in terms of economic or social class distinctions would be relatively meaningless inasmuch as the Indian-mestizo dichotomy of twenty years ago has blended into a continuum that is characterized by increasing cultural homogeneity (Bushnell and Bushnell 1969, 1971). Nevertheless, our subjects do present a range of characteristics and family backgrounds including relative affluence and impoverishment (insofar as these are meaningful distinctions within the framework of a subsistence economy), literacy and illiteracy, and instances of some Matlatzinca still spoken in the home versus Spanish as the sole language — this despite the fact that the twenty-two families represented by our subject population are located, for the most part, in or near the central area of Atzingo.

NATURE OF THE INTERACTION

The doll play sessions gave us an almost ideal opportunity to observe at first hand the modes of interrelating between and among children in general and siblings, cousins, and neighborhood friends in particular. The fact that a number of subjects participated more than once provided additional occasions for us to note how the same individual related to previous playfellows, to new ones, or to both.

We were, frankly, rather surprised at the generally good-natured, amicable, cooperative nature of the children's interaction. It is true that there were frequent instances of rivalry and competition but these were generally of short duration and low intensity or else were handled in the context of joking, teasing, or mock contention. Even boasting, showing off, or accusation were most often playfully carried out, sometimes in exaggerated form for dramatic effect. Children's feelings seldom appeared to be hurt. While passive compliance or withdrawal into inactivity were common responses for some, these seemed to be more a function of personality and age than of feelings of humiliation or fear of failure growing out of the interplay with other children.

Patterns of dominance and submission emerged in a number of the sessions. An older brother or sister might set the tone, dispense toys, and encourage play, even directing the nondominant children to carry out this or that action in accordance with some developing master plan or overriding interest of his or her own (see Appendix A and B, Session 6; also Appendix A, Session 14). Any covert resentment that might have been experienced by younger children was not apparent. On the contrary, in such situations the more passive participants seemed to look to the dominant one for guidance, support, and sometimes vicarious enjoyment. While dominance did tend to be a function of age, this was not necessarily the case as when a younger child was more able or experienced than an older one (Appendix A and B, Session 10), or when a pair or trio of children took center stage, as it were, because of their enthusiasm and involvement in an ongoing sequence of play activity (Appendix A, Session 12; Appendix B, Session 1).

Sex was not a necessary correlate of either activity level or dominance, with boys or girls in the ascendency depending again upon age and personality variables. There were a number of instances in which traditional sex roles influenced the alignment of participants within a play session. However, interaction between boys and girls in joint endeavors was also frequent, and cross-over to opposite gender-related activities, i.e. boys carrying out domestic routines (Appendix A and B, Session 11), girls engaged in vehicular play (Appendix A, Session 22), was commonplace in the absence of children of the opposite sex or in the event that those present were largely passive.

The fact of close relationship as with siblings or cousins seems to have encouraged parental sanction for participation and probably more importantly, to have facilitated play by providing a degree of security that permitted the children to be at ease during the session, at least with each other if not always with us. We were struck with the closeness (not necessarily to be equated with emotional warmth) within families compounded, it seems, of familiarity, friendship, propinquity and the mutual necessity for good working relationships. This, we strongly suspect, may account for the very low incidence of overt sibling rivalry, especially of a hostile nature. In fact, what may be said of close kin seems also to apply, though no doubt to a lesser degree, to acquaintanceships among the children generally. In a sense, the village itself with its small, largely fixed population and its continuity through the centuries may be viewed as somewhat akin to a family, requiring viable modes of interacting and at least outward manifestations of consideration and cooperation. Be this as it may, none of our participants was ever excluded from play by others, shunned in a session, or deliberately ridiculed or devalued regardless of his actions. Tolerance seemed the rule with regard to interruptions or demandingness by small children, the incapacities of a deaf-mute boy, or the backwardness of inarticulate, inept older subjects.

The quality and tenor of sessions varied widely. A few were brief and anxiety-laden while many more were protracted, eventful, and obviously enjoyable for the participants. A considerable degree of blandness or even boredom marked certain sessions but usually the tone was not sufficiently pervasive to affect all subjects and one or more was usually willing or eager to continue. Levity and even boisterousness and hilarity tended to be generated by a relatively small number of children, especially several-time players (i.e. Pepita, Juana).[3] Their mirth or extravagance was sometimes infectious, carrying over to other players and sometimes other sessions. While repeat performances sometimes resulted in heightened or more elaborated activity (Appendix A, Sessions 7, 8), for certain children a follow-up session was essentially a "rerun," as if they had played themselves out the first time (Appendix A, Sessions 17, 18).

THE SELECTION AND USE OF PLAY MATERIALS

Initial responses to the toys ranged along a continuum represented by grabbing and claiming at one extreme and at the other by passively sitting or standing until a toy was proffered. Many of the children looked to their fellow players, especially if older, more assertive or previously initiated, for cues as to how to begin. Once a toy or several toys had been selected, there were various options open for a child (apart from that of simply watching others). For example, he could immerse himself immediately in intense, absorbed activity with the materials, he could enter into interplay with other subjects, or he might proceed in a tentative, exploratory manner.

We conceived of play activity as falling into several categories or "levels," roughly comparable but by no means consistent with develop-

[3]   Pseudonyms have been substituted for the real names of children who participated in the project.

mental stages. Obviously, there are no sharp delineations between these categories, which often overlap, and shifting between them was probably more the rule than the exception. Nevertheless, it was usually possible for us to differentiate such types of play as simple holding, identifying, categorizing and organizing, manipulation, thematic play, and dramatic elaboration. Limitation to a single kind of play was relatively rare except in the case of very young children and in many instances a progression, not always steady, was discernable in the course of a session that involved all or most varieties of play from inspecting and sorting and organizing to the development of thematic routines, or imaginative, dramatic sequences.

Needless to say, the personalities of individual children determined to a considerable extent their approach to the play situation and their utilization of the materials. The behavior of some was stereotyped, imitative or perseverative (i.e. Justo, Session 10) while that of others was comparatively free, spontaneous or even labile (Pedro, Session 11). We have elsewhere (Bushnell and Bushnell, in press) referred to a rigidity-flexibility dimension which characterized the defense and control mechanisms of our TAT and Rorschach subjects, some of whom also participated in the play project. It seems that the relative degrees of constriction and resourcefulness of children at play can be similarly conceptualized.

Apart from such basic characterological differences, there were certain tendencies which San Juan children shared though with variations attributable to personal style. Possessiveness, for example, was a prominent feature of many sessions. Some subjects would clutch a single toy and be most reluctant to give it up. Others reached for as many as they could, gathering in items almost indiscriminately or perhaps according to some preferred category, i.e. animals or kitchen utensils. An extreme form of possessiveness was hoarding. Girls seemed particularly given to this pursuit either as an end in itself or as a preliminary to setting up a particular array of toys. The more constricted hoarders simply sat with a lapful of objects or a pile in front of them which they guarded jealously while more imaginative players incorporated their cache into a play sequence, i.e. piling items on a table and pretending to sell wares. Although a number of the subjects rarely verbalized at all or only to a slight extent, their more vocal counterparts referred to "my sewing machine," "my dishes," or "my airplane." Perhaps the ultimate in possessiveness was manifested by the concealing and stealing of small toys which some of the children found irresistible. Especially popular were the hand-painted native pottery, babies and bottles, and diminutive animals such as squirrel, calf, dogs, and cat, probably not only because they were small enough to be easily taken but also because of an inherent appeal.

The dolls were very rarely identified according to family role or relationship although it was often quite clear from the context that one was a mother, another her baby, and so forth. Even so, the most common designation for figures was "the man," "the woman," "the little boy," "the drunk," "the shepherd," etc.[4] Similarly, direct terms of address between dolls were never used except for an occasional formal "señor" or "señora." Direct verbalization between dolls was also almost nonexistent. Thus, while it might be apparent from the play that a mother figure was indicating that it was time to eat or to go to bed, this was almost never expressed in doll conversation although from time to time it was expressed as a running commentary: "Now they are eating;" "she is teaching the children." It occurred to us that one reason for the third-person narration might have been a wish, on the part of some children at least, to assist us in obtaining a complete record of their activities! Nonetheless, the lack of direct verbal interchange between dolls and the absence of terms of familiarity or endearment were noteworthy features of the play. Incidentally, the lack of conversation between dolls is not to be equated with silence on the part of the children who were sometimes exceedingly noisy and verbal during the session.

Although the children generally appreciated the clothing of the dressed dolls, occasionally even extrapolating from the *huaraches* and old-style pants (*calzones*) to the identification of the doll as a *Guarín* or *Chalmero*, there was no appreciable difference in use between the Mexican figures and others not culturally modified. In fact, neither size nor age seemed to be consistent determinants with regard to assignment of roles. The dolls listed in the Inventory as mother and father were, indeed, used as adults but so too were the brother and sister as well as the small children dolls on many occasions. The father and a small girl (particularly the one carrying the baby) might be seen as man and wife ("man with his woman"). Naked babies were commonly used as drivers and pilots because they could be fitted into a vehicle. Or a group of infants and small children might serve as adult mourners at a wake because they were easier to place around the table. As for the animals, distinctions were usually made between wild and domesticated ones but as the supply dwindled such differentiations were overlooked.

Favorite toys were usually selected in accordance with sex role and

---

[4]   The Henrys (1944: 32) noted a similar phenomenon among Pilagá children. When they named dolls after specific members of the child's family, routine, depersonalized play gave way to intense, emotion-charged sequences. Although our procedure did not employ a naming technique, affect-laden play is prominent in many of the protocols.

when younger and/or passive children were offered a plaything, usually by a sibling or cousin, it was almost invariably sex-appropriate thereby reinforcing traditional roles. In their play girls were generally more inter-action- and people-oriented and boys more construction- and repair-oriented but these interests are probably simply correlates of culturally-defined social and work syndromes.

INTERESTS, CONCERNS, AND PREOCCUPATIONS AS REFLECTED IN THE CONTENT OF THE PLAY

It seems reasonable to assume that play centering on domestic and out-door activities which comprised a substantial portion of our response data is largely reflective of daily life in the village. At first glance it might appear that these data would contain little of consequence but such an assumption would be erroneous since activities of this order are clearly of considerable interest to the children! If nothing else, the avidity with which they entered into the business of daily living attests to the success of the socialization process. Beyond this, they appeared to derive a meas-ure of security and satisfaction from the structure and routine of the familiar, commonplace aspects of their milieu. Occasionally there were actions suggestive of nurturant and succorant concerns, i.e. picking fruit, feeding a baby, a baby dying of starvation, but the repetitive serving and eating of food was generally so embedded in the performance of domestic pursuits that it proved difficult to establish identifications and to attribute dynamic motivation or need.

Cleanliness and grooming, akin to domestic life, are of interest prima-rily because they are of such slight concern to the children. This appears to be a reasonably accurate reflection of the real-life situation where facil-ities are minimal and occasions for cleaning up or dressing up are infre-quent. Use of the brush, comb, and mirror seemed to be more a matter of enjoyment of the miniature toys themselves than an integral part of the family routine.

Explicit sexual activity nowhere appears in the protocols. There were a scant half-dozen allusions, sometimes humorous and sometimes mildly embarrassing to the children, to males and females in close juxtaposition (sleeping, dancing, facing each other), but most interest in this area was confined to peeking at underclothes or bare bottoms. In a few instances the snake seems to have been used in a context suggesting symbolic sexuality, i.e. girl in bed with snake, snake entwined in girl's legs, but in the preponderance of incidents involving the snake we felt such an interpretation was not warranted, with aggression being the dominant theme.

Although we have disavowed an interest in quantification, there is no doubt that the sheer weight of numbers is sometimes revealing in itself, even apart from a consideration of the qualitative features of a given content category. Such is surely the case with respect to themes of violence and aggression and, to a lesser extent, death and funerals, drunkenness, suspicion and robbery. It is our hope that a reading of the summaries of sessions (Appendix A) and the selected protocols (Appendix B)[5] will convey an impression of the extent to which the children of Atzingo experience their world as threatening and hostile, and the people on whom they must rely as only semi-dependable sources of security and supplies, whether tangible or emotional. The drunken father figure and, less frequently, the mother is, of course, a realistic representation of the home life of many children. Thus the recurrence of the theme might be taken simply as reflective of the cultural reality. However, it may well also embody other dynamics, for example, the wish to render the threatening, punitive father pitiable, ludicrous and impotent. The sequence in which the father doll is converted from a drunk to a saint and finally to a dead policeman bespeaks the ambivalence which children feel for the paternal figure (Appendix A, Session 2). Although the image of the mother was more stable in that she typically fed her family, cleaned the house, put her children to bed, and sometimes grieved over her dead husband, never once in a play session did she embrace her children or openly express affection toward them, a finding paralleled in the TAT stories (Bushnell and Bushnell, in press).

Returning to the violence-aggression motif, it might be pointed out that, while the identification of a given child with a particular doll or animal figure may or may not be clear, the frequent and often multiple commission of overtly aggressive acts during play suggests that the child's own aggressive impulses are often being acted out or projected onto some aspect of the environment. Such a hypothesis does not seem to us to contravene the realistically-based concerns of village children, growing out of the undercurrent of hostility and the sporadic violence that are woven into the fabric of San Juan existence. Just as in real life, the make-believe aggression can and does take a variety of forms.

---

[5] The five protocols in Appendix B, while reflecting these and other aspects of world view, were selected to illustrate, in addition to content, variability along several dimensions, i.e. range of play from active, intense involvement to passive, constricted or low-key participation, simple holding and manipulation versus thematic and dramatic sequences, cooperation and competition, the diversity of age, sex and group size, dominance patterns, individual differences in personality, ability, interests, and the like.

Wanton acts of destruction are legion: the truck mows down animals and people; the car rams through a line of school children; corrals, walls and furniture are leveled. Viciousness characterized many themes of violence: animals are hacked to death or cut open; a dog bites a baby; a woman beats and shoots two children. Morbidity intrudes into a number of sessions: the snake eats the corpse of the mother; the tiger will eat the baby; an ox eats a dead man. Stabbings, shootings, and killings may be intentional or accidental: a hunter attempting to shoot a deer kills a girl carrying an infant; one man dies in a gunfight over the killing of a cow; a woman dies of stab wounds. Rage may be expressed in impulsive outbursts: a dead father is beaten across the face; a man thrown from his horse stabs it to death in anger; a mounted cowboy tramples a snake that has startled his horse. Hostility and aggression may also be handled through various defensive maneuvers, for example, through sublimation (men and boys go hunting); displacement (attacks and assaults are carried out via the snake or vehicles); denial (the mother cannot feel the snake's bite because she is dead); undoing (the fatally injured crash victims are brought back to life); rationalization (the children are summarily taken away in the patrol wagon because they are "bad").

Incidentally, though the agent for violence and aggression is most often a male doll, a predatory animal, or a reckless vehicle, girls as well as boys frequently engaged in play involving hostile, violent, or sadistic themes with such tendencies well developed, even rampant, in children as young as seven years.

As for the cultural reality, suffice it to say here that during our first stay in Atzingo, we witnessed gunfights, attended first the funeral of the victim of a passion killing and then another growing out of the consequent blood revenge, recorded other violent deaths including a decapitation and the ax murder of a woman by her husband, experienced the tensions of smouldering family feuds, ministered to the machete and knife wounds of drunken brawlers, consoled a child cruelly beaten with a knotted rope across the face by his mother, and weathered the anxiety arising out of a threat to burn down our house when we declined to become *compadres* with a man whom we scarcely knew or liked. During our 1970 field work, we and sometimes various of our subjects had occasion to observe within the vicinity of our house a man slashing open the belly of a possum-like animal that he had clubbed to death, poking out its unborn young, chopping off the tail, and pushing the parts into the *barranca*; a youth amusing himself by shocking chickens and dogs with a fallen live wire; the severe whipping of one of our nine-year old participants by her father for accidentally breaking a *pulque* pitcher; and a twelve-year old subject seeking sanctuary with us to escape the wrath of his drunken father.

Lest the impression be conveyed that the San Juan child is merely replicating his culture through the medium of play rather than also projecting intrapsychic impulses, wishes, conflicts, and anxieties, it should be pointed out that mass slaughter, wholesale destruction and the omnipresent danger of marauding serpents are clearly products of fantasy.

While death as a consequence of accident or aggression was dramatized by both sexes, the interest, even preoccupation, with funerals seems to reside largely with girls, perhaps because the main burden of funerary detail falls to women in the culture. The repetitive, ritualistic quality of such death scenes seemed with certain subjects (i.e. Appendix B, Session 6) to be almost compulsive in nature, suggesting that the enactment and re-enactment served a counterphobic and mastery function *vis à vis* the inevitable series of first-hand involvements with death with which every San Juanero must contend.

Themes of punishment (in contrast to direct retaliation) are rare in the protocols, particularly in view of the myriad provocations and numerous infractions that occurred. It is therefore not surprising to note the absence of manifest guilt or remorse. For our subjects there was little or no indication of an awareness of such unacceptable impulses as overt sibling rivalry, rage toward parents and, speculatively, incestuous wishes, and therefore presumably no concomitant sense of guilt. Play seems to have served as an arena for the expression of repressed feelings of this kind. Thus, the mass slaughter of children or the snake crawling into the cradle to bite the babies = elimination of siblings; the eradication of mother or father through drunkenness or death = fury with parents; the placing of brothers and sisters or parents and children together in bed = potential for sexual intimacy.

Vigilance and suspicion were rather common as elements of play and, for the most part, centered on relatively affect-free precautionary measures even though these were associated with fears of robbery, loss or escape of animals, impending danger or unspecified threats. The routinized nature of these measures suggest a kind of warding-off operation. Related to themes of vigilance are a basic characterological mistrust and wariness, quite evident also on the basis of observation, that typify a great many adult villagers and quite a number of our child subjects. With the Rorschach test this tendency took the form in some cases of obsessional hypervigilance and oppositionalism while with others it was manifested chiefly as a generalized evasiveness and guardedness (Bushnell and Bushnell 1973).

CULTURE, COGNITIVE ORIENTATION, AND CHARACTER

It would be tempting to conclude that the projective doll play technique has recreated a San Juan child's-eye view of his world. To some extent this is in fact the case. However, life in Atzingo consists of more than daily routines, the threats and hazards of both the predictable and the unexpected, or the crises brought on by accident, injury or the demise of family, friends, and foes. Missing from the picture are significant aspects of the culture, though whether for lack of interest, defensive reasons, or a failure to resonate with underlying needs is not always clear. The entire fiesta system that provides the peak occasions in the annual round (at least for adults!) is conspicuous by its absence. We were surprised, for instance, that with all the fence building and the availability of toy horses, riders, and cattle no child or group chose to create a corral for the *jaripeo* sport of playing and riding the bulls. Similarly, they could easily have enacted nativity and *posada* scenes, or decorated and blessed the animals as their parents do year after year. While the cross, candles, and flowers regularly elicited funeral sequences, there was no reference to the role of the Church or the *mayordomía* system in the community (although the Amish doll with her black garb once served briefly as a nun and on another occasion was identified as a *padre*).

Except for the many variations on the theme of guarding, grazing, and transporting of livestock, the technology of the subsistence economy was sparsely incorporated into the play with but one allusion each to driving a tractor, plowing with an ox team, planting, and contraband lumbering. The processes involved in producing the mainstays of the diet such as *tortillas* and *pulque* were not depicted. Areas of particular ethnographic interest to us, i.e. polygyny, witchcraft, and beliefs concerning folk illness and curing, which are becoming increasingly sensitive and taboo subjects in the village were never touched upon in the play although we were able to probe somewhat into these matters through conversations with individual children and to determine that they still impinge, sometimes directly, on their lives.

For the most part, what has been said here with respect to the content of the play sessions applies also to the stories produced in response to the TAT cards (Bushnell and Bushnell, in press). There were rather striking parallels between the two sets of data in the selection, whether conscious or otherwise, of motifs for inclusion or exclusion despite the obvious differences in the stimuli and a 5-year higher median age for TAT subjects. The conclusion seems inescapable that when presented with an opportunity for the relatively free expression of fantasy, the young people of Atzingo reveal certain over-valent preoccupations, often of a dysphoric nature, to the virtual exclusion of hopeful, optimistic, trusting, and loving concerns. Although there are culturally-sanctioned structures and occasions, particularly within the family and the *compadrazgo* network, for some degree of satisfaction of needs for security, identity, relatedness, and camaraderie, by and large the society offers minimal support or reinforcement for openness, sustained intimacy, or the development of a basic confidence in self and others. Since such positive attributes rarely emerged (in either doll play or TAT) in the form of expectations, aspirations, or wish-fulfillment, it begins to appear that the emphases on passivity, fatalism, mistrust, hostility, and morbidity must increasingly come to dominate and shape character and cognitive orientation as the enculturation process proceeds.

SUMMARY

In deciding to include doll play in our battery of projective tests, we were guided by several considerations, chief among which was the desire to employ a loosely-structured technique suitable for use with children that would facilitate the expression of a wide range of individual interests, concerns, preferences, and modes of behavior. Compared with the relatively high degree of structure and task specificity of our other psychological tools, doll play provided a casual, relatively relaxed atmosphere which generated a maximum of expressive, reflective, and projective responses.

Being well acquainted with the reserve and caution of the people of San Juan Atzingo from our previous fieldwork, we rejected the idea of individual play sessions in favor of a group approach that not only encouraged participation but also provided data not obtainable from the testing or observation of single children. Thus we were able to record the interaction of subjects, note the degree of competition and cooperation, and observe the choice of play partners and patterns of dominance and submission.

A total of 64 children ranging in age from two to sixteen took part in one or more of 23 play sessions. Subjects were, for the most part, siblings, cousins, and close neighbors, a replication of natural play groupings. Despite the factor of self-selection, our subject population constituted a reasonably representative sample with regard to age, sex, and socioeconomic variables.

Notwithstanding some squabbling and minor annoyances, the relation-

Plate 1. Village children engaged in play session with miniature toys

Plate 2. Family portrait of principal dolls

Plate 3.   Reconstruction of domestic scene with drunken father oblivious to surrounding activities

Plate 4.   Ambulance rushes to typical crash scene

Plate 5.   Children watch angry pursuit of stolen animals

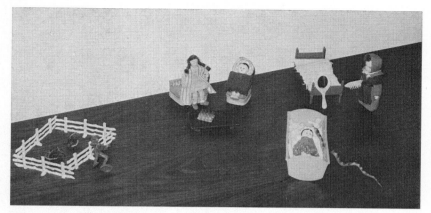

Plate 6. Household unaware as snake attacks sleeping children

Plate 7. Typical burial sequence following highway accident

Plate 8. Corral scene combines both banal and aggressive themes.

Plate 9.   Outraged owner draws gun to shoot hunter who has accidentally killed cow

Plate 10.   Woman grieves over body of her dead husband

ships among participants were generally amicable, cooperative, and tolerant. Overt sibling rivalry was little in evidence although mock or playful competitiveness and teasing appeared both in doll play and in interaction.

In the sessions there was a heavy emphasis on the routines of daily life, particularly as these relate to culturally-defined sex roles. Themes of hostility, violence, drunkenness and death were abundant. Mistrust, guardedness, and suspicion were revealed both through play and the behavioral characteristics of certain children. Nevertheless, many of the play periods were marked by interest and involvement, good humored fun, hilarity, and peaks of excitement.

The findings derived from projective group doll play corroborate to a significant extent those obtained from our other tests, especially the TAT in relation to thematic content, and the Rorschach with respect to personality dynamics.

Although the administration of play materials in an ethnographic setting has remained in a kind of anthropological limbo, we would like to suggest on the basis of our recent field experience that this technique merits reconsideration as a productive adjunct to studies in psychological anthropology.

AFTERTHOUGHTS

Whenever a particular theory, orientation, methodological approach or specific technique falls into disuse or fails to catch and hold the imagination of the members of the professional guild, it is not unreasonable to ask the question, Why? Doll play as an anthropological tool is certainly one such case in point, a stepchild of culture-and-personality (dating that far back!), neglected or overlooked, if not actually ignominiously dismissed. However, like a child, it might respond and flourish when viewed with respect, treated with care and patience, and (anthropomorphizing still further) permitted to take shape in the context of specific field conditions and a given cultural milieu.

What has been for us one of the major attractions of doll play as a method, namely, its great flexibility, has undoubtedly been a deterrent to others, particularly during an era when the emphasis in psychological anthropology has been moving in the direction of obtaining comparable cross-cultural data with techniques that lend themselves to systematization, standardization, and replication. Clearly, such goals might be set and met for doll play but the brief and checkered history of its anthropological application would tend to obscure this possibility. We hasten to add that we personally have no present inclination to pursue such an undertaking but mention it for the sake of those colleagues who might be so inclined. Our own proclivities — and this is the beauty of doll play as an adjunctive technique — lead us to prefer using it flexibly and adaptively, noting whatever data present themselves, testing out hypotheses, following up hunches, and exercising a combination of clinical judgement and ethnographic awareness in assessing, evaluating, and interpreting the results.

While we consider our doll play technique as "free" and "projective," it is obvious, of course, that just as children are not really projecting on a blank screen during play with toys, neither are we as observers, recorders, and keepers of the playthings able to maintain an ideally free-floating state of attention, much as we might like to. Recognizing these limitations, we nevertheless strove to "get into" the perceptions, feelings, and experience of the children as they played. Parenthetically, our use of the Rorschach and the TAT has followed along more time-worn paths but even here we tend to understand and analyze the data in much the same qualitative and experiential manner.

Although we have developed a kind of phenomenological-dynamic approach which is characterized by casting a wide net, so to speak, there is no reason why doll play should not prove equally, perhaps much more, useful when directed at a specific problem or focused upon a limited set of variables. Therefore psychocultural ethnographers in search of a problem or those with problems in search of a technique might do worse than to consider adapting doll play to their needs and incorporating it into their field technology — in the urban ghetto as well as the nonliterate hinterlands. The materials are relatively inexpensive, easy to carry, probably intrinsically interesting to people of various ages, climes and circumstances and, at least for us, enjoyable to administer. Further, no special training is prerequisite nor adherence to any particular psychological persuasion.

We have considered the intriguing possibility that the selection and manner of employing doll play may be to an extent a function of the researcher's own personality! In our own case, our preferred orientation places us toward one pole of the rigorous-nonrigorous continuum. (We admit, however, to feeling comforted by the knowledge that we have reams of data from our other projective tests for backup as well as our files of traditional ethnography.) A fringe benefit of our avowed flexibility is the "privilege" of largely bypassing those perennial questions of validity and reliability, reflection vs. projection, reality-irreality, and similar sticky problems. However, we are fully cognizant of the importance of these issues and hope that in the future other investigators aligned along different points on the continuum will address themselves to their resolution and will design their doll play research accordingly.

APPENDIX A: SUMMARIES OF PLAY SESSIONS

Table 1. Toy inventory

Dolls

Father (5½″)	2 Little boys (3″)
Mother (5¼″)	2 Little girls (3″) (1 carrying baby on back in *rebozo*)
Son (4¼″)	2 Babies (naked, sitting position)
Daughter (4¼″)	Hunter with rifle
Amish woman (5″)	2 Cowboys (1 with guitar; 1 reaching for six-shooter)

Animals

2 Horses	2 Dogs
Burro	Cat
2 Cows	Giraffe
Calf	Tiger
3 Pigs	Deer
2 Lambs	Squirrel
	Snake

Vehicles

Sation wagon	Airplane
Dump truck	Tractor

Furniture and furnishings

Bed	Kitchen table
Mattress with removable cover	2 Metal chairs
2 Blankets	2 Plastic chairs
2 Baby blankets	1 Wooden chair
Dresser	Cupboard
Night stand	Stove
Cradle	Sewing machine
2-piece sectional sofa and hassock	Bathtub
Coffee table	Washbasin
Table (with hole in center)	

Assortment of plastic plates, cups, saucers, silverware, teapot, tray.

Assortment of Mexican pottery bowls, mugs, plates, *cazuelas* (cooking dishes), *sartén* (frying dish).

Miscellaneous

Plastic trees or bushes	Mexican chocolate stirrer
2 Small baskets of flowers	Strainer
2 Baskets	Bottle brush
Palm broom	2 Baby bottles
Petate	2 Candles

Table 1 (continued).

Scissors	Cross
Hair brush	Pistol
Comb	20 Fence sections
Hand mirror	Firewood
Case of soft drinks	Small puff of lamb's wool
Dishdrain	Small puff of cotton

Table 2.   Age and sex of subjects

Age	Male	Female	Total
16	1	1	2
15	2	1	3
14	1	4	5
13	2	1	3
12	8	2	10
11	1	2	3
10	1	1	2
9	2	4	6
8	4	2	6
7	4	3	7
6	2	2	4
5	1	3	4
4	2	2	4
3	1	2	3
2	0	2	2
	32	32	64

Table 3.   Frequency of participation

Number of subjects	Number of sessions	Number of participations
45	1	45
13	2	26
2	3	6
2	4	8
–	5	–
2	6	12
64		97

SESSION 1

PARTICIPANTS   Octavia – 16F   cousin to sibling group
Fedora   – 14F ⎫
Eduardo – 12M ⎪
Juana   – 9F ⎬ siblings
Pepita   – 7F ⎭

TENOR OF SESSION   Delight and hilarity amidst intense prolonged activity.

NATURE OF INTERACTION   Good-natured sharing, vying, teasing, and histrionics.

CHARACTERISTICS OF PLAY   Selection and claiming of favored toys; experimental manipulation and fortuitous events often combine to trigger dramatic themes, sometimes in unlikely juxtaposition.

CONTENT
Domestic activity   Mother and daughter go to bed; baby placed in cradle; two 'women greet each other; old man and woman are sleeping; coffee served in cups; mother counts animals and her eleven children; kitchen organized; table is set; *pulque* served in mugs; dishes are arranged and rearranged in cupboard; mother sits at sewing machine; mother carries market basket.
Outdoor activity   Animals placed in long line, one jumps over gully; livestock are sleeping; corral built; little girl is shepherdess; station wagon loaded and driven; furniture hauled in truck; animals enclosed in new corral; plane is flown; people crowded into truck for pilgrimage to Chalma.
Sexual interest   Boy and girl dolls examined beneath clothing, lack of underwear noted (laughter); husband and wife dance face to face; peeking under mother's skirt.
Criticism and punishment   Woman ignorant of sewing machine must be instructed; woman told she doesn't take care of children properly; naughty children put in patrol wagon (truck); woman threatens to call police when things disappear; angry woman calls police over theft of animals; complaint filed with *delegación* (officials) when toys stolen.
Illness and accidental injury   Baby is hurt; man wounded on forehead; hair of women 'burned,' head covered in shame.
Vigilance, suspicion, and apprehension   Sleeping shepherdess awakened to guard animals; animals counted; drunk woman fails to tend animals.
Aggression and violence   Tiger is going to eat the baby; truck runs over baby, knocks over animals; plane knocks man down; station wagon rams fence, strikes children; pig carries off baby; corral knocked over; truck runs down group of people, then animals; first man, then woman, fall from back of careening truck; girls grab toys from each other, slap in jest; group of people riding in back of truck fall out.
Robbery   Household items stolen from woman; animal theft; girl robbed of possessions.

Drunkenness   Man and woman fall down because they are drunk; drunk man falls into cradle with two infants; drunk woman at table falls from chair; drunk is hauled away in truck; police unable to respond when summoned because they are drunk.

Death and funerals   Deer dies; wanton slaughter of children, adults, and livestock by vehicles.

COMMENT   Both mother and father figures negligent, inept; dual character of authority reflected in punitive police patrol and impotent drunken police.

SESSION 2

PARTICIPANTS   Raquel – 12F ⎫
Justina – 7F ⎬ siblings ⎫
Jacinta – 5F ⎭   ⎬ cousins
Fedora – 14F ⎫   ⎪
Juana –   9F ⎬ siblings ⎭
Pepita – 7F ⎭

TENOR OF SESSION   Reserved self-consciousness followed by buoyant activity.

NATURE OF INTERACTION   Two younger girls of first sibling group scarcely respond to directives of eldest; second sibling group plays freely among selves and engages others with partial success.

NATURE OF PLAY   Organization and utilization of materials by category gives way to imaginative, melodramatic sequence when second group arrives.

CONTENT

Domestic activity   Meal preparation and serving; family brought inside because of rain.

Outdoor activity   Corral-building; shepherding; vehicles parked by trees.

Personal grooming and cleanliness   Baby toileted; girls pretend to brush own hair.

Criticism and punishment   People tied in "patrol" truck, taken away.

Vigilance, suspicion, and apprehension   Father armed with pistol.

Aggression and violence   Snake eats animal; snake eats corpse of mother; snake and tiger fight; truck wreck; teasing and threatening with snake.

Drunkenness   Man is drunk; woman is drunk.

Death and funerals   Drunk becomes El Santo Entierro in "coffin" (bed) with candle; saint becomes policeman who dies; mother dies of grief for dead husband; stuffed into coffin (crib) with flowers at head; woman and baby die, are buried.

COMMENT   Ambivalence toward father reflected in successive roles as drunk, saint, and dead policeman.

SESSION 3

PARTICIPANTS   Armando – 4M ⎫ siblings
               Prudencia – 2F ⎭

TENOR OF SESSION   Shy passivity.

NATURE OF INTERACTION   Boy makes several unsuccessful attempts to interest sister in toys.

NATURE OF PLAY   Brief and highly restricted examination and manipulation of toys.

CONTENT   Miscellaneous — vehicles driven and loaded with a few objects.

COMMENT   Session conducted with mother present; two-year-old remained standing near her holding or sucking small toys; brother confined play space to radius of arm reach.

SESSION 4

PARTICIPANTS   Augusto – 13M ⎫
               Eduardo – 12M ⎬ cousins
               Arnaldo – 12M ⎭

TENOR OF SESSION   Moderate level of activity, interest and involvement.

NATURE OF INTERACTION   Generally cooperative but some underlying rivalry; mixture of individual activity with joint endeavors.

CHARACTERISTICS OF PLAY   Identifying, examining, sorting, and commenting upon toys gradually leads to sequences of activity with occasional dramatic incidents.

CONTENT

Domestic activity   Arranging furniture; setting table, greenery added; utensils put on stove; mattress put on bed; *petate* placed in crib; girl uses sewing machine; floor swept with broom; fire fanned with *aventador*; man walks with wife and baby.

Outdoor activity   Large fence constructed to enclose all toys; gate opened and closed for vehicles; truck filled with animals, driven to pasture; plane flown, landed inside corral; cowboy rides horse; truck driven to work project; *petates* offered for sale; price of plane discussed; offer to buy cow; truck sold.

Personal grooming and cleanliness   Mother carries hair brush to mirror, given comb to comb hair.

Sexual interest (symbolic)   Snake entwined in girl's legs; girl in bed with snake.

Criticism and punishment   Animals on sides called lazy because not eating; policeman stops truck because of nine-year old license plates.

Vigilance, suspicion, and apprehension   Armed guard rides truck to protect animals; child directs another to close corral gate before animals escape; man notes cowboy's gun, arms self with pistol.

Aggression and violence   Plane knocks down boy; truck crashes into father; plane wing knocks over cowboy and horse; snake dropped across face of father, bites him; snake put in bed, girl gets in, is bitten; snake coils around another girl's legs and bites her.

Drunkenness   Drunken father falls down; drunk man slumps on chair.

Death and funerals   Woman carries candle because someone has died.

SESSION 5

PARTICIPANTS   Octavia   – 16F ⎤ siblings ⎤
                Arnaldo   – 12M ⎦   ⎥
                                           ⎬ cousins
                Fedora   – 14F ⎤   ⎥
                Eduardo   – 12M ⎥   ⎦
                Juana   – 9F ⎬ siblings
                Pepita   – 7F ⎦

                José   – 12M   cousin to both sibling groups above.

TENOR OF SESSION   Playful and relaxed; interruptions tended to disrupt play sequences and groupings.

NATURE OF INTERACTION   Cooperation; playful rivalry; some attempts at dominance by more assertive children; gradual division by sex into two play groups.

NATURE OF PLAY   Claiming, hoarding, and trading toys; systematic manipulation, frequently repetitious and imitative; fragmentary episodes of thematic play.

CONTENT
Domestic activity   Mugs put on shelf, flowers on buffet; family placed at table to eat; family scene enclosed by fence to represent house.
Outdoor activity   Truck driving, fence sections loaded and hauled; corral-building; airport outlined by fence sections; plane flying; cars pushed back and forth; road repair; animals placed in "forest."
Sexual interest   Examination of bare-bottomed doll (giggles).
Vigilance, suspicion, and apprehension   Girl instructs younger child to guard her toys while absent because "everyone around here is a thief."
Aggression and violence   Repeated head-on car crashes; cars knock over toys of others; plane flies into brim of boy's hat; truck runs over father; snake bites cow; snake threatens family.
Drunkenness   Father is drunk.
Death and funerals   Dead man placed in improvised casket, flowers and cross at head, *comadrita* brings basket of green branches.

SESSION 6

PARTICIPANTS   Felipa – 13F ⎫
                      Lucia   – 11F ⎬ siblings
                      Concha – 9F   ⎪
                      Cisco   – 7M ⎭

TENOR OF SESSION   Serious, sustained intensity during lengthy session.

NATURE OF INTERACTION   Oldest girl quietly dominant with others compliant and cooperative.

CHARACTERISTICS OF PLAY   Imaginative use of toys and diverse themes with frequent return to a central motif.

CONTENT

Domestic activity   Dishes and furniture arranged; soft drinks served at table; sweeping and clean-up; "nun" eats, sleeps; mother feeds children; mugs of coffee served; girl uses sewing machine, scissors; child put to bed; mother cooks, retires; brothers and sisters put in one bed, mother and babies in another; mother and son have soft drinks; mother takes basket to buy bread.

Outdoor activity   Plane flown; corral building; animal stalls constructed; truck driving, fence sections loaded and hauled; boy on horseback chases bull (cow); people driven in station wagon; animals transported by truck; guitar player sings by corral; truckload of people driven to Chapultepec Park to see animals; corrals repaired; man drives car to work; horses and cowboys taken by truck to work on corral.

Personal grooming and cleanliness   Comb and brush placed beside bed; mother combs girl's hair, places her before mirror; mirror inserted into table to make dressing table; after sleeping, girl combs hair before mirror; child goes to toilet (wash basin), mother places cotton beside toilet, tells child, "clean yourself;" infant wiped with cotton which is thrown in "garbage;" mother wipes feet on *petate* before getting into bed.

Schooling   Nun instructs children in catechism; girl is teacher to children.

Illness and accidental injury   Boy run over by truck, taken by ambulance (station wagon with cross placed on top) to nurse ("nun"), cotton used to treat patient who recovers.

Vigilance, suspicion, and apprehension   Pistol under father's arm; boy walks around guarding corral; man watches over sheep.

Aggression and violence   Hunter shoots deer; snake bites deer; cowboy gunfight; snake shot with pistol; child knocks over fence; child threatens and jabs at sister with snake; driver wrecks car and kills boy; snake crawls over bed to bite girl.

Drunkenness   Man (father doll) drinks too much *pulque*, passes out; "the father of all the children is drunk" (again).

Death and funerals   Cowboy dies in gun fight; fallen cowboy seen as dead; fallen squirrel declared dead; fallen animals in corral hauled away for mass burial; passenger dies in fall from plane; boy killed when thrown from horse; little boy dies in car wreck; dead girl laid out with cross and candles at head, carried on top of car to cemetary for burial, cross placed on grave, mourners served drinks at wake; funeral for old man attended by mourners who are transported by truck; girl who died of snake bite laid out on table with cross and candles, bereaved gather to pray, procession to cemetary with body on station wagon and truck load of mourners, candles and cross left on "grave;" similar funeral for small boy dead of unspecified cause.

COMMENT   Repated and elaborated treatment of burial rituals and funerary trappings suggests attempt to master morbid preoccupations and anxiety over death and aggression.

SESSION 7

PARTICIPANTS   Rolando – 9M ⎱ siblings
　　　　　　　　Plácida – 7F ⎰

TENOR OF SESSION   Quiet, busy involvement.

NATURE OF INTERACTION   Cooperative sharing of toys.

CHARACTERISTICS OF PLAY   Parallel play according to traditional sex roles; examination and collection of toys gradually shifts to fragmentary dramatic play.

CONTENT
Domestic activity   Meals cooked and served; dishes washed; floor swept; furniture arranged; use of sewing machine; family groups put to bed.
Outdoor activity   Corral building; use of vehicles to transport fence sections, animals.
Personal grooming and cleanliness   Woman combs hair before mirror.
Aggression and violence   Hunter shoots animals; snake bites hunter; cowboy kills snake with knife.

SESSION 8

PARTICIPANTS   Rolando – 9M ⎱ siblings
　　　　　　　　Plácida – 7F ⎰

TENOR OF SESSION   Sustained activity with occasional peaks of excitement.

NATURE OF INTERACTION   Amicable cooperation except for annoyance when sister knocks over corral with skirt for third time.

NATURE OF PLAY   Dramatic play.

CONTENT

Domestic activity   Children assigned chores — sewing, sweeping, cooking; table set for meal-time; family retires; baby bottle fed.
Outdoor activity   Corral-building, animals to be sold hauled in truck.
Personal grooming and cleanliness   Woman uses comb and brush; babies bathed; child washes hands.
Schooling   Teacher lines up children single file; pupils seated in classroom.
Vigilance, suspicion, and apprehension   Knife carried in truck to kill animals as necessary; animals guarded; cowboy and father stand watch.
Aggression and violence   Tractor destroys corral; hunter shoots animals, tosses them into truck; cowboy thrown from horse, kills horse with knife; snake attacks animals; dog jumps on horse, horse drops dead; "revived" horse stabbed to death by cowboy; animal killed by corral falling over; car runs over snake; car rams through line of school children.
Death and funerals   Baby dies of starvation; hunter intending to shoot deer kills girl carrying infant; cross, candle, floral spray placed beside body of girl.

COMMENT   Concern over impulse control suggested by compartmentalized structure of corrals; one animal per unit except for pig and sheep because "They won't fight." Extent of underlying aggressive tendencies evident in rampant destruction that emerges in this second session.

SESSION 9

PARTICIPANTS   Inés   – 10F ⎱
               Evangelina – 8F ⎰ siblings
               Esmeralda – 3F
               Yugurta   – 9F
               Fedora   – 14F ⎱ cousins ⎱
               José   – 12M ⎰   ⎰ cousins
               Jonás   – 6M ⎱ siblings ⎰
               Paula   – 3F ⎰

TENOR OF SESSION   Constriction, furtiveness, passivity contrast with assertiveness and dominance of late arrivals.

NATURE OF INTERACTION   Negligible for original group; passive compliance *vis à vis* newcomers.

CHARACTERISTICS OF PLAY   Prolonged sitting, staring at toys; gradual acquisition of piles of toys; clutching, clinging, minimal manipulation; active pair immediately initiates replication of scenes from prior play sessions.

CONTENT
Domestic activity   People and household furnishings arranged in neat, tightly-organized scene; family members identified.
Outdoor activity   Corral building, animals and vehicles enclosed; animals hauled in truck, dumped in corral.
Death and funerals   Death scene set up with man laid out, candles and cross at head.

COMMENT   In all, three groups of children participated; small brothers and sister entering play group near close remained peripheral and were largely incidental to session.

SESSION 10

PARTICIPANTS   Justo – 15M ⎱ cousins
　　　　　　　José – 12M ⎰

TENOR OF SESSION   Slow-paced, low-keyed, desultory with occasional moments of heightened interest.

NATURE OF INTERACTION   Predominantly amiable parallel activity; younger, more able and sophisticated boy corrects, instructs, demonstrates, and initiates to little avail.

CHARACTERISTICS OF PLAY   Considerable searching, sorting, and random manipulation; brief, semi-thematic episodes.

CONTENT
Domestic activity   Fencing employed to outline dining room and bedroom, minimal furnishings.
Outdoor activity   House area converted to corral by substituting horse and cow for furniture; children look through fence at animals; cowboy rides horse, sings; snake draped in tree inside corral; path cleared through toys for roadway; trucks driven, loaded, furniture delivered; hand mirror stuck in truck cab as rear-view mirror; cars speeded across floor; plane flown.

Personal grooming and cleanliness   Girl given "hair cut" with scissors.
Aggression and violence   Station wagon runs over deer; snake coils around father and bites him; hunter aims rifle at standing cowboy, then turns to aim at mounted cowboy; repeated collisions between cars; attempt to cut off head of snake.

COMMENT   Older boy scarcely able to engage in meaningful play, exhibits frequent, incongruous juxtaposition of toys.

SESSION 11

PARTICIPANTS   Pedro   – 12M ⎫
               Rufino – 9M   ⎬ siblings
                             ⎭

               Emiliano – 10M ⎫
               Gustavo – 8M ⎪
               Estela   – 6F ⎬ siblings
               Celina   – 4F ⎭

TENOR OF SESSION   Quiet, guarded beginning with build-up of intensity.

NATURE OF INTERACTION   Girls passive, apathetic; boys compete, cooperate, joke.

CHARACTERISTICS OF PLAY   Various routine, narrative, and dramatic scenes underway concurrently; girls hold and handle minimal number of toys, watch boys.

CONTENT
Domestic activity   Household furnishings arranged; tables are set; people placed in beds; meal served; sweeping; cotton represents food in serving dish placed on table before men; woman stirs food in *cazuela*; baby put in cradle; yard is swept; family eats breakfast; sewing with machine; children sleeping (in tub, bed); sequence of dinner, bedtime, breakfast; man smokes "cigarette;" candle set up on table to light kitchen, later re-lighted; soft drinks are served; woman serves dinner, then sweeps; friends sleep in bed, family asleep on *petate*.
Outdoor activity   Hunter and animals placed in woods; teepee-shaped houses constructed of fence sections; plane circles, lands; dump truck and station wagon driven, dolls inserted as drivers; cows graze; zig-zag fence built; animals put in corral; child slides down sloping side of house; pilot added to plane, passengers added to station wagon, vehicles driven;

horse back riding; animal pen set up, animals added; two animals "yoked" together with candle across backs, man drives team of "oxen;" man lies down in truck to sleep; man and woman ride in truck to Mexico City and back; plane flies to meet them; guitar player sings, takes plane to Acapulco; plane flies to United States; station wagon travels with hunter on top; animals sleep in back of truck; plane flies to Monterrey and back; damaged plane repaired.

Personal grooming and cleanliness Boy's hair combed; later combed again.

Sexual interest Man drives to Mexico City with woman (laughter, embarrassment); P: "I am going to bed." E: "With your woman!" (laughter).

Illness and accidental injury Car turns over, three injured; plane crashes en route to Guadalajara, victims taken to hospital, served meal.

Vigilance, suspicion, and apprehension Man guards animals in corral; dog barks at (wild) animals; man arises, goes to check his livestock.

Aggression and violence Hunter shoots animals; snake bites boy; hunter shoots giraffe, tiger; dog bites baby; driver threatens to dump truck load of people; hunter kills more animals; giraffe stabbed in chest with knife.

Death and funerals Acapulco plane crashes into hillside, three dead; snake bites family sleeping on *petate*, all die (later "revived").

SESSION 12

PARTICIPANTS   Modesto – 16M
Ricardo – 15M ⎫
Segundo – 8M ⎬ siblings
Emiliano – 10M ⎫
Gustavo – 8M ⎬ siblings

TENOR OF SESSION   Busy; activity-oriented; overlapping, often initative, sequences.

NATURE OF INTERACTION   Cooperative, good rapport despite age.

CHARACTERISTICS OF PLAY   Wide utilization of toys; many climactic episodes frequently lacking antecedent development.

CONTENT

Domestic activity Meal prepared and set on table; mat sewn on sewing machine; child sent to market with basket; utensils put in cupboard;

candle set up to light kitchen; table set and cleared; "fire" built and fanned; floor swept.

Outdoor activity   Corrals and small pens constructed, animals enclosed; animals escape, damaged fence repaired; truck gets stuck in mud; station wagon driven to Mexico City; plane flown to United States; dump truck used in road repairs made; animals hauled in truck; corral swept; truck tips over; additional road repair; round trip flight to United States; tree grows in corral; station wagon goes to Vera Cruz, truck to Cuernavaca, plane to Acapulco; car tips over; individual compartments constructed for animals.

Personal grooming and cleanliness   Girl's hair combed and brushed; woman's hair "cut" with scissors; child takes bath in tub; baby bathed; baby uses "toilet."

Sexual interest   Boy and girl sleep in bed together (laughter).

Illness and accidental injury   Truck accident injures two; woman struck by truck, injured.

Aggression and violence   Snake bites man who collapses knocking over fence permitting animals to escape; hunter shoots deer; man shoots giraffe with pistol; man stalks and kills tiger; woman previously injured by truck struck down again; snake strikes at man; hunter attacked by snake; woman hits, then shoots children; snake bites boy; truck crashes into corral, kills pig, carcass eaten by dog; people sleep in bed unaware of snake under mattress; burro hacked with knife.

Robbery   Cow and burro stolen, driven away in truck; child boasts he has stolen snake.

Drunkenness   Man is dead drunk.

Death and funerals   Woman without apparent provocation kills two youngsters with pistol; two injured in overturned truck, later die; two killed in plane disaster; cowboy shoots and kills animals; plane crash kills woman; snake glides into tub, kills bathing child.

COMMENT   Themes reintroduced from prior session by two brothers (E. and G.) sometimes reiterated, sometimes intensified.

SESSION 13

PARTICIPANTS   Modesto   – 16M ⎤
               Leonardo – 12M ⎬ siblings
               Mario   – 8M ⎦
               Andres   – 13M ⎤
               Miguelito – 8M ⎦ siblings

TENOR OF THE SESSION   Enjoyment of toys partially overcomes self-consciousness and constriction.

NATURE OF INTERACTION   Primarily parallel play with activities of oldest frequently focus of interest.

CHARACTERISTICS OF PLAY   Brief, unconnected thematic episodes produced by eldest; others collect, organize, imitate.

CONTENT
Domestic activity   Room outlined by fence sections, furniture and people added; table set, family eats.
Outdoor activity   Fence building and repair; animals put in corral; livestock transported by truck; people given ride in back of truck; plane flies to Acapulco; truck driven to Mexico City; station wagon piled with diverse items.
Sexual interest   Boy and girl standing face to face kissing; (symbolic) girl in bed with snake under mattress with tail sticking out.
Illness and accidental injury   Truck tips over injuring load of passengers.
Aggression and violence   Hunter shoots deer; truck runs over woman; snake bites man; belly of pig cut open with knife; horse bitten by snake; tiger attacked with knife; man stabbed.
Death and funerals   Woman dies of stabbing.

COMMENT   Most themes introduced by oldest boy represent importations from prior session in which he was relatively passive in contrast to more active and imaginative children.

SESSION 14

PARTICIPANTS   Julio   – 14M ⎫
              Bolivar   – 12M ⎪
              Inocencia – 7F ⎬ siblings
              Herminia – 5F ⎭

TENOR OF SESSION   Reserve, self-consciousness, minimal to moderate involvement.

NATURE OF INTERACTION   Younger children dominated by oldest brother; passive compliance.

CHARACTERISTICS OF PLAY   Dramatic play by eldest only; others observe; slight inspection and collection of toys; hoarding by youngest girl.

CONTENT
Domestic activity   Meal preparation; infants put to bed; baby and little boy bottle-fed.
Outdoor activity   Planting, corral building.
Sexual interest   Giggling over bare-bottomed doll.
Criticism and punishment   Criticism of mother figures for neglect of baby.
Vigilance, suspicion, and apprehension   Man guards car.
Aggression and violence   Snake bites animals; hunter aims at animal; hunter shoots cowboy; ox eats dead cowboy; snake bites ox.
Robbery   Thieves haul cattle away.

SESSION 15

PARTICIPANTS   Augusto – 13M
              Bonita   – 11F ⎫
              Elisa   – 9F ⎬ cousins
                              ⎭

TENOR OF THE SESSION   Relatively brief; subdued but interested participation.

NATURE OF INTERACTION   Oldest deflects potential friction by suggesting and encouraging cooperation and sharing.

CHARACTERISTICS OF PLAY   Routine activities loosely strung together.

CONTENT
Domestic activity   Dishes organized in cupboard; table is set; woman cooks dinner at stove; mattress added to bed, bouquet put on night stand; small brother and sister placed in cradle; baby wrapped in blanket, given bottle; sewing with machine.
Outdoor activity   Hand mirror placed in truck as rear view mirror; spinning of plane propeller; horseback riding; animals grouped together.
Personal grooming and cleanliness   Boy takes bath in tub; baby placed on toilet (wash basin); 11-year old pretends to brush hair of 13-year old.
Sexual interest   Giggling over toileting and females astride horses.
Aggression and violence   One child "bites" another with snake.
Drunkenness   Father doll put to bed, described as "drunkest man of all" (by comparison with cowboys).

COMMENT   Covert sexual interest suggested when 13-year old boy spreads flexible legs of mother and daughter dolls to straddle horses (contrary to acceptable riding practice for women).

SESSION 16

PARTICIPANTS Leonardo – 12M
Eduardo – 12M ⎤
Juana – 9F ⎬ siblings
Pepita – 7F ⎦
Grecia – 5F ⎤
Ambrosio – 3M ⎦ siblings
Robertico – 11M

TENOR OF SESSION   Good-natured enthusiasm despite occasional interruptions and confusion.

NATURE OF INTERACTION   Girls generally cooperative; boys engage in parallel or peripheral activities.

CHARACTERISTICS OF PLAY   Thematic play ranging from routine to melodramatic.

CONTENT
Domestic activity   Tables set with dishes, family meal served; baby bottlefed; family retires for night in bed.
Outdoor activity   Truck loaded with furniture; miscellaneous objects piled on top of station wagon; vehicles driven, traded; corrals constructed for animals; table converted to market stall, small items offered for sale; small child rides burro; snake placed in tree.
Personal grooming and cleanliness   Baby toileted.
Aggression and violence   Dead father beaten across face using chocolate stirrer as club; teasing and threatening of group with toy pistol; pistol placed on dead father's chest, declared to have shot himself.
Death and funerals   Body of father placed on bed, candles nearby; grieving mother flings self across corpse; later mother returns to resume weeping.

COMMENT   12 year-old deaf-mute boy enjoyed play; received toys from others upon demand. Other 12 year-old boy entered group belatedly, acted out hostility to real father from whom he had been hiding all morning by savagely beating father doll.

SESSION 17

PARTICIPANTS   Isidra   – 14F   cousin of sibling group
               Maria Ventura – 8F ⎤
               Cornelia   – 6F ⎬ siblings
               Manuel   – 4M ⎦
               Celina   – 4F   'half'-cousin of sibling group

TENOR OF SESSION   Protracted silences, evident discomfort, guarded interest.

NATURE OF INTERACTION   Watching and waiting; passive acceptance of dominance of 14-year old girl and noisy intrusions of 4-year old boy.

CHARACTERISTICS OF PLAY   Holding and sitting; collecting of random items; aimless stacking; fragments of scenes and themes; low incidence of active play except for activity with vehicles.

CONTENT
Domestic activity   Mattress placed on bed, little boy put to bed; baby seated on chair, adults stand at table; small garden area fenced, trees added; girl in tree gathers fruit, basket below; little boy lies on couch; baby placed in cradle; plates, spoons placed on tables; little boy put on *petate* on floor; woman replaces boy in bed.
Outdoor activity   Vehicles driven with motor noises; cowboy rides horse; plane carried in truck; plane flown; "bus" (truck) driven to Mexico City, driver calling out stops en route — Santa Lucía, Santa Marta, Santiago; "contraband lumber" hauled in truck, load falls out; cow grazes.
Vigilance, suspicion, and apprehension   Cowboy guards animals.
Aggression and violence   Hunter on top of station wagon poised to shoot.
Death and funerals   Cowboy and horse fall, cowboy dies.

COMMENT   Oldest girl did not enter directly into play but served as a mother surrogate, quietly issuing directives, encouraging, instructing, correcting, suggesting, and announcing end of session.

SESSION 18

PARTICIPANTS   Maria Ventura – 8F ⎤
               Cornelia   – 6F ⎬ siblings
               Manuel   – 4M ⎥
               Grecia   – 5F ⎦

TENOR OF SESSION   Unimaginative and joyless; sporadic interest alternating with boredom.

NATURE OF INTERACTION   Parallel activity-inactivity; minor squabbles over possessions.

CHARACTERISTICS OF PLAY   Random and semi-categorical collecting and hoarding; scattered uneventful sequences and situations.

CONTENT
Domestic activity   Doll with baby laid on *petate*; little boy placed in cradle; sweeping; baby wrapped in blanket replaces child in cradle; furniture lined up; mother in cradle feeds baby with bottle; table with hole designated toilet; girl in tree picks fruit for family.
Outdoor activity   Tractor and truck driven; tractor used in road repair; plane flown; vehicles enclosed by fence, fence built around orchard and garden area, trees and flowers added, animals kept outside; snake wanders in garden; cowboys and little boy look at animals; damaged fences repaired.
Personal grooming and cleanliness   Woman combs hair.
Sexual interest   Man lies in bed facing woman.
Aggression and violence   Man run over by truck.

SESSION 19

PARTICIPANTS   Juana Marcos – 7M ⎫
            Grecia   – 5F ⎪
            Ambrosio – 3M ⎬ siblings
            Maximina – 2F ⎭

TENOR OF SESSION   Quiet, reserved, exploratory.

NATURE OF INTERACTION   Minimal; toys handed to each other but play seldom mutual.

CHARACTERISTICS OF PLAY   Handling, and miscellaneous stacking, loading and grouping; occasional sex-appropriate activity.

CONTENT
Domestic activity   Dolls piled in cradle, covered with blanket; chairs

lined up; plates put in basket; father added to cradle; woman placed in bed.

Outdoor activity   Truck driven; plane flown; truck loaded, driven about, occasional item unloaded; man rides tractor; station wagon driven.

Aggression and violence   Snake threatens father.

SESSION 20

PARTICIPANTS   Juana – 9F ⎱ siblings
               Pepita – 7F ⎰

TENOR OF SESSION   From concentrated attention and focused activity to rowdy fun.

NATURE OF INTERACTION   Close cooperation interspersed with sibling rivalry, authentic and mock.

CHARACTERISTICS OF PLAY   Situational melodrama plus interludes of bargaining, trading, and vending.

CONTENT
Domestic activity   Table set, chairs pulled up, family seated; kitchen utensils collected and stored; children tucked in bed with blanket, babies placed in crib; dolls get up, go to table; three sisters get into bed.
Outdoor activity   Six adjoining pens constructed, one animal placed in each; later second animal added to each pen; road construction equipment (tractor) driven; truck loaded with animals; vendor sells wares.
Personal grooming and cleanliness   Babies given bath.
Criticism and punishment   Girls criticize each other — "You have many things, I have nothing." "Better this way" (takes over snake and demonstrates); intervention to correct aim of hunter; "I can do it better" (seating doll more securely on tractor).
Illness and accidental injury   Effort to cure victim of snake bite.
Aggression and violence   Snake bites cowboy from behind, hunter shoots snake; snake crawls through bars of crib to bite two babies; cars run over cowboys; animals spilled out of speeding truck; truck rams into fences; car hits family.
Death and funerals   Dead father placed in casket (tub), blanket drawn up over face, two candles placed at head, floral offerings added, wife cries over body; hit-and-run victims piled in casket; dead child brought

to weeping mother; poor family buried without benefit of flowers or candles; babies bitten by snake die; mother of three sisters dies.

COMMENT   Notwithstanding prior participation, sisters heightened enjoyment of session by embellishing old themes.

SESSION 21

PARTICIPANTS   Anastacia – 14F ⎫ step-sisters
                  Jesucita   – 12F ⎭
                  Federico – 5M   half-brother to Anastacia on father's side
                                            half-brother to Jesucita on mother's side

TENOR OF SESSION   Tense, anxious, and abbreviated.

NATURE OF INTERACTION   Girls confer, mostly in whispers; occasional exchange of toys.

NATURE OF PLAY   Brief, hurried examination, collection, and manipulation of limited number of toys.

CONTENT   Miscellaneous — furniture loaded into truck; several dolls placed on chairs; animals heaped together.

COMMENT   Children seem to have participated without parents' permission in the course of performing errands. Anxious, furtive behavior apparently related to long-standing feud between this family and relatives in neighborhood. Session broken into two equally skimpy segments by three-hour-interruption.

SESSION 22

PARTICIPANTS   Anselmo   – 12M ⎫ siblings
                  Silvano Mateo – 7M   ⎭
                  Juana   – 9F ⎫ siblings
                  Pepita   – 7F ⎭

TENOR OF SESSION   Consistently high level of activity and absorption; build-up of emotional intensity.

NATURE OF INTERACTION   Sibling groups play side by side according to prescribed sex roles; when boys depart, girls take over vehicles; engage in closely coordinated activities.

CHARACTERISTICS OF PLAY   Highly-articulated, routine sequences yield to drama, melodrama, recklessness, and excess.

CONTENT
Domestic activity   Two tables carefully set; meals prepared; families come to tables; food served; plates counted; dishes traded; *pulque* served; kitchens reorganized.
Outdoor activity   Truck driven; corral built, filled with animals; animals loaded in truck, hauled away.
Criticism and punishment   Man will file complaint over slaying of cow.
Vigilance, suspicion, and apprehension   Plane searches for missing animals; grand-daughter afraid of falling from back of truck because of reckless driving.
Aggression and violence   Tiger eats dead calf; snake bites burro; hunter shoots snake, then cow; angry owner of cow has gun fight with hunter; truck crashes into kitchen; repeated head-on collisions between vehicles, cars wrecked; truck runs over snake.
Robbery   Animals stolen, trucked away.
Death and funerals   Hunter dies in gunfight; truck loaded with dead people; mourning widow falls from truck, dies; candle placed upright among bodies; additional corpses laid on top of station wagon; funeral procession; grandmother dies in fall from truck; granddaughter and others also killed in same manner; bodies laid out on ground side by side, covered with shroud (blanket); bodies placed in "casket," recovered with shroud.

SESSION 23

PARTICIPANTS   Cecilia   – 15F ⎤
               Faustina – 14F ⎥ siblings
               Cesar   – 6M ⎥
               Anselmo – 12M ⎦

TENOR OF SESSION   Slow-moving, constricted, passive; silence punctuated with whispers.

NATURE OF INTERACTION   Limited cooperation within sex groups; possessiveness by girls.

CHARACTERISTICS OF PLAY   Examining, collecting, hoarding; scattered, minimally-developed sequences; selection of toys by traditional sex roles.

CONTENT
Domestic activity   Kitchen furnished; table set; dishes and utensils sorted; cooking at stove; bedroom, sitting area arranged; little girl put to bed on mattress in cradle; mother lies down; mother and daughter eat at table; table cleared, dishes stored in basket; people seated on chairs.
Outdoor activity   Corral built, animals enclosed; cowboy drives station wagon; corral enlarged; tractor delivered by truck to corral; cowboys and animals loaded and carried in truck.
Sexual interest   Underwear of girl doll hurriedly examined.
Aggression and violence   Hunter aims at snake; truck runs over snake; station wagon runs over snake; hunter aims at cowboy on horse; snake thrown into corral; snake pinned under fence section; to kill snake that frightened horse, angry cowboy jumps horse over fence into corral, lands on snake.

APPENDIX B: SELECTED PLAY PROTOCOLS

SESSION 1

Octavia – 16F
Fedora   – 14F
Eduardo – 12M
Juana   – 9F
Pepita   – 7F

The four girls begin the session. They kneel down to examine the toys. Fedora handles several of the dolls and says, "What a big family!" The others begin identifying various items. Pepita picks up the doll carrying the baby in her *rebozo*. "I like this one the best." Fedora: "I like the little sewing machine the best." She holds it, examines it carefully and turns the wheel. Juana says that it's time to put the baby to bed, picking up a small, naked baby and placing it in the cradle. Pepita lays the doll holding the baby on the bed. Juana, observing that the animals are on their sides, says, "The livestock are sleeping." Fedora begins to set the animals upright. Juana: "One of the animals has jumped over the *barranca!*" Fedora moves the tiger across the floor. "The tiger is going to eat the little boy!" She next picks out the truck from the pile of toys, loads the sewing machine into it and gives it a push. The truck first runs over a baby and then knocks over several animals to the delight of all.

Juana and Pepita attempt to stand up the dolls. They are especially interested in the clothing of the family dolls. Octavia tentatively picks up the father. "This man is a *Guarincito* (backward Indian)." Juana examines a boy doll and then a little girl. "Look, she has no pants!" The girls laugh. "The *señora* (mother doll) has braids." Juana looks under the mother doll's skirt but makes no comment.

Fedora arranges the animals in a long line. Pepita looks into the dish cupboard. She picks up two dolls and has them embrace. "These two women are greeting each other." Juana sees that the mother and son dolls have fallen over and says that these people are both drunk.

Fedora has completed a corral and filled it with animals. She and Juana begin to push the station wagno back and forth across the floor to each other. When the fence is knocked down there is general laughter. "The animals will escape!" On another pass the station wagon knocks down two children. More laughter. Fedora tries to stuff objects into the station wagon without success. The fence is repaired and a girl doll is set up to be the shepherd. Pepita spins the propeller on the plane and flies it briefly. Juana takes it over announcing that the plane will knock down the *señor* (father doll). Fedora manages to get a pig through the window of the station wagon, then puts a small tree through the open windshield. She gives the car a push. "Let's hope that it misses the corral. *Ojala!*" Laughter when the fence goes down. "Look, the deer is dead." "The pig is carrying off the baby!"

Eduardo arrives. The children begin naming and teasing. "Pepita is the doll with the baby!" "Fedora is *La Borracha* (the drunk woman)!" "Octavia is the mother." "Eduardo, this is you!" (father doll). They laugh.

Juana puts the mother and father dolls in bed. "The two old people are sleeping." Pepita collects dishes. "Now we will have coffee." Fedora pushes back the bonnet of the Amish doll and discovers that she has no hair except for a forelock. "Her hair was burned off and she covers her head because she is ashamed." Juana is called by her mother and leaves. Pepita complains that her deer has fallen over and the squirrel as well.

She puts the doll with the baby in bed again. Eduardo sits holding the plane. Fedora pulls the tree out of the station wagon, then loads the truck with the sewing machine and also the bed which falls off. She rams the truck around knocking over people and animals. Eduardo fingers the tree. Juana returns and sits up the babies that have been hit by the truck. Pepita says that one of them has been hurt. Juana: "What has happened to the shepherdess? Where is she?" Pepita: "She's sleeping." (tipped over). A doll is placed near the animals to keep watch.

Juana says, "This drunk [father doll] is going to go to sleep." Her mother calls her again and she goes reluctantly. Pepita continues. "Yes, the *señor* is drunk! He has passed out" (falls into the cradle containing two babies). Fedora moves him into the bed. "He's very drunk." Eduardo reaches across the play area to wiggle the arm of the inert father doll. Pepita looks closely: "The *señor* has an injury on his forehead."

Juana returns and has the mother doll who is standing in the corral count animals, then children. "This woman has eleven children." Fedora plays with the stove and sets the table with dishes. Pepita puts a doll at the table. "This boy is eating." Octavia adds chairs and seats babies around the table. She puts a pottery mug at each place. "Each will have a *jarrito* of *pulque*." Juana sets the case of soft drinks in the center of the table. "These are *refrescos*. You don't know how to take care of children!" Fedora arranges dishes in the cupboard. Octavia asks how to light the stove. Eduardo slowly pushes the station wagon back and forth. Pepita brings the mother doll to the table. "*La Borracha* fell down from the table. She can't go out to watch the animals." Juana knocks down all the animals in the corral. "They all fell down, every one. They're tired."

Fedora begins to collect furniture and cars saying, "These are mine!" Juana piles up dishes. "These are mine!" Fedora calls out, "Buy them if you want them!" Eduardo plays with the tiger in his hand. Octavia rebuilds the corral and insists that all the animals be kept inside. Juana stands the animals up within the fence. Fedora appropriates Juana's dishes and fills the cupboard. Eduardo tries to perch animals in the tree. Fedora puts small dolls in the truck and tells the others that "These are bad children who are being taken away in the patrol wagon." She then puts a basket on the arm of the mother doll. Octavia puts dishes and utensils in the basket, teasing as she says, "Here goes Fedora!" All stop to listen to voices of men on a truck that has stopped down the road. Eduardo runs out. Fedora attempts to fit a small doll into the washbasin, using it as a toilet. Pepita puts the mother doll at the sewing machine. Fedora says that the woman doesn't know how. Octavia: "Here. I'll have the drunk show her how." Fedora leaves momentarily and when she returns says accusingly, "I'll call the police because you're stealing my things!" Juana echoes her. "Someone has stolen all my animals!" All four girls start grabbing for toys. Each makes a pile in front of her. Fedora: "Call the police! I'm getting mad!" Juana: "Look, the police are drunk!" She indicates the father doll lying face down in bed. Fedora says to Pepita: "You are keeping my stove?" Pepita replies with mock-innocence, "What stove, *señora*?" The girls continue to grab and trade toys. Octavia tells Pepita that she should go to the *delegación* (local officials) because her things have been stolen.

Juana piles dolls in the truck and they fall out as it careens around. All laugh. Octavia stands up the father doll and says, "This is Juana's husband! They are dancing." Juana pretends to dance with him by moving his arm up and down. Octavia begins another corral. Juana reloads the truck with dolls and pushes it. "One woman fell off. Now a man fell off." Pepita sing-songs, "This is my bed because it is my bed!" Fedora and Pepita discover that Juana has a secret cache of toys hidden in a basket and force her to distribute them among the rest. When Juana tries to claim some for herself, Fedora pushes her away. Juana retrieves the truck and lays a doll in the back. "They are going to carry this drunk away." Pepita flies the plane around in the play area. Juana adds dolls to the back of the truck and says they are *Chalmeros* (pilgrims on their way to the shrine at Chalma). Octavia grabs dolls away from Juana who retaliates by grabbing animals and fence sections away from Octavia. They slap at each other's hands. Fedora says boisterously, "You're all drunk!" Pepita feigns hiccups and staggers into children and toys. The hilarity increases and the session is ended.

SESSION 6

Lucía   – 13F
Felipa   – 11F
Concha – 9F
Cisco   – 7M

The three sisters select toys to set up a household scene. Felipa stands up the mother doll. Concha collects dishes and puts them in the cupboard. Lucía begins to fit together fence sections to mark off house walls. Cisco picks up the plane and flies it with a boy doll balanced on the wing. Felipa builds a small corral and Cisco comes to help. He drives back and forth with the truck delivering fence sections. Within the corral Felipa builds separate compartments to serve as animal stalls. Concha arranges a kitchen and stands dolls up at the table. Lucía opens and closes the oven door. She and Concha whisper. Concha puts some of the dishes into the stove. Felipa tells the younger girls that there is more furniture for the house. She adds the bed, night-stand and washbasin to the crowded room. Lucía rearranges the walls to enlarge the house. Felipa puts the Amish doll to sleep on the bed, then has the mother doll wake her. Dolls that have been seated at the table are served soft drinks. Cisco places the sewing machine with the other furniture, opening and closing the lid. Felipa puts animals into their stalls and puts the snake in the far side of the corral. She sticks the pistol under the father doll's arm, stands him outside the house, and sends a small boy off to guard the corral.

Felipa lays a small child on the coffee table and places the cross at its head. "Rest in peace." Lucía brings two candles and leans them against the improvised bier. Cisco, who has been watching, picks up the plane, puts it down, then drives the truck. Felipa loads additional animals into the truck and directs Cisco to drive them to the corral. He unloads the giraffe and places it upright straddling the snake. "Look, it's riding the snake." Felipa takes the giraffe away and puts it in another corner of the corral. Lucía sets up the hunter to shoot the deer. Chico mounts the brother doll on the horse. "He is chasing the bull [cow]." Felipa stuffs first one baby and then another through the open windshield of the station wagon. Cisco politely requests one of the babies. Felipa replies, "No, they are all going to the cemetery." She transfers the dead child from the house to the top of the station wagon where the body is adorned with the two candles. After driving a short distance, she puts the dead doll on the floor and places the cross at its head. "Finally she is buried." Felipa returns to the house and has Lucía assist her in setting the table with cups, plates and bottles. "Now they are going to eat. Give everyone who has come to mourn something to drink."

Felipa gets the Amish doll up, saying that she is going to do the housework. Furniture is pushed together and Concha sweeps. Felipa arranges the small dolls around the "nun" (Amish doll). "The Sister is teaching the doctrine of God to the children." Concha pretends to use the sewing machine and Lucía hands her the scissors.

Felipa brings in another dead child and lays it on the bier with candles lying at the sides. "Here is another dead one, a little boy." Cisco appeals to Felipa, "Lend me the pistol." She replies with feigned courtesy, "One moment, señor" but overlooks the request. He toys with the plane propeller. Felipa puts the nun at the table to eat with the children. The mother doll goes back and forth from the stove to the table while serving the meal. Lucía asks, "Where is the *señor*?" Felipa, indicating the father doll, responds, "He is out guarding the sheep." Cisco stands up and yawns. Concha drives cars along the far side of the room. Lucía sits and watches. Felipa picks up the snake and has it bite the deer. Then she sets up the cowboys who shoot at each other. One falls dead. Cisco notices that several of the animals in the corral have fallen over. "These animals are dead." He drives the truck over to collect the carcasses. Felipa drives by with the dead boy on top of the station wagon. Cisco requests one of her candles for his dead animals but is turned down. He dumps the animals out of the truck unceremoniously and declares that they are buried. Felipa proceeds to the "cemetary" with the little boy.

Lucía puts the comb in the brush that lies beside the bed, then begins to put the mugs on the coffee table. Felipa takes over and sets up the people in chairs around the coffee table. She seats a doll at the sewing machine, adds the scissors. Concha looks on. Lucía stands the mother doll at the stove. Felipa leans the father doll against a chair. "This man is drunk. He drank too much *pulque*."

Cisco works on the corral fence. He looks at the remaining fallen animals and says to himself, "Yes, they are still dead." He sees the brother doll lying on the floor. "He fell off his horse. The horse threw him and he is dead." His sisters pay no attention to him. Cisco picks up the pistol. "This will kill the snake!" He aims at the snake. "Now he is dead." Felipa puts the guitar player out by the corral to sing. Lucía, pointing to the man killed in the gunfight, says, "The one who was shot is still here." Instead of responding, Felipa begins another funeral. "This old man has just died." She puts a small doll and candle on top of the station wagon. "His *compañero* (father doll) is going to the cemetary." The station wagon with the corpse and the truck loaded with people form the funeral procession. Upon their return, Felipa transforms the mourners into a group preparing to go on an outing. "They are going to see the animals in Chapultepec Park." A number of animals are moved across the room and set up under two trees. The dolls are driven to the Park, taken from the truck and set up to view the animals. The nun has been brought along to help with the children. Felipa starts putting the dolls back into the truck for the trip home. "It won't hold everyone." She makes two trips.

Cisco reports to no one in particular that the squirrel is dead. Concha stands up as if to leave. Felipa forces one of the babies into the plane. Cisco follows her lead and stuffs a baby into the station wagon. "The driver had a wreck. This little boy is dead." He pulls the doll from the car and offers it to Felipa who ignores him. She begins playing in the house area while the other children, who are becoming tired and bored, mostly watch. She puts a boy to bed. "He is going to go to sleep." She seats a baby in the washbasin. "He is going to go to the toilet." Then she combs the hair of one of the girl dolls. The mirror is propped against the foot of the bed and the girl placed in front of it. Concha leaves the group and goes outside. Felipa places cotton near the "toilet." "That is to clean yourself." She then sticks the mirror upright through a hole in the table to make a dressing table. Cisco stands up and idly pushes the truck back and forth with his foot. Lucía straightens the corral fence and watches her older sister. Felipa moves the mother doll from the table, tells her to wipe her feet on the petate beside the bed, and puts her in bed. The small dolls are set up in a semi-circle with the sister doll standing in the center. "You are to be the teacher to the children." Cisco coasts the station wagon across the floor to Lucía who drives it briefly. Cisco goes outdoors to look for Concha. Felipa continues her monologue. "Now the *señor* has gone outside to work. This boy is the last one to eat." She rouses the mother doll out of bed and brings her to the table where she and the boy have a soft drink. The Amish doll is put into the bed with a child on each side. "They are all brothers and sisters." The mother doll is placed in the cradle with two babies. "She is resting with her children." Cisco and Concha return. Cisco knocks over the fence. He and Lucía argue over the corral and ownership of the animals. Lucía prevails and heaps the fence sections in a pile. She puts the animals and snake in the truck and drives it around, finally rolling it to Cisco who dumps out the animals. Concha stands watching. Cisco jabs the snake at her foot. "It's going to bite you!" Concha pays no attention but begins to build a fence. Lucía comes over to help but Concha tires and goes back to stand by the door. Lucía constructs a square enclosure. She puts a horse and cowboys in the truck and rolls it to Cisco who drives it aimlessly.

Felipa gets all the dolls up. The sister doll combs her hair before the mirror. Lucía enters into the play, using the cotton to wipe the baby after toileting. She throws the cotton into the "garbage" (dishdrain). Felipa hangs a basket over the mother's arm so that she can go and buy bread. The snake is brought into the house by Felipa where it crawls across the bed toward a girl doll lying on the *petate* on the floor. Felipa: "The snake has bitten the girl!" The cross is placed on top of the station wagon to convert it to an ambulance. Felipa drives it over to pick up a little boy whom Cisco has run over with his truck. The victim is delivered to the coffee table where he is cured by the "nurse" (Amish doll) who uses bits of cotton in the treatment. Felipa asks for and gets the truck to take the patient home. "Now he is all well."

The girl who has died of snakebite is now laid out on the coffee table with a candle beside her. Felipa has the bereaved gather around the body and pray. The dead girl is carried to the roof of the station wagon and candles placed on top of her body. The truckful of mourners follows the funeral car to the graveyard. Felipa lays the deceased on the floor with the cross at the head and candles lying across the body. After the ceremony those in attendance are returned by truck.

The three younger children using fence sections have built a series of compartments but leave them empty. Cisco flies the plane, a baby falls and he hands the dead infant to Felipa who, as usual, fails to react. She is setting up a new bedroom. "The nun is sleeping." The father doll is lying on his face. "This man is drunk — the father of all the children."

Cisco and Concha say good night and leave, followed by Lucía. Felipa realizes that she has to stop playing since it has grown dark and she must accompany the younger children home.

SESSION 10

Justo – 15M
José – 12M

Justo sits on his haunches and watches José poke through the toys. José offers him the station wagon. Justo sees the snake, picks it up, turns it over, and pushes it through the rear window of the station wagon which he then drives on the floor in front of him. When he removes the snake, he sees that the station wagon is coming apart. He sets it down and watches José who has begun to work on an oval-shaped enclosure using the fence sections. José places a small chair inside the fence and then parts of the sectional. "This is going to be a bedroom and a dining room." He selects a few other pieces of furniture from the toy collection and shows Justo the dresser, demonstrating how the drawers pull in and out. He sets it in his house along with a bed. Then he examines the sewing machine and shows Justo how the wheel and treadle move. He puts it in the furniture grouping and adds the coffee table. Next he places a tree in the center of the table. "This is a *florero* (vase or pot of flowers)."

Justo gets on his knees and clears an area through the jumbled toys and drives the truck toward José. José finds the hand mirror and inserts it into the cab of Justo's truck, creating a rear-view mirror. José: "Wait a minute." He removes the "bouquet" from his table and puts it in the back of the truck. He takes over the truck, drives it around and eventually delivers the tree back to his house, returning it to the table. Justo fumbles with the broken station wagon trying to fix it but José takes it away from him and readily snaps it back together. Justo next experiments with fitting the bed into the truck. José again intervenes and jams the bed into the back of the truck which he then turns upside down to prove to Justo that it can't fall out. He removes the bed and throws it onto the pile of unused toys.

The boys idly sort through the toys and converse, frequently in whispers. José identifies various family dolls. "I wonder if somebody is missing." He finds a cow and a horse and puts them inside his fence, removing the furniture. Justo returns to his original place, sits, and stacks the plane and snake on top of the station wagon beside him. He yawns and watches José. José puts the guitar player on the horse and sets up the hunter with his rifle aimed at the cowboy. Justo reaches over and turns the hunter toward the mounted cowboy. "No, it's better this way," says José and he switches the hunter back to the former position.

The boys pick up and handle two or three of the smaller dolls. Justo: "This one has a baby. Let's take it out." José: "You can't because it's glued in." He stands the figures around his corral so that they are looking through the fence. He adds a pig and a tree to the corral and then drapes the snake in the branches of the tree.

Justo sits and spins the wheels of the dump truck to see if they move freely. He begins to drive it but José interrupts. "Give me my car." Justo hands it over and José inserts a baby doll as the driver, making sure that Justo notices. Justo takes the station wagon and runs over the deer, dragging it along underneath the car. Both boys laugh. José takes the snake out of the tree and winds it around the waist and arms of the father doll. "He's going to get bitten!" Justo reaches into the corral, picks up the pig, and gives it a ride on the hood of the station wagon. José calls Justo's attention again to the mounted guitar player. "Look, the cowboy is singing as he rides along on his horse." Justo watches with only slight interest, then turns back to his station wagon. He holds it and looks at it from several angles. "It doesn't have any license plates." He puts it on top of the plane and looks at José questioningly. José objects. "They would tip over that way. The plane wouldn't be able to fly." He hands Justo back the station wagon, picks up the plane, blows on the propeller, and briefly demonstrates how an airplane banks and turns.

José lapses into silence and sits spinning the wheels of the truck which he holds upside down in his hand. Justo engages in sporadic, random play. He places a tree on a table, replaces it with a small child, and then tosses them both away. He piles parts of the sectional on the roof of the station wagon and adds a burro to the top of the load. He drives it slowly back and forth without moving from his spot on the floor. He watches José who finally sets down the truck. Justo takes it and loads it haphazardly with the sewing machine, sectionals, washbasin and bed, one on top of the other. José comments, "That's a furniture truck." Justo adds a small boy to the top of the load. He drives and the boy falls off. He ignores the doll and substitutes a tub on top of the load.

José picks up the scissors and pretends to cut the hair of the daughter doll. He sets her aside. Justo watches to see what José will do next. José unwinds the snake from the body of the father and tries to cut its head off with the scissors. Failing, he turns to Justo. "Give me the truck." He takes it and dumps out the contents, takes the station wagon in his other hand and clears a path through the toys by pushing them aside with the bumpers of the two vehicles. "Let's play." He then shows Justo how to coast the cars so that they collide. He hands Justo the truck and their cars crash several times. Laughter follows when the cars are upset. After a short time, however, they tire of the game. José offers to put the toys away. He opens the doll box and starts putting the family members into it. Justo places the station wagon on top of the truck and rolls the doubled-up vehicles a short distance, then he tries to balance the plane on top of the cars. José continues to put the toys away. Justo stands up and watches but makes no move to help. José finds a tiny pottery mug and tosses it into the air, trying to catch it in his open mouth. He finishes packing away the toys and tells Justo that they are ready to go.

SESSION 11

Pedro   – 12M
Rufino   – 9M
Emiliano – 10M
Gustavo – 8M
Estela   – 6F
Celina   – 4F

The two girls watch shyly as the boys grab for vehicles. Having claimed one each, their attention is caught by other items. Pedro kneels, collecting fence sections. He takes the table and stands the guitar-playing cowboy on it. Rufino gingerly picks up the snake, then puts it down. Pedro reaches over to touch it. Gustavo squats as he rolls the truck toward Pedro. Emiliano opens up the sewing machine to inspect it. Rufino reaches for it but is ignored by Emiliano. Pedro finds the mirror and puts it on his table. Emiliano sets up one of the trees and Gustavo sets up the other. The girls remain sitting on the floor somewhat outside the circle. Estela reaches for the dish cupboard and sets it upright. Celina watches. Rufino puts the mattress on the bed. Emiliano searches out animals, some of which he places near the hunter. Gustavo also collects animals. Pedro hands him the father doll which he stands up.

Pedro puts dishes on the table while Emiliano inspects the stove. Pedro reaches for Rufino's bed into which he puts the doll carrying the baby. Rufino, on his knees, flies the plane over the toys with a hissing sound. Estela has a basket of flowers and a dish on the floor in front of her. Celina reaches for the dish but Estela puts it in her cupboard. Rufino draws up pieces of the sectional to the table. Pedro sticks a candle upright between bottles in the case of soft drinks in the center of the table. He sets around spoons and bowls. The two little girl dolls are put to bed.

Pedro, Rufino and Gustavo start building "houses" by placing fence sections on end, two in teepee shapes and one resembling an A-frame. Gustavo's structure falls down and he patiently rebuilds. Rufino flies the plane, landing it gently in a cleared space in the center of the play area. Pedro takes over the plane and flies it noiselessly. Emiliano has been setting his own table and preparing a meal. He now turns away from the kitchen and drives the dump truck. Gustavo drives the station wagon. Estela sweeps the floor in front of her with the broom. She puts the bouquet and dishes into the cradle with Celina participating slightly. Estela hands the daughter doll to Celina, then piles spoons on the cupboard shelves. Gustavo turns the wheel on the sewing machine. Pedro puts a fluff of cotton into the *cazuela* (cooking dish) and brings it to the table. "This is the meal." Emiliano demands, "Give me a *cazuelita*, too." Estela hands him hers. Pedro places the two cowboys at the table to eat. Emiliano pretends to comb the hair of a little boy. Pedro walks the father doll. "Here goes Gustavo." General laughter. He then takes a basket from the girls without protest on their part. He puts it beside the doll with baby near the table. He gives the mother doll the *cazuela* and a spoon. "She's making the dinner." Gustavo says, "If I am the father, you are the mother!" More laughter.

With their meager possessions in front of them, the girls sit watching the boys and play sporadically. Estela holds two family dolls. Celina puts a baby in the cradle. The boys busy themselves with outdoor activities. Gustavo drives the station wagon with a baby on the front seat as driver. Pedro inserts a baby in the plane as pilot. Gustavo and Emiliano trade the station wagon for the truck. Rufino discovers the scissors and tries to cut various objects including the plane wing. He gives up and joins Pedro in corral building. They make a zig-zag fence by forcibly interlocking the ends. "Here are the penned-in animals." Emiliano turns from a "forest" scene where the hunter has shot a tiger and other animals beneath the two trees, to demonstrate for the boys the correct method of fence assembly, i.e. standing the sections on their bases. Pedro builds another teepee-shaped structure and slides a baby down the sloping side. Gustavo has constructed the corral anew. "I am guarding the animals." Pedro sweeps energetically around the corral, then hands the broom to Estela who also sweeps, then gives it to Celina who imitates. Estela: "Whose broom is this?" Gustavo: "It's mine."

Emiliano puts small dolls in the station wagon. "I am the driver." Rufino flies the plane with a doll (brother) projecting through the windshield. Emiliano: "Here I go on my horse!" He dismounts the little boy from the horse and picks up the snake and jabs it at the doll. "This snake is biting me!" Rufino asks for the snake but gets no response. Pedro has been placing dolls on chairs around the table. "They are having breakfast." Each of the boys has his own pile of toys before him. The girls share their small collection but spend increasingly more time watching the others play. Pedro: "Here is the dog barking at the animals in the woods." Emiliano: "I am shooting the animals." He aims the hunter's gun at the giraffe and tiger. Gustavo drives the father and daughter dolls around in the back of the truck. Pedro, who has been flying the plane, offers to trade the brother doll for the father doll and is refused.

Celina gets up and starts to leave the circle. Emiliano coaxes her back with a small doll. She sits down and with Estela places several dolls in and out of the cradle aimlessly. Emiliano operates the treadle of the sewing machine. Gustavo continues to drive the truck with its passengers, then trades with Rufino and flies the plane. Pedro places a candle across the necks of two cows standing side by side to make a yoke. "This man is going to work." He positions a small boy doll behind the animals. "The man is driving the ox team. *Arre!*" Estela holds the mother doll and Pedro remarks that she is preparing a meal. Gustavo places pieces of the sectional in the back of his truck to serve as benches for his passengers. "Off I go." "With your woman!", adds Rufino, referring to the male and female dolls. All laugh. Gustavo appears embarrassed. Pedro: "Look. The dog is biting the baby!" Emiliano combs the little boy doll: "Now I'm combing my hair." Pedro says, "I am going to bed." "With your woman!", teases Emiliano. More laughter. Gustavo, who has been driving his truck on the periphery of the circle says, "I'm going to lie down and sleep in my truck." Pedro pretends to light the candle. "The candle is illuminating the kitchen." Emiliano stands up a boy doll. "Now I'm awake. I'm going out to check my animals. Good, they are all right." Gustavo announces from the sidelines, "This truck is going to dump out the people," but instead he rearranges the dolls and continues to drive. Celina whines for the comb. Estela asks Emiliano to give it to her but he ignores the request. All laugh uproariously when Celina farts loudly. "Who shot it off?" "Yes, who is shooting rockets around here?"

Pedro stands up the guitar player. "Here is a performer singing." He places the singer and cowboys on the plane straddling the fuselage. They take off. "The performers are on their way to Acapulco." He flies the plane holding on to the precariously balanced figures and hits a box at the side of the room. "They crashed into a hill and fell off." Emiliano tips over the station wagon. "The car has been wrecked. Three are injured." Pedro: "My plane crashed over here. There are three dead people." Gustavo drives up with his truck. "I just got back from Mexico City." Rufino says, "I am tired of watching the animals. I'm going to lie down." He lays a boy on the *petate*. Emiliano puts several dolls into the tub, using it as a bed. "They're sleeping." Pedro places two small dolls in the bed. "Here, too, they're sleeping." He picks up the plane again. "We are flying to the United States." Gustavo tips the truck over. "The truck has had an accident. Two are dead."

Pedro awakes the sleeping dolls and brings them to the table. "Here they are having breakfast." Gustavo places a tiny piece of rolled-up paper to the father doll's mouth. "This man is smoking." "Yes," says Pedro, "it is you!" Laughter. Gustavo: "They have now finished break- fast here, too, and are going north." He drives the station wagon away with the hunter on top. Pedro, at his table says, "They are relighting the candle because it blew out. Now they're going to have a soft drink." Celina stands up again and moves away from the play. Gustavo says to Celina. "If you don't want this . ." He takes her doll. Estela has piled the Amish doll across the mother doll on the floor in front of her. She watches the boys. Emiliano urges Estela to play but to no avail. He turns to the corral and rearranges some of the animals. Gustavo and Rufino argue briefly over extra fence sections. Gustavo spreads fencing across the back of the truck and lays out several animals on top. "They are sleeping." Pedro returns to his plane. "I'm flying to Monterrey. And now I'm back." Emiliano repositions the hunter near the trees. "He's shooting the giraffe and the tiger." Turning to Rufino, Emiliano says, "Lend me your knife." Rufino complies and Emiliano hacks at the underside of the giraffe held upside down in his hand. He then returns the knife.

Pedro has reset the table. "This woman will serve the meal soon. Right now she is sweeping." He puts a girl doll through the motions. Gustavo says, "I'm going to shut my animals in the corral." Emiliano trades a giraffe for a cat with Rufino. Pablo puts the cotton in the *cazuela*. "Here is the *sopa* [rice dish]." Pedro puts two dolls to bed. "Now we are going to sleep, me and a friend." He asks Estela for the *petate*. Emiliano interrupts. "No, give it to me!" Estela throws it to Emiliano. He places a baby, the hunter, and a girl doll on the *petate*. "They are sleeping." Then he puts the snake on top of the sleeping people. "They have been bitten!" He has the snake glide away. Pedro flies the plane out of the circle and returns driving the truck filled with dolls. "The plane to Guadalajara crashed. Here are the dead." He puts the bodies in the "hospital" (bed). Emiliano says "These people are dead, too, because of the snake." Pedro brings the damaged plane in for repairs. Pedro: "Now they are going to serve the injured people their meal." He moves the table and dishes to the bedside. Emiliano, referring to the snakebite victims, says, "Now they are revived." He stands the figures upright. The session is terminated.

SESSION 19

Juana Marcos – 7M
Grecia   – 5F
Ambrosio   – 3M
Maximina   – 2F

The boys each select a vehicle. Ambrosio begins driving the truck while Juan Marcos flies the plane. Grecia and Maximina sort through the toys, picking up and putting down small items which catch their fancy. Grecia examines the sewing machine, sets up a tree, and piles dolls into the cradle. She then hands the cradle to Maximina. Juan Marcos lays fence sections across the roof of the station wagon. Ambrosio loads furniture and pieces of fence into his truck and drives with one hand steadying the load. He stops to pick up the plane which he hands to Juan Marcos. "Here's your plane." Juan Marcos sets it down to one side of him and stands up the giraffe which he has discovered. He has begun an enclosure to which he returns, continuing his work. Ambrosio drives by with the truck load saying, "Here is another one" as he takes a fence section from the truck and offers it to Juan Marcos.

Each girl has a small collection of toys before her. Maximina, with her feet tucked under her, reaches for more dolls, then adds silverware and fence sections to her pile. Grecia lines up chairs side by side to form a row.

She reaches over and takes the cradle from Maximina's collection and empties it. She sets it near the chairs. Then she lays the *petate* on top of the dresser which is lying on its back thus making a platform bed. She stands up the father doll and reaches for the snake which she places on the floor facing toward him.

On the far side of the room Ambrosio is driving both the station wagon and the truck. He takes a chair from his load of furniture and says to Juan Marcos, "Here is a chair." Grecia puts the mother doll and a small girl into the cradle. She covers them with a blanket. She sets up the cupboard, then seats a tiny baby in a cup (potty?) and sets it on the upside-down coffee table. She shows Maximina the chocolate stirrer.

Ambrosio picks up the snake and dangles it in front of Grecia. "Drop it!" she says, and he does. "Is it true that it doesn't bite?" She turns back to her domestic scene. The Amish doll is lying sideways across the bed. Grecia brings a piece of sectional close to the bed and pushes it under the doll's head which was over the edge. She switches the *petate* from the dresser to the table with the hole in it.

Juan Marcos drives the tractor across the corner of the room to join Ambrosio. He picks up the guitar-playing cowboy and forces him onto the tractor seat. Ambrosio puts the washbasin upside-down on the roof of the station wagon but then tosses it aside. He drives in the direction of the girls, finds the cross and hands it to Grecia. She stands it up on the top shelf of her cupboard. She adds the father doll to the mother and child in the cradle but it tips and he falls out. She tucks a pottery dish under the rocker to steady it and then replaces the father. Ambrosio loads the case of soft drinks into his truck and drives away. Maximina, who has been watching, takes the basket she has held in her lap and places it on the floor. She lays sections of fence across it as the mother arrives to take the children home.

REFERENCES

BARNOUW, V.
  1963 *Culture and personality.* Homewood: Dorsey Press. (Revised edition, 1973.)
BUSHNELL, J., D. BUSHNELL
  1969 Gente de razón y guarines en San Juan Atzingo: un ensayo psicoanalítico sobre la coexistencia de un estereotypo social y un patrón homogéneo de cultura en un pueblo mexicano. *Anuario Indigenista* 29:317–329.
  1971 Sociocultural and psychodynamic correlates of polygyny in a highland Mexican village. *Ethnology* 9:44–55.

BUSHNELL, D., J. BUSHNELL

1973   "Rorschachs of Indian-mestizo youth: selected case studies from a Mexican village." Paper read at XIV Interamerican Congress of Psychology, São Paulo, April 14–19.

i.p.   Character and cognitive orientation in the TAT responses of children in an indigenous Mexican village. *Proceedings, XIII Interamerican Congress of Psychology*, Panama City, December 1971.

HAWORTH, M.

1968   "Doll play and puppetry," in *Projective techniques in personality assessment*. Edited by A. Rabin, 327–365. New York: Springer.

HENRY, J., Z. HENRY

1944   *Doll play of Pilagá Indian children*. Research Monograph 4, American Orthopsychiatric Association.

HONIGMANN, J.

1954   *Culture and personality*. New York: Harper.

1967   *Culture in personality*. New York: Harper and Row.

HSU, F.

1972   *Psychological anthropology*. Cambridge: Schenkman.

LANDY, D.

1959   *Tropical childhood*. Chapel Hill: University of North Carolina Press.

1960   "Methodological problems of free doll play as an ethnographic field technique," in *Selected papers of the Fifth International Congress of Anthropological and Ethnological Sciences*. Edited by A. Wallace, 161–167. Philadelphia: University of Pennsylvania Press.

LINDZEY, G.

1961   *Projective techniques and cross-cultural research*. New York: Appleton-Century-Crofts.

MURPHY, L.

1956   *Personality in young children*. New York: Basic Books.

RITCHIE, J.

1957   *Childhood in Rakau: the first five years of life*. Victoria University Publications in Psychology 10. Wellington, New Zealand.

RÓHEIM, G.

1941   Play analysis with Normanby Island children. *American Journal of Orthopsychiatry* 2:524–549.

1962   "The western tribes of central Australia: Childhood," in *The psychoanalytic study of society*, volume two. Edited by W. Muensterberger and S. Axelrad, 195–232. New York: International Universities Press.

Dreams as Charismatic Significants: Their Bearing on the Rise of New Religious Movements

VITTORIO LANTERNARI

Dreams may be scientifically analyzed from physiological, psychological, sociological, or anthropological viewpoints. Those of us who take an anthropological outlook must face a fundamental problem: that of the cultural value of dreams. Such a problem needs a preliminary explanation. The cultural value of dreams may have two different interpretations, which are interrelated, depending on which of two possible criteria is used to measure the dream-culture relationship. On the one hand, the culture/tradition has a deterministic influence on the dreams, or on the thematic contents of the individual dream. On the other hand, the individual dream has a deterministic influence on the preservation or the creation of that culture, i.e. in maintaining traditions and introducing innovations. A closer look reveals that the two aspects of this relationship are closely connected. For if a dream can contribute to keeping alive or strengthening tradition with respect to individual behavior and decisions (in some cases the dream itself inspires such decisions), then the dream is a "product" of the culture/tradition and, at the same time, one of its determining factors — i.e. it is both cause and effect. It is better, however, to distinguish between the two aspects of the above relationship: first, we have "culture versus dream," i.e. the cultural determinants of the dream; second, "dream versus culture," i.e. the determining influence of dream on culture.

The dream accounts of Nzema religious leaders were gathered by the author during field work in Ghana in 1971. Information on Kapo's movement in Jamaica and the account of Kapo's dream were collected by film-producer A. Pandolfi in 1972 (on the basis of some indications provided by the author) and were kindly put at the author's disposal.

As far as the first aspect is concerned, the determining influence of the cultural background, of traditions, ways of life, and beliefs, on the configuration of individual dream experience may be taken for granted. A comparative analysis of the dream contents of the average representatives of different cultures and societies would be enough to prove the determining influence of culture on the dream-themes, once we have excluded individual psychological factors. Therefore, we will take a closer look at the second aspect of the relationship and consider the the ways in which individual dream-experience acts as a determining factor in the preservation and creation of cultural patterns.

At this point an important distinction must be made between what is officially known as modern society, i.e. urban and industrial, and traditional societies, i.e. preindustrial, underdeveloped or developing. Rural and marginal groups and classes in modern society should also be associated with the latter because they have many substantial similarities in experience, cultural attitudes, and value systems. This distinction directly concerns the cultural value of dreams in the two types of society or social group. There is an increasing tendency in "modern" society to consider dreams as indicators of certain unconscious or latent contents of the individual psyche, to be used as scientific and therapeutic tools in psychological, psychiatrical, or psychoanalytical diagnosis and treatment. Thus, a dream is regarded as a symbolic document which, once in possession of a psychologist or a psychoanalyst, becomes a basic tool for identifying individual psychic traumas and for the choice of a liberating therapy. This, then, is its real cultural value in "modern" society which is entirely different from that ascribed to dreams in traditional societies.

In traditional societies, and partly also among certain marginal and subordinate groups in "modern" society, dreams have the generally accepted function of "setting the foundations" for an individual's fate through the very symbols they express. The dream establishes a direct relationship between the dreamer and certain supernatural forces and beings belonging to the local cultural tradition, which the group recognizes as having an independent existence, a typically creative potentiality, and an authority which is capable of conditioning human behavior. As I have already pointed out in another article (Lanternari 1966), when, through the dream experience, the dreamer comes into contact with these typically creative, sacred forces and beings, he, in turn, acquires a creative, sacred power. Thus, from his dream the individual draws the certainty of a favorable fate, a reason for self-confidence, inspiration for his decisions and actions and, therefore, his self-identification. Thus, in traditional societies, the individual enters the "sacred sphere" through his dreams. These dreams become an extremely significant, charismatic type of experience, and they act as a guarantee of an individual's fate within the limits of certain traditional value orientations. There is a close psychological and cultural link between dream and myth. Both appear as models and paradigms of cultural elements — dream in relation to the individual, and myth in relation to the society as a whole. If a dream is the archetype of the individual's fate, a myth, then, is the archetype of the entire culture. In certain cases the two are identified together, both linguistically and in psychological experience; this is revealed by the famous example of the Australian natives who use the word *alchera* to indicate both the time of mythical origin and the period of time in which a dream occurs, with the relative events.

In my essay I identified certain categories of recurring dreams and/ or visions in traditional societies: the prophetic dream, the magical-shamanic dream, the initiation dream, and the mystical dream. But if by "mystical dream" we mean that in which the dreamer believes he has captured the original source of an exceptional, let us say charismatic, power, then it becomes a general category, within which the other types of dreams and/or visions, referred to above, form specific subcategories related to the different circumstances and personal roles. Naturally, in traditional societies and in certain subordinate groups of modern society, a dream and /or vision has an important function as a periodical confirmation of the relationships existing between individual and cosmos, between present reality and mythical origins, and between the sacred and the profane. The dream finds its position within the dialectical relationships of man and world, history and myth, the living and their ancestors which permeate the existence of people belonging to such groups and/or societies.

But the function of a dream is also important in relation to cultural change. In fact, the mystical dreams of founders of new religions contain elements of a symbolic system which differs from the traditional one. Such dreams in themselves reflect strongly charismatic personalities; sociologically speaking, this implies an exceptionally creative capacity. As has already been pointed out by Kluckhohn (1942), it is in cases like these that individual dreams become the source of a "private ritual" which, in turn, will be elevated to the role of a new "group ritual," having been socialized through the dreamer's individual influence on his group. But we believe that it also becomes a "group myth," in relation to the charismatic dreamer's personal prestige. In other words, the founder's dream becomes the starting point of a process of "cultural creation." It can give rise to a new type of culture and to a renewal of the world view and of tradition through the foundation of new socioreligious movements.

In those cases with which we are better acquainted, the innovative dreams are stimulated by the dreamer's personal contact with Christian culture. We are not taking into account the very many "dreamers" or "dreaming prophets" who were responsible for movements such as the Ghost Dance, the Sionist Churches of South Africa, the Cargo Cults of Melanesia, the messianic war movements of Polynesia, etc. (Lanternari 1960, 1963). We will simply refer to certain dreams of religious founders of the Nzema people in Ghana. These dreams contain both traditional themes and elements derived from models of Western culture, particularly from the Bible and from Christianity in general. The following examples illustrate how an individual dream can act as a decisive factor in the process of cultural change.

The cases reported here refer to dreams which reflect a crisis within a traditional society and give rise to socioreligious movements. I will begin by describing a series of dreams personally narrated to me by the founder of the Action Church among the Nzema of Southwest Ghana, Mr. Moses Armah. The Action Church is a new spiritual church founded in 1948, and is now widespread throughout Nzemaland of Ghana. Its rise is tied to a series of dreams experienced by its founder, a former Methodist imbued with a number of religious influences from the Bible, from the Hindu prophet Paramahansa Yogananda, and from the English theosophical writings of H. T. Hamblin. Mr. Armah was induced by these dreams to found the new Christian cult, which differs from both traditional religion and from the syncretic cults, namely Water Carriers or Twelve Apostles' Church, which sprouted from the prophet William Harris's movement in the Ivory Coast and are now diffused among the Nzema people. Mr. Armah was born in 1908.

It was in 1941. One night I dreamt and saw Jesus personally. He was walking on something like a bridge. A big house was nearby. I had the house in front of myself, and the bridge on my side. I was standing there. I saw Jesus personally and he was walking like a person. He was a person, and he was clothed with a blue cloth. The wind was blowing; he was walking and his hair were all on his back. I was looking at him, and he was turning slowly. At a moment he gazed at me and I fell down. I put up and saw that he had gone. "This is Christ, he is going." Now Jesus returned again. He looked at me: as soon as my eyes met his, I fell down: three times. After this I could not see him again, and I came out of the dream. At that time

I had not yet thought of founding a new Church. This is the first dream I had.

Then Mr. Armah had a second dream.

The second dream was that I dreamt that from my hair was growing a bunch of banana. It grew and became mature. Then I saw somebody cut it down. That banana was "longhands" [there are two kinds of banana]. I saw on the way come to get them plucking them to eat. But the person came and said: "Don't eat!" Then he brought me another kind of banana, the short one, which I ate. He told me: "Don't eat the long one, but eat this." Then I came out from the dream. I was puzzled. From that day I dreamt that long banana, each time I smell it I vomit. I don't touch it at all. At first I did not understand the meaning of the bunch of banana. But now I understand it. Should I found this church. The banana bunch was the symbol of the new church. Eat the short one means found the new church.

After a period spent in reading the Bible and other experiences, Mr. Armah had a third dream.

It was a light. I was sleeping; then I saw a light. Then I began to read the Bible. After that my heart started to shake, and I began to sing. After the dream was over, I was singing . . . . Then I came out and I go to sing and go from place to place, always singing. I turned on the back of my house. I felt that I was singing and that I should sing all the time. In the morning I could not chop [eat], but sing. My wife began to worry. She made me to chop, but I said no. I was singing. My heart was very joyful as I was singing. Then my wife went to say: "You are reading books, books, books, you are crazy." I left eating, always singing. While I was singing, my wife thought: "Something happened to my husband." My wife thought that I was getting crazy. But it was joy, that: joy, joy. I could not sleep, too. Then I went on singing again and again for three days. Then I began to cool. From that day I had a change of my mind. "The church I was belonging to does not fill my heart. The church does not give me the things that are now good. I shall found a church. I shall found a new Church."

The themes of the three dreams act as private myths for the foundation of a new religion. As far as the individual is concerned, we can speak in terms of "conversion," but the myths will then pass from private experience to group ritual experience. Jesus, appearing as a new figure in the first dream, will become the central figure of the new church. The refusal of the first kind of banana and the choice of the second kind corresponds to the abandoning of the old religion and the birth of the new one; the prophet's untiring song and the Bible become the central elements of the group ritual which, in fact, calls for a great number of choral songs inspired, as in the dream, by joy, exultation, and Bible reading. Private myth passes into group ritual in another sense, too; after his dream, Armah officially became a healer, curing the sick through prayer, and this becomes an essential feature of the new cult.

Something similar also happened to the cofounder of the Action Church, Mr. Andoh. Already a Catholic, Andoh practiced the sacrifices and rituals belonging to the traditional religion, worshipping the *awosonle* spirits. But having received certain religious scripts from Armah, the very same which had stimulated the latter's revelation, one night he had a vision. "A street full of light" appeared to him, and he heard "a voice telling me, 'This is the way'." After this experience, Andoh ceased to follow traditional rituals, now bitterly refused and condemned by the Action Church, and he too obtained the power of curing the sick through prayer. Once more, the dream's charisma, symbolized by the "light," reappears as a foundation myth. Ritual activity of the Action Church is centered on reading of the Bible, sermons, dances, and songs inspired by joyous feelings. The notion of a divine spirit which inspires man is fundamental in it. This spirit is manifested through the enthusiastic behavior and sentiments of followers, and by no means through possession, glossolalia, and shaking, as happens among Nzema Pentecostals.

Nevertheless, the Action Church and Pentecostal Churches have something in common. All of them emphasize the presence of a divine spirit inside the follower's soul; in all of them a drastic demarcation is felt between the "obscure" time before conversion and the "luminous" time after conversion, between a false "heathenism" and the "true religion of Christ." The demarcation line is made, for every individual follower, by a dream-experience, and/or sometimes by a healing experience. The latter happens every time a person, possessed by evil spirits and/or a bad illness, is healed by other people's prayer and faith. In all spiritual churches like the Action Church and Pentecostals, prayer-healing or faith-healing, as much as dreams and visions, operate as charismatic significants. Common followers as well as leaders can share both kinds of gifts. But the dreaming activity of charismatic leaders is more widespread and intensive.

Another example of a new religion founded as a result of a prophetic dream among social groups living in precarious conditions has recently occurred in a poor Negro neighborhood in Kingston, Jamaica. It is the Afro-Christian religious movement created by the prophet Kapo. The following dream account was directly recorded by the ethnographic filmproducer A. Pandolfi, to whom I had given certain indications regarding aspects of the local religion. Having had a somewhat superficial Christian education during childhood, Kapo still felt deep down the influence of African religiousness. This was probably due to the Jamaican environment, in which the Rastafarian back-to-Africa movement flourished side by side with a Garveyan-inspired "autonomous Copt Church" and other Afro-Christian cults, such as Pocomania and Revival Zion Cult, which were largely based on possession, trance, ecstatic dances, and healing practices. All these cults are a syncretic and tendentially escapist expression of the reaction of the poorest Negro classes (who have been living in a state of social emargination since colonial times) to the privileged conditions of the whites and of the black bourgeoisie. In some cases, as in Kapo's movement, there is a genuine rediscovery, or rather recovery, of the messianic and millenarian value of original Christianity, such as was being spontaneously relived by the prophet and his followers.

Through his dream Kapo knew he had a mission to accomplish: that of teaching his people a new religion. In the first dream Jesus appears to him and orders him, after having "annointed" him, to act as his representative on earth. This is his story:

When I was twelve years of age, I was put on to this way of Christianity, and develop afterwards into art. When I was twelve years of age I dreamt one night that I saw a man. He was not a white man, and he was not a very dark man. But he came and he took me from my father's home, down a glade, underneath a white coco tree. Reaching the white coco tree, he asked me the question if I know who he was. I told him "no." He asked me a second time, and then a third time, and I remember that I said to him "If I know who you was, I would have told you." He said, "My name is the Lord Jesus Christ," and he took a bottle from his pocket, about the length of my hand, and he annoint me from my head down to my foot. And then he said I was to go and tell the Nations, my mother and also my father, that he, Jesus, was in need of them . . .

A second dream soon follows the first.

The following night I dreamt that I saw a garden; the garden was a half-moon shape, wider than this yard here. Seventy-two angels were sitting around the edges of that half-moon garden, and seventy-two chairs were set by the edges around, and there were seventy-two little tables, there were seventy-two trumpets, and I was led into the middle of the garden and put on a chair to sit, by the Head, one of these angels. Then they began to play on their trumpets a very wonderful song. I couldn't retain or remember anything about the melody of that song. Before waking in the morning, I was told by the angels that I was to go and tell my mother and my father, my sisters and my brothers and the people around, that Jesus was in need of them. I got up and I did this in the morning and my father and my mother began to feel now that something was wrong with me. But nothing was wrong. But all this comes up about after visiting a revival meeting about three nights before the time when the vision came unto me. And it keep going on like that until I was commissioned to go out and preach the gospel. I preached for about twenty-five years before I became an artist. And while I became an artist I prayed. . . . I never liked the idea of seeing some of the ministers just sit down in those days and they never work, and then they have a fair salary. So I believed to myself that if I put my shoulder to the wheel I could be happy more than burdening the people's shoulders. Well, what came up out of that prayer, I found myself scraping on a stone. On that stone a face came out and then I cut eyes and nose and mouth.

As we can see, for Kapo, art accompanies and completes the activity of a religious preacher and founder. It, too, is a sign of the charisma, to the same degree as that of the mystical dream he had received. "I believe," says Kapo, "that there are many ties between spiritual life — i.e. the Church — and art. I think that art does much for the spiritual Church." Thus, the movement founded by Kapo has the same connotation of "spiritual church" which is typical of Ghanaian and many other African churches. The prophet's dreams betray the influence of the "revelation:" the "twelve years of age" of the first dream, and the "seventy-two angels with trumpets" of the second one. In the actual cult the faithful pray and sing in expectation of universal renewal, which they feel is at hand; this will be followed by the resurrection of the dead, peace and unity in the world, and mystical enlightenment. Under the prophet's guidance the faithful reach a state of mystical exaltation, during which they call out to the spirit to come, and finally fall into a trance. The strong rhythm, the rocking of the body, the flowing arm movements, the continuous summoning of the spirit, the choral songs, and the dances are all ecstatic techniques which help bring on the final, collective trance. In this way, the cult helps its followers overcome the feeling of existential precariousness that results from the conditions of underdevelopment, misery, and social subordination in which they live. Here again we have another case of "Africanized Christianity," as that of the Ghanaian Action Church mentioned above. In such cases, the old African possession cult was tied to a series of beliefs involving divine figures of an ambivalent nature, i.e. possessing both good and evil powers, but, in fact, provoking a condition of suffering during possession.

Today, the cult is fused together with, and at the same time substituted by, a cult of the Spirit, which is experienced as a source of uniquely joyous and exalting redemption. Particular importance seems to be attached to the role of Jesus, who appears in the founder-leader's visions as a bringer of "light"; this symbolizes a psychologically liberating experience which can be easily recognized in the mystical, enthusiastic, and choral character of the ritual activity. Jesus, the light, the burning fire, and the joyous song are all recurring themes in a great number of foundation or "conversion" dreams. They are the symbolic expression of, and are tightly linked with, the expectation of a forthcoming deliverance from impending evil, in other words, from the frustrating conditions of misery, isolation, and social emargination which become all the more explosive when compared to the conditions of other, privileged groups. In this sense, the founder's dream activity acts as an explosive outlet for all the frustrating experiences accumulated by the individual himself and by the group of which he is the exponent and interpreter.

The pattern of the burning fire (symbolizing the light and the Spirit) also comes from the Bible. This is clearly illustrated by the dream of a young Puerto Rican Pentecostal minister, recorded by me in 1965 in one of the store front churches of Harlem, New York City. Ten years before, he had had a dream which determined his fate. Here is his story:

I was at home one night, sleeping next to my wife; it was almost sunrise when all of a sudden I was woken up by a bright flame burning in front of me in the room. Frightened by this sight, I called out to my wife to get up because a fire was burning the house. But my wife, having woken up, could see nothing: neither fire nor light. At a certain point a voice spoke to me from the depths of the flame, saying: "Go to Minister XY; he will explain everything to you and tell you what to do." The next day, frightened and shocked by this vision, I did as I had been told. The Pentecostal minister whom I visited calmed me and explained that the fire was that of the Holy Spirit, and that I should rejoice, for God had touched me.

Since then this man, who had an unfortunate family situation (he was the father of two paralytic boys) and who, together with his group of Puerto Rican fellow immigrants, had always sought in vain the meaning of life and an impossible social self-identification in the immense city of New York, was able to take over a socially recognized role as minister of a cult. He found his self-identification within the group of Puerto Rican Pentecostal followers, whose ritual gatherings express an intense community feeling. "Before that time," he said, "I was a nonentity. Now it's all over."

In these different individual experiences the patterns of the dream and/or visionary themes are clearly taken directly from the visions of Moses, in which the angel of God appears to the prophet inside a tongue of fire (Exodus 3, 1–8); or from the "Transfiguration," in which Christ Himself appears to the Apostles transfigured and shining brightly like the sun (Matthew 17, 1–3); or from the conversion of Saul of Tarsus, with the apparition of a great celestial light (Acts 9, 3–8); or, finally, from John's "Revelation," with the apparition of the golden candlesticks and the sound of the trumpet (Revelation 1, 10–12).

Another example of an enlightening, revelation type dream appears in the following story of a Pentecostal minister from a small town in the "Subappennino Irpino," an underdeveloped area of southern Italy. (The data were collected during field research by a student of the University of Bari). Euplio Aucello, a Pentecostal minister from Anzano, passed from Catholic indifference to active participation in the Pentecostal movement through a series of dreams which, together with an assiduous Bible-reading, dominated his life from adolescence onwards. At the age of eighteen, during a fit of depression in his search for the truth, he was praying to God when he had his first vision. "The room I was in was suddenly filled with light and the bust of a smiling man appeared in the balcony opening, gently calling me. My heart was filled with joy." This was the beginning; having met a community of Pentecostals, he joined it enthusiastically and suffered the Fascist persecutions of Italian evangelists which were later continued by the postwar Christian-Democratic governments. He was put in prison for having refused to give up the cult, and there he had a new vision: "The whole room was filled with light and the words 'you will be released' appeared in golden writing on the wall in front." In fact, he was almost immediately released from prison.

On different occasions other visions followed, accompanying the minister's passionate proselytism and prayers. At one time, Jesus' two hands appeared to him, bigger than life-size, each respectively overhanging the crowds of male and female faithful ("brothers" and "sisters"); at another time, he saw the number "10," the mysterious meaning of which was revealed exactly ten months later, when at the very same hour he received the "gift of the Spirit" — that is, he began to "speak tongues." At yet another time, after a doctrinal discussion with one of his followers, at the end of which neither had succeeded in convincing the other nor in convincing himself of being in the wrong, the minister was depressed and grieved; during the following cult he had a vision in which he saw a bicycle whose wheels, tied together with an iron chain, seemed to be striving to turn in vain. According to Aucello's interpretation, the wheels were the two arguers and the chain was Satan, binding them. Thus, he prayed to God to free his "brother" first and then himself; and as a matter of fact, he saw first one wheel, then the other being released and beginning to turn.

These dreams and/or visions, including all those received by the prophets mentioned above, together with shamanic and initiation dreams and others in general, all show how the unconscious-irrational and conscious-rational elements are strongly linked together. Moreover, it is only after it has been interpreted that each individual dream of this kind becomes of particular importance for the dreamer and, therefore, for the group to which it is communicated; it is thus that the dreamer becomes aware of its symbolic value. The dream's interpretation, either by the dreamer or by others, is based on rational and partly conscious, sociologically significant criteria, while the dream-material is of an irrational and completely unconscious nature.

Among the Nzema, for example, when Armah says to himself and to others: "The banana tree meant that I had to found a new church and abandon the old one," he is acting under a rational, sociologically significant stimulus. This stimulus helps him solve an individual crisis and at the same time solve a social crisis of the group that he feels he is representing; as a matter of fact, he opens up new possibilities for the traditional culture, and he discovers a new path for his own social ascent, contributing toward the creation of a new elite. The same can be said about Euplio Aucello's visions of Christ's hands or of the bicycle, etc. It is not through their raw, "neutral," oneiric material that we come to know about these visions, but only after they have acquired a cultural significance through the dreamer's interpretation. For the latter and his followers, such visions help explain the dreamer's charismatic role and his new status as interpreter-minister of the cult. The sociological significance of this fact is that it gives the dreamer an exceptional social prestige. The same holds true for the mystical/prophetic dreams and/or visions of all religious founders and for the traditional shamanic or initiation dreams. In each case, the dream and/or vision indicates a polyvalent function. It is a source of self-confidence as well as a means toward a special kind of prestige and consequently, toward a leadership position of one kind or another. It is a source of self-identification both on a psychological and social level.

This helps explain the structural continuity and the original close relationship existing between innovative dreams and traditional dreams of a prophetic and/or shamanic nature. This can be seen, for example, in a number of traditional dreams recorded among the Nzema. The following examples show how an individual becomes aware that he is being "called" to become a *komenle* (fetish-priest or priestess) through dreams. It is the case of *komenle* Hannah Kofi and of *komenle* Komili Akye Mokoah.

Here is the story told by Hannah Kofi, wife of the *ninsili* [native doctor] Kofi, in the village of Qpokazo, when she was asked what had made her decide to become a *komenle*.

I was born in Enchi, I was a Methodist but now I am a *komenle*, that is, an interpreter of the *awosonle* [traditional divinities]. When I was in Enchi I fell sick with an illness which lasted five years: I was sick in my whole body, even in my heart. Thus a woman of that place, who was also ill, went to a man who was a healer and this was Kofi (now my husband) and he had come from the village of Qpokazo to heal the sick. I was therefore introduced to Kofi and he said he would try to cure me. My whole body was trembling. My mother had taken me to other *ninsili* more than once, but it was Kofi who discovered the real cause of my illness. He is also a fetish-priest. He carried out *adunyi* [a divination ritual]. What was the cause of my illness? Kofi said that I would have to become a *komenle*. This is what had happened: when I was a child, my father had a "cottage" near the Duwasua river, roughly three miles from Enchi. I normally went down to the river to fetch water. I knew nothing. At that time I used to go to church, I was a Methodist and I did not like these things. Later, when I was pregnant with my first child, I was in bed one night when I had a vision. A woman came towards me and said: "I like you very much, Hannah. If you won't do what I tell you, I will make you die. You must interpret my words and my will. You shall be my *komenle*." She told me her name: she was the river *bosonle* [singular of *awosonle*] whom I had gone to fetch water from as a child. Since that time, the *bosonle* had noticed me and loved me. That is what Kofi the *komenle* understood, and he told me that if I wanted to be cured I should "pacify" the *bosonle*. Thus I married Kofi and together with my husband I went to pacify the *bosonle* by pouring libation and making sacrifice of a sheep and some chicken. It was the *bosonle*'s love that caused my illness, until I became her *komenle*.

Another similar example is that of *komenle* Akye Mokoah from Aiyinasi. The first part of the story was told by her mother.

When my daughter was a child of seven I placed her in the care of her grandmother (my mother) who lived in a village on a side road branching off from the Atuabo-Aiyinasi road and who had a groundnut plantation. The girl was in the plantation when someone told her to fetch water from the nearby river. She went with three friends. As soon as she reached the river, being a little behind her friends, she heard a voice from the river calling her name. She turned round and saw a woman sitting on a stool [the stool is a symbol of power], just like the *bosonle* in the small statue [the *komenle* is holding the small statue]. The woman held in her hands some pounded herbs [used as medicines by the *ninsili* and *komenle*] and two small coins — a one-shilling piece and a threepence piece [the smallest coins used by the Nzemas]. The woman said: "Take these things and go cure people!" But the girl was frightened and ran away. Then the woman threw the herbs and coins at her from a distance. The girl fell down in a faint. Frightened, her friends left her there and ran to warn the village that their friend had fallen and was "dead." People ran to the place and carried her home. A *ninsili* and a *komenle* were asked to visit her; they cured her and she was better. But they said that once she would be grown up she would become a *komenle* of that very *bosonle* who had possessed her on that occasion. For a long time nobody thought about what had happened on that occasion. Being a Catholic Christian, I did not give it much thought either. Things changed when my daughter got married.

At this point the *komenle* herself picks up the story.

After I got married I gave birth to six children, all of whom died one after the other. I had to discover the cause of all those deaths. I went to the *komenle*. The *komenle* said that unless I made up my mind to become the *komenle* of the *bosonle* Azira (for that was her name), I would continue to lose every one of my children. Thus I began to practice as this *bosonle*'s Azira's *komenle*. And in fact, after that, I had another three children, and they are all alive. Thus I began to heal people who come to me to be cured from their illnesses.

The girl's dream and/or vision contains the symbols of power (stool) and of social ascent (medicinal herbs and money).

The above examples show the dream and/or vision as a decisive factor in the personal fate of an individual, according to the traditional Nzema religious system and custom. Illness and death may produce an individual crisis from which the priestly "calling" and, therefore, salvation may be determined through the dream and/or vision. In fact, being a *komenle* means repeating the archetype experience of the individual's first vision and possession, at every public ritual performance, thus repeatedly renewing ties with the original source of charismatic power and social prestige. Dreams and/or visions form, as we have seen, constant "patterns" both in traditional and modern Nzema religious systems, of which the Action Church is an example.

If we are considering mystical dreams and/or visions (i.e. those in which the dreamer is convinced he has gained control of the source of some extraordinary charismatic power) in relation to the process of cultural dynamics, then it is possible to distinguish two different patterns of mystical dreams and/or visions: (1) a traditional pattern, and (2) an innovative one. The themes of the first type of dream and/or vision stem from a heritage of ancestral beliefs, myths, and mythical figures, i.e. traditional values, practices, and world view, the importance of which is thus confirmed. In relation to the process of cultural dynamics, they therefore assume a conservative function. A number of themes in the dreams and/or visions of the second type, however, belong to a different culture with which the dreamer has come into contact. Figures, beliefs, and myths, which have nothing to do with the dreamer's cultural heritage, are reshaped and reinterpreted in an original way. These processes are the result of unconscious psychic operations made by particularly sensitive individuals after the shocking experience of cultural clash; they occur particularly when the individuals are faced with new cultural models and new, fascinating existential perspectives, however disintegrating they may be.

From the analysis of founder-leaders' dreams and from the study of the sociocultural role of the dreams themselves we learn that the acculturation process has important roots in the activity of the unconscious. The syncretic tendency, too, largely stems from the activity of the unconscious; the contents of the dream and/or vision are its initial expression.

If it is true, then, that culture reflects the creative quality in man as a rational member of a given society, we must not forget that a considerable amount of this creative activity is deeply rooted in the irrational unconscious. The product of such irrationality, however, is immediately, consciously re-elaborated by the individual who selects, interprets, and uses it, both personally and on a group level. In fact, the dream which the dreamer "reveals" to his people is sooner or later consciously selected, interpreted, and adapted by the dreamer himself. It is, therefore, halfway between rationality and irrationality, the unconscious and consciousness, subjectivity and objectivity, and becomes a means through which the individual may achieve active social participation as interpreter and exponent of his own group, while the latter will find its frustrations, needs, and expectations symbolically expressed in the "prophet's" dreams or in the ensuing myths and rituals.

REFERENCES

BURRIDGE, K.
  1969   New heaven, new earth: a study of millenarian activities. Oxford: Blackwell.
CLEMHOUT, S.
  1966   The psycho-sociological nature of nativistic movements and the emergence of cultural growth. Anthropos 61(1–2):33–48.
FABIAN, J.
  1966   Dream and charisma: "theory of dreams" in the Jamaa movement (Congo). Anthropos 61(3, 6):544–560.
FRIEDLAND, W. H.
  1964   For a sociological concept of charisma. Social Forces 43(1):18–24.
KLUCKHOHN, C.
  1942   Myth and ritual: a general theory. Harvard Theological Review 35:45–79.

LANTERNARI, V.
1960   *Movimenti religiosi di libertà e di salvezza dei popoli oppressi.*
Milano: Feltrinelli. (English translation 1963: *The religions of the
oppressed.* London: McGibbon and Kee, and New York: Knopf.)
1966   "Il sogno e il suo valore culturale dalle società arcaiche alla società industriale," in *Il segno e le civiltà umane.* Bari: Laterza.

LEWIS, I. M.
1971   *Ecstatic Religion.* Harmondworth: Penguin Books.

OOMMEN, T. K.
1967   Charisma, social structure and social change. *Comparative Studies
in Society and History* 10(1):85–99.

PEEL, J. D. Y.
1968   Syncretism and religious change. *Comparative Studies in Society
and History* 10(2):121–141.

SCHIAVONE, S.
1969   "I Pentecostali di Accadia e del Subappennino Irpino." Unpublished Ph.D. thesis, Bari.

Northern Algonkian Cannibalism and Windigo Psychosis

CHARLES A. BISHOP

The purpose of this paper is to put the phenomenon known as "Windigo" psychosis into historical perspective by relating it to cultural and ecological changes, and by so doing, gain perspective on existing psychodynamic, physiological, and functional interpretations.

Since Teicher's (1960) compilation and analyses of Windigo case materials, much has been written on the subject (Parker, 1960; Fogelson 1965; Rohrl 1970, 1972; Hay 1971; and McGee 1972). Although these analyses involve examples taken from early accounts of traders or missionaries, in addition to more recent ones collected by professional anthropologists, most descriptions of the Windigo phenomenon are torn from their sociological and ecological context in an attempt to arrive at some general explanation. Thus, examples have been drawn from such widely separated groups as the Montagnais-Naskapi, Swampy and Woodland Cree, Northern and Southern Ojibwa, and Micmac, and extending over a three-century period. Such analyses imply that differences among these groups, and over time, can be ignored in favor of a generalized portrait of Northern Algonkians. Thus, Hay (1971: 2) states: "I have therefore treated conclusions based on the most thoroughly studied group, the Ojibwa, as applicable to the people of all the northern Algonkian-speaking groups."

Such a conclusion is rendered untenable in view of recent evidence indicating considerable variability among different sub-arctic groups and

I wish to thank the governor and committee of the Hudson's Bay Company for permission to cite from their records. The research for this paper was supported by grants from the National Museum of Man, Canada.

for the same groups over time. For instance, ethno-historical data pertaining to the Northern Ojibwa (Bishop 1970, 1972) show that their culture in the eighteenth century was different from that of their nineteenth-century descendants (from whom most cases of Windigo psychosis are drawn). What needs to be examined are the data pertaining to the different Northern Algonkian peoples, over time, to note changes which might help account for why most cases occur during the nineteenth century. Teicher, it should be noted, does offer a few comments on the possible effects of acculturation, as, for example, the use of silver bullets (1960: 3) or wooden stakes (1960: 72, 95) to kill Windigos (both used to kill vampires by Europeans), or the crucifix used by a priest to cure one person (1960: 38–39). However, he rather unjustifiably concludes that cases recorded by the Jesuit missionaries during the seventeenth century "establish without question the aboriginal nature of the illness" (1960: 107). Fogelson, however, notes (1965: 77) that the early examples from the seventeenth and eighteenth centuries are aberrant. As he states: " ... more interesting to note is the absence in these early accounts of characteristics which were later associated with the Windigo being: as his gigantic stature, his anthroprophagous propensities, and his symbolic connection with the north, winter, and starvation."

Most scholars, however, have accepted the phenomenon (including the causative factors) as aboriginal, preferring to examine it in terms of psycho-dynamic and sociocultural factors (Fogelson 1965: 74). Although insightful, these studies have not allowed for possible alterations which could be related to cultural and environmental change. While several persons (Cooper 1933: 20–24; Hallowell 1934: 7–8; Teicher 1960: 110; Parker 1960: 609; and Landes 1968: 13) have noted that a fear of starvation and hunger anxieties were intimately related to the psychosis, thus inferring that ecological conditions were involved, they prefer to accept the environment as a constant, albeit a harsh one, in their interpretations. Parker would even rule out the environment as a necessary precondition (1960: 618–619), for although food scarcities created great anxieties, this alone was insufficient to account for behavioral abnormalities, since the Eskimo and Northern Athapaskans, who both lived in a harsh environment, lacked such a cannibalistic creature, a point questioned by McGee (1972: 245). Rather, Parker indicates that cultural and psychological factors are more important in analyzing cannibalistic behavior. While none would deny that these were not involved, it is ludicrous to equate the environment and ecological relationships of Athapaskans, Eskimos, and Northern Algonkians. Furthermore, it is just as erroneous to assume that environmental conditions in the sub-arctic never changed (Bishop

1970). This being the case, one would expect that the food supply at any given time would be a critical factor in determining whether cannibalistic behavior would occur.

Another view of the etiology of the Windigo is suggested by Fogelson (1965: 74) who suggests that the physiological reactions leading to the behavioral manifestations classified as Windigo psychosis may have been produced by "drastic dietary change, chronic or periodic mineral or vitamin deficiency, or perhaps consumption of toxic food substances ..." and possible genetic factors. Rohrl has taken this suggestion seriously in her analysis of a nutritional factor in the etiology of the disorder. Certainly the use of bear fat and nutritious forms of food to cure Windigos is suggestive, even though such a practice may have been rare (Brown 1971: 20). However, the rarity of the practice could, in some cases, reflect availability. Nevertheless, the fact that most sub-arctic Indians appear to have relished fats is strong argument that a nutritional factor was involved in the psychosis whether or not Indians explicitly used fats as a cure. McGee's evidence (1972: 244) that the early historic Micmac possessed the Windigo syndrome despite consuming quantities of moose grease does not necessarily refute this, but rather points to the Indian view of the beneficial effects of fats on general health and welfare. Evidence pertaining to the mid-nineteenth century Northern Ojibwa indicates that Indians who survived on hare and fish throughout most of the winter eagerly looked forward to the spring when fat geese and beaver could be obtained.

Was the Windigo aboriginal? Teicher (1960: 107) cites two incidents occurring during the seventeenth century among the Montagnais as conclusive evidence of the aboriginal existence of Windigo psychosis. In order to evaluate this conclusion, it is necessary to examine these examples within the particular environmental context in which they occurred, and in relation to the early Jesuit literature pertaining to Algonkian religion.

The earliest incident happened near Three Rivers, Quebec, during the winter of 1634–1635, and was recorded by Father Le Jeune. A man, his wife and their sister-in-law contemplated killing their brother who, they feared, would attempt to eat them. He was described as being: "half-mad; he does not eat, he has some evil design" (Thwaites 1896–1901: VIII, 31–33), all typical Windigo symptoms (Landes 1938: 25–26). The critical issue, then, does not involve the authenticity of the incident, but rather the conditions which precipitated it.

By the 1630's, the subsistence base of the Montagnais near Tadoussac and Three Rivers had been drastically disrupted by trade and environmental depletion, processes that had been going on for at least 100 years. Although the fur trade was of minor importance during the early sixteenth century, by 1550 Tadoussac at the mouth of the Saguenay River had become the site of an annual rendezvous where Algonquins and Montagnais brought their furs to exchange for European wares (Rich 1967: 8). For the next fifty years intermittent trade continued so that by the time that Samuel de Champlain and François de Pontgrave reached Tadoussac in 1603, European trade goods had spread far beyond the territories of the Indians who were in direct contact with the French. Tribal boundaries had been disrupted and Indian groups were competing to obtain advantageous positions in regard to the distribution of trade materials. The position of the Montagnais as middlemen close to the St. Lawrence was partially broken when trading centers were established at Quebec, Three Rivers, and Montreal, which attracted large numbers of Indians from miles around. Local bands meanwhile were growing increasingly dependent upon European wares, including foods. Father Pierre Biard noted (Thwaites 1896–1901: III, 106–107) that many Indians by the 1610's had grown fond of such foods as peas, beans, prunes, and bread. Indeed, by the 1620's much of their aboriginal material culture had been replaced so completely that the Indians had grown dependent upon French substitutes (Thwaites 1896–1901: V, 97). Indians were able, however, to maintain a semblance of independence so long as they could acquire large game animals, especially moose. Throughout the 1620's, during the summer months the Montagnais at Tadoussac subsisted on smoked moose meat supplemented by European foods (Thwaites, 1896–1901: IV, 203). However, moose (and caribou) were being extensively exploited by the French for their meat and hides so that they had grown scarce in some regions by the 1630's. So had beaver, another food source. By 1610, the trade in beaver pelts had become a serious business (Leacock 1954: 10–11) with between 12,000 and 15,000 skins being traded annually (Thwaites 1896–1901: IV, 207). This had drastically reduced the beaver supply near the trading centers and Le Jeune feared (Thwaites 1896–1901: VIII, 57) that "they will exterminate the species in this Region." Indians accustomed to donations of French foods and thoroughly immersed in the fur trade began to have difficulties in supporting themselves on local game resources. During the winter of 1633–1634, Father Le Jeune reported (Thwaites 1896–1901: VI, 61) that the Montagnais around Three Rivers were dying in great numbers from starvation and disease. That year, Le Jeune wintered with a band of Montagnais who were hunting on the south side of the St. Lawrence where game was thought to have been more abundant. A rumor spread by other Indians may also have been a factor for the movement. According to Le Jeune (Thwaites 1896–1901: V, 103), the Montagnais reported that:

two or three families of Savages had been devoured by large unknown animals which they believed were Devils; and that the Montagnais, fearing them, did not wish to go hunting in the neighborhood of Cape de Tourmente and Tadoussac these monsters having appeared in that neighborhood.

The fact that the animals involved were "unknown" by the Indians suggests that a specifically named cannibal giant was lacking, especially when it is considered that the Jesuits were quite meticulous when recording details about Indian religion. The spread of the rumor in this case may have been an attempt by one group to maintain control of what remained of the game supply about Tadoussac by frightening off others.

Starvation had thus become a real threat to those Indians located near French centers. Although Le Jeune reported that the Montagnais had dispersed to hunt moose, caribou, and deer in November 1634, he feared that the famine that winter would be even worse than the year before (Thwaites 1896–1901: VIII, 29). Already there were reports of cannibalism: some Indians near Tadoussac were reported to have eaten each other, while those who visited the French were described to be as "flesh-less as skeletons."

There is also evidence that the altered environment and pressure on food resources had modified Montagnais social organization. Groups and segments of groups appear to have been roaming about indiscriminately in search of food, while rules of hospitality and sharing, although still important, were collapsing under conditions of extreme duress. For instance, Le Jeune reported (Thwaites 1896–1901: VII, 49) that Indians who were unable to obtain food became despondent until a critical point was reached when each person would try to "save himself who can," abandoning all common interests.

It seems that environmental conditions had deteriorated to the point where famine cannibalism among some groups was a distinct possibility. It was, then, within this ecological setting that Le Jeune reported the symptoms of the individual believed by recent scholars to have been suffering from Windigo psychosis. Although the behavior is not surprising, given these conditons, the relationship between the symptoms and a specifically named cannibal giant is not mentioned. This, of course, does not deny the existence of such a mythological being. Although nowhere is the term "Windigo" used by the Jesuits, nor can such a term be found in the Jesuit *Relations*, it seems that the Indians did, in fact, have a concept of a cannibal giant. For example, Le Jeune relates (Thwaites,

1896–1901: VI, 175) that the wife of Manitou was "a real she-devil" who feeds upon the flesh of men "gnawing them upon the inside, which causes them to become emaciated in their illnesses." Thwaites also mentions a female monster called Gougou, taller than the masts of ships, who dwelt near the Bay of Chaleurs and who carried off and devoured men (II, 301). But the focus of the Windigo psychosis for psychosociologists is not the existence of a giant who literally eats people, but the belief that people become spiritually devoured and then become the carrier of the canni-balistic evil. Given this distinction, there is no concrete evidence that the early historic Montagnais categorized a specific pattern of human behavior as Windigo madness. The historical data, then, have been selectively used to support *a priori* assumptions that the Windigo psychosis (as opposed to other forms of psychosis) was aboriginal. For example, Teicher (1960: 76–77) gives as evidence an incident that occurred near Lake St. John in 1660–1661. There the Indian deputies of the Jesuits were supposedly seized with madness and a desire for human flesh for which they were put to death by others. The Jesuits go on to say, however, that: "This news might well have arrested our journey if our belief in it had been as strong as the assurance we received of its truth" (Thwaites, 1896–1901: XLVI, 263–265). The missionaries were able to continue and baptize the Indians without further ado. It is important to note that the deputies had gone to summon Indians who resided near James Bay. This would threaten the trade monopoly of the Lake St. John Indians. They thus may have spread the rumor to prevent the Jesuits from continuing on their journey; or they may actually have murdered the deputies lest they reach the Indians to the north.

Turning next to the Cree of the Hudson and James Bay area, parallel developments can be noted. The Cree who became attached to the coastal Hudson's Bay Company posts during the late seventeenth century exhibited a relatively poor ecological adjustment from the beginning. These large trading posts such as Fort Albany, York Fort and Moose Factory represented points of convergence for large numbers of Indians. Thus, game which was hunted for both traders and Indians alike, dwindled rapidly near these centers within a few years after their establish-ment. The relative poverty of the coastal area except during the goose-hunting seasons, and the dependence of the Cree on trade goods and store foods in winter kept many Indians in an area where food was scarce and which may have been abandoned in the winter in aboriginal times. Starving Indians who resorted to the post in winter had to be maintained on oatmeal, peas, or surplus geese and fish. For example, according to Anthony Beale in March 1706, many Indians "are all so hungry that they are ready to Eate one another, so that now heare are 20 that wholely lies on the Factory" (Hudson's Bay Company Archives, B3/a/1). Cases of death by starvation are also fairly numerous. In 1707, Beale wrote that "3 or four familys of Indians ... has perrished this Winter by Reason there was but Fuew Beasts" (B3/a/2).

The first explicit mention of an evil deity called Windigo appears among the York Fort Cree (Fogelson 1965: 77), suggesting a Cree origin for the term. There are also several early examples suggestive of Windigo behavior. Nevertheless, the archival data are often ambiguous. For instance, is the following an early example of Windigo behavior, or simply a case of an individual running amok and killing his wife (a not unknown occurrence in other societies)?

... one of our home Ind Lyes about 20 miles to the Southward Distracted or Lunatick, and hath Murder'd one of his wifes and would the other had she not ... made an Escape to our hunters ... wch hath soe terrified them tt th'y will not tarry there longer, but intend to Pitch under Gunn Shott of the Factory (Joseph Myatt, Fort Albany, 1723, Hudson's Bay Company Archives, A3/2/11).

Other similar examples were recorded during the eighteenth century. At Fort Severn in 1774, William Falconer reported that a Cree

threatned to stab his wife last night, and would have kill'd some of the other natives had they not bound him both hand and foot: he has appeared melancholy for some time past, and the Natives say he has several times been insane of late (Hudson's Bay Company Archives, B198/a/19).

The other Cree asked that the traders put him to death lest he kill people, a request denied although the traders did tie him up. The following day, however, he escaped and "frightened the other natives out of the Tent." He was recaptured but his relatives split his skull with a hatchet. Falconer then asked them why they killed him, to which they replied that they were afraid he would escape. Once having killed him they were now afraid, however, that:

he would get out of his Grave and come back and kill them. ... Their Superstition leads them so far as to imagine People deprived of reason stalk about after death, and Prey upon human flesh, such they say are Witik's (i.e., Divils). In the month of February Ab. 1772 the above unhappy man was so distress'd for food that he kill'd his own Sister and her Child (Hudson's Bay Company Archives, B198/a/19).

This is an important example for it clarifies several points. First, assuming that the 1772 murders were cannibalistic, it is to be noted that there was a direct causative link between subsistence conditions and the original cannibalistic act. Second, in this case the person became a Windigo

AFTER he had consumed human flesh. Cannibalism is NOT evidence of Windigo behavior. It is the pernicious craving for human flesh that indicates the presence of the Windigo. This supports Speck's data (1935: 43) that Windigo behavior occurred only after the cannibalistic act. Teicher's hypothesis (1960: 113) is that belief determines behavior, that is, one believes in cannibalistic monsters and thus can behave as a cannibalistic monster. Yet the belief that a person could be transformed into a Windigo cannibal had to exist *a priori* in order for such a cannibal to identify with the Windigo.

Once the belief arose that humans could transform into Windigos, especially under the very real threat of starvation, it became possible for persons at a later time to become Windigos without actually engaging in cannibalism, and even in times when there was no real food shortage. Yet the belief that a human could "become" a Windigo seems to appear and intensify in direct correlation with a growing fear of starvation in an environment depleted of food, and under fur trade conditions where the quest for pelts stresses individualism over cooperative kin bonds. There is good evidence that the poverty of the environment about the trading post led to a weakening of social bonds which could have been a factor in alienation and a result of anomie. Under these new emergent conditions (which began in the late seventeenth century for coastal Cree groups) the belief in, and fear of, the Windigo expanded so that the potential of becoming one became very real. Yet the catalyst for the development of Windigo behavior was the decimation of game and the dependence on the trading post, and thus it had a firm ecological basis.

Evidence to support this view may also be found in materials relating to the Ojibwa. Nowhere in the early Jesuit accounts relating to the Ojibwa and Ottawa is there a specific devil form recognizable as the Windigo, a rather remarkable fact considering the apparent preoccupation in the nineteenth century with the phenomenon. The argument earlier stated for the Montagnais, that a pre-contact cannibal giant did exist, but that there is no evidence that this monster was associated with a pattern of deviant behavior focusing on a lust to eat human flesh, holds for the Ojibwa as well. There seem to be several reasons for this.

The early literature for the Ojibwa strongly suggests that they had institutional patterns whereby cannibalistic impulses could be directed toward non-Ojibwa. They also appear to have had well-developed techniques of social control within groups. In aboriginal times and for a considerable period after contact, the threat of starvation for most Ojibwa was non-existent. Indians lived on a variety of foods in summer and on large animals in winter. Dollier and Galinee, near Sault Ste.

Marie, in 1669–1670 state: "Meat is so cheap here that for a pound of glass beads I had four minots of fat entrails of moose, which is the best morsel of the animal. This shows how many these people kill" (Kellogg 1917: 207).

Game was indeed abundant in all areas as evidenced by the fact that over 600 moose were reported killed south of Lake Superior in 1660 while Nicolas Perrot reported that 2,400 were killed on Manitoulin Island alone in 1670–1671 (Blair 1911: I, 221). Such devastations, however, took their toll so that by the middle of the eighteenth century, the area near Lake Superior had been virtually depleted of large fauna. Further north, however, the big animals lasted somewhat longer and were in such numbers that groups of 30 to 50 Ojibwa could remain together the year round. The real decline of big game in northern Ontario can be directly traced to the period of intensive competition between the Northwest Company and Hudson's Bay Company, lasting from the 1780's to 1821. This period saw the rapid depletion of game of all sorts through over-hunting to supply traders and Indians alike. By the time of the amalgamation of the two companies in 1821, large animals and beaver were virtually extinct while Indians had grown dependent on store goods for both survival and trapping (Bishop 1972). The large bands of the eighteenth century had atomized into family units for most of the year to maximize efforts in the quest for food and furs.

After 1810, starvation for the Northern Ojibwa became a real threat and it is at this point that the earliest cases of famine cannibalism were reported. Former cooperative sharing patterns among large numbers of kinsmen were impossible where families had to disperse in quest of small non-migratory fauna such as hare and fur-bearers. It was within this context during the nineteenth century that the classic examples of Windigo behavior were recorded among the Northern Ojibwa. There is evidence that the Windigo cannibal myth became increasingly significant to Indians as the threat of starvation intensified. For example, Charles McKenzie of the Lac Seul post recorded the arrival in July 1837 of over 100 Indians who were fleeing in terror from a Windigo which several had reported seeing at their lakeside summer camp (Hudson's Bay Company Archives, B107/a/16). They camped next to the store, posted guards, and for a week the medicine men engaged in conjuring to ward off the evil monster. The trading post, then, where food could be obtained in times of need, had become a symbol of protection against the evil cannibal giant. Need one search far for the pragmatic base of this symbolism?

McKenzie was able to piece together a description of the Windigo and it is of interest that there was a certain amount of disagreement among the

Indian hunters on his anatomical characteristics, suggesting perhaps the relative insignificance of the Windigo myth in earlier times. Nor is the portrayal involving a being covered with hair and lacking heels simply a replica of a large person.

Windigo behavior has been defined as a behavior syndrome diagnostic of a psychosis focused on cannibalism. However, despite the horror and repugnance expressed by Indians, the data demonstrate that cannibalism was potentially normal behavior in an abnormal situation in the face of starvation. The desire for self-preservation cannot be interpreted otherwise. It is thus necessary to distinguish between famine cannibalism and Windigo cannibalism: The former occurs under conditions of extreme famine; the latter may be exhibited in times of plenty as well as during food shortages. The person who believes that he is becoming a Windigo, or who is thought by others to be a potential or actual Windigo, either expresses his cravings or exhibits behavioral characteristics within the expected frame of reference for "normal" Windigo actions, and is treated or eliminated. Hence, both symptoms and cures are culturally defined.

In this sense, Windigo behavior is culturally expected behavior, given the environmental and social conditions mentioned. Teicher (1960) and Landes (1938) have implied that the belief in a Windigo is normal but that the behavior of human Windigos is psychotic. Thus, experience has led Americans to believe that a man may take a gun and shoot people randomly on a city street, but the killer's behavior is nonetheless considered psychotic and abnormal. The behavior dyad is interpreted within the existing belief system, and the relationship becomes reciprocal and mutually reinforcing. Furthermore, new forms of behavior precipitated by environmental changes and contact throughout the sub-arctic were likely appraised within the pre-existing belief system and operated to modify, intensify, and elaborate the corporate elements.

In conclusion, it is conjectured that the belief in a Windigo cannibal among Northern Algonkians was aboriginal and became extended to include situations arising out of famine cannibalism concomitant with the dreadful fear of starvation. As famine became endemic to successive groups of Northern Algonkians, cannibalism became a constant social threat. The psychologically feared, nutritionally derived, and ecologically imposed behavior became culturally identifiable as the "Windigo lunacy." Mythological stories of the Windigo provided the base point for transferring behavior characteristics from the supernatural to the human world. Just as the Windigo in myth was an anti-social being, so was any person who, for physical, social, or cultural reasons, expressed a desire for human flesh. The coalescence of myth and behavior gave rise to the practice of killing actual or potential HUMAN Windigos with no necessity to justify the act. Thus, it was through both increasing occurrences of human cannibalism and the extension of the belief system to include this stress-induced behavior, that human Windigos and the concomitant psychosis were invented. The catalyst for these developments, however, and if one likes, the ultimate determinant, was a dwindling game supply, intensified fear of starvation, increased dependence on trade goods, and weakened cooperative bonds in an atomizing social structure.

This interpretation, based on historical-ecological data, is not intended to supplant any current psycho-cultural "explanation" but is designed to offer specific ethno-historical evidence which allows the investigator to tie real cultural and environmental changes to the development of a real belief-behavior system.

REFERENCES

BISHOP, CHARLES A.
  1970   The emergence of hunting territories among the Northern Ojibwa. *Ethnology* 9:1–15.
  1972   Demography, ecology, and trade among the Northern Ojibwa and Swampy Cree. *The Western Canadian Journal of Anthropology* 3:58–71.
BLAIR, EMMA H., *translator and editor*
  1911   *The Indian tribes of the Upper Mississippi Valley and the region of the Great Lakes*, two volumes. Cleveland: Clark.
BROWN, JENNIFER
  1971   The cure and feeding of Windigos: a critique. *American Anthropologist* 73:20–22.
COOPER, JOHN M.
  1933   The Cree Witiko psychosis. *Primitive Man* 6:2024.
FOGELSON, RAYMOND D.
  1965   "Psychological theories of Windigo 'psychosis' and a preliminary application of a models approach," in *Context and meaning in cultural anthropology*. Edited by Melford E. Spiro, 74–97. New York: Free Press.
HALLOWELL, A. I.
  1934   Culture and mental disorder. *Journal of Abnormal and Social Psychology* 29:1–9.
HAY, THOMAS, H.
  1971   The Windigo psychosis: psychodynamic, cultural, and social factors in aberrant behavior. *American Anthropologist* 73:1–19.
HUDSON'S BAY COMPANY ARCHIVES
  1870   Manuscripts in Public Archives of Canada, Ottawa.
KELLOGG, LOUISE P.
  1917   *Early narratives of the Northwest, 1634–1699.* New York.

LANDES, RUTH
1938   The abnormal among the Ojibwa Indians. *Journal of Abnormal and Social Psychology* 33:14–33.
1968   *Ojibwa religion and the Midewiwin.* Madison: University of Wisconsin Press.

LEACOCK, ELEANOR
1954   *The Montagnais "hunting territory" and the fur trade.* American Anthropological Association Memoir 78.

MC GEE, HAROLD F.
1972   Windigo psychosis. *American Anthropologist* 74:244–246.

PARKER, SEYMOUR
1960   The Wiitiko psychosis in the context of Ojibwa personality. *American Anthropologist* 62:603–623.

RICH, E. E.
1967   *The fur trade and the Northwest to 1857.* Toronto: McClelland and Stewart.

ROHRL, VIVIAN
1970   A nutritional factor in Windigo psychosis. *American Anthropologist* 72:97–101.
1972   Comment on "The cure and feeding of Windigos: a critique." *American Anthropologist* 74:242–244.

SPECK, FRANK
1935   *Naskapi.* Norman: University of Oklahoma Press.

TEICHER, M. I.
1960   *Windigo psychosis: a study of a relationship between belief and behavior among the Indians of Northeastern Canada.* Proceedings of the 1960 Annual Spring Meeting of the American Ethnological Society. Seattle: University of Washington Press.

THWAITES, R. G., *editor*
1896–1901   *The Jesuit relations and allied documents*, seventy-four volumes. Cleveland: Burrows Brothers.

VAYDA, ANDREW P.
1970   On the nutritional value of cannibalism. *American Anthropologist* 72:1462–1463.

American Indian "Social Pathology": A Re-examination

MICHAEL W. EVERETT

Jerrold Levy and Stephen Kunitz (1971) have recently proposed that anthropologists significantly revise their theoretical notions regarding acculturation stress and "social pathologies." In an elegant fashion, the authors persuasively argue that on American Indian reservations (1) contemporary social pathologies — arbitrarily designated as homicide, suicide, and problem drinking — may not be evidence of disintegration due to acculturation stress, but instead may merely reflect traditional pre-reservation patterns of conflict and disruption, and (2) acculturation stress may affect the rates and patterns of traditional pathologies only sparingly and somewhat irregularly, such that both remain relatively stable and persist over long periods of time.

Comparative data, based on numerous studies and years of research, are presented for two Southwestern Indian groups — the Navajo and Hopi — and it is revealed that despite major differences vis à vis social integration and disintegration, contemporary pathological behavior is not notably different from descriptions of traditional antisocial behavior.

With the exception of Hopi cirrhotic mortality figures, rates have not increased. Moreover, the patterning of these pathologies appears to reflect traditional modes of coping behavior and adaptation to stress.[1]

Field research upon which this work is based was supported by grants from the U.S. Public Health Service (MH17923-01) and the University of Kentucky Research Foundation during the summers of 1970 and 1971. Drs. Keith Basso, Robert Weppner, Jerrold Levy, and Philip Greenfeld read an earlier version of this paper. Their assistance is gratefully acknowledged. The author, however, takes full responsibility for the present form of the paper.
[1] The authors did discover some pattern changes in suicide between age level and

The notion that "cultural persistences" or "survivals" may be apparent in or dominate human existence is not a novel idea in anthropology, nor has it been totally ignored in recent studies of American Indian social pathology. Brown (1970), for example, has conceptualized Rio Grande Pueblo social disorders in these terms. Papago drinking behavior is analyzed within this kind of paradigm by Waddell (n.d.). Graves (1970), on the other hand, contends that Navajo Indian urban drinking can be understood without reference to cultural background. Both positions are extreme, both require substantial testing and corroboration, and both are insufficient as explanatory models in and of themselves. The canon of simplicity favorably supports each of these theoretical positions. But methodologically and substantively, both are untenable.

In order to convincingly demonstrate that contemporary American Indian social pathologies are, in fact, reflections, not of ongoing acculturation stress but of traditional pathological patterns, it is necessary to do two things. First, the traditional patterns must be isolated so that it can be reliably argued that they are free from Anglo influence and evidence of internal stress and disorganization or anomie. Where early ethnographies are not available or where analysis of oral tradition is impossible, this can be an exceedingly difficult task. One method of simplifying the problem is to use a pre-reservation/reservation dichotomy. Yet this discrimination is useless if no information about the character of Anglo contact in early reservation times is available. Levy and Kunitz (1971) present no pre-reservation pathological data, nor do they attempt analysis of legend or myth (however, see Levy 1965). All of their data derive from early reservation days, a time when relative deprivation and social pathology would be expectably great (see Dozier 1966; Aberle 1966). Thus, based on these data, the least we can say is that early reservation rates have persisted into recent times in a somewhat stable fashion and are similar to presumed pre-reservation rates. Yet it is possible that acculturation stress has exerted a constant influence on reservation rates regardless of what traditional rates may have been.

The second requirement for a non-acculturation theory of social pathology is proof that no significant developments in patterns of pathology, however they are defined, occur during periods when rates are stable. If significant variation occurs, and it can be readily explained in acculturation terms, the theory is untenable. This, also, can be a difficult task. On the one hand, notable variation in recent pathologies

degree of violence and evidence for acculturational stress as well as old patterns to account for the present situation (Jerrold Levy, personal communication).

simply may not be apparent, based on the data gathering and analytic techniques utilized. On the other, an association between such variation and some trend or event defined as acculturative may reflect nothing of causal or explanatory importance.

Perhaps more importantly, even when evidence of variation is present, some investigators argue that it can be justifiably ignored if a theoretical bias warrants such tretment. This is especially the case where diverse types of data are concerned. Cognitive sorts of information, wherein native categories and meanings are utilized, are frequently viewed as incompatible with documentary, statistical data whose validity has been measured in terms of "empirical" reality (see Pelto 1970). And yet it is often this added conceptual dimension which enables us (1) to perceive significant pattern variation in "pathological behavior" as defined by the investigator and (2) to view "social pathologies" in culturally meaningful terms (Everett 1970, n.d.; Douglas 1967; Topper n.d.).

The purpose of this paper is to demonstrate that social pathologies — defined in both behavior-statistical and cognitive terms — may well reflect dominant cultural themes over long periods of time, but that these pathologies are also subject to significant modification due to acculturation pressure, however this be defined. Data are presented from two Western Apache Indian groups. A comparative strategy is employed to contrast White Mountain and San Carlos Apache pathological behavior. The two groups exhibit marked cultural, linguistic, and genetic affinities. Yet the early history of white contact (ca. 1875–1915) and concomitant acculturation processes for the two groups are notably divergent. Present day acculturation processes are almost identical. Rates and patterns of pathological behavior — here defined as homicide and suicide — could logically vary from one group to the other and from early reservation times to more recent ones. However, it is expected that (1) there will be a marked difference in rates and patterns between the two groups in early reservation days due to divergent acculturation processes, (2) there will be little differences between the groups with regard to contemporary rates and patterns as a result of similar acculturation experiences, and (3) the present-day rates and patterns of both groups will be notably different from those of early reservation days because of the changing character and intensity of acculturation processes on the two reservations. In an attempt to test the particular features of this model, a detailed analysis of one type of pathological behavior — suicide — is presented as it occurs among the White Mountain Apache. First, let us examine the historical and acculturational matrix.

THE SAN CARLOS/WHITE MOUNTAIN DICHOTOMY

Those aboriginal Southern Athabaskans labeled "Western Apache" are identified by Goodwin (1935: 55) as "Apache peoples who lived within the present boundaries of the State of Arizona during historic times, with the exception of the Chiricahua, Warm Springs, and allied Apaches, and a small band of Apaches known as the Apache Mansos, who lived in the vicinity of Tucson." The Western Apache were divided into five major and 20 minor territorial groups. The three most populous groups were the White Mountain, Cibecue, and San Carlos, totaling approximately 3300 individuals (Goodwin 1942: 60). Despite a tremendously diverse natural environment, ranging from low desert foothills to high mountain valleys, most Western Apache groups developed a similar subsistence system, characterized by seasonal exploitation of wild foodstuffs like mescal, acorns, and pinyons, small game (primarily deer), and domestic plants such as corn and beans (see Buskirk 1949; Griffin, Leone, and Basso 1971). With the advent of the horse, plunder from raids on Mexican villages diversified the subsistence system, strengthening it especially during drought years (see Basso 1971).

The 1850's saw Western Apaches in direct contact with Anglo-American military forces. "Pacification" campaigns, in the wake of unsuccessful extermination attempts, were aimed at halting hostilities between Apaches and other Indian groups in the Southwest and northern Mexico (see Thrapp 1967; Ogle 1970). The Western Apaches, who only raided periodically and who possessed a viable nonraiding economy, were not primary targets for these campaigns; their nonfarming relatives, the Chiricahua, were not so fortunate. In the 1860's and 1870's, the reservation system was offered as an answer to hostile Indian relations. Traditional Indian groups were to be confined within specific territorial boundaries (Ogle 1970; Spicer 1962). Initially, containment and control were the goals of the reservation system; subsequently, the "civilizing" of the "wild tribes" became its aim.

These responsibilities were given to military and civil authorities located at strategic garrisons in San Carlos territory near the Gila River and in the northern White Mountain district (Clum 1936; Ogle 1970). From the beginning, Apache-Anglo relations in these two regions differed, though geographically, only about sixty miles separated them. These differences can be seen most clearly in regard to confinement or incarceration and subsistence activities (Everett 1969).

In the mid-1870's, General George Crook proceeded to forcibly concentrate and detain all Western Apache groups (together with many

Yauapai) on the Southern San Carlos Reservation. In 1875, 1800 Apaches from the Northern White Mountain and Cibecue groups were removed to San Carlos, bringing the total number of Indians incarcerated there to more than 4000 (Spicer 1962). A census and tag band system and an Indian police force were instituted. Daily roll calls and travel permits were established. With travel virtually nonexistent, rations had to be issued (Ogle 1970; Davis 1929). Yet Indian agent John Clum permitted several groups of White Mountain Apaches to locate several miles away from the San Carlos groups and to travel frequently to their northern homeland (Clum 1936). By 1883 most of these people had been allowed to return permanently to this region and by 1890 had resumed their old life of hunting, gathering, and small-scale agriculture (Spicer 1962: 256). The bands remaining at San Carlos were under constant travel restrictions except for employment purposes. At Camp Apache in the White Mountains, however, Apache bands roved freely in traditional subsistence pursuits as late as 1902 (U.S. Commissioner of Indian Affairs 1902).

Differential confinement acted to produce very dissimilar reservation subsistence systems for the two Apache groups. At San Carlos government farmers attempted to transform Apaches into full-time agriculturalists. They worked unsuccesfully in the arid river valleys of the Gila drainage, however, and rations had to be issued (Spicer 1962: 256). As a result of Anglo farming activities upstream, the Gila slowed to a trickle and successive droughts caused continual crop failure. Rations were intermittently cut to force Apaches into farm labor. When this strategy proved unsuccessful, Apaches were urged to become wage laborers in surrounding Anglo farming and mining areas. By 1913 most of the available work force was engaged in farming, mining, and railroad, dam, and road construction work (Adams and Krutz 1971; Getty 1963). By 1925 almost the whole reservation was under lease to Anglo cattlemen.

However, at Camp Apache (later Fort Apache) in the White Mountains, no rations were ever issued regularly except to the sick and aged. Since White Mountain Apaches were not concentrated near the military post but remained seasonally nomadic, forcible farm labor was out of the question, except at Turkey Creek where Geronimo and hostile Chiricahua were settled (Davis 1929). Some Apaches did voluntarily work fields in the region, but most continued to exploit traditional economic resources (Spicer 1962). On a voluntary basis wage labor, of a sort, became a viable alternative to raiding and rations: Apaches filled hay and wood contracts for the military post on a seasonal basis, providing these materials in exchange for both cash payment and commissary privileges (see Reagan 1930, Ogle 1970). Never was there any systematic attempt to forcibly supplant this diversified economy with one which was predominantly wage labor oriented.

Apache-white relations during this early reservation period were equally divergent. At San Carlos a constant state of regulatory supervision prevailed. An Apache police force, organized by the agent, enforced local drinking prohibitions, even where drinking was an appropriate part of traditional socioceremonial practices (see Clum 1936). Authority shifted periodically from civil to military officials, with Apaches caught constantly in bitter civilian-military policy disputes (Harte 1973; Ogle 1970). In addition, regular contact with non-Indians was established quite early and continued to accelerate; San Carlos Apaches increasingly served as wage laborers in surrounding farming districts, construction areas, and mining towns — for the same Anglos responsible for the lack of water and encroachment on reservation lands. One result of this contact was the opportunity to obtain the liquor that was prohibited on the reservation. Bootlegging became prevalent and every year Anglos, Mexicans, Blacks, and Chinese were prosecuted for providing Indians with alcoholic beverages (U.S. Commissioner of Indian Affairs 1897).

At Fort Apache regular supervision of Indians by civil and military authorities was virtually impossible due to incessant population movement over rough and distant terrain and low manpower at the military post. The Indian police force was quite ineffective and attempts to halt the production and consumption of alcohol were futile (U.S. Commissioner of Indian Affairs 1903; Wharfield 1965). In addition, civilian-military conflicts similar to San Carlos prevailed prior to 1875 and from 1883 to 1885 (Thrapp 1967). Despite the tag band system and attempts at military control, White Mountain Apaches vigorously resisted, withdrew from, or voluntarily accepted Anglo domination. The Cibecue Creek fight and subsequent attack on Fort Apache in 1881 threatened the tenuous Anglo hold on this region (Wharfield 1971; Thrapp 1967). Even well after the turn of the century, Apaches interacted only intermittantly with Anglos (Wharfield 1965). Missionary accounts which date from this period support this view (William Kessell, personal communication). When they wished, Apaches seasonally worked on hay and wood contracts and some farmed near the fort. They had little contact with local whites, though they did occasionally steal cattle from nearby ranchers who were expelled from the reservation in 1883. Commercial liquor was bootlegged by local whites onto the reservation, but not regularly (Richard Cooley, personal communication). In general, early attempts by soldiers, teachers, doctors, farmers, and missionaries to bring about changes in White

Mountain Apache life styles appear to have met with limited success

PRE-RESERVATION/RESERVATION SOCIAL PATHOLOGY

Virtually no reliable data exist to indicate the prevalence of social pathology in pre-reservation days. Early accounts of Apache life all date from the period of military contact in the 1870's and 1880's. The same is true for civil government authorities, whose reports began appearing annually after the establishment of the reservations. Not so easy to evaluate are the attempts in the 1930's by anthropologist Grenville Goodwin to reconstruct traditional Western Apache culture. Much of the memory culture material he gathered dates from the 1870's and even earlier (Goodwin 1942; Basso 1971). Many events are described as pre-reservation in character, and ethnographic descriptions are generalized to include pre-reservation times. Only homicide — culpable as well as justifiable — can be reliably identified prior to Anglo contact. Unfortunately, almost no pre-reservation information on suicide exists.

Early reservation data on social pathology are quite tenuous (but see Levy and Kunitz 1969). At best, annual agency reports indicate a minimum rate of occurrence for both homicide and suicide due to vested governmental interest in making everything appear as placid as possible. Between 1898 and 1904, the physical anthropologist Hrdlicka (1908) provided data on homicide and suicide for both San Carlos and White Mountain Apaches, data which was contradicted by Goodwin's material. Indian agent Albert Reagan (1930), stationed at Fort Apache in 1901, wrote of White Mountain Apache killings which were only minimally substantiated by annual reservation reports for that period. Beginning in the 1920's and 1930's, Anglo physicians and government agents filed death certificates on all Apache deaths, accidental or otherwise. Since criminal records on both reservations were either non-existent or incomplete, only medical authorities possess anything approaching a reliable account of homicide and suicide events. Actual reporting of these varied so much that identification of an event as intentional or accidental or as homicide or suicide BY ANGLO AUTHORITIES must be considered suspect, unless verified by Apache informants. In summary, only superficial homicide data exist for pre-reservation Western Apaches, while both homicide and suicide are reported, though quite unreliably, in early reservation days. Even recent Anglo accounts of intentional deaths are not suitable for discerning accurate rates or patterns of social pathology. Let us look first at homicide.

KILLING AND HOMICIDE

Big Owl was the son of Sun. It was he who had been killing all the people on the earth. On account of this the boy had gone to his father and asked permission to kill Big Owl. He said, "Big Owl is no good, and he is killing lots of people. For this reason I want to kill him." "Why do you talk this way? He is your own brother," Sun said. The boy wanted to kill his own brother, and because of this, our people did the same way. They still kill their own relatives sometimes (Goodwin 1939:10).

This passage from Apache mythology illustrates two important features of homicide. First is the significance of revenge as a motive. Rationale for Apache homicide seems to vary along the parameters of culpability and justification mediated by the notion of revenge or retaliation. By definition, it is wrong for Big Owl to go around killing people and his brother is therefore justified in retaliating by killing him.

For the period 1850–1935, Goodwin (1942: 390–425) lists eighty-five deaths for twenty-four homicidal events. More than half (53 or 62%) of these are characterized as retaliatory killings for a previous death. The average is from two to three deaths per event, but one feud accounted for thirty-three victims. Initial homicides were commonly motivated by gambling arguments, jealousy over women, and rape, while subsequent killings were in retaliation for the original death. The notion of "getting even" governed retaliatory and feud killings (see also Basso 1971). Regardless of the appropriateness of the initial homicide, subsequent killings could be considered justified. Even if compensation had been paid in a homicide litigation, a retaliatory killing, on the part of the offended kin group, was always a possibility. There was a tendency, however, for some initial killings, precipitated by witchcraft accusations or evidence of incest, to be considered justified and not appropriate for subsequent retaliation. Thus, it is virtually impossible to separate culpable from nonculpable Apache homicide in early reservation days.

Second, according to Goodwin, social relations between homicide victim and offender may be quite varied. On a severity scale, the killing of a person by his clansmen or blood relatives was considered most inappropriate.[2] Yet such an instance was less likely to call for revenge than if the homicide cut across clan lines. On certain occasions, some individuals turned "renegade," frequently after killing a kinsman. Expecting no mercy, they killed indiscriminately until they were killed or captured and

---

[2] The apparent contradiction between this principle and the desire of Sun's son to kill his brother in the myth of Big Owl is noteworthy, especially in view of the increasing trend toward intra-kin homicide in recent times.

incarcerated (see Goodwin's account in Basso 1971: 200–203). Only six or seven percent of the homicides listed by Goodwin (1942) consisted of kinsmen killing each other (two among White Mountain Apaches). In a number of cases, these were considered justified because of a grave infraction of standards of conduct such as incest by the victim. Only two cases of spouse homicide are recorded in this corpus (one for White Mountain Apaches). Of sixty-eight White Mountain Apache homicides, only three of the victims were female; there is not a single female offender in this sample.

Figuring homicide rates for early reservation days is extremely difficult in view of the unreliability of reporting and our inability to distinguish culpable from nonculpable deaths. Goodwin's corpus totals 85 deaths, 68 (80 percent) of which occurred among White Mountain Apaches — a significant proportion in itself. In another account (Basso 1971), Goodwin lists several San Carlos homicides, most of which are indistinguishable from those in this (1942) sample. It is impossible to group these two sets of homicides by year; they range from as early as 1850 to about 1935. Assuming an average of one per year for the White Mountain population, which averaged 2179 over this period of time, we arrive at a rate of about 46 per 100,000.[3] The San Carlos population averaged 1925 during this time. There are eight homicides for 85 years or .09 per year, which is 5 per 100,000. The total average population for both reservations is 4699; at one homicide per year, this is a rate of 21 per 100,000.

A somewhat more accurate strategy is possible based on annual reports of the Indian commissioner (U.S. Commissioner of Indian Affairs 1873–1906). These reports list a total of 119 killings, none of which are distinguished as culpable or nonculpable. Thirty-seven occurred at San Carlos, thirty-six among White Mountain Apaches and forty-six unspecified as to location. It is virtually impossible to cross-check Goodwin's list with this one. Some events are undoubtedly identical; the majority may well be different, given the discrepancy in both total and reservation figures between the two lists. Figured for both reservations (total 1890 population = 4120), the homicide rate is 3.72 per year for 32 years or 90 per 100,000. The White Mountain rate (1890 population = 1897) is

---

[3] The use of average measures here is questionable. But without year-specific dates for homicides, it is necessary. Average population measures are even more tenuous, for though the average population between about 1880 and 1935 is 2,179, the range is from 1,599 to 2,525, with rates of 63 and 40 per 100,000, respectively. The same can be done for San Carlos figures. But with incomplete data, the use of range measures is more misleading than the average ones. The same applies to other cases where rates are calculated over long periods of time.

1.12 homicides per year or 58 per 100,000. The San Carlos rate is 49 per 100,000.

Recent homicide data for Western Apaches are somewhat more reliable than in earlier periods. It is highly unlikely that violent deaths go unreported nowadays. Retaliation and feud killings are not nearly so prevalent as they used to be. But Apaches are rather acutely aware that homicide is unlawful and that punitive sanctions can be expected for such offenses via the Anglo legal system which operates on Indian reservations. Thus, attempts are frequently made to label a homicide nonculpable or either as a suicide or an accident. For example, five deaths labeled suicide in the White Mountain Apache U.S. Public Health Service Hospital (PHS) records are identified by informants as probable homicides. San Carlos data are not as complete as those for White Mountain Apache (see Everett 1969). Between 1957 and 1968, PHS records indicate fifteen homicides. With a population estimate of 4000 in 1969, the average per year is 1.25 or 30 per 100,000. Records contain no mention of the homicide offender or his motive, but they do indicate that eight of the fifteen homicide victims were female, a marked shift from the earlier paucity of White Mountain Apache female victims.

For White Mountain Apaches homicide figures contained in PHS medical records can be cross-checked against informant data for most of the forty-four year period (from 1927 to 1971) for which there is any information. A total of seventy-three homicides occurred during this period, an average of 1.66 per year or 23 per 100,000, based on a population average of 4261. Yet these figures are misleading due to the long time span over which reporting controls do not exist. If we take the last ten years, 1962–1971, for which good reporting controls are available, an annual average of 1.90 obtains; with a population of 5998 in 1969, the White Mountain Apache homicide rate becomes 32 per 100,000. Interview data provide information on both sex and kin relations of victim and offender, in addition to indicating motivation for the act. Of the seventy-three homicides, thirty-five of 48 percent are females. Only sixty of the homicides have a known offender; fifteen or 25 percent are females. Consanguineal kin relations occur in sixteen or 27 percent of the sixty cases (seven of these are parent-child, four are siblings), while twenty-one or 35 percent involve spouses. Motives for White Mountain Apache homicides range from gambling arguments and interference in quarrels to jealousy, with the latter as the dominant factor. Only one of the homicide events can be described as retaliatory, although five involved multiple victims and three involved homicide followed by suicide.

Summarizing these homicide data meaningfully is exceedingly difficult.

Table 1. White Mountain and San Carlos Apache population figures from annual reports of the U.S. Commissioner of Indian Affairs (1878–1928) and of the U.S. Bureau of Indian Affairs reservation superintendents (1934–1971)

Date	Population San Carlos	White Mountain	Total
1878–1883	1,150	1,599	2,749
1890	2,223	1,897	4,120
1901	2,542	1,952	4,494
1904	2,275	2,085	4,333
1906	2,202	2,072	4,274
1911	2,201	2,344	4,545
1919	2,515	2,466	4,981
1927	2,537	2,648	5,185
1928	2,545	2,656	5,201
1934–1936	2,674	2,525	5,199
1953	3,971	3.738	7,709
1968	4,000[1]	5,998	9,998
1971	4,079	6,230	10,309

[1] Estimate 4,335 in 1965.

This is especially true with regard to rates per 100,000 population. In addition to the limitations of reporting already discussed for the several sets of homicide information, population figures are equally unreliable (see Table 1). Census data were obtained at irregular intervals. Goodwin (1942: 582–587) notes that early government census figures suffer from under-reporting but proceeds to discuss Apache band and group affiliation regardless of reservation residence. This constitutes a real problem for those White Mountain Apaches who remained at San Carlos (primarily at Bylas) after the others returned to the northern reservation. At San Carlos in 1874, Tonto Apaches and San Carlos Apaches were placed on the reservation together, large numbers of the former group continuing to live in a state of mutual unfriendliness long into the twentieth century. Goodwin's data do not indicate this admixture accurately. Thus, no single set of homicide or population figures can be considered accurate and undistorted. Table 2 summarizes these data. It is noteworthy that, despite Goodwin's low 1850–1935 San Carlos figure and the low PHS average (1927–1971) for the White Mountain group, homicide rates have remained relatively stable for both White Mountain and San Carlos Apaches with a decline of more than a third in each group over the past 100 years.

Western Apache homicide patterns present the same kind of changing configuration over time. Tables 3, 4, and 5 indicate that a major shift has occurred with regard to the sex of homicide victims and offenders. This shift seems to characterize both White Mountain and San Carlos Apache

Table 2.   Western Apache homicide rates from various sources (figured per 100,000 population)

Source	San Carlos		White Mountain		Total	
	Number	Rate	Number	Rate	Number	Rate
Bureau Indian Affairs						
1873–1905	37	49	36	58	119[a]	90
Goodwin						
1850–1935	8	5	68	46	85[b]	21
Public Health Service						
1927–1971			73	23		
Public Health Service						
1962–1971			19	32		
Public Health Service						
1957–1968	15	30				
Public Health Service						
1962–1968	10	35	18	43	28	40

[a]   Includes 46 unspecified as to location.
[b]   Includes 9 cases unspecified as to location.

Table 3.   Sex of White Mountain Apache homicide victim

Source	Sex Male	Female	Unknown	Total
Goodwin				
1850–1935	65	3	0	68
Public Health Service				
1927–1971	37	35	1	73
Total	102	38	1	141

Table 4.   Sex of San Carlos Apache homicide victim

Source	Sex Male	Female	Unknown	Total
Goodwin				
1850–1935	4	1	3	8
Public Health Service				
1957–1968	7	8	0	15
Total	11	9	3	23

Table 5.   Sex of White Mountain Apache homicide offender

Source	Sex Male	Female	Unknown	Total
Goodwin				
1850–1935	68	0	0	68
Public Health Service				
1927–1971	45	15	13	73
Total	113	15	13	141

Table 6. Social relations between White Mountain Apache homicide offender and victim

Source	Spouse	Relation Consanguine	None	Unknown	Total
Goodwin 1850–1935	1	3	58	6	68
Public Health Service 1927–1971	21	16	20	3	60[a]
Total	22	19	78	9	128

[a] Does not include 13 unsolved homicides.

homicide, although complete data for the latter are lacking. The emergent patterns involve the increasingly frequent appearance of females, primarily as homicide victims, but also as offenders. The change is accompanied by a similar transformation in the social relations obtaining between actors in the homicide event (see Table 6). Early data indicate that non-kinsmen, specifically nonclansmen, killed each other at a high rate. More recently, however, victim and offender tend to be either spouses or close consanguineal kin.

Clearly, Western Apache homicide patterns, as well as homicide rates, exhibit early periods of relative stability followed more recently by marked transformation and change. There is little or no difference between White Mountain and San Carlos Apache groups in this regard. To what degree does Apache suicide follow a similar course of development?

SUICIDE

There is even less evidence for pre-reservation or aboriginal suicide than there was for homicide. The only actual suicidal event referred to in Apache mythology is an attempt which occurs in the tale "Lost with Turkey." The account (from Goodwin 1939: 63–68) begins this way:

Long ago they say. There was a young man living, about eighteen years old. He was living with his father and mother and sisters and brothers. This young man was a real gambler. He played all the time. This way he started in to play hoop and poles with another fellow. First, he bet his moccasins, then his leggings, then the rest of his clothes, and finally his hair. He lost everything and had to come home without anything. When he came home, his father and mother got after him, also his brothers, and made trouble with him about losing everything that way. They said to him, "You have not done right. You lost your shirt, moccasins, leggings and all, and besides you lost your hair and had it cut off close to your head. So we don't want you to live here any more.

You better go someplace else." This man had a pet turkey and that was all he had. So now he left his people and started off, taking his turkey with him.

After the two had gone for a way, they came to a great river and stopped on its bank. Then this man thought, "What shall I do? All my relatives are mad at me. Where shall I go?" After a while, he thought, "I will look for a log, a big dry one, and make a hole inside it and go in and plug the ends up with pitch and then roll into the water and let it carry me as far as it goes."

At this point, Goodwin, in a footnote, says that

The young man's desperation because of the attitude of his relatives toward him is quite typical of these people. When one's relatives no longer want one or cease to show signs of affection and fulfillment of obligations, no situation could be worse and it can easily end in a suicidal gesture or actual suicide.

The account ends with the young man returning to his people, gambling again with his original adversary, and emerging the victor.

In terms of how a suicide gesture (or, for that matter, an actual suicide) affects the survivors, especially in view of their initial responsibility for the act, it is interesting to examine the section of this myth recounting the young man's return to his kinsmen:

They had forgotten all about him by this time. As he was coming, only one, his younger sister, saw him. "There is my brother coming here," she said. Her father said to her, "He is dead almost a year now, so don't think he is alive. Don't talk about him." Then the girl said, "I am telling the truth, my brother is coming close now." "Don't say that. He's been dead a long time. We don't know what happened to him," her father said. The man was getting close now, and his sister said again, "I say true. Step outside and look at him." So the father said, "Let's see," and he sent another child outside to see if this was so. This one said, "She is right. She told the truth. My brother is coming back here." Now the father and mother stepped outside in front of their doorway. When he got there, all his family grabbed him and cried over him because he was home again (Goodwin 1939:67).

It is important to note that anger is replaced by grief after the antagonists realize their folly. The young man is rejected. Distraught and in desperation over this unnatural and intolerable state of affairs, he tries to kill himself. When he returns unexpectedly to his kinsmen, he is met with affection and happiness. So glad are his relatives to find him alive, after an ostensible suicide, that no mention is made of the factors which earlier led to the gesture.

None of the suicides mentioned by Goodwin (1942) can be identified as pre-reservation, although the one attempt he recounts could have taken place during this time due to its co-occurrence with a raid into Mexico (1942: 209). This is the only attempt listed by Goodwin. Moreover, he describes only two successful suicides, covering the period 1880 to about 1935. The female death is the single such event Goodwin recorded. Nowhere does the author provide evidence that male suicide or attempted suicide *per se* were at all prevalent. In view of his exceedingly detailed accounts of Western Apache homicide, for the same time period, it is highly likely that, in fact, self-destruction was a rarity.

Annual reports of the various Indian agents for both Apache reservations support the view that Goodwin's record is a reliable one. Two suicides, one in 1894 and the other in 1902, are reported for the White Mountain region. Only one suicide in 1892 is listed for San Carlos. No mention is made of the sex of the victims or the setting of the events (U.S. Commissioner of Indian Affairs 1892, 1894, 1902).

In an unpublished study of North American Indian suicide, Smith (1941) utilized firsthand reports solicited from reservation Indian agents. Presumably, the suicide events listed in her report are identical to those contained in annual reports of these agents to the Indian Commissioner. Smith lists two suicides prior to 1900, one for White Mountain Apaches (1889) and one at San Carlos (1884). Three suicides (1891) occurred off-reservation at the territorial prison where three men were incarcerated and due to be hung the next day. They strangled themselves rather than submit to execution. This was also the pattern in the other San Carlos suicide (1884) in which a man killed a suspected witch and was then jailed. He stabbed his wife, then killed himself. The White Mountain Apache suicide was a male jealous of his young wife. Smith also identifies Goodwin's single female suicide as occurring in 1921.

Observations on Apache suicidal behavior were also made by the physical anthropologist Hrdlicka between 1898 and 1904. Hrdlicka (1908: 171) writes,

Among the White Mountain Apache one or more cases of self-destruction occur every year. The means vary. Some individuals accomplish their purpose by means of a knife, others with a rope, gun or poison, and some jump from a cliff. The main cause of self-destruction is despondency, or, as the Apache expressed it "his people would not give him anything in his need;" "all her relatives dying, she would die also," etc. A man may kill himself when his wife dies, or a wife may take her own life when her children die, and sometimes suicide occurs during intoxication.

On the San Carlos reservation suicide is rare. Only two definite instances could be learned of by the writer. In one three men prisoners who were to be hanged the next day strangled themselves in the prison by tying cords about their necks, while the second case, which occurred about ten years ago, was that of an old woman who had an altercation with her daughter and in the following night strangled herself with a rope.

Hrdlicka's San Carlos data match Smith's description of the three prisoners who strangled themselves. But Hrdlicka's second case is not mentioned by Smith. It may be the same as the 1892 suicide listed in the report to the Indian Commissioner. (Note also the discrepancy here with regard to Goodwin's recognition of only a single female suicide.) The estimate for White Mountain Apache suicide is quite puzzling. By pooling all data sources, only four suicides for the White Mountain Apache Reservation between 1880 and 1902 are revealed. Presumably, Hrdlicka is referring to suicide events during his tenure in the region, which would mean at least one per year for six years. How reliable such a figure is must remain open to question, especially in view of the controverting evidence from three other sources.

Early reservation suicide rates, due to the unreliability of data and the small number of actual cases reported, do not reflect even the limited accuracy of homicide rates for the same period. Three sources — annual reports of the Indian Commissioner, Goodwin (1942), and Smith (1941) — list nine separate suicides for the period 1880–1904. Hrdlicka's figures, corrected for the probability that his four San Carlos suicides are included in other sources, yield an estimate of at least six suicides. The total of all four sources for both reservations, then, is between nine and fifteen, depending upon how reliable one believes Hrdlicka's White Mountain data to be. Between 1890 and 1906, Western Apache population averages were as follows: San Carlos, 2322; White Mountain, 1973; total, 4,296 (see Table 1). With an average annual rate of between 0.37 and 0.62, the suicide rate per 100,000 for both reservations is between nine and fourteen. Individual rates for San Carlos are calculated on the basis of five suicides over twenty-four years, an average of 0.21 per year, which yields a rate of nine per 100,000. Between four and ten suicides occurred among White Mountain Apaches over this period. At an annual average of 0.17–0.42, the rate per 100,000 is between nine and twenty-one (see Table 7).

In terms of pattern, early Apache suicides are not too revealing. Reports of the Indian commissioner do not specify sex of victim or motive. Goodwin's 1880 suicide involves a young man who is rejected by his brother in an argument over liquor. Smith notes that all four of her suicides were males. Three killed themselves apparently to escape punishment for homicide. Jealousy is also noted in one case. Hrdlicka lists the same three male suicides for San Carlos, but notes an additional female suicide. He identifies no specific White Mountain events, but mentions that both men and women committed suicide as a result of despondancy and grief. Thus, at least twice as many males committed suicide as females, though the proportion is probably much larger (five

Table 7.   Western Apache suicide rates from various sources prior to 1905.
(figured per 100,000 population.)

Source	San Carlos Number	Rate	White Mountain Number	Rate	Total Number	Rate
Bureau of Indian Affairs						
1873–1905	1	2	2	4	3	3
Goodwin						
1880–1900	0	1	2	1	1	
Smith						
1880–1900	4	7	1	2	5	5
Hrdlicka						
1898–1905	4	7	6[a]	13	20	10[b]
Total	5	9	4–10	9–21[c]	9–15	9–14[c]

[a]   Estimate.
[b]   Includes White Mountain estimate.
[c]   Corrected from all sources.

to one without Hrdlicka's estimate). Of seven suicides for which data are available, four were by hanging or strangling, two by shooting, and one by stabbing.

Recent suicide figures for Western Apache are available through a number of sources. Goodwin (1942: 209, 342) notes one female suicide (at San Carlos), identified by Smith (1941) as occurring in 1921. Smith lists nine suicides (six for White Mountain Apaches) since 1900 for both reservations. Only one of these was female. U.S. Public Health Service records show seventeen suicides for San Carlos between 1958 and 1968. This is an average of 1.54 per year for eleven years or 37 per 100,000 (population estimate 4000 in 1969). Seven of these or 41 percent were females. Techniques for self-destruction appear to be sex specific. Table 8 indicates that immolation or burning was the only method utilized by females, while males resorted to shooting, burning, hanging, and railroad trains.[4] PHS records make no systematic mention of motive for these cases.

White Mountain Apache suicide data are more complete and more reliable than the San Carlos material (Everett n.d.; Bartell 1966). PHS records list sixty suicides between 1924 and 1971. Informant testimony reveals some interesting discrepancies. One new suicide, for which there are no medical records, is identified. One death listed as an accident in the records is identified as a suicide by informants. In addition, of six

---

[4]   Bodies are discovered along the railroad tracks leading through the reservation. Some deaths are thought to be intentional, where individuals simply lay down across the tracks and await the next train. Others are most likely accidental, as when an intoxicated person, walking along the tracks, passes out in the path of an oncoming train.

Table 8.   San Carlos Apache suicide by sex of victim and method
(From PHS medical records, 1958–1968)

Method	Sex Male	Female	Total
Shooting	3	0	3
Burning	2	7	9
Hanging	2	0	2
Train	3	0	3
Total	10	7	17

deaths listed as suicides in the records, five are labeled homicide and one accidental. Thus, Apache informants identify fifty-eight suicides for the forty-seven year period of 1924–1971.[5] The population average over this period is 3,602, yielding an annual average of 1.25 and a rate of 33 per 100,000. In view of the long time span and the large population increase, calculating rates at ten year intervals is perhaps more revealing. Table 9 shows a range of suicide rates from seven per 100,000 between 1922 and 1931 to a rate of thirty-two per 100,000 for the most recent decade, with peak rates during the period 1940–1960.

Table 9.   White Mountain Apache suicide rates by ten-year intervals, 1922–1971 (figured per 100,000 population)

Time	Number	Population Estimate	Rate
1922–1931	2	2,648	7
1932–1941	8	2,525	32
1942–1951	13	3,100	42
1952–1961	16	3,738	45
1962–1971	19	5,998	32
Total	58	3,602[a]	33

[a]   Population average.

Information on suicide patterning among White Mountain Apaches is quite detailed, providing data on sex, age, marital status, method, and motive. With regard to sex of victim, there is a marked skewing toward males; almost 70 percent of the fifty-eight suicides are males. Yet beginning in the early 1950's, female suicides approach the male rate and exceed it in the 1960's (see Table 10). The age of the suicide victim varies considerably, depending upon the time period. Early suicides (pre-1950) appear scattered between the ages of fifteen and fifty-plus, while more recent ones are weighted toward younger age categories; 65 percent of the suicides between 1952 and 1971 are below the age of thirty (see

[5]   On the basis of strong evidence, presented in Everett (n.d.), it is probable that these revised figures reflect actuality.

Table 10.   White Mountain Apache suicide by sex of victim in ten-year intervals, 1922–1971

Time	Sex Male	Female	Total
1922–1931	2	0	2
1932–1941	7	1	8
1942–1951	12	1	13
1952–1961	10	6	16
1962–1971	9	10	19
Total	40	18	58

Table 11.   White Mountain Apache suicide by age of victim in ten-year intervals, 1922–1971

Age	Time 1922–1931	1932–1941	1942–1951	1952–1961	1962–1971	Total
15–19	0	4	2	6	4	16
20–24	0	0	3	3	5	11
25–29	0	0	0	2	3	5
30–34	0	0	1	1	4	6
35–39	1	3	4	2	0	10
40–44	0	0	1	2	0	3
45–49	0	0	0	0	1	1
50 plus	1	1	1	0	2	5
Unknown	0	0	1	0	0	1
Total	2	8	13	16	19	58

Table 12.   White Mountain Apache suicide by marital status of victim in ten-year intervals, 1922–1971

Time	Marital Status Married	Single	Other	Total
1922–1931	2	0	0	2
1932–1941	5	3	0	8
1942–1951	8	4	1	13
1952–1961	8	7	1	16
1962–1971	11	7	1	19
Total	34	21	3	58

Table 11). Marital status of suicides has also undergone some shift over the past fifty years. Prior to 1950, suicides tended to be married, whereas subsequently the proportion of married to single suicides is almost equal (see Table 12).[6] Perhaps most striking of all are the changes which have occurred with regard to method of self-destruction. Four techniques have been utilized: shooting, burning, hanging, and stabbing. All but two

[6]   This shift cannot be explained by recent changes in marriage patterns (see Everett n.d.).

Table 13.   White Mountain Apache suicide by method in ten-year intervals, 1922-1971

Time	Method Gunshot	Burning	Hanging	Stabbing	Total
1922-1931	2	0	0	0	2
1932-1941	7	0	1	0	8
1942-1951	11	1	0	1	13
1952-1961	9	7	0	0	16
1962-1971	10	9	0	0	19
Total	39	17	1	1	58

Table 14.   White Mountain Apache suicide by motive in ten-year intervals, 1922-1971

Motive	Time 1922-1931	1932-1941	1942-1951	1952-1961	1962-1971	Total
Argue with spouse	0	1	3	3	8	15
Argue with kinsman						
Parent	0	1	2	5	1	9
Sibling	0	1	0	2	2	5
Other – consanguine	0	0	1	1	3	5
Other – affine	0	0	1	0	0	1
Sub-total	0	2	4	8	6	20
Argue with non-kinsman						
Friend	0	0	0	0	1	1
Other	0	0	0	1	1	2
Sub-total	0	0	0	1	2	3
Grief over death of relative	0	2	0	0	0	2
Escape consequences of behavior						
Homicide	0	1	4	0	0	5
Assault	0	1	2	1	0	4
Jail	0	0	0	1	0	1
Other	0	0	0	0	1	1
Sub-total	0	2	6	2	1	11
Chronic illness	1	1	0	0	0	2
Unknown	1	0	0	2	2	5
Total	2	8	13	16	19	58

instances are either shooting or burning (see Table 13). What is revealing is the clear sexual dichotomy apparent in these two methods. Of eighteen female suicides, only two utilized methods other than burning. All male suicides but two are by shooting. Finally, a shifting pattern of suicide motive can also be seen. Table 14 indicates that 60 percent of all White Mountain Apache suicides occur as a result of arguments with spouses or close consanguineal kinsmen. It is noteworthy that since 1932, the proportion of argument motives to other forms of provocation has doubled.

Summarizing Western Apache suicide data by rates must be done with extreme caution, due to the inconsistencies in records of early accounts.

It is clear, however, that virtually no evidence exists which would permit a determination of the incidence of pre-reservation suicide. Even recourse to Apache mythology provides little illumination relevant to aboriginal self-destruction. Early accounts of suicide prior to the twentieth century are almost impossible to verify. Even Goodwin's data are suspect in view of controverting evidence from other sources. To a lesser extent, this is also true of recent suicide data. Government records do not suffer from the kind of under-reporting they once did. But discrepancies do exist between these accounts and those of Apache informants.

With these caveats in mind, the following conclusions with regard to suicide rates appear warranted. First, the overall Western Apache suicide rate has almost doubled since the 1880's, increasing from a maximum of 14 per 100,000 to a current rate of about 30 per 100,000. Second, San Carlos Apache suicide rates have increased almost fivefold over the past 100 years. Table 15 indicates that pre-1900 rates were in the neighborhood of eight per 100,000, while subsequent rates are between 37 and 42 per 100,000. Finally, suicide is a much more stable phenomenon for White Mountain than for San Carlos Apaches. Between 1880 and 1930, White Mountain rates remained below 10 per 100,000, and probably much less than that. Beginning in the mid-1930's, the rate quadruples and then levels off at about 32 per 100,000. Thus, suicide rates have increased for both Western Apache groups. Unfortunately, data on rates of increase are unavailable for San Carlos.

Patterns of Western Apache suicide present similar configuration changes. Sex of suicide victim is clearly a variable subject to fluctuation over time. Table 16 indicates that marked shifts have occurred over the past 100 years. Prior to 1900, most Apache suicides, especially at San Carlos, were males. Hrdlicka's estimate of high female rates are unsubstantiated. Beginning in the 1950's, females increasingly resorted to self-destruction. Comparable data are lacking for San Carlos, but the thirty year period prior to 1950 among White Mountain Apaches saw nineteen suicides, only two of which were female. Both reservation patterns are comparable for the 1950's and 1960's — females committing suicide almost as frequently as males.

Accompanying this shift to female suicide is a similar trend toward a sexual dichotomy in methods of self-destruction. This is more marked for White Mountain Apaches than at San Carlos. All early White Mountain

---

[7] This range is based on figures contained in annual reports of the Commissioner of Indian Affairs for both groups in order to compensate for presumed under-reporting. Goodwin's data for San Carlos, because they are so far out of line with these figures, have been discarded.

Table 15.   Western Apache suicide rates, 1873–1971 (figured per 100,000 population)

Source and time	Rate San Carlos	Fort Apache	Total
Bureau Indian Affairs			
1873–1905	2	4	3
Goodwin			
1880–1900	0	2	1
Smith			
1880–1900	7	2	5
Hrdlicka			
1898–1905	7	13[a]	10[a]
Sub-total	9	9–21	9–14
Public Health Service			
1958–1968	37		
Public Health Service			
1922–1931		7	
1932–1941		32	
1942–1951		42	
1952–1961		45	
1962–1971	42[b]	32	
Sub-total		33	

[a]   Estimates.
[b]   PHS (1962–1968).

Table 16.   Western Apache suicide by sex of victim, 1880–1971

Source and Time	San Carlos Male	Female	White Mountain Male	Female	Total Male	Female
Goodwin						
1880–1900	0	0	1	0	1	0
Smith						
1880–1900	4	0	1	0	5	0
Hrdlicka						
1898–1905	3	1	3[a]	3[a]	6	4
USPHS						
1958–1968	10	7			10	7
USPHS						
1922–1931			2	0	2	0
1932–1941			7	1	7	1
1942–1951			12	1	12	1
1952–1961			10	6	10	6
1962–1971	7[b]	5[b]	9	10	16	15

[a]   Estimates.
[b]   PHS (1962–1968).

suicides are by shooting. This trend continues for males, but when females begin killing themselves, they do so by burning. San Carlos males do not prefer any single method and have even utilized railroad trains in recent times. Females at San Carlos, however, immolate themselves, as do

White Mountain females. As a technique for self-destruction, this method is not known prior to the 1950's for either reservation (see Table 17).

Finally, the variable of motive or provocation must be considered. Early San Carlos suicides are apparently motivated by (1) desire to escape the legal consequences of one's behavior and (2) grief over the death of a kinsman. At the White Mountain reservation, however, arguments with spouses and siblings provoke self-destruction. Recent data for San Carlos are not available, but at least one suicide was motivated by an argument with a close kinsman. White Mountain Apache suicide motives display a shifting pattern, from a distribution consisting of (1) escape consequences of illegal behavior, (2) argument with kinsman, and (3) argument with spouse to one dominated by arguments with close consanguineal kin and spouses (see Table 18). Precisely what the dynamics of this configuration are will be examined below.

Table 17. Western Apache suicide by method, sex of victim, and date

	San Carlos 1873–1905		San Carlos 1958–1968		White Mountain 1873–1905		White Mountain 1922–1951		White Mountain 1952–1971		Total	
Method[a]	Male	Female	Male	Female	Male	Female	Male	Female	Male	Female	Male	Female
Gunshot	0	0	3	0	2	0	20	0	18	1	43	1
Burning	0	0	2	7	0	0	0	1	1	15	3	23
Hanging	3	1	2	0	0	0	0	1	0	0	5	2
Rain	0	0	3	0	0	0	0	0	0	0	3	0
Stabbing	1	0	0	0	0	0	1	0	0	0	2	0
Total	4	1	10	7	2	0	21	2	19	16	56	26

Hrdlicka also mentions jumping off cliffs and poison. His estimate is not included in the White Mountain data.

WHITE MOUNTAIN APACHE SUICIDE: THE NATIVE VIEW

An attempt has been made to demonstrate changing rates and shifting patterns of social pathology, namely, homicide and suicide, for two Western Apache groups, changes which can be linked, not to traditional modes of integration-disintegration, but to variables imbedded in the acculturation process. Sometimes the changes are only minimal, at least as reflected by rates figured per 100,000 population. But this is misleading, since even today neither Western Apache group numbers over 6500 individuals. One way to compensate for the shortcomings of this analytic strategy is to add to it a cultural or cognitive dimension in which informant testimony and conceptualization, rather than documentary evidence

Table 18.   Western Apache suicide by motive and date

Motive	San Carlos 1873–1905	1958–1968	White Mountain 1873–1905	1922–1951	1952–1971	Tot
Argue with spouse	0	0	1	4	11	16
Argue with kinsman						
Parent	0	0	0	3	6	9
Sibling	0	0	1	1	4	6
Other – consanguine	0	1	0	1	4	6
Other – affine	0	0	0	1	0	1
Sub-total	0	1	1	6	14	20
Argue with non-kinsman						
Friend	0	0	0	0	1	1
Other	0	0	0	0	2	2
Sub-total	0	0	0	0	3	3
Grief over death of relative	1	0	0	2	0	3
Escape consequences of behavior						
Homicide	4	0	0	5	0	9
Assault	0	0	0	3	1	4
Jail	0	0	0	0	1	1
Other	0	0	0	0	1	1
Sub-total	4	0	0	8	3	15
Chronic illness	0	0	0	2	0	2
Unknown	1	16	2–8[a]	1	4	24–
Total	6	17	4–10[a]	23	35	83–

[a]   Based on Hrdlicka's estimates.

obtained from Anglo observers, plays a definitive role. As already indicated, this is a productive approach in the analysis of White Mountain
Apache suicide (Everett n.d.). A brief exposition of this strategy adds
strength to our argument regarding the shifting nature of Western Apache
social pathology.

White Mountain Apaches are very much aware of the changing character of suicide. This awareness is expressed in the form of explanations as
to why suicide should be more prevalent in some communities than in
others and why some people resort to self-destructive gestures while
others do not. The case of community A, with the highest incidence of
suicide, is accounted for by the general "backwardness" of the community
and the fact that intermarriage occurred between these people and the
hostile Chiricahua Apaches in the 1880's. Community B has the second
highest rate of self-destruction. The following tale is used to explain the
situation:

X was the son of a chief. One time he was driving a brand new car which
belonged to his brother. A Cibecue boy was riding with him. It overturned
near the old sawmill in North Fork, and the boy was killed. Everyone blamed X.

The dead boy's relatives from Cibecue came to North Fork and asked for that car. X's brother told them no. So the medicine men from Cibecue worked witchcraft on the North Fork people so that they would all die from things like suicide and killing, all the way down to the last one. Then nobody would be left. At this time, there were many people living there. Now there are few. The medicine men in Cibecue are still powerful.

Two informants indicate in more specific terms some of the causal variables involved in the self-destructive process:

This new generation is something else, something different. In the old days, everything was dry, no liquor, everyone was too hungry. Now they do it because of drinking. Some people are jealous, men, women. Drinking makes trouble for everyone. A lady is seen with another man, she will burn herself.

It's mostly the kids these days that kill themselves. They do it because of lack of discipline. They go from family to family. Apaches are not used to bad words. Working people might be cussed out by their boss. Then they just walk off the job. They have not grown up with these hard words. That is the way with these kids. Their folks scold them for doing something. They throw up to you what you are, like if you are missing an arm, or if you limp, or if you are absent-minded. Apaches are like that. Whatever vour personality is, whatever you are, people kid you about it. Sometimes parents really ride kids hard. Then, the kids say, "Don't talk to me that way. I don't like it. If you don't stop, I'll kill myself."

Apaches label suicide *atiziste* and define it as a voluntary, intentional killing of one's body. The person who destroys himself is usually considered rational and "does not care for his life." Informants agree that the reason the suicide victim "does not care for his life" is to be found in the conditions which provoked the act. With few exceptions, recent suicides occur as a reslt of *ilkkedidii* (bad talk) between the victim and another individual. In the past exceptions to this rule were (1) grief over the death of a kinsman, (2) fear of punishment for a criminal or negatively sanctioned act, and (3) chronic illness. Thus, Apaches expect contemporary suicidal events to exhibit the notion of "bad talk." If a death does not, it becomes difficult to interpret as suicide and may be labeled a homicide or an accident.

Conflict between spouses is a common motive for suicide. Frequently, the trouble results from jealousy, as in the case of A, an eighteen year old girl:

A was married to my son. They have two kids and live with us. There was a dance at the community building. A's husband was dancing with another girl. A came home and took a small can of kerosene from the house. She walk over there between these two trees. She pour it on herself and then burn herself. She must have been jealous. She was not drinking because she belong to the Miracle Church.

Considerable diversity characterizes suicide generated by conflict between consanguineal kin. Sometimes siblings are involved, as in the following instance:

B was my 24 year old brother. He was living with my husband and me. He went over to his brother's camp to watch them play cards. No one would give him a drink. B asked his brother. He said no and talked bad to him. B left and came back here. Only the kids and me were here. He told me that he was feeling bad because his brother talked against him. He took a rifle and said he was going to take it back to the owner. Then he shot himself.

Other kinsmen may just as easily function as antagonists in the conflict which produces a suicidal gesture. According to one informant,

C was my wife's son. He was about 15 years old. He was trying to ask for a drink from his mother's sister, right across the road. She told him no. He told them he was going to go home, get his gun, and kill himself. He got a 30.06 and shot himself in the forehead.

In a number of cases, self-destruction results from a desire to escape retribution for illegal actions. Most of these instances involve "bad talk" which generates physical violence or homicide. An informant described one situation in this way:

D was my 21 year old brother. We were all at our brother's place after a drinking party. This woman was telling bad stories about him, really criticizing him. He really got mad at her. He hit her, beat her up, and knocked her down. He thought he killed her. D left after he hit that woman. He went back to his mother's camp and shot himself.

Why should suicide constitute a legitimate response to "bad talk?" Apaches explain this in terms of aggression. When an individual is provoked by an antagonist, he becomes angry and wishes to retaliate, to "get even." Goodwin (1942: 550) describes this phenomenon as a pervasive theme in traditional Apache interpersonal relations (see also Bartell 1966). It is apparently the case that the more angry an individual becomes at his adversary, the more he desires to hurt him, which could result in anything from assault or homicide to suicide. One informant put it this way:

In the old days, a person could murder someone he was mad at. But now he will be arrested and punished. Now the only way to show a person how much he has hurt you is to go kill yourself. That will show him.

The hurt referred to here takes the form of recognition on the part of the antagonist that he is responsible for the victim's death. Most of the time this awareness cannot be defined, for the suicide victim structures the act

in such a way that no mistake can be made as to its meaning. One informant described the following instance:

E lived with her parents. She was about 17. She was staying with her boyfriend
at her mother's camp. Her mother did not want them together. She and E
fought, and she ran the boy off. After she burned herself, E said to her parents,
"I hope you are happy now as I won't be seeing him anymore."

Note also the public announcement of the impending act in case C cited
earlier.

It is important to realize that Apaches readily identify the suicide
configuration abstractly, i.e. as a possible outcome of ANY event which
involves "bad talk." This is especially true of parents who wish to
reprimand their children for inappropriate behavior. The reactions of
the antagonist in a conflict situation can be of paramount importance
vis à vis the course of action pursued by the potential suicide victim.
Where retaliation is sought, and the antagonist — either knowingly or
otherwise — remains passive, suicide is likely to follow. But if the antagonist makes an effort at reconciliation, the act may be averted. The
initiative for reconciliation may be taken by the potential suicide victim
who chooses only to attempt suicide and thereby manipulate his adversary. It is noteworthy that most attempted suicide results from the obvious nonlethal application of several common techniques, such as drug
overdoses (involving "cold" pills and vitamins), minor burns, and superficial knife and gunshot wounds. After such an attempt, the person
responsible for "bad talk" acquiesces and a reconciliation occurs, as in
the following case:

F burned herself after an argument with her husband. He lost his job and
started drinking. He beat her. Since she burned herself, they have gotten back
together because he feels very sorry for how he treated her and he has gone
back to work and is supporting his family.

More often than not, the suicidal gesture is superfluous. For some
antagonists, even the remotest possibility of such an event calls for
conciliatory action. The problem, of course, is that only the potential
suicide victim can determine the outcome of the conflict situation. Those
ultimately responsible for the act cannot predict its result with certainty
and are usually not willing to gamble. The threat of a possible suicidal
gesture is utilized to great advantage by some individuals, as indicated in
the following account by the mother of three teenagers:

It's really hard when you have teenagers. They think they are so grown up.
They want everything we didn't have as kids. You just don't know what
they're going to do. When they're big, you can't stop them. So you try to give
them what they want, like these motorcycles. If you don't, they'll say, "I'm

going to kill myself." You really get afraid of them. If you talk to them or beat them, they get mad and kill somebody or themselves.

By way of conclusion, the following is apparent from an examination of present-day White Mountain Apache suicide behavior. Apaches possess and utilize in their daily routines a set of standardized expectations and explanations with regard to suicidal events. These clearly date from around 1950 and are quite ineffective in accounting for suicide prior to that time (Everett n.d.). Thus, the cultural significance or "meaning" of such behavior has obviously undergone some important shifts over the past forty years. Apaches themselves explain these changes in terms the anthropologist usually labels "acculturation."

SUMMARY AND CONCLUSION

Substantively, this paper deals with two categories of information. The first subsumes those factors relevant to what Aberle (1966; see also Dozier 1966) has called "relative deprivation" and is couched essentially in historical terms dealing with early confinement and economic assimilation. Aboriginally, all Western Apache groups were quite similar in almost every respect. Yet the early history of these groups in their relations with Anglo-Americans and with each other is quite divergent. Raiding into Mexico and inter-group warfare were forcibly halted, and many thousands of Western Apaches, together with hostile Chiricahuas, were incarcerated at San Carlos under a rigid military and civil regime. The traditional Apache life style ceased, and the impounded groups were forced to adapt to demands imposed by the Anglo world. For San Carlos Apaches this became a permanent state of affairs, as cattle-raising, wage labor, and welfare came to dominate the economic scene. Apaches at San Carlos were compelled to participate in the Anglo way of life, albeit at its margins, and their degree of participation can be viewed either as succesful adaptation to changing conditions or as resistance to assimilation into the mainstream of life in the white world (see Adams and Krutz 1971).

The period of incarceration at San Carlos was only a brief — however traumatic — inconvenience for White Mountain Apaches, who shortly returned to their northern homeland and resumed, almost without interference, a traditional life style, devoid only of its militaristic features. These Apaches continued to be hunters, gatherers, and subsistence farmers well into the twentieth century, making only minor concessions to Anglo government personnel, educators, missionaries, and the like. Relative deprivation vis à vis Anglos was apparently an insignificant phenomenon for most groups, which managed to remain somewhat isolated and impervious to white influence until only a few decades ago.

To be sure, the differences apparent in the early acculturation experiences of the two Apache groups are not great, and subsequent Apache-Anglo interaction is quite similar for all Western Apaches, such that few significant differences obtain in the contemporary acculturation configurations of the two groups. We have argued that rates and patterns of pathological behavior — at least homicide and suicide — can be readily accounted for in terms of these acculturation similarities and differences.

The second category of information dealt with in this paper, and that which is most relevant to this argument, is data on social pathologies, namely, homicide and suicide. Central to the thesis of this paper is that reservation rates of pathology are higher than pre-reservation rates. In addition, it is necessary that reservation patterns of pathology be different from aboriginal ones. In view of the data presented here, neither of these propositions can be satisfactorily supported. The only aboriginal data on social pathology comes from Goodwin (1942, Basso 1971). This information implies that only homicide was prevalent prior to the establishment of reservations. Mythological data lend some support to this contention.

Reservation rates and patterns of pathology are difficult to evaluate, especially in the early days when several sources provide obviously biased or contradictory data. These data indicate that homicide rates for both Apache groups were relatively high — between 49 and 58 per 100,000 (see Table 2). This can probably be accounted for by the disruptive period of incarceration on this reservation in the 1870's and the relative deprivation generated in that hostile environment. Subsequently, both reservation rates decline by about a third. The situation on the White Mountain reservation is not surprising, for the continued isolation and lack of control in this region clearly lent themselves to a diminished rate of acculturation stress and thus of interpersonal violence. Why San Carlos rates should have declined as well is unknown at present; perhaps it was not so much Anglo domination as it was the sudden shift from confinement to almost total economic absorption prior to the depression. Once the incarceration situation was relaxed and voluntary economic alternatives developed, sources of cross-cultural conflict also diminished.

This explanation takes account of one of the primary pattern shifts which are evident in the Apache homicide data. Feuds, in which clan relatives united with each other to avenge the death of a kinsman, characterize early Western Apache homicide events. This was primarily a male-oriented activity, and few females were involved. Over the past 100 years, however, this pattern has changed radically, such that females are now equally involved in homicide activities as victims and, to a lesser extent, as offenders. In addition, recent homicides tend to occur between individuals who are either close consanguineal kinsmen or spouses. San Carlos data are incomplete, but seem to reflect similar pattern shifts. This changing configuration appears to be resulting from an increasingly serious disjunction in the Apache kinship system in which kin obligations become less effective for cooperative action and contribute more to the disaffection of kinsmen. Without support from consanguineal kin, marital relations — never as strong as family ties — are allowed to deteriorate unimpeded. In an economic environment where traditional forms of social organization are no longer adaptive (at least in the widest sense), it is not surprising to see pathological behavior such as homicide in this context.

Self-destructive Western Apache behavior is apparently subject to similar acculturation vicissitudes. Early information on suicide is extremely unreliable. No evidence exists to suggest anything but low rates in pre-reservation days. Early reservation data are contradictory, but suggest that San Carlos rates were higher than White Mountain ones, both in the neighborhood of five to ten per 100,000. For White Mountain Apaches, at least, these lower rates persisted into the 1940's, at which time they, along with San Carlos rates, display a phenomenal increase, anywhere from triple to quadruple the original rates. The overall increase is significant, as is the stability on the White Mountain reservation both prior to the 1940's and subsequently.

Much illumination is cast upon these problems by resort to information on patterns of self-destruction. What is perhaps most striking in these data are the shifts in sex of suicide victim and motive. In the past, males killed themselves for a variety of reasons, most of which could be labeled nonaggressive. However, recent suicides on both reservations are characterized by males and females destroying themselves in equal numbers. Among White Mountain Apaches the act is aggressive, retaliation for a real or supposed offense committed by an antagonist who is either a spouse or a close kinsman. Similar changes have occurred with regard to method and age of suicide victim.

Are there features in contemporary acculturation processes which can account for these changes? As Western Apaches entered the twentieth century females remained solidly entrenched in a domestic structure supported by a complex network of kin relations (Goodwin 1942). But domestic harmony gave way to discord as sex roles became less and less differentiated. Women went to school with men, were exposed to the same sets of Anglo ideas, and yet did not have access to the same channels for expressing newly developed needs (see Parmee 1968). Kin obligations became more disruptive, and marital relations more precarious. It is in this changing atmosphere — beginning in the late 1940's and early 1950's — that females begin resorting to self-destruction as a legitimate means of conflict resolution. That these conflicts are being expressed at increasingly earlier ages is reflected in the youthfulness of recent suicide victims — and problem drinkers (Everett 1973).[8] Apache conceptualization substantiates this explanatory model in almost every respect, with emphasis on the shift in meaning which is reflected in these processes.

Returning for a moment to the question of rates of suicide, it is noteworthy that San Carlos and White Mountain figures are so similar. Both were low in early reservation days, Hrdlicka's Fort Apache data notwithstanding. Increases are fairly regular, insofar as information is accessible. Without data for San Carlos prior to the mid-1950's, comparative statements are difficult to make. It appears that current rates for both Apache groups range from 32 to 42 per 100,000, with San Carlos rates somewhat higher than White Mountain ones. Recall that this was not the case with regard to homicidal behavior; San Carlos rates are slightly lower than those for White Mountain Apaches.

Pathological behaviors are not isolated and independent elements. They are constellations of functionally interrelated units, each of which contributes some portion of meaning to the others. Such is the case with Western Apache homicide and suicide. Not only do the two (increasingly) occur together in a single event, but when they are plotted independently, they tend to covary. Relative to time, early reservation homicide rates are high and suicide rates are low, while current homicide rates are low and suicide rates high.[9] But considered over the past 100 years, San Carlos homicide rates are relatively lower than White Mountain ones, and San Carlos suicide rates are somewhat higher than those of White Mountain Apaches. The discrepancies between the two reservations are probably not significant, but recent cross-cultural research suggests the possibility that homicide and suicide may covary (Bohannan 1960; Palmer 1965). A comparison of White Mountain Apache homicide and suicide rates by ten-year intervals from 1922 to 1971 tends to support this contention (see Table 19). From the mid-1930's on, whenever suicide rates increase, homicide rates decrease, and *vice versa*. Thus, it would appear — though

---

[8] It is noteworthy that recent Phoenix Indian Boarding School records indicate all Apache attempted suicides are female.
[9] The decline in homicide rates over time is interesting in view of findings to the contrary by Nash (1967).

Table 19.   Comparison of White Mountain Apache homicide and suicide rates by ten-year intervals, 1922–1971 (figured per 100,000 population)

Time	Population Estimate	Number Homicide[a]	Suicide	Rate Homicide	Suicide
1922–1931	2,648	2	2	8	7
1932–1941	2,525	14	8	56	32
1942–1951	3,100	12	13	39	42
1952–1961	3,738	9	16	24	45
1962–1971	5,998	27	19	46	32

[a]   Does not include five unidentified by date and four listed as homicide in PHS records but identified by informants as suicide or accidents (see Table 2).

sufficient evidence is not yet available — that Western Apache homicide and suicide are functional equivalents of some sort, at least to the degree that (1) they do covary by rate over time and reservation, (2) they are today defined by Apaches as retaliatory reactions to conflict and antagonism, and (3) they both exhibit similar pattern shifts since early reservation days (see Everett n.d.).

An attempt has been made, on the basis of a rather lengthy exposition, to determine the exact nature of two major forms of social pathology among Western Apaches. Any corpus of such data is amenable to at least two explanatory models: one emphasizing the persistence of aboriginal pathologies, the other stressing the notion of acculturation and relative deprivation due to Anglo influence. As Levy and Kunitz (1971) point out, anthropologists may have taken the latter for granted far too long without examining the possibility of the former's existence and/or explanatory potential. We have argued that neither model is sufficient to account for sociopathological behavior in the most productive way. The Western Apache data tend to support this position. Aboriginal rates of homicide may well have been high, but there is no evidence to support such a claim for self-destruction. Regardless, there have been notable changes — either increases or declines — in the rates of these pathologies over the past 100 years. Moreover, radical shifts in pattern and meaning have occurred in the Apache homicide configuration as well as in suicidal behavior.

The particular acculturation model initially constructed to account for Western Apache social pathology has fared moderately well:

1. It was anticipated that since early acculturation experiences were different for the two Apache groups, there would be marked differences in early rates and patterns of pathological behavior. Data are available for homicide and suicide only. In both instances, no significant differences are apparent in patterns of these forms of social pathology on the two

Apache reservations, while White Mountain homicide rates are somewhat higher and suicide rates relatively lower than for San Carlos Apaches. 2. It was expected that there would be no differences between the groups with respect to contemporary rates and patterns of pathology because their recent acculturation experiences are essentially similar. This is in fact the case with regard to suicide and to homicide patterns, but not for rates of homicide and suicide; White Mountain homicide rates are relatively higher than San Carlos, while suicide rates are somewhat lower. 3. It was assumed that if there were significant changes in acculturation experiences for both Apache groups since early reservation times, these would be reflected in changing rates and patterns of pathology over the past 100 years. This is verified for rates and patterns of homicide and suicide on both Apache reservations and constitutes a more significant discovery than the relative differences between the two Apache groups in regard to rates and patterns of social pathology (see Table 20).

It might be argued, since the direction of rate changes and the character of pattern shifts are essentially similar for two groups whose aboriginal

Table 20.   Comparison of rates and patterns of major Western Apache social pathologies

thology	San Carlos Early Reservation	Contemporary	White Mountain Early Reservation	Contemporary
ɔmicide	High rates; patterns similar to early White Mountain ones.	Low rates; patterns different from early reservation ones, but similar to White Mountain patterns.	High rates; patterns similar to early San Carlos ones.	High rates; patterns different from early reservation ones, but similar to contemporary San Carlos patterns.
icide	Low rates; patterns similar to early White Mountain ones.	High rates; patterns different from early reservation ones, but similar to contemporary White Mountain patterns.	Low rates; patterns similar to early San Carlos ones.	High rates; patterns different from early reservation ones, but similar to contemporary San Carlos patterns.

cultures are similar but whose early acculturation experiences were divergent, that indeed acculturation variables are irrelevant; in the least, they are sometimes overridden by elements of traditional Apache culture. Certainly, this seems to be the case with the traditional Apache notion of "getting even," which has recently changed character, but nevertheless is readily recognizable as a dominant theme in contemporary Western Apache culture. The same is true for rates of pathology in relation to other American Indian groups: they are unquestionably high and have been since early reservation times (see Levy and Kunitz 1971). But, at the same time, the Western Apache data provide support for both a persistence and an acculturation explanatory paradigm. Thus, it would appear that what we see in the Apache case is an intricate and complex relationship between acculturation experience and traditional cultural elements, for which it is virtually impossible to construct a simplistic explanatory model.

Unraveling these complex interdependencies is not especially useful for either the understanding, treatment, or prevention of contemporary American Indian social pathologies. Western Apache verbal and cognitive data suggest that at any one time there exists a set of prevailing expectations and explanations for such behavior. Frequently, it is difficult to tap these, as in the case of homicide, which is illegal and subject to punitive sanctions. At other times, investigators discard them as subjective and thus unreliable obfuscations of some as yet undiscovered empirically verifiable reality lurking below the surface of human consciousness. Yet awareness of these conceptual data is imperative if really effective preventive "mental health" programs are to be established. They simply cannot be ignored. At this level, meaning, not rates per 100,000 population, is of paramount importance, as the case of White Mountain Apache suicide so clearly demonstrates. As these meanings inexorably change, pattern transformations become significant, for a few contemporary pathologies are best interpreted as persistences from earlier periods, while others reflect as yet unknown semantic and cognitive shifts. Whether these are simply permutations of a basic cultural theme or by-products of acculturation processes matters little in the search for viable therapeutic and preventive strategies. Cultural heritability is a timeworn notion which will require some refurbishing before it becomes a serious contender in our attempts to account for American Indian social pathology.

REFERENCES

ABERLE, DAVID F.
  1966   *The peyote religion among the Navajo.* Chicago: Aldine.
ADAMS, WILLIAM Y., GORDON KRUTZ
  1971   "Wage labor and the San Carlos Apache," in *Apachean culture history and ethnology.* Edited by Keith Basso and Morris Opler, 115–134. University of Arizona Anthropological Papers 21.
BARTELL, GILBERT
  1966   *Apache suicide patterns: affective magical acts.* Proceedings of the Thirty-Sixth International Congress of Americanists. Spain.

BASSO, KEITH H., *editor*
1971 *Western Apache raiding and warfare: from the notes of Grenville Goodwin*. Tucson: University of Arizona Press.

BOHANNAN, PAUL, *editor*
1960 *African homicide and suicide*. Princeton: Princeton University Press.

BROWN, DONALD N.
1970 "Law and disorder in an Indian pueblo." Unpublished manuscript.

BUSKIRK, WINIFRED
1949 "Subsistence economy of Western Apache." Unpublished doctoral dissertation, University of New Mexico, Albuquerque.

CLUM, WOODWORTH
1936 *Apache agent: the story of John P. Clum*. Boston: Houghton Mifflin.

DAVIS, BRITTON
1929 *The truth About Geronimo*. New Haven: Yale University Press.

DOUGLAS, JACK D.
1967 *The social meaning of suicide*. Princeton: Princeton University Press.

DOZIER, EDWARD P.
1966 Problem drinking among American Indians: the role of sociocultural deprivation. *Quarterly Journal of Studies on Alcohol* 27:72–87.

EVERETT, MICHAEL W.
1969 Cooperacion en el cambio? El caso de los apaches occidentales. *Anuario Indigenista* 29:97–107. Mexico.
1970 Pathology in White Mountain Apache culture: a preliminary analysis. *Western Canadian Journal of Anthropology* 2(1):180–203. Edmonton.
1973 "Anthropological expertise and the 'realities' of White Mountain Apache adolescent problem drinking." Paper presented at the annual meeting of the Society for Applied Anthropology, Tucson.
n.d. "Conflict, adversaries, and retaliation: suicide among the White Mountain Apache," in *Cross-cultural studies in suicide*. Edited by Ari Kiev. In preparation.

GETTY, HARRY T.
1963 *The San Carlos Indian cattle industry*. University of Arizona Anthropological Papers 7.

GOODWIN, GRENVILLE
1935 The social divisions and economic life of the Western Apache. *American Anthropologist* 37 (1):55–64.
1939 *Myths and tales of the White Mountain Apache*. Memoirs of the American Folklore Society 33.
1942 *Social organization of the Western Apache*. Chicago: University of Chicago Press.

GRAVES, THEODORE D.
1970 The personal adjustment of Navajo Indian migrants to Denver, Colorado. *American Anthropologist* 72:35–54.

GRIFFIN, P. BION, MARK P. LEONE, KEITH H. BASSO
1971 "Western Apache ecology: from horticulture to agriculture," in *Apachean culture history and ethnology*. Edited by Keith Basso and Morris Opler, 69–76. University of Arizona Anthropological Papers 21.

HARTE, JOHN BRET
1973   Conflict at San Carlos: the military-civilian struggle for control, 1882–1885. *Arizona and the West* 15 (1):27–44.

HRDLICKA, ALES
1908   *Physiological and medical observations among the Indians of southwestern United States and northern Mexico.* Bureau of American Ethnology Bulletin 34. Washington, D.C.

LEVY, JERROLD E.
1965   Navajo suicide. *Human Organization* 24 (4):308–318.

LEVY, JERROLD E., STEPHEN J. KUNITZ
1969   Notes on some White Mountain Apache social pathologies. *Plateau* 42(1):11–19.
1971   Indian reservations, anomie, and social pathologies. *Southwestern Journal of Anthropology* 27(2):97–128.

NASH, JUNE
1967   Death as a way of life: increasing resort to homicide in a Mayan Indian community. *American Anthropologist* 69(5):455–470

OGLE, RALPH
1970   *Federal control of the Western Apaches, 1848–1886.* Albuquerque: University of New Mexico Press.

PALMER, STUART
1965   Murder and suicide in forty non-literate societies. *Journal of Criminal Law, Criminology and Police Science* 56:320–324.

PARMEE, EDWARD
1968   *Formal education and culture change.* Tucson: University of Arizona Press.

PELTO, PERTI
1970   *Anthropological research.* New York: Harper and Row.

REAGAN, ALBERT B.
1930   "Notes on the Indians of the Fort Apache region," in *Anthropological Papers of the American Museum of Natural History* 31(5):281–345. New York.

SMITH, ELNA
1941   "Suicide among Indians of the United States since reservation life began." Unpublished manuscript.

SPICER, EDWARD H.
1962   *Cycles of conquest.* Tucson: University of Arizona Press.

THRAPP, DAN L.
1967   *The conquest of Apacheria.* Norman: University of Oklahoma Press.

TOPPER, MARTIN D.
n.d.   "Drinking and male adolescence: the Navajo experience," in *Indian drinking in the Southwest: An anthropological perspective.* Edited by Michael Everett and Jack Waddell. In preparation.

UNITED STATES BUREAU OF INDIAN AFFAIRS RESERVATION SUPERINTENDENTS
1934–1971   *Annual Reports: Fort Apache and San Carlos Reservations.* Unpublished manuscripts.

UNITED STATES COMMISSIONER OF INDIAN AFFAIRS
1878–1928   *Annual reports.* Washington: Government Printing Office.

UNITED STATES PUBLIC HEALTH SERVICE
1927–1971   White Mountain Apache United States Public Health Service hospital records.

WADDELL, JACK O.
n.d.   "Drinking and friendship: the Papago experience," in Indian drinking in the Southwest: an anthropological perspective. Edited by Michael Everett and Jack Waddell. In preparation.

WHARFIELD, HAROLD B.
1965   *With scouts and cavalry at Fort Apache.* Tucson: Arizona Pioneers' Historical Society.
1971   *Cibecue Creek Fight in Arizona, 1881.* El Cajon, California.

PART THREE

Formation of Dominance Hierarchies in Young Children

DONALD R. OMARK, MONICA OMARK, and
MURRAY EDELMAN

The formation of social groups is one of the many possible responses which organisms can take to lessen environmental pressures like predator attacks, severe climatic changes, and so forth. If we assume that social groups are phylogenetic adaptations to those pressures, then the internal organization of the group should reflect adaptations that will tend to preserve group social structures. Some of these adaptations should be accessible to study by human ethologists. The more traditional ethological approach would be to seek adaptations in the overt behaviors exhibited by members of the group. Overt behaviors can be examined through a variety of techniques (Altmann 1973). Human ethologists have opted for a highly refined catalogue of behaviors (Blurton Jones 1972; McGrew 1972), while primatologists have employed similar catalogues as well as total group measures of behavior (Kummer 1968; Carpenter 1964). The present paper will report on a modified use of Kummer's nearest-neighbor-method of recording social interactions and spacing patterns. These results will serve as background for the findings of the perceptual portion of the study.

A more radical approach would seek adaptations in the ways in which group members structure their perceptions of group organization. The latter approach provides the major focus of this paper, reporting on a three-culture study of young children who range from kindergarten age through third grade. The area of perception has not been extensively

The results reported in this study were supported in part by contracts from the Office of Education and the National Institute of Education. The opinions expressed here are not to be taken as reflecting the views of either of these. For help in coding data and reading the manuscript we thank Janet Bare, Ken Rabb, Rita Sussman and Gay Ummel.

explored by human ethologists, although one of the earliest ethological investigators in the field did suggest its importance (v. Uexkull 1957). The basic concept is the *Umwelt* which refers to the perceived and conceived world of the organism. An animal's *Umwelt* includes both the objects and social beings necessary for its survival and reflects the evolutionary process through which the species has become adapted to its own ecological niche. The way an organism structures its perceptions is viewed as open to natural selection, especially to that selection which will foster the maintenance of the group (Omark and Ziegler 1965; Edelman and Omark 1973b). Humans are the only primates which can be questioned directly about their perceptions and this was the method adopted for the present study.

Within the areas of both action and perception an additional factor appears when studying the young of any species: the process of developmental change. For interrelated group-living organisms, the reproductive success of the group replaces individual reproductive success as the measure of evolutionary survival. The total group structure is the unit which is selected for or against. A major developmental factor would then be the young organism's ability to move toward and integrate itself into the total group structure. This means that at every age social actions both by and toward the young organism should lead toward preserving its contact with the social group. Selective pressures should operate to produce behavioral and perceptual adaptations that are appropriate to the age of the organism and aid its social interactions.

An example of this continuing social contact can be seen in the weaning process that occurs in many primate species. The infant is first attached to the mother and protected directly by her. As he is weaned his actions shift from being oriented primarily towards mother to being oriented towards peers. Within very broad limits, even with very quick and severe weaning, contact is not lost with the group, but simply shifts from attachment to one individual in the group to attachment to many others. The process occurs within a protective system that is also shifting. At first protection is given by the mother and then by sub-adult and adult males. It is not until the juvenile is older and more independently viable that emigration from the group might occur.

The hypothesized perceptual changes that might occur during the weaning process start from a base condition where attention is primarily directed towards one other — the mother. The next phase seems to be one of size differentiation between mother and her cohorts, and small juveniles. Attention is increasingly directed toward the latter. The *Umwelt* of the juvenile has expanded along at least a size dimension and possibly an activity dimension, if this is what attracts the juvenile's attention to other juveniles. Once in the peer group the next major perceptual change appears to be a differentiation between others, based on their relative abilities. With time this produces the perception of a dominance hierarchy with the elements of seriation, transitivity, and in-group out-group categories. This perceptual and conceptual world rapidly expands as coalitions, friendships, and other relationships are added.

While the juvenile progresses through this series of stages in which his *Umwelt* becomes increasingly differentiated he is also being increasingly confronted by his peers. His actions are frequently blocked, thwarted, and redirected. Under these conditions escape from the immediate situation may occur but escape from the total group is rare. After momentary flight the juvenile returns to the peer group and continues his encounters with them. This sort of action pattern seen in other primates as well as human children led to one area of speculation in the present study.

The hypothesis under study was that juveniles have perceptual adaptations that enable them to confront their peer group instead of fleeing permanently from it. Until an individual's position was secure within a group, possible perceptual structures that would preclude escape would take the form of inaccuracies in perceiving relative positions of others, and inaccuracies in perceiving the position of the self. The first part of the hypothesis was confirmed for an American sample of nursery school and kindergarten aged children. The children's perceptions of relative positions of others improved rapidly with age and these earlier results will be compared to Swiss and Ethiopian results in the present paper (see Edelman and Omark 1973a). Inaccuracies in self perception did not improve as quickly in the American sample (Omark and Edelman 1973). While with increasing age each child came to place himself nearer the position assigned to him by his peers, when there was disagreement between pairs of children as to their relative position each child would rank himself higher. This tendency to "overrate" one's own position is viewed as a perceptual adaptation that enables each child to continue to confront his peer group. Examples of this overrating will be presented below from the three culture samples.

DESCRIPTION OF SAMPLE

Repeated observations and a variety of tests were gathered from approximately 450 American, 250 Swiss, and 250 Ethiopian children. The children ranged in schooling from nursery school through third grade. The American sample was taken from a private middle-class school, the Swiss from a public suburban school outside Zurich, and the Ethiopian sample from a public school in a large farming village with a population of approximately 2000.

In the following study the results are reported by grade level for the purpose of making comparisons in terms of the approximate amount of time during which the children were interacting in large peer groups. This does not mean that the same grade children are of the same age. In America children start kindergarten at approximately age five. The children in each succeeding grade are then $5+n$, where $n = $ the grade. In Switzerland the children start kindergarten at age five but they stay two years, hence the age at each succeeding grade is $6+n$. In Ethiopia the Swiss (or European) rule is followed, but because many of the children have to care for flocks, crops, younger siblings, and so forth, until the younger siblings are big enough to do this, the older siblings may not start school until they are twelve or more. Twelve and thirteen-year-olds are started in first grade, while children fourteen or older are started in third. These older children are permitted to move ahead as rapidly as they are able to complete the year's work. The average ages for the Ethiopian classes, as well as the range, are compared below in Table 1 with the typical age for the other cultures.

Table 1. Comparison of the age of children in the American, Swiss, and Ethiopian samples

Grade	American age	Swiss age	Ethiopian average age	Range
N	3–4	–	–	–
K	5	5–6	–	3–6
I	6	7	8.2	6–12
2	7	8	9.8	7–13
3	8	9	10.9	8–17

The hierarchical data for the various samples are strictly by grade level since the question about hierarchical status that will be examined refers to the class that the children are in currently. The above description of the Ethiopian sample indicates that there is a wide age range in any class and the expectation would be that the older children would be viewed as tougher. The detailed analysis of this expectation will be published later but let us describe here why this only partially occurs. A phenomenon that appears in primate troops (see Chance and Jolly 1970) also occurs with the human groups that we observed. There is a definite tendency for similar aged children to play together. In most cultures, as in our American and Swiss samples, this is probably due to familiarity — one simply plays with those in his own class. He only infrequently contacts a younger or older sibling and their playmates. In Ethiopia the children again seemed to segregate by ages, probably determined by activities being engaged in by the various ages. In terms of any hierarchy then, the oldest children were not interacting directly with the youngest children in their class and hence had not established a position relative to the younger class members.

Because of the age range in any Ethiopian class it was also difficult to tell what class any particular child occupied when he was observed on the playground. To compensate for this, the observed children were given an assigned grade based on their age which would be equivalent to the American sample (and one year younger than the corresponding Swiss sample). While birthdates are not recorded in most villages in Ethiopia, one of the same methods for determining age for admission to school is used in both Ethiopia and Switzerland and this was taken as the age of the child for comparative purposes.[1] Ninety-five percent accuracy was achieved between the ages we assigned and the various teachers' estimation of age.

OBSERVATIONS AND TEST METHODS

Playground Observations

A technique developed by Kummer (1968) for observing social relationships among Hamadryas baboons was modified for use with children. This technique will be referred to as nearest-neighbor-method. A scoring sheet was used and is included at the back of this paper (see Criteria for Observations in the Appendix). In particular, the four categories of behavior that were recorded on the sheets were: (1) the first, second and third neighbor of the child being observed, (2) the relative distance between the child and each of his neighbors, (3) the type of interaction, if any, occuring between the child and his neighbors, and (4) the activity level of the child during a portion of the observation period. A first neighbor is defined as the child spatially closest to the child being observed, the second neighbor as second closest, and so forth. The obser-

---

[1] In Germany and Switzerland a child is said to be physically mature enough to enter school if he or she can reach over their head with their arm and touch their opposite ear. This typically happens by age seven. The same criterion is used in Ethiopia.

vation period for each class was the morning or afternoon recess period, fifteen to twenty minutes in length. In America the classes tended to stagger their recess periods so that normally an entire class could be observed without confusion. In Switzerland and Ethiopia, where the children were of more than one grade level the size differential between the children permitted recording to continue. In the few instances when more than one class of the same level were on the playground the children were recorded as being in kindergarten, first grade, and so forth, and not in a particular class. The reliability of this method (95 percent accuracy) was checked with the teachers before actual recording began.

To be sure of observing each child the number of boys and girls in a class were noted as they came onto the playground. The child to be observed was selected by dividing the playground into two. A boy and a girl were observed on one half, and then a boy and a girl were observed on the other half. A short description was made of each child so that he or she would not be observed twice. The child was selected (from a listed predetermined random order), watched for approximately ten seconds to familiarize the observer with the situation, and then his interactions, distance from neighbors, and so forth were recorded as completely as possible for the instant following the end of the ten-second period. The distance covered — the activity level of the child — was recorded during the subsequent thirty-second period.

This present study was an attempt to relate children's grouping tendencies to the actions performed by other ground-dwelling primates. The types of interaction which occured on the playground are grouped categories of behavior rather than descriptions of finely detailed physical movements as found in an ethogram. There are two reasons for this procedure. First, the broad patterns, together with the children's perceived hierarchies would be sufficient to generate hypotheses about both children's and primates' group behavior that could be examined in more detail later. Second, an ethogram is meant to be a nearly exhaustive portion of an organism's behavioral repertoire. Hence, the preparation of one is fairly time consuming. Since the rules of data collection require that the definitions of the behavior patterns be complete before data collection begins,[2] the present study served as a time for

---

[2]   The logic behind this "rule" is that the apparent first appearance of a new behavior pattern in the middle of a study might lead one to want to begin recording its occurrence, use it for showing differences between groups, etc. In fact, it might have appeared earlier but it simply took some time before the investigator became aware of it. Hence, its sudden inclusion might weight against a group where it had occured but had not been noticed. Scoring from filmed records obviates this problem.

preparing the ethogram while collecting other data that could be immediately analyzed. The ethogram was then used on the Swiss sample and will be reported later. The categories of behavior listed under Criteria for Observations (see Appendix) were chosen to be broad enough to give a feeling of what occurs on the playground while still indicating areas where sex and age difference might be profitably explored with the finished ethogram. For already completed human ethograms the reader is referred to Blurton Jones (1972) and McGrew (1972).

Hierarchy Test

The existence of dominance hierarchies in primate troops is generally inferred from the physical encounters which occur between troop members. The recording of aggressive encounters on the playground only indicated that boys fought more than girls. A hierarchy could not be derived from these observations because the individual children involved were not recorded (except in the Swiss sample, results to be reported later). Instead of making more detailed observations we questioned the children about the dominance hierarchy which they perceived within their classrooms. The basic question asked was "Who is the toughest?"[3] Two different forms of the test were used, depending on the age of the children.

In kindergarten (American and Swiss samples) the children were photographed and snapshot size pictures were made of each child. On the day of the test each child was individually taken out into the hall. He was shown the photographs of his classmates, placed horizontally on a bench or on the floor. The photographs were arranged in alphabetical order by first name.

The instructions were: "I'm going to ask you some questions about your classmates. The first question is about toughness. Now what is another word for tough?" (If the child had trouble answering he was told "Do something tough.") "Now let us look at the first child in the row. If that child is tougher than you, turn his picture over." After the child acted, the experimenter made sure he understood the question. The experimenter then repeated the question with each picture until he was confident that the child understood the task. Then he said "Now continue on down the row, turning over the picture of each child that is

---

[3] Other questions were "Who is the smartest, nicest, and has the most friends"? Of these "toughest" had the earliest and highest dyadic agreement. Research is continuing in this area.

tougher than you". From first through third grade (in all three cultures) a paper and pencil test was used. The children's names were listed alphabetically down the side of a sheet of paper. The paper was cut so that tabs with each child's name could be easily torn off. The children were also given a sheet of paper with the numbers one through the size of the class listed down the left-hand side. The children were told to "Look through the list of names and tear off the name of the child who is the very toughest in the class. Place that name beside the number one. Now look through the list and find the next toughest child and place that name beside the number two, etc".

In Switzerland and Ethiopia the instructions were translated into the native dialect. A short story preceded the above instructions to define the word "toughest." The story was basically that money or candy was thrown from a passing car or carriage toward a group of children who were standing and watching it pass. One of two named children simply stood and watched while the other named child pushed his way forward through the crowd and got most of the money or candy. We then asked the children in the classroom, "Who was the toughest?" They answered this without error. The story and other instructions were translated from English into dialect by one group of teachers, and translated back by a separate group, modified, etc. until the original English reappeared. The scene described was common in both the Swiss village, where candy is thrown out by the bride and bridegroom on their wedding day as they drive away; and in the Ethiopian village, where the Emperor comes through once a year and throws out money. This had happened shortly before testing began.

Results

Selected results are reported below. The American portion of this study is described in full in Omark (1972) and Edelman (1973). Only the results from early in the school year are presented from the Swiss data. Comparisons between this early data and that obtained later in the school year will be reported elsewhere. Due to computational difficulties, only partial results can be reported on the Ethiopian hierarchical data. These, too, will be reported in more detail at a later date.

The significance levels reported below were derived only from the American data, unless otherwise indicated. Most of the patterns found in the results from the other two cultures were very similar to the American results. With the exception of the playground observations on the

Swiss kindergartens the sample sizes were sufficient to assume that statements about sex and developmental differences are equally applicable in all three cultures. Deviations in the patterns are noted in this paper, and relevant significance levels will be presented for all three cultures in a further paper.

Playground Observations

From the observations of nearest neighbors on the playgrounds it was found that boys associated with boys, while girls tended to be near girls. As can be seen in Table 2, the only reversal in this pattern occurs in the Swiss kindergartens where the number of observations was

Table 2. Distribution of the children's nearest neighbors (NN = 1, 2 and 3 combined) as a percentage of the total observations on each sex

Child observed	Nearest neighbors	Grade				
		N	K	1	2	3
America						
Boys	Boys	49	65	74	66	–
	Girls	30	28	22	29	–
	Teachers	20	6.5	4.1	5.2	–
	n obs.	105	211	181	84	–
Girls	Boys	29	40	20	39	–
	Girls	49	49	70	52	–
	Teachers	22	11	10	8.6	–
	n obs.	95	195	217	86	–
Switzerland						
Boys	Boys	–	66	64	–	85
	Girls	–	34	36	–	13
	Teachers	–	0	1	–	1.4
	n obs.	–	27	62	–	72
Girls	Boys	–	48	28	–	14
	Girls	–	44	69	–	79
	Teachers	–	8.4	2.7	–	7
	n obs.	–	16	60	–	58
Ethiopia						
Boys	Boys	63	71	63	77	81
	Girls	35	28	35	20	17
	Teachers	2.7	1.1	1	2.5	1.5
	n obs	61	62	65	65	65
Girls	Boys	23	21	25	32	28
	Girls	72	73	74	65	69
	Teachers	4.7	3.2	1	2.5	3.1
	n obs.	63	62	65	65	65

small. The affinity for like sex neighbors appears earliest in the Ethiopian data (nursery school) with the boys in the other two cultures reaching similar levels by kinderkarten. The neighbors of girls in America and Switzerland are not predominantly girls until first grade.

Part of the reason for the appearance of boys as neighbors of boys earlier than girls with girls can be seen in a different type of measure made on the American sample (Omark and Edelman 1973). The size of the group children associated with was observed and it was found that in the grades after nursery school the sizes of boys' groups were larger than were girls' groups (both in terms of the maximum and average group size). The groups increased for both sexes as they matured, but the boys' rate of increase was higher. Overall, the boys tended to move in large swarms, while the girls generally associated in groups of twos and threes. The combined percentages for the three nearest neighbors (Table 2) reflects this phenomena of boys being in large groups earlier. A chi square for children being with a like-sexed FIRST nearest neighbor (NNI) is very significant ($p \leqslant 0.005$) even in the Swiss kindergarten classes. Girls are with a girl very early, while boys are with a group of boys.

As in private groups girls were seen to be near teachers a significantly larger percent of the observations than were the boys ($p \leqslant 0.005$, America). As with the American data the results for the other cultures indicate that the girls' rate of association is twice as high as the boys' (see Blurton Jones 1972). The primary trend in the American data was towards fewer contacts with adults with increasing age. The other cultures indicate that trend may be curvilinear with a low point in first grade and increased contact, especially for the girls, towards third grade.

Physical interaction, such as playful wrestling, holding hands, engaging in a group game, or throwing a ball to one another increases with age for both sexes in the American and Swiss data (Table 3). In contrast, the Ethiopian children exhibit two trends. The boys show a decline in first and second grade as they enter classes which have a wide age spread (see sample). The girls show a dip in kindergarten but otherwise maintain approximately the same level of interaction. A more refined analysis of who the children were playing with and what kinds of interactions were occurring will be reported later. As can be seen in Table 3, with only one exception (the small Swiss kindergarten sample) the boys are physically interacting with more of their second and third neighbors, in all of the cultures, than are the girls. This again reflects the larger size groups with which the boys are involved.

In the American sample the girls were significantly more verbal across the grades than were the boys ($p \leqslant 0.005$). The same finding would

Table 3. Percentage of the observations in which children were physically interacting with each of their three nearest neighbors (The number of observations is the same as in Table 2.)

Grade	Nearest neighbor	Sex of observed child					
		America		Switzerland		Ethiopia	
		Boys	Girls	Boys	Girls	Boys	Girls
N	1	23	14	–	–	36	33
	2	6	6	–	–	18	13
	3	1	3	–	–	16	6
K	1	15	9	33	50	31	29
	2	10	6	4	31	24	5
	3	7	4	0	10	13	3
1st	1	36	13	30	30	26	45
	2	31	8	13	13	10	12
	3	28	6	11	7	6	2
2nd	1	51	32	–	–	23	38
	2	48	25	–	–	10	12
	3	44	21	–	–	9	5
3rd	1	–	–	42	40	35	42
	2	–	–	30	24	23	10
	3	–	–	28	9	14	5

appear to apply in the other cultures (Table 4). As was found for physical interactions, verbalization among girls can be seen to be directed primarily toward the first nearest neighbor, with the marked exceptions of the Ethiopian kindergarten and Swiss third grade girls; all of the boys equal or exceed the girls' verbalizations with the combined second and third neighbors.

Across all grades the American boys were significantly more aggressive than the girls ($p \leqslant 0.009$, Table 5). This result should be even more significant for the other two cultures. While the aggressiveness of American boys followed a curvilinear pattern that peaked in kindergarten and first grade and then declined, the results of the other two cultures indicate that another high point may occur in third grade. Whether this continues or declines requires further research. The reverse curve that appeared for American girls appears to be repeated in the other cultures. Since different factors were involved in the school related formation of these groups in the three cultures (see sample) the similarities between the boys' aggressive patterns, and between the girls' aggressive patterns, suggest that there may be: (1) an age related factor operating, or (2) an experiential factor based upon time spent in large peer groups.

Both the Swiss and Ethipian data on aggression (Table 5) appear much higher than the American sample. The authors feel that this should

Table 4. Percentage of the observations in which children were talking with their nearest neighbors (The number of observations is the same as in Table 2.)

Grade	Nearest neighbor	Sex of observed child					
		America		Switzerland		Ethiopia	
		Boys	Girls	Boys	Girls	Boys	Girls
N	1	31	40	–	–	13	29
	2	14	14	–	–	10	6
	3	5	4	–	–	7	2
K	1	55	56	37	63	19	40
	2	27	29	29	31	8	31
	3	13	13	19	13	8	16
1st	1	57	62	23	30	22	26
	2	33	26	30	23	12	11
	3	15	13	22	13	3	8
2nd	1	33	54	–	–	23	25
	2	29	32	–	–	14	6
	3	18	12	–	–	12	8
3rd	1	–	–	29	41	25	35
	2	–	–	14	41	12	12
	3	–	–	14	28	9	8

Table 5. Percentage of observations in which aggression occured between the observed child and his neighbors (The number of observations is the same as in Table 2.)

Grade	Sex of observed child					
	America		Switzerland		Ethiopia	
	Boys	Girls	Boys	Girls	Boys	Girls
N	3	4	–	–	13	5
K	7	1	4	0	23	2
1	6	1	16	4	16	2
2	2	3	–	–	12	9
3	–	–	16	6	20	8

not be taken as indicating that either the Swiss or Ethiopian children are more aggressive than American children. Rather, it shows the grossness of this behavior category. All hitting, pushing hard, pulling toward hard, and so forth, were recorded as aggression if they occurred without a smile or laughing. The presence or absence of the latter "friendly" components of behavior may be culturally related and hence raise or lower the apparent occurrence of aggression. The observations were consistent within each culture so that the developmental patterns should be comparable even if the levels of occurrence may not be. More detailed ethological observations are indicated in order to separate out the culturally related behaviors from the more universal behavioral characteristics. The Swiss children were examined in more detail and will be reported later. The reader is referred to Blurton Jones (1972) and McGrew (1972) for further ethological observations of children of the type that it is hoped will appear for other cultural groups.

A number of other measurements were obtained on the playground. The results which follow are for the American sample, but an initial examination of the other cultures indicates that the same directionality will occur. For all grades from nursery school through second grade the boys were more active in terms of the total distance covered during a thirty-second observation period ($p \leqslant 0.005$). Boys also maintained a greater distance between themselves and other children ($p \leqslant 0.05$), and between themselves and teachers. If opposite sex neighbors happened to occur they were significantly farther apart than same sex neighbors ($p \leqslant 0.001$).

Hierarchy Test Results

In studying children's perceptions of dominance hierarchies, the following are the major questions: Where are they in the hierarchy; Do pairs of children agree about their position; Can they accurately perceive others; and How do they perceive themselves? These questions will be explored in terms of sex differences, developmental changes, and cultural effects.

POSITION WITHIN THE HIERARCHY   Each class tested was asked to arrange the students in their class in a hierarchical order on the basis of "Who is the toughest?". The relative hierarchy formed by the averaged scores assigned to each child resulted in hierarchies in which boys were placed at the top, girls near the bottom, and considerable overlap in the middle. The results for each culture can be seen in Table 6. This configuration occurred in all three cultures at the youngest age tested (nursery school in America, kindergarten in Switzerland, and first grade in Ethiopia) and continued through the third grade. This is the same pattern found in many primate troops.

The American data covers the broadest range of grades and an examination of it shows that there is a developmental change between nursery school and kindergarten, with even fewer girls appearing near the upper end as the children get older. A similar shift occurs in the Ethiopian data between first and second grade. The shift might occur later in this

Table 6.   Dominance hierarchy distribution of children by quintile rank at each grade level (in % of each sex)

American sample

Grade	Sex	Quintile rank					
		N	1	2	3	4	5
N	Boys	22	27	23	23	23	5
	Girls	19	5	5	26	26	37
K	Boys	69	29	35	25	10	1
	Girls	47	0	2	13	46	40
1	Boys	54	31	35	22	7	4
	Girls	50	4	6	12	36	42
2	Boys	55	25	38	25	5	5
	Girls	45	4	0	13	33	49
3	Boys	38	32	42	16	8	3
	Girls	36	0	0	25	33	42

Swiss sample

Grade	Sex	Quintile rank					
		N	1	2	3	4	5
K	Boys	–	–	–	–	–	–
	Girls	–	–	–	–	–	–
1	Boys	30	40	37	23	0	0
	Girls	30	0	3	17	40	40
2	Boys	29	34	38	14	10	3
	Girls	24	0	0	29	33	38
3	Boys	35	31	34	31	3	0
	Girls	28	4	4	7	43	43

Ethiopian sample

Grade	Sex	Quintile rank					
		N	1	2	3	4	5
1	Boys	18	22	17	33	17	11
	Girls	14	14	29	0	29	29
2	Boys	19	37	21	11	21	11
	Girls	22	5	18	32	18	27
3	Boys	34	35	18	21	15	12
	Girls	29	3	21	21	24	31

culture because the Ethiopian children's first experience with large groups did not occur until first grade. In Switzerland even the young kindergarten boys were already perceived to be near the top of their hierarchy. No age change occured between the sexes. The Swiss kindergarten children remained together for two years with new children starting each year. Hence there always existed an established hierarchy which might have marked the experimental change found in the other two cultures. The "new" kindergarten children will be examined separately at a future time. Agreement on the total hierarchy did change however and this will be examined next.

Because of technical difficulties, the following sections will be limited to comparisons between the American and Swiss grade school results. The Swiss kindergarten and Ethiopian results will be presented at a later time.

AGREEMENT ON THE PERCEIVED HIERARCHY   The basic unit of analysis for the hierarchy test was the dyads of established dominance. The percent of dyadic agreement was formed by taking those pair where both children agreed on who was the dominant child and dividing by the possible dyads from the class. For example, if John said that Bill was "tougher" than John, and Bill said that Bill was "tougher" than John, this pair was said to be an established dyad on "toughness."

Following the ages suggested by Piaget, it was hypothesized that the school child (age seven) could readily perceive a hierarchical relationship, and hence would have a higher dyadic agreement than the pre-chool child. This was tested on the kindergarten through third grade American sample. In examining all of the possible dyads within each class it was found that there was highly significant linear trend ($F = 79.2$, $p \leqslant 0.0001$), with the largest jump in agreement on relative status occurring between kindergarten (40 percent) and first grade (62 percent). This large increase in percent of dyadic agreement corresponded to a similar increase on a smaller sample where the underlying cognitive level was measured (see Edelman and Omark 1973b). Children seemed to develop a consistent perception of their dominance structure at the same time as they were developing the logical operations of seriation and transitivity.

In Figure 1 this same trend toward increasing agreement with increasing age is also evident in the Swiss sample. The American sample is composed of four classes at each grade except third which has three classes. The Swiss sample has two chasses at each grade level, and hence its curve is not as regular as the American. It should be noted that the Swiss were tested both early and late in each school year, while the American sample was only tested late in the year.

The Swiss change in agreement across first grade is equivalent to the American shift from kindergarten to first. The "early" Swiss and the "late" American samples should be approximately the same age, but their percent of dyadic agreement is not the same, so this agreement is

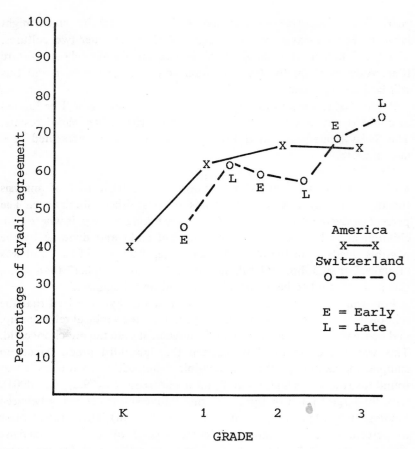

Figure 1.   Percentage of dyadic agreement in a class across cross-sex and same-sex pairings for "toughest"

not simply a maturational phenomena. The "early" Swiss have had two years since most of them went to nursery school, but the low level of agreement shown by both groups indicates that even two years of experience was not sufficient. It would then appear that the change to the more structured environment of first grade aids in the increase of perceptual awareness of peers' status relationships, despite the fact that physical encounters are sharply curtailed.

As an alternate explanation, the marked increase in agreement found at the end of first grade may be the result of an interaction between a certain level of conceptual maturity and some finite amount of experience. In essence, when a child's perceptual and conceptual *Umwelt* has matured to the stage where it can assimilate status relationships from the social environment it will be able to do so, and, perhaps without too much experience being necessary. The following comments on the relationship between playground behavior and agreement on the hierarchy may help indicate how much experience is necessary at different ages.

In the American sample the peak in agressive encounters on the playground for the boys extended across kindergarten to first grade, and the children's perceptions of dominance relationships appeared to follow from this experience. As discussed elsewhere, the younger nursery school children fought much less and were almost unable to form a hierarchy (Edelman and Omark 1973a). They gave extremely self-centered responses, almost always placing themselves first or second in any hierarchy, but experiences in kindergarten and first grade seemed to structure their perceptions in a way that substantiated the view that a dominance hierarchy existed within each classroom. For the older Swiss children an aggressive peak occurred early in the first grade and their perceptual agreement followed within the same school year. The children, of course, perform the actions which they then perceive, and the performance is probably amenable to cultural influences. But as a first approximation it is estimated that at least half a year's experience is necessary before agreement will be reached in seven to eight years olds, and a year's experience will be needed in a six to seven year old group.

The second grade decline in the Swiss data was due to one class that apparently could not resolve its status differences. This class was not part of the observational schedule but extemporaneous observations by both the observers and other teachers indicated that this class had a higher frequency of fighting than the other Swiss classes. This was the only class in which the percent of agreement declined across the school year.[4]

The literature on primate social life indicates that: (1) males generally rank higher than females, and (2) a well-developed hierarchical structure is common among males but not as common among the females in primate groups. Hence, it was hypothesized that most agreement on "toughest" would be between boy-girl pairs, followed by boy-boy pairs and then girl-girl pairs. This hypothesis was clearly confirmed for the American and Swiss samples as seen in Figure 2. Boy-girl pairs had

---

[4] A similar phenomenon was reported for a third grade American class which contained a number of boys who, in separate earlier classes, had been found to be at or near the top of their respective hierarchies. This class remained disrupted throughout the school year despite the presence of a very experienced teacher. In both of these classes lack of stability in their classroom hierarchies appeared to interfere with the attainment of educational objectives. This interrelationship merits further research.

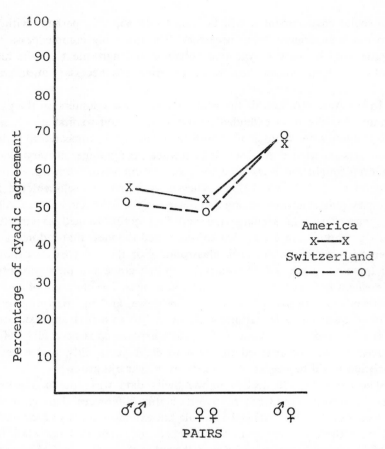

Figure 2.   Percentage of dyadic agreement for same-sex and cross-sex pairs across all grades

an agreement ranging from 68 percent to 69 percent (Swiss figure is first), boy-boy pairs in the two cultures were 51 percent to 55 percent, and girl-girl pairs were 48 percent to 52 percent. For the American sample the difference between cross-sex dyads and boy dyads was highly significant ($F=16.5$, $p \leqslant 0.0008$), as well as the difference between boy-boy and girl-girl dyads ($F=5.02$, $p \leqslant 0.036$). The Swiss sample should approximate these results.

Accuracy of Perception

The percent accuracy of perception measures the child's perception of dominance in those dyads of established dominance of which he is not a member. This is formed by counting the number of correct choices of the dominant child in the dyads of established dominance and dividing by the total number of dyads where choices were made. The average percent accuracy for boys and girls in each class for same-sex and cross-sex dyads was used for the analysis.

In the American sample it was found that both sexes had the most accurate perception of the dominance relationships in boy-girl pairs ($F=44.0$, $p \leqslant 0.0001$), followed by boy pairs ($F=23.4$, $p \leqslant 0.0001$), and then girl pairs (Edelman 1973). This is the same order as found for percent of agreement in both the American and Swiss samples (Figure 2). Table 7 shows that the Swiss boys and girls each exhibit the same di-

Table 7. Percentage of the dyads of established dominance accurately perceived by Swiss children (all classes combined)

Early in school year Pairs Perceived	Perceiving children Boys	Girls
Boys with boys	78.5	74.4
Girls with girls	55.4	63.4
Boys with girls	86.0	82.4
Late in school year Boys with boys	85.1	84.4
Girls with girls	67.5	71.3
Boys with girls	89.9	87.6

rectionality in accurately perceiving dominance relationships, and this relationship occurs both early and late in the school year.

Although different pairs are more accurately perceived, Figure 3 shows that the accuracy of the PERCEIVERS is as high for girls as it is for boys. This occurs in both the American and Swiss samples. For the American children this amounted to no difference in accuracy of perception between the sexes ($F=1.17$). That the upper end of the hierarchy is more accurately perceived, and that both sexes are accurate perceivers, supports the parallel to primate social structure suggested by Chance and Jolly (1970), that stable group functioning is dependent upon all members of the group paying attention to the dominant members.

Figure 3 also indicates that there is a developmental increase across the school year in overall accuracy of perception. The Swiss children are also higher than the American children. This may be due to the fact that Swiss children remain together through the first three years of school and hence have more opportunities to observe pair relationships. Across the grades in the American sample there were relatively insignif-

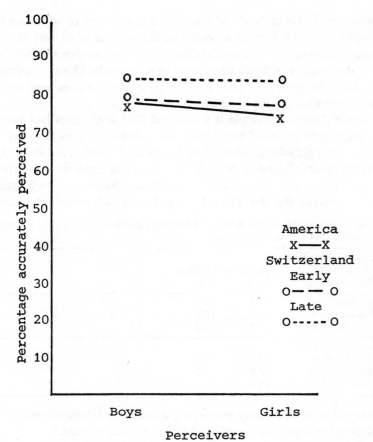

Figure 3. Accuracy of perception for boys and girls rating same-sex and cross-sex pairs on "toughest"

icant developmental changes in accuracy of perception, while major changes occurred in the Swiss sample which again may be related to total time together. The details of this developmental trend will be presented later.

Overrating

As juveniles of other primate species are weaned from their mothers they move towards their peers. Weaning always extends over a period of time and the young can be seen moving back and forth between the mother and a "juvenile cluster," but with increasing amounts of time being spent near the other juveniles. This cluster gradually differentiates into like-sexed groups: the males engaging together in rough-and-tumble play, while the young females sit and groom other young females or try to hold the infants who are still associated with adult females (Chance and Jolly 1970).

With children the formation of peer groups occurs when they are sent to school. The association of children with like-sexed partners appears as early as nursery school — the human weaning period — with girls quietly engaging in conversations (and grooming) with other girls, while boys are engaged in rough-and-tumble play with other boys. These analogous behavior patterns are the precursors for entrance into each group's hierarchical structure.

An important consideration during this developmental process is that both boys and juvenile males have to survive aggressive encounters with others without resorting to permanent escape from their group. The task is only slightly less severe for the young females of the many species which have either female hierarchies or total group hierarchies. Escape beyond the group is an unsatisfactory solution in terms of primate and human groups at their present stage of evolutionary development.

One behavioral solution to the problem of establishing and maintaining a position within a group's social structure was evident on the playgrounds observed. Children play, and fight, with similar aged children. This occurred even in the mixed-age classes in Ethiopia. This segregation by age and size limits aggressive encounters to a physical scale which most children are capable of tolerating. The same phenomena occurred during our observations on juvenile Hamadryas baboons. In general, young males and females do not attempt to enter the adult hierarchy, but rather establish a position among their peer group cohorts.

Although this behavioral solution limits the severity of aggressive encounters, a continuing aggressive experience might lead some children of juveniles to flee their group of peers. This might be especially true for the individuals at the bottom of any hierarchy who perceive themselves as continuously losing encounters. One perceptual and conceptual solution to this problem — an age related structuring of a child's *Umwelt* — was suggested by the work of Piaget and others.

Young nursery school aged children were found to be egocentric in that they had difficulty in recognizing that an object which they were viewing, such as a picture, might not be visible to someone else. They would nonetheless proceed to discuss the object as if the other could see it. In essence, they could not imagine themselves in the position of the other. We hypothesized that not only could they not conceptualize the relationship of another to the self, but also that they lacked an accurate self-perception in relation to the other.

This lack of an accurate self-perception was readily apparent when testing nursery school children. When pairs of children were questioned as to who was tougher, both would shout "me" even after one of them had just lost an encounter (Edelman and Omark 1973a). Similarly McGrew (1972) found in his study of preschoolers that it did not seem to matter in terms of children's subsequent behavior if they lost an encounter to another child of lower status than themselves (status being determined by number of successful bouts between children). If, in fact, young children generally perceive themselves as "winning" despite frequent experience to the contrary, then we would hypothesize the existence of a perceptual or cognitive structure which serves the function of promoting entrance into a hierarchically structured social group.

A heightened estimation of the position of the self vis-à-vis others was termed "overrating." It has already been shown that agreement between pairs of children increases with age so that the amount of overrating was examined in those pairs where disagreement still occurred. Of these remaining pairs both children could say that the other was tougher, or both could say that the self was tougher. A disagreeing pair where both children said the self was tougher was termed overrating and the percent of overrating is formed by taking all of those pairs and dividing by all of the pairs in which disagreement occurred. Because of the increased number of aggressive encounters experienced by boys it was hypothesized that they would more frequently overrate their position than would girls.

Figure 4 shows the comparison of the amount of overrating between same and cross-sexed pairs. Both the American and Swiss samples exhibit the same pattern. For the American data boys were found to overrate in comparison to other boys significantly more than girls overrated themselves with other girls ($p \leqslant 0.006$). Eighty to ninety percent of the American boys' pairs where disagreement occurred overrated themselves from kindergarten through third grade. The range for the Swiss boys was 97 to 100 percent within the various classes.

Two slightly different forms of the hierarchy test were given to the American and Swiss samples. They resulted in the same pattern between the sexes, but different developmental trends were produced. The boys in both cultures maintain a high rate of overrating across the grades, and the Swiss girls are fairly consistent (in first grade, 89 percent; in second, 92 percent; in third, 86 percent). In contrast the American girls' amount of overrating changed markedly (K, 98 percent; first grade,

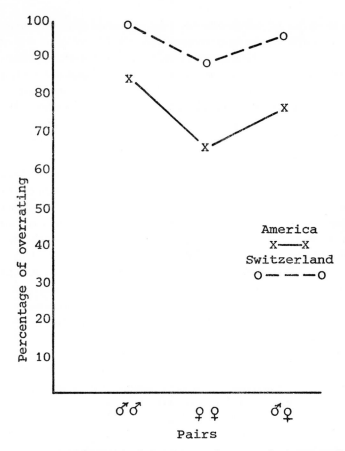

Figure 4.   Percentage of overrating for same-sex and cross-sex dyads across all grades

28 percent; third, 81 percent). It was originally hypothesized that the girls' shift from overrating in kindergarten to underrating in first grade might have been due to their response to adult authority, i.e. an attempt to be "good," or it might have been a withdrawal from the rough-and-tumble world of the boys — a time for watching and learning about others. Whether this difference between the girls in the two cultures is simply an artifact of the tests given or is due to some other factor will be explored further.

CONCLUSIONS

Young children's social behavior in all three cultures exhibited patterns of similarity, both to each other and to a generalized primate paradigm. These similarities were most evident with sex differences in the size and composition of the children's groups, their amount of association with an adult, and the levels of activity and aggressive actions. The children's perceptions of dominance hierarchies within their classrooms resembled the hierarchies derived from the actions of primates where males are at the top, females at the bottom and considerable overlap in the middle.

Detailed examination of the perceived hierarchies were limited to two cultures — American and Swiss. In both of these it was found that: boys had more agreement on their portion of the hierarchy than girls, and boys are tougher than girls (which had even more agreement for both sexes). Despite the apparent lack of contact between the sexes during play periods, the children's direction of attention included the opposite sex. It was found that each sex could accurately perceive the hierarchy created by the opposite sex. Boys were more involved in aggressive encounters and an apparently necessary corollary of this was that the boys overrated their own status position. Swiss girls were almost as high as the boys in overrating their own position, but American girls went through a period of underrating. Questions were raised about this difference and future research is planned.

From an ethological perspective the interplay between cognitive development and social experiencing would be expected to have phylogenetic as well as individually historic components. Since a social world is a prime necessity for humans and other primates, adaptations for adequate survival in relation to that world would be expected to have occurred through the process of natural selection. In essence, this means that a child's development, including his perceptual and cognitive development, should be expected to exhibit characteristic behavior and thought patterns which enable him to adequately function in the particular social world which each age encounters. From the increase on agreement on a status hierarchy with age, it can be seen that a child's *Umwelt*, aided by experience, expands as he or she gets older. In contrast, that portion of the *Umwelt* which includes the self may resist experience in a way which facilitates a child's entrance to his peer group.

The way children conceptualize their world at each age level can then be seen not only in how they manipulate sticks, volumes, or masses but also in the way they interact with and perceive their social world. The amount of agreement about one aspect of the children's peer groups that was found at a very young age indicates that their ability to seriate appears as early for social interactions as it does for the physical world. Another portion of the study indicates that this also occurs for transitive relations and that a great deal of emotional involvement is attached to perceptions of social interactions (Edelman and Omark 1973b). Agreement about the structure of the social world even occurred where direct interaction was very limited as in the low level of interaction found between boys and girls on the playground. Children's abilities to pay attention to others is viewed as a very necessary adaptation that enables them to organize and develop their cognitive abilities. The age changes that occur in these abilities are seen as adaptations that enable the children to continue to move towards peers without being swamped by information and experiences that they are not yet able to assimilate.

If ethology has a message that is relevant for child development, it is that a broader perspective needs to be taken when viewing development. This perspective has to include what the child brings to each encounter with his environment from his phylogenetic past. The question to always ask is "Why does this child act the way he does?", and to look for the answers in more than just immediate cause-and-effect relationships.

APPENDIX: CRITERIA FOR OBSERVATIONS

	Dist.	Verb.	Agg.	Imit.	Int.	Comments
x—N2						
N2						
N3						
Dist. Cov.						
Other						

Explanation:
x   – The child being observed.
Dist. Cov. – This is an activity score and is an estimate of the total distance covered by the child during the 30 seconds he is observed.
N1, N2, N3 – These are the three nearest neighbors, spatially, to x. They may or may not be interacting.
Dist.   – This is the distance which each is from x. This will be recorded as:
            ($<1/3$ m.) C – actual contact with x.
            ($<$ 1 m.) T – within touching distance if both N and x raised their arms, but not touching.
            (1–2 m.) S – normal speaking distance
            ($>$ 2 m.) Y – yelling distance

Verb. – A check is put here if X or N is talking during the observation period. If direction of communication can be determined, an arrow is inserted in the box, e.g. → means x talks to N; = means both are talking to each other.

Agg. – A check here means that an obvious physical aggressive encounter took place, e.g. hitting, punching, pulling down. If the fighting is onesided, an arrow indicates the attacker.

Imit. – A check here indicates imitative behavior, e.g. two or more engaged in the same kind of action, at the same time.

Int. – Interaction is occuring between x and N, but it is not aggressive or imitative. Describe under comments.

Comments – These lines are for comments about the gestures, imitative actions, etc. Interactions will be briefly described here.

REFERENCES

ALTMANN, J.
1973 Observational study of behavior: sampling methods. *Behaviour.*
BLURTON JONES, N., *editor*
1972 *Ethological studies of child behavior.* Cambridge, England: Cambridge University Press.
CARPENTER, C. R.
1964 *Naturalistic behavior of non-human primates.* University Park, Pennsylvania: Pennsylvania State University Press.
CHANCE, M. R. A., C. J. JOLLY
1970 *Social groups of monkeys, apes and men.* New York: Dutton.
EDELMAN, M. S.
1973 "Peer group formation in young children: perception." Unpublished doctoral dissertation, University of Chicago.
EDELMAN, M. S., D. R. OMARK
1973a Dominance hierarchies in young children. *Social Science Information* 12(1).
1973b "The development of logical operations in the social world – an ethnological approach." Paper presented at the SRCD meeting in Philadelphia.
KUMMER, H.
1968 *Social organization of Hamadryas baboons.* Chicago: University of Chicago Press.
MC GREW, W. C.
1972 *An ethological study of children's behavior.* London: Academic Press.
OMARK, D. R.
1972 "Peer group formation in young children: action." Unpublished doctoral dissertation, University of Chicago.
OMARK, D. R., M. S. EDELMAN
1973 "Peer group interactions from an evolutionary perspective." Paper presented at the SRCD meeting in Philadelphia.

OMARK, D. R., J. ZIEGLER
  1965 "The Umwelt." Unpublished manuscript.
V. UEXKULL, J.
  1957 "A stroll through the worlds of animals and man," in *Instinctive behavior*. Edited by C. Schiller. New York: International Universities Press. (Originally published 1925.)

Aggression in the !Ko-Bushmen

I. EIBL-EIBESFELDT

The question of whether the aggressive behavior of man is solely a result of learning processes, or whether phylogenetic adaptations pre-program it to any significant extent is a matter of controversy. Proponents of the learning theory of aggression repeatedly point to the existence of non-aggressive peoples (Helmuth 1967; Schmidbauer 1971b, 1972; Montagu 1968). These statements, however, do not stand critical examination. The allegedly peaceful Eskimos actually perform a rich variety of aggressive acts although most tribes settle their disputes in a fashion that does not result in bloodshed. The tribes of Siberia, Alaska, Baffinland, and Northwest Greenland settle their disputes by wrestling, and occasionally one gets killed. The Eskimos in Central Greenland slap each others' faces; in West and East Greenland song duels are favorite mens of settling disputes. The Kwakiutl Indians have been described as a people lacking the "instinct" to fight and are well known for their Potlatch Feasts during which the chiefs compete fiercely to outdo the guests by destroying valuables. Their songs are aggressive and they call it a fight. It is difficult to understand how one could possibly come to the conclusion that these people lack aggression.

The myth of the aggressionless society is old — it actually dates back to Rousseau — and has popped up again and again. Nansen, by creating the myth of the aggression-free Eskimos, wanted to create a favorable picture of his beloved people. Koenig pointed to this fact in 1925:

Um zunächst einmal das letztere [the alleged peacefulness] zu beleuchten, so ist seine Quelle, auf die er dieses Urteil über das Volk stützt, einzig und allein Nansen. Dieser hat aber die Eskimos im Naturzustand nur sehr wenig kennengelernt und sein moralisches Urteil über sie — das er besonders in seinem

"Eskimoleben" kundgibt — ist durchaus tendenziös gefärbt, da er Mitleid erwecken wollte.[1]

Although this correction was published in 1925, the myth is not at all dead. On the contrary: in blaming our industrial-achievement society for all aggression, the members of hunting and gathering societies are depicted as the noble, noncompetitive, and therefore nonaggressive savages. The argument runs like this:

If human aggressiveness is a phylogenetically determined disposition, then it must be especially evident in those cultures which characterized the stage occupying 99 % of the human evolutionary timetable. The stage here in question is designated as the Stone Age, characterized by the patterns of roaming hunters and gatherers. If such groups of hunters and gatherers had existed for approx. one million years, one can assume that the psychological and physical properties of [present] man became deeply ingrained at this time. The mere ten thousand years in which man became a farmer could have hardly changed the genetic biological basis of the human. If there exists any reason to assume that the life patterns of hunters and gatherers were stamped into our heredity, then the theory of an inborn, aggressive drive would have some support. If it could be proved to the contrary that hunters and gatherers in general are more peaceful than the latter, [are] more highly developed culture forms, then the hypotheses of an aggressive drive would be totally unbelievable (Schmidbauer 1971b: 41).

After this introduction Schmidbauer concludes on the basis of the data of cultural anthropology, that the majority of hunters and gatherers are notably unaggressive and most notable that they would not defend territories.[2] The statement is not at all based, however, on a thorough count of the known hunters and gatherers and an examination of their aggressiveness. It is based on a selection of some allegedly nonaggressive hunters and gatherers. In addition to the Eskimos, the Hadza and the Bushmen of South Africa are cited as examples. In doing so, Schmidbauer primarily relied on the articles by Lee and DeVore (1968). In one of the papers, Woodburn (1968) claims that the Hadza defend no territories, show no aggression, and also live in open groups. Woodburn, however, studied

---

[1]   To focus on the latter — the alleged peacefulness — the only source that this opinion is based on is Nansen. However, he got to know very little about the Eskimos in their natural state and his moral point of view is tendentious in order to arouse sympathy, as he stated himself in *Eskimoleben.*

[2]   In a recent publication Schmidbauer admits that territorial defense occurs; what is lacking, however, is a "territorial imperative," pressing the hunters and gatherers toward conquest of new, already occupied areas. Again this seems a simplifying statement. But since it was a journalist who coined the term "territorial imperative" and since Schmidbauer has never seen a hunter and gatherer so far, I do not feel obliged to try to understand what he actually means. If he implies that hunters and gatherers would never fight for the possession of territories, i.e., under population pressure, he certainly jumps to conclusions. So far there are no facts backing such a statement.

this group in 1958 and the following years when the group, which had formerly occupied approximately 5,000 square kilometers of land, was pressed into an area of 2,000 square kilometers. As a result, they were certainly uprooted and, consequently, changes in their original behavior and social structure were to be expected. Indeed, Kohl-Larsen, who visited the Hadza between 1934 and 1936 and later between 1937 and 1939, recorded in this connection a noteworthy story told him by a Hadza friend. The protocol of August 7, 1938 reads as follows:

In the old times the Hadzapi fought among one another. One tribe which was located in Mangola went to another tribe over in Lubiro. When they arrived there, a man was picked out. He went to the Lubiro band and said: "We have come to you today to fight you!" Now someone from the Lubiro tribe said: "Yes, if you have come here to wage a war with us, we are satisfied." The people in Lubiro came together and discuss among each other. They pick a man who is to fight with the man from Mangola. He is chosen, each of the men get two sticks. With them they beat each other. If no one is victor over the other, both tribes begin to battle each other with arrows and spears. As they are battling each other, an old woman steps out of the crowd and out of the other crowd an old man. Both of them place themselves in the middle of the two fighting tribes and say: "Sit down and rest a bit!" Having rested a bit, they begin hitting each other again. They fight each other for a long time. When one tribe is beaten, they run away. The others, the victors, follow them a stretch, then go back again into their camp and sleep. The next day the tribe that won goes to the losers. They stay overnight with them. In the morning all the strong men and youths go hunting. When they kill a few animals, they take its meat, which is fatty, and sit down and eat it. Only the men may be around then. If a woman goes to the men, she can be killed. However, if the woman has a child which she carries on her back, she pinches him so he cries. When the men hear a crying child they cannot hit the woman. When they [all] eat the meat the friendship between them is re-established. Having lived many days like this and seeing that they are living for no good purpose [no work and nothing to do], they look for another tribe to fight with. They hit each other so badly that a few people often are killed. Whoever loses goes then into the big crowd of the victor (Kohl-Larsen 1958: 35).

The protocol is noteworthy not only because of its numerous interesting details but also because it demonstrates that it is a grossly false generalization to conclude, on the basis of the current behavior of the Hadzas, that they, or hunters and gatherers in general, were originally peaceful peoples.

THE CONTROVERSY ON BUSHMEN TERRITORIALITY

In recent publications (Sahlins 1960; Lee 1968; Schmidbauer 1971a, 1971b, 1972) the Bushmen have been referred to as living in open, non-exclusive bands and as not expressing territoriality in the sense that it is usually defined, namely, as intolerance confined to space. For example this is explicitly stated by Lee concerning the !Kung:

The camp is an open aggregate of persons which changes in size and composition from day to day. Therefore, I have avoided the term band in describing the !Kung-Bushmen living groups. Each waterhole has a hinterland lying within a six-mile-radius which is regularly exploited for vegetables and animal food. These areas are not territories in a zoological sense, since they are not defended against outsiders (Lee 1968: 31).

Such statements are puzzling in view of the overwhelming evidence, published by older authors, on the territoriality of the same Bushmen. Thus Passarge describes the !Kung-Bushmen as bellicose and emphasizes that not only the bands, but every family, owns its particular collecting grounds. He writes:

Die Einteilung der Buschmänner in Familien ist bereits seit langem bekannt .... Dagegen habe ich noch nirgends eine Notiz darüber gefunden, daß auch der Grund und Boden gesetzmäßig verteiltes Eigentum der Familien ist. Das ist aber ein Punkt von ungeheurer Wichtigkeit. Denn erst bei Berücksichtigung dieser Tatsache kann man einen klaren Einblick in die soziale Organisation der Buschmänner gewinnen (Passarge 1907: 31).[3]

Von Zastrow and Vedder report that the Bushmen are not allowed to hunt or collect food in the land of another band:

Wo das Buschmanngelände noch nicht in Farmen aufgeteilt ist, sondern Sippengebiet sich an Sippengebiet schließt, weiß jeder Buschmann, daß er in fremdem Gebiet nicht jagen oder Feldkost sammeln darf. Wird ein Wildjäger angetroffen, so hat er sein Leben verwirkt. Es ist damit nicht gesagt, daß man ihn auf jeden Fall umbringt. Die Blutrache ... hält vielleicht davon ab ... (Von Zastrow and Vedder 1930: 425).[4]

Lebzelter reports of the great distrust the !Kung show when meeting members of foreign bands:

Jeder Bewaffnete, dem sie begegnen, gilt von vornherein als Feind. Fremde Stammesgebiete darf der Buschmann nur unbewaffnet betreten. Selbst am Rande der Farmzone ist das gegenseitige Mißtrauen so groß, daß ein Buschmann, der als Bote auf eine Farm geschickt wird, in deren Bereich eine andere Sippe

---

[3]   The classification of Bushmen into families has been known for a long time. Despite that, nothing has been found to show that land is distributed according to law. However, this is a fact of enormous importance, because it leads to a clearer understanding of the social organization of the Bushmen.

[4]   Where the Bushmen's land has not yet been divided into farms — but band areas follow band areas — every Bushman knows that he must not hunt nor collect "veldkos." If a poacher is caught, he may forfeit his life although this does not necessarily follow. Vendetta may prevent this.

sitzt, den Fahrweg, der als eine Art neutrale Zone gilt, nicht zu verlassen wagt. Nähern sich zwei fremde bewaffnete Buschleute einander, so legen sie zunächst auf Sichtweite die Waffen ab (Lebzelter 1934: 21).[5]

Similar reports can be found by Brownlee (1943), Vedder (1952), and Wilhelm (1953). Also Marshall reports on territoriality:

The !Kung say that one cannot eat the ground itself, so it does not matter to whom it belongs. It is these patches of veldkos that are clearly and jealously owned and the territories are shaped in a general way around these patches .... The strange concept of ownership of veldkos by the band operates almost like a taboo. No external force is established to prevent one band from encroaching in another's veldkos or to prevent individuals from raiding veldkos patches to which they have no right. This is just not done (1965: 248).

Von Tobias emphasizes that the Bushmen strictly move within their territory:

Territoriality applies among bands of the same tribe and between different tribes. Intribal bounds are sometimes reinforced by social attitudes, such as the traditional enmity between the Auen and Naron. Under special condition such as an abundance of food these bounds and the accompanying enmity are forgotten (Von Tobias 1964: 206).

In view of all these reports we have to assume that the group studies by Lee no longer show the typical pattern, probably because of acculturation. In addition, they may not have been aware of the possible existence of a nexus system, which bonds several bands to a larger unit in the !Ko-Bushmen.

TERRITORIALITY AMONG THE !KO-BUSHMEN

The !Ko-Bushmen belong to the central Kalahari. Bushmen live in the area south of Ghanzi. Many of the bands are still living as hunters and gatherers. Heinz gave a detailed report on them (1972), and I had the opportunity to visit repeatedly one of his groups in 1970, 1971, and 1972, and live with them while documenting unstaged social interactions on film. These studies not only shed light on Bushman aggression and aggression control, but also contribute to the more general area of phylogenetic adaptations in human aggressive behavior.

Territoriality among the !Ko-Bushmen has been dealt with extensively

[5] Every armed man is considered an enemy. The Bushman must enter other tribal territory unarmed only. When a Bushman is being sent as a messenger to another farm, the mutual hostility will not permit him to leave the street which is recognized as some kind of neutral zone, even at the boundaries of the farm zone. If two Bushmen are approaching each other, their arms will be put down within range of sight.

by Heinz (1966, 1972). I will therefore review his findings. My observations are in complete agreement.

Heinz distinguishes three levels of social organization: (1) the family and extended family, (2) the band, and (3) the band nexus. All these units have a definite pattern of bonding and spacing. The seating arrangement of family members around the fireplace is less formalized than in the !Kung (Marshall 1965). The wife can sit anywhere on the house side of the fire. But the proper place, according to Heinz, is at the right side of her husband. Parents settle at least twelve meters away from their married children and the entrance is always arranged in a way so as not to allow them to watch their married children sleeping.

Though all band territory is accessible to everyone in the band, nevertheless, the family's area of activity is recognized. When hunting alone, a man is expected to hunt on the side of the village on which his house is built, a rule applying to women collecting veldkos (wild food) or firewood as well. Only collective activity — which is most prevalent — breaks this rule (Heinz 1972).

Heinz reports, furthermore, that the bands periodically split into family groups, each family then moving to a family place which is respected by the others.

While families have no direct territorial claims, the band definitely has. A band considers a piece of land as its territory. Control over it is exercised by the "head-man" (Heinz 1966, 1972) on behalf of the band and a group of old men and women acting as consultants. The band hunts and collects wood and *veldkos* within its territory. In case of emergency they may ask for permission to hunt and collect in another band's territory. To members of the same nexus permission is normally readily granted.

I consider the nexus system to be Heinz's most important discovery, since it may explain, at least to a certain extent, how some of the controversial statements about Bushmen arose. The nexus constitutes a group of bands. Members refer to themselves as "our people." The people are bounded by friendship and kinship ties, by ritual bonds (e.g., by gathering for trance dances) and marriage within the nexus. The band nexus is a territorial group which is more exclusive than the band territories. The nexus territory is demarcated from those of another nexus by a strip of no man's land, which is generally avoided by the members of both sides. It would not occur to a !Ko-Bushman to seek permission to hunt in the land of another nexus.

Access to territory is acquired by birth, by admission to a band, or by marriage. If the parents come from different bands, dual band membership is the result. When he marries, the groom resides for a certain period of time with the bride's band and has access to this territory. Thereafter, the couple moves to the man's band, where the bride receives access to the band's territory. "It is this phenomenon which gives parents rights in each other's land, and which is transmitted to the children and which might in certain cases blur band territoriality" (Heinz 1972).

PATTERNS OF AGGRESSIVE BEHAVIOR

Being interested in the universals in human behavior I spent many hours studying and filming unstaged social interactions. In all, approximately 12,000 meters of 16-mm film were taken on the !Ko-Bushmen, and about 2,000 meters on the !Kung. On the basis of this documentation it can be proved that: (1) aggressive behavior patterns are fairly frequently observed, and (2) many of the patterns are identical in form with those observed by people in other cultures in the same context.

Aggressive acts in this context are defined as all those that lead to spacing or to the establishment of a dominance-subordination relationship. Whether or not the person involved hurt another person physically does not enter the definition, nor do we incorporate the "intent." If one were to speak of aggression only when damage results one would have to omit all the patterns of aggressive threat and other ritualized patterns of aggression. I see no reason to do this.

SIBLING RIVALRY

Intersibling rivalry can be observed at a very early age. I documented a most dramatic example during my stay with the !Kung. The parties involved were two brothers. The younger was about one year old, the elder perhaps five years old. The elder was evidently seeking bodily contact with the mother but her attention was concentrated on her smaller son whom she nursed exclusively. The elder son tried fairly frequently to harm his younger brother. He attempted to scratch and beat him on several occasions and tried to poke him with sticks (Plate 1a-c). The mother had to be on the alert to keep both brothers from fighting. The elder brother also tried to interfere with his younger brother's play, teasing him, for example, by taking his toys and throwing them away. But the younger brother too was aggressive. While drinking he was observed to give his brother a well-aimed kick with one foot. The elder brother certainly was suffering a good deal, and in his frustrated efforts to seek contact with the mother, he often cried. His mother did not respond very eagerly to these efforts. She allowed contact when her small son was away on a playing excursion, but she did not invite it; rather she seemed fed up with him. Less dramatic cases of sibling rivalry were observed in the !Ko-Bushmen. In view of the fact that hunters and gatherers are so often reported to grow up without any frustration, these observations are important in correcting such ideas. In general, babies show aggressive behavior at a very early age. A ten-month-old boy used to attack other babies, for example, by pushing them over and by scratching them (Plate 2). (For further examples see Eibl-Eibesfeldt 1972).

AGGRESSION IN GROUPS OF PLAYING CHILDREN

Playful Aggression

Patterns which normally lead to spacing subordination and the cut off of contact are often performed during play. Although the motor patterns in such a case are often difficult to distinguish from genuine aggressive acts, additional signals like laughing and smiling allow us to recognize that the aggressive interaction is actually play. And so does the fact that the roles of attacker and defender or pursuer and pursued change freely.

Serious Aggressive Interactions

Serious aggressive interactions are fairly common within groups of children playing. The acts of aggression are: slapping with the palm, beating with a stick or another object, throwing objects toward a child, throwing sand, punching with the fist, kicking with the foot, pushing the other with one or both hands, ramming a child with the shoulder, pushing the hip, pinching, biting, pulling hair, scratching, wrestling, spitting, stealing objects (Plate 3). All these patterns have been described in detail in my monograph (Eibl-Eibesfeldt 1972). There are further significant patterns of threat and submission: When threatening, the person stares at the opponent and frowns and clenches the teeth, often exposing them at the same time. Sometimes a hand, with or without an object, is raised. Both opponents may become involved in such a threat stare-duel. Such display can lead to the submission of one, then the loser lowers his head, tilts it slightly, and turns sideways. At the same time the child pouts. This behavior strongly inhibits further aggression. But that is not all: one can

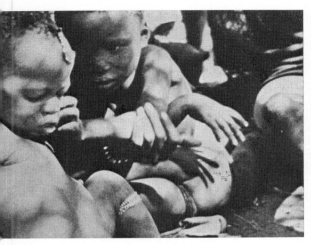

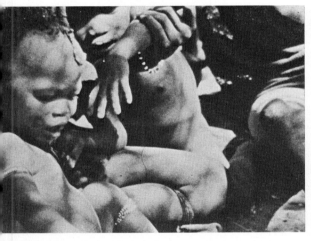

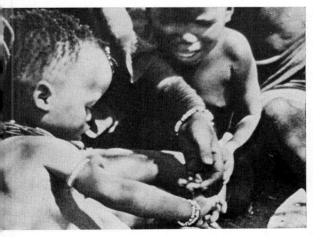

Plate 1. Sibling rivalry in the !Kung-Bushmen. The elder brother (in the background) tries to scratch the younger (1a). The mother interferes by pulling the attacker's hand away and warding off further attacks with her hand (1b). The elder brother cries in evident frustration (1c).
(From a 16-mm film, HF 41, by the author.)

Plate 2. Attack of a ▮
about 11 months old a▮
a baby girl who tried ▮
take an object from hi▮
hand. The boy pushes ▮
girl over and scratches▮
at the same time.
(From a 16-mm film, ▮
by the author.)

Plate 3. Girl about t▮
throw a stick toward a▮
(From a 16-mm film, ▮
by the author.)

Plate 4. Boy threat st▮
at a girl. She is poutin▮
(From a 16-mm films, ▮
and HF 3, by the auth▮

5a

Plate 5.   a. Pouting Bushman girl
            b. Pouting Waika-Indian
(the man wanted to have a ride in
our boat. His request was refused.
From a 16-mm film by the
author.)

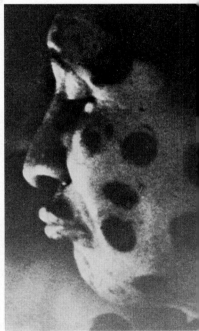

Plate 6.   Three girls mocking the
author by lifting the genital apron.
The author was filming with a
mirror lens. When he looked up,
the girls stopped their mocking.
(From a 16-mm film, HF 1, by the
author.)

5b

Plate 7. Posturing of a mocking girl. Situation as in Plate 6.
(From a 16-mm film, HF 1, by the author.)

8a

8b

Plate 8. Genital presenting by a girl (8a, b). Situation as in Plate 6.
(From a 16-mm film, HF 1, by the author.)

observe that the aggressor quite often tries to comfort his victim, seeking friendly contact. The victim normally responds to it only after a certain lapse of time. At the beginning, he responds to the effort by clear cut-off behavior, that is, by turning away. Another aggression-inhibiting behavior is crying. Both submissive behaviors are to be found in all cultures I have visited so far (Plates 4 and 5).

Aggressive interactions are fairly common in groups of children playing. Within 191 minutes I counted, in a group of seven girls and two boys, 166 aggressive and defensive acts: slapping, punching with the fist or beating with an object (96 times); kicking with the foot (23 times); throwing (8 times) and a number of other acts. Ten times a child cried loudly during this observation period, which indicates clearly that many of the aggressive acts lead to serious conflicts. Only about one-third of the interactions were clearly playful aggression by the criteria mentioned above. Not all play sessions are disturbed by so many aggressive acts. Another time twelve children played for 88 minutes together and 7 aggressive acts were counted.

QUARRELS BETWEEN CHILDREN

Quarreling about the Possession of Objects

Children like to play ball with melons and the ball is often the object of a quarrel. In particular, boys try to rob others of the ball. Pursuits and fights for and in defense of the object develop. The loser often shows all the signs of serious anger and sometimes even cries. Children rob each other also of other objects, sometimes even of food which is considered a more serious offense.[6] Robbing another child of an object is often a means to tease a playmate and entice him into a fight.

Punishment for Offenses

Older children often interfere with the quarrels of their younger playmates, e.g., by punishing the attacker. In one play group the oldest, pre-pubertal girl regularly acted in such a way that she practically controlled the play activity. She initiated many of the play activities and demanded

---

[6] Refusing to share food is an offense which invites punishing attack. Once a girl gave a morsel to an eight-month-old baby, expecting that it would return part of it. The baby crawled away with all of it and immediately was beaten by the girl.

obedience. If a child was breaking a rule of the game or behaving in an unskilled way, she attacked. We called her the *Spielleiterin* [play leader] for this reason.

Demonstrative Aggression

The *Spielleiterin* sometimes attacked another child without evident reason. In the morning, when she came to the group of children who were already assembled, she kicked the melon out of the hand of a child, or boxed another, and indeed all the children showed signs of respect for her by approaching and showing their melons, even at the danger of being robbed of this prized object. It seems to me that the function of this aggression is to achieve and keep rank and respect, which is a prerequisite for functioning as a mediator and soothing quarrels between the other playmates.

Unprovoked Spontaneous Attacks

Children often attacked others without apparent reason. The patterns were of particular interest since it was evident that a child is inhibited against starting a full attack against an innocent bystander. If a child seeks a fight he incites it by a pattern of provocation. Teasing, by offering something and withdrawing it when the other child tries to grasp it, is a common way. A slight slap, a kick, showing the tongue, or stealing an object and throwing it away are all typical, small insults which provoke the other. And once he attacks, a heavy retaliation follows. It appears that the provoking child seeks an excuse to attack by the provocation of aggression, which allows him then to retaliate.

Retaliation

Retaliation is the regular answer to an attack. This retaliation need not follow immediately. I observed once that an attacked boy went into the bush, broke off a branch from a small tree, and returned after some ten minutes to retaliate.

Escalation of Play

Rough-and-tumble play occasionally developed into a fight. If one child accidentally or by intent hits the other slightly more than expected, he invites retaliation and a fight may start.

QUARRELS BETWEEN CHILDREN AND ADULTS

Children sometimes responded violently when parents admonished them. Once a girl was scolded by her father for carelessly kicking a pot, causing part of its content to spill. The girl then grasped the pot and threw it against the floor, spilling all of its content. The father did not say anything further. On another occasion a girl kicked her mother with her foot, after she had been scolded for her greedy begging for food. Once a girl robbed a small boy of a piece of meat. The boy cried out and his father came, took the meat back to the boy, and slapped the girl slightly on the head. The girl retaliated by throwing sand at the man, who in turn slapped her a second time. This did not subdue her at all, for she answered by throwing sand after him again when he left. A final example: A man hid a little object to prevent a baby from swallowing it. The baby and another boy, about six years of age, were searching for the object. They were searching the man's body with much laughter when the man and the little boy started in a playful manner to exchange slaps. This escalated, however, and when the man slapped harder, the boy started to cry, ran away, and returned with large bones and horns of antelopes, threatening to throw them at the man. At this moment the boy's father intervened, and calmed his son.

AGGRESSION IN THE ADULT

Within a band, aggressive behavior of the adult is under good control. The cultural ideal of the Bushmen is indeed a peaceful life. Should tension arise between two families of one band, the problem is solved by splitting up. One family moves for a while to another place and this relieves the tension (Heinz 1966, 1967). I myself had no opportunity to observe serious, but only playful, aggression between adults. Young men wrestle, married couples engage in teasing and mock fighting. An element of aggression is certainly to be observed in the numerous games. Heinz noted that males tease and maltreat "underdogs," that is, low-ranking members of the group. Verbal threats of murder are often uttered ("I will kill you with my medicine"). Males, after insulting each other, occasionally use their weapons, and Heinz reports a case of manslaughter. He also describes the temper fits which occasionally overcome the Bushmen: "An angry Bushman finally settles down with a face that shows an unbelievable degree of anger. It takes very little for this anger to cause a wrestling and punching encounter with sticks and knobkerries. If the reasons are serious, the fight will deteriorate into one in which knives and spears are used...." (Heinz 1967: 6). Married couples fight for reasons of jealousy, and so do women. Adultery may lead to bloodshed among the males.

TEASING AND MOCKING

By teasing and mocking, group homogeneity is enforced and an outlet for aggression provided. Heinz describes the existing mocking relationship in detail, so I shall confine myself here to a discussion of some patterns of mocking. These patterns are activated by individual behavior that deviates from the group's norm. By this mocking the outsiders come under pressure to conform. Mocking certainly has an educational function. It takes the form of imitating the behavior which provoked the hostility of the group, and thus ridiculing it. I also found that female genital display, showing the tongue, and showing the rear are used during mocking. Several ways of female genital display can be observed. Children repeatedly mocked me while I was filming with my mirror lens. They imitated my behavior and if I did not pay attention they approached dancing and singing and when near, lifted their genital apron (Plate 6). Often the girls posed with their hands on their hips, posturing in a characteristic way with the legs (Plate 7). In addition to this frontal genital display a genital display from the rear was observed. The mocking girl turned the rear toward the person and bent deeply (Plate 8). The pubic region was exposed in a very conspicuous way, particularly since this race — as a characteristic feature — shows a strong lordosis. It is noteworthy that the enlarged *labia minora* contributes to the marked visibility of the vulva. I assume that this posturng is homologous to primate sexual presenting; in fact the Bushmen copulate from the rear, lying on their sides.

The widespreaid use of patterns of sexual presenting (Eibl-Eibesfeldt 1972) in mocking displays may be explained by the fact that sexual inciting is taboo, except under certain circumstances. To use it outside its original context is therefore a demonstration of disregard. Not to be confused with the pattern of genital presenting are patterns of showing the rear. This pattern is used more often as an aggressive threat. I observed that girls mocked boys that were teasing them this way. They shoved sand between their buttocks, then, approaching the boys, they turned, bent over, and let the sand go as if defecating. Sometimes wind was passed. Both are clear indications that this pattern is a ritualized form of defecation.

Tongue showing is another pattern used in mocking. It is difficult to interpret, since it occurs in various forms. In derogatory tongue showing, the tongue is stuck out and turned down, as if the person were about to vomit. Spitting can even occur in this context, and the German word *spotten* [mocking] is related to the word *spucken* [spitting]. There exists, furthermore, a sexual tongue flicking, and to complicate matters further, there exists a friendly tongue showing derived from licking. I want to mention, however, that the tongue flicking is often used in a teasing fashion.

DISCUSSION

The much cited cross-cultural "evidence" for man's primarily peaceful and nonaggressive nature proves, on examination, to be a weak point in the environmentalists' argument. Among others the Bushmen certainly do not lack territories nor do they fail to be aggressive. Even within the band numerous aggressive acts can be observed. The situations and most of the movement patterns are identical with the aggressive patterns in other cultures. They are universals, and although the similarity of many of the movements can be explained on a functional basis (hitting, kicking, etc.) and thus be acquired independently in a similar way, this certainly does not hold for the more elaborate aggressive displays, such as the facial expressions of threat, the threat stare, the patterns of submission (pouting, head-lowering, gaze avoidance, crying) or some of the patterns of mocking (genital presenting, tongue showing). We can assume that many of these patterns are phylogenetic adaptations ritualized in the service of spacing and aggression control.

It is true, however, that Bushmen are not bellicose. Their cultural ideal is peaceful coexistence, and they achieve this by avoiding conflict, that is, by splitting up, and by emphasizing and encouraging the numerous patterns of bonding. This way they achieve a peaceful life. Most of the socialization of aggression takes place within the groups of children at play. In interaction with others, children learn to control their aggression. It should be mentioned that many of the patterns of bonding and the urge to bond are inborn to man. Man is, so to speak, by nature a bonding as well as a spacing creature. Culture puts emphasis on one or the other and may unbalance man, for better or worse. The Bushmen certainly belong to those people whose culture shapes man according to a peaceful ideal. What is striking when observing the Bushmen is not their lack of aggression, but their efficient way of coping with it. Friendly bonding behavior predominates in the interaction of adults and these people spend many hours a day grooming each other, chatting, sharing the pipe, and playing with their children, to mention a few of these social interactions. Since wood and food gathering consume only two to three hours a day for the women, and since men hunt only occasionally, the Bushmen have plenty of time for intimate social interaction. One could say that these people have more time at their disposal to be "human" in a friendly way while we are losing this capacity to a greater and greater extent.

REFERENCES

BROWNLEE, F.
   1943   The social organization of the !Kung-Bushmen of the North-Western Kalahari. *Africa* 14:124–129.
EIBL-EIBESFELDT, I.
   1970   *Ethology, biology of behavior*. New York: Holt, Rinehart and Winston.
   1972   *Die !Ko-Buschmanngesellschaft: Agressionskontrolle und Gruppenbindung. Monographien zur Humanethologie 1*. München: Piper.
HEINZ, H. J.
   1966   "The social organization of the !Ko-Bushmen." University of South Africa, Department of Anthropology.
   1967   *Conflicts, tensions and release of tensions in a Bushman society*. Isma Papers 23. The Institute for the Study of Man in Africa.
   1972   Territoriality among the Bushmen in general and the !Ko in particular. *Anthropos* 67:405–416.
HELMUTH, H.
   1967   Zum Verhalten des Menschen: die Aggression. *Zeitschrift zur Ethnologie* 92:265–273.
KOENIG, H.
   1925   Der Rechtsbruch und sein Ausgleich bei den Eskimo. *Anthropos* 20: 276–315.
KOHL-LARSEN, L.
   1958   *Wildbeuter in Ostafrika: die Tindiga, ein Jäger- und Sammlervolk.* Berlin: Reimer.
LEBZELTER, V.
   1934   *Eingeborenenkulturen von Süd- und Südwestafrika*. Leipzig: Hiersemann.
LEE, R. B.
   1968   "What hunters do for a living," in *Man the hunter*. Edited by R. B. Lee and I. DeVore, 30–48. Chicago: Aldine.
LEE, R. B., I. DEVORE
   1968   *Man the hunter*. Chicago: Aldine.

MARSHALL, L.
1961   Sharing, talking and giving: relief of social tensions among !Kung-Bushmen. *Africa* 31:231–249.
1965   "The !Kung-Bushmen of the Kalahari desert," in *Peoples of Africa.* Edited by J. G. Gibs. New York: Holt, Rinehart and Winston.

MONTAGU, M. F. A.
1968   *Man and aggression.* New York: Oxford University Press.

PASSARGE, S.
1907   *Die Buschmänner der Kalahari.* Berlin: Reimer.

SAHLINS, M. D.
1960   The origin of society. *Scientific American* 204:76–87.

SCHMIDBAUER, W.
1971a   Methodenprobleme der Human Ethologie. *Studium Generale* 24:462–522.
1971b   Zur Anthropologie der Aggression. *Dynamische Psychiatrie* 4:36–50.
1972   *Die sogenannte Aggression.* Hamburg: Hoffmann und Campe.

TOBIAS, P. V.
1964   "Bushmen — hunters — gatherers: a study in human ecology," in *Ecological studies in southern Africa.* Edited by D. H. S. Davis, 196–208. Chicago: Aldine.

VEDDER, H.
1952–1953 Über die Vorgeschichte der Völkerschaften von Südwestafrika. *Journal of the South West Africa Scientific Society* 9:45–56.

WILHELM, J. H.
1953   *Die !Kung-Buschleute. Jahrbuch des Museums für Völkerkunde in Leipzig* 12:91–189.

WOODBURN, J.
1968   "Stability and flexibility in Hadza residential groupings," in *Man the hunter.* Edited by R. B. Lee and I. DeVore. Chicago: Aldine.

ZASTROW, B. VON, H. VEDDER
1930   "Die Buschmänner," in *Das Eingebornenrecht: Togo, Kamerun, Südwestafrika, die Südseekolonien.* Edited by E. Ewerth and L. Adam. Stuttgart: Strecker und Schröder.

Films

EIBL-EIBESFELDT, I.
1971   HF 1 !Ko-Buschleute (Kalahari) — Schamweisen und Spotten. *HOMO* 4:261–266.
1971   HF 2 !Ko-Buschleute (Kalahari) — Aggressives Verhalten von Kindern im vorpubertären Alter, Teil I. *HOMO* 4:267–278.
1971   HF 3 !Ko-Buschleute (Kalahari) — Aggressives Verhalten von Kindern im vorpubertären Alter, Teil II. *HOMO* 4:267–278.
1971   HF 41 !Kung-Buschleute (Kungveld) — Geschwister Rivalität. To be published.

Cultural Variability in the Structuring of Violence

M. ESTELLIE SMITH

Though little has been done on a comparative analysis of violence it appears logical to assume that there are cultural forces which pattern the expression of violence — i.e. that the violent behavior in which individuals or groups engage is not random in its expression but is structured by cultural bases. Northern New Mexico offers a situation wherein members of three distinct cultures seem to demonstrate cultural variability in response to the "need" for violent behavior.

The three groups are not only culturally diverse but the data are drawn from three temporally distinct eras. The Amerindian community of Taos Pueblo is examined during the contact period (essentially the seventeenth century); the Spanish-Americans of Taos Valley are of primary concern during the eighteenth and nineteenth centuries; and the last group — a multitude of Hippie communes scattered throughout the valley — is viewed during a brief decade in the mid-twentieth century.

Taos Pueblo, with a strong, highly explicit theme emphasizing non-violence, was pressured by the in-migration of both precontact Indians and, later, the Spanish into offering positive sanctions to violence in order to survive both marauder and conquistador. The frontier settlements of the first Spanish settlers had to minimize the potential destructiveness of internal violence in a situation where survival demanded that a premium be placed on violence as a favored means of coping with a hostile environment. Finally, in the late 1960's approximately twenty Hippie communes

An earlier format of this paper was presented at the 1972 Annual Meeting of the American Anthropological Association, Toronto. My thanks to Esther Goldfrank, Stanley Diamond, and anonymous members of the audience for helpful questions and comments.

(with over 2,000 members) were forced to recognize that, despite their philosophy of love and peace and brotherhood, they must deal with intense violence in order to survive local hostility.

The need to change a cultural leitmotif and integrate a new element of violence so as to control the "environment" varied in all three cases; the culturally patterned response will be examined and compared.

Several caveats must be emphasized concerning the limitations of this analysis. For example, it is not within the scope of this paper to deal with a general examination of violence (particularly its causes) despite the pressing need for such a review. It must be pointed out however that much of the currently existing material deals with conflict rather than with MODES of violence PER SE. The normative or equilibrium approach argues that conflict and aggression are dysfunctional and focuses on techniques for restoring peace.

A survey of the causes is needed to bring some order into what is (rather appropriately) the chaos of the field. The genesis of conflict and aggression has been proclaimed as: (1) sociological (the need for stability, the expression of social ills, an agent of change); (2) psychological (the quest for power, the expression of activities by charismatic leaders or an *agent provocateur*); (3) ecological (population pressure, subsistence needs); (4) biological (the physiologically based effects of crowding); (5) economic (a search for scarce goods and/or a market for surplus goods); and (6) ideological (defensive, ameliorative, divinely inspired, teleologically imperative). Perhaps, too, it is time for social scientists to examine social scientists and these various theories and explanations which they propound. By probing the subculture of those who explore conflict, aggression, and violence we may be able to determine the who, what, where, and when of the various positions and analyses — and thus arrive at the why of the current "state of the art."

It has been argued that anthropologists have a disciplinary bias toward the normative approach (cf. Coser 1954: 24) and there is, to be sure, no great wealth of material available. However, studies on factionalism (e.g. French 1948; Fenton 1957), warfare (e.g. Bohannan 1967; Otterbein 1965, 1968a, 1968b, 1970), law (Hoebel 1954; Gluckman 1956), and government (e.g. Barth 1959; Leach 1954) indicate that we have not committed ourselves to the emphasis on stability and consensus to the degree with which we have been charged.

It is true, though, that it is essentially the sociologists and political scientists (especially in recent years) who have presented the functional approach as an argument for the positive exercise of conflict. Coser (1954: 157) maintains that, "What threatens the equilibrium of a structure is not conflict as such but the rigidity itself which permits hostilities to accumulate and to be channeled along one major line of cleavage once they break out in conflict." Lundberg (1939, passim) argues that, while abstinence from communication is the essence of conflict situations, violence itself is a form of communication which is essential when the social structure will not permit other modes of message-transmission. George Sorel (1950, passim) suggests that violence is not only a way to establish and preserve group identity and cohesion (as a result of internal agreement on the form and focus for violence) but also that the conflict itself acts as a cohesive agent for those against whom the violence is directed. Finally, Simmel argues that once even a hostile relationship between two groups is established (barring, of course, total elimination of one of the parties!) other interactional links will follow (1955: 35).

Most studies of conflict and aggression, then, tend to deal with violence as incidental and ameliorative techniques of primary concern. Some few (e.g. Marx, Lundberg, Simmel, Sorel, Fanon, and Mills) perceive the process as fundamentally necessary for a system in a dynamic state of equilibrium.

It must be emphasized at this juncture that a study of conflict is an analysis of only one kind of violence, seen from a particular aspect. Conflict is a clash between opposing forces and necessarily involves at least a dyad, members of which are complementarily ACTIVE. It is most often the result of AGGRESSION (best defined as "a unilateral show of hostility or violence"), a process which implies at least one active and one PASSIVE participant in an asymmetrical dyad. Violence (an intense form of hostility) may take the form of either aggression or conflict. Further, violence need not be defined as limited to the act of bodily harm; if the modern techniques of the twentieth-century cold and hot wars have taught us nothing else, they have demonstrated that violence may exist at a high level of intensity despite an overt state of physical "peacefulness" (see Figure 1).

A methodological point also needs to be made: I do not intend to argue for consensus for, like Marx, I believe consensus to be an "idealization of coercion" (an attitude possibly resulting from my study of pueblo governing), whether that coercion be based on pragmatic necessity or sociocultural controls. Further, consensus is usually a falsification or reality based on conscious models. Neither will I make a case for violence as a positive social agent (though the study of the Penitentes owes much to Gluckman's argument [1963: 126–127] that the sort of conflict which produces fissioning is avoided through the institution of ritualized violence).

Such discussions, again, while crucial, cannot be brought to the fore without a lengthy examination of areas more appropriately explored in

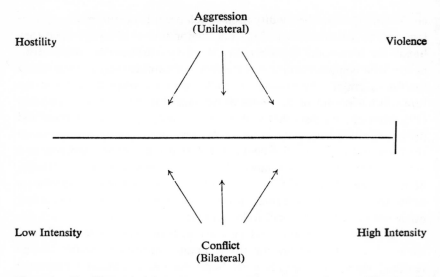

Figure 1.   Hostility and violence are extreme points on a continuum. When hostile behavior reaches a critical point of intensification it takes on a quality which shifts that behavior into another categorical range which is more properly defined as "violence." Though many will object to this sort of intuitive model it can only be defended on the grounds that we have still not solved the problem of "How many hairs make a beard?"

This schematic presentation (only tentatively formulated) assumes that aggression and conflict may (a) occur at any point on the continuum; (b) have both etic and emic dimensions; and (c) be viewed as situated differently on the scale by the opposing participants.

a discussion of the philosophy of science. The data that follow are little removed from the raw state of collection and demonstrate, essentially, only the cultural variability of human societies under stress and strain.

The major thrust of the paper is to demonstrate that violence does contain consensual aspects — the type of consensualism that is designated as "culture" or "patterned behavior." It is assumed here that societies must provide their individual members with needed techniques of defense/attack (however these are defined and perceived, and whether at the psychological or sociocultural level of expression). Thus, there must be agreement as to (a) what is aggression; and (b) what modes of violence are acceptable techniques for channeling violence. All violence occurs within a system of customs, norms, laws, and values. The absolute essence of internal cohesiveness is predominant agreement regarding the degree to which endogenous volence can extend — temporally, socially, and (physically) destructively.

The ethnographic data demonstrating response variability by the representatives of three different cultures under examination here show very clearly how particularistic is the structuring of violence. However, one of the aspects of the study which has shown little change (relatively speaking) is the locale. All three groups are found in the same setting. Taos Valley is located high in the Sangre de Cristo Mountains, a range which is a spur of the Rocky Mountains. At an altitude of almost 7000 feet, the valley lies bounded by both barren mesas and fir-treed slopes. The Rio Grande has cut a deep gorge only a few miles from both the town and the Pueblo of Taos.

Prehistoric Indians, fur traders, Spanish settlers, artists, tourists, and Texans have all found the area one of the most attractive in the Southwest. Summers are cool (the temperature is rarely beyond the eighties — and even in July and August some nights are cool enough to light *piñon* fires) while winters are relatively mild and snow usually stays on the ground for only a few hours. The land, rich in game and wild plant food, has proved a fertile spot for the crops of the valley people. Unlike much of the Southwest, water is usually abundant and only the most severe droughts affect subsistence patterns, though as little as twenty miles to the south crops may be totally lost and cattle die by the hundreds for lack of sufficient moisture.

The present village site of the Indian community of Taos Pueblo has been located in approximately the same spot since about A.D. 1250. Even the most modern and cynical present-day Taos Indians admit to a special feeling about the land — the mountains, the valley itself, and the many historical locations in the area such as Blue Lake, which are linked to the native ceremonial system. While the pueblo has been the scene of bitter internal conflict, I have never heard anyone disagree with the statement made by one informant that, "... it never feels right to fight that way in this place. Things should be quiet and good — like the valley almost tells us to be."

Benedict's commentary on the Puebloan peoples (1934: 62–120), though justifiably criticized for certain weaknesses, seems to me to be essentially accurate in its characterization of the IDEAL Puebloan individual as "... a person of dignity and affability ... [A]ny conflict, even though all right is on his side, is held against him" (1934: 95). Citing Bunzel to support her thesis she goes on to say that a good person has "... a yielding disposition ... a generous heart ... is a nice polite man [who] never gets into trouble ... never betray[s] a suspicion of arrogance or a strong emotion" (1934: 95–96). And, finally, "... [A] man sinks his activities in those of the group and ... is never violent ... moderation is the first. The fundamental tabu ... is against any suspicion of anger. Controversies ... are carried out with an unparalleled lack of vehemence ... [Pueblo Indians] do not contemplate violence [because] the Pueblos provide institutions that effectively minimize the appearance of a violent emotion" (1934: 101–103).

Now, granted that this is an over facile characterization (and, in fact, is not supported by some of Benedict's own data), few Southwestern anthropologists would argue that this is not a meaningful statement of the ideal values of Puebloan culture; it has, in many forms, been repeated to me over and over at all of the pueblos of the Rio Grande Valley.

How then, given this statement of nonviolence as a *sine qua non* of pueblo life, did the Taos respond to invasions of their territory by Athabascan and Spanish foreigners? Here was a situation which, for most people, would certainly require a violent and aggressive response.

The precontact Athabascan invasions presented no real stress for change; the Taos either fled or retreated behind the walls of the upper floors of their multistoried pueblos. This was a relatively effective defense because the Athabascans were only hit-and-run raiders, primarily seeking food from the usually bulging maize granaries. But this proved an inappropriate technique for handling the Spanish who had guns, horses, armor — and an obvious strategy of long-range settlement and gain. They came to conquer, to enslave, and to homestead, permanently. Flight proved unfeasible, and the pueblo architecture was no defense against Spanish tactics.

After the initial shock, the Taos must have seen how much more the Spanish feared the tactics of the nomadic Indians. The settled Indians also quickly learned that, though radically different culturally as the Indians might be — one society from another — the Spanish viewed all Indians as "the same" in comparison to Europeans. Tactics borrowed from the Athabascans and other non-puebloan Indians not only might be "untranslatable" in purely pueblo terms but (obviously) could be seen to be not totally satisfactory when employed by the nomads themselves. But they were a model for a conflict response. Thus a kind of cultural duality was introduced which even today leads many anthropologists to talk of "Plains-type anomalies among the Puebloan peoples." The peaceful pueblo Indians superficially adopted, BUT DID NOT INTEGRATE, the cultural style of raiding nomads. But I believe this to have been only an experiment in coping techniques.

Only a few generations after the original Spanish *entrada* in 1598, the pueblo peoples saw that the individual and sporadic attempts by each village to rebel against Spanish rule accomplished little except a response of brutal retaliatory suppression. Led by a cabal at Taos, all of the pueblos united to obliterate and expunge the Spanish forever. Such unity among atomistic villages, such absolute and bloody violence from peaceful farmers could only be temporary — the result of an impermanent rejection of all that pueblo culture represented so that the world could once again be brought into focus. Had the world turned upside-down? Then perhaps the way to right it was to turn upside-down also.

In the revolt of 1680, the Spanish were forced south to El Paso, the only time in North American history that Europeans were ever successfully removed from a major area of occupation.

But like the so-called Clowns — societies whose members act as agents of social control among the Puebloans, correcting and policing villagers at ceremonial times — they had to become non-Puebloan (i.e. "non-human") in order to use violence. A mask had to be worn. Just as the ceremonial violence of the figuratively "masked" native priests and literally masked clowns is seen as being done by beings who, for the moment, are not within the normal structure, so the Puebloans, to become violent, also sought to assume another identity, to become someone else completely even though temporarily.

Violence was compartmentalized. During the 1680 revolt the mask was that of the nomadic Indians. Later, following the reconquest the Taos adopted another mask — that of the Spanish — and began acting as auxiliary forces of the Spanish in attempts to subdue the raiders. Now they used Spanish weaponry, military tactics, and military titles, were listed with European names, even (if records are to be trusted) spoke Spanish to each other while on military duty. From this point on violence (excluding both the ritually sanctioned and individually focused covert attacks which were internally centered) was always perceived as being externally located, and foreign in style.

In sum, the only way in which the Taos could engage in a defensive war was to become non-Taos. A kind of cultural schizophrenia was established and compartmentalization was the result. I would suggest that this plurality of identity in plural societies is a very common adaptive strategy for the subordinate group. The closed corporate community of the pueblos demands more identity dichotomization than other more interdigital social groups in the United States. Puebloans have only accreted, not integrated, elements of European culture into their own.

Thus, even today, when factions engage in violence within the pueblo, the violence is apparently erratic, unstructured, disorganized, and of short duration. The non-Indian community of the valley is often bewildered by the fact that a long-smoldering dispute, after it finally flares into overt violence, will cease to be even a topic of conversation at the pueblo in a matter of hours — even though no settlement was reached on the problem which apparently led to the conflict in point. The point is that communal violence is an accretive element and, as such, appears to be unpredictable in its genesis as well as impossible to sustain.

Covert and subtle though it may be there is a kind of "natural" tempo which can be perceived in the seemingly unscheduled conflict that afflicts Taos Pueblo and perhaps it is this which ultimately makes, say, factionalism among the Indians more capable of *post facto* explanations by the local population than what appears to them to be the unnatural "scheduling" of the violence of a Penitente meeting.

Many have argued that the Spanish of northern New Mexico are cultural anachronisms. It is maintained that this is due primarily to the fact that the mainstream of change and innovation (not to mention bureaucratic contact) acted as bastions where their inhabitants could retain many of the features of the seventeenth-century Spanish peasant base whence the original settlers sprung. The first Spanish to move into the area were aggressive individuals; they had to be in order to face living on the furthermost limits of what was already the frontier of Spanish settlement in the New World. There was constant fear of Indian "treachery" from both the settled Indians and from the raiders who were drifting into the northern reaches in their southward move from the Plains.

This, then, was a selected population, a group of immigrants who could face the threat of Indian attacks and possible torture, captivity, rape and even death. It was not the more effete population of the south nor even the frontier "aristocracy" of Santa Fe. Most were crude people, prepared to face violence because they themselves found violence a bearable constant state. Cultural selectivity operated to attract, maintain, and equip for survival only those individuals who were determined not to perish or be frightened into retreat. But this same selectivity also produced a problem for the internal cohesiveness of the Spanish community. Aggressiveness is not a trait which can be channeled in one direction only: the very person who could survive the rigors of outpost life and Indian warfare was just as likely to engage in behavior detrimental to the well-being of his neighbors and community. There were various aspects of social dysfunctionalism in such internecine conflict and, most importantly, the population needed all the internal cohesiveness it could muster in order to maintain maximum joint defense against both nature and human foes.

The difficulties were further compounded by the fact that the area was short of military and clergy. The presence of the latter in particular was crucial to the maintenance of peace since it was the power of the Church which acted as a strong force to restrain disruptive behavior and work for the continuance of traditional Hispanic culture.

Following the reconquest of the area by de Vargas in 1692 a request was issued for the establishment in the region of the Third Order of St. Francis, an organization of laymen whose Rule of Life had been established by St. Francis in the thirteenth century so as to accommodate secular figures who wished to work for the amins of the order. (The First Order of Franciscans consisted of monks; the Second Order, Poor Clares, of nuns.)

The Franciscans played an important role in the establishment of Spanish rule in the New World, but both history and a sea change seem to have affected the entire order after the sixteenth century. The guidelines laid down by St. Francis underwent great change and, in the New World especially, the rule of self-discipline gave way to excesses of self-punishment — often of the cruelest and most senseless variety. Toribio de Benavente, speaking of seventeenth century Mexico, (Steck 1951: 143–144), wrote that, "... every Friday of the year and on three days of the week during the Lent they take the Discipline in the churches ... some disciplined themselves with wire scourges and others with cords ... [others] ... carry the cross."

As late as 1833 only three episcopal visits had been made to New Mexico and even the records of 1850 show only ten priests serving the entire area of New Mexico (de Baca 1954: 55). These few men could not (and often would not) discourage behavior which time would show was repugnant to Rome. Although the apparent rationale of de Vargas' attempt to establish the Third Order was a belief that such an organization would serve both as a supplementary rule of social order and a technique whereby the few Franciscans could serve as an institutional nexus which would link together the isolated mountain villages, the results were not as expected. For example, although technically it was the First Order whose members were canonically allowed to direct the activities of the Third Order laity, the Third Order became an organization so independently powerful, and functionally so far removed from the original structure that, for a time, the Church rejected their presence and members were even excommunicated.

The Third Order (later, in New Mexico, to become Los Hermanos Penitentes de la Tercera Orden de San Francisco) did perform practical tasks relevant to village affairs and leadership but their secular role became inextricably intertwined with their own revisionist view of the proper functioning and ultimate aim of the order. It was at this point that self-punishment became an expressive mode for the leitmotif of violence which was so dominant in the lives of these frontier people. The tortures to which members would submit themselves were ingenious, cooperative, and imaginative: whipping by yucca whips, rolling on spiny cactus, kneeling in red ant hills, the holding of candles until they burnt to the flesh, crucifixion (though, theoretically, never deliberately until death), and other acts of piety and atonement for the sins of the mind and the flesh were performed so as to attain an ecstasy of agony.

I would suggest that the impetus for and extensiveness of membership, and the historical durability of the society may all be explained by the argument that the folk of these isolated communities recognized, albeit largely out of awareness, the need for a set of controls of potential for violence by individuals who lived removed from most punitive restraints of ethical, hieratic and secular controls. Internal peace was maintained by the redirecting of the potential for unpredictable, personally-impelled aggression.

The redirection took the course of historically familiar and socially controllable, patterned self-violence and, perhaps most importantly, a self-violence which was based on an exploration of one's sins against God's code and one's fellow men. The violent acts of the brotherhood were condoned because they not only served to maintain what was considered a necessary orientation toward the practice of violence but also controlled that violence within the internal network. When one considers that the Indian wars of the Southwest did not end until the late nineteenth century and that Anglos — particularly Texans — are even now an economic threat, it is not difficult to see why the Spanish could not afford to relax their belief that violence, from and toward those who would oust them from their precarious perch, was an ordinary fact of everyday existence.

It is this historical background which would seem to explain the important role played by Hispanic-speakers in the dissolution of the majority of Hippie communes during the 1960's. Not only were Hippies just another variety of "Anglo outsider" (whom Hispanos saw as threatening their way of life in the valley), they were especially vulnerable because of their philosophy and the category into which they were put by "respectable" Anglos.

The Hippies as such are a phenomenon of the mid-twentieth century, not only in North America but also in other areas of the world. The life style they propound, however, is not unique to these times; there have been those before who preferred the life of wandering monks and scholars, of hobos and bohemians; one does not have to stretch an analogy to be able to draw parallels between present-day communes and various utopian communities, particularly those of nineteenth-century America. It is not in point here to discuss the reasons for their recent, brief florescence, of the "call of the lemmings" which drew over 2,000 of them to the Taos area.

Although there were only three communes left by 1972 (and these had shrunk considerably in membership) there had been as many as twenty during the brief decade in which they had flocked to what some called "The Second Valley of Buddha." Taos became known as the "in place" on the circuit — a kind of nature-lover's Haight-Ashbury. Further, it was touted as a place where drugs were available without too much difficulty, especially peyote. (Many had read the various accounts of the Native American Church and knew that Taos Pueblo was the only one of the nineteen Pueblos ever to have had an explicit involvement in the ritual use of the hallucinogen.)

There is no question in the minds of the local people that it was the vigilante activities of the predominantly Spanish population which drove the majority of commune members away from the valley. Yet, when the original Flower Children had begun drifting into Taos they were viewed with amusement or condescending acceptance by most of the residents, whether Indian, Hispano, or Anglo. Taos had been a noted art colony for over half a century; in the town of several thousand people there are usually about sixty galleries, some doing a business of over $100,000 a year. Writers, musicians, potters, and silversmiths all combine to give Taos "atmosphere." As a local popular song puts it, "You can be anything that you want to be/In Fernandes de Taos by the Rio Grande." People remarked that Hippies added more color to an area already attractive to tourists for its bohemian flavor. *Taoseños* had been complaining for many years that the true flavor of Taos, established during the twenties and thirties by such international figures as D. H. and Frieda Lawrence, Dorothy Brett, and Mable Dodge, was fading. The artistic and/or intellectual cliques of the town claimed that Taos was becoming a "Tawdry Texas Tourist Trap," dominated by neon-embellished motels, souvenir shops, and drive-in hamburger stands. Thus, the initial Hippie invasion reaffirmed this group's rather unrealistic perception of Taos — a place where the avant garde flourished, and the Babbits of the world were properly scorned. The philosophy of "do your own thing" was shared by both and provided a bond which later proved the first — and last — time of defense for most Hippies.

For the others in Taos the Hippies brought hopes of a new wave of national fame and increased prosperity. After all, "everyone knew" they'd drift on after a few days or weeks. In the meantime, tourists continued to flock in and head for the plaza to see "the weirdos" in their "strange apparel and their foolish ways."

This also reaffirmed the cultural identity of all three ethnic groups in Taos. They laughed as they saw the Hippies and tourists eye one another; each whispered asides of ridicule to their own. Only The *Taoseños* were superior in this world of rocks and bermudas, love beads and tattered shifts. The one real bond among the three cultures of Taos — a belief in the "specialness" of all who lived in the valley — was shown as all locals united in reasuring each other that the golden years were about to be revived.

For a while, then, the residents and the Hippies had a kind of symbiotic relationship and the Hippies were viewed as merely one more "type" of the sort that had always been attracted to Taos and that would bring money in as well as assist in attracting the tourist trade — especially Texans, Oklahomans, and Kansans — which provided a major part of the valley's income.

Unfortunately for the Hippies, however, the general tightening of the economy in the late 1960's was also felt in Taos. Taos, like many resort areas, had continued to raise prices throughout the affluent years — "going for what the traffic will bear" — and suddenly, people didn't "do better" than they had the year before, a pattern which had been consistent since the late 1940's. Searching for a rationale, many valley residents began to complain that Hippies were getting so numerous that they were driving the conservative middle-class tourists away. "They don't want to come into a place that's got those dirty smelly long-hairs around. Hell! People don't dare bring their families here anymore because of drugs and all that sex right out in the open!"

The Spanish were not only hit first and hardest by the economic pinch; they were also the ones most threatened by the new set of values presented by this "peculiar breed" of essentially affluent Anglo young people. How much of their perception was true is not in question here; it is enough to say that they believed the worst.

Two more elements ware added to the situation. By 1969 people in the valley were talking of a Hippie invasion: "They say that 5,000 [10,000, 20,000, 100,000] are going to invade the town this summer! They're just going to take over!" "Yeah, I heard that a bunch of the Hells Angels are coming here to beat the crap out of 'em. And that leaves us in the middle!" Some fuel for this rumor (and it proved to be nothing more) was added by the fact that the Hippies had not just "drifted" through but had begun buying up property and establishing permanent communes. And, finally, there was an outbreak of hepatitis which was of epidemic proportions in the Hippie population.

Comment by a Spanish-American businessman:

They come in dirty, living like animals, talking sex and dirt, and high on drugs most of the time; and they're bad examples for our kids. They go around half-dressed — when they aren't swimming naked at the Hot Springs, where any of our kids can see them any time!

Comment by an Anglo businesswoman:

They really treat their own kids terribly. I've seen them give hard drugs to little ones not even in school yet. They don't feed them, or wash them. They aren't decent human beings — the way they neglect their own children and bring them up like animals.

Comment by an Anglo waitress:

They're crazy! They drop out of school and then live off their parents. And all that disease! Hepatitis and God knows what else! We try to bring our kids up to live decent lives and then they see some rich kid from back East come in and run around in junk clothes, with bare feet, tossing away everything his family worked so hard to give him. What's happening to the world? Has everyone started to go crazy?

Comment by a Spanish-American high school student:

They dodge the draft; they use money from home to buy those dumb bells, and psychedelic clothes, and lights, and incense and stuff like that. Then they line up for our food stamps. One more way you Anglos screw us Spanish — coming and going.

Comment by a Taos Pueblo farmer:

They come in with their dirt and they put their feet in our stream that we get our drinking and cooking water from — and they bathe in it. Why, we use that there stream and we have rules about how to use it. Who are they that they can come out here and do that like they belong in the pueblo? And they ask us for peyote. And even our young kids they ask for drugs. And they try to get them to have "Indian nature ceremonies" with them. They ridicule us with their dime-store Indian clothes, and then they act like they think we should welcome them. We don't want those pseudo-Sioux [a derogatory term for any romantic Anglo who tries to dress or adopt tribal ways].

The scene was set for violence and it began on a small personal scale. At first, there were isolated incidents involving individuals; a beating, a robbery, some roughhousing in a local bar. The next phase involved raiding the communes, searching out females for a crowd rape, and imposing more severe beatings. Attacks could employ as many as fifteen to twenty men and not uncommonly consisted of seven or eight who carried knives and/or guns.

By 1969 several attacks had been made upon a cooperative store at the edge of town by men in pickup trucks, who fired shotgun blast at the storefront; there was open boasting by some individuals of the extent and supposed effectiveness of their vigilante activities; students told how a few teachers in the high school were urging their classes to help in the effort to get rid of the Hippies: and a widening circle of fear and fear of involvement was demonstrated by the genuineness with which people would caution friends to avoid certain parts of the back areas when rumors circulated or a particular vigilante strike to be made that evening. One particularly gruesome incident centered on a local group stopping a long-haired, bearded Hippie just off the central plaza and demanding that he "come along and get his hair cut." Repeated demands — and repeated refusals — resulted in the boy being held while kerosene was dumped over his head and then set fire.

Through all of this the response of the Hippies — transient or commune members — tended to be defensive and pacifistic. They continued to try and maintain their unstructured, open-encampment life, and seemed to make a conscious effort to treat the attacks as individually motivated, not a reason for them to become prejudiced against a class or group of people in Taos generally. The turning point appeared to have come when Dennis Hopper (of Hollywood's "Easy Rider" fame) bought a luxurious house in Taos.

He brought with him a retinue which included what several in Taos unkindly called "his drugstore cowboy sycophants." Who sought out whom is difficult to say but Hopper was soon championing the Hippie cause. A group of locals "mixed up" with Hopper and his crowd one evening, and though Hopper was later to have legal difficulties as a result, it was said that he and his group claimed it had been a vigilante attack and announced that henceforth they would carry shotguns and rifles in their vehicles at all times. People talked of how Hopper was boasting that he would "break the back" of the anti-Hippie forces.

The commune members were now faced with a dilemma: should they support their champion (if such he actually was) and in so doing deny the principles upon which their communities and their new value systems were founded? Or should they let him fight THEIR battles alone?

For many the problem was unsolvable. The dilemma and/or the terrorism was too much and by summer of 1970 at least half of the communes had disappeared, their members simply taking to the road to find a new paradise — "maybe in Montana or up north somewhere." Some of the remaining commune members began carrying shotguns in their pickups (though whether the guns were even loaded is not known for sure).

The vigilantes, however, argued that their program was showing results and continued the attacks with no let up. The major difference was that there were fewer communes and stray Hippies against whom they could direct their efforts and this meant greater concentration against the few.

The denouement was now at hand. Commune members began to talk of vigilantes (for the most part Spanish-Americans) as "naive dupes of the Anglo Establishment." They were laying the psycho-cultural groundwork to fight not "the beautiful common folk," whom they had come prepared to love for their Hemingwayesque "simple grandeur," but rather the traditional enemy of both Hippies and minorities, now perceived as being at the root of their problem:

Man! Like, don't you see? It's the old divide-and-conquer routine. They've lied to these people; they've gotten to them the economic way — firing anyone who showed a decent attitude and scaring the rest into going after us. Like, it's the almighty buck still running things.

Once this rationale was established the commune members finally appeared able to begin using the guns to defend themselves and began setting up armed guards around the communes. Though possibly unrelated to the harassment, the communes also began selecting the individuals whom they would admit to membership to the communes, and aggressive remarks began to replace the former "peace and love" phrases. It seemed that they were now able to use (or threaten to use) violence without perceiving it as an abrogation of their pacifistic belief system. They were not shooting at Hispanic brothers; they were hitting back at those "Tio Pepes who had betrayed their own kind to work as Anglo dupes." The Hippies saw themselves as defending not only their own homesteads but the homestead — the freedom and democracy — of the oppressed as well. They were not shooting at individuals; they were attacking the aggressors (now impersonal and dehumanized) and fighting for everyman.

The threat of violence now became too pervasive for all but the most stalwart commune members and by the summer of 1971 there were only a few communes left — perhaps as few as three but no more than five or six. Those that remained had changed considerably in character. They were secretive and remote, highly structured in organization (by comparison, that is, to what had been intended as an open-commune life style), and restrictive in membership. Those who remained were there only because "they loved peace so much they would fight to preserve it." Thus, they fell back on a traditional American rationale for instituting and maintaining violence (or the threat of it), "the preservation of TRUE peace." Those who were unable to adopt this new strategy simply left — another trait within the American historical tradition; many of our immigrants had fled their European homelands to avoid the conflicts (and, often, conscription) of nineteenth-century continental life.

Has this material given us any insights into the nature of violence? And, if so, do those insights have any pragmatic value? Or, to ask a question which is stylistically more *au courant*, are these data relevant?

The foregoing material has demonstrated that real or perceived situations structure the form which violence will take. The primary significance of the data lies in the model for categorizing violence which has evolved in the course of the study. It is clear that all three groups varied in what I am calling their channelization process. The Indians compartmentalized (to use Dozier's term 1961: 150–151, 175–178), the Spanish intensified, and the Hippies transformed.

The first process allows a group to separate out violence from the "normal" cultural totality; the second technique allows an existing element of the system to be extended while mainaining supportive ties with the rest of culture; and the third rationalizes goal alteration. There may be a fourth process, codification (not illustrated here) in which violence becomes mutated into a "nonviolent" aspect (as language is encoded into writing) and represented by games, play, legal actions, verbal exchanges, and so on.

The data graphically illustrate that violence — like such patterns as seating habits, humor, sex, proxemics, and social control — is culturally patterned. Different groups will not perform the same acts of violence in the same style as will other groups in similar situations. Once stated, the point seems too simple, almost a truism. Yet a survey of the literature reveals that the obvious has tended to be overlooked; indeed, many have proceeded (e.g. in the fields of international negotiations, ethnic relations, penology and criminology, and the analysis of violence generally) as if it were not so.

It seems not unreasonable to argue that it is necessary to make an examination of such details as the structuring of violence; its accepted and ignored forms; the variations between those techniques which are considered suitable in particular circumstances for groups — and for individuals; styles which are considered "legitimate" for the elite and for the folk; the personnel involved; how violence is legitimized; and the cognitive categories which differentiate physical and psychological violence, aggression and conflict, terrorism and sadism — to list only a few.

We might ask, for example, if headhunting, corporal punishment, the battered-child syndrome, games and play of various types, ceremonial sacrifice, hunting for sport, and suicide are "the same kind" of violence — if indeed we even agree that they are all forms of violence. Is there a subculture of violence (as some have suggested) — and what does that mean? Is it a universal that when conflict occurs between two or more groups each will hold the emic view that it is exogenous in nature? Or do some groups (as, apparently, do some individuals) see the generating of violence as a positive good — something to be sought after for the stimulation or the constant renewal that it brings?

It is very easy to be trapped into making glib and superficial statements about violence; though I have tried to avoid it I'm sure this paper is not innocent of them. Yet, we are in too great a state of naïveté. To give only one example, one need only take an objective look at the amount of ink spilled concerning the relationship between the internalization of violence by an individual and his exposure to violence via the mass media. Yet no one has explored the correlation between such exposure and the presence of a large segment of American youth who are altruistic and pacifistic, nor that other segment who are altruistic and revolutionary (or counterrevolutionary, for that matter). (For a recent discussion on this see Larsen 1967.)

It would be interesting to explore the hypothesis that violence becomes increasingly depersonalized (though with wider-ranging implications), as one moves up the economic scale in his society. Conversely, is it true that the less access one has to scarce goods the more individualized, immediate, and narrow is the expression of violence? If this hypothesis were valid would the cause be related to the degree of power which one has in initiating, sustaining and terminating group violence? We have no accepted classification of the forms of violence, sexual or age variation, or even the degrees of acceptability of various kinds of violence. If violence is a fact of societies; if, as many would argue, it is increasing and the number of individuals being recruited into organizations dedicated to violence is multiplying, then surely a clearer perspective is required.

In short, considering how significant a part of behavior is violence, there is little known on the subject. The material which has been reviewed here makes no attempt to being statistically grounded, or being socioculturally conclusive. It is presented in order to point up the tremendous deficiency and limitations that exist in our studies despite a wealth of data on the structure of social systems and the cultural glue which holds such systems together. It may be argued that violence is a warning signal of social ills and, as such, we should not strive to eliminate a valuable — perhaps necessary and structurally irreplaceable — element. But few would argue the desirability of limiting uncontrolled expansion of violence to a point at least slightly less than that of total endemic conflict. One hopes that increased attention to the study of violence will enable man to control his innate capacity for absolute oblivion.

REFERENCES

BARTH, FREDRIK
   1959   *Political leadership among the Swat Pathans.* Monograph of Social
          Anthropology 19. London: London School of Economics.
BENEDICT, RUTH
   1934   *Patterns of culture.* Boston: Houghton Mifflin. (Mentor edition, 1946.)
BOHANNAN, PAUL
   1967   *Law and warfare: studies in the anthropology of conflict.* New York:
          The Natural History Press.
COSER, LEWIS
   1954   "Toward a sociology of social conflict." Unpublished doctoral
          dissertation, Columbia University.
DE BACA, FABIOLA CABEZA
   1954   *We fed them cactus.* Albuquerque: University of New Mexico Press.
DOZIER, EDWARD P.
   1956   *The functions of social conflict.* Glencoe: The Free Press.
   1961   "Rio Grande pueblos," in *Perspectives in American Indian culture
          change.* Edited by Edward H. Spicer, 94–186. Chicago: University of
          Chicago Press.
FENTON, WILLIAM N.
   1957   *Factionalism at Taos Pueblo, New Mexico.* Bureau of American Ethno-
          logy, Anthropological Papers 56. Reprinted in BAE Bulletin 164:
          297–344. Washington, D. C.: U. S. Government Printing Office.
FRENCH, DAVID H.
   1948   *Factionalism in Isleta Pueblo.* New York: American Ethnological
          Society.
GLUCKMAN, MAX
   1956   *Custom and conflict in Africa.* London: Basil Blackwell. (Barnes and
          Noble edition, 1967.)
   1963   *Order and rebellion in tribal Africa.* Glencoe: The Free Press.
HOEBEL, E. ADAMSON
   1954   *The law of primitive man.* Cambridge, Massachusetts: Harvard Uni-
          versity Press.
LARSEN, OTTO, *editor*
   1967   *Violence and the mass media.* New York: Harper and Row.

LEACH, EDMUND
1954   *Political systems of highland Burma.* London: Bell.
LUNDBERG, GEORGE A.
1939   *Foundations of sociology.* New York: Macmillan.
OTTERBEIN, KEITH F.
1965   Conflict and communication: the social matrix of Obeah. *Kansas Journal of Sociology* 3:112–128.
1968a   Internal war: a cross-cultural study. *American Anthropologist* 70:277–289.
1968b   *Cross-cultural studies of armed combat.* Studies in International conflict, Research Monograph 1. *Buffalo Studies* 4(1):91–109.
1970   The evolution of war: a cross-cultural study. *Behavior Science Notes* 4:221–236.
SIMMEL, GEORG
1955   *Conflict and the web of group-affiliations.* Translated by K. H. Wolff and Reinhard Bendix. Glencoe: The Free Press.
SOREL, GEORGE
1950   *Reflections on violence.* Glencoe: The Free Press.
STECK, F. B., *editor and translator*
1951   *History of the Indians of New Spain,* by Toribio Motolinia de Benavente. Academy of American Franciscan History, Documentary Series 1. Lexington: Franciscan Academy.

A Consideration of Feud
and Conflict in a
Mediterranean Island Society

ALEXANDER LOPASIC

The area we are dealing with is the central part of the island of Sardinia known as Barbagia, which has a pastoral economy and a land-holding system. Land is held either by individuals or by communes and is rented to shepherds for a fixed period of time, usually for a year, and then renewed if the parties agree.

Barbagia is the most mountainous part of Sardinia and includes the highest mountains of the island, such as Monte Genargentu (1834 meters) or Sopramonte (1463 meters). The largest part of the area is covered with pastures known as "pascolo brado" (wild pastures) covered with small shrubs and macchia grazed by large flocks of sheep, goats, and some herds of cattle. It represents the chief means of existence for the population.

This explains the importance of pastures which are sometimes hired at high rates, creating one of the sources of tension between the pasture owners and their tenants. Some of the pastures are of low quality and the quality of most of the pastures often depends on the weather conditions of a particular agricultural year — the shepherds who rent them rarely improve the pastures.

The so-called "hunger for pastures" in Central Sardinia is partly related to this indifference toward improvement held both by owners and tenants, and the insufficient and uneconomic utilization of pastures has contributed toward their insecure position, particularly of the better ones which are subject to trespass, burning, and stealing or destruction of flocks.

Though the rental rates for communal land are relatively low and though the quality of land varies from region to region, the attitude toward communal land upkeep does not vary much from that for privately rented land. Because communal land belongs to everybody, and therefore nobody in particular, it is often badly neglected. Some communes have tried to improve their land but have encountered strong opposition from the shepherd-tenants who believe that some of them would profit more than the others. In particular, the shepherd-tenants have opposed the land-irrigation programs proposed by the local and regional authorities.

Another obvious difficulty is the extreme fragmentation and diminution of the landed property due to the traditional inheritance laws, according to which the inherited land is divided equally among all the children. This results in the atomization of the smaller and medium properties. The inheritance laws occasionally cause tensions among the inheritors, and conflicts and vendettas are the result of such family tensions. Quite recently a man stabbed a relative for refusing him the use of a passage which his family has enjoyed for half a century.

Shortage of water is one of the traditional plagues of the island which has been eased to some extent by the creation of artificial lakes and the regulation of rivers. However, abundance of water is still considered a great advantage which might be trespassed upon and misused when the owner is absent. Artesian wells and water-wells are therefore well guarded.

Because of the harsh climatic conditions in the mountains, a large number of shepherds leave their villages and in the winter move with their flocks to pastures with a milder climate in Campidano or Baronia. Richer pastures with more water and a milder climate has made Campidano very important to the shepherds from Barbagia, especially to those from the higher villages such as Fonni, Ollolai, or Gavoi.

In the past, the presence of half-nomadic shepherds from the mountains in Campidano has sometimes led to robbery-expeditions or the famous "Bardanas" (e.g. the one performed by about 100 Orgosolo outlaws against Tortoli in 1894). Fear of the mountain population is well expressed in a Campidano saying: "Leave your horses in the stables as the mountain people are coming, those wearing leggings." Today, these tense relations between the highlanders and the lowlanders are diminished due to recent purchases of land by enterprising shepherds from some of the highest villages in Barbagia. However, high costs of hiring pasture in Campidano even today result in tensions and conflicts between some landed proprietors and their highland-tenants.

A classic source of tension in a shepherd society is, of course, cattle stealing. Some statistics indicate a decrease in cattle stealing, but as no complete figures exist (only a part of the thefts are reported), no definite evidence can be offered. Stealing, as a mark of personal courage and arrogance, is appreciated by the people of Barbagia. In the past a person who did not engage in such enterprises was not considered a worthy marriage partner. A girl's relatives would say: "He is not good enough to steal even a lamb," and refuse the suitor. Such enterprises are dangerous but at the same time fair, as the owner has the opportunity to defend himself and his flock. If the animals were stolen in his absence it is considered even worse for him.

Increasing one's status through stealing is one of the ways in this egalitarian society that an individual can improve his social position and become the centre of a clique, which will try to imitate his example and contribute to the prestige of the able and brave cattle-thief. But, of course, his position and life might be endangered by the envy of others or by the cattle owner's wish to retaliate.

The idea of reciprocity is important, and if somebody has 20 sheep stolen he will try to retaliate by stealing 30 or 40. To outdo one's opponent is an important aspect of such retaliation. He can do better, he is braver and more courageous, therefore he has the right to more respect and will enjoy higher prestige. It is a continuous contest in a society where neither nature nor neighbours are particularly generous. Stealing itself is not considered a grave offence, but shooting and casualties may occur on both sides if the owner is encountered.

Cattle and sheep may also be killed, as a retaliation for some old standing offence. The culprit will be watched by relatives and friends of the enemy, and when the opportunity comes they invade his pen and kill a number of animals either by cutting their throats with a gardening-knife or by shooting them with a gun. Cases of 100, 200, or 300 sheep being killed are not unusual.

Such killing of animals, if done on a large scale, can easily destroy the livelihood of a shepherd, who in turn will try to retaliate. This leads to long-standing feuds, often to blood-feuds, as the injured person will mobilize all his friends and relatives to find out who the offender is. The killing of a bull or a ram is considered a particularly severe offence and must be paid for in blood, for it is considered that the offender wanted to destroy the owner's flock by destroying the "seed" of the flock.

Generally speaking, loss of sheep and cattle leads to mobilization of friends and relatives and puts into action a mechanism of mutual help from individuals who might easily become involved in feuding relations with the offender, his relatives and friends. It can lead to a series of mutual hostilities, some of long duration.

The social structure is based on a bilateral kinship system and strong kinship ties between members of 3–4 generations' depth of linear and collateral relatives who normally exchange help and hospitality on different occasions.

Artificial kinship ties are extended to the godfather who is considered to be a person of confidence and who stands up for his godchild in different life situations, particularly if the godson and his family need help. This includes helping in a search for stolen animals, financial help, and protection of the godson in time of danger. Offending a relative is considered bad, but offending the godfather would mean in practice offending the godson and would demand retaliation. It might end with a few punches, but in serious offences it could end in bloodshed.

Villagers tend to keep on good terms with their neighbors with whom they may exchange small favors and help, but in serious matters it will be the family which will decide the action. This includes retaliation in cases of offence, and it will be the family that will decide what action is going to be taken and when. The men take action, but much of the instigation is done by women, who are fairly independent, particularly among the shepherds where they make many decisions in the absence of their shepherd husbands. There are occasional cases of women taking retaliatory action; e.g. a mother revenged herself for the murder of her son by killing a brother of the offender. However, such cases are rare. Children are normally exempt from retaliatory actions, but a few cases of killing children as a vendetta are reported. Such actions are considered particularly vile and provoke a very negative reaction. One of the famous Barbagia bandits was killed a few days after he killed a child of one of his opponents because of a vendetta.

Normally retaliation does not take place immediately. The vendetta has to grow and ripen; it has to be and will be done, but when is decided by the avenger. It is also wise to wait, as the police might easily suspect a person who was known to be on bad terms with the victim. In addition, the waiting tends to put the opponent at ease, and after years he may forget the danger. A recent case is of a vendetta killing after 18 years. Awaiting the right opportunity to vindicate oneself is another reason for delay. The opponent's life habits and movements are carefully watched and then at the right moment the retaliation will take place. Big feasts such as Christmas, Easter, or the Patron Saint Day are used for such a purpose, as it hurts the victim, his family, and relatives much more.

There are two types of vendetta. One is the BLOOD-FEUD vendetta usually performed in retaliation for another killing. The killing of male animals, as already mentioned, demands retaliation in blood as well; likewise the destruction of entire flocks or a large part of them. Such vendettas might go on for a long time but their continuation will depend on family members' wishes. Some long-standing feuds have ended after a male member of one side married a girl from the opposite camp. In some cases the third or fourth generation might lose interest in the vendetta and decide to stop. Even so, they might avoid each other in private and/or in public. Lack of confidence might easily remain between such feuding families for a very long time, even if no hostile action takes place. There are cases of flare-ups of old rancors after many years, and here the smallest offence or provocation might be responsible.

One of the most famous of such long-standing feuds in Barbagia was between the two families in Orgosolo from 1900 to 1917, resulting in 25 dead, many wounded, and considerable material damage on both sides. It involved a number of other families, creating a real civil war between the two factions. It lead eventually to harsh punitive actions by the police and, in 1917, to a peace-treaty between the two sides in which a large number of people and authorities participated as guarantors. The last stroke was provoked by a dispute among a rich land-owner's inheritors, but the main reason was the retaliation in blood for one of the relatives killed in a dispute. Blood demanded blood and the chain of blood and other retaliations followed. Another such long-standing feud took place in another Barbagia village — one opponent's family tried to implicate their enemy in a murder of one of their relatives and when this failed they tried to show that he kept a large amount of ammunition and arms for large-scale outlaw action. The whole dispute took years.

Bad relations between two villages can be responsible for a blood-feud. Regular stealing of animals might provoke a murder which is paid for by bloodshed. A visit of a shepherd to a friend living in a hostile village might provoke a fight and a knifing. This leads to retaliation and in some cases to death. The way to further retaliation lies open.

Particularly in the past, broken promises of marriage, especially if aggravated by the girl's pregnancy, have lead to open hostilities and revenge in blood. In one famous case it was the girl herself who took action and killed her fiancé. In another case, a refused lover sang a song of contempt for the girl at the village piazza and as it touched the honor of the family he was killed by the girl's relatives.

Another offence provoking retaliation by blood is false testimony, either helping to condemn an innocent or helping to condemn the accused. Both such actions were considered to be the result of revenge and are considered as offences of extreme gravity.

Arson is another grave offence. It is regarded as a sign of complete disrespect and an open challenge, as are killing of male animals, false testimony, and destroying entire flocks. It might be answered by another example of arson, but more easily by revenge in blood.

The second type of vendetta is retaliation of a different kind which DOES NOT INVOLVE KILLING. It follows the logic of retaliation but it is not considered so grave as to demand bloodshed. In these cases intermediaries may step in. In blood-feuds such intermediaries would not intervene, as blood-offences are considered to be the problem of the opposing parties in which intermediaries cannot intervene. Cases in which intermediaries may act are inheritance disputes, boundary disputes, stealing of animals on a small scale, personal offences of minor importance, and some disputes over profits and money. In some of these cases the public authorities may make use of such intermediaries and in most cases their decision is accepted.

However, some of these minor incidents of revenge may provoke retaliation on a large scale which may develop into something more serious. For instance, continuous stealing of sheep or cows might end with bloodshed. Smaller offences and disputes might be settled but confidence is not always restored. Unwillingness to grant a favor is often one of the results. In the past, certain churches were considered to be "neutral territory" and were used as meeting places for feuding parties. They would approach the church from different parts and then meet at the entrance. No police or other intervening parties were allowed in such churches. This method excluded, however, blood-feuds.

Feuds certainly create tension between individuals, but relatives also can be easily involved on both sides. However, that does not mean that tension is always visible. A feud can exist for a long time without anything in particular happening, and then one day erupt in open retaliation, possibly creating troubles in the daily life of the village. Certain actions, like the recent large-scale stealing of animals in a village in Barbagia, have provoked a collective action and a practical mobilization of the entire male population; in this case they demanded punitive action against the neighboring village from where the cattle thief came. Eventually the police had to intervene.

The feud is related to both levels of the social organisation of which the individual is a part; namely, that of the family, with its extended family affiliation, and that of the village, which is composed of a number of such families. This also means that the feud is a part of these two loyalties and, to be more precise, an expression of them, a demonstration of both loyalties toward the internal and the external group: the family and the village. Traditionally, bad relations may exist between the villages of Bitti and Orune, Fonni and Orgosolo, Ollolai and Gavoi, etc., and such enmities might take different forms: e.g. occasional fights between groups of youngsters or shepherds, disputes over minor issues like whose costume is the more original, or a more permanent tension between shepherds and cattle owners. In instances where feuds involve bloodshed, loyalties are clearly on the side of each individual's own village. This does not mean that bad relations exist between all villagers, as good friendships might exist between individuals of such traditionally feuding villages. It does mean that in such cases the old rancor would prevail and put such friendship aside; even if only for a while.

The feud is certainly a powerful way of keeping the group together: either the smaller extended family or the larger village. When somebody dies, particularly from violence, there is a large-scale attendance at the funeral; and if a member of a village is a victim of the opposing village, the participation would have great significance. The funeral, thus, reinforces the importance of family and village ties. Also, the victim represents a permanent demand for vindication even if retaliation takes a long time. He exercises a pressure on individual members of the group. He forces the individual to participate in action, whatever it may be.

Today, a feud is very much a diachronic phenomenon; some individuals may avoid action by going from the village, either to continental Italy or abroad (to the Common Market countries). They may also forget to retaliate and the old rancor may be forgotten. However; flare-ups are always possible.

I have spoken a great deal about shepherds; but the traditional code of behavior of others is similar, even if some points of tension, such as disputes over pastures or cattle-stealing, may be absent or irrelevant.

We can now turn for a moment to feud as it exists in some other Mediterranean societies. Limited literature in the field does not permit me to go into details, but two points can be discussed briefly.

The existence of "eternal feud" between Bedouin groups in Cyrenaica was postulated by E. Peters who studied them in the first years after World War II. The study shows feud as it exists in a pastoral North-African society and is therefore of some interest as a comparison to a traditional pastoral but bilateral Mediterranean society. The idea of the "eternal feud" is known in Central Sardinia. However, the "ideal pattern" is today weakened by the diminishing influences of the extended family and avoidances of old rancors through emigration, etc. There are cases where the opponents have met to discuss the results of such old enmities should they continue and have then decided to stop.

The theory of realistic and nonrealistic conflict was developed by Black in his recent thesis dealing with different Mediterranean societies. He refers to disputes over cattle, water, or boundaries as realistic; disputes over honor, however, as less realistic. In the Sardinian case these categories cannot always be separated, realistic being mixed with the nonrealistic. Nonrealistic reasons like honor, prestige, hatred, or envy may be, however, more decisive and prominent. A dispute may easily start for very realistic reasons but develop into a nonrealistic one and be pursued with great vigor as a matter of loyalty to the traditional values of a shepherd society.

Culture and the
Expression of Emotion

E. RICHARD SORENSON

Culture, as the selectively patterned realization of basic human potential according to the social and physical parameters of a milieu, may modify the expression of such subcortically programmed neurophysical mechanisms as those of emotion. These neurophysiological "universals" may be common to all men regardless of differences in culture and background, as Darwin (1872) thought; but, at least in part, culture seems to pattern their expression.

Work with D. C. Gajdusek suggested that such patterning of human response emerges in the growing child as his central nervous system is differentially programmed by the various social and physical experiences provided by different cultures (Sorenson and Gajdusek 1966). With Paul Ekman a cross-cultural comparative study of facial expressions of emotion among culturally isolated peoples was initiated at my field station in the Fore region of New Guinea. From this study we concluded that there are universals in the facial expression of emotion (Ekman, Sorenson, and Friesen 1969). Here I review that work in greater detail and in the light of more complete data to suggest how cultural forces may act to modify and stereotype such neurophysiological universals.

This study grew out of earlier work by Tomkins, Ekman, and Friesen on recognition of facial affect by Westernized college students (Tomkins 1962, 1963; Tomkins and McCarter 1964; Ekman and Friesen 1969a, 1969b).

At Yagareba village, in the South Fore region of New Guinea, we developed the initial data collection procedures. A Fore sample was obtained. I then extended the sampling to a gathering group in the Sepik Hills region of New Guinea and a settled agricultural group in Borneo.

The Fore were a remote isolated people with no contact with the outside commercial or technological world until the mid-1950's. It was not until 1957 that the first government patrol post was established in their region. Up to that time the Fore had remained an isolated primitive people using bows and arrows. They had no metal, no cloth, no concept of money, and possessed a culture quite different from the people of the Western world. A last vestige of a once more common way-of-life, the Fore were a proto-agricultural people possessing a kind of socioeconomic organization which followed hunting-gathering and preceded settled agriculture (see Plates 1 and 2). Penetrating a fringe pioneer region extending southward from a large deforested Eastern Highlands core, the Fore verged onto vast regions of unexploited virgin rainforest. An informal socio-political structure facilitated flexible segmentation — a practice well-suited to opportunistic exploitation of new lands.

In the 1960's changes in the Fore life-style began to occur rather quickly. Unusually adaptive, the Fore were quick to shed their indigenous practices to adopt an emerging market culture similar to those forming throughout the Highlands around access to Western economy under the aegis of Western government.

At the time of this field work, some Fore were in daily contact with Western government officers, missionaries, and scientists (and their families); some worked as servants and day-laborers in or around Western households or communities; others had lived as workers on Western-administered plantations outside the Fore region. These Fore had a chance to learn the facial expressions used by Westerners. But there were also Fore who had remained apart from these Westernizing influences. Some had remained largely in their isolated hamlets and had not had an opportunity to become acquainted with the typical facial expressions of Westerners. These individuals met our requirement of VISUAL ISOLATION (i.e. they had not had sufficient direct experience with alien people or their pictorial media to have learned their culturally specific language of facial expression).

The different degrees of acculturation possessed by the Fore made it possible to divide our subjects into three groups: most acculturated, less acculturated, and least acculturated.

With the help of Wayne Dye, a linguist of the Summer Institute of Linguistics who spoke Bahinemo, I was able to extend this study to another kind of New Guinea group, one more visually isolated than the Fore, one relying primarily on a gathering economy. The social organization and ecological setting of these people differed from that of the Fore (see Plates 3 and 4).

We interviewed the Bahinemo subjects in two distantly separated regions: (1) Wasui Lagoon to the north of the central Sepik River, and (2) Muli village on a hillock surrounded by sago swamps between the headwaters of the April and Korosameri Rivers. The Bahinemo at Wasui Lagoon had only recently moved down from the hill region; but, since they arrived, they had been in frequent contact with Mr. Dye, his wife and children, and occasionally, with traders and government officers. Muli village was completely isolated; no Westerner had yet been there, although some of its residents had been out to villages in contact with the outside. We found Muli by random searching from the first helicopter to be used in this region and landed there without warning in the company of a Bahinemo speaker from Wasui.

We were much less familiar with Bahenimo behavior and culture than any of the other groups studied. It was a culture which had not yet been reported. Unlike the situation in the Fore, I had no well-known native assistants to depend on and to explain the task. And, more than the Fore, the Bahinemo had not had experience with ethnographic interviews. Furthermore, Caucasian faces were still unfamiliar; some wondered why the white man appeared angry much of the time. Also, unlike the Fore, there was a reticence associated with socioideological secrecy as a means of maintaining group solidarity.

The Borneo sample was made possible by the cooperation of Kent Stauffer, at that time a Peace Corps volunteer working among the Sadong Dyaks in southwest Sarawak. He spoke the Bidayuh language of this group of Hill Dyaks and assisted in the sampling.

The Sadong were not as visually isolated as the Fore, but they were still living in their traditional longhouses and maintained their traditional settled subsistence agricultural way-of-life (see Plate 5). One man spoke a little English, most men spoke some Malay, and several had seen motion pictures at Serian, a small commercial center about a day's walk from their longhouse. Women and young children, for the most part, spoke only Bidayuh. Most school-aged children were learning to speak English and Malay in a school established six years earlier.

In sampling we relied on photographs selected on the basis of Sylvan S. Tomkins's work defining primary affect states. We limited ourselves to seven basic emotions: happiness, fear, anger, surprise, sadness, disgust, and contempt. The final set of pictures was selected from more than 3,000 affect photographs, collected primarily by Tomkins, on the basis of high agreement among American college students on the emotion expressed (see Plate 6).

We devised three basic data-gathering methodologies. Two of these were based on native responses to our affect photographs; the third was based on pictures we took of natives posing affect expression.

Ekman preferred an interview technique adapted from Dashiell (1927) and Izard (1971) based on simple stories designed to connote specific emotions (Method 1). I favored a technique where the subject was asked to respond with an affect term from his own language as he looked at a single picture (Method 2). These two approaches had different merits and weaknesses.

METHOD 1   On the basis of knowledge of Fore culture, short stories were devised to portray a particular emotional state in Fore daily life. For example, theft or deliberate injury to someone's pig would be certain to cause anger. Thus, the story connoting anger was about a man whose pigs had been injured by another. The subject was asked to point to a picture, out of a set of 2 or 3, which showed how the owner of the pig felt. No verbal response was required. This, we felt, was an easier task than having to respond with a spoken answer.

The outstanding weaknesses of this technique were the difficulties of (1) devising stories in an alien culture which we were sure unambiguously reflected the emotions we had in mind, and (2) controlling the testing situation.

Neither Ekman nor Friesman (who participated in the second field trip) knew Melanesian-Pidgin or Fore. My own Melanesian-Pidgin was good; but I was not up to making myself understood in Fore beyond the simplest messages or to follow native discourse. Therefore, we had to rely on Fore translator-assistants to explain the task and relate the stimulus stories; communication between the translator-assistants and subjects was unmonitorable. In view of Fore communicational conventions, it was likely that at least some responses were influenced by feedback between translator and subject. No Fore, even the school boys who had begun to learn a little English, could be expected to have sufficiently internalized our Western concepts of a testing situation to avoid "leaking" information. The suggestion that free exchange of information was "cheating" was quite alien to the Fore concept of cooperative relationship. Thus, the best we could do was to continually impress our assistants with the importance of not discussing the pictures with the subjects, telling them what pictures to select, or to suggest key features to watch for. The effect of our cautions is unknown.

METHOD 2   We showed a set of photographs of facial affect one at a time. Only the social scientists, a single Fore assistant who had worked

Plate 1. The Fore setting. Vast stands of virgin rainforest cover much of the mountains which the Fore call their home. As these proto-agricultural people continue to move into the virgin lands with gardens and hamlets, irregular clearings of varying size develop to punctuate this rain forest. Abandoned gardens are replaced by unproductive grasslands. Above, a serpentine path of abandoned grasslands winds through unclaimed virgin forest to current sites of settlement and gardening (top, right). At the extremity of one such path, a typical hamlet-garden complex sustains the lives of the Fore who have settled there (top, left). Hamlets are small (top, left; bottom, left and right), a consequence of the continual segmentation by which the Fore take advantage of new lands. A virgin environment of this sort favors a dispersing society, like that the Fore have evolved, characterized by small groups of close friends and kinsmen breaking away from earlier communities to take advantage of new lands. Exhausted lands are left behind. Incompatible people move in different directions. Social organization based on informal unbinding relationship is advantageous in such a setting. Personal rapport, tacit understanding, trust, and intimacy emerge as principles of group solidarity — not formal kinship with graded responsibilities, codified obligation, or principles of conduct.

Plate 2. Fore proto-agricultural associates. Midway between hunting-gathering and settled agricultural societies, the Fore proto-agriculturalists form small, closely interacting groups of voluntary associates. Subsistence gardening is the basic economic activity, and daily life revolves around the hamlets and their outlying gardens. Hamlets are self-sustaining and require little from other regions. Relationships within these groups of associates are cooperative and consensual; labor and food are shared rather than garnered.

Above, two women with their children leave the sweet potato garden they have been cultivating cooperatively, to return to their hamlet with bags of vegetables under their bark capes (top, left). Hamlet mates begin to return to their hamlet as the mid-afternoon clouds gather; some have already begun preparations for the major daily meal (top, right). Men place bundles of vegetables in a collective cooking pit for an informal community feast (bottom, left). Women sit together to prepare vegetables to cook in the pit (bottom, right).

Plate 3.   The Bahinemo of Wasui Lagoon.   Within the last generation Bahinemo
from the difficult to reach Sepik Hill region have left their isolated interior villages to
settle near the Sepik River on Wasui Lagoon. The newest of these communities is
Hahamsuwe (top, left) which has been settled only in the last few years by immigrants
from remote Gahom village to the north. Wagu village (top, right) has been settled for
a longer time and for 3 years prior to this study has been occupied half of each year by a
linguist-missionary and his family. The Bahinemo are relative newcomers to extensive
canoeable waters, and their dugouts are much cruder than those of the Sepik River
villagers. However, young children are quickly learning the dynamics of canoe handling
by experimentation and exploration (bottom, left). Sago is the dietary staple, and the
collection of it from wild sago palms and its preparation occupy much of the women's
time. A favored preparation is as a gelatinous sticky substance (bottom, center, and
right).

Plate 4.   The Barinemo of the Sepik Hills.   In Muli village, isolated deep in the Sepik Hill region, first contact with Westerners was made during this study. Landing by helicopter in this village which had not yet seen Western man, we found it deserted, but with fires burning in the houses. A full day of shouts into the surrounding forest by our Bahinemo assistant from Wasui Laboon brought a few frightened, wary men to the edge of their village clearing. Gifts of steel axes and bush knives brought shouts which brought more men and boys. Within three days nearly 30 individuals returned to the village. Above, a woman proffers food to a hamlet mate (top, left). Women and children return to a women's house (top, right). A recently initiated youth and an elder watch the Western intruders (bottom, left). A woman carrying a child in the typical Bahinemo fashion passes a funeral platform on which a body is decaying (bottom, center). Women and girls stare at the activities of their Western visitors (bottom, right).

Plate 5. The Sadong Dyaks of Borneo. About a day's walk from Serian, Sarawak, is this Sadong community of Bidayuh-speaking Hill Dyaks. Living together in the single longhouse which comprises their community, these Sadong, like their Dyak neighbors, have evolved a formal kinship system which defines relationship by responsibility and authority. The over 150 individuals living in this single house are in daily contact with their kinsmen with whom they cooperate in community affairs and in gaining their daily livelihood. Most of these Dyaks have adopted elements of Western dress, although a few maintain a Malaysianized style.

1-4

5-8

9-12

13-16

17-20

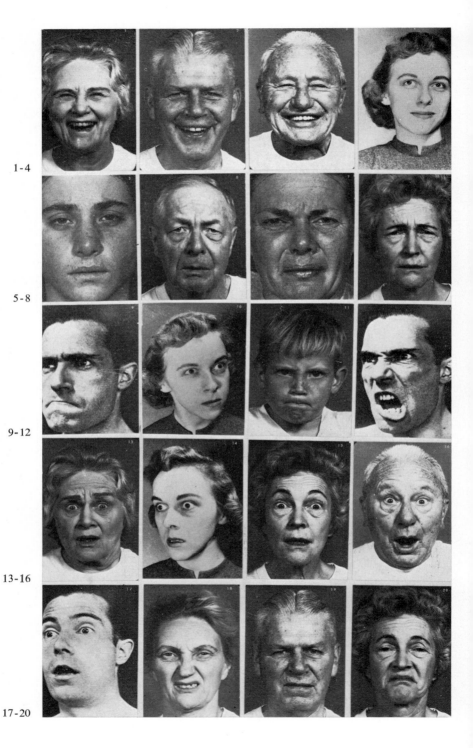

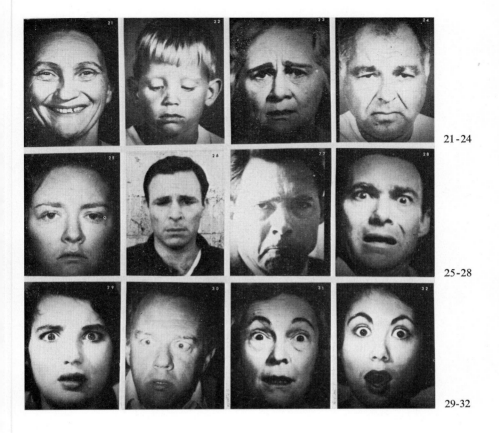

21-24

25-28

29-32

Plate 6a and 6b. The facial expressions of emotion. With the affects displayed having been defined by high statistical agreement among American college students, these photographs, primarily from the collection of Sylvan Tompkins, were shown to non-Western subjects in New Guinea and Borneo in an attempt to see if they agreed with Westernized peoples on the affect displayed. In this study we limited ourselves to the following affects: Happiness (1–4, 21), sadness (5–8, 22–26), anger (9–12, 27), fear (13, 14, 28–30), surprise (15–17, 31, 32), disgust (18–19), contempt (20).

Plate 7. A Fore expression of anger. Under the conditions of Fore social organization, the expression of anger is often like that of sadness. The above expression of anger posed by a Fore native was shown to other Fore natives who agreed that it represented anger. A few said it was sadness.

Plate 8. Anger expressions among the Sadong. The kind of community life practiced by the Sadong makes direct expressions of anger a threat to the group. Young children can be seen displaying an expression of anger recognized across all cultures tested. However, by the time adolescence is reached the expression of anger within the kinship residential collective is typically that which is socially approved. Above, we asked two brothers to pose facial expressions of emotion. When the young boy (left) displayed the unsanctioned expression he was reproved by his older brother who then demonstrated the "correct" way to express anger (right). However, both of these expressions are recognized by most Sadong as representing anger.

with me for several years, and the subject were present during the testing. The Fore assistant explained the task to the subject in the Fore language before the testing began. The social scientist showed the pictures, one at a time, and waited for the subject to give the affect term he thought best described the expression displayed in the picture. The Fore assistant remained silent while the pictures were being shown. He was positioned so that he could not see the pictures.

The subject responded to each picture with a single affect term in the Fore language. When terms we did not know were elicited, they were added to our list of Fore affect terms. When the response was not an affect term (e.g. "she is just looking," "he is ugly," "he is stupid," etc.), an affect term was requested. This worked well in the majority of cases.

The advantage of Method 2 was that it considerably reduced the translator's influence on the subjects' responses. He did not even see what pictures were being shown and remained silent during the testing. He was present only to explain the task to the subject and to occasionally explain to the social scientist the meaning of a novel response or a new word. The weakness of this method, however, was that it required a spoken response among a people who were not familiar with question-and-answer as a means of communication. Among Fore direct questions were usually considered hostile provocations and answers were not expected.

METHOD 3   We asked a native in each of the cultures to "act" or pose the facial affects we were investigating. Later, other natives in the same cultures were asked to tell us what affect the pictures connoted. Those pictures which received a significant degree of agreement among these native judges are now being presented to American high school students to see whether they recognize the same affect expressions.

The results of Methods 1 and 2 are presented in Tables 1 and 2.

Our greatest difficulty stemmed from the need for formal interview sessions involving question and answer. In the small peer groups comprising traditional Fore society, there was little indigenous need for an interrogative approach to communication. Fore social horizons did not extend much beyond one's small community where daily familiarity in a commonly understood milieu since childhood led to an understanding and intimacy which minimized the usefulness of formalized interrogative discourse. Human interaction was based largely on common feeling, personal rapport, and familiarity. Subtle interactive behavior, not questions or demands, communicated needs, desires, and interests.

Table 1.   Responses to pictures of facial affect: Method 1

Emotion connoted by story	Fore adults		Fore children[a]	
	Percent correct choice	Incorrect choices by frequency	Percent correct choice	Incorrect choices by frequency
Happy	92	sad, anger, disgust, fear, surprise	92	sad, anger, disgust, surprise
Sad	79	anger, disgust, fear, surprise, happy	81	anger, disgust, fear, surprise
Anger	84	sad, disgust, fear, surprise	90	sad
Disgust/ contempt	81	sad, surprise	85	sad
Fear	80	sad, disgust, anger, happy, surprise	93	sad, anger, disgust

Number of adult subjects = 189.
Number of child subjects = 130.

[a]   Prepubescent.

Indeed questions, like demands, were an indication of alienation and often treated as insults.

Apparently because the interrogative style had not evolved as a significant part of the Fore communicative repertoire, many of our subjects displayed uncertainty, hesitation, and confusion. Some were completely tongue-tied; others trembled and perspired profusely, or looked wildly about. The least acculturated were most afflicted; they often seemed bewildered, even fearful, in the face of the kind of interrogative communication which Westerners take so much for granted.

In the broader view the confusion and nervousness, which marked the interview situation, had its roots in the social organization. Economically opportunistic and socially egalitarian, the continually dispersing small bands of Fore proto-agriculturalists had no chiefs, patriarchs, medicine men, priests, or the like, to whom anyone was accountable. Solidarity and allegiance stemmed from personal familiarity and regard. Bad feeling led to segmentation and divergent settlement.

Thus, in order to gather data from our New Guinea subjects, we had to bridge a major cultural barrier to communication — a barrier more fundamental than difference in language alone.

With interpersonal communication among the Fore, and probably the Bahinemo as well, differing so markedly from the Western style, we were, in effect, extending to an alien culture a communicative technique

Table 2. Responses to pictures of facial affect: Method 2

Emotion seen in picture	Fore Group A (most contact)		Fore Group B (less contact)		Fore Group C (least contact)		Bahinemo	Sadong
	P^1	F^2	P^1	F^2	P^1	F^2		Bidayuh
Happy	99 h	82 h	92 h	67 h 18 an	87 h	60 h	Anger a generalized response.	92 h
Fear	46 f 31 an	54 f 25 an	37 f 21 an	30 f 20 an	36 h 33 f	23 f [a]	No clear mode of response to	40 f 33 su
Disgust	38 d 21 pa	39 c 21 pa	41 an 23 pa	24 h 22 c	26 h 22 an	23 h [a]	specific pictures	26 d/c[b] 23 h
Anger	56 an 22 f	50 an 25 f	56 an 16 f	49 an 29 c	51 an 25 h	48 an [a]		64 an
Surprise	38 su 30 f	45 f 21 an	34 an 28 su	31 f 27 h	33 su 33 an	31 h 26 su		36 su 23 f
Contempt	29 an 21 sa	36 an 29 c	40 d 27 an	28 c 26 an	33 an 25 d	27 an [a]		
Sadness	55 sa 23 an	56 an [a]	37 sa 27 an	57 an 13 f	43 an 26 h	53 an [a]		52 sa

[1] = Pidgin   Number of Fore subjects = 100.
[2] = Fore   Number of Bahinemo subjects = 71.
            Number of Sadong subjects = 15.

Group A: Experienced at least one year of government or mission schooling, spoke Melanesian-Pidgin well and dressed in Western shorts.

Group B: Had lived away from the Fore region on a government station, mission station, or plantation for more than 4 months, wore cloth, spoke moderate Melanesian-Pidgin, and had not had more than one year of mission schooling.

Group C: Had not left the Fore region for more than brief visits of a few days, never worked for Westerners, spoke little, if any, Melanesian-Pidgin, wore traditional dress.

[a] No clear second mode.
[b] Disgust and contempt were combined for the Sadong.

specific to our own culture. This caused interviewing dissonances not faced within the Westernized world where interrogative discourse has waxed under a system of institutionalized education.

Among the Fore this problem was partially ameliorated by the eagerness with which this economically opportunistic people were ready to change their activities and beliefs according to the Western model. This new way-of-life, they believed, was the key to obtaining lavish shipments of extraordinary goods and material of the sort which so dramatically blessed the alien newcomers to their lands.

Because of such cargo-cult beliefs, both native assistants and subjects were generally eager to do things in the Western way. This greatly enhanced our relations with them, but it caused other kinds of difficulties: like other things Western, our pictures and procedures were the subject of considerable interest and active discussion by the behaviorally alert Fore. They were quick to seize on the subtlest cues for an indication of how they should respond and react. This undoubtedly skewed our results, particularly those of Method 1, toward ideas of appropriateness developed by both the translator-assistants and the Fore subjects. A distinct probability is that the views of our English-speaking school boy assistants are reflected to some degree in the results.

That we used pictures of Caucasians to elicit responses from visually isolated non-Caucasian peoples also intruded uncertainty into our results. Some of the more haphazard responses may have been due to the strangeness of our pictures among people who had seen very few Caucasians. Among the more visually isolated subjects, these pictures more often caused consternation, laughter, and animated discussion.

The generalized Bahinemo view that our pictures portrayed anger may have been related to their view of the white man as being angry much of the time. Possibly this view developed mythically through grapevine accounts of Western behavior elaborated by a people generally distrustful of strangers. Or it could have stemmed from unpleasant early experiences with Westerners they had met or heard about. It may be significant that a number of Bahinemo men had been taken out to jail for tribal warfare a few years earlier.

But it is also possible that the Bahinemo responses stemmed from a higher than usual sensitivity to expressions of anger. Their small sago-gathering groups would have been vulnerable to anger — more so than the proto-agricultural Fore. But, in contrast to the Fore situation, dispersive segmentation was not such an economically rewarding alternative to social friction. The Bahinemo, therefore, would have reason to be more sensitive to traces of anger and alienation. This may have caused them to focus their attention on the subtle facial consequences of the Western aggressive-competitive social system reflected by our pictures. The less anger-vulnerable Fore could more readily disregard these, particularly in their enthusiasm with the material richness of Western man; and Westerners would ignore it as a constant.

Although the Fore saw anger much less frequently in the pictures than did the Bahinemo, they saw it more often than Westerners. In particular, pictures judged by Westerners to be sadness or fear were frequently thought to show anger by our Fore respondents.

This may be viewed in relation to the kind of social organization possessed by the Fore. In such egalitarian, informally organized small groups, the existential consequences of anger would be more acute than in societies less personally based; both sadness and fear would more often be corollaries of anger (See Plate 7).

In our own Western culture, we need only to reflect on the expression of anger between lovers, or between a mother and child, to see how such expressions of alienation may trigger pangs of sadness among people closely tied by personal bonds. Because the Fore society is so informally organized, its members would be more susceptible to such consequences of anger than people in societies where relationship and responsibility are stabilized by a more formalized kinship structure.

In such loosely organized societies as the Fore, the existential consequences of anger could also engender fear. In our own culture a dependent's anger against those who nurture him may be mingled with fear. Where security and well-being depend on bonds of warmth and trust, anger threatens the sense of identity and future and may, thereby, create a condition of existential fear. Social order among the Fore was more susceptible to this.

Sadong social organization provides a distinctly different setting. Formal kinship principles and convergent residence could concentrate a hundred or more individuals in a single communal longhouse. Like the Fore, the Sadong depend on crops to sustain themselves. But unlike the proto-agricultural Fore who continuously disperse into new virgin lands, the settled agricultural life and activities of the Sadong are circumscribed by surrounding Dyak communities. Thus the Sadong had to rely upon and to defend their traditional lands from encroachment. Given this situation it was to their advantage to maintain a large-group solidarity resistant to disruption. Formal kinship bonds facilitated this; centralized residence expressed it.

With group structure stabilized by formal interpersonal relationships, the power of anger to provoke existential crises was reduced among the Sadong. With the group-shattering potential of anger reduced, their expressions of anger were less likely to have correlates of despair and fear of the sort Fore would experience. However, in this kind of setting, uncontrolled expressions of anger would still diminish solidarity and make the community more vulnerable to outside encroachment. This may be the basis of the culturally approved expression of controlled anger which chidren learned as they grew up (see Plate 8).

CONCLUSION

The significant agreement by Fore, Sadong, and Westernized observers on the emotions expressed in our pictures leaves little doubt that some degree of universality exists in the facial expression of emotion. Statistical analysis of this data in comparison to other data from Westernized groups by Ekman and his colleagues is convincing on this point (Ekman, Sorenson, and Friesen 1969; Ekman and Friesen 1971; Ekman 1972; Ekman, Friesen, and Ellsworth 1972). Ekman's more recent report (1973) that Heider has obtained supporting data from the isolated Dani of West Irian is further evidence of universality.

At first glance the Bahinemo responses seem to challenge this view. Yet a failure of an alternative clear mode of picture specific response to emerge from the Bahinemo suggests the problem is not one of a different system of recognition. Furthermore, a preliminary study, now underway, shows that American high school students agree with Bahinemo on pictures taken of Bahinemo actors expressing emotion. The difficulty here seems to have stemmed primarily from using pictures of Caucasians, although use of interrogative procedures unfamiliar to the Bahinemo and the unavailability of skilled translator-assistants may have contributed to the indeterminacy of these results.

The complicated matter of applying testing procedures developed in one culture to isolated alien cultures rules out precise statistical comparisons. Thus, even though our findings clearly indicate pan-culturality, we cannot assume they reveal the actual degree or limits of panculturality.

The data also reveals some cultural influence on the recognition and expression of emotion. The frequent Fore responses of anger to our pictures displaying sadness and fear is the clearest example to date of culturally specific influence on the recognition or expression of emotion.

Parallel studies of human behavior and social organization among the Fore (Sorenson 1971, 1972, i.p., n.d.) provide a basis on which we can now begin to explain such influences. It is clear that the informal dispersive social organization of the Fore makes their groups vulnerable to anger and provides an arena in which sadness, anger, and fear are frequently associated. We can also see how the formal centralized social organization of the Sadong reduces vulnerability to social disruption of the kind inherent in Fore social organization, and gives rise to a culturally distinct expression of controlled anger which does not interfere with the requirements of group stability or strength.

Clearly, there are universals in the facial expression of emotion; but, just as clearly, culture and social organization may pattern the expression of these universals. Further work is required before a more specific definition of the limits of universality can be developed.

REFERENCES

DARWIN, C.
1872 *The expression of the emotions in man and animals.* London: John Murray.
DASHIELL, J. F.
1927 A new method of measuring reactions to facial expressions of emotion. *Psychological Bulletin* 24:174–175.
EKMAN, P.
1972 "Universals and cultural differences in facial expressions of emotion," in *Nebraska Symposium on Motivation.* Edited by J. K. Cole. Lincoln: University of Nebraska Press.
1973 "Darwin and cross cultural studies of facial expression," in *Darwin and facial expression: a century of research in review.* Edited by P. Ekman. New York: Academic Press.
EKMAN, P., W. V. FRIESEN
1969a "Origin, usage, and coding: the basis for five categories of nonverbal behavior," in *Lenguaje y communication social.* Edited by E. Veron, et al. Buenos Aires: Neuva Vision.
1969b The repertoire of nonverbal behavior. *Semiotica* 1:49–98.
1971 Constants across cultures in the face and emotion. *Journal of Personality and Social Psychology* 17:124–129.
EKMAN, P., W. V. FRIESEN, P. ELLSWORTH
1972 *Emotion in the human face: guidelines for research and an integration of findings.* New York: Pergamon Press.
EKMAN, P., E. R. SORENSON, W. V. FRIESEN
1969 Pancultural elements in the facial expression of emotion. *Science* 164: 86–88.
IZARD, C. E.
1971 *Face of emotion.* New York: Appleton-Century-Crofts.
SORENSON, E. R.
1971 "The evolving Fore: a study of socialization and cultural change in the New Guinea Highlands." Unpublished doctoral dissertation, Stanford University, Stanford, California.
1972 Socio-ecological change among the Fore of New Guinea. *Current Anthropology* 13:349–383.
i.p. "Ecological disturbance and population distribution in the Fore region of New Guinea: a proto-agricultural phenomenon," in *Aspects of Oceanian cultures world.* Edited by W. E. Sibley. World Anthropology. The Hague: Mouton.
n.d. "The edge of the forest: land, childhood, and change in a New Guinea proto-agricultural society." Submitted to Stanford University Press.

SORENSON, E. R., D. C. GAJDUSEK
   1966   The study of child behavior and development in primitive cultures. Supplement to *Pediatrics* 37:149–243.
SORENSON, E. R., P. E. KENMORE
   1974   Proto-agricultural movement in the New Guinea Highlands. *Current Anthropology* 15:1.
TOMKINS, S. S.
   1962   *Affect, imagery, consciousness*, volume one: *The positive affects*. New York: Springer.
   1963   *Affect, imagery, consciousness*, volume two: *The negative affects*. New York: Springer.
TOMKINS, S. S., R. MC CARTER
   1964   What and where are the primary affects? Some evidence for a theory. *Perceptual and Motor Skills* 18:119–158.

Strategies for Self-esteem
and Prestige in Maradi, Niger Republic

JEROME H. BARKOW

This paper will not argue that self-esteem is man's primary goal in life —
it will simply ignore most other psychological needs as being sufficiently irrelevant to the understanding of social behavior and sociocultural
change to be safely ignored. The changes under consideration are taking
place in the Hausa town of Maradi, Niger Republic; they provide the
context but not the focus of the present discussion, which will deal primarily with the strategies which some residents of Maradi are currently
utilizing in order to preserve and maximize their self-esteem, and with the
implications of these strategies for future change. The data to be presented are an early product of an ongoing study of Maradi and its inhabitants.

THEORETICAL BACKGROUND[1]

Men have many basic goals or needs and it is sometimes convenient for
the theorist to arrange these in a hierarchy. Near the base of any such
hierarchy will always be found the goals of maintaining and increasing
self-esteem. It is here postulated that only two primary strategies are
available to men in their efforts to achieve these closely-related goals,

This paper is based in part upon one presented at the November, 1972, annual meeting
of the African Studies Association, in Philadelphia. That paper was entitled, "Strategies
for achieving prestige among the Hausa of Niger."
   The author wishes to thank the Canada Council for supporting the research here
discussed. He also wishes to express his appreciation of the co-operation shown him
by the Centre Nigerien de Recherches en Sciences Humaines.
[1]   This section represents a drastic oversimplification of the theory of self-esteem,
prestige-striving, and social change presented in Barkow (1972).

these being (1) the pursuit of social prestige, and (2) the use of distortions of perception of self and environment. The operation of these strategies at the level of the individual will be analyzed and illustrated in a later section of this paper. At this point it will be more useful to discuss their sociocultural implications.

In stable, i.e. slowly rather than rapidly changing, societies, the ultimate social consequence of most available strategies is an increase in that stability — in a sense, that is why these societies are stable. Strategies involving acquiring prestige through subsistence activities best illustrate this point: the young hunter seeks the respect of his fellows by bringing back and distributing game, the pastoralist earns the approbation of others with the increase of his flocks, etc. Such strategies are obviously adaptive for the society as a whole as well as rewarding for the individual. In these traditional, small-scale societies, prestige-strategies tend to be relatively few in number and they are clear and unambiguous. The individual rarely has cause to doubt that success in terms of a given strategy will bring prestige because standards of evaluation of relative standing are never challenged, while contrary sets of standards do not exist (though complementary sets may). Not everyone can achieve "success," but everyone knows how to go about trying to and everyone knows how to recognize it.

What of the individual who fails? If success is clear, then so must be failure. The unsuccessful man falls back on the second primary strategy in the maintenance of self-esteem — the use of distortions of perception. Just as his culture has supplied him with prestige-strategies, so it provides the rationalizations he can use to justify himself in the face of failure. Perhaps his rivals utilized "medicine" against him, or perhaps he violated a taboo and is being punished by a spirit; or perhaps the failure of the crops or hunt or whatever was simply the will of God, beyond the power of mortal man to understand or influence. To paraphrase Spiro's description of religion (1965) as a "culturally constituted defense mechanism," these beliefs are culturally constituted rationalizations serving to protect self-esteem whenever the individual fears he has been unsuccessful in maintaining his social standing. The ego is protected against the consequences of social failure.

Traditional ethnographic language is probably adequate for the description of these stable or slowly-changing societies. Rather than the ethnographer speaking of, for example, an individual following a prestige-strategy of hunting and distributing large amounts of game, he describes the culture as having the value of "generosity." Where an individual chooses to follow an unusual strategy, the ethnographer has his category of "deviant" ready. In a similar fashion, distortions of perception serving to defend the ego are discussed under the rubric of "religion and the supernatural." This kind of vocabulary leads to an image of a culture constructed of such bricks as beliefs and values. However, as long as the society in question actually is reasonably stable, the ethnographer can use his customary language without doing excessive damage to social reality.

Rapid sociocultural change, however, creates difficulties for both ethnographer and individual. To speak of the individual's difficulties first: he may be proud of his success in terms of old strategies, only to find that others — strangers, or even his own children — are utilizing unfamiliar standards of evaluation and thereby withholding their approbation. New strategies come into being — perhaps a non-traditional craft, or the possibility of a different type of education — but these are risky and often not fully understood, and their payoff in prestige is problematic. Choosing is difficult.

As the culture changes, the distortions of perception necessary to protect self-esteem become less standardized and more varied. Rationalization of failure as being of supernatural origin continues to be relied upon, perhaps even more so than previously, but additional defense mechanisms, ones having to do with redefinition of the self and social identity, are now also utilized. For example, an individual failing to achieve prestige in terms of developing modern or urban norms may stress his identity as a traditional man, accentuating those values (e.g. deference towards the aged, hereditary position, etc.) in terms of which he merits respect. He may castigate those successfully utilizing new prestige-strategies as belonging to a separate group or social category, one morally inferior to his own "traditional" group and therefore not to be compared with it.

Similarly, the urban individual successfully following a newer strategy may maximize his self-esteem by taking his fellow urbanites as his reference group and accepting only their criteria for the evaluation of relative social standing as valid, simultaneously de-emphasizing his identification with the more rural members of his original ethnic group. Clothing, coiffure, or other aspects of life style may serve as symbols of the boundaries generated by the aggregative use of differing sets of prestige-strategies. Of course, particular individuals may shift group membership and social (and even psychological) identity from year to year and even situation to situation, these shifts themselves constituting psychosocial tactics in the service of the maintenance and enhancement of self-esteem.

Rapid sociocultural change obliges the researcher to alter his vocabulary and to lower his level of analysis. He now must pay careful attention to the seeming idiosyncracies of individual behavior and his language becomes more processually oriented: he speaks in terms of transactions, situational and network analysis, case studies, etc. Without realizing it, in his desire to understand the motives and goals underlying the actions of individuals he has moved towards a more psychological (or even phenomenological) anthropology (Barkow i.p.).

Men have many motives and goals, but it is neither possible nor necessary for the researcher to attempt to understand all of them. It is here suggested that the individual-level goal most relevant to the analysis of sociocultural change is that of the maintenance and enhancement of self-esteem. It is further suggested that a vocabulary of "strategy" and "tactics" (borrowed from psychologists Miller, Galanter, and Pribram [1960]) is appropriate to an analysis of overt and covert behavior in the service of that goal. For heuristic purposes, it will be necessary to slight the other goals of the individuals to be discussed and to ignore the fact that any given item of behavior may be simultaneously in the service of several motives or even represent a "compromise formation" between partly conflicting goals. Hopefully, this simplified psychology (and when have social scientists used other than simplified psychologies?) will not gravely distort the analyses. However, since the theoretical approach sketched here is discussed more fully elsewhere (Barkow 1972), it will be more profitable at this point to move on to the attempt to apply that approach.

THE TOWN OF MARADI

The individuals whose self-esteem strategies are to be discussed are residents of the Hausa city of Maradi in the Niger Republic. "Hausa" is a term used to refer to a number of overlapping dialects and subcultures primarily found in northern Nigeria and, to a lesser extent, in the adjacent Niger Republic. Though the Hausa are mainly rural cultivators, their strong tradition of commerce has resulted in their language becoming a West African *lingua franca*. While not all Hausa are Muslims, Islamic influence is ancient in Hausaland, particularly in the urban centers of the traditional city-states.

The town of Maradi itself, though not the state that bore the same name, was founded prior to 1830 by the royal refugees of the Fulani-conquered Hausa kingdom of Katsina, and by the region's autochthonous "pagan" Hausa inhabitants.[2] Maradi was built as a walled citadel and was very much a warfare state, its early rulers continually striving to reconquer

---

[2]   The very brief historical background and description provided here is largely based upon David (1964) and Thom (1971).

their Katsina homeland. Intermittent warfare and raiding between Maradi, the Fulani-dominated Hausa states and various Tuareg bands continued until about 1909 and French conquest. Politically, Maradi had been organized along the lines of the old Hausa state of Katsina but, with the coming of the French, power increasingly passed to the new rulers.

The town of Maradi had been built in a valley of the Goulbi of Maradi (*goulbi* refers to a river which runs only during the rainy season). In 1945 the Goulbi overflowed, destroying much of the town. The French authorities forced the Maradawa (inhabitants of Maradi) to move to higher ground nearby where a wholly new city was constructed in 1946, the former site becoming farmland. Though the new city is laid out in a "central circle with streets radiating from it in the form of the spokes of a wheel" and is "reminiscent of Paris and French 19th century urban planning" with its walled compounds of baked clay, Maradi is surprisingly reminiscent of traditional Hausa towns (Thom 1971: 484–486).

Maradi, today the capital of the Department of the same name, has a population on the order of 30,000 (no trustworthy census exists as of this writing). Electricity and potable, piped water are available to those who can afford them, and a considerable number of European-style houses have been built. The city is largely an administrative center but also serves as a conduit for trade with the wealthy Nigerian Hausa city of Kano. The prosperous of the town are invariably either civil servants or merchants. Both groups tend to put their surplus capital into the construction of houses which are then rented to others.

Maradi is described by its older inhabitants as "full of strangers" and, judging from the clearly visible physical expansion of the city (particularly in the Nouveau Carré and Sabon Gari wards), the present period is one of rapid growth. Though perhaps not as ethnically varied as many other West African cities (e.g. Bamako in Mali, Jos in Nigeria, or Niamey, the capital of Niger), it would be a mistake to regard Maradi as homogeneous. Non-Hausa newcomers to the city are drawn from Nigeria, Togo, Upper Volta, Mali, the Ivory Coast, and Dahomey. Though Maradawa generally speak the Katsina dialect of Hausa (with an admixture of Gobir dialect), the accents of Ader, Damagaram, and Agadez are constantly heard on the streets, and the sophisticated Maradawa seem to understand all dialects and accents without difficulty. The various Hausa-speaking groups often differ considerably from one another in cultural detail as well as dialect, and these differences are a common topic of conversation.

There is some specialization of occupation by ethnic origin in the city, carriers of water generally being Ader Hausa, photographers Yoruba, petty traders Hausa from outlying areas, farmers native Maradawa, and schoolteachers residents from other states of the old French West Africa. Authorities complain of an influx of young rural villagers to Maradi, blaming them for what is described as a recent increase in gambling, drinking, and theft. It is impossible to say to what extent these new-comers represent immigrants rather than transients. Employment for the unskilled being scarce — Maradi has little industry — the authorities attempt to round up the itinerant unemployed each year just before the rains, in order to truck them to rural areas where they may at least farm.

Traditionally, in the Maradi region as well as in other parts of Hausa-land, the range of strategies available to maintain self-esteem and increase social prestige was quite limited. For the vast majority of men, prestige came with large harvests. Only through a massive ceremonial distribution of produce (the *dubu*) could a man eventually achieve the coveted title of *sarkin noma* or 'master farmer'. Some, benefiting from an urge to travel and access to capital, could follow a strategy of becoming small traders and then merchants, gaining prestige as they accumulated wealth. A third strategy was open only to those who considered themselves Mus-lim. These individuals could attach themselves to a scholar of the Quran (*mallam*) as his pupil (*almajiri*). Great prestige has long been associated with Islam in Hausaland, especially in the urban areas, where resistance to that religion had early collapsed. A man able to acquire a reputation for Muslim learning could (and still can) count on receiving great respect from others, particularly since the Quran is considered by many to be a more potent basis for sorcery than the herbal knowledge of traditional practitioners (*bokaye*). Though the strategy of seeking prestige through large harvests is presently declining in popularity (and, apparently, in efficacy), those involving commerce and religion are probably more wide-spread today than they were formerly.

Hausa prestige-strategies usually involve the tactic of either becoming or, less often, seeking a client. The rural cultivator without many sons may seek young men — often, but not always, kinsmen — as clients, in order that their labor produce for him the large harvests necessary for social prestige. The initial step in the strategy of commerce often involves becoming the client of a merchant prosperous enough to supply credit to one whom he trusts. The pupil of the Muslim scholar learns from him by becoming, in effect, his client. Even among the aristocracy, the lesser aristocrat gives his loyalty to the greater with the expectation that his patron, in advancing, will in turn advance the follower (Smith 1959). Clientship underlies many Hausa social relationships and is a tactic basic to most of their prestige-strategies.

If the three major precolonial prestige-strategies of Hausaland — farming, commerce, and study — tend to share a single major tactic, that of clientship, failure in following any of these strategies automatically invokes a single major ego defense, that of blaming the supernatural. Poor crops may be caused by the anger of the gods or spirits, or perhaps by the maliciousness of one's sorcery-using enemies. Unprofitable commerce may result from the supernatural machinations of one's rivals, or in their having engaged a *mallam* more proficient than one's own. Even the *mallam* himself may protect his self-esteem in the face of failure by fatalistically ascribing his misfortune to the will of Allah (*ikkon Alla*).

THE THREE MEN

The study from which the data to be presented are taken consists essentially of an attempt to follow the lives of a panel of Maradi residents for some two to three years. Because this project remains, as of this writing, in its early stages, only life-history data are presently available.[3] Though the chief self-esteem strategies of the individuals concerned seem reasonably apparent, the analyses to be presented must be regarded as tentative rather than final. Equally tentative will be the evaulation of the possible sociocultural consequences of these strategies. In order to protect the privacy of the informants, they will be referred to by pseudonyms, and certain details which might serve to identify them will be either altered or omitted.

Though it was argued previously that the prestige-strategies followed by aggregates of individuals can have important sociocultural consequences, it is equally true that some strategies may be purely idiosyncratic and therefore of psychological, rather than sociological, interest. The first informant whose life is to be sketched here, given the cognomen of "Biyu," fits into that latter category.

Biyu is a large, powerfully built man of thirty-three, presently employed as a guard for a government corporation. Some ten years ago, Biyu moved to Maradi from one of the rural hamlets that cluster about the city. His father was of Buzu (Tuareq serf) origin, his mother Gobir Hausa, and they lived by farming in the bush, clearing new land when the fertility of the old would wane. His father's only craft, other than farming, was keeping an occasional horse in order to fatten it and sell it at a profit.

Biyu was the third child born to his mother and, while not the last-born, was the last that lived beyond infancy. Biyu's father had other wives and

---

[3]   Since this paper was written, an unanticipated interruption in funding has forced the abandonment of this project. Salvage operations, however, are under way.

there were always many children in the household. When asked about his childhood, Biyu speaks of what a good farmer he was, of how he always won the boys' hoeing competitions. Biyu is emphatic about how well he was trained as a child, and how well he then trained his younger siblings. He and his siblings received neither Quranic nor secular education.

Biyu was still living in his father's compound when he first married. His bride soon became pregnant but the child died in infancy and the mother returned to her father's compound. Left alone, Biyu went to Agadez and spent two years there working at unloading lorries. He and his wife were divorced soon after his return home and Biyu again went to Agadez, this time staying for only a single year. Back home once more, Biyu was wifeless, a state considered shameful for an adult Hausa man. He moved to Maradi, he explains, in order to earn the money with which to marry.

At Maradi, Biyu soon found work as a guard for a government corporation and within five months was able to marry. Some time later, he added a second wife, eventually divorcing the first. He remains married to his second Maradi wife, though they have no children. Biyu still works as a guard, living in the compound for which he is responsible together with his wife and the son of one of his brothers.

Biyu's duties as a guard are largely fulfilled simply by his living in the compound with his family. He feels free to leave Maradi for days at a time, visiting friends and kin in the hamlets surrounding the city. His pattern of activities resembles that of a young, unmarried man in that he spends much time visiting friends and neighbors, escorting them on their various minor errands. Biyu's friends are farmers, petty traders, and guards like himself. Like his father, Biyu enjoys purchasing a horse and caring for it, hoping eventually to sell the animal at a profit. Each afternoon, Biyu goes to the Maradi racetrack in order to exercise his horse, sometimes racing it against other animals.

Biyu was a difficult informant, sometimes replying evasively or even at random to questions, at other times rambling at great length in a totally disjointed fashion. A research assistant and I took turns in interviewing Biyu, but neither of us felt we ever achieved genuine rapport with him. Many of Biyu's tales must be considered to be fantasy. His style of life and dress show him to be a poor man. Guarding is a very low-paying occupation, and it is doubtful if he makes any profit from his horse-raising — he frequently complains of the cost of the grain the animal consumes. But Biyu claims to be involved in long-distance trading (*fatauci*), and that he owns a house which he rents out. There is ample evidence that these stories are untrue.

Biyu's occupation of guarding is a respected if not lucrative one, and his long tenure at his present post is prestigious in that many would consider it to be proof of his good character. However, his occupation apparently brings him insufficient prestige, for he utilizes two additional strategies to enhance his self-esteem.

One strategy operates on a psychological level and involves constant fantasy and self-glorification. For example, though Biyu may have migrated to an urban area because he was an unsuccessful farmer — his harvests apparently were too scanty to provide him with bride-wealth — he describes himself as a kind of hero with a hoe. If he praises the agricultural ability of a younger brother it is always because he, Biyu, trained him. When asked how he originally found work, first in Agadez and later in Maradi, his reply is that people saw "how good" he was. When he discusses his marriages, he claims to have paid an amount of bride-wealth that can only be described as fanciful. Similarly, he attempts to portray himself as a successful long-distance trader, though interviewing quickly reveals his ignorance of the details of such commerce. Others who know him agree that his tendency towards self-aggrandizement is habitual and not an artifact of the interviewing situation.

Biyu does have another prestige-strategy, however, one which is based on reality rather than fantasy. A horse is a traditional Hausa prestige-symbol and owning one definitely increases Biyu's standing in the community, particularly since it enables him to visit the racecourse regularly and mingle there with the other horse owners, almost all of whom are of higher social standing.

Biyu's self-esteem and prestige-strategies appear to be wholly idiosyncratic and with few social consequences. His occupation is respectable, if not especially respected, and he is extremely fortunate, given Maradi's plentiful supply of unskilled labor, to have it. Realistically, no other strategies are open to him, with the exception of engaging in petty trading — a strategy that would win him no more and possibly less prestige (and income) than he presently enjoys. The social prestige accruing to him by dint of his occupation and his horsemanship apparently does not suffice for him to maintain his self-esteem, and he therefore makes use of covert or psychological strategies. He is not so much rationalizing failure as building a fantasy world in which he is a wealthy merchant, esteemed by all. One has the impression that Biyu himself half believes his fantasies.

If Biyu's strategies have no clear social implications, those of others do, particularly those utilizing strategies involving Islam. Islam in Maradi appears to function as a powerful protector of self-esteem, a point which we can illustrate by comparing the lives of two men, here referred to as

Daya and Shida. These men have quite similar backgrounds, differing chiefly in that Daya received an extensive Quranic education and Shida did not.

Both Daya and Shida are descended from the original founders of Maradi and both are members of the hereditary aristocracy and have relatives who even today hold high position. Both grew up in rural villages and were obliged to work in the fields as boys. They differ, however, in that Daya was taught by a *mallam* from an early age and has never ceased to study Islamic lore. When he was sixteen years old he completed reading all sixty sections of the Quran, and a ceremony (*sauka*) was held to celebrate this accomplishment. Even today, his voice registers pride when he speaks of that ceremony. Shida, on the other hand, was never sent to Quranic school because, he explains, "In those days we didn't recognize how worthwhile it was." Shida is almost twenty-five years older than Daya — had they been born at the same time they undoubtedly would both have received the same Quranic education (or lack of it).

Royal families are often so huge that individual scions profit little from their connection, particularly at the present time when traditional rulers have little remaining power and wealth. Both Daya and Shida, when they reached manhood, were obliged to support themselves. From this point on, their stories diverge.

Daya continued to farm into adulthood, spending mornings in the family's fields and afternoons on his personal farm plot. In addition, he became the *boyi* [servant] of the village schoolmaster, performing such tasks for him as washing clothing and gathering firewood. At the same time, Daya took advantage of a government adult education program to learn to read and write Hausa, though the new knowledge made little difference in his life. Eventually he left his village in order to seek work at Arlit, center of the then newly-discovered Niger uranium fields. He worked there for a year as a *monteur*, a worker on heights, and at the end of that time spent his accumulated wages on gifts to his family and repairs to his rooms in their compound.

At the end of his second year at Arlit, however, he used his savings to travel to Niamey and purchase goods, returning to his work-camp in order to sell them at a profit. He made several such trips, buying in other cities, selling in Arlit. Daya had changed occupations, from that of laborer to that of trader, the occupation he still follows today. At present, Daya lives in an inexpensive rented compound with his two wives and three surviving children. He is a licensed peddler in Maradi, in addition occasionally traveling to Kano, Nigeria, to bring back goods in bulk. Recently, difficulties with customs officials have cost him much of his capital.

He earns enough by peddling a variety of goods — mostly wearing apparel — to feed his family and pay the rent, but complains he lacks sufficient capital to engage in the larger-scale commerce he would prefer.

Though Daya is at present in rather difficult circumstances, he is an extremely proud, almost arrogant man. He criticizes the authorities for their treatment of petty traders, declaring that a peddler has as much status as a functionary — an opinion many Maradawa would not share. He agrees that one must honor the high officials of the land, but he personally reserves most of his respect for the religious figures, the *mallams* and the *imams*. This is not surprising, since, when Daya is not traveling about the city on his bicycle, hawking his wares, he is engaged in some religious activity, studying with a *mallam*, reading a religious text, or praying. He spends at least several hours each day in this manner.

Shida also left home as a young man, though not to work as a laborer. He was first apprenticed to a kinsman, a Maradi tailor. After some five years learning this craft, he was employed by another kinsman as a groundnut buyer in a different city. At the end of the groundnut season he found employment with his host who, as it happened, was also a tailor. After several years, Shida was put in charge of a small cloth shop. He remained in this position for almost ten years, when he quarreled with his patron and returned to Maradi.

Today, Shida is in effect a client without a patron. He and his present wife live in a small inherited compound, together with his mother, a divorced sister, and the sister's daughter. Though he has been married many times, he has no children. The mother and the sister provide the only reliable income in the compound by preparing cooked food (*tuwo*), which is then sold by the latter's daughter. Certain kinsmen provide some help in spite of Shida's having quarreled with them, but the family is distinctly impoverished and would be in far worse difficulties were it not for the inherited compound. Shida spends his days much as Biyu does, wandering about the city and greeting friends and kinsmen. His closest friend is an army veteran with a low-paying but undemanding sinecure of a job.

A relative of Shida's attributes the man's difficulties to his aristocratic origin, his 'nobleman's heart' (*zuciyar sarauta*). The attitude that only ruling is good enough for him has plagued his life, explains this relative, leading Shida to scorn more practical goals. He could never really accept being a tailor or petty trader; these occupations were beneath him. Shida explains that he would be willing to engage in trade if it were on a sufficiently large scale, and that he hopes a wealthier kinsman will provide him with the necessary capital.

The physical contrast between Daya and Shida is striking. Daya is a slim, vigorous man of twenty-eight with an air of energy and confidence about him. He gives the perpetual impression of being in the middle of planning something, and he often is. Shida, on the other hand, is slightly over fifty but appears to be well into his seventies. He is a tall but rather stooped man who adopts a cringing, fawning manner in the presence of someone of higher status, much as a traditional Hausa retainer might with his royal master. Shida's voice is uncertain and indistinct. Though his relative may be accurate in explaining Shida's difficulties as the result of excessive pride, there is certainly no evidence of this fault in his demeanor.

The aristocratic background shared by both Daya and Shida puts them at a disadvantage: in order to maintain self-esteem, they must achieve a status higher than that which might content other men, and they must do this without the benefit of the financial and politcal support their origins might once have conferred. Their lack of French education disqualifies them for the newer positions of status and authority, yet they must live in a world in which minor clerks not infrequently treat the unlettered with arrogance and disdain. Daya has succeeded in finding a strategy which protects his self-esteem. Shida has not.

Daya judges a man's worth by his knowledge of the Quran. Others may hold power and it is necessary to show them formal respect, but their power does not indicate that they are of exceptional merit — only religion can do that. So it is that Daya can state that a petty trader may be more worthy (have more *daraja*) than a functionary, for the thought he has in mind is that it is the trader who is likely to have the greater knowledge of the Quran. And Daya is fully aware that his own religious learning is considerably deeper than that of most of the people he meets, including that of most functionaries. Of course, he must honor the *mallams* and the *imams*, but this he does willingly, for they comport themselves with dignity and show him the respect due a serious student. By taking extent of Islamic learning as his major standard of evaluation of the worth of men, including himself, Daya protects his self-esteem. So successful is this strategy that he can even engage in manual labor and petty trading, his pride secured by his studies of the Quran.

Daya has utilized a psychological, covert strategy for maintaning self-esteem. He denies the legitimacy of standards of evaluation based on mere wealth or French education, and accepts only the one measure by which he himself does well, that of Muslim learning. Shida, on the other hand, never received a Quranic education, and so does not have this strategy open to him. Instead, he must use the traditional Hausa prestige-strategy of seeking to be the client of a wealthy and powerful man. This strategy depends upon the client convincing the patron of his loyalty, obedience, and usefulness. For reasons unknown to us, for Shida the strategy has not worked. One would have expected him to react by becoming a petty trader, the standard occupation of almost every urban Hausa man. However, given his background, such an occupation would apparently have been an unbearable blow to his fragile self-esteem.

The traditional strategies have failed Shida and he has been able to find neither overt nor covert (psychological) alternatives. So, where Daya is at least self-supporting and constantly explores new ways to achieve economic success, Shida lives on charity and the unrealistic hope that further charity will enable him to become a prosperous, respected merchant. By all accounts he is just what he appears to be — a thoroughly miserable man.

But is Islam really the reason for Daya's relative confidence and Shida's malaise? Alternative hypotheses are available: Perhaps the true explanation lies in differing genetic endowments of the two men, or in their different socialization experiences. Perhaps it is Shida's lack of offspring that destroys his self-esteem, or perhaps Daya had the benefit of growing up during a period in which opportunities were more numerous than they had been during Shida's youth. But it seems most plausible that it is indeed Daya's adherence to Islam that protects him from the demoralization and lack of self-esteem which so damages Shida's functioning.

ISLAM AND SELF-ESTEEM

Daya's case suggests that Islam may serve in general to protect self-esteem in the face of rapid sociocultural change. The very existence of the new bureaucratic elite challenges the efficacy of some of the older prestige-strategies. The successful farmer, for example, finds that his large harvests win him far less prestige than they might once have done, and he does not speak French — how can he be admired? The farmer may react in part by choosing a modern prestige-strategy for his children (e.g. sending them to a secular school), but he can hardly follow such a path himself.

If he has had some Quranic education he is likely to use Daya's strategy and strive to increase his Islamic learning while refusing to accept fully the legitimacy of the bureaucrats' demands for respect. We would expect that the more contact he has with members of the new elite, the more likely he will be to react by seeking a strongly Muslim social identity.

Farmers do not, however, usually have very much contact with the new bureaucracy, unless they also happen to be merchants. And it is precisely among the merchant class that ostentatious adherence to Islam is most frequently found, in Maradi. It is also the members of this class who tend to belittle the bureaucrats for their lack of true Islamic learning. However, because the link between Islam and commerce in West Africa long antedates the rise of a francophobe bureaucracy, it would be unwise to conclude that traders are almost invariably pious Muslims solely because they seek to protect their self-esteem.

The idea that Islam serves to protect self-esteem during rapid socio-cultural change may explain the Maradi phenomenon of "tradition replacement." By "tradition replacement" I mean the substitution of an Islamic tradition for a "pagan" one. Thus, even though many informants were raised in areas in which Hausa traditional religion remains strong and in which Islam has made relatively minor inroads, they tended to claim that they and their ancestors had "always" been Muslim. It was only with much reluctance that some individuals would admit that their fathers had indeed performed traditional rituals and sacrificed to the old gods (*iskoki*, s. *iska*).

This reluctance to discuss traditional religion did not appear to be the product of shame at being of "pagan" background, but seemed to stem from a deep emotional attachment to Islam. Many Maradawa appear to be genuinely ignorant of Hausa religion: their psychological as well as social identification is with the nation of Islam. Thus, it would be inadequate to state that the Muslim religion is merely spreading in Hausaland — it is replacing other beliefs. Emotionally and cognitively, if not historically, Islam is becoming the sole "traditional" religion of the region.

This process seems to be at least in part due to Islam's ability to protect individual self-esteem against the onslaught of European-influenced urban values. That colonial conquest and modernization in Hausaland have failed to create even a trace of the cultural demoralization typical of the indigenous inhabitants of North America may well be due in part to Islam's hypothesized self-esteem-protecting qualities.

AN EVALUATION

Since only life-history data are presently available from the Maradi study, the sociocultural-level hypotheses it has already generated cannot be evaluated. It may well be true that Islamization is a prophylactic measure in favor of the maintenance of community mental health in the face of rapid sociocultural change, as the case of Daya would seem to indicate; but an analysis of a single case is not enough evidence.

It is appropriate, however, to evaluate the assumption that the kind of psychology necessary to understand sociocultural change is a psychology of self-esteem and social prestige. This assumption is contrary to the subsistence or materialistic psychology basic to such social science fields as Marxist theory, economics, and ecological anthropology. But men simply do not work to maximize their economic benefits, any more than they try to maximize their physical comfort.

Africa provides us with examples of individuals who stint on food to the point of malnutrition in order to purchase garments dreadfully unsuited to the local climate.[4] In the case of Shida, fear of loss of self-esteem prevented him from engaging in the only activity by which he might at least have been able to feed his family, that of petty trading. Daya devoted time to religious activities he would otherwise have spent in peddling his goods. Though he complained of lack of capital, much of his earnings were given away as alms (*sadaka*).

Materialistic psychology, the assumption that men seek to maximize their material resources, seems to work in only two cases. The first involves ostentatious or conspicuous consumption. We often seek social prestige by competing with our fellows in the consumption and display of symbols, and some of these symbols are usually material goods. But only by interpreting this consumption in terms of social prestige do we understand why some goods but not others should be sought after, or why intangibles, the intangibles having to do with repuation, should be pursued with an even greater avidity than that involved in material acquisition.

The second case in which materialistic psychology seems to work is that of the genuinely needy man. His behavior is indeed to be explained in large measure by his desire for material goods. But once he has been fed and warmed, his actions grow immediately inexplicable except in terms of his strategies for maintaining self-esteem. It is true enough that a man without material goods is hungry. But a man without self-esteem is mad.

It is hoped that this paper has demonstrated that it is possible to understand the behavior of individuals in a context of rapid social change by analyzing their strategies for the maintenance and enhancement of self-esteem; and that these strategies themselves shed light on the nature of sociocultural change.

[4] For the reader unconvinced that only a psychology of self-esteem maintenance and social prestige enhancement can adequately explain economic behavior, I suggest he see the issue of *Tiers-Monde* devoted to the "Economy of Ostentation" (Poirier 1968).

REFERENCES

BARKOW, JEROME H.
1972   "Anthropological man strives for prestige." Paper presented at the May, 1972 symposium, "Fringe Theory in Anthropology." Oswego, New York.
i.p.   Darwinian psychological anthropology: a biosocial approach. *Current Anthropology.*

DAVID, PHILIPPE
1964   Maradi, l'ancien état et l'ancienne ville: site, population, histoire. *Documents des Etudes Nigeriennes* 18.

MILLER, G. A., E. GALANTER, K. H. PRIBRAM
1960   *Plans and the structure of behavior.* New York: Holt, Rinehart and Winston.

POIRIER, JEAN
1968   L'économie ostentatoire: études sur l'économie du prestige et du don. *Revue Tiers-Monde* 9.

SMITH, MICHAEL G.
1959   The Hausa system of social status. *Africa* 29:239–252.

SPIRO, MELFORD E.
1965   "Religious systems as culturally constituted defense mechanisms," in *Context and meaning in cultural anthropology.* Edited by M. E. Spiro. New York: The Free Press.

THOM, DERRICK
1971   The city of Maradi: French influence upon a Hausa urban center. *Journal of Geography* 70:472–482.

Fatalism and Type of Information Sensitivity

RICHARD P. NIELSEN

Fatalism, as measured by Rotter's "internal-external locus of control scale," is the degree to which a person generally believes that events affecting his life are largely determined by other forces rather than by his own efforts.

High fatalism is considered a problem for the following reasons: (1) Fatalism inhibits learning of problem solving information compared to descriptive information (Seeman 1962, 1963; Green, et al. 1966). (2) There is a high incidence of high fatalism within lower socioeconomic groups, groups that particularly need to be motivated (Rotter n.d.; Rogers and Svenning 1969). (3) The incidence of high fatalism in the general American population appears to be increasing (Harris Survey 1972; Throop and MacDonald 1971).

The purpose of this paper is to examine behavioral science theory concerning fatalism, and to develop and test which types of benefit explanation information are more effective in forming positive attitudes among high fatalists towards attitude objects. This paper attempts to demonstrate that under certain information stimuli conditions, the conclusions of several authors quoted below concerning the role of communications in causing positive responses among fatalists should be modified. For the sake of brevity, the only authors I refer to specifically are Green, et al. (1966), Grunig (1971), Rogers and Svenning (1969), Rotter (n.d.) and Seeman (1963). The conclusions of these authors which should be modified are illustrated and noted in the discussion section.

However, before reviewing selected aspects of behavioral science theory concerning fatalism, it is important to establish that the researchers cited within the fields of psychology, sociology, communications, and management are referring to the same general variable I have called "fatalism."

As a psychologist, Rotter (n.d.: 1) defines internal-external locus of control as "the degree to which the individual perceives that the reward follows from, or is contingent upon, his own behavior or attributes versus the degree to which he feels the reward is controlled by forces outside himself and may occur independently of his own actions." Rotter developed his "I–E scale" to measure this variable.

As a sociologist, Seeman (1963: 270; 1971: 135) defines powerlessness alienation as "the expectancy or probability held by the individual that his own behavior cannot determine the occurance of the outcome, or reinforcements, he seeks." Seeman uses Rotter's I–E scale to measure this variable.

Within communications research, Rogers and Svenning (1969: 273) define fatalism as "the degree to which an individual perceives a lack of ability to control his future. Hence fatalism is a sort of generalized sense of powerlessness, one of the five dimensions of alienation postulated by Seeman." However, rather than using the Rotter scale as Seeman did, Rogers and Svenning, in their Colombian studies of fatalism, developed and used their own scale based on earlier work done by Seeman and Rotter. Among one of five decision types conceptualized by Grunig (1971: 585) in his Colombian studies, is fatalism; he says "in fatalism, alternatives are not considered because the individual believes that he cannot control his destiny, but instead thinks it is controlled by supernatural or other outside forces." Grunig does not use a social-psychological scale to measure fatalism.

Green, et al. (1966) in their consumer information seeking experiment refer to the variable "fatalism" and use Rotter's definition of internal-external locus of control as well as his I–E scale to measure fatalism.

The types of information this paper is concerned with are: reward enumeration; reward explanation; explanation of immediate-society rewards; explanation of future-society rewards; explanation of immediate-individual rewards; and explanation of future-individual rewards. Reward enumeration information is a statement of several good qualities associated with an attitude object. Reward explanation information is an explanation of how rewards can be received through an attitude object. Immediate-society reward explanation information is an explanation of how rewards can be received immediately by society through the attitude object. Future-society reward explanation information is an explanation of how rewards can be received in the future by society through the attitude object. Immediate-individual reward explanation information is an explanation of how rewards can be received immediately by the individual through the attitude object. Future-individual reward explanation information is an explanation of how rewards can be received in the future by the individual through the attitude object. In the studies reported in this paper several different examples of each type of information were presented to people for their responses.

HYPOTHESES

Since low fatalists have a history of being rewarded for their own actions and have learned to believe that they can gain rewards through their own behavior (Rotter n.d.) they should respond positively to those alternatives which the information indicates have more rewards associated with them. Since high fatalists have a history of not being rewarded for their own actions and consequently have learned to believe that they cannot gain rewards through their own actions, there should be little motivation for their taking the effort to positively respond to information that promises rewards. Therefore, it is hypothesized that: (1) High fatalists respond less to reward enumeration information than low fatalists.

Because of the high fatalist's history of not being rewarded for his own actions, he learns to believe that there is a weak or non-existent cause-effect, "get/want" (Lerner 1967), relationship between his actions and rewards. Information that explains how there is a cause-effect relationship should be more effective than information which only states without any causal explanation that rewards will flow from his behavior. Therefore, it is hypothesized that: (2) High fatalists respond more to reward explanation information than to reward enumeration information, and the differences in the responses of high and low fatalists are less in response to reward explanation than to reward enumeration information.

There is a negative relationship between fatalism and deferred gratification (Bialer 1962). Since the high fatalist has learned to believe that he cannot control events, he perceives a higher risk in postponing gratification. Therefore, it is hypothesized that: (3) High fatalists respond more to immediate than to future reward explanation, and the differences in responses of high and low fatalists are less in response to explanations of immediate rewards than to explanations of future rewards.

Since high fatalists have learned to believe that they cannot control rewards within the environments in which they live, they should have little confidence that benefits accruing to society will reach them. Therefore, it is hypothesized that: (4) High fatalists respond more to information that explains how the individual can attain benefits than to information that explains how the society can gain rewards, and the differences in responses of high and low fatalists are less in response to explanations of individual than to society rewards.

It is also hypothesized that: (5) High fatalists respond more to immediate-individual reward explanation than to future-society reward explanation. Since this hypothesis is a combination of hypotheses (3) and (4), it should hold if these hypotheses do. Finally, is hypothesized that: (6) Fatalism explains more the responses to the set of theoretically derived information stimuli than education, income, and age characteristics.

METHODOLOGY

In the magazine advertisement field experiment two hundred adult residents from Champaign and Urbana, Illinois were selected in a clustered random sample. An overview of the procedure used in the data collection follows. First, each subject was shown eight magazine advertisements for different products. One hundred different magazine advertisements from twenty different magazines were responded to. Advertisements were randomly assigned to people. Second, each person was asked to evaluate each of the products advertised on seven point semantic differential, very bad-very good scales. Each person was also asked to indicate his intention toward buying or trying the attitude objects in the advertisements on seven point semantic differential, very unlikely-very likely scales. Third, people were asked to evaluate on seven point scales: how much each advertisement explains the benefits of the attitude object; and, how many benefits of the attitude object are claimed or implied in the advertisements. Fourth, people completed a short form of Rotter's I–E scale. Hypothesized differences in responses to reward enumeration and reward explanation information were tested with paired t tests.

In the type of reward explanation study two hundred different adult residents of Urbana and Champaign, Illinois participated in a field experiment and were selected in a clustered random sample. In both studies, of those people asked to participate the response rate was over 90 percent. An overview of the procedure used in the data collection follows. First, people completed a short form of Rotter's I–E scale. Second, subjects responded to questions about their income, education, and age. While subjects were filling out these questions the interviewers classified subjects as high or low fatalists according to whether they scored on the top or bottom half of the Rotter scale. Third, each person was shown one of the four types of reward explanation information for the theater, state social services, and consumers unions. Each person responded to a total of three information stimuli of the same type of reward explanation. Twenty different examples of each type of reward explanation information for each of three attitude objects were randomly assigned to subjects. Fourth, subjects were asked to indicate their intention toward supporting the attitude objects on seven point very likely-very unlikely semantic differential scales. Hypothesized differences in response to the different types of reward explanation information were tested with paired *t* tests. The hypothesis about whether fatalism, income, education or age characteristics most explained the responses to the set of theoretically derived types of reward explanation information was tested with canonical correlation analysis. Canonical correlation was used rather than multiple regression because the hypothesis is concerned with explaining responses to a set of information stimuli rather than to single types of information. Canonical analysis attempts to answer the questions: first, are the responses to the set of information stimuli dependent on the fatalistic, education, age, and income characteristics of people; and second, which of the independent variables of fatalism, age, income, or education contributes the most in explaining the relationship between the set of responses to the different types of information and the set of people characteristics (Green, et al. 1966).

RESULTS

In two previous field experiments conducted in Utica and Syracuse, New York, and in one laboratory experiment conducted in Syracuse it was found that for the nutritional, reading, and political behaviors considered, reward explanation information motivated high fatalists more than reward enumeration or conformity information. In addition, it was found that the differences in responses of high and low fatalists to reward explanation information were less than for reward enumeration and conformity information.

The information stimuli, which acted as the independent variables manipulated in these three studies were constructed by the author. The purpose of the magazine advertisement field experiment conducted in Illinois was to test the results of the previous three studies with subjects from a different part of the country with actual commercial and possibly more realistic information stimuli not constructed by the author, e.g. the one hundred magazine advertisements.

Table 1.   Means of responses to different types of information

		High fatalists		Low fatalists
Field experiment with magazine				
Advertised attitude objects				
Reward explanation				
Evaluation of attitude object		5.47		5.61
Intention toward attitude object		5.18		5.06
Reward enumeration	2[a]			
Evaluation of attitude object		4.41	1[a]	5.31
Intention toward attitude object		3.97	1[a]	4.92
Type of reward explanation				
Field experiment				
Immediate-individual reward explanation				
Theater		5.12		4.81
Consumer unions		5.85		5.10
State social services		5.71		4.65
Total		5.57		4.85
Immediate-society reward explanation				
Theater		4.28		5.02
Consumers unions		3.74		4.96
State social services		3.96		4.23
Total	5[a]	3.99		4.73
Future-individual reward explanation				
Theater		3.88		5.10
Consumer unions		4.13		5.07
State social services		4.10		4.55
Total		4.03		4.90
Future society reward explanation				
Theater		1.97		4.75
Consumer unions		2.04		4.84
State social services		1.83		4.01
Total		1.93		4.53
Total immediate reward explanation	3[a]	4.77		4.78
Total future reward explanation		2.98		4.71
Total individual reward explanation	4[a]	4.79		4.87
Total society reward explanation		2.96		4.63

[a]   Significant difference at p less than 0.05. 1, 2, 3, 4, and 5 are hypothesized differences (1), (2), (3), (4), and (5).

Hypotheses (1) and (2) were supported. The hypothesized differences were significant at p less than 0.05 (see Table 1). High fatalists responded more to reward explanation information than to reward enumeration information and the differences in the responses of high and low fatalists is less in response to reward explanation compared to reward enumeration.

It was also found that the degree of positive responses to all information types was higher for attitude object evaluations than for intentions toward attitude objects. This is to be expected since the constraints on evaluation are probably less than such constraints on intentions. However, the hypothesized pattern held for both.

On the basis of this study and the three previous studies referred to above, it was concluded that reward explanation information is an effective means for inducing positive responses among fatalists. We then decided to investigate what types of reward explanations were more effective in inducing positive responses among high fatalists than other types of reward explanation information.

Hypotheses (3) (4) (5) and (6) were supported. The hypothesized differences were significant at *p* less than 0.05 (see Table 1). High fatalists responded more to immediate reward explanation than to future reward explanation, and the differences in responses of high and low fatalists were less in response to explanations of immediate rewards than to explanations of future rewards.

High fatalists responded more to information that explained how the individual can attain benefits than to information that explains how society can gain rewards, and the differences in responses of high and low fatalists were less in response to explanations of individual rewards than to explanations of society rewards.

High fatalists responded more to immediate-individual reward explanation than to future-society reward explanation, and the differences in the responses of high and low fatalists were less in response to immediate-individual reward explanation than to future-society reward explanation.

These findings held for all types of attitude objects studied.

In addition, the responses to the set of information types were dependent upon the fatalistic, education, age and income characteristics of subjects, and fatalism contributed most in explaining the relationship between the set of responses to the set of theoretically derived types of reward explanation information and the set of consumer characteristics (see Table 2).

Table 2. Canonical output for type of reward explanation field experiment

Canonical correlation	0.7761
p less than	0.01
df	200.00
Eigen values of dependent variables: responses to different types of reward explanation information	
Immediate-individual reward explanation	−0.5471
Immediate-society reward explanation	0.1842
Future-individual reward explanation	0.2659
Future-society reward explanation	0.4725
Eigen values of independent variables	
Fatalism	−0.7451
Income	0.4087
Education	0.3649
Age	0.3129

DISCUSSION

These findings demonstrate that under reward explanation information stimuli conditions in general, and under immediate-individual reward explanation information, stimuli conditions in particular, high fatalists responded positively. The field experimental conditions manipulated were type of information content, while significant changes in social structure during the few hours of the field experiment were unlikely to have occurred and accounted for the positive responses. The only systematic changes occurring in the field experiment were types of information.

These findings should be interpreted within the context of the following previous research in psychology, sociology, management, and communications. In his studies of hospital and prison situations, Seeman found that high fatalists were aware of less problem solving information than descriptive information about the institutions they were in. Seeman interprets these findings to mean that high fatalists do not seek or respond positively toward information that would help them function productively. Green, et al. (1966) in their experimental consumer behavior study found that fatalism was negatively related to prepurchase information processing. They interpreted this finding to mean that making available problem solving information to high fatalists does not induce them to utilize such information. Grunig, in his Colombian study, concludes generally that "For the typologies with available opportunities, communication behavior was an important determinant of the typology; for those without opportunities it was nonexistent. Communication behavior and its concomitant socialpsychological variables are a function of the situation in which an individual performs" (Grunig 1971: 597). More specifically, Grunig states that with respect to his fatalism decision type "information seeking does not occur" (Grunig 1971: 585). Rogers and Svenning (1969), in the three Colombian villages they studied, found that fatalism was negatively related to communications and modernism variables such as literacy, mass media exposure, empathy, cosmopolitanism, innovativeness, aspirations, achievement motivation, and political knowledgeability.

The communications variables investigated in the studies of the above authors are different from the variables I investigated. Rogers studied mass media exposure of fatalists. Grunig investigated the subjects people sought information about, the sources they sought it from, the perceived usefulness of the information received, and the socioeconomic situations of different groups of people. Seeman and Green also studied the subjects people recalled and sought information about.

My study investigated different types of information, the "how" of what was communicated as well as the subject of the information. It is worth stating what should be obvious: response to communications is a function of how something is stated and explained as well as the topic of the communication, the perceived usefulness of the information, the communication channel, the socioeconomic situation of the people being communicated with, etc. Message content includes the subject or topic of communication as well as how the subject or topic or idea is explained.

When the immediate-individual benefits of an attitude object are explained to high fatalists, they positively respond to such information content across subjects of communication. Therefore, the conclusions of the above authors concerning the causes of positive responses to communications among high fatalists should be modified to include how a message is presented.

The question might be asked: does type of reward explanation change a person's fatalism? The answer is probably no, as personality traits are not subject to easy changes. However, this does not reduce the significance of these findings. We have learned more about how to explain a behavior to a high fatalist within the context of his experience and personality with resultant positive responses. It is not necessary or even desirable to change the personality and character of people in order to encourage changes in their behavior. It should also be kept in mind that when one explains the immediate-individual benefits of an attitude object to a high fatalist, that the attitude object have in fact immediate-individual benefits.

The question might also be asked: did the immediate-individual reward explanation messages induce large motivational changes among high fatalists? The response variables investigated were verbal at one point in time, rather than overtly behavioral over long periods of time. The findings would have been more significant if the latter could have been investigated. However, with the exception of the Green experiment and the Syracuse experiment where the response variables were overtly behavioral, all the above studies were limited to verbal behaviors in short time periods.

The purpose of this discussion has not been to argue that message content is more or less important than situation, media, source, or subject matter. Such a debate is less important than learning how effectively to include and then combine all these relevant communications variables when communicating with and motivating fatalists.

REFERENCES

BIALER, I.
1962   Conceptualization of success and failure in mentally retarded and normal children. *Journal of Personality* 54:197–202.

GREEN, PAUL, MICHAEL HALBERT, PATRICK ROBINSON
1966   Canonical analysis: an exposition and illustrative application. *Journal of Marketing Research* 3:32–39.

GRUNIG, JAMES
1971   Communications and economic decision-making processes of Colombian peasants. *Economic Development and Cultural Change* 19(4).

HARRIS SURVEY
1972   *Alienation in America*. New York: Louis Harris.

LERNER, DANIEL
1967   "International cooperation and communication in national developments," in *Communication and change in the developing countries.* Edited by Daniel Lerner and Wilbur Schramm, 102–128. Honolulu: East-West Center Press.

ROGERS, EVERETT M., LYNNE SVENNING
1969   *Modernization among peasants: the impact of communication*, 273–290. New York: Holt, Rinehart and Winston.

ROTTER, JULIAN B.
n.d.   *Generalized expectancies for internal versus external control of reinforcements*. Psychological Monographs, General and Applied 80(1): 1–36.

SEEMAN, MELVIN
1962   Alienation and learning in a hospital setting. *American Sociological Review* 27:772–782.
1963   Alienation and social learning in a reformatory. *American Sociological Review* 69:270–284.
1971   The urban alienations: some dubious theses from Marx to Marcuse. *Journal of Personality and Social Psychology* 19(2).

THROOP, WARREN F., A. P. MAC DONALD, JR.
1971   *Internal-external locus of control: a bibliography*. Psychological Reports 28, Monograph Supplement (1-V28):175–190.

PART FOUR

PART FOUR

The Social Perception of Illness in Some Tunisian Villages

JOEL M. TEITELBAUM

The problem of this paper is to describe and explain illness beliefs and practices among village dwellers in Tunisia. Twentieth-century literature on disease hardly deals with this phenomenon (Montague 1970: 250–260). Although in the past medical historians took note of these facts, current workers have ignored the point of view of the patient in his social context (Gallagher 1957: 1). My investigation shows a strong awareness of illness and health as integral parts of social relations and reveals people's preferences for various forms of medical care. The poor response among rural people in Tunisia to government attempts at health delivery services may be influenced by such preferences and beliefs (Tomiche 1971: 16–21).[1]

The population studied resides in a few villages in the Sahel, the east-central Mediterranean littoral of Tunisia, and consists of dense agglomerations of craftsmen and petty agriculturists. They and their offspring have experienced rapid technological and social changes during the French Protectorate period and especially since independence from France in 1956, in the struggle for which many villagers took an active part (Stambouli 1964).[2]

[1] The humoral theory of disease discussed in this paper was in widespread use around the ancient Mediterranean littoral of Europe, North Africa and the Middle East. Arab physicians early on employed its precepts with some success. However, in modern times the medical profession in Tunisia has disabused itself of these "unscientific" notions and replaced them with so-called scientific medicine without taking into account the persistence of a belief system involving humors among their patients in society.
[2] Support for my first study in 1964–1966 which resulted in a doctoral thesis at the University of Manchester (Teitelbaum 1969) came from a fieldwork grant and predoctoral fellowship with the U.S. Public Health Service, NIMH. The return visit in 1971–1972 was sponsored by the Institute of International Studies, U.S. Office of Education in which I was designated as a Fulbright, Faculty Research Abroad Fellow from West Virginia University.

Yet, French physicians practicing in the larger cities of Tunisia are much preferred to Tunisian doctors in nearby towns. French medicine still carries great prestige in Tunisia. The least trusted doctors are Tunisians, especially if they are Muslims. Things European, particularly French, are considered to be modern or high-class and termed *suri*. Its opposite, that which is traditional or common, is called *'arbi*. Depending on the context, French (modern) or Tunisian (traditional) forms are chosen and sometimes they are combined. In health matters villagers look toward the most advanced medical aids and have recourse to traditional cures simultaneously.

A second element influencing medical choice is the universal preference for the private practitioner over the "free" doctor provided by the government for the medically indigent. Although most village dwellers qualify for medical indigency cards, they believe that a doctor who receives no fee will not provide adequate care. Tunisian doctors (and eastern European physicians) participate in the state-run free medical clinics in the villages each week. This may account in part for their lower prestige. The highest prestige is attached to physicians who charge the highest fees, use the most modern techniques and are of greatest social distance from the community.[3]

A doctor is viewed as having performed a good medical examination if he employs shiny, strange-looking diagnostic instruments and particularly if he touches the patient firmly with his hands in affected portions of the body. Those physicians who rush patients through and do not "lay hands" on them, epitomized by the overburdened doctors at free government clinics, are suspect. If some direct verbal communication occurs, even in broken Arabic and French, the doctor is appreciated far more than one who relies upon the assisting nurse for translation of symptoms. Private physicians are preferred for their helpfulness not only in treating disease, but in providing medical certificates of health and disability used in obtaining employment, entering school, or gaining compensation for health damage. Thus visits to a doctor are combined with social ends, although it may appear that a person has traveled to a distant city, waited perhaps for hours, and paid fees to correct some organic complaint.

An ill person is attended by his close kin and upon request may be

---

[3]   The ranking of physicians by nationality is not overly rigid. Individual practitioners build a clientele from the villages and any doctor who permits a large margin of interpretation in the explanation of symptoms and is sympathetic to his patients is appreciated. It may be that linguistic and cultural differences between the village patient and the foreign doctor encourage this rapport when the physician is not rushed or overwhelmed with waiting patients.

transported to a city hospital or a doctor's clinic by taxi or bus. The nearest hospital and doctor's office is in a market town a few kilometers away, and another hospital is in the district seat some fifteen kilometers distant. But village people prefer to drive about forty kilometers to the regional hospital and doctor's clinics in the provincial capital city, where they believe better care is to be found. Time and cost of the travel involved are not thought wasted or urgent; rather the further away the city and the more prestigious the physician visited, the greater the social weight of the patient's condition in the eyes of the community.

Illne s behavior varies according to the ascribed and achieved status of the person. Few people go to the doctor regularly; wealthy families have better access than poor people. For the most part, village men avoid preventive care, while the women routinely use the community dispensary for minor health needs. There are separate entrances and waiting rooms for men and women at this type of facility to accommodate the customary shame and avoidance behavior which characterizes social relations between the sexes in a community. In city clinics these social distinctions are not overtly followed. At the village level, children are the most regular recipients of health care. Parents of both genders lavish concern by word and amulet on their children, whom they watch anxiously for the first sign of illness and for whom they fear the presumed harmful effect of the Evil Eye — the jealousy and hostile sentiments of unrelated others (Spooner 1970: 315).

In general, the beliefs about the causes of illne s (except among a few highly educated persons), do not involve concern about infection or contagious disease. Most village people are not aware of the germ theory of disease. Although household cleanliness is a moral and religious virtue, family members do not use separate utensils. It is believed that members of a kin group who dine together should eat from the same large dish, using the fingers of the right hand. When in use, cutlery is shared and people drink water from the same tin cup.

This commensal type of meal is justified in terms of interpersonal social relations: close friends and kinsmen cannot "give" one another sickness because they must like one another and do not harbor feelings of ill will towards each other. On the other hand, strangers, known enemies and persons of low social standing in the community are considered potentially harmful dining companions and are avoided. Incompatible social position is believed to create health risks affecting the organic health of the people involved. The air is also held to be a primary source of illness, particularly colds. Although aversion to dirt is morally good, sneezing, coughing and spitting are not thought to transmit disease.

After the common cold, the most frequent type of illness noted is sickness of the "blood". It is a strongly psychosomatic affliction thought to be created by anger and dismay which makes the blood run too fast and spoils it. As a result of "bad" or "black" blood, a person may sicken in the heart or head or other portions of the body. Bad blood can be either too strong or too weak. This belief appears to be a combination of pathophysiology based on ancient humoral theories of disease and a folk version of modern medical knowledge about high blood pressure and nutritional disease deficiencies.

Blood affliction is thought to be caused by the disruption of essential interpersonal social relations among networks of people in the community. Thus human emotions and sentiments are tied to the circulatory system of the body. The heart is considered to be the source of good and evil feelings (white and black), which responds organically to moral problems. Strong emotions affect the flow of blood by increasing or decreasing the heartbeat, and blood which has circulated too rapidly due to emotional hypertension turns "bad"; it may rise to the surface of the body causing headaches, sores, and pains. This "rotten" blood is removed by bleeding and cupping techniques. Sores and skin problems are dealt with by scrubbing the body vigorously at the public bath in an attempt at purification of skin and blood.

Anger is considered the major cause of rotten blood. Outbursts of anger enfeeble the individual and bring on fatigue much as do shock and overexertion. In cases of acute weakness after a display of anger a person is rushed to the hospital complaining of a "broken heart", due to the rapid pounding of his blood. A wise doctor asks the patient if he has been angry recently, and if so, usually prescribes a sedative and some sugary placebos.

Although some people do indeed suffer from high blood pressure and must follow special diets, the folk explanation of this is that the regime is intended to "thin" or weaken the excess blood so that a bout of anger will not break the patient's heart. Plethora of blood is dangerous, as is lack of blood (anemia) which is believed to cause wasting-away disease. Vitamin preparations are sought out in the belief that they strengthen weak blood. The outward signs of good health are firm fatty limbs and a fleshy face. Plumpness is preferred and slimness viewed as unhealthy.

The psychosocial element in this set of "causal" beliefs is that "anger in the blood" is preceded by worry, and a man who constantly worries is considered a prime target for blood affliction. Worry causes anger in people with a plethora of blood. In those who lack blood it depresses the appetite and leads to thinness and weakness. A worry-free attitude is associated with corpulence and good health. For example, wealthier people are thought to have fewer worries (about money matters) than the poor and thus to have good appetite for health-giving fattening foods such a meat and oil, which they can afford to purchase more easily also.

Poor people are known to substitute excessive quantities of cheap red peppers for expensive meat in their diet. Peppers are believed to excite the blood and produce anger more quickly, thus making poor people more susceptible to blood afflictions. Peppers are also thought to increase sexual libido and thus account for the larger number of children among the poor which compounds their poverty and makes for more worries. These notions form a vicious circle as a folk theory of the roots of economic status difference associated with health and illness. Ability to pay for prestigious doctors and medication and to eat strengthening expensive foods are the key to understanding social stratification and standing.

The blood-affliction beliefs are linked with the field of small-scale social relations within the community. Close kin or associates who have broken customary obligations are thought to bring on worry and anger in the affected person. Furthermore, to have someone close to you who harbors ill feelings towards you is immoral and a source of active concern as it can disrupt daily life. Expected norms of behavior are interpreted in terms of sentiments of love, hate and jealousy and if someone acts disrespectful or shameful so as to hurt the feelings of a companion the latter may sicken with the blood affliction from worry and anger.

Treatment by a physician is a partial means of obtaining relief from the symptoms of the illness, as well as a device for demonstrating to others the gravity of the affliction. Visits to religious shrines such as *marabouts* (saint's tombs) and watering places widely known for their curative properties afford physical and emotional relief and also serve to communicate the immediacy of the problem to kin and friends in the community. These visitations are social acts which correspond to the value system of the community. Thus the tendency to expend time and money by leaving the village for treatment reflects the seriousness of the social breach which is thought to have caused the affliction and weighs the standing and other status components of the invalid and the person (or persons) who has wronged him on the scale of communal values.

Real recovery can come only when the person who incited the afflicted one to anger or worried him excessively, comes to beg forgiveness, make amends and acknowledge customary duties. If these acts are refused the illness may persist and visitors to the sickbed, who according to custom must come to wish the invalid well and demonstrate their good will toward him, are told the story of how he has been wronged and who has "sickened" him. Usually the accused "sickener" is noticeably absent among the stream of visitors. This accusation is terrifying, but not unusual. Through the medium of gossip the story grows and may become a social issue which requires resolution at a larger group level such as between families or kin groups. Thus illness behavior is associated with social disruption and the cure must include a reordering of human relationships and a redress of offended sentiments in order to be complete, as shown in Figure 1 (Gluckman 1955: 23).

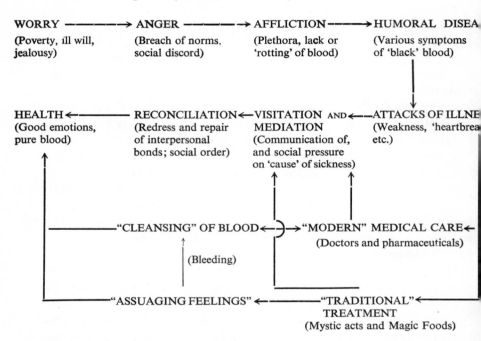

Figure 1.   "Causes" and "cures" of illness in Tunisian villages

An intermediary, related to both the invalid and the accused, often attempts to bring them together and reconcile their differences. This is done by means of a ritual handshake before which the mediator takes an oath before God which compels the two to resume relations or risk committing the sin of offending the Deity. A formal time for such reconciliations in the community at large is at the mosque during the celebration of the *Aed Es-Sghrir* after *Ramadan* when all men are expected to resolve their grievances toward one another accumulated during the past. Reconciliation permits the afflicted person to recover worry-free health. Should he later contract an illness he will not attribute it to the person with whom he has become reconciled. Even if the original disease becomes chronic or fatal, a reconciled individual escapes the stigma of having "killed" the afflicted one. When death occurs he is not believed to be burdened with mystical retribution, and he can attend the funeral ceremonies and beg forgiveness of the deceased's soul on the same basis as other persons in the latter's social network. However, if reconciliation is not achieved beforehand, the accused "killer" may suffer community-wide reprimand for years and his family may lose honor in the eyes of others. Thus the social pressures toward repair of fractured social relations are strong and persistent and involve a combination of medical care and mystical recourse, as well as the intervention of others in the community.

In short, beliefs about illness and improper human conduct call for a cyclical system of perceptions which fit neatly into the framework of modern medical practice and tend to employ doctors for social ends. The humoral theory of disease through blood affliction gives a personalized causation theory to complement scientific explanation with accounts of the why and the particularity of an illness. This *post-hoc* system of belief incorporates disease into the small-scale social context of kin groups and communities, and tends to reinforce the constraints surrounding the application of customary norms of behavior. The basic framework of belief is taken for granted by most villagers. Those few who through outside education are led to question it skeptically are discounted by the convinced majority. I myself found it necessary to express health problems in this idiom rather than try to give so-called scientific explanations of the causes and cures of disease. In this paper I have followed the pattern of beliefs and practices and analyzed them as a model of perceptions attached to the social context they encompass.

REFERENCES

AMMAR, S.
1970   *En souvenir de la médecine Arabe.* Tunis: Bascone et Muscat.
BOTT, E.
1957   *Family and social network.* London: Tavistock.
DEMEERSEMAN, A.
1967   *La famille Tunisienne et le temps nouveau.* Tunis: Maison Tunisien de l'Édition.
DESPOIS, J.
1955   *La Tunisie orientale, Sahel et basse steppe.* Paris: P.U.F.

DURKHEIM, E.
1893　*De la division du travail social.* Paris: Alain.

DE MONTETY, H.
1958　*Femmes de Tunisie.* Paris: Mouton.

EVANS-PRITCHARD, E. E.
1963　*Essays in social anthropology.* London: Faber.

FERCHIOU, SOPHIE
1969　Différenciation sexuelle d'alimentation au Djerid (Sud Tunisien). *l'Homme* 1969: 64–85.

GALLAGHER, CHARLES F.
1957　Modern medicine in North Africa. *American Universities Field Staff Reports* N. Af. CFG-2.

GLUCKMAN, M.
1955　*Custom and conflict in Africa.* Oxford: Blackwells.

MALINOWSKI, B.
1948　*Magic, science and religion and other essays.* Glencoe: The Free Press.

MONTAGUE, JOEL
1970　Disease and public health in Tunisia: 1882–1970: an overview of the literature and its sources. *A current bibliography on African affairs* volume 4, series II: 250–260.

SPOONER, BRIAN
1970　"The evil eye in the Middle East," in *Witchcraft, confessions and accusations.* A.S.A. Monograph 9: 311–319. London: Tavistock.

STAMBOULI, F.
1964　*Ksar Hellal et sa région: contribution à une sociologie du changement dans les pays en voie de développement.* Thèse de 3e cycle: U. de Paris.

TEITELBAUM, J. M.
1969　"Lamta: leadership and social organization of a Tunisian community." Unpublished Ph. D. Thesis, University of Manchester.

TOMICHE, F. J.
1971　Tunisia: how to make the most of health services. *World Health* December, 1971: 16–21.

Culturally Contrasting Therapeutic Systems of the West Sepik: The Lujere

WILLIAM E. MITCHELL

Cultures are never neutral about human existence. Inasmuch as cultures are arrangements for living, each has opinionated beliefs about what is correct and proper, what is deviant and wrong. It is this strongly ethical stance about how to live that permeates cultural behavior. It is also the ability to arrive at varied and often conflicting ethics that so vividly distinguishes humans from other primate species. So within any one culture the "good" and the "bad" are polarized opposites yet, paradoxically, therein lies the intimacy of their ontological relationship. For knowledge of what is good and bad is a contrasting process; one helps to define and determine the other.

The behavioral dialectics that derive from these beliefs about the good

The research on which this paper is based was made possible by a grant (Number 1 RO1 MH 18039) from the National Institute of Mental Health. I am grateful to the following institutions and governmental departments for facilitative support and to their staffs for countless personal courtesies: Papua New Guinea Office of the Administrator; Papua New Guinea Department of Public Health and Department of Social Development and Home Affairs; West Sepik District, Lumi Sub-District and Edwaki Base Camp offices; Christian Missions in Many Lands; Franciscan Catholic Mission; National Archives of Papua New Guinea; Commonwealth Archives Office of Australia; New Guinea Research Unit, Research School of Pacific Studies, Australian National University; Department of Anthropology and Sociology, University of Papua New Guinea; Department of Anthropology, American Museum of Natural History; Wenner-Gren Foundation for Anthropological Research; and the University of Vermont. I also am grateful to Wakau village for hospitality and fellowship, to Oria for teaching me much about Lujere culture, and to Dr. Rhoda Metraux for her careful reading of this manuscript and helpful suggestions. Some of the material in the paper was first presented in talks to the Department of Social and Preventive Medicine, University of Papua New Guinea; Department of Behavioral Science, Pennsylvania State University College of Medicine; and the Department of Psychiatry, Tufts University College of Medicine.

and the bad are at the affective core of each culture. They are reflected in the everyday behavior of every man, every woman, every child, and are formally realized in cultural customs of great emotional and dramatic intensity. In this sense cultures are massive morality plays that embrace all aspects of life — how I am born, where I may sleep, whom I may love, when I may weep, and how I shall die. If I do not follow the lines, if I deviate markedly by design or by accident, a prompter will attempt to save my bad performance — and the play. Just so cultures invent ways to remedy the bad, to correct or eradicate what threatens the good life, and to conserve the cherished concepts and behaviors, the organisms and the things of which cultures are made.

But what happens when two cultures with contrasting traditions about the good and the bad come into continued contact? Are the remedial systems for changing the bad to the good — always a major cultural preoccupation — complementary or in conflict? And what is the systemic nature of this relationship? Is it a simple and separable interface, or do discordant values and behavior become intermeshed in the lives of the people and, if so, with what consequences for the individual as well as the culture?

These were some of the broad questions I asked as a way of orienting my research in Papua New Guinea on culturally contrasting therapeutic systems. The two-year expedition (May 1970–May 1972) was carried out among two cultural groups of the West Sepik District: the *Wape*, a people of the Torricelli Mountains, and the *Lujere*, who live in the vast swamplands of the upper Sepik River. Joyce Slayton Mitchell, my wife, and I worked with the Wape for about a year and a half; thereafter I completed my field work among the Lujere (November 1971–April 1972).

Remedial actions directed toward individual human beings tend to take one of three therapeutic modes, viz. they are intended to instruct, to punish, or to heal. The three modes are alike only in their goal — to change the bad to good. Their strategies for inducing change are radically different. But these therapeutic modes are not necessarily mutually exclusive and two — or all three — may be implemented simultaneously. In our own society a person may be jailed (punished), while in jail he may attend vocational training classes (be instructed) and participate in group psychotherapy (be healed), all in an effort to make him over into a law-abiding good citizen.

Instruction attempts to induce a positive change by teaching; punishment, by inflicting suffering; healing, by alleviating suffering. The therapeutic mode chosen to correct a particular deviation will depend upon the culture's values and the specific circumstances of the offending case.

But it is the cultural rationale for the intervention, not the intervention itself, that classifies the therapeutic act. For example, amputation may be either a punitive or a healing intervention depending upon the therapeutic intent of the operation. So it is not enough to know only the therapeutic act; its intent must be ascertained as well.[1]

In this paper I limit my analysis to those therapies available to the Lujere that express an intent to HEAL. Punitive and instructional therapies, although existing among the Lujere and important for a full understanding of their therapeutic system, are not considered. Because the general features of Lujere culture have not been described, I shall first present these data and then describe consecutively the indigenous and the introduced healing therapies that are directly available to the Lujere. Finally, I shall discuss these contrasting therapeutic traditions for insights into their present functioning and their implications for theories of cultural change.

I first began to learn about Lujere culture while I was living among the Wape people in the village of Taute. The Lujere, a cultural group of about 3,000, live from two to three days' walk south of the Wape in the great grass and rainforest swamps of the Sepik River and its tributaries, the Yellow and Sand Rivers that help to carry away the heavy rainfall of the Torricelli range (see Map 1). In fact, the Sibi River, which I looked down upon from my house on the Taute ridge, eventually empties into the Yellow River. If the day was clear and I looked south toward the Sepik, I could also see the smoke rising from the burning grasslands, smoke from the seemingly perpetual fires set by the Lujere to keep the plains open or to facilitate a hunt.

The Wape have only a scanty knowledge of the Lujere and before Europeans came into their mountains they had no contact with them at all. Then after World War II, Lumi station was established in the midst of Wapeland, and Lujere men came to the station, infrequently to be sure, to sign on as laborers for the island copra plantations or to respond to requests from the Australian administration. From the Wape I learned that Lujere men dwell apart from the women in large men's houses and that their land is enviously alive with the birds, pigs, and cassowaries which they hunt. The Wape also told me that the Lujere are even more avid hunters of people as unrivaled practitioners of a type of murderous witchcraft called in Melanesian Pidgin, *sanguma*.[2]

---

[1] For example, the *Hastings Center Report* (1973:16) cites a new law in Libya permitting a surgeon to amputate a criminal's right hand for stealing and his left foot for armed robbery.

[2] Melanesian Pidgin is the major *lingua franca* for Papua New Guinea and is also

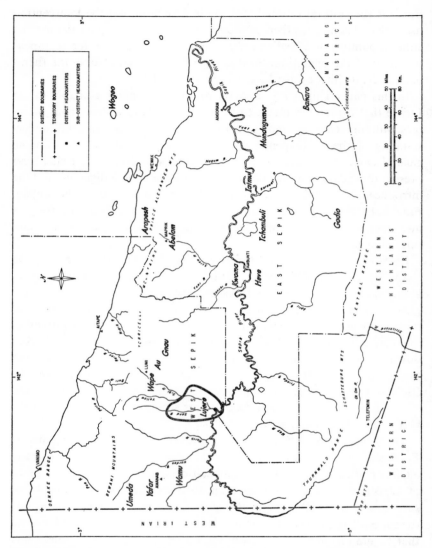

Map 1. The approximate territory of the Lujere people in geographic relationship to other Sepik Basin cultures with intensive ethnographic studies

This was one of the principal reasons I decided to work among them. The Lujeres' alleged obsession with witchcraft, their interesting environ-

called Pidgin English, Melanesian Pidgin English, and Neo-Melanesian (cf. Mihalic 1971.)

mental niche, and the fact that they and their immediate neighbors were ethnographically unknown made them an intriguing group to study. In addition, it was clear that they were sufficiently different from the Wape to engender stimulating comparisons. Two reconnaissance visits to the Lujere convinced me that my interest was well-founded and of the feasibility of working among them.

The Lujere have no name for themselves or their language. The Wape usually refer to them as the "swamp people" and the government as the "Yellow River people," but in my publications I shall call them the "Lujere," a word in their own language meaning "people."[3] Laycock (1968) calls their unrecorded language Namie and most recently (Laycock i.p.) classifies it as one of three languages of the Yellow River Family. Namie also belongs to the Middle Sepik Super-Stock (along with the Ndu, Sepik Hill, Nukuma and Yerakai language families) and the large Sepik-Ramu Phylum stretching westward from the mouths of the Sepik and Ramu Rivers to the Indonesian border. But geographically the Lujere are a linguistic cul-de-sac far upriver from the other Middle Sepik Phylum languages and they are surrounded by other linguistic groups.[4] The linguistic evidence as well as their mythology indicate that they have migrated upriver to their present location. However, the Lujere have few marked cultural similarities to the cultures of the Middle Sepik Phylum, e.g. the Abelan, Iatmul, and Kwoma; culturally they appear to be more closely related to their present neighbors to the West.

I settled in the Lujere hamlet of Wakau (population 125) near the Sand River and on the western edge of Lujere territory. Wakau is one of four geographically separate hamlets comprising the village of Iwani; Mauwi, situated atop a hill, is considered the mother hamlet from which the other three Iwani hamlets originated. Iwariyo is located at the western base of the hill; Okwam, the most recent hamlet to be established, is located on the Sepik River near the mouth of the Yellow River, a four-hour walk away. Wakau, a forty-five minute walk from Mauwi, is situated in sight of the Sand River on a slight rise in the swamps at the edge of a small wet plain. No one knows when Wakau was established; it happened too long ago.

---

[3] J. K. McCarthy (1936:12) in one of his Yellow River patrol reports suggested the term "Yuan" after the native word the Lujere people use for that waterway. However, this usage was never adopted. For a brief summary of his 1935 patrol among the Lujere see McCarthy (1963:161–164).
[4] For recent maps showing the Namie language in relation to other Sepik Basin languages see Conrad and Dye (i.p.) and Laycock (i.p.).

LUJERE-EUROPEAN CONTACT

In 1884, Germany acquired the north-eastern portion of the New Guinea mainland as a colonial possession and named it Kaiser-Wilhelmsland. But it was not until shortly before World War I that any extensive exploration of the upper Sepik basin was undertaken. At that time several successive scientific expeditions were sent into the field to explore this unknown region of the world. Although the principal purpose of the expeditions was geographic exploration, cultural artifacts also were collected for German museums.

In 1910, the first of these expeditions, led by Leonhard Schultze, went far up the Sepik River, passed the Lujere territory but apparently made no contact with them (Schultze 1914). In 1912-1913, an even larger expedition that explored the upper Sepik region did make some superficial contacts with the Lujere. Richard C. Thurnwald, the first anthropologist to work in the Sepik Basin, was a member of this expedition to the German-Dutch border. In the course of his many impressive pioneering explorations he entered Lujere territory to explore and name the Yellow and Sand Rivers (Behrmann 1917: 54). However, his relationship with the Lujere seems to have been limited to barter for food (Thurnwald 1916), as he published no ethnographic observations about them. This lack of interest apparently was mutual, for the Lujere today have no memory of or tradition about his visit. In spite of the fact that Thurnwald ascended the Sand River to the foothills of the Torricelli Mountains and, going and returning, passed directly through the Wakau bush, my informants now know nothing of what must have been an extraordinary event in the lives of their forebears. This lack of interest in the past is also evident in the shallow Lujere genealogies.

At the outbreak of World War I Australia took control of German New Guinea. Exploration abruptly ceased and the only foreigners to enter Lujere territory were Malay bird-of-paradise hunters from Dutch New Guinea. This was nothing new, for Malays had made hunting forays into the Sepik swamps for many years. Almost twenty years passed before the Lujere were visited by their first Australian government officer. In 1930, a government patrol led by E. D. Robinson — known more familiarly to old New Guinea hands as "Sepik-Robbie" — visited the lower Yellow River and was "accorded a friendly reception by all the natives" (Robinson 1931: 9). But a laborer recruiter apparently had preceded the government, for when Robinson again visited the Lujere he reports (Robinson 1932: 7) that twenty-four men and one woman recently had returned from completing three-year contracts at the Alexishafen Mission on the north coast near Madang. These Lujere had gained a speaking knowledge of Melanesian Pidgin and Robinson was thereby able to collect the first sketchy data on their customs. Although incomplete, his tentative findings are supported by my own research.

In 1934, Robinson made the first overland patrol from the New Guinea coast, beginning at Aitape, crossing the Torricelli Mountains and Wape territory and then following the Yellow River to its conjunction with the Sepik. On this patrol Robinson (1934) further established friendly relations with previously uncontacted people, including other Lujere. On Robinson's recommendation (1932: 5–6) a Base Camp was established on the south bank of the Sepik near the mouth of the Yellow River to bring the Lujere and their Sepik neighbors under government control. For the Lujere the task was not difficult. J. K. McCarthy, a government officer with wide experience of New Guinea peoples, observed on his inspection of the Base Camp in 1936 that there was no inter-village warfare or raiding among the Lujere and he commented that "the people are the most peaceful that I have ever met" (McCarthy 1936: 20). Before it was abandoned during World War II, the Yellow River Base Camp became famous as the most isolated station in the Territory, where unruly young officers were stationed to contemplate their misdeeds. During the war, occasional Allied patrols moved through the area but the few Japanese patrols operating in the Torricelli Mountains never ventured into the Lujere swamps.

After World War II, Lumi Patrol Post was established in the Torricelli Mountains and in 1949 a patrol officer made his first visit to the Lujere. Since then the Lujere have been administered from Lumi with one patrol through the area every year or so. In recent years the Lujere have pressed for their own government station, and in April 1971 Edwaki Base Camp with a resident patrol officer was established near the Yellow River in the middle of Lujere territory.

As McCarthy's early report indicated, the Lujere people did not fight among themselves. They did, however, participate in back-and-forth raids with the tribes around them. They were not cannibals; when the Lujere ambushed and killed an enemy the left arm of the victim was severed at the elbow and brought back to the village to be exhibited in the center of the clearing as proof of the killing. To the booming of great slit gongs, now rotted and gone, the people paraded and sang through the night.

The tribes across the Sepik were cannibals. When raiders captured a Lujere villager, they would tie him alive to a pole like a pig and carry him away to be butchered, cooked, and eaten. From the mid-1930's on, intertribal peace was gradually established over the area although occasional killings continued. Even as recently as 1962 men from the Lujere village of Tipas on the Sepik ambushed and killed a neighboring tribesman to the east over a marriage dispute.

The government also succeeded in changing the Lujere's mortuary customs. Formerly, the body was placed on a platform within the village to decay, but burial is now universally practiced. Of much greater significance than any government intervention was the opportunity brought by private enterprise for men to sign up as contract plantation laborers. Traveling far from their villages, Lujere men saw their first towns, learned how to work for Europeans, and earned money to buy their coveted goods. Although it has been forty-five years since the first Lujere men went away to work on plantations as laborers, this still is their only important source of cash income.

The Lujere were under government influence and control for many years before any attempt was made to Christianize them. In 1958, the Sola Fida missionaries with the help of many Lujere built a small station and air strip near Edwaki village between the Yellow and Sand Rivers. In 1960 the Sola Fida Mission turned the station over to another group of evangelical missionaries, the Christian Brethren, who are registered with the government as the Christian Mission in Many Lands. Since that time the Brethren usually have had one or two missionary families in residence at the mission station. Their work consists primarily in: (1) personally carrying the Christian message into the villages, (2) conducting Bible and Pidgin literacy classes on the station for young men, (3) teaching domestic skills to the women, (4) helping supervise the Standard I and II English primary school, and (5) providing health services for pregnant women and small children. The influence of the mission is strongest among the hamlets close to the mission station. Throughout the rest of the Lujere territory traditional ceremonial life continues much as before. Iwani village, however, is considered by the mission to be the village that is least interested in and most resistant to their teachings and services.

LUJERE CULTURE

The Iwani hamlets are, traditionally, and continue to be discrete political entities except in matters that concern relations with the government. In these matters a government appointed headman and his assistant are charged to act as intermediaries between the government and the villagers. But the appointees' influence begins and ends there. The effective linkage among the Iwani hamlets is not the superimposed headman system but the network of kinship and marriage that ties the villagers' lives together with lines of reciprocal obligations.

The Lujere settlement pattern is semi-sedentary. Although each family belongs to a specific hamlet, much of the year is spent dispersed in various hunting camps and the hamlet is not visited for months at a time. When they are living in the hamlet the men live separately from the women, just as the Wape had told me, in a large house. This men's house is primarily a dormitory, not a ceremonial center. Lujere ceremonial life, as we shall see, is very limited in comparison with that of such Sepik cultures as the Abelam, the Iatmul, and the Wape. Women and children live in separate houses, where the wives of two close lineage mates may perhaps share a single dwelling. But when a Lujere family leaves the hamlet for a hunting expedition into the bush, the family — a man, his wife, and children — travels together and lives together in a single house.

The traditional covering for men is a small gourd penis sheath; women wear a string skirt that leaves the thighs bare. But cloth clothing has been introduced and the two types of covering are seen together everywhere. Small children continue to go naked.

The Lujere are only sometime agriculturists. Their gardens are small, unfenced, and untended; they produce bananas, some sugar cane, and an occasional taro or sweet potato that the wild pigs have carelessly bypassed. Their subsistence is based upon hunting and the processing of sago. Fish are trapped in the many small waterways or are poisoned with pounded derris root. Men hunt, women process sago. In fishing and agriculture the division of labor is not so marked, and is more of a cooperative venture. Although each hamlet has a few domesticated pigs they are unimportant in cultural terms or as a source of protein.

Marriage is almost exclusively by sister exchange, but elopement is sometimes a successful alternative for a man who has no female relative to give in exchange for his wife. Although polygyny is permitted, it is unusual. In Wakau, all of the marriages were monogamous. Marriage with first cousins is forbidden and marital residence is virilocal. Cousin kin terms are Hawaiian; unusual for a Sepik culture but not for New Guinea (cf. Pouwer 1967: 89). The small patrilineages control access to the community's strategic resources and are combined into patriclans. Genealogical knowledge is meager, tending to be limited to those kin the informant has known personally. Because of the high incidence of death in young adulthood, the network of living kin is small. In Wakau no child had a grandparent alive in the village and similarly no married man had a living father. Europeans familar with the Lujere attribute the high

incidence of early adult deaths to periodic influenza epidemics and pneumonia. The Lujere have their own interpretation: witchcraft. The Lujere
call a witch or *sangumaman* (Melanesian Pidgin, cf. Steinbauer 1969: 166)
nakworu in their Namie language. It was one of the first Namie terms I
learned and certainly one that I shall never forget.

LUJERE THERAPIES

Witchcraft

Some situations in life must be personally experienced in order to plumb
their peculiar emotional depths. Among these, I place at the top of my
list, living in a witch-ridden culture. Instruction or vicarious knowledge
simply is not enough. Although I had read numerous anthropological
accounts of witchcraft and had lived with two other Sepik societies, the
Iatmul and Wape, I was utterly unprepared for the affective impact of
living in a society riveted together by witchcraft beliefs. Certainly my
own interest in witchcraft was scientific and my attitude objective. But
once I had settled among the Lujere my emotional experience became
detached from that sober reasoning and I drifted into a sentient state I
had not known since childhood. I experienced a sensitization to the
unseen and the demonic that had been prefigured by ghostly tales of
terror told among children under a street lamp on a hot Kansas night.
  Beginning with my first night in Wakau, and quite against my rational
will, my adult feelings about witches began to change. As the men left
me that night they cautioned me to fasten my door securely and to call
out loudly if I heard anyone moving outside or within my house. Witches,
they said, often steal into villages at night to attack a sleeping victim.
They did not want this to happen to me. I silently looked around. The
entire back portion of my temporary residence was rotted away and I
could not tell where the forest ended and the house began. Until that
moment I both thought and felt that I was immune to the predations of
anybody's witches. But the Wakaus were teaching me differently.
  This is a paper about therapeutic systems and, in particular, about the
healing therapies of the Lujere. But to understand the single most important type of Lujere therapy we first must understand Lujere witchcraft.
In the following account of Lujere witchcraft I distinguish witchcraft
from sorcery in accordance with the distinction first made by Evans-
Pritchard (1937) and more recently explicated by Middleton and Winter
(1963). In this usage witches are personifications of evil; they possess

"mysterious powers unknown and unavailable to ordinary people: it is this which sets them apart" (Middleton and Winter 1963: 8). In this sense witches are extraordinary individuals — Middleton and Winter would say "abnormal" individuals — within the communities where they live and, depending upon the culture, they may be male or female, child or adult. But regardless of culturally determined requirements such as sex or age, it is the witch's special pernicious powers that separates him from others. The practice of sorcery, however, is not restricted in this way. Sorcerers, unlike witches, do not have extraordinary and mysterious powers; their ritual techniques for evoking evil are potentially available to all. Thus "a sorcerer's capacity to harm ... depends on his ability to control powers extrinsic to himself; whereas a witch ... possesses powers — inherited or acquired — as an intrinsic part of his or her person" (Glick 1972: 1080).[5]

Lujere witchcraft can be characterized by the way a witch murders his victim; it is representative of a generic type of witchcraft I shall call "*sanguma* witchcraft." Although the specific details vary among cultures, the general procedure for a *sanguma* witchcraft murder is as follows: (1) the victim is rendered unconscious, (2) his skin is cut, (3) the incisions are healed without scars, (4) returned to consciousness he is without memories of the assault, (5) he becomes progressively ill, (6) he dies. The assertion is also frequently made that once a person is attacked in this way death is inevitable.[6]

[5] Some anthropologists, following Evans-Pritchard's description of Zande witchcraft beliefs (1937), restrict the term "witch" to someone who is innately and involuntarily possessed of evil and mysterious powers. In reviews of Evans-Pritchard's work, Middleton and Winter (1963) and Mair (1969) suggest it is a witch's possession of evil supernatural powers, not how he came by them, that is the essential characteristic of a witch. Unlike the ordinary mortal, it is a witch's sinister powers, perceived by his fellow-villagers as inherent to his very being, that "sets him outside the pale of common humanity" (Mair 1969:22). It is this usage that I have adopted for this paper.
[6] *Sanguma* is a Melanesian Pidgin term translatable as 'witchcraft' and refers especially to the supernatural form of murder described here. It is distinguished from *poison* (sorcery) that refers to destructive spells anyone may learn. But it should be recognized that the term *sanguma* has not at all times and in all places met the criteria set forth here; e.g. the Rao of the Madang District use the term for demon-induced illnesses (Stanhope 1968:139), and Mead (1947:419), working with the Arapesh of the East Sepik District in 1932, defined it as "a form of combined sorcery and divination, associated with pointing bones, burial of exuviae, and possession by a spirit of the dead." According to Höltker (1942–1945:213), *sanguma* is derived from *tsangumo* (cf. Vormann and Scharenberger 1914:180), a term in the Monumbo language located on the coast in the northern Madang District. The nearby Tangu language has a similar term, *ranguma* (Burridge 1960:59–71, 1965:224–249). Both terms refer to the type of supernatural murder already described. Mead (i.p.) has recently critically discussed *sanguma* as a cultural trait of the Sepik area.

Sanguma witchcraft is widely distributed throughout Melanesia and aboriginal Australia. It was first described by Codrington (1891: 206–207) under the term *vele* from Savo Island in the Solomon Islands. Seligman (1910: 170-171) independently, it seems, described a similar phenomenon called *vada* among the Koita people in the Port Moresby region.[7] Fortune (1932: 284–287) later cited *vada* as analogous to what the Dobu call *wawari*. Among the Waropen of Geelvink Bay in the western part of New Guinea, *sanguma* witchcraft is termed *sema* (Held 1959: 258–262), and on Wogeo Island off the north-central coast it is called *yabou* (Hogbin 1970: 148–156). On the New Guinea mainland it is also reported, for example, among the Iatmul (Bateson 1958: 58–61) and the Wam of the East Sepik District (Schofield and Parkinson 1963: 30–33), the Telefomin of the West Sepik District (Simpson 1954: 228–231), and the Daribi (Wagner 1967: 51–55) and the Gimi (Glick 1967: 41–42) of the Eastern Highlands. Both Elkin (1964: 282–310) and Warner (1958: 194–206) give graphic accounts of *sanguma* murders among Australian aborigines.

When an anthropologist first moves into a village there is a considerable period during which both he and the villagers, strangers, mutually test the extent of each other's trustworthiness. The issues of trust are many but I am concerned here only with witchcraft. New Guineans know that these activities are outlawed and that individuals convicted of them will be jailed. Yet they are a viable part of village life. The question therefore arises: how much can you tell this new inquisitive European?

As I have indicated, the Wakaus were quick to clue me into the dangers of predatory witches. But their references to witches from the surrounding hamlets and other villages were always vague. I was given no names. As to Wakau witches, no, we had none. The fact that I could not obtain data on actual persons designated as witches, together with my own skepticism about the logical possibility of *sanguma* murders, initially led me to wonder if Lujere witchcraft was not just part of a belief system that explained sickness and death. In other words, there were probably neither Lujere witches nor witchcraft murders.

One afternoon when the village was almost deserted a bright-eyed boy from Mauwi hamlet whom I knew stopped to watch me work. I was typing an interview and we chatted sporadically as I worked. Sometimes I took advantage of these moments of quiet intimacy to ask about problems troubling me in my research. I asked him who were the *nakworu*

---

[7] Burton-Bradley and Julius (1965:15) provide a brief description of *sanguma* witchcraft for the Koitapu village of Baruni (Port Moresby) that indicates the persistence of *sanguma* beliefs in urban areas.

Plate 1. Kaigu, a famous and feared *nakworu*, begins treatment of Maruwami, a young married woman of Wakau hamlet, by examining her paining chest. The author's European-based diagnosis was pneumonia.

Plate 2.   Probing his patient's breast, Kaigu attempts to locate the noxious substance shot into her by a ghost or witch.

Plate 3.   The patient cries out in pain as Kaigu continues to probe deeply within her body. Male relatives attend her.

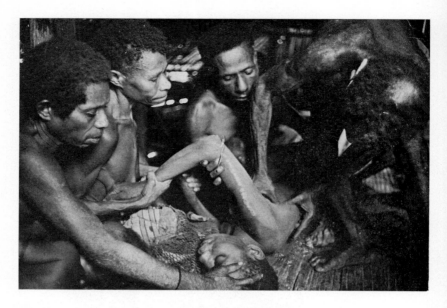

Plate 4. The patient is physically restrained by relatives including her mother as the *nakworu*'s treatment continues. Here he mends bones broken in the alleged attack by pressing them together.

Plate 5. Locating a noxious substance, Kaigu pulls it from the patient's skin with shredded sago leaf fibers bespat with betel juice. Before recovering the patient also was treated by other *nakworu*, exorcised during two *aiwar wowi* curing festivals, and given a course of drug therapy by the author.

Plate 6. An *aiwar wowi* curing festival in the village of Gwidami concludes with exorcism rites for a woman (seated left with back to camera) and a man who also is a *nakworu* (standing facing camera). The four decorated bamboo trumpets carried earlier by the dancing trumpeters are in the foregound. The style for the elaborate trumpet on the right was recently imported from the foreign village of Tila in the swamps west of the Sand river.

Plate 7.   A masked *na wowi* figure enters the plaza of Mauwi hamlet to dance around a patient afflicted by a sore. The painted headdress is trimmed with chicken feathers.

Plate 8. Two young men waiting their turn outside the village to don the *na wowi* costume practice the difficult phallic movements characteristic of the *na wowi*'s dance.

men in Wakau. Counting them on his fingers he named four of my new
friends and, as we continued to talk, he have his version of how a *nakworu*
is initiated into his killing art. But it was his information about actual
witches, men I personally knew, that subsequently changed the focus of
my questioning and in the weeks that followed the facts about Lujere
witchcraft gradually unfolded before me.

The status of *nakworu* is self-chosen. A young man wishing to become
a witch first approaches a known witch, usually an agnate, and seeks
instruction. If the witch accepts him, the novice agrees to pay him about
$A2 and a time is set for a secret meeting in the forest. At this first meeting
they catch a lizard, cut its skin in several places and remove bits of the
flesh. Then the wounds are pressed together and the lizard's skin becomes
whole. It scampers away after it is marked to die the following day. When
the witch and the novice return the next day they find the lizard dead.
They repeat the same process on a dog and, if it is successful, the witch
announces that it is time they killed a human and an old woman is
chosen.

With humans the process becomes a bit more complex. The old woman
is garroted to unconsciousness. Slits are made on the fleshy parts of her
upper and lower arms and the inner section of her thighs and calves and
slivers of flesh are removed. Then a slit is made on each side of the victim
between her breast and arm pit and the blood is drained into small
bamboo vials. The wounds are closed, the day is set for the old woman's
death, and she returns to the village in a dazed state and without memory
of the attack.

After she dies the novice's training is complete. The new witch then
begins a career of killing that, paradoxically, gives him the power to cure.
So to understand Lujere therapy we must relinquish the Western conscious image of the healer as a kind and benevolent person. Lujere therapists are not benign; they are witches. The popular term "witch-doctor"
fits them perfectly for Lujere therapists are both killers and curers.

Still, I had no documentary evidence of a witchcraft murder. All the
recent deaths I inquired about — with the exception of a single infant
killed by a ghost — were said to be the work of witches. But no convincing evidence, such as a reported observation of a witch's attack on a
person, was forthcoming. Then I learned from the villagers that three
important Iwani witches were jailed in 1961 for the *sanguma* murders of
two old women of Iwariyo hamlet. Only one of the three witches was still
alive, but I knew him well and often observed him curing. It was said
that the three men had entered the women's house while they were alone
in the hamlet and had strangled them into unconsciousness. But when the

witches attempted to revive their victims, they discovered they had already killed them. The murderers were later caught, tried by the Papua New Guinea Supreme Court, and sentenced to jail for four years. Interestingly, there is no reference to witchcraft in the Supreme Court documents on the case. The reasons given by the Court for the killings were that the old women were social nuisances and that the social organization under which the people lived was deficient.[8]

The Lujere are not keen-minded ontologists and I never succeeded in getting an account that succinctly spelled out the connection between witchcraft murders and the power to heal. But the relationship is essentially a mystical one wherein the spirits of dead victims give the witch supernatural powers denied to ordinary men. These powers permit him to look into a person's body, identify the cause of a sickness and remove it. The same powers enable the witch, when he wishes, to fly through the air like a bird.

The first evidence to others that a man has become a witch is when he begins to exercise his curing role. From then on until his death he is known as a *nakworu*. But the new witch is not instructed in curing as he is in killing. Having gained the power to cure is all that is important, for he has witnessed the actual techniques of curing since childhood.

It is unusual for a witch to be consulted unless the illness is a serious one and the patient is confined to the village. Treatment is frequently in the patient's own house but sometimes word goes around that an important witch from another village is at the men's house and patients are brought to him for treatment. In these "clinics" he sees each patient separately and is paid from one or two shillings to two dollars for his services, depending upon the seriousness of the illness. But a witch also retains the right to deny treatment. If he is angry at a potential patient or considers him near death and beyond his curing powers, he may refuse to undertake treatment. The patient's family will then try to enlist the services of another witch.

Treatment sessions, especially when they have the character of a clinic, are important social occasions. The witch arrives in the village with

[8]   I am grateful to Assistant District Commissioner Peter Broadhurst. Vanimo Sub-District, for locating the relevant court documents on this case. Actual accounts by Europeans of *sanguma* attacks with good supporting evidence are rare. The best account is given in Dutch by Koster (1942–1945), for many years a missionary on the coast in the northern Madang Distrinct. Dr. Risto Gobius of Wewak kindly translated the article for me. In a personal communication, Dr. S. C. Wigley of Port Moresby sent me photographs of three x-ray films of a man from the Ambunti area admitted to the Wewak General Hospital in 1956 showing long wires inserted into the mediastinum and abdomen during a *sanguma* attack. The wires were removed successfully by Dr. A. A. Becker who was at that time the Medical Officer in Wewak.

several companions, all of whom are fed in the men's house by the family requesting his services. The village men gather together and, sitting on the floor in the Lujere fashion, smoke, chew betel nut, and visit. As they talk, handfuls of sago-leaf fibers pressed into loose balls are passed among them. The men chewing betel nut spit repeatedly into the balls until they are almost dripping with the bright red spittle. There is no special reason for this procedure except that this is the way it is done. The explanation, "It is what our ancestors taught us," was one I heard repeatedly among the Lujere whenever I probed for interpretations or meanings of culturally stereotyped behavior. The Lujere are men of action concerned with the present act. How it came to be or what is its ultimate meaning were questions guaranteed to bore them and, if pressed for answers, noticeably irritated them. The manifest and socially obvious meaning was sufficient explanation and they eventually trained me to somewhat inhibit my propensity to ask questions that apparently struck them as frivolous or stupid.

A patient entering the men's house for treatment goes to the witch and either sits or lies down near him. The witch asks a few questions about the location of the pain and then begins to examine the patient's bare skin with his hands in the region of the pain as in Plate 1. He does a great deal of probing and kneading of the skin (see Plate 2) as he attempts to find the cause of the sickness. Most therapists are fairly careful, but if the probing is done roughly as in Plate 3 it can be an extremely painful process, and children and young women often scream in pain and fright as the witch's strong fingers probe deeply into and under tender body areas. A protesting patient is restrained by relatives and the treatment and screams continue (see Plate 4).

When the witch locates an offending entity under the skin he grips it tightly within his fingers, pulling the skin away from the body. Then, taking the betel-bespat fibers in the other hand, he grasps the afflicted skin and by pinching, pulling, and shaking the skin he expresses the noxious substance, whatever it is, into the fibers (see Plate 5). Rising, he carries the fibers outside and disposes of the offending substance out of sight of observers. This process may be repeated numerous times until the witch believes he has removed the cause of the sickness. Rarely are patients or observers shown what was removed or told exactly what it was. The stock reply is that it is "something bad" and whether its nature is spiritual or corporeal no one seems able to say or to be concerned about. There were a few instances, however, where a witch did remove some object, e.g. a bit of razor blade, nail, or hair and, producing it from the fibers showed it to the patient before taking it outside for disposal.

Another cause of sickness that witches treat is "broken bones." This diagnosis pertains especially to the many bones of the upper body that are cracked or broken by invisible arrows shot into the body by ghosts or witches. These are repaired by the witch by pushing the fractures together with his fingers. Witches may sometimes perform other therapeutic acts as well. Muscle soreness is treated by simple massage and babies diagnosed in a position improper for birth are said to be turned by massage and external manipulation.

Whatever the treatment, once it is completed the patient expects to improve almost immediately. If he does not, he will send for another witch, a process that continues until he either begins to improve or becomes unconscious and dies. During three days of acute illness one boy whose illness I was following was treated by five different witches before showing signs of improvement. A witch, however, usually does not treat himself or members of his immediate family but seeks the services of other witches. Nor will he treat a person whose sickness he has caused.

But the work of witches is not all killing and curing. The packets of flesh and blood collected from their victims are sold to bring men and their dogs luck in hunting. Another reason that helps maintain the witchcraft complex is that each community needs a complement of witches not only to cure and further hunting prowess, but also to protect the villagers themselves. For when the alarm is given at night that a witch is lurking in the nearby forest, it is the village witches armed with bow and arrows who go to the attack and shoot arrows into the wooded darkness.

Some witches practice curing assisted by one or more female ancillary therapists and, just as the therapeutic prerogatives of a European nurse are circumscribed, so are theirs. Wakau does not have a tradition of woman therapists, but I observed several of these women assisting witches who had come to Wakau for curing sessions. Although these women do not have a special name, as the *nakworu* does, they undergo a special initiation ceremony to obtain their power to help the witches heal.

A woman who wishes to gain this power goes into the river accompanied by her husband or a close male relative. Then men who are upriver begin to run through the forest yelling and frightening ghosts into the river where they are swept downstream toward the woman. If a ghost enters into one of the women undergoing the ceremony she begins to shake violently and is held by her male attendant to save her from drowning. Leaving the river, the party returns to the village and, with the other villagers, sing and dance all night. After this the initiated woman has the power to assist a witch cure and remains subject to mild, although infrequent, shaking fits caused by the ghost within her.

As far as I could learn or observe, these women have a single therapeutic task. When the witch has located the noxious agent, his assistant receives it into the bundle of sago fibers and carries it outside to throw away. These women, like the witches, are paid for their services but proportionately lower.

Ritual Curing Festivals

In the previous section I have mentioned that ghostly spirits, called *agwai,* are sometimes the cause of sickness treatable by a witch. But the term *agwai* is used in at least two ways. One type of *agwai* is the ghost of a dead person. The other is the spirit of a supernatural being called *wowi.* Although a witch may remove objects shot into a patient by a ghost, he can only diagnose — not treat — a *wowi*-induced sickness. When the *agwai* of a *wowi* enters into a person's body, it grabs some organ, e.g. the heart or lungs, and so causes a sickness that can be cured only by exorcising the *agwai.* These exorcisms are ritual curing festivals carried out by ordinary men, not witches. These ceremonies generally include the entire community who are usually joined by relatives of the afflicted person from other villages.

The Wakaus have curing ceremonies for three different kinds of *wowi,* viz. *aiwar wowi, na wowi,* and *agwai wowi.* This is not the place to go into detail about each ceremony but I shall summarize their salient features. The *aiwar wowi (aiwar* is not translatable) is related to sicknesses where shortness of breath is a prominent symptom. Toward sunset the women and small children leave the village and the patient is seated on the ground in the village clearing. If the patient is a woman, her head is covered for she may not see the ceremony. Bamboo is lighted and its explosions announce the beginning of the ceremony. Three or four men carrying bamboo trumpets decorated with leaves and feathers and bespat with sacred ginger enter the clearing. Dancing together in a close line they first advance toward the patient and then retreat, stopping periodically to blow into their trumpets. Two or three other men, usually the patient's close relatives, attend the patient and a variety of rituals may be carried out (see Plate 6), including rubbing the patient with the trumpeters' sweat, daubing parts of his body with caly or paint, and making small incisions on his legs. At the conclusion of the rituals the trumpet-dancers leave the clearing and the women return to the village to distribute food to the participants and guests. After eating — it is dark now — the villagers dance and sing until dawn, circling the patient who sits by a fire with relatives.

The *na wowi* (*na* = sago) and *agwai wowi* ceremonies are usually performed, respectively, to cure sores and loss of weight. The *agwai wowi* ceremony is rarely performed and I did not see it. But I was told that it is very similar to the *na wowi* ceremony. For a *na wowi* curing festival the villagers gather toward sunset in the village clearing with the patient sitting in its center. The sound of hand drums signals the beginning of the ceremony and two masked figures — the *na wowi* — enter the clearing (see Plate 7) and repeatedly circle the patient. Each of the two performers wears a four-foot painted head mask made from the wide base of sago palm stems and decorated with feathers. His body, excepting his naked frontal area, is hidden by sago-leaf strands that reach to his ankles. Hanging from his neck and resting on his chest is a small net bag fringed with Job's tears seeds (see Plate 8). His erect penis is sheathed by a foot and a half long gourd phallus and he carries a small hand drum up near his head. As he circles around the patient the phallus soars upward striking the seeds on his chest with a clack as he simultaneously strikes the drum. The two figures are joined in their stately dance by younger villagers who follow after them. If a performer feels that he is losing his erection he leaves the clearing and another man assumes the costume and returns to the clearing. Children are warned by their mothers not to stare at the figures' oscillating phalluses to insure their dancing longer. Just before dark the two *na wowi* leave the clearing and the villagers and their guests have a small feast. Unlike the *aiwar wowi* flute men, the *na wowi* masked figures may be viewed by women during the ceremonies. This is because a dancing *na wowi* was first discovered in the forest by two women. On seeing the women, he flew away and they claimed the phallus and costume he left behind for their own. But as they never succeeded in imitating his exotic performance, they gave the dance and costume to their husbands who performed it perfectly.

After the feast, villagers, again primarily the younger adults and children, sing throughout the night until dawn as they trot back and forth across the clearing in front of the patient. At daybreak the masked figures again enter the clearing and dance around the patient until one, going up behind the patient, kneels with the headdress above the patient who is then smeared with some of the paint from the mask. The two *na wowi* retire and the exorcism ceremony is completed. In both the *aiwar wowi* and *na wowi* ceremony the prerequisites for participation are technical rather than privileged. The *aiwar wowi* men must be able to dance in unison and blow their flutes; the *na wowi* men must be able to maintain an erection and dance with a drum and a gourd phallus. In neither ceremony is there an initiated priesthood whose members alone can perform the rites as among the Wape.

Home Remedies

Other than the healing by witches and the curing festivals, there is a third and very important form of healing among the Lujere. This consists in the use of home remedies for everyday therapies. These remedial treatments are performed by the patient himself or by a member of his family for minor ailments or before a progressive sickness becomes grave.[9] For example, a woman whose legs ache may ask her sister-in-law to incise them to allow the bad blood to bleed away. Or a father with a screaming baby may cut down a black palm tree in the middle of the night because, earlier, he inadvertently stepped upon a branch that fell from it. Then at night when the wind blows the palm's branches, his baby will cry and only silencing the palm will quiet his child. Another reason for a crying baby is that the ghost of one of his dead grandparents has returned to the village to see him. The crying father must blow into each of the child's ears at the same time imploring the ghost to go away and leave the child in peace.

If a man's body aches from hard labor he will ease the pain by applying a counter-irritant of stinging nettles. Or a case of tinea may be treated by crushing a shoot of a *moru* shrub mixed with lime to smear over the affected areas.

EUROPEAN THERAPIES

Aid Post Clinic

The descriptive data presented on the Lujere's three types of indigenous therapy are brief and incomplete but sufficient to document the available modes of therapeutic intervention before these were augmented after

---

[9] The Lujere operationally distinguish between those illnesses that are obviously external and visible to the eye (e.g. sores, wounds, and injuries) and those internal illnesses (e.g. pain, fever, and malaise) that are felt but are not visually focale. The former type, unless the patient becomes critically ill, tend to be treated by home remedies and the latter type by a witch.

contact with the Australian government and the Christian Brethren Mission. At the time of my field work, the Lujere had direct access to European medicines and therapies via two types of Western-trained health professionals, the Aid Post Orderly and the Maternal Child Health Nurse.

An aid post orderly usually works alone in a medically isolated village where he provides the only immediate resource for the simpler forms of scientifically based medical practices. He is literate in Melanesian Pidgin and has completed a two-year training course of didactic lectures and supervised work on hospital wards and in clinical laboratories. In Pidgin he is called *doktaboi* and his training is primarily in principles of hygiene and public health and in first aid procedures, including the treatment of wounds, burns, fractures, asphixia, shock, hernia, fits, fainting, dislocations, sprains, and bruises. He also learns to diagnose and treat some of the many tropical diseases of the skin and other common illnesses and injuries.[10]

At the conclusion of his training he becomes an employee of the Public Health Service and is assigned to an aid post in a rural village. Provided with a uniform and medical supplies, he often must make his own way to the assigned village, perhaps one he has never visited before, where the language and customs are strange to him. There he is responsible for the health of the villages in his vicinity and is expected to visit each of them occasionally. The Public Health Service does not provide his aid post or house; he must arrange with the village officials to build these for him and to provide him with food or a garden where he may grow his own.

An orderly is expected to maintain regular clinic hours and to complete and forward records to his supervisor. There were two government aid posts among the Lujere and each had auxillary buildings where patients could stay overnight. The aid post used by Wakau was established in 1967 and is located near the mission air strip about a two-and-one-half hour walk from the hamlet. It is staffed by a Lujere man with kin ties to Wakau. Before the aid post was built the mission had provided similar medical services within its own compound.

---

[10]   The training and skills for an aid post orderly are described by Fowler (1960) and some points of strain in the APO system are discussed by Mitchell (1968). In 1965, the Department of Public Health decided to phase out the aid post orderly health role and closed the government's training schools. Missionary medical facilities, however, continued to train some aid post orderlies. The government's closing of their schools was widely criticized by some of the country's health officers; e.g. Radford (1971:14), who sees the APO training program as "a top priority in planning the allocation of resources for a successful future health service." After I left the country in 1972, the government reversed its policy and reopened one of the APO training schools at Mt. Hagen.

MCH Clinic

The Maternal Child Health (MCH) nurse is a member of the Christian Brethren Mission, but her work is subsidized by the Department of Public Health. During the dry season she flies into the area from Lumi each month. Trekking on foot to the villages, she examines pregnant women and small children, maintains childhood growth records, gives immunizations and medication, and teaches and advises mothers in the care of their children, especially regarding problems of diet and hygiene.[11] MCH clinics are held in about half of the Lujere villages and women in surrounding villages are also notified and invited to attend with their children. Mothers and children needing nursing care are referred to the small MCH ward at the mission which is supervised by one of the woman missionaries who is a nurse.

I have mentioned the MCH clinic as one of the two direct sources of European medical care for the Lujere. Many Lujere women participate in the clinics but the Wakau women did not. One of the reasons, an important one, is that the Wakaus rarely allow European expectations to disrupt their semi-sedentary living pattern. Only the sanction of a jail sentence succeeds in getting the Wakaus to attend the patrol officer's annual census of the hamlet. MCH nurses have no such sanction to require attendance at their clinics, so the Wakau women rarely attend. And because the Wakaus have shown a complete lack of interest in the clinic, they are no longer notified when it is to be held. So the MCH clinic, as such, is not a significant therapeutic service for the Wakaus, and I shall have little to say about in the discussion that follows.

CULTURALLY CONTRASTING THERAPEUTIC SYSTEMS

In this paper I have presented data on five different modes of therapeutic intervention directly available to the Lujere. Three are rooted in the traditional culture, viz. treatment by witches, curing festivals, and home remedies. The other two, treatment by aid post orderlies and at MCH clinics, are rooted in European culture. In the following discussion I shall focus on these five therapeutic modes primarily from the perspective of the client population, i.e. the Lujere people, in particular the residents of

---

[11]   These services are described in more detail by Biddulph (1969:129–137).

Wakau hamlet. I shall then conclude with some general comments on the relationships between the indigenous and the introduced therapies.

In order to clarify similarities and differences between these culturally contrasting therapeutic systems, a classification of types of possible healing techniques is helpful. For the typology set forth here, I am indebted to Rena Gropper's classification (1967), but mine differs from hers in a number of ways.

The major types of healing techniques identifiable cross-culturally may be briefly identified as follows:

1.   MEDICINAL TECHNIQUES: introduction of the *materia medica* into the patient's body, e.g. orally administered medicines, injections, inhalations, enemas, ear and nose drops, etc.

2.   SURGICAL TECHNIQUES: cutting or penetrating into the patient's body, e.g. lancing, acupuncture, bloodletting, amputation, trepenation, circumcision, etc.

3.   PHYSICAL TECHNIQUES: physical and mechanical manipulation of the patient's, body, e.g. massage, exercise, bonesetting, tourniquets, trusse, traction, application of ointments, poultices, nettles, etc.

4.   RITUAL TECHNIQUES: appeal to a supernatural agent, e.g. exorcism, prayer, sacrifice, etc.

5.   AVOIDANCE TECHNIQUES: patient is instructed to abstain from or avoid specified foods, substances, organisms, places, etc.

6.   RELATIONAL TECHNIQUES: the use of specially structured human relationships to alleviate the patient's suffering, e.g. psychoanalysis, amicatherapy, psychodrama, family therapy, etc.

Table 1.   The variability of healing techniques utilized in the therapeutic modes available to the Lujere, West Sepik District, Papua New Guinea

Healing techniques	Lujere therapies			European therapies	
	Home remedies	Witches	Curing festivals	Aid post clinics	MCH clinics
	(1)	(2)	(3)	(4)	(5)
Medicinal	×			×	×
Surgical	×			×	×
Physical	×	×		×	×
Ritual	×		×		
Avoidance	×			×	×
Relational					

Table 1 shows in tabular form the different patterns of healing techniques according to the therapeutic modes available to the Lujere. The therapies with the most similar profiles are home remedies (Lujere) and aid post clinics and MCH clinics (European). All three employ a wide variety of healing techniques, except that the European therapies, grounded as they are in experimentation and clinical empiricism, exclude ritual techniques, whereas certain home remedies consist of private ritual treatments in which ghosts or a *wowi* spirit are invoked and asked to depart from the afflicted person's body. And just as the curing festivals use only ritual techniques to heal, witches use only physical techniques. Through the use of certain physical techniques and by virtue of his special powers, only a witch is able to remove the noxious substances intruded into a patient's body by other witches and ghosts.

Also of interest is the fact that home remedies and curing festivals may be performed by ordinary people; no apprenticeship to learn the techniques is required as in the case of witches, aid post orderlies, and MCH nurses. And of the three types of professional curers among the Lujere, the witch has the highest status as a practitioner. This is, as I shall show later, because he alone is able to satisfactorily explain or diagnose the cause of a serious illness and proceed to cure it. This helps explain why home remedies and aid post and MCH clinics, even with their vast array of healing techniques, are considered therapeutically inferior to a witch's treatment for serious sickness. As in most therapeutic systems, it is not technical versatility but diagnostic skill that is ultimately valued by the society.

None of the therapies, it will be noticed, use relational healing techniques. These techniques, it seems, are more characteristic of technologically complex cultures, where deviant acts and feeling states, such as unhappiness and despair, are sometimes culturally defined as illness. But in Lujere society the patient-therapist relationship itself is never, in and of itself, conceived of as the curing agent. Nor has this technique been introduced as a part of the aid post and MCH clinics' armamentarium. Among the Lujere it is the concrete act performed by the witch, orderly, or nurse that is considered efficacious, not the patient's relationship with the therapist.

Finally, though in the absence of reliable counts, my observations on the differential usage of the five therapeutic modes suggest that home remedies, witch cures, and the aid post clinic are utilized most frequently and in that order. The usage frequency lessens significantly for curing festivals — the Wakaus had two in the six months I lived with them — and the MCH clinic.

As a student of Lujere therapeutic systems it was my methodological intention to interfere as little as possible with the Wakau villagers' resort to curative practices. I had not come to New Guinea to study myself as a practitioner of Western medicine. As most New Guineans expect any European among them to provide some medical aid, I announced to the Wakaus I had few medicines with me and that the aid post orderly at the air strip was both better supplied and better trained to treat them. So, unlike many anthropologists, I took my place in the village without a formal curing role. However, I also knew that no European raised as I was can endure to watch severe suffering or death if he has the means of effecting a cure. Later, I shall give an instance of the type of health emergencies in which I intervened.

Just as we do not feel a pressing psychological need for a definitive diagnosis for every sore muscle, diarrhea attack, or headache, neither do the Wakaus. They treat themselves much as we do, perhaps with rest or a home remedy learned from their mothers. Or they may go to the aid post because the orderly has medicine that is known to heal, for example, an ulcerating sore or eradicate a feverish headache. Only ambulatory patients, a girl with a badly abcessed hand, a man with recurrent diarrhea, or a mother who can easily carry her sick infant go to the aid post clinic. A person too sick to walk is never carried to the aid post for treatment. This initially shocked me, for while I was living with the Wape I was accustomed to seeing the gravely sick, even the dying, carried into Lumi for treatment. But the Wakaus' lack of interest in carrying patients to the aid post is not out of a lack of concern for the patient's welfare or because the long walk to the post through deep swamps is an arduous one. I have seen patients who fell ill in a bush hunting camp carried much greater distances and through more difficult terrain to return them to their home village for treatment. The reason the severely sick are not brought to the aid post is that the orderly is not considered an appropriate therapist for a critically ill person. His healing techniques, like home remedies, are sufficient for minor illnesses and accidents but not for a patient whose life is endangered.

First and foremost an orderly simply does not have the training to cope with a major illness. In Lujere cultural terms, his diagnostic ability is completely unconvincing. The germ theory of disease, which the orderly has learned and on which his treatments are based, is outside of Lujere culture and has absolutely no explanatory power relevant to Lujere theories about sickness. Rarely does the orderly even try to communicate the theory to his patients. For a people living in a world where violent witches, ghosts and sorcerers are rampant, the idea that sickness is caused by tiny impersonal "snakes" is quite beside the point. However, the orderly is valued as a dispenser of free European medicines that are often very helpful in curing minor illnesses where cause is not an issue and in relieving symptoms of a major one. So in major sicknesses his interventions are therapeutically limited because he has not attained the knowledge and power to diagnose the CAUSE of an affliction and remove it. When a loved one's life is endangered by sickness the family turns to a trained and proven expert, a witch — not an aid post orderly — who can provide a sensible and definitive diagnosis in Lujere cultural terms and proceed to eradicate the causative agent.[12]

Another point on which the European and Lujere therapies differ is the frequency of treatment for serious illnesses. According to Lujere belief, if one receives the CORRECT treatment, then one treatment is all that one needs. The same treatment is not repeated over and over. If the patient does not improve after a treatment he changes therapists or the therapist modifies his technique for a subsequent treatment. For example a witch, having failed to cure a young Wakau man in a daytime treatment, told him he would like to try the same treatment at night. The evil substance was eluding him in the daytime, the witch explained, but at night he would grab it unawares. Treatments based on European medicine, however, often consist of taking the same medication not once but several times a day and even continuing over a period of time. Obviously, this attenuated approach to serious healing does not inspire confidence in the practitioner of European medicine.

The conflict between the Lujere belief about the efficacy of a single curative treatment and European use of repetitive treatments was a source of despair to me in those numerous instances where I intervened with medication in an attempt to save a person's life. These were all, according to my European-based diagnosis, pneumonia patients who were being treated exclusively by witches or exorcism ceremonies. I always offered medication to these patients, but the response to my offer varied. Some simply refused it, others wanted only a portion of what I offered, others took the medication a few times and then stopped; none completed a standard treatment course. Some, I learned, accepted the medicine apparently just to please me and then secretly disposed of it.

Linked to their belief that any truly effective treatment for eradicating the cause of a serious illness should be a single one is a belief that although European medicines may at times be dramatically helpful, they are poten-

---

[12] That the indigenous healing system provides a more satisfactory explanation for the patient than that given by introduced European medicine is, not surprisingly, a general finding of culture-contact studies, cf. L. R. Schwartz (1969), Peck (1968), and Stanhope (1968).

tially lethal as well. Swallowing too many pills or capsules may destroy your inner body. So in the face of these beliefs my attempts to help the seriously sick were of very limited effectiveness. While a bottle of tetracycline capsules lay idle in my house I watched, angry and frustrated, as two of my friends died.

No student has yet attempted to work out a general paradigm on how culturally contrasting therapeutic systems operative within a single culture change through time. The cross-cultural data are too meager, the multiplicity of socioeconomic and political factors too complex. But the Lujere findings presented here appear to be prototypical for at least one important initial contact period between culturally contrasting therapeutic systems in a situation in which a primitive culture is in benevolent vassalage to a politically dominant industrialized culture. It is a type of contact relationship characterized by mutual autonomy of the indigenous and introduced therapies. For when we compare Lujere and European healing systems the most obvious finding is that each has remained inviolate. Neither has been altered noticeably by contact with the other; each continues to follow its own rationale and treatment schema. Only in the person of the Lujere aid post orderly are both systems separately operative as conceived by each of the originating cultures. Nor have the Wakau villagers innovated any alternative therapies based on cultural syncretism as described for Manus (T. Schwartz 1962; L. R. Schwartz 1969) and the Wape (Mitchell 1973). Especially in the case of the Manus, Christian cosmology and moral concepts about the good and the bad have extensively influenced therapeutic beliefs and practices in a succession of cults and in the Paliau political movement. But the Lujere have not moved into this kind of syncretic period of therapeutic change.

Some of the factors contributing to the persisting cognitive and structural separateness of the Lujere and European healing systems have been alluded to in this paper in various contexts. Let me summarize them here.

First, a general point is that marked change in any group's indigenous healing system through cultural contact is usually slow to transpire. Concepts and beliefs about sickness and its treatment are personally learned at an early age through intense experiences of sickness and suffering and these primal fears and hopes of childhood imprint the personality forever inhibiting change.

More directly relevant as an explanatory point is that although the Lujere have been under the direct political influence of Europeans since the 1930's, actual inter-cultural contact has been very sporadic and superficial. With a relatively small and scattered population geographically isolated off the Sepik River in inhospitable and economically destitute swamps, the Lujere, both figuratively and literally, are a back-water culture in terms of European interests. For example, before the establishment of the Christian Brethren mission and the even more recent Public Health Service's aid post, the only contact with European medicine occurred every year or so when a government patrol, including a health officer, set out from Lumi to visit the distant Yellow River villages. Then sores were dressed, injections were given, and an occasional order was given to carry a patient, frequently a child, to Lumi for treatment. More than one Wakau father was jailed for failure to comply. But the patrols made no impact on indigenous healing techniques and little on health practices beyond the burial of the dead. The mandatory latrines are still rarely used.[13]

Similarly, the influence of Christian teaching has been culturally insignificant, so that basic concepts about life, sickness, death, and a person's relationships to others remain unaltered. One or two missionary couples, however ardent their faith and energetic their effort, can have only limited influence on a widely dispersed alien population of thousands who live, for much of the time, in isolated family hunting camps. Another argument, not pursued here, is that Lujere culture itself has a structural and cognitive resiliency that tends to minimize the threatening dissonances which occur when radically divergent cultures meet.

To date no New Guinea society has completely abandoned its traditional healing therapies in favor of European therapies with their professed impersonal theories of causation. But we can hardly expect it to be otherwise. The religious chapel that is an integral part of almost every American community hospital attests to the fact that impersonal "scientific" theories of disease causation and secular therapies do not always meet the explanatory and treatment needs of patients and their families. As Christians readily turn to thought about God, Who both gives and takes away life, and appeal to Him to perform a healing miracle when sickness threatens life, so do the Lujere find explanatory comfort in their beliefs, centuries old, that promise surcease from suffering by the extraordinary powers of a witch's hand.

---

[13]   But one significant service of the Public Health Service was its yaws erradication patrols that practically eliminated this dreaded disease in the Lumi Sub-District.

REFERENCES

BATESON, GREGORY
1958 *Naven: a survey of the problems suggested by a composite picture of the culture of a New Guinea tribe, drawn from three points of view* (second edition). Stanford: Stanford University Press.
BEHRMANN, WALTER
1917 Der Sepik (Kaiserin-Augusta-Fluss) und sein Stromgebiet; geographischer Bericht der Kaiserin-Augusta-Fluss Expedition, 1912–1913. *Mitteilungen aus den Deutschen Schutzgebieten* 12.
BIDDULPH, JOHN
1969 *Child health for health extension officers.* Port Moresby: Department of Public Health, Territory of Papua New Guinea.
BURRIDGE, K. O. L.
1960 *Mambu: a Melanesian millennium.* London: Methuen.
1965 "Tangu, Northern Madang District," in *Gods, ghosts and men in Melanesia.* Edited by P. Lawrence and M. J. Meggitt, 224–249. Melbourne: Oxford University Press.
BURTON-BRADLEY, B. G., CHARLES JULIUS
1965 *Folk psychiatry of certain villages in the Central District of Papua.* South Pacific Commission Technical Paper 146:9–26.
CODRINGTON, R. H.
1891 *The Melanesians.* Oxford: Clarendon Press.
CONRAD, ROBERT, WAYNE DYE
i.p. "Some language relationships in the upper Sepik region of Papua New Guinea," in *Aspects of Oceanian cultures.* Edited by Willis E. Sibley. World Anthropology. The Hague: Mouton.
ELKIN, A. P.
1964 *The Australian Aborigines.* Garden City: Doubleday.
EVANS-PRITCHARD, E. E.
1937 *Witchcraft, oracles and magic among the Azande.* Oxford: Oxford University Press.
FORTUNE, REO
1932 *Sorcerers of Dobu: the social anthropology of the Dobu Islanders of the Western Pacific.* New York: E. P. Dutton.
FOWLER, F. R.
1960 *Aid post medical and hygiene training book* (in Melanesian Pidgin). Port Moresby: Public Health Department, Territory of Papua New Guinea.
GLICK, LEONARD B.
1967 Medicine as an ethnographic category: the Gimi of the Eastern Highlands. *Ethnology* 6:31–56.
1972 "Sorcery and witchcraft," in *Encyclopedia of Papua and New Guinea.* Edited by Peter Ryan, 1080–1082. Melbourne: Melbourne University Press.
GROPPER, RENA C.
1967 "Toward a universal comparative medicine." (Unpublished mimeograph.).
1973 "Marcus Welby, Executioner." *Hastings Center Report* 3:16.

HELD, G. J.
1959   *The Papuas of Waropen.* The Hague: Martinus Nijhoff.

HOGBIN, IAN
1970   *The island of menstruating men: religion in Wogeo, New Guinea.* Scranton: Chandler.

HÖLTKER, GEORG
1942–1945   "Forward," in *Sangguma* of de Sluipmoord op de noordoostkust van Nieuw-Guinea. By G. J. Koster. *Anthropos* 37–45:213–224.

KOSTER, G. J.
1942–1945   *Sangguma* of de Sluipmoord op de noordoostkust van Nieuw-Guinea. *Anthropos* 37–45:213–224.

LAYCOCK, DONALD C.
1968   Languages of the Lumi Subdistrict (West Sepik District), New Guinea. *Oceanic Linguistics* 7:36–66.
i.p.   "Unstudied ethnographic areas of the Sepik Basin, New Guinea," in *Language in anthropology*, volume four: *Language evolution.* Edited by William C. McCormack and Stephen Wurm. World Anthropology. The Hague: Mouton.

MAIR, LUCY
1969   *Witchcraft.* New York: McGraw-Hill.

MC CARTHY, J. K.
1936   *Report of patrol to the Yellow River Base Camp, Sepik Division.* Department of Territories, Patrol Report from Territory of New Guinea. Accessioned as 13/26 Item 20. Commonwealth Archives Office.
1963   *Patrol into yesterday: my New Guinea years.* Melbourne: F. W. Cheshire.

MEAD, MARGARET
1947   The Mountain Arapesh: 3. Socio-economic life, 4. Diary of events in Alitoa. *Anthropological Papers of the American Museum of Natural History* 40:163–419.
i.p.   "A re-examination of major themes of the Sepik area, Papua New Guinea," in *Aspects of Oceanian cultures.* Edited by Willis E. Sibley. World Anthropology. The Hague: Mouton.

MIDDLETON, JOHN, E. H. WINTER, *editors*
1963   *Witchcraft and sorcery in East Africa.* London: Routledge and Kegan Paul.

MIHALIC, F.
1971   *The Jacaranda dictionary and grammar of Melanesian Pidgin.* Port Moresby: Jacaranda Press.

MITCHELL, WILLIAM E.
1968   "The *doktaboi:* a medial medical role in New Guinea." Presented at the Eight International Congress of Anthropological and Ethnological Sciences, Tokyo.
1973   A new weapon stirs up old ghosts. *Natural History* 82:74–84.

PECK, JOHN G.
1968   "Doctor medicine and bush medicine in Kaukira, Honduras," in *Essays on medical anthropology*. Edited by Thomas Weaver, 78–87. Athens, Georgia: University of Georgia Press.

POUWER, J.
1967   "Toward a configurational approach to society and culture in New Guinea," in *Behavioral science research in New Guinea*, 77–100. National Research Council, Publication 1493.

RADFORD, ANTHONY J.
1971   "The future of rural health services in Melanesia: with particular reference to Niugini." Presented at the Fifth Waigani Seminar on Change and Development in Rural Melanesia, Port Moresby.

ROBINSON, E. D.
1931   *Annual report of Sepik District 1930–1931*. National Archives of Papua New Guinea.
1932   *Patrol report: Ambunti to the Sepik-Dutch border, and approximately 10 miles of the Yellow River*, number A4 of 1932–1933. Sepik District, Department of Territories. Accessioned as 13/26 Item 14. Commonwealth Archives Office.
1934   *Patrol report: overland from Aitape through Wapi area to headwaters of Yellow River and down Yellow River to Sepik River*, number S.D. 1/1934–1935. Sepik District, Department of Territories. National Archives of Papua New Guinea.

SCHOFIELD, F. D., A. D. PARKINSON
1963   Social medicine in New Guinea: beliefs and practices affecting health among the Abelam and Wam peoples of the Sepik District. *Medical Journal of Australia* 1:1–8, 30–33.

SCHULTZE, LEONHARD
1914   *Forschungen im Innern der Insel Neuguinea (Bericht des Fühers über die wissenschaftlichen Ergebnisse der deutschen Grenzexpedition in das westliche Kaider-Wilhemlsland, 1910)*. Berlin: E. S. Mittler & Sohn.

SCHWARTZ, LOLA ROMANUCCI
1969   The hierarchy of resort in curative practices: the Admiralty Islands, Melanesia. *Journal of Health and Social Behavior* 10:201–209.

SCHWARTZ, THEODORE
1962   The Paliau Movement in the Admiralty Islands, 1946–1954. *Anthropological Papers of the American Museum of Natural History* 49:211–421.

SELIGMAN, C. G.
1910   *Melanesians of British New Guinea*. Cambridge: Cambridge University Press.

SIMPSON, COLIN
1954   *Adam with arrows: inside New Guinea*. London and Sydney: Argus and Robinson.

STANHOPE, J. M.
1968   Competing systems of medicine among the Rao-Breri Lower Ramu River, New Guinea. *Oceania* 39:137–145.

STEINBAUER, FRIEDRICH

1969   *Concise dictionary of New Guinea Pidgin* (*Neo-Melanesian*). Madang: Kristen Pres.

THURNWALD, RICHARD

1916   Vorstösse nach dem Quellgebiet des Kaiserin-Augusta-Flusses, dem Sand-Fluss und dem Nord-Fluss bis an da Küstengebirge. *Mitteilungen aus den Deutschen Schutzgebieten* 29:82–93.

VORMANN, FRANZ, WILHELM SCHARENBERGER

1914   *Die Monumbo-Sprache, Grammatik und Wörterverzeichnis.* Anthropos-Bibliotek, volume one. Vienna: Mechitharisten-Buchdruckerei.

WAGNER, ROY

1967   *The curse of Souw: principles of Daribi clan definition and alliance in New Guinea.* Chicago: University of Chicago Press.

WARNER, W. LLOYD

1958   *A black civilization.* New York: Harper and Brothers.

The Dynamics of Therapy
in the Lower Zaire

JOHN M. JANZEN

This essay seeks to elucidate the patterns of folk therapy among KiKongo-speaking people of the Lower Zaire in Central Africa. One representative case is drawn from a larger study to elaborate a processual-generative model of the therapeutic process. This focus — on case histories and process — is felt to be particularly pertinent today in view of the gradual yet pervasive changes that have taken place in African society as a result of mission and colonial intrusion, and the attendant internal evolution of the society.

Today, one finds forms reminiscent of earlier native therapy and Western medicine intertwined complexly in peoples' lives. In the north bank Manianga region where research was conducted, by Dr. William Arkinstall and myself in 1969,[1] the rural population of about 120,000 persons enjoys access to three local hospitals and a variety of smaller dispensaries, as well as, through migration and travel, constant and active exposure to facilities in surrounding cities. Most of these are today staffed by Western-trained Africans. Despite this active medical Westernization and modernization, echoes of rituals of social redress and cults of affliction (cf. Turner) in connection with illness are never far in the background. The challenge presented by this institutional multiformity (Janzen 1969a: 70) is that of laying bare the existing structure of contemporary therapy, as well as the zones of tension and change.

[1] Research was carried out with Dr. William Arkinstall of the Royal Victoria Hospital and McGill University, Montreal, in 1969, under a grant from the Social Science Research Council. Acknowledgement is due the African participants who literally suffered our scrutiny, and participants in my seminar at McGill University, 1971–1972, whose generosity in ideas and discussion helped spawn most of the analytic ideas of worth in this paper.

It is imperative that the researcher work out a careful methodology. It is risky to rely on indigenous explanations of the normative system to obtain an accurate description of what is happening. Fieldwork experience demonstrated that people normally explain their therapeutic system either by an account of the traditional system of diviners and healing cults, or by an assertion that only the Western hospitals and dispensaries are nowadays used. As it turns out, neither ideal system corresponds to what most people in fact do when they become ill, nor explains the dynamics of the tacit contemporary system. Instead, then, of looking to normative explanations or specialists' techniques to account for the institutional structure of contemporary therapy in Kongo society, we turned to extended case studies drawn primarily from a single restricted population. Over a period of ten months, in an area where we had both been known previously, as field anthropologist and medical doctor respectively, we studied first-hand a dozen cases. Though this method limited our scope in terms of total cases — we also did hospital surveys and censuses of healers' clients — we were able in these cases to observe in depth the dynamic quality of decisions, and, by comparison of the cases in their natural career over time, to elicit the social-cultural structure of therapy.

Out of the many types of illnesses and illness care that BaKongo recognize and require, our attention was drawn particularly to the problematic cases which did not readily respond to first treatment, as conventional ills like wounds, recognized contagious illnesses, or common influenzas might. This focus, of course, further biased our selection of cases toward those implicated in social conflict and witchcraft suspicions. These, though, were precisely the cases which revealed the full latitude of contemporary therapeutic structural alternatives, AND the contradictions in terms of the structure. Characteristically, each case (patient) would initially signal significant illness behavior such as withdrawal from work, complaints, and spontaneous private visits to a local dispensary or hospital. Such behavior would evoke an indulgent response from certain kinsmen and other peers who, if the case did not respond eventually to treatment, would rally to help in a more active way. In the ensuing dialogue, diagnostic discussions, decisions for action, and prognosis, we observed a case-by-case definition of the therapeutic process.

The character of therapy, and its distinctiveness from similar processes such as litigation and ceremony, has received considerable attention in both social science and medical writing. There are those who have seen "therapy" or "medicine" as an ethnographic category quite discrete from other areas of behavior (e.g. Mechanic 1962; Glick 1967). Such static taxonomies elicited consciously from informants do not serve the present purposes very well, for reasons noted above, and because of the dynamic nature of therapy itself. More promising for present purposes is another perspective which looks at the whole question of the characterization of therapy, in terms of open and closed social-cultural forms. Thus, if ceremony is defined as behavior without choice and option (cf. Frake 1969a), and litigation as behavior in which options are consciously entertained and voiced, the therapy and illness resolution would fall between these two poles as behavior that occurs within the latitude provided by certain mutually exclusive courses or "cures." This has led to analysis of therapy in terms of "indeterminate" logical models like Markov chains, and "determinate" forms such as stochastic processes (Attneave 1969; Frake 1969a).

In Kongo culture the native descriptive labels *mbukulu* and *ndyakusunu* are recognized as referring to "therapy" (Janzen 1969b). But this conceptual discreteness does not reveal that processually there is a constant overlapping and interdigitation of categories which consciously-elicited inquiries cannot study. Therapy and litigation have in common the underlying quest for the elimination of social dissensus and conflict. Thus, when sick behavior is signalled (by passivity, complaint), others, particularly the legal possessor or guardian, press for an analysis of the case. It is in this debated diagnosis, particularly of the "complicated" cases that absorb so much time, that we can find the synthetic classification of disease and therapy we are seeking.

By far the prevailing direction of these illness etiology hypotheses has to do with a breach of norm somewhere in the close proximity of the sufferer, e.g. adultery, incest, childbirth without adequate marriage payment, insubordination, ingratitude, envy, etc. As this happens, the distinction between "crime" and "illness" becomes very thin; the concern extends to individuals who have "violated" themselves and suffered the consequences. The etiological concern may be directed toward spirits in need of placating. This is a rare illness hypothesis, though it probably was more common in the past. As one healer told us, wherever people speak of spirit in connection with illness, there is a human being lurking behind it.

In any event, our attention here will not be directed at understanding the outer zones of belief in disease etiology so much as the inner dynamics of decision-making within the group that forms around a sufferer to work out a course of healing. This group (occasionally a single individual) we will consider as a kind of illness and therapy managing field that entertains alternatives and reaches decisions having to do with purposive action. Usually it includes the sufferer, to a degree, and most of the time the specialist who is consulted. In Kongo society, the managing group is mostly composed of close kinsmen of the sufferer. The model of the therapeutic process which we shall develop later, while grounded in the ethnography of this egalitarian therapy management, also applies, with slight modifications, to the prevailing hierarchic and asymmetric structure of therapy in highly professionalized Western medicine. A specific case will serve to illustrate this point.

THE CASE STUDY

Nsimba is a male nurse who, at the time of this observation in 1969, was in his early twenties. As a member of an elite group in the society, he is subject to the dictates and pressures of professional requirements, achievement orientation, and salary dependence. As a resident and employee of a mission station, he is exposed to a further set of expectations related to Western Christianity and the way it interprets family structure and interpersonal behavior. Neither the professional nor the mission status, however, makes him impervious to the traditional sector of his society with its kinship loyalties based on seniority and ascribed roles. Nsimba's case reflects his particular response to a number of predicaments of the elite in contemporary Zarian society. That these have an influence on his illness, and the way it was worked out, is obvious from the start. This is all the more true since, upon graduation from nursing school, he returned to his home community to hold his first nursing job near his paternal and maternal families.

The mission where Nsimba had attended secondary school, and where he had received initial experience in nursing, sent him to a superior training school in 1965 to further develop his skills. He did quite well in school, and when he returned to the mission in 1967 everyone was anxious to have him back to fill a place in the understaffed medical facility. He was, in fact, appointed head nurse in charge of the dispensary, a busy place with 50 general and 20 maternity beds, and many outpatients daily. His responsibilities were compounded by the fact that there were no doctors in the close vicinity to whom he could refer, and the dispensary often had seriously ill patients. Another hospital a half-hour's drive away lacked a doctor at the time; the closest doctor was a day's drive away.

Nsimba's staff at the time of his appointment consisted of a European midwife, two aide-*accoucheuses*, three nurse aides, and an elderly male nurse who, without any formal training, had served the dispensary faithfully for fifty years. In recent years, this man had opened an "unofficial" private dispensary in his village. For this reason, and because of his prominent position as clan headman and his access to medicines, he was a powerful and influential figure in the community. When Nsimba assumed his new position, he criticized the older man for some mistakes, and the mission decided to retire him prematurely with full pension several months short of his sixty-fifth birthday. This he regarded as an affront and an insult after fifty years of dutiful service. Later events reveal that he held Nsimba responsible for this turn of events, although at the time all seemed to have gone well. In all other respects, though, Nsimba seemed to adjust well and to prosper. Though his wife had suffered a miscarriage and did not consider herself too well, he had a family and was considered a successful and reliable person, well adjusted to his new position.

It was something of a surprise when, in December 1968, over a year after beginning his job, Nsimba began to complain of complications in a simple urinary infection he had himself diagnosed and treated with antibiotics. When he felt he was not improving properly, he left his work temporarily to consult European doctors at the hospital, a long day's drive distant, where he had trained two years earlier. There he received further antibiotics for his infection. A new diagnosis was made, and a small operation performed in order to biopsy a swelling in his groin which had been present since 1961. He was slow to recover, and continued to complain of abdominal pain and to walk with a marked limp, apparently due to pain following his surgery. No further diagnoses were made at the hospital; the biopsy was not helpful and did not indicate a disease.

After recovering from his minor surgery, but still unwell, Nsimba went to Kinshasa to be with his father and several maternal uncles. Shortly after arrival there he began to suffer intense headaches, and his kinsmen feared for his life. They returned him to the hospital, a day's drive from Kinshasa, but the headaches did not disappear. His relatives attending him took him back to Kinshasa to a prophet-seer (*ngunza*) from Nsimba's own rural area, who lived and worked in the capital. The seer analyzed the case through many questions to the kinsmen and the sufferer and established to his satisfaction that the illness was due to "evil acts" *(mavanga mambi)* perpetrated upon him by others. Also, he suggested that there was "a snake" involved in the case; this cause was dismissed as insignificant when Nsimba could think only of ordinary encounters with snakes. (The term *mavanga mambi* is a euphemism, one of many, for witchcraft-induced illness, also spoken of as a category of illnesses caused "by man," in contrast to those caused "by God," or natural.)

The discussion by Nsimba's kinsmen and the seer about evil acts or "others getting their hands on him," dwelt on two kinds of concerns. The one had to do with the persistent demands of his maternal kinsmen upon his salary or his services. Those residing close to the dispensary expected him to pay their bills, or to treat them gratis. An unpleasant exchange had occurred in November 1968 between Nsimba and an aunt over the treatment of three children, when he was paid for only two. He felt the demands to be unreasonable, since he did not earn a lot, and had a hard time maintaining his own wife and children. The seer and the relatives, however, tended to minimize the role of this kind of tension on his illness. They concentrated, rather, on the relationship of Nsimba's immediate clan section to his father's group, which had, in the past, been in slave-master relationship respectively, and the animosity this had produced between them. Nsimba's maternal grandmother had been bought as a child by his paternal group. In 1958, when the matrilineally-derived slave line that ensued had become numerous, they, failing to win their freedom in the customary fashion of ransom payment, had taken the case to court and won, with the obligation to pay a "dry pig" in cash for their ransom. The paternal (master) group retained a begrudging view of the settlement. To end the affair, Nsimba's maternal group, in 1959, supplemented the payment in an out-of-court arrangement. Nsimba's illness now reopened suspicion of lingering animosities. The seer pointed to other illnesses and hardships in the matrilineage, and suggested that there was need for a reunion of the two groups, and for the former masters, Nsimba's father's group, to ask pardon of their former slaves. A meeting was arranged.

Meanwhile, Nsimba's condition remained unimproved. He, together with his father and a maternal uncle, journeyed two days' distance to the paternal village where the two clans were to meet. The meeting went as planned, with Nsimba's paternal clan asking his pardon, which he gave; they, in turn, blessed him, for which he thanked them. There was no appreciable improvement in Nsimba's condition. He had been taking aspirin all along, but this only made him dizzy. At one point shortly following the meeting with the paternal clan, he became delirious and spoke incoherently. He requested that the mission vehicle come to get him, so he might see his newly-born daughter. His kinsmen again feared for his life, and he expressed the thought later that he feared he would die. When he did arrive at the dispensary, he was complaining of dizziness and severe headache. Thorough medical diagnosis at this point revealed no physical findings, though he improved with symptomatic therapy at the dispensary. The headache continued.

At that point, Nsimba said he could not return to his job, although from a medical viewpoint he might have been able to. He expressed the desire to work with the mission organization, but only if he were transferred to another dispensary. If this could not be worked out, then he would, he said, find a nurse's job with another organization.

Together with his father and another kinsman, Nsimba then sought relief for his headache from a regional school teacher who doubled as a reputed healer of head pains, in particular a malady known as "split-head" (*mumpompila*) which afflicts mainly children, but occasionally adults. Nsimba was diagnosed as having this, and took the prescribed treatment: a head pack of plants from the water and from the land, moistened and crushed together in a compressed pulp, kept on the head for four days. After this treatment, Nsimba reported, he felt somewhat better.

But he did not yet return home, nor did he return to work. Together with his father and mother, his mother's brother, and a sister, he consulted a self-styled prophet-healer for a ten-day supportive retreat at the prophet's village in the company of a dozen or so other pilgrims. The prophet regarded himself as a visionary, and during independence politics had been coopted as provincial deputy, on which basis he had served as court-curer in prominent Kongo politicians' families. Now secluded in his village, he saw a steady stream of clients who stayed as long as a month. The regime of treatment to which Nsimba and his kinsmen — who were also held to be sick — submitted began and ended with a ritual bath. During the treatment they were not to bathe at all. This was common treatment for all serious cases. Nsimba's actual illness, said the prophet, was "head pressure" (*nkatanga*), a disease comparable to rheumatism which "sapped the intelligence." The prophet refused to investigate the social implications of Nsimba's illness, contending that the other specialists who did this provoked animosities among kinsmen. His treatment consisted of prayer, laying on of hands, and healings. He did not deny the possibility of illness resulting from "others," but insisted that this was not his approach, a stand that seemed to us inconsistent with his later actions. All visiting sufferers, and collectivities of sufferers like Nsimba and his group, attended nightly worship and healing services at which there would be hymn singing, preaching, blessing, praying and laying on of hands, and anointing with oil. After finishing this ten-day regime Nsimba felt sufficiently improved to return to work at the dispensary.

He was not prepared for the "message" awaiting him. In a bottle "planted" in his house he discovered the Kongo equivalent to a threatening anonymous telephone call: a bottle fetish containing a twist of tobacco, several peanuts, a few blades of grass, and a slip of paper with a girl's name inscribed on it. Although he discarded the bottle with its contents down the toilet, its connotations frightened him badly. The tobacco was interpreted to mean he would continue being dizzy; the peanuts, that he would no longer be able to have children; the grass, often a sign of life and hope, here, because it was crimped and mutilated, that his life too would be "cut"; and the girl's name, that he would become involved in a scandal. Quickly he returned to the prophet-healer whom he had just visited, and the prophet divined for him the name of the responsible party, although this was not disclosed to us. Coincidentally or not, shortly thereafter a group of mission personnel formed a delegation on Nsimba's behalf, going to see the retired nurse with whom Nsimba had had problems before. This delegation, we may point out, took the initiative for the visit, though Nsimba agreed with their motives. They asked the elder nurse "what he wanted," though they carefully avoided accusing him of having "planted" the fetish in Nsimba's house. He apologized for his ill-will toward Nsimba, and the mission delegation in turn assured him that no ill will had been intended in his early retirement.

Now Nsimba improved, at least to the extent that he could begin work on a partial basis. He still hoped for a transfer to another post within the mission organization. This desire was submitted formally to a meeting of mission-related medical personnel in late June of 1969. They promised to meet his request as soon as it could be arranged. The meeting was in the form of a conference-retreat with business, meditation, and fellowship among peers mixed together. Later Nsimba said he had enjoyed it greatly. In early July he was back at work in the dispensary. The headaches had disappeared. It is not clear at the time this is being written up whether he was tranferred or not.

ANALYSIS

This case is no better or worse than others we worked with in elucidating some of the dynamic features of Kongo therapy. Beneath the case-study method, there rests the assumption that "the case" is a significant whole that somehow reveals the workings of people in society. We may then open the analysis by raising the question one might naturally ask before such a case: in what sense, and why, is the case ONE illness, and not just thirteen separate episodes? The most convincing argument for considering it as a single illness unit is social-structural: it constitutes a related sequence because the sufferer and his kinsmen begin to act differently towards each other at the outset, and continue to do so until the twelfth or thirteenth episode (Figure 1). Above all, Nsimba's status as "sufferer" *(mbevo)* is defined by his withdrawal from work, and the others' permission to allow him this. Quite passively, he permits his kinsmen to step in voluntarily

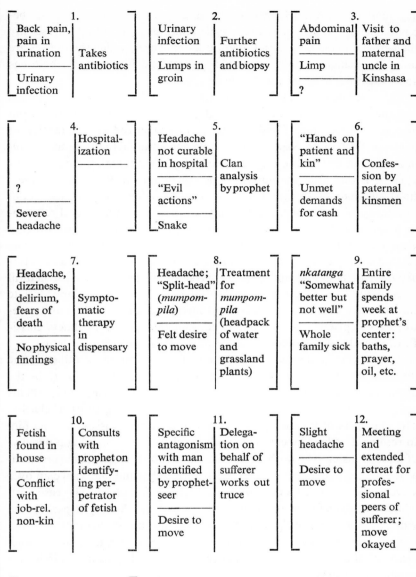

Figure 1. Successive episodes of case from late 1968 till about August, 1969. Middle line of each episode-frame indicates distinction between diagnosis (on left) and therapy (on right). Note multiple diagnoses in most frames; these refer to severally-held alternatives by the group, but may correspond to factions or segments of therapy-managing group.

and manage his quest for well-being as they see fit. This is unusual behavior for a normal young male. Role relations and mutual statuses are then crucial in defining a unit of episode-sequences, which themselves are units. To generalize this, we would suspect that illness everywhere has some identifiable set of social signals.

There is, however, much more to the social-structural aspect of illness and therapy here than the consensual "sick role," to take a phrase from Parsons (1951), which Freidsen has recently amended as "imputation of deviance" (1970). In Nsimba's case, role and status actually define the illness content, and set the stage for the therapy. What makes the case complicated is that after the initial physiological ailment (e.g. urinary infection) all kinds of further symptoms and therapies are generated, both physiological and social. Analytically, we cannot impute causal relationship between the two, as the indigenous therapy does. But we observe clearly a sort of "inverse psychosomatic"[1] process that permits us to correlate a variety of symptoms and illnesses with a variety of social-structural concerns. Thus a second level of analysis parallel to the social-structural is required, pertaining to the classification of the illness and its appropriate therapy. The case thus requires us to invoke variables explaining the sequence of episodes, on the one hand, and the systems of illness classification and social structure, on the other. We begin with the latter.

At least three different role and status features can be identified in the illness as it unfolds. Nsimba is, first of all, encumbered in his work by the disparity between his professional, salaried role in the dispensary, and his obligations to his kinsmen, who expect of him nothing short of charity. The managers of his therapy consider this a marginal issue, leaving him to resolve it as best he can. He tacitly resolves it by obtaining a promise of a job transfer. The problem focused on by the therapy managers, initially, is the conflict between Nsimba's paternal clan and maternal clan over slavery and ransom money, with him right in the midst. The ease with which Nsimba's father negotiates this part of the therapy is perhaps an indication of how it weighs on him, personally; but it also indicates that it is a non-issue, easy to resolve because no longer a burning issue. Nsimba's illness is here analyzed as resulting from his membership in two conflicting groups.

A third social-structural issue of perhaps more substance involves the

---

[1] This term was originally proposed by Dr. Don Bates, Chairman of the History of Medicine Department, McGill University, to indicate the way that simple initial physiological symptoms generate sociological and other difficulties. Turner and Gluckman's thesis, discussed elsewhere in the paper, addresses this issue in another way.

discrepancy between Nsimba's interpretation of his role as professional in the dispensary and the senior nurse's self-image and role definition as a fifty-year-long employee. The first is based on criteria of education and standards of medical care; the second on age, seniority, and patronage in the community. The contradiction between the two role definitions is probably more responsible than anything else for Nsimba's protracted "illness"; for though we cannot extract exact physiological symptoms from the social factor, it is clear that these social-structural components involved him in interpersonal conflict. The fetish of malice that appears at the close (Figure 1, Episode 10) and the quick response by Nsimba's peers in forming a reconciliation group between him and the senior nurse, indicates that this was also their perception of the case. For Nsimba to criticize the old man for his mistakes, even in the name of good health care, violated his definition of the nurse's role by invoking another; such was the basis of the structural contradiction. Two important considerations flow from this fact, the first having to do with social structure and illness, the second with decision-making in the therapeutic process.

The transition from the old nurse's regime to Nsimba's regime involved a structural shift in or redefinition of the position of the African male nurse in a mission dispensary setting — from repetitive choices and decisions within the parameters of seniority and patronage, to novel options related to health care standards and educational levels (Fortes 1949; Nadel 1957: 134–136). Generalized to the entire society, this shift would have had revolutionary implications. In the microcosm of a single case, it merely wreaked havoc in two private lives and caused concern in those around them. The case is instructive in that it echoes the precedent in Kongo society of structural conflict or transition being expressed in disease. Most of the traditional "cults of affliction" recruited individuals from similar contradictory positions in society, realigning their lives so they could cope with the contradiction permanently, usually readjusting the individual's role from that of sufferer to doctor in the cult.

What is unique to this case, and innovative for the modern context, is the composition of a traditional therapy-managing group recruited from professional peers and employers and not from the sufferer's kinsmen. Episodes 11 and 12 (Figure 1) involving Nsimba's non-kin peers thus exhibit the same kind of decision-making as the informal "managerial" group comprised of his father and mother's brother (Episodes 3 to 9). The delegation that visited the senior nurse after the discovery of the fetish (Episode 11) had its own reasons for taking the initiative, growing out of the employer's sense of concern for having precipitously retired an old hand. But the outcome was beneficial for Nsimba's therapy, and demonstrates the dynamics of what will be termed the "managing group" in the therapeutic process.

From an analytical perspective, the managing group is a multi-dimensional social system with potentially shifting membership, operating within a social field (Lewin 1951) to determine the course of therapy by its choice and decision. It is the focus of decision, whether we consider early episodes where Nsimba is diagnosing himself, or later episodes where he is in the hands of a professional physician, or the remaining episodes where he shares decision-making responsibility with kinsmen, peers, and a variety of specialists. We can expect the decisions reached to reflect the nature of the social field and the "managing group" within it, including the slightly anomalous instances in which an individual like Nsimba diagnoses and treats his own case. This, too, is part of the social system.

The theoretical implications of this perspective are crucial, and set apart what is being tried here from much of the writing devoted exclusively to therapy in Western societies. This is so not because Western society is unique, which it is not, but because theory inspired from that context alone demonstrates an overly limited perception of the social context of therapy. This can be illustrated by Nsimba's case, which begins as he makes a therapeutic decision bearing on his well-being. The case is not typologically unusual because of this; it is not essentially different from self-diagnosis and treatment in our society. It is important to consider the first step (Figure 1) as the beginning of the composite illness because it is there that role-stereotyped behavior begins, inspired by the sufferer's self-diagnosis. This contrasts to the way in which both Parsons (1951) and Freidson (1970) write of illness, an imputation of social deviance and recognizing the onset of the "sick role" as the first consultation with a medical professional. Since Henderson's important article calling the patient and doctor a social system (1936), most sociological writers have identified illness and illness behavior with some contact between patient and the medical profession. Not only does this perspective prove useless in comparative work; it undoubtedly limits the analysis of illness and therapy features in Western society too. Other writers (e.g. Twaddle 1969; Stoeckle, Zola, and Davidson 1963; Butler 1970) have been more sensitive to the variety of factors and influences outside of the patient-doctor relationship to the determination of illness and therapy processes.

In Nsimba's case, the conventional patient-consults-doctor format is present only in Episodes 2, 4, and 7 (Figure 1), and even there with growing undertones hinting of doubts in the profession's competence in his particular case. In most of the episodes we find a combination of kinsmen in consultation with a very passive (i.e. sick-defined role) sufferer choosing and deciding the course of therapy. But overall, within the managing field, decisions shift from individual to collective foci, hierarchic to egalitarian group formation, and specialist-prone to participatory involvement, depending on which of these variables are selected in combination.

Once the choice and decision process is identified within such a shifting therapy management group, itself drawn from a social field, it becomes clear why so much time is taken up in Nsimba's case preparing or conditioning for decision-making. Of all the possible forms the therapy management field may take, the Western professional model of hierarchic asymmetrical relations, making the doctor far more powerful than his client, is no doubt the most efficient in terms of decision-execution, although structurally undermining the "rights" of the client in the process (see Freidson on this issue).

The form seen in Nsimba's case, by contrast, is more cumbersome, requiring consensus and overall agreement between the participants. While this form has its advantages, in that all parties concerned are represented, it is vulnerable, as a choice- and decision-making group, to internal dissension and conflicting opinions. In Nsimba's case, at least, several episodes (3, 5, 6, 9) are devoted to shoring up the decision-making group so it can get on with its business. To put it idiomatically in Kongo terms, the illness spills over into group-decision dynamics, embracing indecision as part of the disease. We see this clearly in the episodes (5, 6, 9) in which wider harmony is sought through group therapy. At one point (Episode 9) Nsimba's entire nuclear family and his mother's brother, are "in therapy," receiving treatment for specific individual and general group problems.

The native model of socially-caused illness should here be distinguished from the analytic model of choice and decision in the therapy management field, to understand better just what factors necessitate expansion of the field, or as in the case of the just-cited group therapy, consultation of an outside ritual expert. Brodsky (1970) has described the decision-making system of clinics in this light, including professionals, and patients and their families. Simple procedural and routine tasks require FOCAL decisions that go little beyond the individuals carrying them out. Issues that go beyond the common, believed-in procedures of therapy require EX-TENDED decisions, and these necessitate a broader consensual basis including the therapist, patient, and usually more individuals. Issues that involve not just the disease therapy in a restricted sense, but other aspects of the patient's (and doctor's) physical, psychological, social-structural domains require COMPREHENSIVE decisions that involve major long-range plans (Brodsky 1970: 559–565). The shift from individual to collective role-relations corresponds to a need for focal, extended, or comprehensive decisions imposed by the case's preconditions. Applied to Nsimba's case, it is evident that the managing field required would contract, expand, and shift composition, depending on the participants' perception and involvement in the case at a given moment.

These role shifts in the "consultation interface," as Brodsky speaks of the locus of therapeutic decision, can be identified in more dynamic terms as shifting levels of consensus and dissensus of the decision-making group within the managing field. The work of Gluckman (1965) and Turner (1957) on litigation, ritual, and therapy has developed this perspective largely as a result of their interest in accounting for ritual in social organization and law in Africa. The perspective also serves well in accounting for the role combination shifts within the therapy managing field in Kongo society. Conflict that is not worked in an ad hoc interpersonal fashion, states Gluckman, will be submitted to the existing judicial mechanisms in society, but only as long as the contenders subscribe to common norms or common values or value hierarchies (Gluckman 1965: 241; Turner 1957: 126). Where conflict and dissensus go beyond the boundaries of norm and value to the "deeper level," precipitating dispute over unshared norms, there is likely to be recourse to ritual, or help outside the contesting group. Choice and decision-making follow this same expanding rhythm in the therapy-managing field. As long as broad common diagnoses are shared, by the managing group, the details will be worked out by manipulating the therapy to include all seriously entertained alternatives, even if sequentially. If the dispute crescendoes to involve basic norms and values, an outside specialist is sought who strives to reorient the field to common terms. This acceleration to ritual or mystical treatment in Nsimba's case marks the transition from his problem as a "disease of God" to a "disease of man." The former can be treated readily, even by Europeans; the latter requires mystical intervention. Gluckman's theory, as useful as it is, ignores a very real eventuality, namely, that contenders will commit themselves to all-out conflict, or a state of mystical aggression.

The tension expressed between Nsimba's maternal and paternal groups as an outgrowth of his initial illness may be interpreted in the light of the preceding paragraphs. Recourse to investigation and confession served to work out agreement on tactical matters in his therapy. Recourse to prolonged common ritual by his family (including the mother's brother) reinforced common norms and values, and allowed the group to find common terms in illness. But the illnesses at that point reflected what we earlier called inverse psychosomatics, with the psychosomatic entity abstracting and projecting the dissensus within the immediate community and finding a cure for them (Turner 1957: 126).

It is in choice and decision during the heat of crisis, illness and therapy, that the genuine values and models of reality emerge, and the degree of their integration with social structure can best be noted. The spiral of appeals to "comprehensive" levels of decision (Brodsky), requiring common norms and values (Gluckman, Turner), reveal what, in a given case, are the negotiated working ideas current in a changing society. Taxonomy-eliciting methods that follow self-conscious, context-free inquiries are of little help here, even though they may be sensitive to the processual flow of events (Frake 1969a; Metzger and Williams 1963). The very indeterminancy of therapy as an independent type of activity, making it more like a Markov chain in which the probability of an episode is a function only of the outcome of the preceding events (Frake 1969a: 481–482) than like ceremony or predictable linguistic syntax, requires methodological attention to the context of choice and decision.

Table 1. Partial application of model to case

Variables		Successive episodes of case:	
		$\doteq 4$	$\doteq 5$
1. *Social Structural:*			
formation of therapy-managing group	egalitarian	—	+
	hierarchic	+	—
participants' roles (in relation to sufferer)	maternal kin	—	+
	paternal kin	—	+
	non-kin	+	+
	specialist	+	+
position of sufferer in decision-making group	peripheral	+	+
	integral	—	—
position of specialist in decision-making group	peripheral	—	—
	integral	+	+
character of decision	concensual	—	+
	dissensual	+	—
type of therapist consulted (or therapy undertaken)	prophet-seer (*ngunza*)	—	+
	prophet-healer (*ngunza*)	—	—
	herbalist (*nganga mbuki*)	—	—
	M.D.	+	—
	dispensary nurse	+	—
	(etc., open-ended to be limited to actual therapeutic choices)		

Variables		Successive episodes of case:	
		∓4	∓5
2. Evaluational and Classificational:			
consistency of evaluation	agreement	−	+
	disagreement (and alternatives)	+	−
type of illness (allowance for euphemisms of main types)	"Of man"	−	+
	"Of God"	+	−
	(open-ended to include all identifications in diagnostic discussions)		
therapy required for case (including alternatives entertained)	divination (examin.)	−	+
	indigenous plant cure	−	−
	prayer	−	−
	ritual ablution	−	−
	hospitalization	+	−
	surgery (open-ended, but to include all cases suggested or identified in diagnostic discussions)	−	−
cost of therapy	expensive	+	−
	inexpensive	−	−
	gratis	−	+
distance travelled	far (one day or more)	+	+
	near (less than day)	−	−
mode of travel	walk	−	−
	vehicle	+	+
3. Personal Psychological Judgment of Therapy	effective	−	−
	ineffective	+	+

Choice and decision in therapy are most appropriately seen to operate against a backdrop of three variables (Table 1). The social-structural variables, which we have demonstrated at some length, are obvious. The second variable is that of evaluation and classification of the illness, and its appropriate therapy, which always occurs in a social-structural context. Thirdly, the variable of the protagonist's own response usually overrides the other two, because it itself mediates the course of illness. Freidson put it this way:

Organically, diseases have onsets, climaxes, and outcomes that, during any single course, pass through identifiable stages marked by stable configurations of signs and symptoms. This movement is also to be observed in human efforts at finding meaning in experience. In medicine, the physician's diagnostic (or labelling) behavior may also be seen to have a course, moving from one diagnosis ... to another in the process of trying to find a consequential method of management: some diagnoses are imputed only after all others have yielded negative results (1971: 240).

The degree to which the protagonist's response is mediated by his place between the illness and the social process of diagnosis (labeling), on the part of what we expand to call the therapy managing-group, is always mitigated by considerations of need and resource. Barth's notion of the entrepreneurial choice based upon successive transactions within the channels of social structure and economic value, can be adapted to this context (Barth 1966: 5–6). The cost of therapy, and the extent of energy expended, is often a quality-control against a superficial taxonomy of the phenomenon. This was brought home to me one Sunday morning as I walked fifteen miles in the rain with a clan on its way to a prophet-seer in search of solution to a difficult illness problem.

THE MODEL

The therapeutic process can best be thought of then as a sequence of episodes generated by a decision-making group (operating within a field whose sub-sets vary and realign at successive moments) of those concerned with the welfare of the sufferer(s) in their midst. Such a group — the "therapy-management group" — may be tightly structured by kinship ties, as in much of Nsimba's case, or it may be loosely structured, as are the relationships between a medical professional and a patient-client. It may be hierarchic and asymmetric, or egalitarian and symmetric.

Crucial to this model of the therapeutic process is the fact that although a degree (or level) of consensus is necessary for purposive common action, dissensus either at a focal, or a more inclusive, range generates the next therapeutic episode. Certain exceptions, such as failure to reach even the slightest common accord over basic values, could paralyze action and render the model invalid. But already the fact of common concern for a sufferer, or a torn community, provides a common bond. Within that minimal tie of community, the variables of (1) social structure, (2) evaluation classification, and (3) individual psychological criteria of effectiveness, offer domains for agreement and disagreement in perceptions for common action and alternatives. This is true whether the alternative is conceived by an individual who is rationally plotting the course of his own treatment, by dissenting clansmen of separate factions, by the dissatisfied client in the hands of an authoritarian professional, or by the perplexed professional coping with an unintelligible or difficult case. Therapy is always in this sense "participatory." But it embodies the type of decision-making that creates majority/minority alternatives, the former of which is acted upon immediately, and the latter abstracted, and through projection deferred into a near or indefinite future (Kolaja 1968: 66–70). Such alternatives, and often a plurality of options, will emerge internal to the therapy-managing group in terms of the three main variables of social structure, evaluation and classification of the problem, and the personal satisfaction of the "protagonist(s)." In the case of each of the variables there will be, at any given point in the managing group or field, consensus or dissensus. There may be general consensus in all but one area, let us say the cost, and if there is dissatisfaction over the course of solution, another step will be indicated that follows the "minority" opinion. Or, if there is consensus in all areas but the choice make-up of the decision group (social structure), this dissatisfaction leads to a subsequent stage along the lines laid out by the "minority" opinion. Thus, anything from dissensus between doctor and patient, to factional cleavage in a clan, to ineffectual therapy and patient dissatisfaction, will generate a further episode.

The first several "episodes" in Nsimba's case involve a dual diagnosis by Nsimba himself: the one a symptomatic "back pain" and pain in urination, the other an analytic "disease entity" diagnosis of urinary infection. Being a graduate nurse, he applies what to him is appropriate therapy, antibiotics. However, he does not improve as quickly as he expects to (Table 1, Variable 3), and consults another therapist, this time European (Variable 1). Partly on his own instigation, partly on the diagnosing physician's, the mutual "group" diagnosis is amended to include the lumps in his groin. Both diagnoses are treated, the infection with a continuation of antibiotics (the first episode), the lumps with a biopsy. Again Variable 3 comes into play, in Nsimba's estimation that he is not improving. This time, though, rather than consult another Western-type physician, he, with the help of kinsmen (Variable 1), reassesses his general condition and changes the basic direction of the therapy (Variable 2). Thus the sufferer's original evaluation is amended, modified, complemented, and revised in the light of subsequent episodes of therapy.

A corresponding realignment of the managing group (Variable 1) grows out of negotiation and transactional bargaining over these and more material considerations (see Edgerton 1969; Barth 1966). This happens as alternatives to initial therapeutic disappointment and mis-application are sought. Self-therapy and rational scientific therapy having been exhausted, the perception of "illness" develops apace with the realignment and expansion of the therapy management group. Since the expanded group of Nsimba's father and mother's brother is a responsible and competent one, an attempt is made to incorporate dissensual parties and opinions, rather than to seek premature and restricted consensus of the case, based

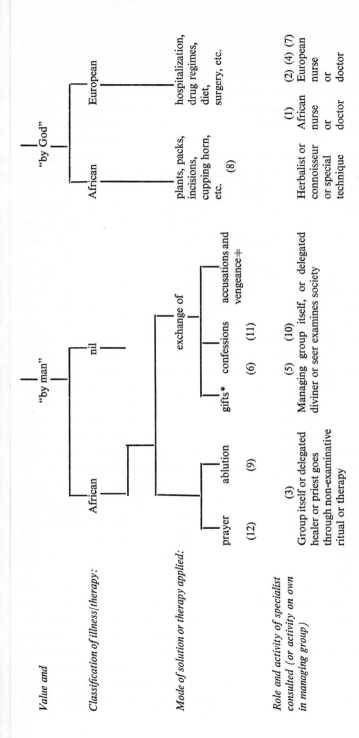

Figure 2. Partial synchronic outline of social-structural and value/classification variables in case study. Numbers in parentheses indicate sequential stages of Nsimba's therapy course. Cost and energy assessment variables not shown. (*) Indicates the mode of solution used at earlier date by sufferer's clan to obtain freedom and full health from master clan. (#) Indicates technique of aggression magic used against sufferer.

on exclusion of differences. It is thus necessary to expand the group to the two clan groups, and to "agree to agree" on the basic relationship, before Nsimba's diagnosis can be reconsidered.

In many Western contexts this desire to achieve conjunction would probably be worked out differently, and we may parenthetically explore the lines. Applying our model to the typical case of dissensus between a doctor who is a professional — well entrenched in a code and practice — and a patient, we would rarely find the latter openly negotiating or bargaining with the former. There would, however, be a relational system, and very likely both would have a diagnosis of the problem at hand. The patient's would be symptomatic and "folk"-informed; the professional's systematic but esoteric, and largely incommunicable to the patient. This may account, but only in part, for the failure of many M.D.'s to share their information with the patient fully. If we consider the case, however, from the viewpoint of a participatory managing group, as we have been developing it, dissensus and disjunction between the two roles over any one of the major three variables — social structure, evaluation and classification, personal criteria of success — would generate a further therapeutic episode around alternative combinations. Very likely the dissatisfied patient would assert his alternative choice by seeking another therapist of the same kind. This contrasts to the Kongo case in which (see Figure 2) the analogous instance generates a visit to another kind of therapy. This is so because the Western therapy-managing field for decision is asymmetrical, with the therapist enjoying a higher status than his client. Accordingly, his diagnosis prevails in any given episode. The only outlet of the client's "minority" diagnosis, by Western customary and legal admission, is for him to find another specialist who will agree with it, and treat it as such. Only by re-defining the illness as "crime" can (and does) the Western medical profession impose its therapy upon the patient (Freidson 1970). This is evident in rulings on heroin addiction at the present, and on alcoholism in the past. In both instances the potential for therapeutic legalism emerges from the hierarchic structure of the therapy-managing group.

Persistent differences of opinion in the Kongo type of therapy-managing group, as we can well see from Nsimba's case, do not create the same kind of inflexibility. Rather, the obverse kind of predicament results. Because the therapy-managing group is egalitarian in structure, social differences tend to proliferate alternatives of therapy types. The forces of colonization, missionization, and urbanization have contributed to this. Unlike Western medicine, in which disjunction leads the dissatisfied patient to seek another therapist of the same kind he sought previously, in

Kongo the tendency is to seek another kind or class of therapist; not because the therapist was incommunicative or disagreeable — the therapy was after all negotiated — but because the mutually agreed-upon course of therapy wasn't "successful." The same kind of rationale seems to carry over into the native perception of Western medical specialists in Kongo society. Failing to communicate their information to the patient, in keeping with the expectations of negotiated therapy, they virtually generate easy-to-comprehend alternatives such as "split-head" (Episode 8) or "rheumatism of the head" (Episode 9). The ensuing classificatory proliferation of therapies and sub-therapies has resulted in a tremendous waste of human time and energy, as individuals seek satisfaction within the terms of the synthetic system, pervaded as it is with contradictions and inconsistencies. The obvious tactical solution to this problem, and to the proliferation of folk therapy types, is for medical authorities to take seriously their tacit role in the managing group and negotiation to explain scientific therapy in terms of the system, so that it becomes a successful, communicated alternative.

It should be clear that the concrete case method is needed in this situation to discover contemporary perceptions of disease and therapy. The model developed only sketchily here provides for an inductively-generated classificatory synthesis that is in fact an enlarged native classification in the process of absorbing Western medicine (as perceived by Africans). On the basis of alternative cognitive categories and social courses entertained in actual decisions, it is possible to establish several levels of variables. The model can be used to anticipate the logic of memory exercised by actors. And while this plotted memory is by no means totally predictive, we can successfully anticipate certain overriding ideas that appear in sequentially-ordered patterns. For one thing, the evidence from our cases permits us to say that in successive therapeutic episodes a different (rather than same) class of specialists will be consulted (Figure 2). This seems to be correlated, as suggested, to the social-structural variable of egalitarian, negotiated decision in the therapy managing group. Secondly, all cases move from the general evaluative category of natural illness, caused "by God" to that of illness caused "by man," as disjunction (disagreement in diagnosis or outside existing conflict) persists in the therapy-managing field group.

It is premature, on the basis of one case, to go beyond these generative rules of Kongo therapy. The method developed, though, provides an avenue for systematic study of social institutions and orders of thought in a problematic setting, and is immune to the query of whether it is the RIGHT or REAL structure, since it is the inductively-derived order generated by alternatives considered in concrete decisions. As further cases are added to the analysis, a representative pattern will emerge.

REFERENCES

ATTNEAVE, FRED
1969   *Application of information theory to psychology.* New York: Holt, Rinehart and Winston.

BARTH, FREDRIK
1966   *Models of social organization.* Royal Anthropological Institute, Occasional Paper 23.

BRODSKY, C. M.
1970   Decision-making and role shifts as they affect the consultation interface. *Archives of General Psychiatry* 23:559–565.

BUTLER, J. J.
1970   Illness and the sick role: an evaluation in three communities. *British Journal of Sociology* 21:241–261.

EDGERTON, ROBERT
1969   "On the recognition of mental illness," in *Changing perspectives on mental illness.* Edited by S. Plog and R. B. Edgerton. New York: Holt, Rinehart and Winston.

FORTES, MEYER
1949   "Time and social structure," in *Social structure: studies presented to A. R. Radcliffe-Brown.* Oxford: Clarendon Press.

FRAKE, CHARLES
1969a   "A structural description of Subanun 'religious behavior'," in *Cognitive anthropology.* Edited by S. Tyler, 470–486. New York: Holt, Rinehart and Winston.
1969b   "The Yakan concept of litigation," in *Law in culture and society.* Edited by Laura Nader, 147–167 Chicago: Aldine.

FREIDSON, ELIOT
1970   *Profession of medicine: a study of the sociology of applied knowledge.* New York: Dodd, Mead and Company.

GLICK, L. B.
1967   Medicine as an ethnographic category: the Gimi of the New Guinea highlands. *Ethnology* 31.

GLUCKMAN, MAX
1965   *Politics, law and ritual in tribal society.* Chicago: Aldine.

HENDERSON, L. J.
1936   The patient and physician as a social system. *New England Journal of Medicine* 212:819–823.

JANZEN, JOHN M.
1969a   "The cooperative in Lower Congo economic development," in *The Anthropology of development in sub-Saharan Africa.* Edited by David Brokensha, 70–76. Lexington: University of Kentucky Press.
1969b   Vers une phénoménologie de la guérison en Afrique centrale. *Etudes congolaises* 12:97–114.

KOLAJA, J.
  1968   Two processes: a new framework for the theory of participation in decision-making. *Behavioural Science* 13:66–70.
LEWIN, KURT
  1951   *Field theory in social science.* New York: Harper.
MECHANIC, D.
  1962   The concept of illness behavior. *Journal of Chronic Diseases* 15:189.
METZGER, D., G. WILLIAMS
  1963   Tenejapa medicine I: the curer. *Southwestern Journal of Anthropology* 19:216–234.
NADEL, S. F.
  1957   *The theory of social structure.* New York: The Free Press.
NASH, J.
  1967   The logic of curing behavior in a Maya Indian town. *Human Organization* 26: 132–140.
PARSONS, T.
  1951   *The social system.* New York: The Free Press.
STOECKLE, J. D., I. K. ZOLA, G. E. DAVIDSON
  1963   On going to see the doctor; the contributions of the patient to the decision to seek medical aid. *Journal of Chronic Diseases* 16:975–989.
TURNER, V. W.
  1957   *Schism and continuity in an African society.* Manchester: University of Manchester Press.
TWADDLE, A.
  1969   Health decisions and sick role variations: an exploration. *Journal of Health and Social Behaviour* 10:105–115.

Suffering as a Religious Imperative in Afghanistan

ROBERT L. CANFIELD

An Old Man at a Shrine

In front of a famous shrine in central Afghanistan I encountered an old man, a Hazara (an underprivileged ethnic group), slumped against the trunk of a large tree, weeping. I discovered that he had come to this shrine from a great distance to obtain the healing of his only surviving son. In the city where he lived a doctor had told him that the child had an advanced case of tuberculosis and gave him no hope of recovery. So the man had brought the boy to this shrine, hoping that somehow God would work a miracle of healing. Instead, the boy had died.

Moreover, now that the boy was dead, the bereaved father was trapped here because of a bureaucratic technicality. His son's death had to be recorded, lest in a few years the government require him to produce his son for service in the army, but he had no money to pay a government clerk the customary tip to ensure registration of the death. Because he was obviously very poor none of the officials would take an interest in him. He was surviving for some days by staying with some relatives, and begging. The relatives were even poorer than he, he said, and anyway they were only distant relatives. Of his close kinsmen all were dead. He was alone.

The sufferings of this man were multiple. He was broken hearted at the loss of his only surviving son. He was deprived of raising up progeny, something highly prized in this society, and consequently of any security in old age. Moreover, he was alone, without a close kinsman, no one permanently to live with, scarcely anyone on whom to rely for succor and comfort, even less for social and economic security. And upon all this was compounded the insult of governmental insensitivity and petty corruption. He suffered the emotional shock of a loved one's death, the social loss of his future security and — unable even to pay the fees for registering his son's death — the grinding humiliation of poverty.

This is a study of suffering in Afghanistan. It has been customary for anthropologists to study religion as essentially a cultural or ideological phenomenon. Anthropologists commonly have tried to show how a people's culturally conditioned interpretations of suffering direct them to certain forms of religious ritual and magical curing. For such an approach the variables that critically "explain" the diversity of religious forms are cultural. Spiro, for example, subtitled his book (1967) "a study in the explanation and reduction of suffering," but scarcely mentions the actual conditions of suffering in Burma. Similarly, Turner (1968) was not so concerned with the concrete circumstances of suffering among the Ndembu as with their cultural orientation toward their suffering.

This paper has a rather different focus. It points out the real conditions of suffering in order to suggest that suffering materially influences social relations. Cultural resources, i.e. systems of belief and ritual, provide the tool kit for dealing with suffering, but suffering itself, by its imperious presence in real life, makes these resources desperately important. To the peasants of Afghanistan suffering is a material condition strongly inducing them to seek efficacy through the religious and magical services provided by religious specialists; suffering, therefore, is one factor in maintaining a set of social relations.

This of course is not a novel argument,[1] but it is presented as a reminder that to explain religious belief and practice we must not only look at cultural orientations but also at the actual conditions of distress inducing people to look for religious answers and to pay for religious services. Where we find people carrying on religious activities in earnest we are well advised to take note of stressful circumstances that may be incentives for religious observance. But suffering in other cultures must be looked for. If the forms through which suf-

---

[1]   An inspiration for this view of suffering has been Max Weber (see Gerth and Mills 1958:270–725). Belshaw (1967) presents a thorough and sympathetic description of economic hardships among the peasants of Fiji. I am grateful to Mary Farvar for pointing out to me that while in Egypt Elizabeth Fernea (1970), despite her educated disinclination, felt impelled by the urgent sickness of her child to accept and use an amulet.

fering is expressed among another people are unfamiliar, certain aspects of their suffering can evade us. It is easy to grasp that in our own society people in many walks of life have problems; ethnocentric notions may obscure our sensitivity to the kinds of burdens that people in other cultures bear. We are apt to suppose that if they do not complain as we do, they must not suffer as we do.

Another reason for this study of suffering as an impingement on social relations is that I want eventually to explain why religious leaders in Afghanistan, "mullahs," are so important. They are indeed very important. Many of them are relatively well off by Afghan standards and a few, the great "saints," are wealthy by anyone's standards. They are also influential. Religious leaders are everywhere highly esteemed, the most powerful of them being carefully respected by the Afghan government. This respect is not without reason: the power of mullahs was dramatically evinced in 1929 when an eminent saint in the country, eventually with the support of many other religious leaders, instigated a popular insurrection that overturned the ruling monarch.

Their influence has continued to be felt since then, though contained by police control. In 1958 when King Zaher Shah took measures to allow the veil to be removed from Afghan women, the secret police quietly rounded up key religious figures and imprisoned them for a time. Even so, despite four decades of growing government control of religious leaders and two decades of Western secular influence in Afghanistan, mullah influence has not declined. In fact, recently there has been a resurgence of religious fanaticism and a corresponding rise in the power of mullahs.

There have been large demonstrations of mullahs in Kabul, the most notable being against the use of a term of religious veneration for Lenin in a government newspaper. Also, there have been a number of xenophobic acts of violence, probably induced by religious fervor (cf. Dupree 1971a). And in the last national election persons associated with eminent mullahs and conservative religious interests seem to have gained in numbers at the expense of modernist-secular-istic candidates (cf. Dupree 1971b). So a student of Afghanistan life and affairs has good reason to ask what the factors are that make religious personages important, why wealth flows to them, and why their opinions exert so much influence.

There are a number of factors involved, of course, but the one I can describe here is the sufferings common to the populace. If there were space I would demonstrate that the sufferings of many people in Afghanistan are so severe, so real, so inescapable that they are happy to pay dearly for the spiritual and emotional support provided by religious leaders. Here I can only present the data on their physical sufferings and economic distresses and affirm that they induce this effect.

PHYSICAL DISTRESS AND ITS PSYCHOLOGICAL IMPLICATIONS

Physical Infirmities

Until very recently descriptions of health conditions in Afghanistan were based on only impressionistic information. The most common serious diseases formerly were reported to be malaria and tuberculosis (Simmons 1954:173) but the World Health Organization has announced the eradication of malarial mosquitoes (Smith, et al. 1969: 104). Tuberculosis remains highly frequent. A tuberculine survey conducted in 1949 yielded a reaction rate of 85 percent in persons of twenty-three years or older, indicating a high incidence of tuberculosis exposure (Simmons 1954:173).

Simmons indicates that smallpox (of which there were 1,290 reported cases in 1951), measles, and whooping cough are endemic and occasionally reach epidemic proportions. He also indicated that "syphilis and gonorrhea are prevalent. . . . The highest rates of infection are encountered in Kabul and in the border towns, particularly in Herat and Jelalabad; the lowest in the central highlands" (1954: 174a). Cholera, typhoid, rabies, and typhus *(exanthematicci)* also occur in high frequencies (Berke 1946). An immunological survey in 1967 revealed the incidence of positive poliovirus antibodies in children over five years of age to be more than 90 percent (Sery, et al. 1970). Moreover,

undernutrition and avitaminosis are prevalent. Rickets is common among children of the poorer families in the cities and towns. Osteomalacia is frequently observed among the women . . . . Vitamin A deficiencies are prominent, especially in remote districts in the country and southern provinces. Minor manifestations of vitamin C deficiency are widely distributed . . . . Goiter is endemic in foci in the Amu Dariya river valley in the northeast (Simmons 1954:176).

While medical services have been improving, a growing body of solid statistics indicates that health conditions continue to be generally

Table 1. Most frequent conditions diagnosed in clinics of the Ministry of Health in selected areas of central Afghanistan (from MAP 1967)*

Conditions diagnosed:	In Obey (Herat Prov.)	In Rukha-Panjsher (Kapisa Prov.)	In Dehrahood (Urozgan Prov.)	In Urozgan (Urozgan Prov.)
Total number patients seen	1,146	1,408	1,155	1,225
Gastro-intestinal				
Number of patients	496	721	559	922
Percent of clinic	40.6	51	48.4	74
Ophthalmological				
Number of patients	236	272	158	140
Percent of clinic	20.6	18.4	13.8	11.2
Pulmonary				
Number of patients	165	103	131	88
Percent of clinic	14.4	6.9	11.4	7.2
Pulmonary and extrapulmonary TB				
Number of patients	86	29	53	56
Percent of clinic	7.5	1.9	4.6	4.6
Orthopedic				
Number of patients	147	205	144	155
Percent of clinic	12.8	14	12.5	14.4
Dermatological				
Number of patients	93	156	100	122
Percent of clinic	8.1	11.2	8.7	10

* Only the most frequent disease categories are reproduced here. The percentage figures indicate the percentage of persons having a disease in each category. Because a number of patients had more than one infirmity, there were more cases reported than patients examined, so the percentages never total 100 percent.

poor. Statistics from the 1967 and 1969 reports of the Medical Assistance Program (MAP), are indicated in Table 1. These are mainly based on personal histories and physical examinations done in field-clinic situations. (Worms, for example, were only diagnosed on the basis of their having been seen in stools; laboratory examinations would certainly have revealed a higher incidence of both intestinal parasites and tuberculosis.)

A high number of the diseases encountered were seriously debilitating: out of the five most prevalent diseases — i.e. intestinal parasites, trachoma, chronic pulmonary disease, bacillary and amoebic dysentery, and tuberculosis — all but the first seriously impair health (MAP 1969:7). Among the less frequent diseases not indicated in

Table 1 were the following serious infirmities: acute and chronic otitis media (3.8 percent), tapeworm (3.1 percent), leprosy (2.1 percent), and osteomyelitis (1.9 percent) (MAP 1969:9). A leprosy survey in the schools of Hazarajat during the summer of 1969 yielded the number of leprosy cases in the districts indicated as shown in Table 2 (MAP 1969:16).

Table 2. Number of positive tests for leprosy among students in three districts

	Students	Positive tests
Yak Awalang	983	9
Panjaw	992	10
Lal-o-Sarjangal	716	2

A report on the sorts of opthalmic diseases found in four areas of Afghanistan is summarized in Table 3.

Incidence of child mortality is high (see Table 4). In 1969 MAP published a four-year summary of the mortality and survival rates of children under five. Out of 18,854 children born to the 3,564 mothers interviewed, 9,565 were still living, indicating a mortality rate of 49.5 percent. In Hazarajat the mortality rate was 50.4 percent.

The Mystery of Infirmity

The above disease categories are of course our own, not those of the local populations. The persons suffering from these ailments have scarcely any sense of what is wrong with them. They typically describe their ailments only in general terms — as aches here and there, in the head, back, leg, side, etc. Also, they have little recollection of the history of their discomfort.

I met a man, for example, whose arm had been broken and remained unset; the broken part now flops loosely from his elbow. He said it had been very painful for a long time but eventually it began to feel better. He didn't know why he could no longer use it. A man blind in one eye told me he had no idea why it had become blind; he simply woke up one morning and noticed that he couldn't see out of it. (Being a farmer and illiterate, he probably did not strain his eyes sufficiently to notice that one eye was failing until it was almost gone.)

A man told me he had once washed his newborn child in the river — an icy mountain stream. For some reason, he said, it died soon afterwards; he supposed he shouldn't have washed it there. Thus,

Table 3. Incidence of ophthalmic diseases encountered in selected areas, in percent (from Barclay 1969)*

	Baghlan	Bost	Kandahar	Jalalabad
Trachoma	33	17	23	18
Leuconia	32	24	15	21
Cataract	14	14	11	19
Conjunctivitis (non-specific)	7.5	11	9	11
Glaucoma	6.5	6	5	3
Absolute glaucoma	–	–	2.5	1.5
Trichiasis	5.5	5.5	9	0.7
Paunus	7.7	2.5	6.5	2.5

* For the same reasons as noted on Table 1, these percentages do not necessarily total 100.

Table 4. The mortality rates of children to five years of age in selected areas of Afghanistan (from MAP 1969)

Place and province	Number of women questioned	Total live births	Total now living	Percent of Mortality
Mohamand-Dara (Nangarhar)	54	278	143	48.6
Kaja-Khogiana (Nangarhar)	42	216	122	45.6
Obey (Herat)	183	1,071	453	57.7
Rukha-Panjsher (Kapisa)	29	175	73	58.4
Dehrahood (Urozgan)	76	475	264	44.5
Urozgan (Urozgan)	105	556	293	47.3
Chowki (Kunar)	147	684	416	39.4
Sharan (Kunar)	136	641	352	45.2
Total	772	4,096	2,116	48.4

lacking an understanding of anatomy and of the most elementary processes of physiology and disease, they seem not to know or perceive the natural causes for diseases and physical discomfort.

A lamentable consequence of this ignorance is the neglect of certain injuries that normally would be minor, but owing to improper care become serious. This is noticeably true of skin abrasions which are seldom washed clean, for soap is rarely used except to wash clothing, as it dries out the skin. A boy's leg, for example, which had been only slightly cut in a fall against a rock had become septic. A blister on a man's hand became badly infected and then was further infected by an unsanitary cowhide glove that was fitted on his hand to inhibit the swelling. By the time he received medical attention the swelling had crept up his whole arm. Had he not received massive injections of antibiotics, he would have faced the prospect of tetanus.

Ignorance of what is happening to their health often results in people feeling a pervasive anxiety. Fear of the unknown, a common experience, of course, is intensified by their insufficient medical understanding. The narrowness of their technological insights leaves relatively more room for disquietude. Owing to the greater extent of what is unknown, serious harm or illness seems to strike capriciously, with unaccountable severity and irregularity. The tendency therefore is to worry overmuch, to be on edge about relatively harmless misadventures of routine life.

A child in a Hazara family, an only surviving son, had fallen while running and apparently had injured his arm. The boy cried for several hours. A medical examination that evening, however, revealed that nothing was wrong with his arm. Evidently the boy's crying had resulted from his mother's emotional response to his fall: frightened by this fall, she had also cried, and this upset the boy. Having been told that there was nothing wrong, both the boy and the mother felt better, and both were quite well the next day.

Not only illness and injury but also death seems to strike wantonly and without warning. This has been especially so during epidemics. Twice in the living memory of these populations there have been epidemics which struck down persons by the scores. About twenty years ago an epidemic of scarlet fever[2] killed a number of persons. But while many were sick in most households, some families were struck more severely than others. In one household, for example, all but the mother were sick, but they all survived; in a neighboring family six persons died.

In 1915 cholera swept through the entire country with devastating effect; that year is now known as *saal-i-taawan* "the year of judgment." [3] But there was an unevenness in the distribution of the disease. For example, while many communities suffered badly, the Tajik community of Tolwaara, blessed with a pure spring, was scarcely affected.

[2] This is judged only by their descriptions of the symptoms. They called the disease *surkhakaan* which is usually translated "measles," but probably refers to any rash-producing disease.

[3] Jewett records the date precisely for us with the disease reaching Kabul in October 1915 (Bell 1948: 263), though informants could only estimate the date.

Nevertheless the value of the spring in protecting the community from the spread of the disease seems to have been overlooked; people feel that Tolwaara was protected supernaturally because it is surrounded by several shrines, two of which are famous for supernatural power.

The apparent wantonness of death may be further illustrated by a

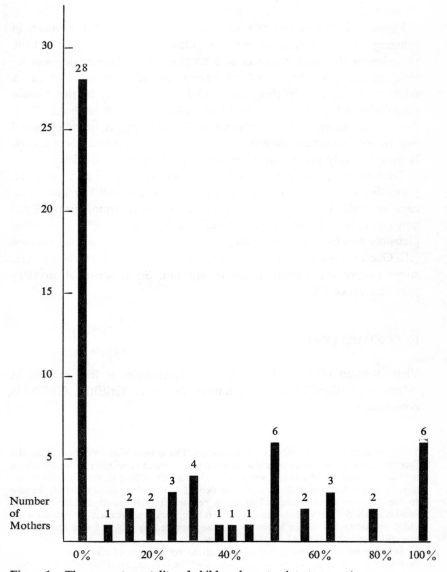

Figure 1. The percent mortality of children born to sixty-two mothers

close look at infant mortality rates in a community of 120 households.[4] In this community I collected data on the birth and mortality of offspring from sixty-two women. These mothers bore 264 live
children, an average of just over three per mother. Of the children
born, eighty-eight had died before puberty,[5] most of them before
reaching five years of age, a mortality rate by the age of puberty of
33 percent.

Figure 1 indicates the relative success of the sixty-two mothers in
bringing their children to puberty. Observe that there is a wide
variation in child-rearing success, a number of mothers having lost no
children and a number of others having lost all of their children. A
third mode in the distribution of child mortality is in the middle
range of roughly 50 percent child mortality in each household. Thus,
the overall average of 33 percent child mortality is not distributed
evenly, some mothers obviously being far more successful than others.
It would clearly seem that some are more blessed than others.

That some people are blessed and some are not is an impression
pervading not only matters of health but of social and economic success as well. Life is as inscrutable as death. Technological explanations being absent, supernatural considerations offer the most
plausible means of understanding the irregularities of personal fortune
(cf. Geertz 1965). In the strange caprice of supernatural powers,
some people are fortunate, some are not. So a sense of mystery
pervades all of life.

ECONOMIC DISTRESS

Visitors often observe that economic deprivation is less evident in
Afghanistan than in many countries of Asia. Griffiths (1967:74)
comments:

---

[4] These data have a number of deficiencies. The census was complicated by the
fact that most of my informants were men who do not remember these details as
well as the women. Moreover, some were clearly not willing to give me this information and either reported no deaths, or denied some infant deaths already known
to me through other sources. For these reasons, I have omitted data on some
mothers, which, for various reasons, I felt were not trustworthy. As my data on
child mortality are rather lower than those reported by MAP, I suspect the data
are still somewhat skewed by these factors.
[5] Informants sometimes found it difficult to recall ages of children. They preferred to use the terms *reeza* "small, infantile" for infants, *xord* "little" for children
under puberty, and *jawaan* "young, youthful" for those over puberty.

The great contrasts between wealth and poverty common to most under-developed countries are scarcely evident in Afghanistan. . . . The signs of disease are plentiful, but the emaciated limbs and swollen stomachs of severe malnutrition are rare. There is some begging, but not the persistent buzzing swarm of importunate human flies common to other Eastern countries.

This kind of observation, though true, should not obscure our perception of the hardships that do exist. We should not surmise that economic distress is not extensive. It is found wherever one looks closely; since Griffiths wrote the above, it has become much more evident. In the marginal agricultural areas, especially in the isolated valleys of the central highlands, poverty is found among peasant landowners; in the great agricultural centers it is found among tenant farmers; and in the cities it is found among day laborers.

Most of the poorest people in the country are Hazaras, an ethnic group distinguishable by Mongoloid features and, usually, Shiite faith (cf. Canfield 1973). The central highland region, from whence they come, is known as the Hazarajat. To illustrate the patterns of economic hardship the following paragraphs primarily describe problems of Hazaras and the Hazarajat, but this is not to imply that only they are poor. In fact, I want to use the Hazaras to argue that the greatest poverty is not in the rural districts — where admittedly it may be severe — but in the lowland plains where populations are more dense and more economically stratified. This generalization applies as much to the lowland territories of Farah, Herat, and Faizabad where few of the poor are Hazaras, as to Kabul, Ghazni, and Mazar-i-Sharif where most of them are. The phenomenon, of course, is not peculiar to Afghanistan.

Highland Peasants

In Afghanistan's diverse terrain there is a relationship between wealth and land ownership in the central plains. Normally collecting heavy snows in winter, the mountains of central Afghanistan are the source of the country's great rivers — the Helmand, Hari, Morghab, Qunduz-Oxus, and Kabul rivers. In their flexuous pursuits of low ground these waters sometimes cascade through precipitous gorges, sometimes pause to wash tracts of alluvial plain. High on the mountain plateaus these plains are no more than narrow glens, but further down they become progressively wider and longer, and some, those at the confluence of the larger streams, serve as major centers of population and wealth. On the fringe of the central highlands the important centers of agricultural abundance are Besud, Uruzgan, Panjaw, Yak Awland, Bamian, and Doshi.

Further down, the waters debouch upon the broad, rich plains which are the great food baskets of the country: Kandahar, Girishk-Bost, Farah, Herat, Mazar-i-Sharif, Qunduz, Koh-Daman, Laghman-Nagarhar. Here in these expansive plains the economically successful, the socially well-placed, and the politically strong have their lands. For as the Afghan state rose to power, those in close relation to the rulership laid claim to the most lucrative territories and they enlarged and increased their lands and profits by investing in expensive irrigation works such as canals and *karezes* (see Humlum 1959).

Thus, the most expansive and rich plains are owned largely by the wealthiest and strongest families. Most of these families are Afghans (Pushtuns), but in the north many are Uzbeks; almost invariably, except for wealthy Shiites who have recently bought into these territories, they are Sunni Muslims. In the smaller agricultural plains of the central highlands, ownership of land also entails relative abundance. Often they are owned by Sunnis, but in some areas by well-to-do Shiites. In the highest valleys and glens, however, where the tracts of irrigable plain are narrow and ownership does not necessarily entail wealth, many of these landowners are poor; most are Shiites.

There is a general tendency for the fortunes of highland peasant cultivators to decline. One reason has been the pressure of Afghan nomads in the Hazarajat. As a reward for service in the defeat of the Hazaras at the end of last century, Afghan nomads were invited by the Amir of Kabul, Abdul Rahman, to graze their flocks in the Hararajat. This provided them opportunity also to sell at highly inflated prices goods obtained in the Indus valley, such as cloth, tea, sugar, and salt. These were sold on credit in the spring when the nomads migrated into the highlands, and were paid for in grain after the autumn harvest. When the nomads moved to the Indus lowlands to winter their flocks they replenished their stocks of goods by selling the grain.

Nomad power over the Hazaras for a time grew to oppressive proportions so that sometimes the peasants were forced to buy goods they did not want (Ferdinand 1962). Peasants told me that sometimes the cloth would be thrown into the house through the ventilation hole in the roof, with the demand that it must be paid for (with interest) the next fall. Fortunately, the government has recently taken a more favorable stance toward the peasant cause and such repressive practices seem no longer to continue. Peasant indebtedness, however, does; around 1960 as many as 60 to 80 percent of the Hazaras in some areas were in debt (Ferdinand 1962).

The fortunes of a highland peasant can also decline because of fortuitous events that upset the delicate balance of resources and labor that enables a peasant to subsist and prosper. An example is the case of Hosain Mamad. Hosain Mamad was at one time quite wealthy, for he was the son of a strong Mir. His land produced, it is said, as much as twenty *xarwars*[6] of wheat, so he was one of the richest persons in his area. He had lots of animals, which helped to fertilize his land. Able to entertain many notables, he once fed several hundred guests when the saint of that area came to visit, an occasion that imparted to him much prestige. He spent his time supervising work on his land and in reading. Unfortunately he had no surviving sons who might have joined in the development and supervision of his economic resources, and only one daughter — a circumstance that eventually caused his good fortune to decline.

He adopted a son from a family having twelve children, but the boy turned out to be deaf and could not do much work. Also, he lost two wives and now has a third. Now in his old age, he has much less land because he had to sell some to purchase his wives. He has fewer animals, and because they provide much less manure for his fields, his land now produces only four or five *xarwars*. Too old to work it himself, he divides the yield half and half with a tenant worker, who, it is said, cheats him because he cannot supervise the work as he once did.

Another factor in the general decline of the highland peasants is the system of partible inheritance common to the Muslim world, whose dynamics are only now roughly understood (Wolf 1966:73–77). According to the requirements of Islamic law, land is divided among plural heirs, twice as much to a son as a daughter, so that no heir receives the entire estate on which the deceased subsisted. As the offspring multiply, after a few generations an heir may not receive a plot large enough for his own subsistence. In Afghanistan, land is so highly valued among the poor that the heirs try to hold the land in common, leaving it to one while the others emigrate. Even then it may not be sufficient.

For example, Khan Ali was a joint heir, with his brother and two

---

[6] Estimates of land size are commonly expressed in terms of the amount of seed that can be profitably sown on it. A *xarwar* is 80 *ser* (Samin and Nielsen 1967). See also Note 7.

male cousins, to a piece of land inherited from his grandfather that was too small to support even one person. In 1967 all of the other co-owners had left the land in Khan Ali's care and found work in Kabul; the brother as a shopkeeper, one cousin as a hired hand, and the other as a driver. Their land consisted of four *sers*[7] of irrigated land, and a quarter *ser* of cultivable dry land; altogether it was worth about 10,000 afghanis (about $250). Khan Ali had one bull, one donkey, and no sheep or goats. In spring 1967 he planted two *sers* of wheat, two *sers* of barley, and the rest in alfalfa. This, I judge from the yield of neighboring plots, would produce at least 1200 *paw*[8] of grain.

As the residents calculate their monthly consumption needs to be a minimum of ninety *paw* of grain per person, his land would in a moderate year produce enough to last Khan Ali, if he consumed it all himself, over thirteen months. This assumes that none of the grain was sold for taxes, paid as debts, or claimed by any of the other three owners. Actually, however, all three of these liens on his yield existed, so that in order to remain viable his yield had to be considerably higher than the average in his area. Obviously he was close to the margin of viable subsistence.

Khan Ali lived alone. The high price of brides had denied him the privilege of a wife, though he was about forty years old. In summer 1967 he ran short of food and money and borrowed a little from neighbors to hold him until harvest. I asked him how he would repay the debt; he didn't know. The following spring he leased the land to a man from outside his valley to pay back his debts.

As the lessee had hired someone else to work the land, Khan Ali took a bus to Kabul. He planned to work as a coolie until he could get enough cash ahead to do something more profitable. Several factors contributed to Khan Ali's economic decline but the critical one was the size of the land left him by his father. The partible inheritance rule eventually carved the land into too small a fragment for it to support even one preson.

The same rule, however, while impartially applied to all classes, has relatively little detrimental effect on the wealthy, for they have benefited more directly from the burgeoning economy in the cities. The growing numbers of heirs in the great families has enhanced, rather than weakened, their strength because as their offspring have increased, their involvement in national institutions has increased. They have dispersed into the many new positions in government, in-

[7]   A *ser* is 16 *paw*, which in English weight is 15 pounds.
[8]   See Notes 6 and 7.

dustry, and commerce that have become available as the nation modernized. These are the families that have gained most from foreign development.

The correct generalization seems to be that to remain viable a rural family must profitably articulate with the national cash economy. Some highland families have been able to do this — but only the rich ones. During the economic surge of the past twenty years these Hazaras have invested in small business activities and have profited greatly. Mir Ramzan Khan is an example.

Mir Ramzan Khan is the oldest surviving son of a formerly powerful Hazara Mir. Like his father, he attempts to mediate disputes among his neighbors and poorer friends, and when necessary he represents them to the government. For these services he receives many benefits, usually informal and unofficial. He is often paid in cash or grain by his clients and they also help his paid servants during plowing and harvest seasons, so he does little of his own work.

He and his younger brother have not yet divided the property they received from their father. It consists of forty *sers* of land (i.e. ten times that of Khan Ali and his three co-owners), on which, in addition to the grain needed for their own consumption, they have planted a number of trees that in a few years will bring several thousand afghanis when sold in Kabul. In about 1965 they purchased a bus which carries both passengers and freight between Hazarajat and Kabul. They have also acquired a *saray*[9] in Kabul which serves as a depot for the bus and its freight.

Mir Ramzan Khan lives on his natal land and in addition to his political activities oversees the cultivation of his land, while his younger brother supervises the bus business and the *saray* in Kabul. Unlike Khan Ali, Mir Ramzan Khan was able to stabilize his already strong position by investing in the national economic network. He and his brother are growing more wealthy.

While only the well-to-do can make such profitable investments, it seems likely that many of the rank-and-file highland peasants will become poorer. This is due to a fourth and more basic factor in the decline of the highland peasant, the general insufficiency of cultivable land. The scarcity of land in the Hazarajat is indicated in the rough data available on nutritional density.

The average amount of cultivated land per Hazarajat resident is 1.78 *jeribs* (about half an acre). The national average is 2.08 *jeribs*. Average amounts

* An enclosed compound in the city, a caravansary.

of cultivated land per operator disclose an even greater discrepancy of 12.07 *jeribs* for the nation at large (Jung 1970:9).

Because of the land scarcity, for more than a century highland peasants have been coming down to the lowlands and the cities during the winter to supplement their incomes (Burnes 1842: 230). Usually they have returned in the spring, but those who obtained steady work have stayed, entrusting their land to relatives, some of them returning home briefly to help with the spring plowing and the autumn harvest. As a result, the summer population of the highlands has been greater than the winter population.

According to a research team that visited Hazarajat in 1968, perhaps as many as 30 to 50 percent of the highland labor force have been seasonally absent. Still, population pressure has not decreased: "Permanent migration does not offset the natural population growth with the result that the summertime population of the [central] region is increasing. Consequently landholdings are becoming smaller and the number of landless families is increasing" (Allen 1963: 2).

Rural Sharecroppers and Urban Day Laborers

The decline of the economic fortunes of the poor land owners eventually forces them, like Khan Ali in the case described earlier, to leave their land permanently. Even so, they are unlikely to sell it; commonly they rent it to a neighbor or mortgage it. Once pried off their land, they seek employment elsewhere. Most go to the cities, but some stay closer home, moving to the nearer lowlands to work as tenant farmers for richer landowners. We shall examine this latter strategy first, using the Bamian valley as an example.

Bamian is a basin-shaped valley in Hazarajat at an altitude of about 6,000 feet surrounded by mountain ridges that reach 16,000 feet. The contracts of tenant sharecroppers in Bamian's lowlands suggest that their incomes are less than many peasant cultivators in the highlands, for there is a rough gradation from lowland to highland in the shares paid to tenants and hired workers. In 1968, with the landlord providing the seed, oxen, and other equipment,[10] share-

---

[10]   Most published reports on tenancy contracts indicate that the tenant receives "one-fifth of the crop if he provides nothing but labor. If he also supplies implements, his share is one-fourth, and if he has draft animals, he gets one-third" (Smith, et al. 1969: 250). This apparently is the case in some major agricultural regions, but even there, the arrangements are probably more flexible.

croppers working in the most valuable lowlands received one-seventh or one-sixth of the crop; those who worked somewhat away from the central plain received one-fifth, those further out and higher up on the slopes of the mountain one-fourth, others somewhat higher one-third, and those in the highest glens of the basin one-half.

The one-half contracts were different in that the worker provided his own oxen and equipment. Also, other considerations besides geographic location affected the arrangements, such as the amount of land worked by the hired hand, the kind of crop, whether other provisions are made for him (such as a strip of land whose yield is entirely his), and the like. Still, the gradation suggests the relative severity of the sharecropping contracts in different places: the lower the lands, the less the share of the tenant.

These data suggest that the peasants who still viably subsist in the highlands are better off than those who have left and acquired work as sharecroppers elsewhere. The matter needs additional research, but however accurate for lowland sharecroppers, the argument seems incontestably true for migrants who have moved to the cities.

They have come because there were more jobs than in their natal valleys, but recently they have been finding that there is a surfeit of workers like themselves to fill those jobs. The vast majority of them are impoverished. This, except for the boom years of the fifties and sixties, has been the common pattern: most Hazaras coming to the cities have been miserably poor. In general, the poverty of the Hazaras has been most severe, not in the distant highlands, but in the cities. The poorest Hazara landowners are found in the highest lands, but the poorest Hazara workers are found in the urban centers.

In competition for work in the cities, they contract to work for relatively little. That the competiton of these migrant laborers for work reduces their wages is indicated by the fluctuation of wages in the cities according to their seasonal influx from the central highlands. Daily wages in Baghlan fall from 30 afghanis in summer to 20 in winter; in Mazar-i-Sharif from 50 afghanis in summer to 25-30 in winter; in Bost from 25 afghanis in summer to 18 in winter (Smith et al. 1969: 303). At these rates, assuming 300 paid days per year (which for most is much too high), a year-round day-laborer would annually receive around 8,000 afghanis (about ($110) in Baghlan, 12,000 afghanis (about $165) in Mazar-i-Sharif, and 6,000 afghanis (about $80) in Bost.

Formerly, when they migrated to the cities, people used to find good jobs. During the fifties and early sixties, when the cities were prospering from massive injections of foreign aid, many Hazara peasants in quest of opportunity rented out their lands to neighbors and moved to the cities. Thus, an important factor in the large Hazara out-migration during that period was the "pull" of outside economic opportunity. More recently, however, fewer of them have been willing to leave; as already noted, those who do so are compelled by straitened circumstances. So, in more recent years it has been due to the "push" of economic difficulties at home. Jung (1970: 11) argues from census data on migrants to Kabul from all regions that "push" factors predominate:

When asked the reason for their migration to the city, 20 percent stated insufficient land; 23 percent meager income; 8 percent unemployment; and 12 percent insufficient employment.

The efflux from the Hazarajat has been accelerating. When Khan Ali left his land and journeyed to Kabul he was not alone. The bus was jammed with dozens of other men like himself, some of them so poor that upon arrival they lacked even the half afghani (half cent) necessary to ride a city bus across town to reach a relative's home. On the basis of Russian estimates and the Greater Kabul Census, Jung (1970) estimates that from 1954 to 1961 an average of 7,600 people per year immigrated to Kabul from all provinces, with the number rising abruptly since then — to 12,000 in 1962, for example, and to nearly 20,000 in 1965. Of these, 31 percent came from the central provinces. By 1969 about 40,000 persons had recently emigrated from the central provinces. Of these 48 percent had been in Kabul for more than five years, 36 percent for one to four years, and 12 percent for less than one year — that is, almost half had been in Kabul for less than five years (Jung 1970: 7). One Hazara clan lived until about fifteen years ago entirely in the central highlands, but today 70 (i.e. 60 percent) of its 114 households live in Kabul.

Most of the Hazara migrants are permanently residing in Kabul, but many of them work only as day laborers and are often without employment. A recent phenomenon in Kabul has been the groups of unemployed Hazara men in the early mornings at central locations where people needing laborers may find them. These are Kabul's poor. In 1968 their services were available at 30 to 50 afghanis per day; few worked every day.

The pull of the cities was strong when the national economy was flourishing but since 1967 it has been faltering, bringing down even further the fortunes of the poor. The main reason for the decline of the national economy, of course, has been the reduction of foreign aid. From 1960 to 1967 annual amounts of foreign aid to the country approached 100,000,000 dollars, but since 1967, despite increased aid from the People's Republic of China, this figure has dropped sharply — to 69,050,000 in 1967–68, to 50,200,000 in 1968–69, and to 44,210,000 in 1969–70 (Newell 1972: 144). The drop in foreign aid has especially affected the Hazaras who were favored by the foreign populations as domestic help. Hundreds of these are now without jobs. Moreover, inflation has continued; the price of wheat per *ser* (a common measure of the economy) rose from 20-25 afghanis in 1960 to 60 afghanis in 1968.

Since 1967 a natural calamity has greatly intensified the suffering. The snow on which Afghan agriculture depends for irrigation water in summer was for three successive years unseasonably light, resulting in one of the severest famines in Afghan history. In the summer of 1972, though a heavier snowfall augured for a better crop, the famine was so severe that in the north riots broke out as farmers demanded food for their families. According to the *New York Times*, November 14, 1972, estimates of the number of deaths reached 80,000.[11]

Meanwhile, uncounted numbers have fled the famine areas to the cities, forming new shanty districts. An informal survey of these people in Kabul revealed that perhaps as many as one-third of their families had perished that year (personal communication). The famine crisis is of course a major calamity, hopefully only temporary, but it is merely an intensified form of hardship already familiar to the poor. For many, economic hardship is today an endemic condition.

The trajectory of the highland peasant, if he is not rich, seems to be downhill. Now the whole economy sags and his prospects seem even worse. Perhaps this is the reason for the concomitant rise in religious fervor in Afghanistan. Even after twenty years of Western secular influence, in Afghanistan the ancient bond between hardship and religion remains vigorous.

CONCLUSION

For the physically afflicted and poor, suffering and hardship belong to the world of real things. Suffering is a material condition with

---

[11]   Some observers feared that during the winter of 1973 as many as 200,000 would die (*U.S. News and World Report*, November 6, 1972). According to personal sources, this figure was much too high. (See also Afghanistan Council 1973.)

which the infirm and the hungry must deal. They must deal with it as they must cope with aridity or heavy snowfalls, government officers or local landlords, the price of wheat or the cost of hired labor. Like each of these circumstances, suffering raises issues — i.e. poses problems and perhaps offers opportunities — which must be coped with or exploited as part of the on-going process of maintaining survival and a degree of comfort and security.

Thus, for the afflicted and poor, religion is not simply a matter of beliefs, customs, and rituals, but it is also essentially one of material efficacy. The services of religious specialists are valued not just because the common people are socialized to value them, as mere cherished traditions of their ancestors, but primarily because their problems constrain them to demand these services. Amid their dilemmas they are willing to pay dearly to obtain a measure of relief — perhaps even deliverance — through the services of their religious leaders. Their sufferings convert their desire for a meaningful existence — a universal concern — into a social force, the pursuit of immediate and substantive efficacy. The need for power to exert influence on social and material exigencies is the mainspring of religious practice and one of the bases for the influence and wealth of Afghan religious leadership. This is what brought an aging man and his dying only son, at the price of their last farthing, to the door of a notable shrine. For the shrine was reputed to have efficacious power, power as specific to the infirmity as streptomycin.

The shrine's failure to deliver shattered an old man's world. Unfortunately I know nothing of what became of him, for he was soon gone — chased away by onlookers who were embarrassed that a foreigner had discovered his plight. One can only imagine how he might have picked up the pieces of his life. But to do this one would need to examine the cultural heritage that both "explained" to him his suffering and offered him a fresh hope, and that will have to be another study.

REFERENCES

AFGHANISTAN COUNCIL OF THE ASIA SOCIETY
  1973   *Newsletter,* January 1973. New York.
ALLEN, P. H.
  1963   "Report on Hacarajat trip." Mimeograph. Kabul, Afghanistan: Agency for International Development.

BARCLAY, A.
1969   Developing ophthalmic treatment in Afghanistan. *Transactions of the Ophthalmological Society,* United Kingdom 89:591–600.

BELL, M. J.
1948   *An American engineer in Afghanistan.* Minneapolis: The University of Minnesota Press.

BELSHAW, C.
1967   *Under the ivy tree.* Berkeley: University of California Press.

BERKE, Z.
1946   Public health and hygiene in Afghanistan. *Afghanistan* 1:1–18.

BURNES, A.
1842   *Cabool: a personal narrative of a journey to, and residence in that city in the years 1836, 1837, and 1838.* London: John Murray.

CANFIELD, R. L.
1973   *Faction and conversion: religious alignments in the Hindu Kush.* Anthropological Papers of the Museum of Anthropology 50. Ann Arbor: University of Michigan Press.

DUPREE, L.
1971a   *A note on Afghanistan: 1971.* American Universities Field Staff Reports, South Asia Series 15(2). Hanover, New Hampshire.
1971b   *Comparative profiles of recent parliaments in Afghanistan.* American Universities Field Staff Reports, South Asia Series 15(4). Hanover, New Hampshire.

FERDINAND, K.
1962   Nomadic expansion and commerce in central Afghanistan: a sketch of some modern trends. *Folk* 4:123–159.

FERNEA, E.
1970   *A view of the Nile: story of an American family in Egypt.* Garden City: Doubleday.

GEERTZ, C.
1965   "Religion as a cultural system," in *Anthropological approaches to the study of religion.* Edited by Michael Banton. London: Tavistock.

GERTH, H. H., C. R. MILLS
1958   *From Max Weber: essays in sociology.* New York: Oxford University Press.

GRIFFITHS, M.
1967   *Afghanistan.* London: Praeger.

HUMLUM, J.
1959   *La géographie de l'Afghanistan.* Copenhagen: Gyldendal.

JUNG, C. L.
1970   *Some observations on the patterns and processes of rural-urban migrations in Kabul.* The Afghanistan Council of the Asia Society, Occasional Paper 2. New York.

MEDICAL ASSISTANCE PROGRAM
1967   *Annual Report.* Kabul: Ministry of Health of the Royal Government of Afghanistan.

1969   *Annual Report.* Kabul: Ministry of Health of the Royal Government of Afghanistan.

NEWELL, R. S.
1972   *The politics of Afghanistan.* Ithaca: Cornell University Press.

SAMIN, A. Q., G. A. NIELSEN
1967   *Conversion factors for agriculturalists of Afghanistan.* Faculty of Agriculture Research Note 2. Kabul, Afghanistan: University of Kabul.

SERY, V., O. THRAENHART, K. ZACCK, S. BROGGER, A. OMAR, A. SABOR
1970   Basis for poliomyelitis surveillance in Kabul city. *Zentralblatt fuer Bakteriologie, Parasitenkunde, Infektionskrankheiten und Hygiene. Abteilung originale medizinisch-hygienische Bakteriologie, Virusforschung und Parasitenkunde* 221:311–318.

SIMMONS, J. S.
1954   *Global epidemiology, a geography of disease and sanitation,* volume three. Philadelphia: Lippincott.

SMITH, H. H., D. W. BERNIER, F. M. BUNGE, F. C. TINTZ, R. SHINN, S. TELEKI
1969   *Area handbook for Afghanistan.* Washington: U. S. Government Printing Office.

SPIRO, M. E.
1967   *Burmese supernaturalism: a study in the explanation and reduction of suffering.* Englewood Cliffs: Prentice-Hall.

TURNER, V. W.
1968   *The drums of affliction: a study of religious processes among the Ndembu of Zambia.* Oxford: Clarendon.

WOLF, E.
1966   *Peasants.* Englewood Cliffs: Prentice-Hall.

Understanding Ritual Process in the Medical Setting

JAY B. CRAIN

A few years ago I had the opportunity of spending a year as an anthropological fellow in the Department of Psychiatry at a large western university. While there I visited many of the medical facilities in the area. One of these visits was to a Veterans Administration Hospital, which operates as a "Dean's Committee" hospital in conjunction with the School of Medicine.

This is a general hospital, with 320 beds about equally divided between the Medical, Surgical, and Psychiatric and Neurological Services. The psychiatric section consists of two twenty-bed locked wards that occupy opposing wings of one floor and function as admission wards. An open forty-bed ward on another floor serves as a convalescing ward, where patients from the admission wards are transferred prior to their discharge.

During my one-day visit to the hospital, I talked informally with various members of the permanent staff and with the psychiatric residents from the university who are assigned to the service for six-month periods. At lunch, one of the nurses casually remarked that there was a "strange" discrepancy between the patients in the two admission wards. Each of these wards had been described by the senior staff as operating as a "therapeutic community," following the orders of the Chief of the Service, who was interested in applying the models of Maxwell Jones (1953) and Harry Wilmer (1958).

The nurse explained that — while the patients were supposed to be assigned to one of the two admission wards on a random basis — the

An early version of this paper was read before a faculty seminar in the School of Medicine, University of California, Davis. I would like to thank Dr. Donald G. Langsley and Dr. Thomas Rhys Williams for helpful suggestions.

"sicker" patients always seemed to end up in the ward on the west end of the building, while the "less schizophrenic" went to the ward on the east. When I asked her to explain this, she said she really didn't understand it, but speculated that the residents, who did the admission interviews, consciously, or even unconsciously, sent the more "acute" patients to the West ward.

Later in the same day, I asked the residents general questions about the admission wards. They too indicated there were significant differences between the patients on East and West. Patients on West were said to be more "regressive" and to exhibit more "acute schizophrenic reactions." The residents were aware of speculation about discrepancies in admission; they denied this could occur, since admissions were done according to a rotation of residents and on the availability of beds. They and various of the other staff offered a general explanation of unknown, but suspected, differences in the regulations and "therapeutic value" between the wards.

Before leaving, I talked with the Chief of the Service about the puzzle with which I had been confronted. He was aware of the speculations and observations I had encountered, but viewed these from his administrative perspective in terms of staff dissension, particularly the residents' well-known dislike of the Veterans Administration hospital system.

He stated that the only unit which operated as a true "therapeutic community" was the forty-bed open ward on the floor below. He was the supervisor for this unit. The two locked wards were only approximations of therapeutic communities, since more "structure" was required to treat the relatively more acutely ill patients that were admitted to these units. He went on to explain that originally the three wards had operated as a three-stage affair, with only the patients with the severest disorders being admitted to the West ward. As these patients became more "integrated" (well), they were transferred to the East ward, and finally to the forty-bed open ward before being discharged.

The change to a two-stage process, with two admission wards, had been completed several years before and he speculated that some of the staff had not yet quite accepted the equivalence of the two wards. He nonetheless assured me that each ward operated formally under the same set of regulations and procedures. If any differences between the patients on the two wards did exist, he felt these were probably reflections of the personalities of the head nurses or individual residents.

I returned to the hospital the next day, determined to make more sense out of the confusing picture that had emerged. This time I wandered wider afield and talked with other hospital personnel. I also spent several hours visiting each of the two wards. By the end of this second day, I had the following picture: (1) not only the psychiatric staff, but individuals throughout the hospital had certain notions that the West ward was somehow a place where "bad" or "sicker" patients were to be found, (2) the assignment of patients to one of the two wards did appear to be on a random basis, (3) the daily operation of the two wards — at least to an outsider — did appear to be quite similar, (4) architecturally the two wards were like mirror-images of each other, with only minor differences, and (5) the picture of the West ward that emerged from comparing the comments I heard was rather inconsistent. One individual would characterize the patients as more acute or schizophrenic, while another described them as more character disorders and sociopathic types — nosological categories at opposing poles in normal psychiatric classifications. There was wide disagreement as to which ward was more structured and which was more therapeutic. The only agreement was on the essential difference between East and West.

My interest was aroused by the ambiguous and obscure nature of many of the statements I had heard. I sensed that these were essentially putative contrasts between ideological structures, not evaluations of rational medical differences. These were not facts, but beliefs. My reading at this time had been increasingly concerned with comprehending the meaning and social significance of ritual and ritual symbolism. I was convinced that the analysis of ritual behavior offered many insights into the understanding of social structure and social processes.

Previously, Erving Goffman (1961a, 1961b, 1963) as well as others (notably Crain 1967) had provided sociological approaches to the description and analysis of social processes in psychiatric settings. I decided to try and apply the body of knowledge gained from the anthropological study of tribal ritual to the understanding of the contrasting ideological structures I suspected underlay the puzzling differences between the East and West wards.

The concept of ritual employed by anthropologists differs from related meanings and usages found in behavioral biology and psychiatry. In a paper presented at a London conference on ritualization in man and animals (Huxley 1966), Edmund Leach stressed that anthropologists are concerned with forms of behavior that are not genetically determined. He classified these behaviors into three main types:

(1) Behavior which is directed towards specific ends and which, judged by our standards of verification, produces observable results in a strictly mechanical way... what may be called "rational technical behavior."
(2) Behavior which forms part of a signalling system and which serves to communicate information, not because of any mechanical link between means

and ends, but because of the existence of a culturally defined communication code... what may be called "communicative behavior."
(3) Behavior which is potent in itself in terms of the cultural conventions of the actors, but not potent in a rational-technical sense... what may be called "magical behavior" (Leach 1966: 403ff.).

Leach proposes to group behaviors of class (2) and (3) together as "ritual," rather than restrict the term, as many anthropologists have, to behavior of a magical or occult nature. In so doing, he focuses attention on the significant functions of the ritual of storing and transmitting information.

This approach is useful. It attempts to bridge an awkward conceptual gap between anthropological studies of ritual in human societies and the recent advances in the description of ritualization in animals by ethologists, since the concept of ritualization as used in the study of signal movements in lower vertebrates refers primarily to the evolutionary changes such movements have undergone in adaptation to their functions in communication (cf. Hinde 1966: 285ff.).

Classing communicative and potent behaviors together as ritual broadens the concept, allowing us to focus attention on the complex interaction between behavior and belief embodied and expressed in human ritual performances. The psychiatric concept of ritual as psychomotor activity sustained by an individual to relieve anxiety differs from ritual as used here primarily in terms of its private, compulsive nature, as opposed to the public, dramatic behaviors that characterize tribal ritual.

While Leach's view implies that ritual does not specify a type of behavior, but rather aspects of almost all behavior, it is relevant to examine those cultural contexts which are most dramatically concerned with the expression of ritual symbols. It is in this regard that the ideas of Victor Turner (1962, 1967, 1968b, 1969a, 1969b) are highly significant.

In Turner's approach to the analysis of ritual symbols, society is viewed as a set of concepts rather than an aggregate of people. The focus of study is on the symbolic representations (*denotata*) of concepts (*significata*) and the way these are interrelated and expressed. The dynamics of this interrelationship constitute the ritual process.

In the ritual process we get a glimpse at the deepest level of human values. As Monica Wilson phrased it:

... men express in ritual what moves them most, and since the form of expression is conventionalized and obligatory, it is the values of the group that are revealed (Wilson 1954: 241).

The symbols and their relations found in moments of ritual are not, however, merely a set of cognitive classifications for ordering social experience; they are, as importantly, a set of evocative devices for arousing and channeling powerful emotions. Ritual is more than the iteration of traditional truth — it is equally a dynamic aspect of social experience.

What are the characteristics of these ritual symbols and what is to be derived from their analysis? Ritual symbols, from what we know from Turner's seminal studies, appear to exhibit three properties (Turner 1961, 1962, 1966, 1967, 1968a, 1968b, 1969a, 1969b):

1. Condensation — ritual symbols are polysemic, representing many different properties or things.

2. Unification of disparate *significata* — various concepts are interconnected by virtue of their common possession of analogous qualities or by association in fact or belief.

3. Polarization of meaning — ritual symbols appear to possess two clearly distinguishable poles of meaning. At one pole, what Turner calls the ideological or normative pole, cluster concepts (*significata*) that refer to the moral and social orders of society, to principles of social organization and to the values inherent in social relationships. At the opposite pole, what Turner calls the physiological, or *oretic* pole, cluster concepts that refer to natural or physiological phenomena or processes.

Ritual symbols are thus capable of conserving and expressing meaning in very special ways. The same set of symbols may be displayed repeatedly in varying contexts, giving the system a high redundancy feature. The properties of condensation, unification, and polarization make any particular symbol or assemblage a sublime instrument for expressing order in a social system which is full of ideological conflict or undergoing cyclical change.

The polysemic qualities of ritual symbols (what Turner calls "multivocal") provide the capability of simultaneously expressing conflicting axioms of social conduct or natural order. Thus, the ritual process may serve to mask conflict between social, moral, economic, technical, or political principles.

Why this redundant, simplistic coadunation of things reason would suppose to be distinct or incompatible? Turner rejects the Freudian notion of neurotic fantasy and suggests that it is an attempt to use the "... esoteric language of ritual to say something significant about the nature and meaning of man" (1968b: 22).

This is plausible when we consider the patterning of ritual activity in human societies. Ritual crops up consistently at those moments of repetitive crisis in human affairs: at birth, death, the onset or ending of disease. More generally, ritual rites of transitions — in individuals, groups, in the relationships between individuals or groups, and in the cyclical fluctuations in the relations between man and nature.

Rituals not only play an important part in the religious processes of human societies, but are found in those secular contexts whose social processes deal with altering social and moral relationships.

A remarkable feature of rites of transition is the fundamental processual similarity they exhibit wherever they are found. This basic ritual sequence was first pointed out by Arnold Van Gennep (1909). Van Gennep was attracted by the formal similarities between the kinds of rites that were performed as people moved across borders or entered the thresholds of houses or temples, and those performed at the so-called "life crises" — birth, initiation, marriage, and death.

He demonstrated a common order or sequencing of these behaviors in various parts of the world. First there is a separation, a removal from the normal state of things of the previous order. This is followed by a liminal or in-between state, where the individual is not what he was before, but not what he will become. The third stage involves the assumption of, or installation into, a new status/condition or a return to a normal state/condition.

During the ritual sequence, particularly during the middle or liminal phase, the individual is comparatively removed or separated from the totality of his normal social personality. His structural attributes as a person (in the sense of Nadel 1951: 92ff.) become reduced or simplified. In medical rites, for example, the individual finds that upon becoming a patient, he is only expected to follow the "doctor's orders." His rights and duties as father, husband, employee, friend, and so on, are put aside, held in abeyance. As attention to structural components of the individual diminish, there is an increase in the symbolic component. Normal events are given new or abnormal significance, contradictory meanings. Quite simple events, statements, conditions, or artifacts become vehicles for polysemic symbols. The patient (initiand, neophyte), in the context in which he is "processed," becomes a template upon which to inscribe ultimate realities which reason cannot fully comprehend nor control.

The patient, who normally experiences "being" in this or that body is confronted with the idea of "having" this or that body; instead of "being" this or that personality, he must examine "having" this or that personality. This new perspective of body and self is accompanied by radical altering of his normal (and "natural") perspectives of which parts of physical and psycho-social self he controls and "understands" and which he does not.

Those culturally significant secular transitions that are marked by elaborate ritual performance in tribal societies are in American society largely in the province of medicine. In our medical system, the context in which patient and physician interact is invariably concerned with processes of transition. Birth, death, the physical trauma and social stigmata of injury, the emotional disturbances of public or private crises, the biological and cultural landmarks of maturation and degeneration — indeed most of those *significata* that symbolically epitomize the meaning and experience of the human condition — fall today within the technical, social, and legal domain of medicine.

The behavioral settings where medicine is practiced involve more than the interaction of medical technique and dysfunctional processes; the clinical context contains sequestered settings for cultural drama laden with ritual symbolism.

The evocative, potent nature of the *significata* and the symbols which mask their opposition, together with the transformation of the client as patient to a state of ritual humility, all serve to make intelligible to the observer the extremely high status and stability of the medical profession.

For the patient, then, entry into the hospital is part of a complicated ritual passage, overseen by a body of technical specialists who are also ritual functionaries. Much of what happens to the patient, together with its explanation, is only fully intelligible when we understand the nature of the communications embodied and expressed in symbols in these contexts of ritual performance.

Such I think is the proper approach to the riddle of the discrepancy between the East and West wards at the Veterans Administration Hospital. The patients and other transitional *personae* entering these two units are exposed to subtly different orchestrations of ritual symbols, whose interaction or *gestalt* yield quite different experiences of what is lumped under the rubric of psychiatric therapy.

Some of these symbols and their oppositions have to do with differences perceived in nature, others are expressions of cultural traditions, while still others embody the internal opposition of natural and cultural — recalling the sensory-ideological polarization Turner has shown to be so characteristic of these polysemic phenomena (1969a: 23f).

I began my study, as had Van Gennep, by an examination of the symbolic characteristics of the doorways and halls — the thresholds through which the patient entered the physical confines of these differing ritual contexts. It is only this aspect of my research that I will describe in this paper.

The hospital building is oriented on an east-west axis, the wings parallel to this line extending from a central core containing administrative offices, elevators, and service areas. An individual entering the floor proceeds from the elevator foyer in the central core through a door with a large glass window and enters an attenuated hallway which terminates at each end in a locked door. These doors mark the outer boundaries of the East and West wards.

A patient entering the East ward will turn left down this hallway and will pass by the open doors of a large office used by the Psychology Service and a smaller office used by psychology interns. During the early hours of the morning nursing shift, when all but emergency admissions occur, these offices are areas of considerable social activity.

A patient entering the West ward will turn right down this hallway and pass by several closed doors. These open onto conference rooms which are not used at this time of day. The west end of the hallway thus is normally devoid of any signs of social activity during a patient's admission.

An individual about to enter one of these units is faced at the end of the hallway with a large steel door containing a small square window. Opening of the door is accomplished with a large skeleton-type key or, lacking this, by pressing a small button on the door jam to alert the nursing station at the far end of the ward inside.

The time of day is significant here in relation to the directional orientation of the hospital. A patient peering in the window of the door of the East ward sees a poorly illuminated hallway ending in an activity room relatively brilliant with the rising morning sunshine. The view through the glass in the door of the West ward shows an even less illuminated hallway ending in a RELATIVELY DARKER activity room.

The combination of sunlight and the arrangement of offices in the central hallway yields the following perceptual oppositions in the natural and social conditions at the thresholds of East versus West: light into dark into brilliance as opposed to light into dark into darker; greater activity into less activity as opposed to no activity into unknown activity.

The symbolic significance of differing sensory impressions of social activity, proximity to conversation, and relative degrees of illumination are not readily susceptible to analysis. Such observations seem relevant, however, in view of the repeated comments of rotating staff and off-ward personnel about the relative gloominess yet higher level of activity in the West ward.[1]

The physical thresholds themselves present the patient-initiand with quite startling symbolic statements. The East ward door is devoid of

---

[1] These were manifest in such associations as "dreary-wild," "gloomy-manic," "quiet-fast."

markings. On the West ward door there are two large colored signs. The largest sign, on the center of the door, warns that "matches [are] not allowed." The smaller sign proclaims "locked ward — ring for admittance."

Now, in both wards matches are not allowed. In both wards the doors are kept locked and an individual without a key must ring for admittance. These and other regulations are explained to each new patient AFTER he has entered the ward. Any matches in the patient's possession are confiscated AFTER he has entered the ward.

A patient being admitted is ALWAYS escorted to the ward by one of the nursing staff and this individual either has a key or rings the nursing station inside. The patient is not asked prior to entering to surrender his matches nor is he given the opportunity of learning, until later in his stay, the use of the doorbell arrangement.

This conspicuous and redundant statement of policy on the West door contains several significant *denotata*. The ritual characteristics of these are manifest in the inherent oppositions they display. The signs themselves are made of colored fiber board with gold embossed lettering. They are faded, somewhat warped, and show evidence of having been there a long time. They are, in fact, remnants of a labelling system that was used in the hospital before plastic engraved signs were substituted. These were apparently the last remaining old-style signs in the hospital.

The conflict embodied in the signs was revealed in the emotional and divergent nature of the attitudes of various staff in response to questions. Significantly, no one was quite certain how or when the signs got there. Their social and artifactual origins, like ritual symbols elsewhere, were shrouded in myth. Some individuals felt they were put up at the behest of the Chief of the Service, others by that of the Head Nurse, still others by an overzealous employee from the Engineering Department. None of the principals in this drama could say how the signs came into being.

One resident reported the attitude he had taken to the signs was to ignore them. He noticed their age and the substantial difference (cf. Turner 1969a: 13) between them and other signs that appeared throughout the hospital. Since their form of construction was obsolescent, he assumed their message was also. To him, the signs were another indication of the antiquated methods he saw as characteristic of the Veterans Administration system.

Why were the signs still there, or at least why had they not been replaced by the now standard plastic signs as had others in the hospital? The engineering people, who had done the sign work, recalled that a nurse or perhaps a nursing assistant had told them to wait on the signs until it had been decided whether they should remain. This incident was not remembered by anyone connected with the ward. No one claimed responsibility for the signs, nor was anyone certain if they should stay up, or what they were really intended for.

The age of the signs, apparent in their condition and substance, seemed to indicate they were no longer functional. Yet they were there — they had not been removed. As I went about trying to follow up the story from the engineering people, the staff readily accepted the idea that some decision should be pending on the signs — they were obviously important — yet no one knew through whom or how a decision would be made.[2]

Several visitors to the ward were not certain if the restriction against matches applied to them or only to patients. Two nursing students also reported this — they were aware that matches were taken from patients after they entered the ward, not outside the door. The manifest form, content, and location of the signs implied to those who saw them many different things.

Since my space is limited, let me proceed to summarize the threshold portion of my research. The signs on the West door exhibited the following characteristics of ritual symbols: (1) they appear in a context of transition — the physical, social, and legal threshold of a ritual unit; (2) they appear in an area/situation devoid of complex focused social interaction (Goffman 1961a: 7–9) and in a locus of reduced (i.e. dyadic) social structure; (3) they exhibit condensation of various beliefs (*significata*) in the juxtaposition of their condition and their discrepancy with the general institutional labelling system; (4) the unification of seemingly disparate *significata* is evident in the conflicting nature of the message and the location of the signs — they are really meaningful only from the OTHER SIDE of the door (staff keep their matches and know how to gain entry); (5) polarization of meaning is evidenced in the opposition of the denotatives "matches" and "not allowed" — the former evoking the sensory images of fire and perhaps self-immolation, the latter in calling to mind social and legal sanction or constraint; (6) finally, the signs are powerful evocative devices, calling forth considerable emotion in the individuals interacting with or about them.

Of what analytical value is this schematic treatment of threshold symbols? It gives some clues to the nature of the total ritual process that is part of the social drama within the West ward. I was later able to confirm that those ritual symbols displaying the greatest polysemy and emotional

---

[2] Four years after my study, a graduate student of mine visited the hospital and reported that the signs are still in place.

potency were "cigarettes" and "patient privileges." The latter concerned a system of graduated rights and duties, the major aspect of which involved permission to leave the ward for short periods.[3] In the relation of these symbols was repeated the opposition of social constraint/obligation to destruction/self-indulgence. This opposition was related, through symbolic unification, with the opposition of staff-patient and inside-outside which was symbolically condensed in the location of the threshold symbols.

In contrast, the symbols expressed in the ritual process of the East ward were dominated by the polysemic symbol "coffee." In interactional terms, cigarettes, patient privileges, and coffee are present as multivocal devices in the ritual behaviors in both wards. Yet comparatively, the wards differ in the amount of real time spent communicating with and confronting these. The symbols also differ in their potency — the evocative potential for calling forth emotion and sentiment.

At one level the threshold symbols can be seen as portraying a concatenation of basic conflicts in beliefs and principles of organization characteristic of a particular time and place. While the "telic structure" (cf. Nadel 1951: 31; Turner 1968b: 3) of the two wards had for some time been equated by organizational changes, the ritual processes within still conserved an historical difference. At a more general level, the polarization of matches (whose corollary is fire/destruction) and constraint (whose corollary is sacrifice/social order) speaks of a timeless enigma of human society — the paradox of turning the obligatory into the desirable (cf. Turner 1969b: 52–53).

This study takes the view that medical personnel are functionaries in a very significant symbolic system — for the patient, themselves, and ultimately, society. At a time of manifest flux in the relationship between medicine and other structures in our society, the understanding of the ritual components of so-called "health delivery systems" can give us a broader human perspective through which to examine traditions and alternatives.

The ritual, as opposed to the rational-technical, aspects of medicine share many characteristics with other curative and transition creating traditions in our own and other societies. Such entities as Christian Science, Synanon, The Family, and various parapsychological and counter-culture oriented "therapy" phenomena have, as functionaries,

---

[3] The patient privilege system was a three stage process: (1) ward restriction — not allowed off the ward, (2) ward privileges — allowed off the ward in the company of a staff member, and (3) hospital privileges — allowed off the ward in the company of two other patients (held jointly responsible for each other's conduct and safe return).

individuals who have been recruited through experiences, "cures," or other individualistic experience.

Generally the openness of recruitment to a system or group appears to be directly related to its perceived significance in the wider society. Thus, closed groups do not have the potential for expanding their social and symbolic base beyond a certain point. From the perspective of the significance and relevance of the ritual experience that occurs in contexts of medical treatment, a wholistic system of medicine such as our own should strive to recruit its members from as many different kinds of individuals as possible. At the same time, the symbolic base (the ritual relevancy) of medicine can be expanded by encouraging the training of medical personnel in a wider diversity of social and cultural contexts.

Medical ritual, not only for patients, but also for medical practitioners, has potency. Medical contexts come to be places where, as Turner describes liminality:

... anything can happen, where immoderacy is normal, even normative, and where the elements of culture and society are released from their customary configurations and recombined in bizarre and terrifying imagery. Yet this boundlessness is restricted — although never without a sense of hazard — by the knowledge that this is a unique situation and by a definition of the situation which states that the rites and myths must be told in a prescribed order and in a symbolic rather than a literal form. The very symbol that expresses at the same time restrains; through mimesis there is an acting out — rather than the acting — of an impulse that is biologically motivated but socially and morally reprehended (Turner 1968a).

As an anthropologist, I view the psychotherapy treatment systems of psychiatry as healing rites or rites of affliction. As theory or clinical practice, psychiatry deals with a basic enigma of social life — the relationship of private motive to public meaning.[4]

If healing means to "encourage people to discharge the obligations of their status well and not seek escape from them" (Turner 1967: 375), then the more widely idealized a set of symbols that can be translated into ritual common denominators of social experiences, the more efficacious will be the healing.

Coffee, cigarettes, matches, and patient privileges are functional in this way in the subtly differing symbolic systems of the East and West wards. The specific constellation of symbols and their evocative potential for the participants were culturally and historically embedded within a particular

[4] The Psychiatric Anthropology Research Project at California State University, Sacramento, the University of California, Davis, and Sacramento Medical Center has explored this question from a variety of angles (cf. Click 1973; Darrah 1971, Herdt 1972).

treatment context. In their oppositions, however, can be seen the mimesis through the pedagogics of liminality of a condemnation of two kinds of separation from communities: (1) "... to act only in terms of the rights conferred on one by the incumbancy of office," (2) "... to follow one's psychobiological urges at the expense of one's fellows" (Turner 1969b: 105).

In today's world of the community psychiatry movement, the sequestered setting of inpatient ritual seems to many to be parochial and unmomentous. Those forms of communication which are potent in the rituals of normative abnormality of healing temple and private rite have not yet been successfully translated into forms which are appropriate to the profane real world. Those of psychiatry who see the world as their ward and the citizen as their patient, must seek a more grandiose metaphor.

REFERENCES

CLICK, CHRISTOPHER G.
1973 "A social approach to dependency need: a ritual illustration." Unpublished Independent Study Thesis, Waseda University.

CRAIN, JAY B., *compiler*
1967 "The ethnography of the mental hospital: a provisional bibliography." Mimeo.

DARRAH, ALLAN
1971 "Ritual aspects of psychotherapy." Unpublished master of arts thesis, California State University, Sacramento.

GOFFMAN, ERVING
1961a *Encounters: two studies in the sociology of interaction.* Indianapolis: Bobbs-Merrill.
1961b *Asylums: essays on the social situation of mental patients and other inmates.* New York: Doubleday.
1963 *Stigma: notes on the management of spoiled identity.* Englewood Cliffs: Prentice-Hall.

HERDT, GILBERT
1972 "Models of ritual: a study of the symbolism of the psychiatric." Unpublished master of arts thesis, California State University, Sacramento.

HINDE, R. A.
1966 "Ritualization and social communication in Rhesus monkeys," in *Philosophical Transactions of the Royal Society of London*, series B, 251(772):285–294.

HUXLEY, SIR JULIAN, *organizer*
1966 "A discussion on ritualization of behavior in animals and man," in *Philosophical Transactions of the Royal Society of London*, series B, 251(772):247–526.

JONES, MAXWELL
1953   *The therapeutic community.* New York: Basic Books.
LEACH, EDMUND R.
1966   "Ritualization in man in relation to conceptual and social development," in *Philosophical Transactions of the Royal Society of London,* series B, 251(772):403–408.
NADEL, S. F.
1951   *The foundations of social anthropology.* New York: The Free Press of Glencoe.
TURNER, VICTOR W.
1961   *Ndembu divination, its symbolism and techniques.* Rhodes-Livingston Papers, 31. Manchester: Manchester University Press.
1962   *Chihamba the white spirit: a ritual drama of the Ndembu.* Rhodes-Livingston Papers, 33. Manchester: Manchester University Press.
1966   "The syntax of symbolism in an African religion," in *Philosophical Transactions of the Royal Society of London,* series B, 251(772):295–305.
1967   *The forest of symbols.* Ithaca: Cornell University Press.
1968a "Myth and symbol," in *International Encyclopedia of the Social Sciences.* Edited by D. L. Sills. New York: Macmillan and the Free Press.
1968b *The drums of affliction: a study of religious processes among the Ndembu of Zambia.* Oxford: Clarendon Press and the International African Institute.
1969a "Forms of symbolic action: introduction," in *Forms of symbolic action.* Edited by R. F. Spencer. Seattle: University of Washington Press and the American Ethnological Society.
1969b *The ritual process: structure and anti-structure.* Chicago: Aldine.
VAN GENNEP, ARNOLD
1909   *Rites de passage.* Paris: Emile Nourry.
WILMER, HARRY A.
1958   *Social psychiatry in action: a therapeutic community.* Springfield, Illinois: Charles C. Thomas.
WILSON, MONICA
1954   "Nyakyusa ritual and symbolism." *American Anthropologist* 56(2).

Sex, Nature, and Culture in Ponapean Myth

J. L. FISCHER

Probably all cultures express in some form an opposition between nature and culture and an opposition between men and women. It is logically possible, then, to align these two pairs of oppositions, associating one sex with "nature" and the other with "culture." Thus one culture might emphasize the role of women as preservers and builders of the home, which is the seat of culture, and contrast this with the role of men as destroyers in feuding and warring. Another culture might emphasize the role of men in providing the political framework within which culture exists and contrast this with the role of women in drawing men back from the larger society to a concern with satisfying basic animal needs for their families. It is the purpose of this paper to describe briefly the traditional attitudes of the people of Ponape, Caroline Islands (Micronesia) as reflected in their myths and folklore, and to call attention to some methodological implications of the ethnographic data.

The people of Ponape speak a single language with recognizable, mutually intelligible dialects, and think of themselves as sharing a single basic culture, although they were divided into five small independent states at the time of first recorded foreign descriptions. The population was also divided among about twenty exogamous matrilineal clans, which continue to persist to the present day but with somewhat less importance. Most of the clans were found in all five states, their relative rank varying locally.

Ponapeans have no words which directly translate "nature" and "culture" but these are useful labels for the anthropologist to use to subsume a series of more concrete oppositions including "human" (*aramas*) and "beast" (*mahn* — includes fish, insects, birds, etc. as well as mammals);

"cooked" (*leu*) and "raw" (*amas*); "land" (*nan-sapw*) and "sea" (*nan-sed*), "cultivated land" (*nan-sapw*) and "jungle" (*nani-wel*), etc. The first of each of these pairs is, of course, "cultural" and the second is "natural."

People are contrasted with animals in that people live most of the time and ought to live according to social rules, many of which are prescribed or exemplified in myths recounting the behavior of ancestors. People who violate these rules are either said to be crazy or evil or to be acting like animals, or all three. People typically live on land as opposed to sea. Cultivated land as opposed to jungle has largely been cleared and planted with breadfruit trees, coconut palms, bananas, taro, yams, etc. People's houses are in the middle of it, while animals live mainly in the sea or jungle.

Nevertheless the distinction between "nature" and "culture" or "beast" and "human" is blurred at times. Many of the clans have totemic animal ancestors and at times Ponapeans will say that a certain animal species is "not an animal; it is really human." The totemic species are believed to share some human behavior at times even today, and in the totemic myths the ancestral animals are said to have at times performed acts which would require temporary human shape as well as human intent. Thus the freshwater eel, totem of the Great Eel clan (Lasialap), is reported to come out of streams to visit the homes of its human relatives at life crises such as birth and death, and is also said to be able to recognize members of the Great Eel clan and refrain from biting them as they bathe or do laundry in the streams. At the same time the eels are reported to occasionally bite strangers, clan enemies, and even spouses of clan members or children of the men, if the spouses and children are not properly loyal and industrious.

The blurring of the distinction between beast and human shows a certain statistical and logical patterning. If we look at instances of reputed transformation from one category to another in myth it appears that there are cases of animals transforming themselves into humans as babies (e.g. the origin of the Bird Clan from sea slugs who came onto land) and humans transforming themselves into animals as old people (e.g. the first ancestress of the Bird Clan on Ponape, who became an insect in her old age; or the last hereditary ruler of the whole island, who leaped into a stream and became a small brightly colored fish on his defeat in battle) but it appears to me that there are no clear cases of transformations either way involving young to middle-aged adults. This would be consistent with a view that the main bearers and defenders of culture are mature adults, and that the very young and very old both lack full participation in culture, the former not having had time to learn the rules and the latter having lost the physical and mental agility necessary to play a fully cultural role.

If we ask about the sex of animals in myths we also observe a distinct patterning. Where sex of animals is specified the animal is usually, though not always, female. Since the clans are matrilineal the immediate animal forbear of the clan is always female. When male animals appear in the clan myths they are secondary, although human males may be important as actors in the myth along with the animal females.

The principal part of the Great Eel myth, for instance, involves a female eel. Briefly, she was raised by a human couple who planned to eat her when she got big. She ate them instead and then traveled here and there giving birth to the human ancestresses of the various subclans of the clan. She bore her first child after a frightful encounter with a demon eel fisherman, and bore other children after marrying a high chief. Eventually she settled at an estuary and began to eat selected human passersby. A magician lured her out to sea, whereupon she traveled to the island of Kusaie (the easternmost high island of the Carolines) and gave birth to more children there. Finally she swam back to Ponape and beached herself in the state of Net, where she bore her last daughter and expired. Her body now forms a long peninsula.

Nevertheless, preceding the account of the female eel there is another section of the myth which tells about a male eel who was in a sense the father of the female eel. This male eel was also raised by a couple who had a daughter. When the eel grew to maturity it started having a love affair with the daughter, who grew thin because of it. The parents therefore decided to eat the eel. The eel overheard their plans and — unlike the female eel — acquiesced in the plot but told the daughter to request the head for her portion and to bury it and watch what came out of the grave. She did so and two kinds of bananas and one kind of breadfruit sprouted from the grave. The female eel whose career is described above hatched from a small stone or seed in one of the bananas. A bird pecked out the seed and defecated it into the lagoon where the human couple who raised the female eel picked it up.

I have told the two sections of this myth out of chronological order, but this is fairly common on Ponape. The part dealing with the female eel is better known and is more elaborate and more directly relevant to the members of the Great Eel clan. While there are similarities between the two sections of the myth, the differences are interesting. The male who is assigned "beast" status in this myth is engaged too intensely in a premarital romance, while the female who is assigned "beast" status is producing offspring, mostly after marriage.

A review of other Ponapean animal myths tends to bear out the conclusion drawn from the eel myth. Female animals are likely to be engaged in child bearing, while male animals are likely to be involved in premarital or extramarital affairs.

Ponapeans have traditionally placed a high value on children. A woman who produced many children was praised. Abortions were discouraged and infanticide was apparently not practiced, even for defective children, in contrast to some other Oceanic societies. Nevertheless the myths suggest that pregnant and nursing females were somehow identified with animals. I believe this makes sense in view of traditional attitudes and practices concerning food on Ponape.

On the one hand, contributions to feasts were important, and raising food and preparing it for feasts were considered primarily the work of men. The emphasis at feasts was primarily on the display and redistribution of food. Most of the food presented at feasts was taken home by the participants and it was considered bad form for men to eat much, especially in public.

On the other hand, men were also supposed to indulge the appetites of their pregnant and nursing wives in order to produce healthy babies and provide abundant milk for them. A man busy satisfying the food whims of his fertile wife would have less time for feast work, which was traditionally the most important kind of service a man could offer his chief: the "great service" (*tou-lap*) as opposed to the "lesser service" (*tou-tik*), which was bravery in war. It seems safe to say that men also had special appetites for foods at times which they did not satisfy because of the cultural restrictions on male gluttony. From the male view, the pregnant and nursing women would appear to be excused from cultural restrictions on eating as well as from the cultural prescription to produce and prepare food in order to indulge their animal appetites.

On the other hand in the case of premarital and extramarital affairs Ponapeans tend to ascribe the initiative to the men, at least in the sense that the men are thought to be generally ready for sex, while it is the role of the women to resist if it is inappropriate for whatever reason. Ponapeans were traditionally fairly tolerant of premarital sex, but parents had definite ideas of who was and was not a suitable potential spouse for their child; infant engagements were sometimes made. Probably parents of daughters frequently disapproved of particular suitors, as they still do today at times. A Ponapean saying, "Men are demons (*eni*) but women make them human," is applied to illicit sexual affairs of various sorts. In this context it is the women who are supposed to uphold the human cultural rules, while men are ready to violate them with the slightest encouragement. Incidentally, there are grounds for regarding demons (*eni*) as halfway between humans and beasts in Ponapean mythology.

In conclusion, it is possible to make alignments between nature and culture, male and female in Ponapean mythology but the alignments differ according to social context and the stage of the life cycle involved. There is the suggestion that infants are somewhat identified with animals regardless of sex and that a similar identification is made for feeble old people. With adults, males are considered more animal-like in the context of pre- and extramarital affairs, while women are considered more animal-like in the context of pregnancy and nursing. Most myths involve only one set of these identifications or associations. Attention to a reasonably large sample of myths is required to develop the complexity of Ponapean traditional thought and attitudes.

PART FIVE

Mental Configurations: An Approach to Guatemalan Culture Change

ALFREDO MÉNDEZ DOMÍNGUEZ and GORDON DARROW

"Ladinoization," urbanization, and modernity have been used as para-meters to measure culture change in the Meso-American area. They all center upon the notion of degrees of similarity of the Indian cultures to an alien pattern and upon outside system influences. Seldom has change been seen as a restructuring process: a process resulting from the possi-bilities of combining elements in culture and mind, whether or not provoked by outside influences, and leading, in any case, toward a non-preconceived pattern.

The frequent empirical conjunction of ethnic mobility, urbanization, and modernity, as described by Redfield (1941), makes the distinction of the three approaches in Guatemala frequently possible only at the theoretical level. The distinction is kept for purposes of pointing out some important issues.

Ladinoization has focused primarily on culture change, less on social variables, and only incidentally on cognitive and attitudinal features. The adoption of material traits, such as dress, has played an important part in the conception of change. The learning of new abilities, such as knowledge of Spanish, is treated also as trait adoption. But while re-nouncing a systemic view and grounding itself ultimately on individual adoption, the ladinoization approach has barely touched upon processes occurring within the individual and the resulting mental configurations.

A similar situation prevails in the social aspects. Thus, the absence of the civic-religious hierarchy is said to signify a high degree of ladinoiza-tion; but only in few cases, and in restricted subjects, is something about the emerging system known. Moreover, it cannot be assumed that its absence implies the emergence of a Ladino society, no more than the adoption of dress or language assures a Ladino way of thinking. Even assuming that much, we have little knowledge of this new system because only one Ladino community has been studied (Méndez Domínguez 1967), and the author has no claim as to the generality of his findings.

The controversies on the universality of Redfield's (1941) findings in Yucatán seem to have dwarfed research in Guatemala on the process and significance of urbanization, leaving our knowledge barely above that of the 1940's. This is an unfortunate circumstance since laboratory conditions are provided by an explosive growth of urban influences and by urban development of many localities.

From Tax's (1959) commentaries on Redfield's work, it can be concluded that certain economic attitudes and practices could not be attributed to modern city living, influence, or imitation. This seems to have been interpreted as a negation of differences between town and city rather than as a challenge to find the actual correlates of urbanization in particular Guatemalan continua.

Insofar as it is known, no serious effort has been made to describe change in Guatemala from a modernity approach. However, a survey of over a thousand interviews in five towns, Indian and Ladino (Méndez Domínguez and Waisannen 1966), provided some of the leads for this study. The propaganda that tinges many works in modernity and modernization deserves no commentary here. The approach, however, furnishes an invaluable methodological contribution: to attempt to describe change from the mental perspective. Only in this sense could this study be said to be one of modernity because it also differs from most of them in its emphasis on cognition rather than on attitudes.

This is a preliminary report based on one of an ongoing sequence of studies attempting to describe the cognitive structure of Guatemalan Indians as they appear at different levels of ladinoization and urbanization. These studies have a triple purpose: first, to reach a deeper and more significant level of change than the simple adoption of material and quasi-material traits; second, to arrive at a sequence or order of change which may serve as a base to draw inferences about mental processes; and third, to discover relations between different social systems and mental configuration types.

This presentation deals only with aspects of the first objective. Specifically, this is a preliminary description of some aspects of the mental configurations as they relate to levels of urbanization and urban influences.

The Theoretical Approach

The frequent preoccupation with mental configurations and processes in the social sciences makes a review of even the major contributions inappropiate in this presentation. Thus, when references are made, they have no other purpose than to clarify particular issues of the present approach. The only claim of novelty concerns the choice of some tactical principles and the application of the resulting model to a particular change process in the Guatemalan region.

The tactical principles used are:

1. The construction of a model conceived only as a first approximation to the mind's operations, to be enriched progressively by theoretical refinements and empirical testing.

2. The postulation of a small number of basic and (conceived as) irreducible processes, which have the potential to account for a large percentage of the mind's content and operations. These processes are those of allocating, comparing, linking, and referring.

3. The basic process should be easy to translate into less abstract derivative forms or to presuppose them without mediation of processes other than those that the model establishes. These derivatives are said to be primary concepts (example: the process of allocating implies or generates the concepts of time and space).

4. The primary derivations should have the potential to be further subjected to other basic processes to generate secondary concepts (example: comparing in space is said to generate, among others, the idea of region and space units and measurements).

5. The primary concepts should have the potential to combine with other primary, secondary, or lower level concepts (example: the conjunction of time and space have the potential to generate certain concepts of velocity). In the same way, ego's reference groups may be said to result from a conjunction of derivatives of the comparing and referring processes.

6. Given that within the model, one could move from very abstract levels to very concrete ones; a choice should be made as to the primary focus of attention. An intermediate level is thought more useful for cross-cultural comparisons. If a high level of concreteness is reached, one ends with comparisons of specific cognitive contents; if too abstract, the possibilities of comparison may be lost in the commonality of the human mind.

7. The level of abstraction should be such as to permit the study of the relation between mental processes and other behaviors.

8. The parameters the researcher uses to characterize the subjects under study should preferably be derived from the same process and model used to depict the subjects' configurations.

Explanations of these principles follow.

The need for parsimony was fully realized and explicitly stated by Kluckhohn while developing a frame for cross-cultural comparison of value emphases as early as 1955. His thirteen axes made possible the construction of cultural profiles. Even this relatively small number would be excessive when the axes are not thought of as independent parameters but have generative properties by their combinations other than the empirical ones in a given profile and when the values in each axis are not of a simple binary nature.

While a large number of axes can thus diminish the usefulness, clarity, and even the complexity of the model, a very limited number also has disadvantages. A risk is taken in this case of increasing the level of abstraction to the point of vagueness or of unduly restricting the area of the mind under study by working at lower levels.

The extreme is reached when mind is equated to a single process. The works of Lévi-Strauss may exemplify this submersion of all processes under one, the operations involved in classification. By this or similar monolithic approaches, one ends up trying to explain the mind by substituting a structure equally large, complex, and undifferentiated as the notion of the mind itself. If what is being attempted is the construction of a model with the power to clarify the nature of mental processes, this procedure is clearly self-defeating. Its application is perhaps better justified in other tactical contexts.

Preliminary thinking leads to the belief that any one of the four processes mentioned under principle two, i.e. allocating, comparing, linking and referring, could be raised to a level of abstraction in which it may constitute the most basic process from which the other three, as well as a more specific meaning of itself, could be conceived as derivations. However, this seems of no practical use. The choice was consequently made of remaining at a lower level of abstraction, with a small number of processes which can be combined within the model to arrive at a large number of derivations.

"Allocating" is understood to be the process of thinking in terms of time and space. Longitude, area, and volume are considered important forms of space, and past and future important features of time. "Comparing" refers to the process of establishing equalities ($=$) and similarities ($\approx$) and their negative forms. These constitute the qualitative forms of comparison. Equality, similarity, and a quantitative dimension of inequality ($>$) and their negative or inverse forms constitute the quantitative forms of comparing. "Linking" refers to connections drawn between two or more elements. These connections could be of the pattern form, "a" with "b," (ab)'; of the action form "a" influences "b," (a→b); of the inclusion form, "a" is in "b," (a)b; and of a developmental form "a" turns into "b," (a...b). "Referring" alludes to the position, departure, point, or focus assumed in a set of relations whose base could be a system of allocation, comparison, or linking or a derivation of them. The three primary persons, "I," "you," and "he" possibly constitute the primary concepts of the process.

The combination of tactical principles four and five above transform the model from a simple scheme that permits a characterization of cells formed by the conjunction of two or more axes in a cartesian form into a model of processes that can generate new axes and new paradigms by itself. Although the possibilities of these principles are not pursued here, they bear directly upon the relevance of the results and will be examined at a later point.

The choice of an intermediate level of abstraction rather than one which focuses on specific content produces different possibilities of cross-cultural comparison. By placing attention upon specific content, one takes the risk of ending up with a multitude of non-comparable descriptions, a kind of "ethnography of the mind." This study places emphasis on processes and on the forms that these processes take. In this regard it differs from many studies in cognitive anthropology which emphasize the content, the parameters, and the structural principles of what are taken to be learned, existing classificatory structures. Rather, it focuses on the processes used by the individual in structuring his world, as well as his preferences among alternative structuring devices within each type of process. There is also an emphasis on change in these forms and preferences. By attending to both mental process and mental change, we expect to arrive at insights into cultural change in Guatemala and mental processes in general.

When external categories are imposed, the question of arbitrariness is likely to be raised; but the final test should be in terms of analytical power. One measurement of the adequacy and completeness of the model should be its capacity not only to give a satisfactory account of the subject's conceptual operations, but to generate the terms the researcher uses to describe these operations as well. Otherwise, one is resorting to a metalanguage consisting of terms existing outside the generative provenance of the model. No satisfactory solution to this problem has yet been developed by the authors although work in this area is in progress. In this study the concepts of extension, abstraction, symmetry, and convertibility are used as descriptive markers to characterize specific modes of use within the basic processes. As the study stands, they constitute a metalanguage, although it is likely that further analysis will reveal extension and abstraction to be derivations of the process of comparison. Symmetry and convertibility may have, in addition, a referential component.

"Extension" refers to the size of a system of allocation and the number of elements put together in a system of comparison and link chains. "Abstraction" refers to the degree of proximity to perceptual data or to material and quasi-material objects. "Symmetry" refers to equivalence or complementation in different axes of the system of allocation, comparison, linkage, and reference. "Convertibility" refers to the possibility of translating values or concepts, without leaving residues, from one system, level of abstraction, direction, or position to another. Some of these concepts have been successfully used by other authors in restricted ways and with different nuances of meaning.

Data on the processes of allocating and comparing are presented in terms of all four of these parameters. Linking is treated only in terms of extension. The data for referring is not as yet analyzed, but a brief discussion of it will be presented later.

Sample Procedures and Techniques

Studies were conducted in six localities during the summers of 1971 and 1972 with the help of members of the staff and students of the Facultad de Ciencia Social of the Universidad del Valle de Guatemala. The communities are: Chipiacul, a hamlet; Santa Catarina Ixtahuacán, Patzún, San Andrés Itzapa, Santiago Chimaltenango, all towns; and Guatemala City. Those listed as towns were chosen because they represent progressive levels of physical proximity to Guatemala City from west to east through the Pan-American Highway and they belong to the same cultural region, the central plateau. Chipiacul, the hamlet, was chosen as representing the lowest level of urbanization. However, a greater city influence was expected in this locality than in Santa Catarina, the most distant community, because of its substantially greater proximity to the city and to the larger town of Patzún, upon which it depends administratively. Patzún itself is the second farthest town from the city in the sample. The Guatemala City subjects are from marginal barrios.

Circumstances in the country and the nature of the study forced a choice of limited non-random samples, nineteen to forty-two individuals in each community. The results cannot be said with certainty, therefore, to be typical of each town's population. Despite this, there are indications that the samples are representative. The peasant character of the communities, excepting Guatemala City, guarantees a high degree of homogeneity with regard to important variables such as level of formal education, economic situation, and occupation within each community.

Comparability between populations was insured by several means. Both ethnic affiliation and sex were experimentally controlled. Only males who claimed to be Indians were interviewed. The application of Cochran's test of homogeneity of variance showed that the sample of the six populations were comparable with regard to age. Since the intellectual sector to which the subject belongs may be important in the answers he gives, care was taken to include members and nonmembers of the intelligentsia. About the same proportion of leaders and nonleaders of agricultural cooperatives and administrative institutions were chosen in each community. An exception to this was Guatemala City, where it was necessary to rely upon a network of acquaintances. In all the communities, including Guatemala City, only Indians born in the locality were included in the sample.

A scheduled interview containing direct questions, pictures, and designs was administered individually. This instrument was enlarged and refined between the 1971 and 1972 field sessions. Consequently, most of the information presented here concerns the three localities studied during 1972: San Andrés, Santiago, and Guatemala City. Information about the other three populations is given in those cases where comparable data exists. The interviews were carried out generally in Spanish, although translators were used occasionally in Santa Catarina Ixtahuacán.

RESULTS

Measurements of Urbanization and Urban Influences

Each community was ranked on the basis of selected characteristics to arrive at a general indication of the levels of urbanization existing within the sample of communities. Distance to the capital, population size, number of resident Ladinos, and the politico-administrative importance of the community entered into this estimation. These variables are thought to account for a variety of diffused but important influences upon the mind of the individual, whose independent weight should eventually be

Table 1.   Measurements of urbanization by locality and size of the samples

| Locality | Measurements of urbanization | | | | |
	Distance to city	Population size	Number of Ladino residents[b]	Politico-administrative importance	Size of samples
Chipiacul	108[a]	470[a]	0	Hamlet of Patzún	19
Sta. Catarina	159	911[b]	11[b] (1.20%)	County seat	25
Patzún	83	6,871[b]	1074[b] (16)	County seat	42
San Andrés	63	5,314[b]	1705[b] (32%)	County seat	28
Santiago	28	4,596[b]	332[b] (7%)	County seat	19
City	—	Above one million	—	Capital of the country	30

[a]   Dirección General de Cartografía (1962).
[b]   Dirección General de Estadística (1971).

determined. Their distribution is shown by community in Table 1, along with the size of each community's sample. As can be seen, no clear sequence emerges when all the variables are taken together, but the best fit seems indicated by the order in which the communities appear in this table. Population actually decreases in the sequence from Patzún to Santiago, but this is compensated for by increasingly closer proximity to the capital and, in the case of Santiago, by its proximity to important tourist stops and regional markets which attract substantial numbers from the city. The low number of Ladino residents in Santiago is therefore felt to be compensated for as well.

Specific urban influences were also assessed. It was found that the number of visits paid to the city varied in the towns studied in 1972 in accordance with the rank-order of urbanization shown in Table 1. See Table 2.

Table 2.   Percentage distribution of frequency of visits to the city by locality

Locality	Never	Twice a year or less	More than twice a year
San Andrés	32	50	18
Santiago	26	21	53

A similar pattern occurs with regard to exposure to selected forms of mass communication. Table 3 shows a progressive increase in the number of hours of daily radio listening from hamlet to city, except for Santa Catarina which does not follow the general pattern.

Exposure to written mass media, i.e. reading of newspapers and magazines, shows lower levels in Chipiacul (52 percent), somewhat higher in Santa Catarina (64 percent), and a little more in Patzún and Santiago (68 percent). The city does not differ considerably. However, San Andrés

Table 3.   Percentage distribution of number of daily hours of radio listening by place of residence

	Number of hours		
Locality	0	1–4	5 and more
Chipiacul	47	53	0
Santa Catarina	32	44	24
Patzún	43	52	5
San Andrés[a]	40	39	14
Santiago	10	69	21
City	0	50	50

[a]   No information is available for 7 percent of this town.

falls out of the pattern of progressive increase by showing a low level (39 percent).

It is concluded, then, that in general the individuals in each sample are exposed to greater local urbanization and urban influences in accordance with the order shown in Table 1.

Measurements of Ladinoization

Language is usually held to be of importance in the ladinoization process. We depend exclusively upon it, because of its close relation to thinking and because it can be measured more objectively than other general indicators such as "way of living." Informants were asked whether they speak a Mayan language or Spanish at home and to read or repeat one sentence in Spanish. The interviewer registered the degree of accent based on vowel pronunciation on a three-position scale: "no accent," "slight accent", "heavy accent." In Chipiacul, Santa Catarina, and Patzún no one spoke Spanish at home, and only a small number spoke it in San Andrés (5 percent) and Santiago (7 percent). In the city this figure increases to 57 percent. The population also differs by "accent," showing a progressive increase of individuals with no accent in Spanish in the communities studied in 1972: San Andrés (7 percent), Santiago (26 percent) and Guatemala City (33 percent).

From these results it can be seen that ladinoization and urbanization are positively related to each other, but this relation is not sufficiently close to warrant the submersion of both into a single process. The small size of the total sample makes it unrewarding as yet to use a statistical procedure to weigh the relative influence upon mental configuration of ladinoization as opposed to urbanization. In view of these limitations, the results are presented exclusively in terms of urbanization. Although it is felt that such variables as amount of formal education, income, and occupation represent concomitant indicators both of ladinoization and urbanization, they are not statistically related here to mental configurations. Those interested in this aspect are referred to the Appendix, where a summary distribution of some of these variables are shown for the three communities studied in 1972.

The Process of Allocating

In the following sections, informants' conceptions of space and time are analyzed respectively in terms of the parameters extension, symmetry, abstraction, and convertibility. Unless otherwise indicated, the data presented are taken from the three locations sampled in 1972: San Andrés, Santiago, and Guatemala City.

CONCEPTS OF SPACE

Extension   Casual observations in 1962 regarding ideas about the size of the stars suggested the existence of differences in the conception of the size of the universe between individuals at different levels of ladinoization. Later research (Méndez and Waisannen 1966) conducted with over a thousand subjects in five communities rendered a positive and significant correlation between literacy and ideas concerning size of the stars. Following these leads, the subjects were asked about the distance to and dimensions of some familiar items in the universe.

Table 4.   Percentage distribution of estimates of distance to the sky by locality

Locality	Distance in kilometers				
	Less than 100	1,000–100,000	1,000,000	Infinite	Does not know
San Andrés	4	25	29	14	28
Santiago	0	16	32	21	31
City	0	27	23	43	7

Table 4 shows the percentage distribution of answers to the question, "How far is it from here to the sky?" Only the farthest town of those studied in 1972 registered a small percentage (4 percent) of individuals who thought this distance to be less than a hundred kilometers. The idea of infinite space increases from 14 percent to 21 percent to 43 percent as one moves from lesser to more urbanized localities. Moreover, Indians in the city seem to be surer of their knowledge than those in the towns.

While only 7 percent answered "do not know" in the city, over a fourth of them in the towns could not give a specific answer.

In addition to this "direct" measurement, a question regarding the size of the stars was administered in the hope of indirectly obtaining further evidence of the conception of total space. This question also differs from the previous one in that the idea of volume is more evident.

The answers to the item "Of what size are the stars?" were almost universally answered in longitudinal terms. Table 5 shows that the per-

Table 5. Percentage distribution of conceptions of the size of the stars by locality

Locality	More than 101 kilometers	100 kilometers– 1 meter	Less than 1 meter	Does not know
San Andrés	25	50	0	25
Santiago	32	32	10	26
City	47	33	17	3

centage of individuals who conceive the stars as very large, more than 100 kilometers in diameter, increases from 25 percent to 32 percent to 47 percent with urbanization.

The percentage of those who think of stars as measuring between one meter to a 100 kilometers is less in Santiago and the city than in San Andrés, the farthest town of the three. However, the percentage of those who conceive them as very small (less than one meter) unexpectedly increases from the farthest town to the city. One-fourth of the informants in both towns were unsure enough on this issue to register "don't know" answers. Perhaps if these people had ventured a guess, the surprising pattern shown in the "less than one meter" column would reverse itself. However, the recurrence of much the same pattern on other issues suggests that the population of San Andrés tends toward greater homogeneity and that, in fact, there may be a division, in both Santiago and the city, into two rather distinct groups.

Symmetry   Two types of symmetry were studied. In the first, the individual has a symmetrical conception of space where he conceives his own spatial position as equidistant to the limits of his total space, when he thinks of himself as being at the center of his universe.

The maximum distance "toward above" was compared with the maximum "toward below" for each individual. Because about 40 percent of the informants in both San Andrés and Santiago could not respond to the question concerning distance "toward below", the remainder of both towns was collapsed into one pool. Only a third of each of the two remaining populations emerged as symmetrical.

The second kind of symmetry, only partially examined here, is based on the individual's notion of his position relative to maximum and minimum space, however these are conceived. If he considers his position as intermediate between these extremes, his conception is symmetrical; if closer to either extreme, asymmetrical. Since the idea of analyzing spatial symmetry in thia way occurred too late to obtain all the parameters necessary, only the notion of minimum space is presented here, with inferences regarding the informant's perceived relation to it. The question was asked, "What is the smaillest thing in the world?" The answers display some interesting twists and are shown in Table 6.

Table 6.   Percentage distribution of types of answers to the question, "What is the smallest thing in the world?" by locality

Locality	Minimal space categories[a]					
	Diffused	Humble	Small animals	Tiny things and animals	Microbes cells, atoms	Does not know
San Andrés	7	18	7	39	0	29
Santiago	0	5	0	63	0	32
City	0	0	0	73	27	0

[a]   See text for explanation of the categories.

A number of informants in San Andrés expressed minimum size by turning to a number of unexpected paradigms. Seven percent of them answered that objects impossible to grasp, such as clouds, ghosts, and fog, were the smallest. Moreover, 18 percent in San Andrés and 5 percent in Santiago resorted to another paradigm, one with connotations of powerlessness: man's insignificance in the universe and possibly man's ugliness in comparison with the rest of nature. For example, a typical answer was: "Man is the smallest thing in the world," meaning the humblest, the lowest.

Only in San Andrés were animals larger than a small insect reported as the smallest things in the world. Small chicks were reported, for instance, with some frequency. A combination of a feeling for beauty and an element of pity may be present in this case. For peasants to answer in this way seems incredible because they are acquainted with all sorts of smaller *animalitos* (little animals) that plague their crops. But many of the subjects were actually bewildered by such a question. Over a fourth of them answered "do not know" in both towns as compared to none in the city.

In contrast to the town pattern, a fairly large percentage (27 percent) of Indians in the city answered that microbes, cells, and atoms were the smallest things in the world, while the remainder also kept well within paradigm based upon purely spatial criteria. Thus, it seems that a large number of people in the towns have not only thought little on the matter, but among those who have, especially in San Andrés, there is a tendency to transfer to tangential paradigms which incorporate moral and attitudinal dimensions.

A complete analysis of this kind of symmetry was prevented in the absence of data concerning the other end of the continuum, the "largest thing in the universe." Despite this, we can offer some tentative conclusions based on the relation inferable between the informant and his notion of the smallest thing. Thus, at least some of the Indians of the city would appear to have a more symmetrical conception of space simply because of their implicit juxtaposition with things as small as atoms and so forth. Additionally, as one nears the city, the progressive increase in the frequency of "tiny things and animals" answers is also indicative of an expansion of the "lower dimension," possibly suggestive of an increasingly symmetrical conception from town to city. Before we can say anything definite regarding this form of symmetry, however, we will have to know something about conceptions of maximum space. As things stand, our only clues about these come from the responses to questions concerning size of the stars and distance to the sky. If we take the informant's idea of distance to the sky as a rough indicator of the minimum magnitudes involved in his conception of the size of large things, it is clear from Table 4 that all informants who responded are working with fairly large magnitudes. However, this does not tell us how they would answer the question, "What is the largest thing in the universe?" If the unusual responses obtained in the towns regarding the "smallest thing" are any indication, we can expect some surprises here as well. For the present, the matter is left with the observation that some individuals appeared to move beyond large space to an ethereal realm (heaven lies beyond the sky) in the same way that they move from small size to ghosts; at both ends of space there is the intangible and possibly the sacred.

Abstraction   Three problems administered in a sequence were to measure degrees of abstraction. The first of them consisted of using a unit of land measurement, the *cuerda*, to determine if the informants had an abstract notion of area. *Cuerdas* vary in size according to the region, but are usually equivalent to 1600 square yards. Previous experience in the field had shown that when peasants are asked about the size of the *cuerda* they frequently respond in terms of a piece of land of equal sides. This suggests that a *cuerda* may be conceived by some as a form-dimension unit, approaching the idea of a concrete object rather than as a shapeless unit of measurement.

Informants were asked first, "What are the measurements of a field one *cuerda* in size?" ("*cuanto mide un terreno de una cuerda?*"). (The answers to this question are presented below under "Convertibility.") Once this information was secured, informants were presented with a perfect square on a piece of paper and were told, "Let us suppose that this is a piece of land, one *cuerda* in size, and that its front measures X (one of the measurements that the informant has already given) and that its side also measures X. Now, are there other fields measuring one *cuerda* but of a different shape?"

Three types of answers were given. Some informants answered that the *cuerda* could be of any shape provided the area size was kept constant. Other informants answered that they would be of different forms, but that these forms were limited. These additional forms were basically of two types. The first, the *cuerda doblada* (doubled) has two of its opposite sides twice the length of a square *cuerda* while the other two sides are only half the length. The second type is the *cuerda sesgada* (inclined), in which the sides are equal and parallel but the angles are other than 90 degrees. Some informants suggested the possibility of *cuerdas doblades* in *sesgada* form. Finally, some informants denied the possibility that a *terreno* (field) of *cuerda* size could be other than a perfect square.

Table 7. Percentage distribution of conceptions of the possible forms of the cuerda by locality

	Possible forms		
Locality	Any form	Limited number of forms	One single form
San Andrés	11	82	7
Santiago	16	74	10
City	20	63	17

Table 7 shows that the number of those answering that the *cuerda* could be of any shape increases from the farthest town to the city (11 percent to 20 percent), although these differences are slight from locality to locality. Most people in all three populations conceive the *cuerda* as a unit of limited numbers of shapes, but the percentage decreases from the farthest town to the city. The number of those who associate the *cuerda* with a specific shape also increases toward the city. This reversal of the pattern does not seem to be accidental. It seems to have deeper roots, as the results of the following two questions will show.

The second problem consisted in showing the informant two rectangles of an equal area but of different shapes. The question was stated as follows, "Are these two *terrenos* the same or not, and how could you find out if they are or not?" There were some individuals who answered the second part of the question "by measuring" and tried to do so, arriving at either correct or incorrect answers. Another group stated literally "*al tanteo*" (intuitively) or (by mental guess), arriving also at correct or incorrect results. Finally were those who stated that they did not know how to resolve the problem. Table 8 shows, contrary to all expectations,

Table 8. Percentage distribution of the approaches to determining if two areas with dissimilar form are or are not identical in area by locality

Locality	Approaches		
	By measure	By guess	Does not know
San Andrés	43	36	21
Santiago	21	47	32
City	37	3	60

that a great number of people of the most distant town tried to measure the rectangles (43 percent), while most people in the city confessed that they simply did not know how to go about it (60 percent). The results for Santiago, which seemingly deviate, offer a key for the interpretation of the pattern. This town tended toward an "intuitive" solution of the problem (47 percent), compared with the predominance of measuring in San Andrés and the confusion of the city Indians. A tentative interpretation could be that the city Indians have "lost" their ability to measure and, not having the opportunity to encounter similar problems, have not developed an intuitive approach as the people of Santiago have. A partial confirmation that such a loss has occurred is indicated by the success achieved by measuring in the three localities. In San Andrés only one tenth (4 percent) of those who measured (43 percent) failed. In Santiago, a fourth failed (5 percent out of 21 percent), and in the city more than a third failed (10 percent out of 37 percent who measured).

The last problem measures the capacity to draw imaginary lines for the purpose of resolving a problem. The subjects were asked to divide a

Table 9. Percentage distribution of procedures used in a problem involving division of an area into three equal parts by locality

Locality	Used imaginary lines			
	Successfully	Unsuccessfully	Intuitively	Does not know
San Andrés	7	11	32	50
Santiago	10	11	42	37
City	13	67	0	20

terreno of an "L" form into three equal areas. Table 9 shows that an over-whelming number of Indians in the city used imaginary lines as a prelimi-nary procedure to measuring (80 percent), although only 13 percent could resolve the problem successfully. In the towns, however, this percentage is low, 18 percent and 21 percent respectively, with 7 percent and 10 percent of successful solutions. The towns greatly rely on *tanteo* to adequately resolve the problem: 32 percent in San Andrés and 42 percent in Santiago. No one in the city attempted to resolve the problem in that way. The column at the right in Table 9 shows those cases when the method of *al tanteo* failed or when the informant confessed his incapacity to resolve the problem before trying.

The results of these three problems seem to indicate an increase in the proportion of people with more abstract conceptions of space as urbaniza-tion increases. However, this conclusion should be modified by two additional statements. First, one can see in the city a parallel increase in the concrete notion of space, suggesting a bifurcation of the population. Second, there is an apparent decrease with urbanization in the ability to resolve problems which involve conceptions of greater abstraction.

Convertibility   Convertibility concerns the ability to transfer units from one frame of reference to another; for example, moving from longitudinal measurements to area to volume and vice versa. If the conceptions of area and volume are not abstract there cannot be convertibility. Field experience had suggested that some measurements of volume are thought of by peasants simply as concrete area measurements of variable thickness. The cubic meter, for instance, is frequently thought of as being one meter by ten to fifty centimeters. A similar procedure occurs with area measure-ments. When the size of the *cuerda* was elicited, a large percentage of answers were in a single longitudinal dimension, i.e. "forty yards": 75 percent in San Andrés, 68 percent in Santiago, and 40 percent in the city. In order to test further the hypothesis of frequent lack of convertibility, the question was asked: "If you found a bunch of firewood spread over the floor, how could you know how many *tareas* it will make?" The *tarea* is a measure of firewood; it is universally known and can be conceived as a volume measurement like the cord. Answers were of four kinds. The first kind was "by piling them and measuring the length, width, and height." This answer was given only in the city (3 percent). A second group answered "by piling them and measuring length and width." Forty-six percent in San Andrés, only 16 percent in Santiago, and 60 percent in the city answered this way. A third group answered "*al tanteo*," "*al ojo*" (by eye), or "by counting the sticks." The overwhelming majority

(84 percent) answered in this way in Santiago, confirming as previously mentioned, a reliance on intuition in this town. San Andrés relies comparatively less on this method, although 58 percent responded in terms of it. The people in the city, on the other hand, rely much less on it (27 percent). Only in the city were there informants who did not know how to resolve the problem (10 percent), again indicating the presence of a population sector deprived of the knowledge of measuring and of the know-how to do it intuitively.

In conclusion, there appears to be little convertibility from longitude to area to volume in all three localities, but the city compares favorably in general terms.

CONCEPTS OF TIME

Extension Time extension was measured making total time roughly equivalent to the life of the universe. The extension of time toward the past was measured by the question: "How long has the universe existed (that is, earth, stars, all that exists)?" Table 10 shows the distribution

Table 10. Percentage distribution of conceptions of the age of the universe in five localities

| Locality | Age in years | | | | |
	Less than 100	100	1,000–100,000	More than 1,000,000	Does not know
Chipiacul	4	7	89	0	0
Sta. Catarina	4	4	88	4	0
Patzún	11	6	77	6	0
San Andrés	4	4	75	6	11
Santiago	5	5	58	6	26
City	0	0	67	30	3

of answers for six towns. The first two columns at the left indicate no major differences with the exception of Patzún and the city. The column indicating "over a million years" shows that the four towns are similar; however, no individuals gave this time length in Chipiacul, the hamlet, and the city shows a substantial increase (30 percent).

The column indicating the range between 1,000 to 100,000 years includes most of the populations and could be considered as residual between the extremes. A further breakdown of this category produced a remarkably constant distribution: 75 percent of responses in each one of the localities was between 1,000 and 5,000 years; the rest were between 5,000 and 7,000. No responses were found in any locality between 7,000 and a million years.

The question, "When do you think that the universe will end?," was intended to measure the extension of time toward the future. The authors were entirely unaware that a surprisingly large percentage of individuals in all localities believe that the world is going to end in a relatively short time, probably by the end of this century. Table 11 shows that this belief

Table 11.   Percentage distribution of conceptions of time remaining to the end of the universe in five localities

| | Future in years | | | |
Locality	Less than 100	100–100,000	More than 1,000,000	When God wishes
Chipiacul	56	44	0	0
Santa Catarina	60	40	0	0
Patzún	36	50	14	0
San Andrés	43	18	7	32
Santiago	21	27	21	31
City	27	47	16	10

tends to decrease with urbanization, although not in a strictly progressive form from town to town.

The column indicating answers of more than a million years shows that, conversely, the idea of a very extended future increases with urbanization. For San Andrés and Santiago there were also large percentages of indefinite answers such as, "Whenever God decides," and "At any moment, maybe soon, if God decides so." These answers decreased in the city and were not found in the three farthest towns, but it is possible that this is due to a greater insistence in 1971 on the part of the interviewers to obtain a specific date than in 1972.

Symmetry   The comparison between past and future for each individual tells us where the individual positions himself: near the center, or toward the beginning or end of all time. Table 12 shows that the first conception

Table 12.   Percentage distribution of symmetric and asymmetric time conceptions by locality

| | | Notions of asymmetric time | |
Locality	Notions of symmetric time	Longer past	Longer future
San Andrés	14	50	4	32
Santiago	21	15	27	37
City	20	57	10	13

barely increases with urbanization, from 14 percent in San Andrés to 21 percent in Santiago and 20 percent in the city. The rest of the cases show asymmetry, and the differences between localities exhibit no particular tendency. It is interesting to notice, however, that in San Andrés as in the city, most people consider the world old and about to finish, while in Santiago the future is either greater than the past or about the same. Whether these similarities at two distinct levels of urbanization are due to social factors concomitant to urbanization or to unknown social variables cannot be answered here. The residual column presents those cases in which no specific date was obtained for either future or past time.

No adequate measurements of abstraction and convertibility for time were included in the study.

The Process of Comparing

Both quantification and classification are thought to constitute forms of the process of comparing. Quantification is analyzed here in terms of degree of extension of numerical scales, some aspects of the degree of abstraction of numbers, and the symmetry and convertibility within numerical systems. Classification is presented in a similar way except that the data for convertibility is still under analysis.

QUANTIFICATION

Extension   The extension of the quantitative scale was measured by the question: "What is the largest number?" It produced the results shown in Table 13. As urbanization increases, there is a decrease in the propor-

Table 13.   Percentage distribution of conceptions of the largest number in existence by locality

| Locality[a] | Largest number | | | |
	Less than 100	1,000–100,000	More than 1,000,000	Does not know
Chipiacul	16	26	53	5
Patzún	9	24	60	7
San Andrés	7	22	54	17
Santiago	0	21	68	11
City	0	10	87	3

[a]   There is no comparable data for Santa Catarina Ixtahuacán.

tion of individuals whose largest number is small: 16 percent in the hamlet, 9 percent in Santa Catarina and 7 percent in San Andrés think the largest number is less than one hundred, while in Santiago and the city no one thinks so. Numbers mentioned in the order of millions, on the other hand, increased with urbanization.

Moreover, the survey indicated that the idea of an infinite sequence of numbers was not held in either Chipiacul or Patzún; while one third (32 percent and 33 percent) of the subjects in San Andrés and the city mentioned the concept of infinity. In Santiago, however, only a low percent (5 percent) mentioned it.

Abstraction   Numbers can be used as nouns, as in "the number 1, the number 2, the number 3," or as adjectives, as in "three apples." They can also be used as abstract symbols with no reference to objects and with meanings that only refer back to the numerical system to which they form a part, as in $5 = 2 + 3$. When numbers are used exclusively in a noun form, their removal produces the category of nothing (example: "Here is a two, if we remove it, what is left?" "Nothing.") When numbers are used exclusively as adjectives, the removal of the objects to which they make reference also produces "nothing" (example: "If you cut these five trees, how many are left?" "None.") But if numbers are thought of abstractly, there is a possibility in both cases of another number which will summarize the end result of the operations conducted: zero. Therefore, the conception of zero can be an adequate indicator of the presence of an abstract notion of number.

Table 14.   Percentage distribution of the presence of the conception of zero and "nothing" by locality

Locality	Nothing	Does not know	Zero
San Andrés	25	32	43
Santiago	5	32	63
City	0	10	90

Table 14 shows the results to the question: "Before the number three is the number two, before the number two there is one; what is before one?" One can see in this table a decline from the farthest town to the city in the distribution of "nothing" as an answer, complemented with an increase in the occurrence of "zero" from 43 percent in San Andrés and 63 percent in Santiago to 90 percent in the city. Although the towns do not differ in the proportion of "do not know" answers, there is a clear decline in this type of answer in the city.

Abstraction was further tested in the context of the use of fractions. We suspected that the idea of a fraction was present in large sectors of the less-urbanized populations only as a concrete representation of culturally

standardized systems of division, such as weight measurement and currency systems; we chose the latter to test this notion.[1] The subjects were
asked three questions in increasing order of abstraction and difficulty.
The first stated: "How much is one-fourth of a Quetzal?" Over 98 percent
of the total sample answered correctly. The second asked: "How much is
six-fourths of a Quetzal?" Only about a fourth of the respondents in both
San Andrés and Santiago correctly answered, against two-thirds in the
city. The third question called for two successive fractioning operations
for which there is no corresponding coin equivalent. It asked: "How
much is a third of a Quetzal?" No single informant was able to give the
correct solution. The best approximations were of the nature, "Thirty-
three cents and there is a penny more in three parts." Counting all
answers within three units above or below thirty-three as correct, the
following results were obtained: only 4 percent in San Andrés and 11
percent in Santiago answered correctly, while 73 percent did so in the city.

Convertibility   A problem was designed to determine whether or not the
subjects had a notion of the possibility of arriving at a given number by
different arithmetical operations. Informants were presented with a
drawing of twenty-five oranges arranged on a piece of paper in five rows
and five columns. The oranges were equidistant from each other. The
informants were asked, "How many oranges are here?" While the subject
pondered the answer, the interviewer registered all clues relevant to his
manner of attacking the problem; and after the answer, he asked the
informant how he had arrived at that number.

The reason for the arrangement in fives is that the *mano* (hand), a five-
unit set, is universally used in Guatemala to count larger fruits and many
other items. Consequently, the problem also provided additional information on concreteness and abstraction. Analysis shows that the
informants proceeded in five different ways:
1.   by an impressionistic and intuitive procedure (*al tanteo*);
2.   by counting one orange at a time (1, 2, 3 ...);
3.   by counting by *mano* (five manos = 25);
4.   by counting in fives (5, 10, 15 ...); and
5.   by counting the oranges in a row and the oranges in a column, then
multiplying one by the other.

Because the unknown number could always be determined by counting
one orange at a time, the use of any other procedure implies knowledge

[1]   In the Guatemalan currency system, the Quetzal (which equals one dollar) is
divided into half-Quetzal bills, and twenty-five-cent, ten-cent, five-cent, and one-cent
coins.

of at least one alternative possibility to arrive at the same answer. But not all of these possibilities are equivalent; some require conversion of results obtained by operations conducted in one framework into terms of another, while others remain within the same framework throughout requiring no conversion. Thus, those who count by fives (5, 10, 15, …) are using the same framework as those counting single oranges (1, 2, 3, 4, …). Both methods use a single ordinal numerical scale; the difference lies only in the size of the interval used to progress along the scale. In both methods, the answer is determined simply by reading off the final value achieved; counting by fives is simply a fast way to arrive at the final value.

The situation is different in counting by *manos*. Here the scale is not equivalent to the one used in counting singly or in fives. Instead it is composed of a consecutive series of ready-made five-units, which are themselves counted by application of another scale, the ordinal, to them (1 *mano*, 2 *manos*, 3 *manos*, …). To answer the question, "How many oranges?," the individual has to convert *manos* to an ordinal number of oranges (5 *manos* = 25). For individuals well-versed in these two frameworks, this conversion is automatic; it does not presuppose a multiplication (5 *manos* × 5 units per *mano* = 25). Rather, it is likely to call for the same intuitive nature as used, say, for conversion from a given temperature in Fahrenheit and Centigrade by a physicist who works daily in both systems, or conversion between dollars and marks by a United States citizen who has resided in Germany for twenty years. It is possible that individuals who reported that they resolved the problem intuitively were also applying this easy type of conversion between hands and individual units.

Multiplication also requires conversion, but of a higher order of complexity, therefore producing a more conscious "operation." This operation begins by converting one row and one column of oranges into ordinal quantities (5 and 5), then relating them to each other in a certain way (5 × 5), then converting the result of this relation to an ordinal figure which expresses the total number of oranges (5 × 5 = 25). It is unlikely that persons using this procedure would not know how to use any of the other procedures mentioned, whereas counting by *mano* does not necessarily presuppose knowledge of multiplication.

Table 15 shows no important differences between localities in their preference for multiplication, but there is a decline in counting by hand from the farthest town (18 percent) to nearest town and city (5 percent and 6 percent). Most informants add in fives, but the percentage of these increase from the farthest town to the nearest town and city. The city also has a larger percentage, although a small one (17 percent) of those who

Table 15.   Percentage distribution of operations preferred in the solution of a counting problem by locality

Locality	Operations requiring conversion		Possible conversion	Operations requiring no conversion		No information
	Multiplying	Counting by *mano*	Intuition	Counting by fives	Counting by ones	
San Andrés	29	18	7	28	11	7
Santiago	26	5	5	42	11	11
City	30	6	0	40	17	7

counted by units, perhaps another example of the counter-pattern present in results previously presented. Only in the towns are there individuals who rely on *al tanteo*. The column at the right includes the small percentages of those individuals who stated that they did not know and those whose procedure could not be determined.

CLASSIFICATION   A noun referring to a material object is a classification of the object's multiplicity of actual and potential occurrences. Other nouns are classifications of purely abstract things, while still others are classifications of classificatory categories of real or abstract objects. Thus, through language acquisition the individual is furnished with at least a rudimentary classificatory pattern, and by learning the rules of this pattern, with the potential of elaboration upon it. This, however, does not preclude the possibility of individual differences in knowledge and use of language, in the capacity to further develop the pattern, and in creating new associations within the pattern.

Because of these circumstances, individuals are likely to differ in the way they see the world: for some it will be fragmented, an unconnected conglomerate of unique objects; others will have a more unified perspective, in which things constitute instances or representatives of classes. If these classes themselves are included in other, more inclusive classes, greater unification will be achieved. As shown below, individuals also differ in other characteristics of their approaches to the classificatory process, such as degree of symmetry, the criteria they use to form classifications, and the referential position they assume with respect to their classifications.

Procedures   The subjects were asked to classify a set of thirty-six animals pictorially represented in natural color on small, commercially-sold individual cards. The animal domain was chosen because it is familiar and presumably important to all groups sampled, and because the test offers more possibilities of being culture-free by not relying on human products. Plants were not chosen because city dwellers are likely to be less familiar with them. The most important features of the set of animal cards used are the following:

1.   The majority were animals familiar to Guatemalans.

2.   Three uncommon animals (peacock, pheasant, and bat) were also used to test the potential inclusiveness of the informants' classificatory systems.

3.   To detect lower levels of associativeness, representations of the same species but of different varieties were used. For example, two kinds of chickens were used to determine whether or not informants would classify them (at least them if not others) in one single group, "chickens." There were also two dogs.

4.   The set was composed of animals of very different kinds: fowls and mammals, domestic and wild, useful and harmful, small and large, and of different colors. The purpose was to facilitate the application of any potential classification system.

Degrees of Fragmentation   Were an informant to classify the animals in thirty-six separate groups, each composed of a single card, we would conclude that, to the extent that his view of the animal realm represents other areas, he has a very fragmented view of the world. We would also have to conclude that his classification is below the level of the most elementary noun classes; below the level of species (in the linguistic, not in the zoological sense). The opposite would be true if the informant divided the cards into a few inclusive groups which were then further subdivided. By counting the number of the most inclusive or primary classes, then, one obtains a rough idea of the degree of fragmentation of the informant's world.

Table 16.   Percentage distribution of classificatory systems by number of primary subdivisions and locality

	Number of primary categories			
Locality	2–3	4–5	6–7	8
San Andrés	29	21	7	43
Santiago[a]	26	16	11	42
City	57	17	20	6

[a]   There is no adequate information in one instance (5 percent).

Table 16 shows that there exists a higher degree of fragmentation in the towns than in the city. While only 29 percent and 26 percent in San Andrés and Santiago used two or three categories to include all animals, 57 percent did so in the city. Moreover, only 6 percent in the city as opposed to 43 percent and 42 percent in the towns used eight categories or more.

Levels of Abstraction Related to the degree of fragmentation, but not identical with it, is the maximum level of abstraction attained in a classificatory system. A coding system was devised to differentiate levels of abstraction.

If the informant puts only one of a pair of like animals in a single-animal class, he has constructed a level zero class. Classes formed of a single species are at level one. A qualitative difference is thought to be introduced when two or more different species are subsumed under the same class; this is level two. A subsequent qualitative difference is introduced when these abstract classes are themselves classed in more abstract groups; this is level three; level four and subsequent levels are formed by repeating this procedure.

A classification's level of abstraction was measured by the highest level attained in the classification. Different levels are frequent within the same system. Table 17 shows a progressive increase from the farthest town to the

Table 17. Percentage distribution of maximum level of abstraction in classificatory systems by locality and level

Localities	0–1	2	3–4
San Andrés	10	58	32
Santiago[a]	5	32	58
City	0	20	80

[a] There is not adequate information for one case (5 percent).

city in the proportion of individuals reaching higher levels of abstraction. Thus, while 10 percent in San Andrés and 5 percent in Santiago ended up at level zero and one, none did so in the city. Moreover, of those attaining these levels, only two individuals were at level zero, both in San Andrés (7 percent). Only 32 percent and 58 percent reached levels three and four in the towns, but in the city this figure reaches 80 percent.

Symmetry This characteristic, which is a complex one, is simplified here to refer to the presence of at least two complementary, mutually exclusive or, simply, parallel classes at each level of abstraction. There is a symmetry, for example, when animals are divided into mammals and non-mammals. But there is asymmetry at the next lower level if the mammalian group is further subdivided into useful animals versus rabbits and lions.

A higher frequency of symmetry was found rather unexpectedly in San Andrés: 50 percent of the classifications as opposed to 16 percent in Santiago and 20 percent in the city were symmetrical. Since lower levels of abstraction are more common in San Andrés (see Table 17), one might hypothesize that, by remaining at more concrete levels, the classifiers leave themselves less opportunity to commit errors in symmetry than those who operate at levels more removed from the objects being classified, thus producing more symmetrical classifications. To test this interpretation we can examine Table 18, which presents the proportions

Table 18.   Percentage distribution of asymmetrical classification systems by level of abstraction and locality

Locality	Asymmetrical systems by level[a]	
	"Low" (0–2)	"High" (3–4)
San Andrés	40	78
Santiago	72	100
City	67	83

[a]   Each figure represents the percentage of all classifications in each location which attained the levels of abstraction indicated and which were asymmetrical.

of asymmetrical classifications occurring at "low" and "high" levels of abstraction in each locality. It does confirm a general tendency toward asymmetry as the level of abstraction increases in each community, but it also shows that both low- and high-level classifications in San Andrés are less asymmetrical than those in Santiago and the city: 40 percent versus 72 percent in Santiago and 67 percent in the city in the low levels, and 78 percent versus 100 percent and 83 percent respectively in the high levels. Thus there is a greater overall tendency toward symmetry in San Andrés, followed by the city; and much less in Santiago.

Criteria   An examination of the classificatory systems show that the criteria used to construct them are reducible to three major groupings: word similarity, morphological characteristics, and relational criteria. There was only one instance when a subject classified two animals in the same group by word similarity, *oveja* (sheep) and *aveja* (bee). The use of morphological criteria is more widespread and closely follows the distribution by level of abstraction: "All are different," (level one); "These have two legs," (level two, three, or four), and so forth.

Relational criteria were not only the most common but also rendered the best possibilities of analysis.

When relational criteria were used, animals were equated on the basis of an identity of relation to a third element or a relation between themselves. Five types are distinguishable; types one and three are subject-centered, the rest, object-centered:

1. Categories formed on the basis of kinds of relation to ego: example, one group is pleasant to ego and another is not (*Estos me gusta, aquellos no*).
2. Categories formed by the mutual or reciprocal relation of two or more animals among themselves: for example, "They like each other," "They fight each other," "They know each other," "One eats the other."
3. Diffused-ego-centered. Categories formed by their relation to humans in general, that is to a pluralized and diffused ego. Three subcategories can be distinguished: usefulness, domesticity and territorial contiguity to man. For example, "These are edible, those harmful to the crops," "These are domestic, those are wild," "These are animals of the *patio*, those live in the wild *monte*."
4. Habitat-centered. Categories formed by a passive relation of animals to a habitat: for example, "These are aquatic," "Those live in caves."
5. Behavioral-centered. Categories formed on the basis of the behavior of the animals: for example, "These hunt," "Their young are born from eggs."

Table 19. Percentage distribution of relational criteria of classification by type and locality

Locality	Types				
	Ego	Mutual relation	Diffused Ego	Habitat	Behavioral
San Andrés	7	20	63	3	7
Santiago	0	22	50	5	23
City	0	5	42	16	37

Table 19 outlines the distribution of these five types of criteria. It shows a reduction in the frequency of criteria of the first three types and a progressive increase of criteria of the last two as one moves from the farthest town to the city. Ego-centered criteria ("I like") were found exclusively in San Andrés (7 percent). The two towns do not differ in the use of mutual relationship criteria (20 percent and 22 percent), but the city shows a sharp decrease (5 percent). There is a slow but progressive decrease in use of criteria of the third type centering in a generalized conception of man as one moves toward the city. The two towns make small use of criteria establishing a passive relation of the animal to its environment (3 percent and 5 percent), while in the city this type gains somewhat more importance (16 percent). Finally, a clear and progressive increase of the use of criteria that center on behavior occurs from San Andrés (7 percent) to Santiago (23 percent) to the city (37 percent).

The Linking Process

Information on the linking process was elicited by the use of sequences of drawings representing elements of the universe and situations of men, as well as by direct questioning. A wealth of material was obtained, most of which is still under analysis. A partial analysis of the returns from one of the series of drawings intended to measure the extension of link-chains is presented here.

The approach to the linking process is set in the context of a theoretical model intended to portray the essential ideational components of man's world. The model is composed of four complementary systems: creative, maintenance, destructive, and social (or human interactive). Each of these systems can have a varying content depending on the culture of the individual, and each can be linked or not, in varying ways and degrees, to all or only some of the others. When all the systems are closely interlinked they constitute a total cosmology. They are not always found in this condition. The number of intermediate possibilities for combination and separation are vast, ranging finally to a hypothetical extreme of complete fragmentation between systems and intrasystemic elements. Regardless of the degree of inter-linking, however, there is always segmentation, a fact which gives rise to the very applicability of such a subdivided model.

The possible uses to which this model can be put are numerous. One important analytical perspective it accommodates is the analysis of the degree of dominance one or more system exercises over others. Most obvious, perhaps, is the model's utility as a framework for comparative purposes, both synchronic and diachronic. In the present context, however, we are referring to the model only in the analysis of one of its systems, maintenance, and in examination of the nature of this systems segmentation, linkage networks, and subsystems.

A fragmented perspective can occur because few ELEMENTS are linked together, or because the NUMBER OF LINKS established between elements is small in relation to the total number of linked elements. The first situation is best visualized as a small number of elements linked in the manner of a chain, one to the next; the second, as a pattern consisting of possibly even a large number of elements, each linked, however, only to a single "central" element, and not to each other. A third possibility exists in which the NATURE of the links is not such as to produce consistent unity between the elements. We are concerned here exclusively with measurements of fragmentation of the first two types, those dealing with the number of ELEMENTS and the number of LINKS.

To obtain such measurements, one of the drawing sequences already mentioned was shown to the informants. It consists of ten drawings depicting what was considered to be a comprehensible link-chain of the maintenance system. The drawings were ordered from left to right on a narrow strip of paper in the following way: an Indian praying, a representation of God, the sun, a pool of water, clouds, rain, an Indian tilling the land, a corn plant, a cow, and an Indian smiling. Informants were asked to tell a real story about the strip. Although the kinds of links called for by the strip may seem obvious, we had reason to suspect that the informants would vary in their approach to the problem.

The possibilities of combination within this link-sequence were calculated with the assumption of only one possible link between any pair of the ten elements. The total possible links (or unique pairs of elements) each informant can make, then, takes the form N (N–1)/, or forty-five possible links. No attempt was made to deal with indirect links or to distinguish between different kinds of links. Thus, an informant would have made all possible links had he narrated a story as simple as the following: "A man prays to God to have sun; the sun heats the water that becomes clouds; the clouds make rain; when the rain comes the man works and the corn grows; now he can feed himself and his cattle; he is happy because of that."

A high degree of fragmentation was found. In San Andrés all the subjects combined were able to connect only 20 percent of the total linking possibilities, or 246 out of 1,260 (twenty-eight informants times forty-five) possible links. In Santiago this percentage was 23 percent (198 out of 355 possible), and in the city, 29 percent (386 out of 1,350 possible).

Moreover, most of the links were made directly between the two extremes of the chain — God (left end), corn and cows (both right end) were linked to happiness (extreme right), with very little integration of the intervening elements in the series, sun-water-clouds-rain. These four intermediate terms were intended to measure the presence of a semi-autonomous subsystem in the form of knowledge of the rain cycle. Actual linkages between these four elements amounted to less than 1 percent of the total linkage possibilities in each of the three localities.

Natural elements, such as the rain cycle, therefore, constitute neither an autonomous nor a semi-autonomous unit, as they do for us, nor do they appear to represent a well-integrated sequence of events within a larger context. However, this part of the maintenance system is segmented in other ways. Some informants said that God provides the sun, water, clouds, and rain, and, without relating them between themselves, proceeded to show how each contributes to man's happiness. Thus, one can think of some degree of unity in the maintenance system. But even God, the most heavily linked element of all, was linked to other elements in San Andrés in only 37 percent of its total possibilities. In Santiago this figure is 35 percent and in the city, 53 percent.

In the picture sequence, the proximity of the elements, "A man praying" and "God," was intended to suggest links bearing upon the idea of man's ability to induce God to produce desirable results. But this kind of link was not very often made. It occurred in 28 percent of all of its possibilities in San Andrés and in 23 percent in both Santiago and the city. When these figures are compared to those for God's effects upon the elements and man's happiness, one finds that there is a residue of 9 percent in San Andrés, 18 percent in Santiago and 20 percent in the city, which may be interpreted as God's acting without the interference of man. San Andrés, then, has the highest "magical quotient," since folk wisdom has it that in almost all cases when God interferes, it is in response or in relation to man's supplications. Man's interference in the maintenance system through praying decreases in Santiago and the city, and God's direct interferences increase.

A second measurement of man's interference in the maintenance system concerns his work. The data show essentially no differences between the three localities: in San Andrés, man's work is linked in 18 percent of its total possibilities; in Santiago, 20 percent; and in the city, 18 percent. These values closely approach those obtained for man's interference in the maintenance system through prayers to God. That is, roughly equal value is placed in all the communities on man's direct and indirect interference, by work and by praying; although San Andrés shows slightly higher values for praying (28 percent) than for work (18 percent), as opposed to 23 percent and 20 percent in Santiago and 23 percent and 18 percent in the city.

As insignificant as man's interference through work is in the chain, it is not low enough to grant the notion of a deterministic view toward nature, as many have. It is enough to remember that even God does not enter into more than 53 percent of all of his possible linkages. Moreover, when man's contribution through work is compared with that of God, its relative importance decreases with urbanization. The differences between God's links and work links are of the order of 19 percent for

San Andrés, 15 percent for Santiago and 35 percent for the city, all in favor of God's contributions. Thus, one can conclude that at least in this respect, there is no greater determinism in the rural sectors than in the city and if anything, the opposite.

The responses obtained differ considerably from locality to locality in whether the various elements are linked or not to the end of the picture sequence, man's happiness. Happiness is linked in 27 percent of its total possibilities in San Andrés, 40 percent in Santiago, and 69 percent in the city. The high figure in the city appears to be based on the belief that each of the other elements in the chain is provided by God directly for the pleasure and happiness of man. Very little linkage exists between these other elements, but they are all separately and heavily linked both to God and to man's happiness. Sun, water, clouds, rain, corn, cattle, God, prayer, and even work are all objects of (or at least linked to) man's happiness; and each of them except clouds and prayer are linked to happiness by more than 70 percent of the informants (Figures 1, 2, and 3). With the substitution of happiness for God, each of them is again linked with God although with lower levels of accordance among the informants. All the natural elements, then, seem to be, as articles of consumption, created by God to be enjoyed by man. Work appears also as an independent activity contributing directly to man's happiness.

In the towns, on the other hand, there appears to be more evidence of a mediating structure between God and happiness (Figures 1, 2, and 3). Compared with the city, there are approximately twice the links between the elements found in the middle of the sequence, sun, water, clouds, rain, plus corn and cattle: 11 percent of all possible links are made between these elements in the city, against 21 percent in San Andrés and 27 percent in Santiago. Work appears linked in a greater extent with other elements while in the city it relates to the natural elements, plus corn and cattle, in only 7 percent of the total possibilities; in Santiago this figure is 18 percent and in San Andrés, 15 percent. The high consensus in the city which produced strong links between each of the natural elements and man's happiness either fall out completely or subside drastically in their frequency of occurrance. Corn, cattle, and God remain frequently linked to happiness but at lower rates of concurrence: between 50 percent and 60 percent of informants mention them, rather than more than 70 percent in the city.

Moreover, there are differences between the towns. In Santiago there are much stronger links between the natural elements themselves than in San Andrés, and there is an explicit connection between them and man's happiness, which occurs only very weakly in San Andrés. In Santiago

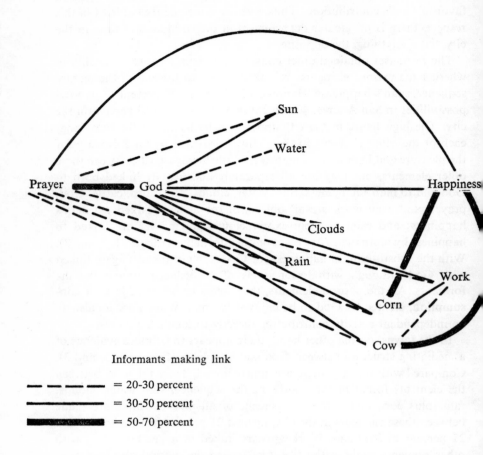

Informants making link

— — — — — = 20-30 percent

▬▬▬▬▬▬▬ = 30-50 percent

▬▬▬▬▬▬▬ = 50-70 percent

work exhibits a moderate tendency (between 20 percent and 30 percent of informants) to be linked with clouds, rain, corn, and God, a group whose elements in turn are directly linked with each other by a 30 percent to 50 percent informant concordance. In San Andrés, work links significantly only with corn and God and to a moderate degree with cattle and prayer. All four of these elements have links to still other elements, but they do not form an interlinked cluster, as is seen in Santiago. As has been previously touched upon, prayer in San Andrés forms a secondary link element after God and happiness, with independent links to sun, God, rain, happiness, work, corn, and cattle, with mostly between 20 percent and 30 percent informant concordance. In contrast, prayer in Santiago has only four significant links.

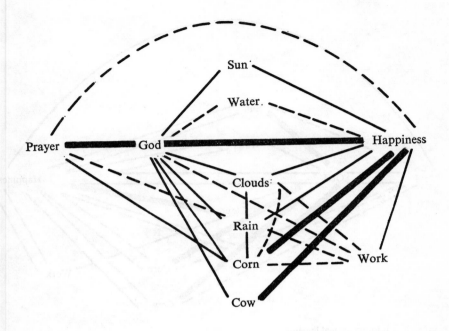

Informants making link

- - - - - = 20-30 percent

——————— = 30-50 percent

■■■■■■■ = 50-70 percent

Despite the tendencies and patterns indicated, both towns and the city appear to have very fragmented organizations for this area of the maintenance system. The towns can be grossly characterized by a scarcity of links, whereas in the city few elements are linked. While the data are lacking to support such an assertion, it is presumed that the difference in pattern between city and towns is at least partially explained by the fact that the Indians in the city have not developed a coherent linkage network encompassing many elements of their maintenance system and have lost whatever links still remain in the towns.

For a schematic view of the major features of each town, see Figures 1, 2, and 3.

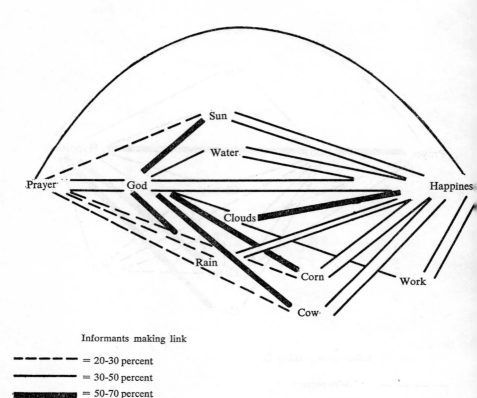

Informants making link

— — — — — = 20-30 percent
—————— = 30-50 percent
▬▬▬▬▬ = 50-70 percent
══════ = 70 percent and more

CONCLUSIONS

Beyond the adoption of material traits and the development of a new social system lies an area of change whose importance cannot be disregarded. Attempts here to depict some of the changes occurring at the level of mental configurations have produced sufficient evidence of the presence of a relationship between some urban variables and the form that certain cognitive processes take. Sample limitations, new and unproven instruments, and an incompletely developed theoretical frame give these results a provisional nature. Despite these problems we believe we have established significant leads for future work.

The general empirical conclusions of this report can be quickly summarized. With urbanization, there is an increase in the extension, symmetry, and convertibility of space concepts, as well as in the extension and symmetry of time conceptions. Conversely, some problems dealing with abstraction of space were better resolved in San Andrés than in more urbanized populations. The extension of numerical scales and abstract handling of numbers also increases with urbanization. Classifications tend to show lower degrees of fragmentation and concreteness and greater asymmetry with greater urbanization. The number of links in a linkage sequence appears to increase with urbanization, but at the cost of an increased emphasis on a more direct relationship between man and God which impoverishes the numbers of links existing between other elements in the system. The town "cosmology," fragmentary as it is, unites a greater number of elements than that of the city.

A description of general patterns associated with the increase of urbanization must take into consideration the presence of individuals that do not fall within the patterns. There is evidence throughout the study that a variable number of individuals in the towns think in ways similar to those of their urban counterparts and vice versa. Moreover, there is also some evidence of a bifurcation within the city's population which produces two contrasting forms of thinking, resulting in some cases in increases in two opposite directions; for example, abstract and very concrete conceptions of area.

The process of referring was not independently treated in this study. There is scarcely any information concerning it. Differences in the position or base from which classificatory categories emerge (i.e. ego, relations among the objects being classified, a diffuse ego, etc.) suggest differences in the referring process. The analysis of time concepts in terms of their symmetry provided some additional information. The extension of total time and space can be seen from a central position or a displaced one. It is likely that the focal position in the first case is ego and in the other a third person, perhaps God. In the link-chain studied there is also evidence of certain differences. The city people see the maintenance system as a direct dialogue with God; the chain centers in "I" and "thou." In the towns the elements in the chain form a mediating structure between man and God. Ego's happiness is seen as a result of a process more or less independent of ego, and not, as a deterministic view would have it, because ego does not contribute to it but, rather, because his contribution is also a part of a larger link system.

In the introduction, it was mentioned that the combinatorial potential of the model is not exploited in this study. To anticipate questions concerning combinatorial aspects, an example will be discussed which shows the model's potential to shed light on mental functioning within and between basic process areas and to make sense of a variety of apparently unrelated issues, not only at the mental level, but also at the social and cultural levels. The example concerns another point mentioned in the introduction: the interplay of elements of the comparing and referring processes in the derivation of the conception of reference group.

On the basis of these results, if it follows the same pattern exhibited in the classification of animals, one would expect that ego's classification of the people in his own social system would tend to be more fragmented, symmetrical, and with fewer levels of abstraction, to the extent that he is less influenced by urbanization. This prediction is at least partially supported by results of a study of subjects' views of social stratification conducted by the senior author in three Ladino communities: a hamlet, a town, and a small city, all in the same general geographical area (Méndez Domínguez 1967). People in the hamlet divided society into rich and poor Indians and rich and poor Ladinos, whereas many informants in the large town and city responded with complicated asymmetrical systems consisting of divisions at several levels of abstraction. The distinctions in the hamlet were oriented around characteristics which had a more static or fixed character (wealth and ethnic identification), while in the town and city they tended to be dynamically or functionally oriented. This kind of division is reminiscent of the one occurring in San Andrés and Santiago for classification by habitat versus behavioral attributes.

Within the Ladino town there were also differences. Some informants based their classifications on either restricted or expanded ego-perspectives. The small number of resident Indians, for instance, divide society into those with whom they enter into a special form of patronage (the "ranchero" system) and those with whom they did not. Although the distinction is socially functional from an observer's point of view, its most important feature is lack of interest on the part of the informants to draw other distinctions within the system on other functional bases. There is a striking similarity between this procedure and the one found in San Andrés which distinguishes between "animals that I like and animals that I don't like." At the other extreme, only the members of the intelligentsia classified their society by assuming an "objective" third-person position, making distinctions which were based on multiple, behaviorally oriented criteria, tending toward a structural view.

But the results of the Ladino study also show that the situation is even more complicated: informants in some social segments will change their reference position while developing different parts of a single classification. In places the classification will be ego-centered, in others, other-centered, and so forth. This does not produce a very consistent scheme, but the changing of position, or transposition, produces a situation in which the individual is able to include himself simultaneously in various groups. This inclusion presupposes claims to the rights and privileges of the various segments into which he includes himself. The fact that transposition occurs does not eliminate the possibility of preferences for given classificatory patterns nor the possibility of differences in the number of alternative patterns one individual uses.

These observations suggest, then, that reference groups are more complex affairs than is indicated by a view which understands them simply as products of classificatory divisions. Seeing them as results of the conjunction of the comparing and referring processes permits a view which makes the dynamics of the social system more understandable and allows such social issues as claims to rights, privileges, recognitions of the claims of others, and conflict to be analyzed in terms of mental process.

A discussion of each of the model's possible derivations is out of place here. But the example perhaps suffices to show that some understanding of social variables, as well as of mental processes, can be derived by proceeding in the manner suggested.

Certain concepts of territoriality, property, and significant time and space, for instance, can be thought of as derivations of the allocating process, with elements of reference, comparison, and linking interfering in different orders and at different levels of the derivation process. Every one of these and other derivations can be thought of, then, as a summary statement of a series of operations which could be approximated by an "operative composition," simulated in the model. The operative composition of a derivate requires time and thought. Once it is derived from the model, it can be submitted to empirical tests to confirm its adequacy. By going back and forth from simulation to empirical data, taking into consideration the various forms that the four processes take, the operative composition could be brought to an acceptable resemblance of the actual mental process. What is suggested is the possibility of a formal analysis of concepts through the model, a sort of mathematics of the mind, whose confirmation should be in the empirical world, a sort of physics of the mind.

APPENDIX

Percentage distributions of individuals with reading knowledge, more than three years of formal education, an income greater than Q50.00 a month, and occupied in non agricultural tasks in the communities studied in 1972.

	San Andrés	Santiago	City
Reading knowledge	62	89	90
Adequate reading ability (by test)	32	58	80
More than three years of formal education	10	26	46
More than Q50.00 monthly income	37	42	68
Non agricultural occupation	18	16	100

REFERENCES

DIRECCIÓN GENERAL DE CARTOGRAFÍA
1962   *Diccionario geográfico de Guatemala,* two volumes. Guatemala: Dirección General de Cartografía.
DIRECCIÓN GENERAL DE ESTADÍSTICA
1971   *VII Censo de población, 1964.* Guatemala: Ministerio de Economía.
KLUCKHOHN, CLYDE
1955   "Toward a comparison of values-emphasis on different cultures." Paper read at the twenty-fifth anniversary celebration, Social Science building, University of Chicago.
MÉNDEZ DOMÍNGUEZ, A.
1967   *Zaragoza, la estratificatión social de una comunidad Guatemalteca.* Guatemala: Tipografía Nacional.
MÉNDEZ DOMÍNGUEZ, A., F. WAISANNEN
1966   "Some correlates of functional literacy," in *Proceedings of the American Psychological Association Meetings.*
REDFIELD, ROBERT
1941   *The folk culture of Yucatán.* Chicago: University of Chicago Press.
TAX, SOL
1959   "La visión del mundo y las relaciones sociales en Guatemala," in *Cultura Indígena de Guatemala.* Guatemala: Seminario de Integración Social Guatemalteca.

Some Filipino (Cebuano) Social Values and Attitudes Viewed in Relation to Development (A Cebuano Looks at Utang-Na-Loob and Hiyâ)

LOURDES R. QUISUMBING

Modernization studies now draw from all social sciences because of the way in which economic, political, and social forces interact in development and modernization. Economists recognize the mutual interaction of economic and noneconomic forces over long periods of time as comprising the essence of development (Dalton 1971). Empirical studies revealing unusual success or unusual failure pinpoint both cultural heredity, and economic and physical environment as factors inducing success or failure (Dalton 1971: 13). It is increasingly apparent that sociocultural dimensions are often instrumental in the success or failure of development programs (Rogers and Svenning 1969: 361); and yet much of the research in less developed nations has been strictly economic in nature, ignoring sociopsychological variables and cultural aspects of the development problem (Inkeles 1967: v). Much more is known about gross national products and per capita income in less developed countries than about perceptions, attitudes, and beliefs of the people (Rogers and Svenning 1969: 361).

Social psychologists and other behavioral scientists maintain that while the process of modernization involves change in technology, in social systems, in political and economic institutions, it also involves change in the attitudes, values, and behavior of people. Whether such changes in people are the cause or effect of technological modernization, it remains a fact that they are important because the beliefs and attitudes of a people play a significant part in determining how readily modernizing trends will spread (Guthrie, et al. 1970: 1). Smith and Inkeles (1966), in presenting the thesis that individual members of a modern society have a certain set of attitudes, values and beliefs, have offered an overall modernity

(OM) scale designed to measure the sociopsychological characteristics of modern man. McClelland (1966) and other authors emphasize the role of individual attitudes and behavior in modernization, claiming that need achievement (*n* Ach) is a precondition to development.

Most social scientists are concerned with national and macro-development, or with impersonal problems and sectors, such as foreign trade and capital formation; and while it is readily admitted that some of the most intractable problems met in modernization exist on the rural community level, less focus is placed on development from below (Dalton 1971: 3). The culture-bound research methodology of social scientists from more developed countries hinders social research in less developed countries because there are important sociocultural differences between these countries and researchers often squeeze less developed countries into their methodological models instead of making new molds to fit the new research situation (Rogers and Svenning 1969: 361–362). The role of the anthropologist in development and the planning of change is imperative, especially at the village level (Sinha 1968).

That development can take place within the cultural context of the people, utilizing their own behavior patterns and value-orientations, is compatible with the theory that it is traditionalism, not tradition, which is a barrier to modernization (Weiner 1966). Traditions are constantly subject to reinterpretation and modification, and as such constitute no barrier (Weiner 1966). This writer adopts the view that development programers would do well to utilize local models and cultural patterns. It is better to explore their positive features, and to introduce innovation by directing, as well as adapting change to existing local value-and-belief systems avoiding incompatibility with the people's norms and practices. There is no doubt, of course, that rational-empirical approaches, like first-hand knowledge of alternative ways of doing and producing things and reduction of the high risks of adopting innovation, as well as power-coercive strategies can effect faster change (Bennis, et al. 1962), but innovation requires new attitudes and skills, and adjustment to existing social structures and cultural expectations creates problems. Understanding and respect for the client's own values and attitudes facilitates the change-agent's choice of appropriate techniques and strategies for effecting change and increases the acceptability of the innovator himself. In personalistic societies like the Philippines, social acceptance of the person must oftentimes precede acceptance of his views and ideas.

That the Philippines is a traditional society undergoing modernization is obvious, but the process is taking place in different regions of the country in varying tempo. Metropolitan Manila, some major cities and their near suburbs manifest clear evidences of urbanization and industrialization. The increasing network of communication and transportation facilities, the building of more roads and bridges, accelerate the rate of change. Notwithstanding this, the great majority of the country depends on an agricultural economy, is rural in orientation, and predominantly traditional in outlook. Values cluster around personalism, particularism, and non-rationalism. The explanation of events tends to be personalistic rather than mechanistic, intuitive rather than scientific, subjective rather than objective. The cultural ethos sustains close personal ties, harmony with nature, not control; smooth interpersonal relations and reciprocity, rather than independence and achievement.

This paper is focused on the analysis of two major themes in Philippine value-orientation; *utang-na-loob* and *hiyâ* in a Cebuano context,[1] on the premise that these themes, because they play a dominant role in Philippine behavior and social organization, can be utilized for development and therefore, should be better understood. Recent studies by social scientists and psychologists have shown the prevalence of these two values among many peoples of the Philippines and their importance as conceptual tools for the analysis and understanding of social interaction (Pal 1958; Lynch 1959, 1970; Kaut 1961; Bulatao 1964, 1970; Guthrie and Jimenez-Jacobs 1966; Landa Jocano 1966; Barnett 1966; Lawless 1966; Kiefer 1968; Hollnsteiner 1970). The existence of equivalents to the terms *utang-na-loob* and *hiyâ* in the different Philippine languages further proves their presence as a Filipino cultural universal.[2]

This study attempts to give further elucidation to *utang-na-loob* as the dominant principle in Philippine behavior and *hiyâ* as the strongest sanction ensuring it. Analysis of Cebuano conversational patterns among the rural folk, especially household helpers, vendors, and small landholders; interviews and group discussions with the writer's students in cultural anthropology on the graduate and undergraduate levels, supported by the writer's actual observation and personal experience, provide the bases of

---

[1] The island of Cebu is located in the central Visayas region of the Philippines. Due to its strategic location, Cebu City is the second largest commercial center in the country. Cebuano-Visayan is spoken by the majority of the people in the Visayas and Mindanao.

[2] Some other equivalents to *utang-na-loob* and *hiyâ* are: *utang-nga-naimbag-a-nakem* and *mabain* (Ilocano); *otang-nalub* and *nabababainan* (Pangasinan); *utang-lub* and *marinê* (Pampango); *utang-na-buot* and *supog* (Bicolano); *utang-nga-kaburut-on* and *awud* (Waray); *kabalaslan-sa-lawas* (debt of one's self) and *huyâ* (Hiligaynon); *buddhi* or *panumtuman* (a remembrance) both meaning a debt which is not to be demanded; *pangdagdag* (the sentiment in the creditor upon the failure of a friend to repay), *way sipug* (*hiyâ*) on the part of the debtor who fails to repay (Tausug).

the conclusions drawn and herein presented. This writer contends that the viewpoint of the participant-in-the-culture provides a deeper insight and adds valuable understanding to such an area as values and attitudes, cultural realities which are difficult to observe, describe, or measure, and are at best FELT and EXPERIENCED. The time has come when the behavioral scientist, especially the anthropologist, should join hands with the trained native to arrive at more reliable conclusions on any aspect of the latter's culture.

Reciprocity or *utang-na-loob* (*utang-kabubut-on* in Cebuano) and *hiyâ* (*kaulaw, ka-ikog, katahâ* in Cebuano), as they operate in Cebuano society, offer fine distinctions and different shades of meaning, an analysis of which reveals their importance as premises and sanctions of social behavior. While reciprocity is accepted as a universal norm, its emphasis and importance in Philippine social life are dramatically manifest and institutionalized in highly specific and patterned ways. *Utang-na-loob*, translated by Hollnsteiner as a "debt inside oneself" and by Kaut as a "debt of prime obligation," is described as a special type of reciprocity which stems from a good or favor received, or a service rendered and which allows no quantification in terms of payment, nor termination (Hollnsteiner 1970; Kaut 1961). This is distinct from *utang*, a simple debt of contractual nature, where terms of payment are specified and exact, and the obligation is terminated upon payment with no emotions involved. *Utang-na-loob* is a unique Philippine pattern of reciprocity, which exists with some interesting, significant, and logically related variations in different parts of the country, in Luzon, in the Visayas, and Mindanao (Kiefer 1968). Kiefer refers to the exchange of gifts and services as conjunctive reciprocity or *buddhi* among the Tausugs of Sulu; and to blood-debts or revenge on the other hand, as disjunctive reciprocity.

Every Filipino is expected to possess a fine sense of *utang-na-loob*, to be keenly aware of his indebtedness and obligations to those from whom he has received favors, by being grateful and by repaying them when possible and at an appropriate moment. Among Cebuanos, an individual possessing *utang-kabubut-on* is admired for his concern and thoughtfulness, his solicitude and consideration for another's needs and feelings. He is a *maayong tawo* (good man), *maantigo mo balus sa iyang mga utang-kabubut-on* (knows how to repay his indebtedness to others). The Tagalogs say he has a *magandang utang-na-loob* (a beautiful sense of gratitude). *Utang-na-loob* is never uttered or referred to in a trivial manner. It reflects a "system of social sentiments," of a deep and strong affective nature and expressively symbolizes a whole configuration of reciprocal obligations (Kaut 1961). Similarly, in Cebuano, the concept of *utang-kabubut-on* implies a complicated network of reciprocal relationships that reflect deep and strong affective sentiments.

Emotions accompanying such indebtedness do not cease upon repayment, since such a debt is never completely repaid. As Cebuanos say it, "*Ang utang-kabubut-on dili kabayran ug salapi hangtud sa kamatayon*; *hangtud sa kahangturan*" (A debt of gratitude cannot be paid with money; it lasts until death or forever). This is truly so, for *utang-kabubut-on* is passed on to one's family and kin, and repayment can be made to any member of the benefactor's reference group, even after his death. Reciprocity takes on different forms and degrees depending on the varying social contexts in which it occurs, the circumstance and the nature of the gift, and the relationship between the giver and the receiver. The degree of indebtedness increases with the intensity of the need of the receiver, the generosity and goodwill of the giver, and the closeness of the relationship between them.

The notion that *utang-kabubut-on* is created only when the presentation of goods and services is UNSOLICITED fails to account for reciprocity in the case of intimate alliances where mutual requesting and accepting can be taken for granted. A favor, good, or service SOLICITED from someone with whom one has close relationships, usually a kin or a friend, also creates a great sense of indebtedness. Here the Cebuano does not speak of a mere *pañgayo* (asking) but a *hangyo* (request) which he expects to be granted. Refusal of a serious *hangyo* hurts the *amor propio* (personal dignity) of the person requesting. An UNSOLICITED offer, however, because it is tendered by a person sensitive enough to see the other's needs, is highly appreciated, and elicits a touching *utang-kabubut-on*. The unsolicited gesture comes from one with whom the receiver has a pre-existing relationship. It is a symbol of affinity which the receiver can accept with confidence.

The assertion that the gift activates a unilateral relationship of indebtedness reversible only by means of a properly offered return gift (Kaut 1961), does not seem very precise in the Cebuano case. While it is true that there is an implied expectation of return, the giver-receiver relationship becomes mutual upon acceptance and the primary concern is not to have the gift repaid but to maintain or strengthen existing ties. The acceptance of the *kabubut-on* (gift of oneself) further implies that the receiver is willing and eager to help the giver when the latter's need for help arises. The receiver may now give something better or more than the original gift; or whatever lies within his means, not as interest on an investment, but as an acknowledgment of goodwill and generosity and a means of reinforcing relationships.

Emphasis on the feeling of uneasiness and the burden imposed on the receiver in the never-ending "see-saw kind of reciprocity" referred to by Kaut and Hollnsteiner certainly misses that sense of self-satisfaction and fulfilment which the receiver experiences when, as he becomes a giver, he is able to repay a socially-expected obligation which he has embraced wholeheartedly. As soon as an individual becomes the recipient of a favor, he willingly takes upon himself not only the obligation to repay but also the duty of seeking opportunities which will allow him to show his gratitude. Repayment is not made at any time. There are proper occasions and necessary circumstances when it is expected, foremost among them being the time when the donor is in need and when the receiver is in a position to repay.

Utang-kabubut-on, translated as "debt of one's volition," expresses this willingness to assume the obligation, the payment of which not only enables one to fulfill a duty but also to form, renew, or strengthen social ties and relationships. *Utang-kabubut-on* is not a mere exchange of gifts or services, but a reciprocal interaction, creating or strengthening social bonds not only between the giver and the receiver, but between their families as well, a process by which the individual can place himself in a secure network of mutual obligation extending even beyond kinship lines.

Because the Cebuano is aware of the social and personal meaning of a gift, he is careful in choosing the person to whom he gives or from whom he accepts a gift. A girl who does not intend to accept a suitor is not expected to accept his gift, especially if it is an expensive one. As Kaut says, acceptance (*pagtanggap*) institutes a virtual contract, but to say that this signifies that the donor can then expect a greater type of return at a later time is to overstate the investment aspect. In fact, when a receiver has the slightest suspicion that this is the motive behind the gesture, he is careful not to accept the favor, and his *amor propio* (sense of personal worth) is hurt.

Care in accepting a gift, *ang pagdawat*, because of its deep significance, carries with it the delicate task of knowing when and how to refuse a gift, *ang pagbalibad*. Rejection of a gift or voluntary aid which is equivalent to rejection of the person of the giver could be an extremely serious act, affecting both the giver and the potential receiver with the unpleasant or bitter consequences of *hiyâ* (shame) or revenge (Kaut 1961). The Cebuano usually feels *kaulaw* (hurt, embarrassment, shame) when his offer is rejected, and *ka-ikog* (complex feelings of consideration, respect, and fear to displease) when he has to refuse a gift.

Intra-familial reciprocity partakes of a deeper meaning and more intense emotionality. *Utang-kabubut-on* to one's parents is permanent and can never be adequately or completely repaid. One owes one's very life and existence to the care and loving solicitude of one's parents. to whom deep and lifetime loyalty is rightfully due. In return, grown-up children, whether married or unmarried, consider it a serious and sacred obligation to take care of their aged, disabled, or needy parents in their own households, where they continue to be respected and consulted. Growing old in Cebu, as well as in almost all parts of the Philippines, is usually much less of a problem than it is in other countries. A Cebuano saying expressing this filial obligation goes this way: one never completely repays or understands one's debt to one's parents until he himself becomes a parent, "*dili gayud kita makabalus sa utang-kabubut-on sa atong guinikanan, hangtud nga kita usab mahimong guinikanan.*" Among siblings and other close kin, reciprocal exchanges are frequent and to be expected. These deepen their interaction and relationship.

Failure to observe the norms of *utang-na-loob* is identified with disloyalty, lack of consideration, negligence. *Walay ulaw, walay ka-ikog, walay ikagbalus,* and *walay batasan* are very strong terms referring to ingratitude.[3] They operate as powerful sanctions.

Utang-kabubut-on to one of a superior status is accompanied by feelings of *ka-ikog* or *katahâ*, a sense of awe and respect. Repayment is not expected in equivalent terms, since one is usually not in a position to make that kind of payment. Thus, personal services are rendered instead. These would consist in assisting at household chores, such as laundry and kitchen work, housecleaning or gardening, in attending to a sick member of the family, or attending to visitors during a *fiesta*, wedding, baptism, burial, and other family social gatherings. Willingness and availability to serve, when needed, count most. Thus, the value of the reciprocation does not lie so much in the material or monetary amount of the gift or in the economic equivalent of the service, but in the timeliness of the help, the goodwill and intention behind the gesture, and the feelings of friendship or loyalty that go with it. Cebuanos do not use the term *bayad* (payment) which suggests a cash amount but *balus*, which is a mutual exchange or personal reciprocation, the giving of self. This explains why the non-reciprocation of *utang-kabubut-on* when the benefactor is in need or when there is an event of significance to celebrate like a departure, an arrival, a birthday, an anniversary, the wedding of a family member and other similar situations, is looked upon as negligence or default. The same applies to non-acceptance or refusal to receive a favor or gift. The refusal amounts to personal rejection.

---

[3] Cebuano terms expressing lack of respect for traditional values and customs.

The norm of reciprocity has been the subject of considerable study and has been established as a universal principle at work in the social order. The *utang-na-loob* manifestations in different Philippine groups possess features characteristically similar to those exhibited in tribal societies and peasant economies, where exchanges are reciprocal gestures conceived as "noneconomic," governed and often instigated by direct social relations, and constrained always by the kinship and community standing of the parties concerned (Dalton 1971: 51).

Each sector implies appropriate norms of reciprocity, which is not always a one-for-one exchange, but a complex continuum of variations in the directness and equivalence of exchange .... Observable at one end of the spectrum is assistance freely given, the small currency of everyday kinship, friendship, and neighborly relations, the "pure gift" Malinowski called it, regarding which an explicit demand for reciprocation would be as unthinkable as it is unsociable — although it would be equally bad form not to bestow similar casual favors in return, if and when it is possible. Toward the middle of the continuum stand balanced exchanges, in which a fair and immediate trade is right behavior, as for example when kinsmen come from a distance seeking food and bearing gifts. And at the far end of the spectrum self-interested seizure, ... (Dalton 1971: 51–52).

The end points of the continuum are referred to as "generalized" and "negative" reciprocities; the midpoint, "balanced" reciprocity (Service 1966).

At this point it may be stated that as the Philippines shifts from traditional to cash economy, it may be expected that *utang-na-loob* as an operating principle of interrelationships and redistribution of surplus goods may decline (Hollnsteiner). Ambivalent attitudes among the Filipinos themselves regard *utang-na-loob* as both an incentive and a deterrent to progress. While Filipino effort continues to be motivated by gratitude to the significant persons in one's life and community projects may still hinge on loyalty to people one is indebted to, there are definite trends towards preference for cash and stipulated payment of goods and services rather than goodwill and smooth relations, reliance on merit rather than on personal influence and connections. Original resistance to such modern institutional practices like insurance, hospitalization, banking transactions, cooperatives, and credit unions is lessening; traditional values, attitudes, and beliefs are undergoing many adaptations to changing conditions. Technological, economic, and political changes penetrate through the whole Philippine social and cultural fabric, even though discontinuities and lags still exist.

Modernization brings about profound changes in traditional settings and social relationships, as kinship units lose their pervasiveness and values become less personalistic and particularistic. But this is not to say that *utang-na-loob* and all the other Filipino personalistic traits will completely disappear, nor to expect that the people will relinquish their traditional way of life in favor of highly impersonal modern attitudes, for as Anderson aptly puts it in his study of Philippine entrepreneurship,

... despite the obvious and oft-cited maladaptiveness of personalism for development (such as red tape, erosion of bureaucratic honesty, encouragement of corruption, undermining of public morality), personalism may on balance provide functions without which development could not take place (without a rather complete structural and ideological revolution). The advantages of Filipino economic personalism constitute another challenge to the ethnocentric fallacy that only Western social forms and psychological conditions give rise to incipient and more advanced economic development (Anderson 1969).

Claude Lévi-Strauss further underscores this writer's viewpoint:

... Societies which are at present engaged in the processes of economic development and industrialization may with the help of their own specific cultural wealth build up their own systems of motivations and incentives; and before these are criticized by reference to criteria peculiar to the industrial societies of the West, they must be subjected to minute examination. They also offer us a rewarding field of study (Lévi-Strauss 1954).

Finally, in discussing the modernization of social relations, Smelser (1966) expresses the danger developing nations face when they conceive speed of economic development to be the only criterion of growth — the too rapid destruction of various forms of social integration taking place at the very high cost of social unrest and political instability that may in the end defeat the very effort to develop (Weiner 1966: 111). In the last analysis, development is for the people, and their choice of priorities should be respected.

REFERENCES

ANDERSON, JAMES N.
  1969   Buy-and-sell and economic personalism: foundations for Philippine entrepreneurship. *Asian Survey* 9(9).
BARNETT, MILTON L.
  1966   *Hiyâ*, shame and guilt: a preliminary consideration of the concepts as analytical tools for Philippine social science. *Philippine Sociological Review* 14(4):276–282.

BENNIS, WARREN G., *et al.*
1962   *The planning of change: readings in the applied behavioral sciences.*
New York: Holt, Rinehart and Winston.

BULATAO, JAIME
1964   *Hiyâ. Philippine Studies* 12:424–428.
1970   "Manileño's mainsprings," in *Four readings on Philippine values*. IPC
2. Edited by Frank Lynch and Alfonso de Guzman II, 89–114.
Quezon City: Ateneo de Manila University Press.

DALTON, GEORGE
1971   *Economic development and social change.* New York: The Natural
History Press.

GUTHRIE, GEORGE M., PEPITA JIMENEZ-JACOBS
1966   *Child rearing and personality development in the Philippines.* University
Park: Pennsylvania State University Press.

GUTHRIE, GEORGE M., *et al.*
1970   *The psychology of modernization in the rural Philippines.* IPC Papers 8.
Quezon City: Ateneo de Manila University Press.

HOLLNSTEINER, MARY
1970   "Reciprocity in the lowland Philippines," in *Four readings on Philippine values.* IPC 2. Edited by Frank Lynch and Alfonso de Guzman II.
Quezon City: Ateneo de Manila University Press.

INKELES, ALEX
1967   "Forward," in *Economic development and individual change: a social-psychological study of the Camilla experiment in Pakistan.* Edited by
Howard Schuman. Harvard University, Occasional Papers in International Affairs 15. Cambridge, Massachusetts.

KAUT, CHARLES
1961   *Utang na loob:* a system of contractual obligation among Tagalogs.
Southwestern Journal of Anthropology 17.

KIEFER, THOMAS M.
1968   Reciprocity and revenge in the Philippines: some preliminary remarks
about the Tausug of Jolo. *Philippine Sociological Review* 16(3–4):
124–131.

LANDA JOCANO, F.
1966   Rethinking "smooth interpersonal relations." *Philippine Sociological
Review* 14(4):282–291.

LAWLESS, ROBERT
1966   A comparative analysis of two studies on *utang na loob. Philippine
Sociological Review* 14(3):168–172.

LÉVI-STRAUSS, CLAUDE
1954   Economic motivation and structure in underdeveloped countries. *The
International Social Science Bulletin* 6(3).

LYNCH, FRANK
1959   *Social class in a Bikol town.* Philippine Studies Program, University of
Chicago, Series 1.
1970   "Social acceptance reconsidered," in *Four readings on Philippine
values,* IPC 2. Edited by Frank Lynch and Alfonso de Guzman II.
Quezon City: Ateneo de Manila University Press.

MC CLELLAND, DAVID C.

1966   "The impulse to modernization," in *Modernization: dynamics of growth*. Edited by Myron Weiner, 28–39. New York: Basic Books.

PAL, AGATON

1958   A Philippine barrio. *Journal of East Asian Studies*. University of Manila.

ROGERS, EVERETT M., LYNNE SVENNING

1969   *Modernization among peasants: the impact of communication*. New York: Holt, Rinehart and Winston.

SERVICE, ELMAN

1966   *The hunters*. Englewood Cliffs: Prentice-Hall.

SINHA, D. P.

1968   *Planned socio-cultural change: myth, possibility or reality*. Proceedings VIIIth International Congress of Anthropological and Ethnological Sciences, Tokyo and Kyoto, volume three.

SMELSER, NEIL J.

1966   "The modernization of social relations," in *Modernization: dynamics of growth*. Edited by Myron Weiner. New York: Basic Books.

SMITH, DICK HORTON, ALEX INKELES

1966   The OM scale: a comparative socio-psychological measure of individual modernity. *Sociometry* 29:353–377.

WEINER, MYRON, *editor*

1966   "Introduction," in *Modernization: dynamics of growth*. New York: Basic Books.

Change in Rank and Status in the Polynesian Kingdom of Tonga

CHARLES F. URBANOWICZ

There is a certain amount of timelessness inherent in some ethnographic reports: a timelessness which stems from the quest of the synchronic description *cum* analysis of culture. This timelessness is present even though I am in agreement with Locher's basic point that "there is a new interest in the relation between anthropology and history" (Locher 1967: 77). Unfortunately, this relationship has yet to be intensified.

Change obviously takes place over time, yet all too often statements in the published accounts have compressed many of the unique aspects of Tongan culture into a homogenized whole. The massive work of Gifford (1929) has various points in it where one is not certain what was aboriginal Tonga and what was the Tonga of Gifford's research period of 1920–1921. In order to describe aboriginal Tonga and analyze changes in Tonga, one must "begin at the beginning" and gather the most reputable information on aboriginal Tonga, i.e. early-contacted Tonga. By itself, twentieth-century "memory culture" of what aboriginal Tonga was like (from which most researchers get their idealistic ethnographic base lines) is not sufficient to say what Tonga was like in the past. Memory culture descriptions,

Funding for the research partially presented in this paper was provided, in part, by an NDEA (Title IV) Fellowship and an NIH Traineeship (PHS Grant No. 5 T01 GM01382–05). Field work was conducted in Tonga from July to October of 1970 and from August to October of 1971. In the intervening months archival research was conducted in the major libraries of Fiji, New Zealand, and Australia, with most of the research being done in the Mitchell Library, Sydney, Australia. Assistance and data provided by all of the individuals contacted in Tonga, especially those connected with the *Komiti Talafakafonua 'o Tonga* (Tongan Traditions Committee), and by the individuals of the research institutions, is greatly appreciated.

in numerous respects, are not superior to reputable eye-witness descriptions of aboriginal Tonga.[1]

CONTACT AND DESCRIPTIONS

Part of the Tongan archipelago was first contacted by the Dutch navigators Schouten and Le Maire in 1616, and various contacts with Europeans followed: 1643 (Tasman), 1767 (Wallis), 1773, 1774, and 1777 (Cook), 1781 (Maurelle), 1787 (La Perouse), 1789 (Bligh), 1793 (D'Entrecasteaux and Labillardière), and 1793 (Malaspina) (see Colson 1885; Tudor 1968: 125–127). These contacts between Europeans and Tongans lasted for periods of a few days to several weeks. The accounts of these men made Europeans aware of Tonga and placed Tonga on Europe's map. The accounts spurred Europeans to send men to proselytize the peoples of the Pacific. Tonga, along with Tahiti, was one of the first island groups to be sent European missionaries in the late eighteenth century.

The first missionaries were of the Missionary Society of London (form-

[1] Tonga, named by Captain James Cook "The Friendly Islands," is composed of some 150 to 200 islands and islets with perhaps only 25 percent of those being inhabited. The islands are a form of raised limestone, or volcanic formations and limestone formations (Anonymous 1944: 16). The most recent work indicates that the total land area of the archipelago is 256.42 square miles, with the Tongatapu Group (the main island of Tongatapu with surrounding small islands but excluding the island of 'Eua) having 100.37 square miles of that total or some 39.1 percent (Maude 1965: 218). Tongatapu Island is approximately 99 square miles in area. The estimated population for the entire archipelago for December 31, 1970 was 86,055 (Tapa 1971: 4).

The territorial boundaries of the Kingdom of Tonga were proclaimed by King George Tupou I to be 15°S and 23°S and 173°W and 177°W (*Tonga Government Gazette*, 2: 55, August 24, 1887). The islands of the Kingdom thus fall within a rectangle of the South Pacific some 596 miles North-South by 264 miles East-West, with the outer islands of the Kingdom being Niua Fo'ou Island to the North at 15°34'S and 175°40'W, and 'Ata Island to the South at 22°20'S and 176°12'W. 'Ata Island is approximately 100 miles southeast of the main island of Tongatapu and Niua Fo'ou Island is approximately 232 miles northwest of the Vava'u group of Islands.

Tonga derived its name from the principal island of the group, Tongatapu Island or 'sacred' Tonga. The *tapu* was probably appended to the Tonga because this island became the residence of the leaders of the archipelago. Tongatapu Island was the focal point for the political and religious system in the archipelago prior to and after European contact. The Polynesians who settled the archipelago appear to have chosen this relatively flat island because of terrain and climate. The middle, or Ha'apai group of islands are a series of low islets. The northernmost island group of Vava'u has relatively high hills, with most of the land being at least one hundred feet above sea level (as opposed to Tongatapu Island which is no higher than two hundred feet along the southern or *liku* coast). Vava'u was, and is, subject to more destructive hurricanes than Tongatapu during the hurricane season and it was only on Tongatapu that relative permanency of Tongan culture and continuity of leadership could be maintained for generations.

ed in 1795 and later termed the London Missionary Society, or LMS) and they arrived at Tongatapu on April 10, 1797 (Benson 1960: 113; Wilson 1799: 96). Ten male missionaries landed and some remained until 1800, but the attempt at religious conversion ended in a debacle. One missionary, Vason, married a Tongan woman and was converted to the *anga-faka-Tonga* or 'Tongan way of life' (Vason 1810). The Wesleyan Missionary Society established a mission station on Tongatapu in August of 1822 manned by one missionary, Walter Lawry, who was accompanied by his wife and several servants (including Europeans and a Marquesan islander) (see Lawry's *Diary* for August, 1822). This attempt at Christian conversion also ended in failure with Lawry being ordered by London to be "removed from Tonga to Van Diemen's Land" (Lawry, *Diary*: July 26, 1823). Lawry eventually left the island in October of 1823, and it wasn't until 1826 that a second Wesleyan mission was attempted in the archipelago. In June of 1826 the Wesleyan missionaries John Thomas and John Hutchinson arrived, with their wives, and this mission eventually proved succesful. From 1826 onwards Tongans entered into sustained European contact.

The various published accounts of the individuals of this period (1616–1826), combined with twentieth-century field work, have allowed us to make inferences about aboriginal Tongan culture (Coult 1959, for example), yet no systematic attempt had ever been made to incorporate manuscript materials into (1) an aboriginal ethnographic base line, and (2) an analysis of changing Tongan culture. What were the processes by which the aboriginal Tongan culture of 1800 developed into the Constitutional Monarchy of 1875?

The date of 1875 is extremely important in Tongan studies, for in many respects the Tonga of pre-1875 was not the same as the Tonga of post-1875. In 1875 the Tongan Constitution was promulgated by the *Tu'i Kanokupolu* King George Tupou I, with the help of European advice. The Constitution was the result of Western influence on Tonga and the culmination of all of the written Tongan law codes in effect in the archipelago since 1839. The date of 1850 given in Murdock's *Ethnographic atlas* (1967) for Tonga, for cross-cultural research of a certain type, can be extremely misleading, for by this time two major wars (as a result of nineteenth-century Western influence) had been fought in the archipelago (1837 and 1840), the Tongan language reduced to a systematic orthography (c. 1830), and a European-induced codified system of laws had already been in effect for certain parts of the archipelago for many years (in the island groups of Vava'u and Ha'apai). Certainly Goldman's most recent work which suggests 1800 as the "terminal date" for aboriginal Polynesian society merits closer consideration than 1850 for Tonga (Goldman 1970: xxviii).

Utilizing 1800 as a reference date for Tonga, one has a dynamically operating and changing Polynesian society, with an elaborate system of rank (based on kinship ties) and status (based on kinship and achievement). Changes in the rank and status systems resulted from Western contact but these have not always been successfully analyzed or reported in ethnographic accounts.[2]

ABORIGINAL TONGA

There are four major titles in Tonga with which we are concerned: *Tu'i Tonga*, *Tu'i Ha'a Takalaua*, *Tu'i Kanokupolu*, and *Tamaha*. When the various missionaries arrived in the archipelago, they grasped part of the cultural system of ranking. The Wesleyan missionary Lawry recorded in his diary for September 13, 1823, that

the following is the order in which the present Chiefs of the Friendly Islands rank, viz: –
1.   Tooitonga [*Tu'i Tonga*]
2.   Tooihatacalowa [*Tu'i Ha'a Takalaua*]
3.   Tooicanacabooloo [*Tu'i Kanokupolu*]

Another Wesleyan missionary, John Thomas (in the archipelago from

---

[2]   The only way in which a researcher can attempt a reconstruction of aboriginal culture is for that researcher to examine the earliest extant documentation pertaining to that culture and then make comparisons between the old information and new information gathered by contemporary field work. Urbanowicz (1972) provides a detailed explanation of the methodology of the documentary research.

Ethnohistorical techniques were used to extract ethnographic information of the past from the documentary materials. Ethnohistory is thus the application of historical method to a body of documents specifically chosen for the construction of an historical ethnography (See Fenton 1962; Sturtevant 1966). The ethnohistorian focuses on the "ethno-" in the term, in presenting an ethnography of a given group of people; the "-history" refers not to the writing of history, but to the application of historical method to gather verifiable ethnographic facts of the past. Ethnohistory is not a study of change per se, although it eventually contributes to studies of change. The term ethnohistory as used by ethnographers is not synonymous with culture history, as the distinguished Pacific historian H. E. Maude has written (1971: 21).

Every ethnographer is, in essence, an ethnohistorian, since every ethnographer must read background material prior to beginning field work and must weigh and assess previous research reports; and every ethnohistorian is at heart an ethnographer, combining archival research with field work among the contemporary people. This is why I went to Tonga. Also see Cohn 1968; Dodge 1968; and Lurie 1961. Original orthography has been maintained throughout this paper.

1826 to 1850 and again from 1855 to 1859) wrote in one of his manuscript accounts:

Formerly there were three ranks of nobles in Tonga to which the term *Eiki* or Lord applied, of these the Tuitonga stood first, then the Tamaha, and next the Hau or civil ruler (Thomas MS. 5:1).

The *Tamaha* was the title given to the female child of the sister of the *Tu'i Tonga*, who herself had the title of *Tu'i Tonga Fefine*. The different ranking of the *'eiki* for Thomas and Lawry stems from the fact that there were *Tamaha* before there were *hau*. Included in the *hau* at various points in time were the titled individuals *Tu'i Ha'a Takalaua* and *Tu'i Kanokupolu*.

The *Tu'i Tonga* was the embodiment of the sacred and the secular in aboriginal Tonga and the nominal leader of all Tongans. In approximately the fifteenth century, however, a division was made between the sacred and secular aspects of leadership and the *Tu'i Tonga* Kau'ulufonua delegated his secular authorities to a brother, and the title of *Tu'i Ha'a Takalaua* was begun. A description from a manuscript account, ostensibly "written by [the last] *Tamaha* Amelia, and begun in May the 27th, day of the year 1844" (Collocott MS. 2: 19) provides some basic information on this title. The *Tamaha*, who was described as "the living oracle of the Tongans" (Thomas MS. 5: 59), probably dictated the account since she was well over sixty years of age in the 1840's. The *Tamaha* spoke of the *Tu'i Tonga* Kau'ulufonua and how "he portioned out to each of his brothers an island to be king over" and how he:

appointed Mougamotua Tui Haatakalaua, and he was to reside at Fonuamotu as he was to be protector of the Tuitonga (as the Tuitongas were apt to be assasinated), and the Tuitonga was safe because his younger brother kept guard over him (Collocott MS. 2:21).

Mo'ungamotu'a was thus the first *Tu'i Ha'a Takalaua*.

In approximately the seventeenth century a *Tu'i Ha'a Takalaua* delegated some of his secular responsibilities to a son, and the title of *Tu'i Kanokupolu* was created. The *Tu'i Ha'a Takalaua Mo'ungatonga* gave his son Ngata the title of *Tu'i Kanokupolu* and also "royal estates at the West end of Tonga [tapu] called Hihifo" (Thomas, MS. 5: 1).

With the *Tu'i Tonga* responsible for the sacred matters of leadership and the *hau* (either the *Tu'i Ha'a Takalaua* or *Tu'i Kanokupolu*, depending on what period one is speaking about) responsible for secular matters, the *Tu'i Tonga* eventually became dependent on the *hau* for his titled position. The *hau* literally had to have the strength and authority to "install" the *Tu'i Tonga* with the title. Consensus and flexibility were always key aspects of aboriginal Tongan culture and a leader needed the support of the people around him. Such support came from numerous plural marriages and successful leadership. Laufilitonga, the last individual to hold the title of *Tu'i Tonga*, was delayed in being appointed to his position in the early part of the nineteenth century because of the inability of a secular ruler to support him. Thomas wrote of the *hau* as King, that:

> It is said had the King's party been succesful in the war in the Anga, it was the intention of the King to have presented his daughter Halaevalu to Laufilitonga as his wife, and to have appointed him to office as Tuitonga but though a battle was fought and many fell on both sides — no victory was gained — The evils they had hoped to have removed were allowed to remain — as the King could not remove them — his daughter was therefore not so given — neither was the chief appointed to office, but remained at Vavau where he had been brought up (Thomas MS. 4:192).

After the separation of sacred from secular matters in aboriginal Tonga, the *Tu'i Tonga* was still esteemed and revered but more as an intercessor with the Tongan deities. Thomas wrote of the *Tu'i Tonga:*

> The office of the Tuitonga was still esteemed, and became one of vast importance, even as the connective link between the gods and the people; he was not a high priest but a friend, or representative of the gods, his office as with his person was considered sacred (Thomas MS. 5:1).

Other eye-witnesses of the early nineteenth century corroborated this, as the Wesleyan missionary N. Turner relates:

> Many were present at the service this afternoon and were very attentive. The Tui Toga was there, who is by birth and rank according to their former superstitions the greatest Man in all these islands. Tho the nature of his office forbids him to have anything to do with public affairs. According to the ancient customs of Toga he is altogether a sacred person (N. Turner, Letter-Journal dated November 29, 1828, reporting events of October 28, 1828).

Eventually, however, as a result of Western contact (specifically the Wesleyan missionaries in the nineteenth century) the position of the *Tu'i Tonga* was totally eclipsed by that of the *Tu'i Kanokupolu*. Laufilitonga, the last *Tu'i Tonga*, had eventually been installed in his office in 1827 and held the title until his death in 1865. Although he requested that a *Tu'i Tonga* be appointed after his death, no such appointment was made by the *Tu'i Kanokupolu* King George Tupou. As a point of fact, at a Tongan parliamentary meeting in 1875 King George Tupou stated:

You must remember that I was conferred with the following two titles during the meeting that was held in Vava'u, Tu'itonga and Tu'iha'atakalaua together with my own title of Tu'ikanokupolu (Hunter 1963:4).

This was the ultimate consolidation of King George's rise to power. A recent assessment by Latukefu of King George, or Taufa'ahau, is worth considering:

It appears, however, that Taufa'ahau's initial acceptance of Christianity was only a part of his general desire to adopt the ways of the white man, his wealth, superior knowledge and weapons of war, and also [incidentally] his religion, to achieve his ambitions (Latukefu 1970:61).

With the eventual decline in the rank and status of the *Tu'i Tonga* and the concomitant rise of the *Tu'i Kanokupolu*, the position of the *Tamaha* also suffered a decline. Where the titles of *Tu'i Tonga* and *Tu'i Kanokupolu* meant that the individual so invested was responsible, respectively, for sacred and secular matters, Thomas has pointed out that in aboriginal Tonga the *Tamaha* "is more a title of honour than office" (MS. 4: 30). Although the *Tamaha* was usually held by a female, Thomas also pointed out that "there may, in the absence of a female, be a male *Tamaha* — which thing has been known to occur, but generally it is a female" (ibid.).

The rank and status associated with that of the *Tamaha* was extremely high in Tongan culture, and early nineteenth-century observers were astute enough to point this out. The French navigator, Dumont D'Urville reported of his 1827 visit to Tongatapu:

all the people of Tonga, without exception, even the touï-tonga and the touï-Kana-Kabolo themselves, had to accord the homage of *moe-moe*, while she was not obliged to honour anyone in this way (n.d.:27).

The *moemoe'i* was the indication of respect that an inferior had to show to a superior, with the inferior person bowing down to touch the head to the soles of the superior person's feet.

Dumont D'Urville, however, was also aware of the fact that by showing deferential respect one did not necessarily acknowledge power and authority, and he pointed out that the *Tamaha* "was reverenced in the islands although she only had any real authority over her personal property and her people in Ardeo" (ibid.). She not only had authority over "Ardeo," or *Ha'ateiho* (an area on Tongatapu), but it also extended into the Ha'apai islands. Of the person designated the *Tamaha*, Thomas wrote:

while it raised the individual in the estimation of all her friends, she was by this means brought so near to the gods, as to be a kind of divinity herself to the people, and was much sought unto as such (Thomas MS. 5:4).

The Wesleyan missionary Webb was quite correct when he wrote that "the *Tamaha* is the greatest personage in the whole group of islands" (Webb, Letter-Journal of March 1, 1843, for the events of August 12, 1842). Where the *Tu'i Tonga* was the representative of the gods on earth, the *Tamaha* herself was virtually viewed as a god.

Although the Wesleyans made numerous attempts to convert the *Tu'i Tonga* Laufilitonga to Wesleyanism, they failed (and the *Tu'i Tonga* became a Catholic); on the other hand, the *Tamaha* converted to Wesleyanism and the missionaries scored quite a coup on aboriginal religious beliefs when this happened. Thomas wrote in his Journal that "Tamma ha has turned to God — also her brother Fehokohaabai, and all the people of Tungua have turned" (Thomas, *Journal 5*, December 12, 1832). Gradually, Tongan culture changed in the nineteenth century under the pressure of the Wesleyan missionaries.

The four titles of *Tu'i Tonga*, *Tu'i Ha'a Takalaua*, *Tu'i Kanokupolu*, and *Tamaha* thus represented the core of titles of aboriginal Tongan culture. From these four titles all other titles developed and as Thomas stated (as cited earlier), "formerly there were three ranks of nobles in Tonga" for whom one would apply the term *'eiki* (Thomas MS. 5: 1). The concept of *'eiki* has changed over time in Tonga, but this change has not always been understood and interpreted by all European observers. Writing of these four core titles in the nineteenth century, one astute eyewitness to changing Tongan culture did comprehend the changes in part:

It may be noticed that the term Eiki applied to the above chiefs and their families almost exclusively in gone by days, and was a very choice word, but of later years it has become more common (Thomas MS. A1961: 7).

In aboriginal Tonga, individuals closely related to the *Tu'i Tonga* were termed the *Sino'i 'eiki*, literally 'the body of the *'eiki*' (Churchward 1959: 430). These included the *Tu'i Ha'a Takalaua*, *Tu'i Kanokupolu*, and the *Tamaha*. In aboriginal Tonga, *'eiki* was a concept of nobility, or noble birth. *'Eiki* is not immediately synonymous with 'chief' as numerous early European observers recorded.

One of the earliest voyage accounts of Schouten and Le Maire from 1616 has *Ariki* for 'King' (Dalrymple 1770–1771: II; n.p.). The various vocabularies connected with Cook's voyages have, for the Tongan vocabularies, *'Eegee* as 'a chief' (Anderson, in Beaglehole 1967: 956),

Agee as 'chief' (Samwell, in Beaglehole 1967: 1045), and *Eegee* as 'chief' in King's 1821 vocabulary (King 1821: 447). Mariner's 1817 edition has *E'gi* as 'a chief; a god' (II: n.p.) and with a cross-reference to 'chief' one finds in Mariner "(a noble). Egi; (chief of a district or island) toói; (supreme chief or king) how" (ibid.). By the time of Mariner's 1827 edition, however, some revisions had been made and for *Egi* Mariner has "a chief; a god; the head man of a party" (1827: II, lvi). This final definition roughly approximates the range of variation on the concept of *'eiki* in aboriginal Tongan culture. Not all 'chiefs' as reported by European observers were *'eiki* to the Tongans and not all *'eiki* to the Tongans were chiefs.

At one point in the past the *Tu'i Tonga* divided his lands between his kinsmen, his *'eiki*. The various *'eiki* established and belonged to their own named groups or *'eiki* of *Ha'a*, a corporate descent group. Various *'eiki* of the *Ha'a* were given titles to represent some specific aspect of the *'eiki*. When the *Tu'i Kanokupolu* Ngata received his title, he gave his own son who was named Leilua the title of *Ve'ehala* which is roughly translated as 'the wrong-footed man.' With the title of *Ve'ehala* went some land on Tongatapu. It is the title of the *'eiki* which passed on to another individual when the *'eiki* was no longer able to perform his duties. The title would not necessarily go to the oldest natural son of the *'eiki*. The title could be passed to a brother of the *'eiki;* the title could go to a son of a sister's child, or the title could go to an adopted son of the *'eiki*. In aboriginal Tonga, succession to titles (and chieftainship) depended on a variety of factors, including a joint decision of the corporate descent group on the ability of the prospective *'eiki*, as well as his age, number of wives, and the number of supporters the *'eiki* could muster if he wanted to be a chief of the corporate descent group.[3]

It cannot be stressed enough that in aboriginal Tonga consensus and flexibility were key concepts. An *'eiki* who wanted to be a chief of a group of people had to have the consent of the people; and a chief also needed the consent of his fellow chiefs. Even the *Tu'i Tonga* could not be appointed to the title without the consent and support of either the *Tu'i Ha'a Takalaua* or the *Tu'i Kanokupolu*. Thomas wrote in his *Journal* that "there is a union amongst the Tonga people, especially the chiefs, so that they consult each other before they determine anything" (February 11, 1826). A *Tu'i Kanokupolu* had to have the support of the various *Ha'a* of Tonga to become *Tu'i Kanokupolu*. Thomas recorded how one individual had given up the *lotoo* or Wesleyan religion:

---

[3] See Urbanowicz (n.d. [1973]) for a description and analysis of aboriginal Tongan adoption patterns and the changes in adoption and inheritance procedures as a result of the Tongan Constitution of 1875.

This evening Hohela came today to say that Tooboo had yielded to give up lotoo and to be made the Tooicanacabola. In a few days time all the old people are to meet at this part [Hihifo on Tongatapu] to make him. This is a serious event (Journal entry of December 1, 1827).

Other nineteenth-century observers also witnessed this "consensus and flexibility" aspect of Tonga culture: Cross wrote how the "Monarch is only a superior Chief, and is absolute no longer than he is supported by others, many of whom have nearly as much power as himself, and in some instances more" (Hunt 1846: 30). One non-missionary observer of 1850 wrote:

The government of the islands is despotic, and not hereditary, but elective in the royal family. The eldest son of the king does not necessarily succeed his father, but another may be chosen from the sons of a former king, or a younger son may be elected before an elder if he be thought to have more capacity for government (Brierly 1852: 98).

Thus an *'eiki* who was chosen as a chief had to have the support of the people. He was a titled *'eiki*.

In aboriginal Tonga, there were also those *'eiki*'s who did not have a title: these would be the *Sino'i 'eiki* for whom genealogical position, and not a mere title, was the important criterion. There were also those individuals who did have a title, yet were not *'eiki*. These would be *matapule* titles — titles given to an individual by an *'eiki*, and the *matapule* title-holder would look after a specific spot of land for the *'eiki*. Finally, in aboriginal Tonga, (as well as today), there was the bulk of the populace: non-titled, non-*'eiki* individuals.

In aboriginal Tonga then, *'eiki* stood for a concept of noble birth and Tongans used the term appropriately. The Tongans would be able to distinguish between: titled *'eiki*, such as the *Tu'i Tonga*, non-titled *'eiki*, a kinsman of the *Tu'i Tonga*, titled non-*'eiki*, a *matapule*, and the non-titled, non-*'eiki*, bulk of the populace. In aboriginal Tonga, then, *'eiki* was a concept of noble birth and not synonymous with 'chief.' In the nineteenth century Thomas wrote:

From this it will be seen that there are very many persons in the Friendly Islands, to whom the term *eiki* applies — persons who have nothing to do with the government of the Islands, but who had to be supported according to their rank, and many of them did receive more than civil respect — they had what may be called divine homage paid them, and some of them appeared to think that that was their proper right and due (Thomas MS. A1961: 16).

CHANGES

With sustained European contact, culminating in the Tongan Constitution of 1875, aboriginal Tongan culture changed. The Constitution was promulgated by the *Tu'i Kanokupolu* King George Tupou with the aid of European advice. King George's refusal to install a *Tu'i Tonga* after the death of Laufilitonga in 1865 has already been discussed. With the Constitution of 1875 King George totally consolidated his position (receiving the titles of *Tu'i Tonga* and *Tu'i Kanokupolu*) and removing the inherent consensus and flexibility concerning the rights of chieftainship.[4] The flexible system of titles and inheritance passed out of existence and a rigid father-to-son inheritance system was initiated. Where before a person received a title because of ability and consensus, now a person received a title because of the law. A completely workable system of status achievement had been removed and in its place a system of ascribed status substituted.

With the Constitution of 1875 King George created the hereditary class of nobles, or *nopele*, who are included in the generic gloss *hou'eiki*. The Constitution created the *'eiki nopele*, but some of these *'eiki nopele* were only *matapules*, or titled non-*'eiki* in aboriginal Tonga, and hence were only *'eiki* in name and not *'eiki* by noble birth.

Prior to the Constitution, no one individual could hold more than one title, since the title-holder was responsible to a specific group of people. Now, as a result of the Constitution there are men holding two titles, the most notable being Honorable Kalaniuvalu-Fotofili, and an individual has to divide his time, and hence his obligations, between two different groups of people.

In aboriginal Tonga, women always had important positions in the society, with the *Tamaha* being the classic example, With the passage of time, the descendants of the *Tamaha* have suffered (Kaeppler 1971: 183), although the *Tamaha* herself had extremely high rank and status in

---

[4] It was not written into the Tongan Constitution that *Tu'i Kanokupolu* King George was given the two titles of *Tu'i Tonga* and *Tu'i Ha'a Takalaua*. King George merely said that he "was conferred" with the two additional titles; however, at the same parliamentary meeting, King George said: "However I now desire to appoint paramount chiefs for these two dynasties as well as the Hangatatupu so I now confer the following titles and they are to be hereditary. (1) Tungi and his descendants to be head of the Ha'atakalaua for ever. (2) Kalaniuvalu and his descendants to be head of the Kauhala'uta [of the *Tu'i Tonga*] for ever. ..." (In Hunter 1963: 4). One of the reasons that this was done was because of the fact that it was eventually written into the Tongan Constitution that if King George Tupou I were to have no legitimate heirs, the "Crown of Tonga" was to "descend to Uiliami Tugi and his lawful heirs" (King George Tupou I in *Tonga Government Gazette*, Volume II; 35E, December 16, 1885, page 1; also see Wylie 1967: I, 21).

Tongan culture. In aboriginal Tonga, the *Tamaha* and her descendants always were well treated.

INTERPRETATION AND SUMMARY

Change obviously takes place over time and to discuss changes in Tonga one must first know what Tonga was like. Tonga is the only Polynesian island group to successfully survive into the twentieth century. It is currently a Constitutional Monarchy under His Majesty King Taufa'ahau Tupou IV. The survival and establishment of the constitutional monarchial form of government was due to a skillful and somewhat bloodthirsty unification of the archipelago in 1852 by King George Tupou, later known as "the First" and a Great-Great-Great Grandfather of his current majesty.

The unification of the archipelago after the final war in 1852 and the subsequent reorganization and codification of the laws along Western European concepts brought about changes which have had ramifications in Tonga to this day. Scarr has shown that Tongans were advised in the nineteenth century that if Tongans wanted to avoid being "taken over" by larger foreign powers, Tonga would have to take on the trappings of Westernization. This Westernization was replete with a "Western facade" of a written Constitution and codified laws (Scarr 1968: 86). Thus the Constitution of 1875 must serve as a landmark for virtually any discussions pertaining to Tongan culture.

In a volume on psychological anthropology, it only seems fitting that there be some psychological aspects to the paper: psychological aspects concerning both the Tongans and the numerous Europeans who have been in Tonga and who have written on Tonga. For aboriginal Tongans, rank was something which came about because one was born into the position. Status could be achieved by means of arranged marriages, skill at leadership or warfare, or anything which would virtually enhance an individual in the minds of fellow Tongans. The family was all important, or the genealogical relationships between individuals of the extended family. In aboriginal Tonga, politics was "kinship writ large," something which seems to exist to this day. The *Tonga Chronicle* of October 17, 1971, had the following statement in reference to the wife of His Majesty King Taufa'ahau Tupou IV:

Queen Mata'aho in an interview with the Singapore newspaper *Straits Times* explained the tradition of the people and the monarchy in Tonga is like one big family with the King and Queen looked on as parents.

This may be how some view the monarchy today, and it would probably be consistent with a statement pertaining to aboriginal Tonga, but it is not how nineteenth-century (and earlier) Europeans viewed Tonga. Alboriginal Tonga WAS an extended family, with virtually everyone being able to trace kinship ties with everyone else. The concept of *'eiki* or noble birth was a perfectly viable one in aboriginal Tonga, for Tongans knew who was genealogically related to whom. The fact that only a proven individual could be made a leader of men in aboriginal Tonga also made sense — but this did not make sense to European observers of the time. The Europeans, with European concepts of government, expected to find an articulating "wholeness" in Tonga; instead, as Wilson's statement makes clear, to their eyes they found chaos:

The Government of Tongataboo is so complex in itself, and the natives' account of it so different, each taking a particular pride in exalting his own chief above others, that it is difficult to come to any certainty concerning it (Wilson 1799: 269).

Cook's ealier statement from 1777 is also in keeping with this approach:

Of the nature of Government we know no more than the general outline, a subordination is established among them that resembles the feudal system; but of its subdivisions of the Constituent parts and in what manner connected to form one body politic I confess myself totally ignorant (In Beaglehole 1967: 174).

Cook was not "totally ignorant" but he was honest in his reporting.

When the missionaries arrived, particularly the Wesleyans in the nineteenth century, they too were confused — but they did something about it: they did not admit to their confusion and set out to convert a culture! They sent back fantastic reports to Sydney and to London and continued to receive money and supplies to "convert" the Tongans. It was a fortuitous moment in 1826 when the Wesleyan missionaries Thomas and Hutchinson arrived on Tongatapu: they brought their own supplies (to augment those abandoned by Lawry when that missionary left in 1823) to convert the Tongans, they capitalized on the Europeans who had been living in the archipelago for numerous years, and they also profitted from the problems of the Tongans. As Thomas relates in his Journal for 1827:

I learn from a young man here, an Englishman, that Tonga at this time is principally in the possession of petty chiefs. Some few years ago the great men departed this life and some were killed — even the King's family now have no power — but these chiefs fought and defended Tonga and they now possess the part they have rescued from their enemies, SO THAT AT THIS TIME THEY SEEM MUCH CONFUSED, HAVING NO HEAD MAN (Thomas, *Journal*, entry of January 30, 1827. Emphasis added.)

Because there was no "head man" or secular ruler, there was no Tongan with the authority to order the missionaries to leave. The mission approach was that of "divide-and-conquer" and they turned Tongan against Tongan — chief against chief. The religious wars of the nineteenth century which resulted from Wesleyan interference in aboriginal Tongan life were notorious for their ferocity. In January of 1837, the Wesleyan missionary Watkin could write of the destruction of the non-Wesleyan-ized-Tongan fortress of Ngeleia and how "one Christian was killed and three wounded more than 25 heathens perished" (Watkin, Journal entry for January 11, 1837). Of the 1840 battles, the Wesleyan missionary P. Turner wrote:

The heathens seem determined to die in their foolishness. I am told that they have made an oath to do so, before they will yield to the Xtns. (Turner, *Journal*, entry for July 19, 1840).

Of the ferocious 1840 wars, Thomas could write that he told the *Tu'i Kanokupolu* Jiosaia Tupou that "the heathens had acted more kind a great deal than the Christians and that they were less disposed for war" (Thomas, *Journal*, entry for August 4, 1840).

Aboriginal Tonga was forcefully pulled into the nineteenth century and more needs to be written on this distasteful period. The demise of aboriginal Tongan culture was clearly visible in 1840 when the Wesleyan missionary John Thomas, probably one of the few missionaries who ever partially "understood" Tongan culture (and who has been ridiculed for it), wrote in his Journal of August 4, 1840, of the titled *'eiki* Ma'afu of the *Ha'a Havea*, a staunch non-Wesleyan-induced pro-indigenous Tongan individual:

Old Maafu is angry and grieved, saying like one of old, "Ye have taken away my gods, and what have I more."[5]

---

[5] Thomas gathered a tremendous amount of potential ethnographic data, most of which (if not all of it) still remains in manuscript form. He realized the problems of data-gathering when he was asking specific questions and the following somewhat poignant statement from his *Journal* of 1858 is worth re-reading: "conversed with a few persons, on some little matters connected with the Tonga history. My matter accumulates — also I hope it is in a way to be corrected before it sees the light — but whatever case I may take, it is scarcely possible to avoid making some mistakes, the more so, as various opinions are formed by various persons on the same subject" (Thomas, *Journal*, entry of February 20, 1858).

REFERENCES

ANONYMOUS
1944 *Pacific Islands*, volume three: *Western Pacific (Tonga to the Solomon Islands)*. London: Naval Intelligence.

BEAGLEHOLE, JOHN CAWTE
1961 *The voyage of the Resolution and Adventure 1772–1775*, volume two. Cambridge: Hakluyt Society.
1967 *The voyage of the Resolution and Discovery 1776–1780*, volume three, part two. Cambridge: Hakluyt Society.

BENSON, C. IRVING
1960 "Missionaries of the South Seas," in *The Pacific ocean: ocean of oceans*. Edited by C. L. Barrett, 113–125. Melbourne: N. H. Seward Pty.

BRIERLY, O. W.
1852 Sketch of the Friendly Islands and Tongatabu. *Journal of the Royal Geographical Society* 22:97–118.

CHURCHWARD, CLERK MAXWELL
1959 *Tongan dictionary (Tongan-English and English-Tongan)*. Oxford: Oxford University Press.

COHN, BERNARD S.
1968 "Ethnohistory," in *International encyclopedia of the social sciences*, volume six, 440–448. New York: Macmillan.

COLLOCOTT, E. E. V.
n.d. *Papers on Tonga, 1845–19?? I–V*. Sydney: Mitchell Library ML MSS. 207.

COLSON, DON PEDRO DE NOVO Y
1885 *Viaje politico-cientifica alrededor del mundo por las corbitas Descubierta y Atrevida almando de los capitanes de navie D Alejandro Malaspina y Don Jose de Bustamente y Cuerre desde 1789 a 1794*. Madrid: Imprenta de la Viuda e Lijos de Abiengo.

COULT, ALLAN D.
1959 Tongan authority structure: concepts for comparative analysis. *Kroeber Anthropological Society Papers* 20:56–70.

DALRYMPLE, ALEXANDER
1770–1771 *An historical collection of the several voyages and discoveries in the South Pacific Ocean*, volume two: *Dutch voyagers*. London: Nourse.

DODGE, ERNEST S.
1968 The American sources for Pacific ethnohistory. *Ethnohistory* 15:1–10.

DUMONT D'URVILLE, JULES S. C.
n.d. Partial translation by Olive Wright of *Voyage de la Corvette L'Astrolabe ... Histoire du voyage, 1826–1829*. Wellington: Alexander Turnbull Library Misc. MS. 1374.

FENTON, WILLIAM N.
1962 Ethnohistory and its problems. *Ethnohistory* 9:1–23.

GIFFORD, EDWARD WINSLOW
1929 *Tongan society*. Honolulu: Bernice P. Bishop Museum.

GOLDMAN, IRVING
1970 *Ancient Polynesian society.* Chicago: University of Chicago Press.
HUNT, JOHN
1846 *Memoir of the Rev. Wm. Cross.* ... London: Mason.
HUNTER, D. B., *editor*
1963 *Tongan law reports,* volume two. Nuku'alofa: Govt. Printing Office.
KAEPPLER, ADRIENNE L.
1971 Rank in Tonga. *Ethnology* 10:174–193.
KING, JAMES
1821 *The three voyages of Captain James Cook round the world. Complete in seven volumes,* volume two. London: Longman.
LATUKEFU, SIONE
1970 "King George Tupou I of Tonga," in *Pacific islands portraits.* Edited by J. W. Davidson and D. Scarr, 55¼75. Canberra: Australian National University Press.
LAWRY, WALTER
n.d. *Diary (February 1818–February 1825).* Sydney: Mitchell Library A1973 (copy also under M.O.M. 134).
LOCHER, G. W.
1967 "Historical and unhistorical anthropology," in *Septième Congres International des Sciences Anthropologiques et Ethnologiques,* volume four, 77–84. Moscow.
LURIE, NANCY OESTREICH
1961 Ethnohistory: an ethnological view. *Ethnohistory* 8:78–92.
MARINER, WILLIAM
1817 *An account of the natives of the Tonga Islands.* ... by John Martin, two volumes. London: James Murray.
1827 *An account of the natives of the Tonga Islands.* ... by John Martin, two volumes. Edinburgh: Constable.
MAUDE, ALARIC MERVYN
1965 "Population, land, and livelihood in Tonga." Unpublished Ph. D. dissertation, The Australian National University.
MAUDE, HENRY EVANS
1971 Pacific history: past, present and future. *Journal of Pacific History* 6:3–24.
MURDOCK, GEORGE PETER
1967 Ethnographic atlas. *Ethnology* 6.
SCARR, DERYCK
1968 *Fragments of empire.* Canberra: Australian National University Press.
STURTEVANT, WILLIAM C.
1966 Anthropology, history, and ethnohistory. *Ethnohistory* 13:1–51.
TAPA, SIONE
1971 *Report of the Minister of Health for the year 1970.* Nuku'alofa: Government Printing Office.
THOMAS, JOHN
n.d. *Journal 1 (1825–1828).* Sydney: Mitchell Library Microfilm FM4/1433 reel 42 (original in London).
n.d. *Journal 5 (April 1832–October 1834).* Sydney: Mitchell Library Microfilm FM4/1434 reel 43 (original in London).

n.d. *Journal 6 (October 1834–March 1838)*. Sydney: Mitchell Library Microfilm FM4/1434 reel 43 (original in London).

n.d. *Journal 7 (March 1838–September 1841)*. Sydney: Mitchell Library Microfilm FM4/1434 reel 43 (original in London).

n.d. *Journal 12 (February 1856–October 1859)*. Sydney: Mitchell Library Microfilm FM4/1436 reel 45 (original in London).

n.d. *MS. 4, History*. Sydney: Mitchell Library Microfilm FM4/1439 reel 48 (original in London).

n.d. *MS. 5, Ranks of chiefs*. Sydney: Mitchell Library microfilm FM4/1439 reel 48 (original in London).

n.d. *MS. A1961, History of the Friendly Islands*. ... Sydney: Mitchell Library A1961.

TUDOR, JUDY, *editor*

1968 *Pacific islands year book and who's who* (tenth edition). Sydney: Pacific Publications (Australia) Pty.

TURNER, NATHANIEL

1828 *Letter-journal* dated November 29 (with entry of October 28, 1828). Sydney: Mitchell Library Microfilm FM4/1417 reel 26 (original in London).

TURNER, PETER

n.d. *Journal (June 11, 1839–April 15, 1840)*. Sydney: Mitchell Library B305.

URBANOWICZ, CHARLES F.

1972 "Tongan culture: the methodology of an ethnographic reconstruction." Unpublished Ph. D. dissertation, University of Oregon.

n.d. [1973]. "Tongan adoption before the Constitution of 1875," in *Adoption and fosterage in Oceania*. Edited by I. A. Brady. Honolulu: University of Hawaii Press.

VASON, GEORGE

1810 *An authentic narrative of four years' residence at Tongataboo*. ... London: Longman, Hurst, Rees and Orme.

WATKIN, JAMES

n.d. *Journal*, two volumes. Sydney: Mitchell Library A834 and A835.

WEBB, WILLIAM

1843 *Letter-journal* dated March 1 (with entry of August 12, 1842). Sydney: Mitchell Library Microfilm FM4/1419 reel 28 (original in London).

WILSON, JAMES

1799 *A missionary voyage to the southern Pacific Ocean, 1796–1798 in the ship 'Duff.'* London: Chapman.

WYLIE, CAMPBELL

1967 *The law of Tonga*. ..., three volumes. Nuku'alofa: Government Printing Office; London: Sweet and Maxwell.

When Brokers Go Broke: Implications of Role Failure in Cultural Brokerage

MICHAEL SALOVESH

> The position of [cultural] "brokers" is an "exposed" one,
> since, Janus-like, they face in two directions at once. They
> must serve some of the interests of groups operating on
> both the community and national level, and they must cope
> with the conflicts raised by the collision of these interests.
> They cannot settle them, since by doing so they would
> abolish their own usefulness to others. Thus they often act
> as buffers between groups, maintaining the tensions which
> provide the dynamic of their actions.
>
> ERIC WOLF[1]

This paper is a study of cultural brokers in action. Ultimately, it is aimed
at the same kinds of questions that Wolf asks in his pioneering article
(1956). Wolf, however, chose to look at cultural brokers as part of an
attempt to understand complex societies at the national level. I will
examine the effects of cultural brokers in a local community. If the
cultural broker is like Janus, then the anthropologist, too, must look
both ways to grasp the import of cultural brokerage. Because I share
with Wolf an interest in learning how the larger society operates, I am
examining the interface between local community and the national-level
society. Wolf's later works (1959, 1969) have pointed the way to national-
level interpretations — a lead that has been followed by many others
(cf., e.g. Banton 1966; Adams 1970; etc.). Studies of cultural brokerage

Fieldwork on which this paper is based took place in 1958–1959, 1960–1961, 1962,
1963, 1968, and 1972. The support of the Social Science Research Council, the Department of Anthropology of the University of Chicago, and the Purdue Research Foundation is gratefully acknowledged.
[1] In: *Aspects of group relations in a complex society: Mexico*, page 1076.

from the local viewpoint are a necessary complement to those which concentrate on the national scene. This paper is such a study.

I begin with a brief overview of the relations between ethnic groups in Venustiano Carranza, Chiapas, Mexico, the town which provides a setting for the brokerage activities examined here. Then follows a detailed examination of the roles played by both an indigenous local leader and an outsider (whose role as conscious agent of directed culture change also involved cultural brokerage). The interplay between these two strong brokers is the center of specific empirical data examined here. Finally, the conflict of brokers and the ultimate "failure" of both of them provide entry into a discussion of the structural implications of role performance and role failure in cultural brokerage.

The cases studied here took place around forty years ago. Why have I not chosen more contemporary cases? The first reason has already been stated by Wolf: "group relationships involve conflict and accommodation, integration and disintegration, processes which take place over time" (1956: 1066). The consequences of the activities examined here, parts of a series of processes in which the local community went through dramatic readjustments in its relationships with outsiders, have had the necessary time to work themselves out. In recent years, culture change has been so dynamic in this community, and so many brokers have arisen and fallen, that it would be difficult to pick up the threads of a single series of events without writing several books of explanation. Even then, the explanation would be as incomplete as the processes themselves. Finally, I have had to face serious ethical problems in examining, for public presentation, the activities of contemporary figures on the local scene.[2] What I write here will shortly become available to officials of national and state government, and to at least some members of the community itself. Although I have closely followed the activities of many cultural brokers in the community during the last fifteen years, I cannot

---

[2]   Three cases from my notes will illustrate the possible drastic consequences, on both brokers and the community, of public knowledge of details of brokerage activities. An Indian who turned cultural brokerage to his own financial profit was repeatedly accused of witchcraft, and eventually killed by other Indians — "coincidentally" at the time when some of the extent of his profit became known. A self-styled "mestizo" go-between was shot from ambush when a powerful rancher learned of the broker's nearly successful attempt to reclaim illegally-expropriated Indian communal lands. A priest who established a school in which Indian and poor Ladino children had a chance to make up for discrimination against them in the official Escuela Federal was "exiled" to a remote, isolated community when his superiors learned about the school. (I hasten to add that this was because church-connected schools are forbidden by law, not because the priest's superiors were opposed to education as such, nor because they favored discrimination.)

allow myself the luxury of publishing the details of their activities now. There is too much danger that they will suffer from my indiscretions. Nonetheless, I cannot wipe out what I know; some of the conclusions presented in the final section of this paper have been shaped in part by my knowledge of recent brokerage relationships.

THE TWO COMMUNITIES OF VENUSTIANO CARRANZA[3]

Venustiano Carranza (formerly called San Bartolomé de los Llanos) has been an important agricultural community in Chiapas, Mexico, since the sixteenth century (see, for example, Gage 1946: 143; Thompson 1958: 139). Cotton was a major cash/trade crop in the sixteenth through eighteenth centuries, and there have been several periods of cattle ranching as a major source of income during the present century, but the products of milpa agriculture have been the prime economic base throughout recorded history. Large surpluses of maize and beans grown in the fertile lands near the Río Grijalva (Río Grande de Chiapa) are exported annually, except in years of severe drought.

Censuses taken in the town at various times from the sixteenth through the eighteenth centuries show a steady growth in population to an apparent peak, in 1778, of at least 4,800 (Trens 1957: 222). The population in the 1930's was something on the order of 7,000; between 1960 and the present, the town has grown from about 10,000 inhabitants to perhaps 15,000 today. (Censuses in the Colonial epoch are notoriously undependable in their precision; my own investigations suggest that there are also gross errors in the reported population of V. Carranza in the decennial censuses of 1960 and 1970. I prefer to avoid the specious accuracy that would be implied by citing the exact figures that appear in published censuses.)

More interesting than the basic population figures is the fact that V. Carranza has been a mixed community, part Indian, part "Ladino," at least since the early 1600's. "Ladino" is the local term for Spanish-speaking individuals oriented to supra-local norms. The term "Indian" is used here to mean individuals whose first language is a native American one — in this community, Tzotzil Maya — and who participate in the affairs of some local, closed corporate peasant community (cf. Colby

---

[3] In the remainder of this paper, I shall use Venustiano Carranza to refer to the town as a whole. When I speak of the Indian community within the town, I follow the practice of Mexico's Instituto Nacional Indigenista and the Museo Nacional de Antropología by calling the Indian community San Bartolomé.

and van den Berghe 1961; Wolf 1957.) Census figures suggest that
Ladinos constituted at least 10 percent of the local population by 1712;
at the turn of the present century, they made up about a third (or less) of
the inhabitants of a temporarily reduced town center. In the early 1930's,
Ladinos were a rapidly rising segment of the population, slightly less
than 40 percent of the total; by 1960, Ladinos made up about half the
population; today, as many as two out of three inhabitants of the town
may be Ladinos. (The recent rise in Ladino population, in both absolute
and relative terms, is due more to in-migration from other parts of the
state than to any differential in reproductivity or mortality rates within
the town.)

In this century, settlement patterns in V. Carranza have gone through
three major stages. Prior to the Mexican Revolution, the bulk of the
population came into the town center only for ceremonial occasions.
(Most of the Indians were bound in debt peonage to owners of outlying
fincas, and many of the Ladinos resided on cattle ranches or plantations
well away from the town.) Military campaigns in the surrounding
countryside around 1917 made a move to some densely-settled center a
practical necessity (See, e.g. Moscoso 1960.) At about the same time, the
Revolution ended the system of debt peonage, freeing the Indians to
return to their old town-center. Finally, heavy Ladino in-migration in
the late 1920's and early 1930's, together with the seizure of much Indian
land within convenient walking distance of the town, led the Indians
(but not the Ladinos) to a divided settlement pattern which continues
to this day. In this pattern, women and children reside in the town all
year long. Indian men, however, follow a typical pattern of leaving the
town on Mondays, sleeping in their distant fields during the week, and
returning to their families on Friday evening. (In Salovesh [1965] I
comment on the effects of this "periodic manlessness" on patterns of
acculturation among the Indians of this town. In that article, I suggest
that the same pattern occurs elsewhere, albeit rarely; and that the effects
of the pattern where it occurs are so important that they justify adding
this category to those established in Tax [1937]. The other patterns I
have described here are what Tax would call a "vacant town" and a
"town nucleus" type of settlement pattern.)

From 1917 to 1934, there were two kinds of formal governmental
structures which reigned in V. Carranza. The first, the Ayuntamiento
Constitucional, was established under the provisions of the 1917 Constitution of Mexico and the dependent provisions of Chiapas state law.
Under the law, this Ayuntamiento (like its predecessors in prior centuries)
was recognized as the legitimate governing body of both the town and

a large territory (now called a *municipio*) surrounding it. V. Carranza was, and is, the *cabacera* (head town or administrative center) of both the *municipio* and an even larger judicial district, governing both the rural periphery and several subsidiary towns. (Among the administrative dependencies of the *cabecera* are the Indian community of Aguacatenango and the Ladino town of Socoltenango.) Until 1934 or 1935, neither the Presidente Municipal nor any members of the Ayuntamiento (the *regidores*, or 'councilmen') were Indians. Since 1936, it has become the custom for one of the *regidores* to be selected from among the Indians of the town center. (The Tzeltal-speaking Indians of Aguacatenango remain unrepresented on, but subordinate to, the municipal Ayuntamiento.)

In parallel to the council and officers recognized as legitimate by state and national law, V. Carranza had a separate Indian Ayuntamiento until 1934. Legally, this Ayuntamiento had no binding jurisdiction as a general governing body, although it could and did control access and title to lands owned communally by the Indians (see *Constitución*, Article 115; *Leyes* 1959, Article 64 et seq.). But the Indian Ayuntamiento functioned extralegally as the basic organ of Indian government. (I use the term "government" in the sense defined in Smith 1956.) This group also served as one of the central foci of the traditional politico-religious hierarchy through which the Indians organized their public life. (Structure of this hierarchy in San Bartolomé is described and analyzed in Salovesh [1971]; for an overview of similar hierarchies in Mesoamerica in general, see Carrasco [1961]).

Two kinds of divisions within the Indian community of San Bartolomé will become relevant later in this paper. First, the community was and is organized into five partially independent groups based on territorial divisions within the town. These groups, *(barrios)* were traditionally in control of separate segments of the communally-owned agricultural lands. Each *barrio* was led by its own "council of elders" (the *principales*, 'principal men,' those who had risen to the top of the hierarchy through service in temporary civil and religious offices). A second kind of internal division within the Indian community was the lingering aftermath of an ancient moiety division. *Barrios* were wholly-included subdivisions of the moieties. In some unspecifiable past, strict moiety endogamy had been practiced, but this custom had pretty much disappeared by the 1920's. (Still, those who wished to marry across the lines of the old moiety division are said to have been required to seek permission of the *principales* of the *barrios* concerned; no such permission was needed for inter*barrio* marriage within a moiety.) Men from one *barrio* found it easy to use lands traditionally assigned to another *barrio* within their own former moiety, but it was extremely rare for a man to make his *milpa* on lands assigned to the opposite moiety, and a complicated process of seeking formal permission was a prerequisite. Since the 1920's, the last vestiges of formal moiety organization, as such, have disappeared. But the old *barrio* allegiances to the former moieties have provided the nucleus for continuing factional alliances in the political structure of the community.

The existence of two separate formal organs of government within V. Carranza was but a reflection of a larger social reality. I have shown elsewhere (Salovesh 1971: especially Chapter 3) that the physical commingling of Indian and Ladino residents within the town does not conceal the fact that for all practical purposes there were two socially separate communities within the town during the time period with which this paper is concerned.[4] Here and elsewhere, when I speak of the Indian community within V. Carranza, I refer to it as the community of San Bartolomé. In many ways, the lives of the Indians of San Bartolomé are very much like those of their Tzotzil-speaking cousins in such better-known communities as Zinacatan (Vogt 1969) or Chamula (Pozas 1959). But the immediate physical presence of such a large proportion of Ladinos within the same town, and the imbedding of the Indian community within a surrounding and superordinate Ladinos community in virtually the same physical space, has led San Bartolomé to a series of unique adjustments to the Ladino world.

Within a period of about five years before and after 1930, the community of San Bartolomé underwent drastic shifts in its relationships with the surrounding Ladino community. The activities of two men, who are called "Bartolo" and "El Maestro" in this report, were central to these developments. Both were cultural brokers; both had careers marked by temporary success, but ultimate "failure" in their brokerage roles. Let us now examine what they did, and how.

---

[4] I have come to speak of the community of San Bartolomé as if it were totally, rather than partially, separate from the Ladino community with which it shares the town of V. Carranza. I thus take the position that relations between San Bartoleños and Ladinos within the town reflect, in microcosm, the relations between isolated peasant communities and the larger national community. (Treating the Indian segment of a mixed community as if it were an independent, isolated community of its own is hardly an innovation in Mesoamerican studies; see, for example, Tax [1953], Gillin [1951], Tumin [1952], etc.)

A *CACIQUE* AS CULTURAL BROKER

Bartolo was born an Indian of San Bartolomé. Unlike nearly all of his contemporaries, however, Bartolo was sent to a school for Indians in another town at an early age, and he remained there at least until his late teenage years. At school, Bartolo gained an excellent command of Spanish, and he became comfortably literate. At the same time, he became fluent in his understandings of how Ladino culture worked — particularly in the political sphere. Later in life, Bartolo's command of spoken and written Spanish and his knowledge of Ladino culture made him unique among the Indians of San Bartolomé.

When Bartolo returned to V. Carranza and San Bartolomé, he was well past the age for service in the bottom level of the politico-religious hierarchy. He did serve, once or twice, as a lower-level *mayordomo* in those groups within the hierarchy that were responsible for the celebration of annual fiestas, but he never rose very high in the ladder of offices and never was a *principal*, in the traditional sense. Instead his literacy in Spanish and familiarity with Ladino ways soon led to Bartolo's appointment as the Secretary of the Indian Ayuntamiento.

The post of Secretary carried no authority in the traditional Indian system. It was customarily held by younger men, who were temporarily excused from service in the fiesta hierarchy during their service as quasi-official scribes. The post was regarded as an onerous burden, which took a great deal of the incumbent's time but yielded no increment of prestige and little other reward save a token salary.

But Bartolo's knowledge of the Ladino world, and his comfort in handling the written record, was far superior to that of his predecessors in the office of Secretary. As broker between the Indian community and the surrounding Ladino world, he was able to use the written record to recover some Indian land rights, and he was an effective representative of Indian viewpoints when minor conflicts between Indians and Ladinos arose. On this base, Bartolo began to build a series of interlocking networks with many of the leaders of the Indian community. Eventually, he forged alliances of mutual obligation and particularly close ties of *compadrazgo* (affinal relationship or work-group association) with major leaders from all five *barrio* territories within the community.

At the same time that Bartolo was building a power base out of his position as Secretary of the Indian Ayuntamiento, he made himself a vital link in communications between the Indian community and agencies of Ladino government and powerful individuals in the Ladino community. Drawing on his connections within all five Indian *barrios*,

Bartolo could deliver labor levies or cash contributions in the quantities requested by Ladino authorities. And, having delivered Indian goods and services in response to the demands of outside authorities, he could later call on those authorities to cut corners in granting permission to the Indians to conduct activities they considered vital. (Law or custom, according to the specific case, called for Ladino authorities to grant or withhold permission for Indians to celebrate a public fiesta, to bring crops into or through town, to send delegations to state or national authorities, to clear trees from *milpas* being prepared for new planting, *ad infinitum, ad nauseam*.) Eventually, Bartolo was able to convert his control of the written record and of access to outside authorities into power that made him the *cacique* (political boss) of the entire Indian community. He exacted a toll of power and prestige from both sender and receiver whenever communication took place between the Indian community and the outside, Ladino world.

Bartolo's position of power ultimately depended on the unique command of communication channels he had taken into his own hands. True, the *principales* of the five *barrios* usually forged interlocking alliances that resulted in a unitary power structure within each *barrio* — but Bartolo's alliances entered into all five *barrios*. Many *principales* were able to join their counterparts in neighboring *barrios* to form larger units of political control by the manipulation of kinship and *compadrazgo* links across *barrio* lines, but the lingering aftermath of the old moiety system stood in the way of expansion of these links to the community as a whole. No *principal* had close solidary links outside the two or three *barrios* of his own moiety, and Bartolo used his own connections to keep such links from forming. A constant struggle over diminishing land resources led the *principales* of the two opposing groups to a strong desire to maintain exclusivity in rights of usufruct on communal lands to their own followers, and Bartolo used his control of the land records to keep the two groups apart.

Another part of Bartolo's control of communication channels came from his personal network of dyadic relationships with powerful authorities in the Ladino world. The most notable of these was his unique relationship with the Secretary-General of the Department of Agrarian Affairs of the national government. This major leader had political ambitions centering on his native state of Chiapas; he later was to move from the Department of Agrarian Affairs to become manager of the National Bank of Ejido Credit, and finally gained election as Governor of Chiapas. In all of these posts, this leader was in a position which could be used either for or against the Indians of San Bartolomé. And whenever an Indian delegation from the community went to see him, in one or another of his official capacities, Bartolo served as spokesman for the group. It was Bartolo who wrote to ask for appointments, Bartolo who controlled the written records, and Bartolo who had the greatest confidence in speaking Spanish with such an important figure. And, whether or not the community could get the actions it sought from the head of such powerful outside organizations, the community under Bartolo's leadership could provide a strong base of apparent popular support for the future of the man who might use his government offices to help them. Bartolo also used his position within the Indian community to form similar relationships with other outside leaders on the local and state levels. In each case, Bartolo's access to those outside leaders was qualitatively and quantitatively far different from that available to any other Indian leader.

Eventually, Bartolo's power within the Indian community was to be sorely tried by events originating outside that community. The ways he moved to meet those challenges, and the effects of his actions on the community as a whole, can only be examined after we have looked at the position of a Ladino cultural broker whose activities complemented Bartolo's for many years.

A TEACHER AS A CULTURAL BROKER

El Maestro was born and raised in Veracruz. He first came to Chiapas as a major in the Constitutionalist forces during the latter part of the Mexican Revolution. Late in the 1920's, he was appointed head of the federally-supported primary school in V. Carranza; soon afterwards, he set up evening and Sunday adult education classes for Indians and Ladinos alike. His classes, particularly those for adults, were El Maestro's platform for the advocacy of political, economic, and social change throughout his residence in V. Carranza.

El Maestro was soon appointed as a local organizer for the "official" political party — called, in its early days, the Partido Nacional Revolucionario, or PNR. In the early 1930's, it was the conscious policy of the PNR to beat swords into plowshares by making teachers out of former Army officers. But the civilian function of these ex-officers was, in a sense, a continuation of their old military missions: as party organizers, their primary duty was to mobilize support for both the PNR and the national government and its programs (see Bosques 1937: 10, 59–61).

Today, San Bartoleños recall that El Maestro's teachings began with a call for unity and solidarity. Many of them quote him as repeatedly saying "now we are a single pueblo, united in the interests of all." From El Maestro's viewpoint (and that of the PNR), the "we" of this statement meant the people of Mexico — but to the Indians of San Bartolomé, the words were taken as a call for cross-*barrio* and cross-moiety unity. Later, when he preached a message of class solidarity for all members of "the agricultural sector" — i.e. *milperos* and agricultural laborers — he was interpreted as supporting the possibility that poor, landless Ladinos be allowed to use Indian communal lands.

In fact, El Maestro's activities took on just such a local flavor. As he built the *campesino* section of the local PNR apparatus, and tried to build local support for the land reform programs of the central government, El Maestro had to break down old allegiances and avoidances. To consolidate his power on the local front, he eventually had to mount a three-pronged attack on the forces of leadership in the Indian community by initiating or promoting changes in labor relationships, in religious participation, and in access to land. In all of these programs, he was at the same time taking power away from the old *principales*, the Indian Ayuntamiento (and Bartolo, its Secretary), and the exclusively-Indian Comité Agrario (the land-holding alter ego of the Ayuntamiento.)

For centuries, Indians in San Bartolomé had been subject to service in unpaid labor levies at the beck and call of Ladino authorities. Allegedly, this service was supposed to be *pro bono publico*, and limited to such work as road-clearing, cleaning streets and public areas, and the like. But it was customary for rich Ladinos to use the system as a means of obtaining free labor on their ranches and plantations. The Indians were not unaware that similar practices had been among the causes of the Revolution, and they had begun to resist Ladino calls for labor levies even before El Maestro's arrival. (Bartolo's rising power, in that initial period of resistance, came from the fact that his community-wide ties with leaders in all *barrios* made him uniquely able to deliver workers in the desired numbers, while *principales* limited to a base of followers in only one or two *barrios* often could not get together an adequate work force when asked to do so.) But it took El Maestro's constant reiteration of the labor articles of the 1917 Constitution to make a convincing case. In 1932, El Maestro — acting on behalf of some members of his adult-education classes, who had been threatened by the Indian Ayuntamiento with jailing for their repeated refusal to contribute labor to public projects — got legal support through his PNR connections. As a result, the labor levy system was officially ended, and future work on public projects became a matter of paid labor.

Prior to El Maestro's arrival, and for some years afterward, Indians also contributed both labor, goods, and money to the fiesta-celebrating wings of their politico-religious hierarchy. From the beginning (which, after all, coincided with a militant phase of anticlerical activities at the national level) El Maestro fought against this. Again, many informants today impute the same words to him, suggesting that he taught the following as a kind of litany: "A man who gives to the fiestas carries a load like a pack animal." (This was an obvious play on the word *cargo*, meaning both 'burden' and 'fiesta office'.) "When he has money, he burns it up in skyrockets and liquor in the fiestas. When you get money, you should save it to buy a burro. Then the animal can do the work of an animal, and you can walk upright like a man. But when you give money or work to the fiesta, then you will remain like an animal, nothing more."

Finally, El Maestro sought to promote class solidarity by opening access to all sections of the Indian communal lands to any member of the community, regardless of *barrio* affiliation, and to poor Ladinos as well. The Indian Ayuntamiento resisted this proposal with all the force it could muster, under the particular urging of Bartolo as *cacique*. At the same time, Indians in general resisted any move to cut down on, or away from, the celebration of fiestas in the traditional way. If San Bartolomé had been isolated from outside forces in these matters, El Maestro's programs would have been an utter failure; but outside forces did operate, dramatically.

In August, 1933, the Governor of Chiapas ordered that all churches in the state were to be closed and locked permanently (Lópes Gutiérrez 1957: III, 449–450). Federal troops acting under his orders came to V. Carranza on November 1st to insure that these orders were carried out. (At the same time, they seized and burned church records, images of the saints, and altar decorations, both from the churches and from attempted refuges in private homes. The day is locally called "the burning of the saints.") The troops remained in the town for several years, serving as the local police force. There was no public celebration of fiestas for the next six years; traditional recruitment to office in the politico-religious hierarchy came to a permanent end.

In February, 1934, Lázaro Cárdenas, President-elect of Mexico, made an unprecedented tour of Chiapas, fulfilling his campaign pledge to visit every part of the country. Cárdenas recieved a San Bartolomé delegation led by El Maestro, the only local leader to be received individually by the President-elect. It is my impression that Cárdenas, himself a general, undertook a private visit with El Maestro as part of his program to unite and continue his hold on former as well as present officers in the military as Cárdenas maneuvered for control of the emerging official party. But back in V. Carranza, local Ladinos took El Maestro's visit with Cárdenas as a signal that he enjoyed the direct support of the President-elect.

On his return to V. Carranza, El Maestro, at the head of a squad of locally-garrisoned Federal troops, released the prisoners who had been jailed by the authority of the Indian Ayuntamiento. He then marched the troops over to the building which had been occupied by the offices of the Indian Ayuntamiento, padlocked the Indian offices, and posted a military guard to insure that the Indian Ayuntamiento could no longer exercise quasi-legal power. He was supported in these actions by the town's Ladino authorities and by most of the Indian pupils of his adult-education classes. The way was now clear for a direct confrontation between El Maestro's followers and those Indians linked to Bartolo, the *cacique*. The arena for this confrontation was to be provided by questions relating to access to the communal lands.

Before examining the most dramatic episodes of confrontation between El Maestro and Bartolo, let us stop to consider whether, and in what ways, El Maestro can properly be considered as a cultural broker rather than a politician, a teacher, or an agent of directed culture change. To a certain extent, anyone occupying one of the latter three roles must often act through means that are indistinguishable from those of the cultural broker. Generally speaking, however, each of these three roles is directed at ends quite different from those of the cultural broker, and brokerage activities are simply one set of means out of many that might be used to achieve the ends implicit in these other roles. The cultural broker, on the other hand, exists — or, rather, persists in his role — only so long as he can keep the cultures he bridges dependent on his services as intermediary. El Maestro's activities as politician were based on his attempts to unite a single segment within the Indian community (and, to a lesser extent, the lower levels of the Ladino community as well), not really to advance the avowed aims of the PNR he nominally served. He took two different attitudes toward teaching: when teaching Ladino children, the occupation from which he derived primary support, he taught to national standards by traditional schoolroom methods, with the end result that at least some of his pupils were able to go on to further schooling on their own. But he did little more for the Indian children in his classes than to keep them in the classroom; he made little or no effort to help them learn Spanish, and did not lead more than half a dozen to even rudimentary literacy in all his years of teaching in the town. His adult-education classes, insofar as they served as something more than a pulpit for message preaching, served to increase the dependence rather than the independence of the students. The new programs and techniques he introduced called for more sophisticated knowledge than he was willing (or able?) to impart for their continuation without the intervention of a cultural broker as intermediary. (I am convinced, but do not have the space to demonstrate here, that this was deliberate policy on El Maestro's part, designed to consolidate his own position.) Finally, the major effect of the cultural changes El Maestro introduced was to cut down on the independent avenues to power and communication formerly available to the Indian community while increasing the community's dependence on his own power through his control of intercultural communication. All of these activities are much more consonant with the classic role of cultural broker, who must struggle to maintain the separation between the groups he bridges, than they are with the other roles El Maestro played.

BULLS AND BEARS: BROKERS IN CONFLICT

The two brokers we have been examining had often taken opposite sides in their approaches to power through control of the gates of intercultural communication. Bartolo had obtained his power through manipulation of the traditional system; El Maestro worked to undercut the traditional system through ending labor levies, fiesta participation, and the authority of the Indian Ayuntamiento. Their struggles came to a head in a continuing conflict over land control.

Until April, 1934, title to the extensive communal lands owned by the Indian community was formally held by a group called the Comité Agrario. Service as a member of the Comité Agrario was coterminous with formal membership in the Indian Ayuntamiento. When El Maestro, aided by Federal troops and Ladino authorities, closed down the Indian Ayuntamiento, its former members continued to serve as the Comité Agrario for a short time. As in the past, the committee members were only nominally in control of that organization; their actions were totally controlled by the body of *principales*. The *principales*, acting through the Comité Agrario, controlled the allocation of use-rights on communal lands and the rental of those lands to outsiders; they adjudicated land disputes between Indians, and represented the Indian community before legal authorities when land disputes arose between Indians and Ladinos. But when the Mexican government adopted a new Agrarian Code in April, 1934 and that Code was implemented by Chiapas law a short time later *(Código Agrario* 1934), the Comité Agrario of San Bartolomé was formally dissolved by law. Its titles and functions were transferred to a new landholding organization called Bienes Comunales.

The first crisis over disputed lands under the Bienes Comunales organization came as that organization was being formed. The old Comité Agrario had rented some fallow lands to a group of Ladino cattlemen, who used the lands for grazing. Bartolo had been instrumental in gaining the approval of the *principales* in this arrangement. Now some Indians wanted to return those lands to cultivation, only to be rocked by the cattlemen's claim that they had purchased, not rented, the land. El Maestro, fully familiar with the legal provisions of post-Revolutionary land acts, knew that it was legally impossible to alienate communally-owned lands. Capitalizing on the impression of power gained through his visit with President-elect Cárdenas, El Maestro sought the intervention of local authorities. At that time, the Ladino Presidente Municipal (roughly equivalent to a combination of town mayor and chairman of a county board) was a man who had several relatives who were landless milpa farmers. The Presidente agreed to recognize the Indian claims to return of their lands, on condition that some of his poorer relatives be allowed to farm on Indian communal land. El Maestro formalized this arrangement by agreeing to use his influence to open full participation in Bienes Comunales to any landless Ladino *milpero*; Bartolo, anxious to bring the rented lands back to Indian control so that he would not be blamed for their loss, joined El Maestro in this commitment. The Presidente then obtained court orders restoring the disputed lands to the control of Bienes Comunales.

In the first elections of Bienes Comunales officers, newly-admitted poor Ladinos joined El Maestro's followers among the Indians in electing an Indian who was fully sympathetic to El Maestro's views as head of the new organization. But several other officers chosen in the same election were *principales* firmly linked to Bartolo, and Bartolo's old job of secretary meant that he still retained physical possession of the land titles, basic documents, and records of the Indian community. The initial phases of internal struggle within Bienes Comunales, then, resulted in no clear advantage for either cultural broker.

Events on the national scene brought strong outside pressure on the newly-formed Bienes Comunales organization. The accelerating pace of land reform under President Cárdenas was pushing Bienes Comunales toward a legal reorganization of its land titles, even though those titles were recognized as valid under the new Agrarian Code.[5] Under Cárdenas's

---

[5] Somehow, against the overwhelming tide of Mexican history between 1847 and the 1911 Revolution, most of the Indian communal lands had remained in the community's

program of land reform, the *campesinos* of V. Carranza were asked to reconstitute themselves as an *ejido*, a form of cooperative landholding group. If a majority of the members of Bienes Comunales agreed to take this step, the former landholding organization would be disbanded and its lands transferred to the *ejido* (cf. Simpson 1937). I will not review here all the ins and outs of arguments favoring or opposing the formation of an *ejido*, in V. Carranza or elsewhere, but a very abbreviated summary may prove helpful to those unfamiliar with the history of this institution in Mexico. (Both Simpson [1937] and Tannenbaum [1964] provide good overviews of the problem from a national viewpoint.)

If Bienes Comunales were to be completely supplanted by an *ejido* under the national program of agrarian reform, the law provided that title to enough land to support the new organization would be guaranteed. Much of the land would, of course, come out of lands to which Bienes Comunales already held uncontested title; but many areas of highly productive land had been alienated from Bienes Comunales control, particularly in areas close to the town. Formation of an *ejido* held the promise of regaining these alienated lands for use by *milperos*. An *ejido*, furthermore, would have access to credit from the National Bank of Ejido Credit, from which Bienes Comunales was effectively precluded. An *ejido* would also be entitled to technical assistance, aid in forming a marketing cooperative, and wholesale buying privileges for a consumer cooperative if the members of the *ejido* decided to form one (*Plan sexenal* 1934: par. 52, 53; *Código Agrario* 1934: Article 148, 153). For *milpero* Ladinos newly given access to communal lands, there was the further advantage that they would be guaranteed legal protection for continued access to *ejido* land, while the original land grants on which Bienes Comunales based its successful struggle for recognition of title to the communal lands had been made "a los Indios nativos de San Bartolomé de los Llanos ..." (to the *Indians* native to San Bartolomé and their descendants).

There would also have been many disadvantages resulting from the replacement of Bienes Comunales by an *ejido*. The promise of restoration of lands close to town carried with it the threat of losing some of the most fertile land in the area, bottom lands along the Río Grijalva that were too far from the town center to be legally assigned to an *ejido* based in V. Carranza. Agricultural land would have to be divided into indivi- dually-held plots, a method of landholding inappropriate to the *milpero's*

---

control (cf. Simpson 1937: 15–55). In 1934 and early 1935, Bienes Comunales sought and received legal recertification of its land titles. (See *Código Agrario* [1934: Art. 27 et seq.] for a statement of the legal grounds for this recertification.)

techniques of shifting cultivation. Furthermore, each member would have to give five per cent of his crops to the *ejido* for the formation of a general fund (see *Código Agrario* [1934: Article 139, 153] for the legal provisions underlying these disadvantages). Most Indians of San Bartolomé viewed the legal formalization of poor Ladino access to Indian lands with suspicion, if not alarm. Finally, in general it could be argued that the Bienes Comunales way of holding the land was closer to tradition, more secure in its operation, and more likely to survive any new shifts which might occur in the national laws than the ways of an untested and unfamiliar *ejido*.

There was no way for Bartolo and El Maestro to remain aloof from this struggle over the landholding organization if they were to maintain their positions as cultural brokers. Whatever was done would require recourse to outside authorities, and if the two cultural brokers did not take part, they ran great danger of losing their previous control of communication between the community and the outside world. In the ensuing events, El Maestro (true to his role as supporter of President Cárdenas) pushed hard for the formation of an *ejido*. Bartolo, seeing a chance to regain some of the power he had lost with the closing of the Indian Ayuntamiento, urged his associates among the *principales* to oppose the *ejido*. Within the Indian community and in Bienes Comunales, Bartolo's views eventually held the field — but most of the Ladino *milperos* and a sizeable minority of the Indians hived off from the community. They petitioned for recognition as a new *ejido*, establishing the town of La Vega del Paso in the fertile bottom lands near the Río Grijalva (see *Código Agrario* 1934: Articles 99–108). By establishing their *ejido* center near the river, the *ejidatarios* obtained title to the best available land base; most of their land was located outside the former territories of Bienes Comunales, but they took a large chunk of the best portion of Bienes Comunales land as well.

El Maestro's partial success in aiding the foundation of an *ejido* contained the seeds of his downfall as a cultural broker. The new community was located some twenty miles away from V. Carranza, and his school duties kept him from close contact with the *ejido*, which contained nearly all his close supporters and those who had been most dependent on his brokerage activities. Eventually, El Maestro's position as a Federal employee got him embroiled in the struggle over the Chiapas gubernatorial elections of 1936. The outgoing Governor's chosen candidate was generally opposed by Federal employees, and Governor Grajales took strong measures against many of them while he still held office. Nonetheless, the candidate supported by Grajales lost the election, and the incoming Governor — Gutiérrez Rincón, Bartolo's old contact in the Department of Agrarian Affairs and later in the National Bank of Ejido Credit — was highly suspicious of those who had retained Federal employment during Grajales's program of persecuting his opponents (see López Gutiérrez [1957: III, especially 457] for an insider's view of this struggle over the 1936 Chiapas gubernatorial succession.) For a short time, El Maestro was put in jail by officials of one side or the other. This made the weakness of his alleged support from President Cárdenas apparent on the local scene. Even worse for El Maestro, most of his strongest local supporters now no longer lived in V. Carranza, and their *ejido* was not as successful as they had been led to hope. (The problems of the La Vega *ejido* were of a piece with those making problems for new *ejidos* all over Mexico; see, for example, Whetten [1948: 216–224], Simpson [1937: 335–353]). As a result, El Maestro was unable to prevent his discharge from the Federal school in V. Carranza; he was forced to leave the town to seek further employment elsewhere.

For a time, Bartolo paradoxically gained new power after his failure to block the formation of the new *ejido*. Many of his most vocal opponents among the Indians were drained out of the community for all practical purposes. Ladino *milperos*, with whom Bartolo had not developed either relationships of control or mutual dependence, were reduced to a very small proportion of those who remained with Bienes Comunales. Furthermore, while the *ejido* had great difficulties in its early years, those who stayed with Bienes Comunales had several comparatively good crop years in a row. Finally, Bartolo's old political patron in Mexico City was now the Governor of Chiapas, and willing to listen sympathetically to requests for assistance from the Indians of San Bartolomé — provided those requests were channelled through Bartolo's intervention. (Symbolically, Bartolo's apparent position of power was reinforced when his daughter received gifts and a congratulatory semipublic telegram from the Governor on the occasion of her marriage.)

But Bartolo's reaccession to power as the acknowledged *cacique* of the San Bartolomé Indians was to prove much more limited than his old powers as Secretario of the Indian Ayuntamiento. One series of events, among many, will serve to show how those limits were made clear. In 1938–39, public legal pressure against the celebration of religious fiestas was considerably lightened. By accident, a majority of the ritual specialists needed for the customary Indian celebrations happened to be inhabitants of Bartolo's *barrio*, and because of his particularly close relationships with the *barrio principales* Bartolo was able to exercise a major measure of control over how and where the ritual specialists would perform. As the fiesta cycle was re-established, Bartolo tried to use this control to dictate the conditions under which fiestas would be celebrated. He asked that the Indians return to the old system of obligatory labor service within the fiesta groups. In 1939, Bartolo became the elected Indian representative on the municipal Ayuntamiento; he used the power of that office to cause the jailing of Indians who would not obey him or the *principales* when labor levies were being assembled. These extralegal attempts to impose control were ended permanently in March, 1940. At that time, outgoing President Cárdenas made a second tour of Chiapas. A delegation of Indian leaders, mostly young men but including a few *principales*, went to a pan-Indian conference called by Cárdenas, and while there they complained that their followers were being forced into labor levies without compensation. On his return, one of the dissident leaders advised the men of his *barrio* to refuse unpaid service in the fiesta organization. Bartolo jailed that leader, but the leader's friends went to the state capital for the assistance Cárdenas had promised. Bartolo's old champion was no longer Governor, and the new Governor issued official orders freeing the dissident leader and jailing Bartolo in his turn. (In the subsequent legal hearing before the Ladino municipal judge, all charges were dropped on both sides, contingent on future good conduct.) After that series of events, Bartolo was replaced by another Indian on the municipal council. From that time until his death in the mid-1940's, the old *cacique* was largely limited to expressing his public position through participation in ritual affairs. Even there, he was reduced to the role of one leader among many. (For example, his name is painted on the doorway of a small church that was rebuilt in 1945 as one of those who contributed to the reconstruction. That is more recognition than was given to most of the participants, who are acknowledged by a collective "y demás otros socios" [and other participants in addition]; but his name is not first on the list of four, and one of the others listed specifically is the same "dissident leader" Bartolo had put in jail in 1940.)

DISCUSSION: "FAILURE" AND "SUCCESS" IN BROKERAGE

The events I have described here, and other similar sequences I have observed in San Bartolomé in more recent times, raise serious questions about how we are to define "failure" and "success" as we examine cultural brokerage in the context of goal-oriented activities. It is clear that much of the literature on cultural brokerage has had a consistent eufunctional bias, despite Wolf's caution that brokers often have to act to "maintain ... the tensions which provide the dynamic of their actions" (1956: 1076). My knowledge of cultural brokerage in San Bartolomé inclines me to believe that those outcomes which are functional in maintaining cultural brokerage as a means of coping with boundary problems at the interface of two cultures may very well be dysfunctional in their effects on at least one of the cultures involved in the contact situation: conversely, it may be that the community's "success" depends on the broker's ultimate "failure." Let us briefly reexamine the two cases cited here to expand on possible applications of these ideas.

El Maestro's role with regard to the Indians of San Bartolomé can be seen from three viewpoints: (1) that of the political party at the national level; (2) of the community; (3) as an example of the interests of a cultural broker. Whichever of these viewpoints one adopts, his activities ultimately resulted in failure. As promotor of the programs of the PNR, El Maestro did succeed in establishing an *ejido*, and in linking *ejido* members firmly to national institutions. But most San Bartoleños remained firmly committed to the traditional forms of community organization by staying with Bienes Comunales. As soon as external pressure was lifted, they returned to the celebration of the old fiesta cycle — modified, it is true, by the removal of such "official" sanctions as the jailing of those who were reluctant to serve, but still a pattern closely similar to that of the old days. The PNR, on the other hand, was firmly anti-Church in its programs. Agricultural productivity remained essentially unchanged despite El Maestro's attempts to introduce technological innovations. Finally, San Bartoleños remained uninvolved in and uncommitted to the idea of participation in the national, state, or municipal communities. From the viewpoint of the local community, El Maestro's activities resulted in a reduction of local autonomy when he closed the Indian Ayuntamiento. The ending of labor levies, viewed by the Indians as a good in itself, nonetheless had the result of removing one bargaining counter which had been an effective means of gaining some concessions from Ladino authorities. As one result, Indians lost the support of formerly sympathetic Ladinos in later land struggles. Finally, the fact that El Maestro was forced to leave the community constitutes sufficient demonstration of his failure to protect his own interests.

Bartolo's career, in the period examined here, was one of a type that could be called a holding action against external forces constantly militating against each position of power he was able to develop. First, the Ayuntamiento which had provided him a base through his post as secretary was dissolved. Indian labor levies, which he was uniquely able to deliver and in exchange for which he was able to gain support from Ladinos to his own advantage, were ended. He was forced to participate in opening Bienes Comunales to Ladino participation — even though he knew full well that these new participants were entirely capable of communicating with outside authorities by themselves, and would have little or no use for his services as intermediary. His later attempts to consolidate control through his election to the Ayuntamiento Constitucional were likewise blocked, ultimately by his removal from that council.

We are not concerned here, however, with the question of whether a particular individual manages to make a success of his chosen activities. In all cultures, some people do better, some do worse, in achieving their own ends. Here, I have been interested in the balance between the personal ends of a cultural broker and the effects of his activities on the communities he bridges. Both brokers we have watched in action here (and their successors in the same community) had ambivalent vested interests. Full promotion of the best interests of the community would have led to the elimination of any need for the services of a cultural broker. If El Maestro had been completely successful, within the framework of the ideas he was supposed to promote for the PNR, San Bartolomé would have become an integrated part of the national community — and the local community of V. Carranza as well. If Bartolo had been completely successful in promoting the ideals of his own natal community (ideals which were obviously impossible of accomplishment), the Indians would have become completely independent of outside, Ladino interference. Every move toward partial accomplishment of these ultimate goals was a move away from the community's dependence on the services of either of the cultural brokers. But if they had been unable to deliver some kind of progress toward BOTH integration and independence, they would have been unable to continue in their roles as brokers through failure to serve the interests of their "clients."

The cases I have examined here, then, are more than detailed examples of how two individuals operated in the context of an ethnically divided town. They suggest that the cultural broker is both more and less than a Janus-like figure, facing in two directions at once. Unlike Janus, who was a keeper of the gates, cultural brokers have their deepest interests in keeping the gates of communication between cultures or between ethnic groups closed. For the broker to succeed AS A BROKER, he must try to control those gates so as to guarantee that only the broker himself may pass them freely. To maintain that sort of control, the broker can only afford to give a surface impression of serving some of the interests of groups operating on both the community and national level. While doing so, the broker who would continue to maintain himself in his brokerage role must ultimately work against the interests of both communities while appearing to serve them.

REFERENCES

ADAMS, RICHARD
  1970 *Crucifixion by power*. Austin: University of Texas Press.
BANTON, MICHAEL, *editor*
  1966 *The social anthropology of complex societies*. A.S.A. Monograph 4. London: Tavistock Publications.
BOSQUES, GILBERTO
  1937 *The National Revolutionary Party of Mexico and the six-year plan*. Mexico, D.F.: Bureau of Foreign Information, National Revolutionary Party.
CARRASCO, PEDRO
  1961 The civil-religious hierarchy in Mesoamerican communities: pre-Spanish background and colonial development. *American Anthropologist* 63:483–497.
Código Agrario
  1934 *Código Agrario de los Estados Unidos Mexicanos*. México, D.F.: Departamento Agrario.
COLBY, BENJAMIN N., PIERRE L. VAN DEN BERGHE
  1961 Ethnic relations in Southeastern Mexico. *American Anthropologist* 63: 772–792.
Constitución
  1962 *Constitución política de los Estados Unidos Mexicanos*. México, D.F.: Librería Porrua. (This document available in many editions, from several publishers; the edition cited is reprinted and redated annually whether or not there have been intervening amendments. No special significance of the particular edition is implied by its citation here.)
GAGE, THOMAS
  1946 *Nueva relacion que contiene los viajes de Tomas Gage en la Nueva España*. Guatemala, C.A.: Biblioteca "Goathemala."
GILLIN, JOHN
  1951 *The culture of security in San Carlos*. Middle American Research Institute Publication 16. New Orleans: Tulane University.
Leyes
  1959 *Leyes del Estado de Chiapas*, tomo I: *Constitución política del estado y leyes*. México, D.F.: Galeza.
LÓPEZ GUTIÉRREZ, GUSTAVO
  1957 *Chiapas y sus epopayas libertarias* (third edition, revised and enlarged.) Tuxtla de (*sic*) Gutiérrez, Chiapas, Mexico.

MOSCOSO, PRUDENCIO
   1960   *El Pinedismo en Chiapas.* México, D.F.
Plan Sexenal
   1934   *Plan sexenal del P.N.R.* México: Partido Nacional Revolucionario.
POZAS A., RICARDO
   1959   *Chamula: un pueblo indígena de los altos de Chiapas.* Memorias del
          Instituto Nacional Indigenista 8. México, D.F.: Instituto Nacional
          Indigenista.
SALOVESH, MICHAEL
   1965   Pautas de residencia y estratificacíon entre los Mayas: algunas per-
          spectivas de Son Bartolome, Chiapas. *Estudios de Cultura Maya* 5:
          318–338.
   1971   "The political system of a Highland Maya community: a study in the
          methodology of political analysis." Unpublished doctoral dissertation,
          Department of Anthropology, The University of Chicago.
SIMPSON, EYLER N.
   1937   *The ejido: Mexico's way out.* Chapel Hill: University of North Carolina
          Press.
SMITH, M. G.
   1956   On segmentary lineage systems. Curl Bequest Prize Essay for 1955.
          Journal of the Royal Anthropological Institute 86:39–80.
TANNENBAUM, FRANK
   1964   *Mexico: the struggle for peace and bread.* New York: Alfred A. Knopf.
TAX, SOL
   1937   The *municipios* of the midwestern highlands of Guatemala. *American
          Anthropologist* 39:423–444.
   1953   *Penny capitalism: a Guatemalan Indian economy.* Institute of Social
          Anthropology Publication 16. Washington, D.C.: Smithsonian In-
          stitution.
THOMPSON, J. ERIC S., *editor*
   1958   *Thomas Gage's travels in the New World.* Norman: University of
          Oklahoma Press.
TRENS, MANUEL B.
   1957   *Historia de Chiapas.* México, D.F.
TUMIN, MELVIN
   1952   *Caste in a peasant society: a case study in the dynamics of caste.* Prince-
          ton, New Jersey: Princeton University Press.
VOGT, EVON Z.
   1969   *Zinacantan: a Maya community in the highlands of Chiapas.* Cambridge,
          Massachusetts: Belknap Press (Harvard University Press).
WHETTEN, NATHAN L.
   1948   *Rural Mexico.* Chicago: University of Chicago Press.
WOLF, ERIC R.
   1956   Aspects of group relations in a complex society: Mexico. *American
          Anthropologist* 58:1065–1078.
   1957   Closed corporate peasant communities in Mesoamerica and Java.
          Southwestern Journal of Anthropology 13:1–18.
   1959   *Sons of the shaking earth.* Chicago: University of Chicago Press.
   1969   *Peasant wars of the twentieth century.* New York: Harper and Row.

PART SIX

Psychological Anthropology: Trends, Accomplishments, and Future Tasks

JOHN J. HONIGMANN

Psychological anthropology, as I conceive it, employs the concepts and theories of psychology (including psychiatry) to study what it assumes to be the individual's significant role in the creation, performance, and maintenance of culture and social structure. From the opposite standpoint, it studies the implications of culture and social structure for the experience of individuals, including their behavior and mental health.

The Long-Standing Interest in a Psychology of Culture

Cultural anthropological theory has for a long time embodied assumptions about the psychological antecedents and concomitants of culture. Such assumptions prevailed among nineteenth-century psychogenic evolutionists who explained worldwide cultural similarities as due partly to the propensity of human beings everywhere to respond to similar experiences in much the same way. Even the later diffusionists regarded culture, its material apparatus and social forms as well as its ideational content, as a psychological phenomenon and therefore defined ethnology as the study of mental life in its overt forms (see, for example, Ratzel 1886: 181; Brinton 1895: 3, 11–13; Powell 1896: 633; Rivers 1924: 3). But rarely,

Originally written in 1972 for the National Institute of Mental Health, this paper has been somewhat revised and extended for this volume. Considerable assistance in revision was furnished by Irma Honigmann, particularly in editing and in assembling the bibliography.

prior to Freud, did anthropologists venture to explore in detail the psychological dynamics underlying culture in order to identify what specific features of man's mental life were expressed in particular cultural traits or institutions. Lacking knowledge about psychological processes, psychogenically minded evolutionists could only ascribe cultural innovations to anonymous individual inventors or to ancient tribal geniuses (Frazer 1910 [1899]: I, 138, III, 9–10; later he repudiated such forms of historical explanation).

Other theorists held culture to be an objective system, external to, and independent of the individual, which followed its own laws and processes (Comte 1911 [1854]: 195ff; Durkheim 1964 [1895]; Vierkandt 1908: 112). As a phenomenon sui generis, culture could, however, influence persons and pattern their behavior and development. This view, fundamental in the work of Ruth Benedict, Margaret Mead, and other pioneers of culture and personality, was first clearly stated in the seventeenth century when Francis Bacon (1937 [1625]) coined the phrase "tyranny of custom" to describe how people dutifully carried out socially required customs that were painful, morally reprehensible, and sometimes self-destructive. (For an earlier statement of the same idea, see Augustine 1972 [ca. 427].) Such customs, Bacon perceived, are often inculcated during early years of childhood when individuals are most pliable. In somewhat similar fashion, Descartes, looking for a basis of philosophical certainty, observed how people are led through divergent experiences in different lands to hold contradictory ideas (Descartes 1960 [1637]). In a passage that could have been written for a twentieth-century anthropology textbook, he maintains that a man of the same disposition would be quite a different person if brought up from childhood among Frenchmen, Germans, Chinese, or cannibals. Seventeenth-century philosophers tended to bemoan the grip of custom or enculturation on the individual because, as they saw it, it stupefied reason, distorted thinking, sanctioned superstitions and prejudices, and made for stupid behavior.

At the present time almost every other article in a journal of anthropology refers to psychological dynamics operative in culture, to the repercussions of culture on the individual, or to the role of individuals in the cultural process. Hence, strictly speaking, there is no discrete field of psychological anthropology. It is, however, customary to distinguish between casual psychological analyses of cultural phenomena and more deliberate, focused research consciously employing psychological theory. In reviewing developments in psychological anthropology (or, as I also call it, culture and personality) during the past quarter of a century or so, I deal mainly with research of the latter type.

OVERALL EVALUATION

Before looking at major trends in the last quarter century of research in psychological anthropology, I will adopt a more general orientation and ask about the contribution of this subfield to two areas in which, I think, it has had an especially pronounced impact: college teaching and the epistemology of anthropological method.

Appreciation of Cross-Cultural Variety

Injected into teaching, the results of culture-and-personality research have quickened several generations of American undergraduate students' appreciation of cross-cultural variety, brought them to realize the relativity of cultural behavior from one society to another, and made them aware of the basic consistency of human nature from one culture to another. Culture-and-personality materials have enabled the student learing anthropology to experience vividly, if through secondary sources, what it is to play another role than his own and what it means to live in another culture. The data of cultural psychiatry have enlarged his understanding of how socially-produced stress can erode the capacity for adaptation and adjustment. College courses in psychological anthropology continue to be popular, and each year's crop of applications for admission to graduate study brings a substantial number from undergraduates who want to work on problems connected with that topic.

Epistemological and Methodological Contributions

The self-examining or reflexive inquiries of anthropologists into how knowledge of culture is acquired and how personal and social factors of the observer affect such knowledge owe a considerable debt to psychological anthropology. Although a reflexive interest in social science goes back close to its beginnings,[1] the first article wholly devoted to anthropological epistemology was a reaction to dismayingly contradictory reports

---

[1] Late in the eighteenth century travelers as well as stay-at-home philosophers realized that in observing another culture one must be on guard against reinterpreting in familiar terms that which is difficult to grasp because it is strange. See, for example, Forster cited in Muehlmann (1968: 61); Forster (1968 [1777]: 13–14); Vico cited in Berlin (1969:84); Herder cited in Berlin (1965:55); and Goguet (1775:364).

resulting from psychological studies of American Indian societies. Conflicting views of personality traits associated with Pueblo Indian culture inspired John Bennett's inquiry (1946) in which he concluded that anthropologists' largely unconscious value preferences are apt to bias the collection and interpretation of empirical data.

The famous "sentiments controversy," which began when Needham (1962) issued his critique of Homans and Schneider's psychological explanation (1955) of matrilateral cross-cousin marriage, resuscitated and invigorated another old, but today still unresolved issue: the appropriateness and logical defensibility of providing psychological explanations for social facts. There is no easy rule to settle the question. Certain psychological reductionisms are now avoided — for example, the Freudian excesses that accounted for money and other cultural traits by characterological factors. Similarly, few will any longer try to account for historically rooted myths and folktales by appealing to psychological traits currently evident in the members of a social system. But it is valid to explain such narratives in terms of pan-human psychological traits forming part of the nature of man, the problem then being to identify those traits in an unambiguous, useful way. One could also explain the decision to tell or reinterpret a folktale or to apply or disregard a social rule by appealing to the motives of persons acting in a specific social situation. The latter is partially what the extended-case method and situational analysis are about (van Velsen 1967).

Another methodological problem stems from the tendency found in much cultural anthropology to make statements about behavior in a social system without attending to variability between the individuals or subsystems that are components of the system. To offset this tendency, psychological anthropologists like Wallace (1952) and Hallowell (1955: Chapter 18) borrowed the use of projective tests from clinical psychology and applied them in fieldwork to determine the extent of intrasocietal psychological variability.

Conducting anthropological research with attention to both the general and variable features of personality has naturally intensified the quantitative and statistical character of anthropology, which is also exemplified in hologeistic cross-cultural research, for example that dealing with the lasting effects of early socialization on personality pioneered by Whiting and his associates (J. Whiting and Child 1953).

Incidentally, the distinction sometimes drawn between the "old" and "new" culture and personality proves to be groundless when one considers the extent to which hologeistic studies have taken over early propositions in psychological anthropology (often based on psychoanalytic theory), operationalized the concepts, and demonstrated relationships cross-culturally that were originally advanced by psychologists, psychoanalysts, and fieldworkers interpreting for single societies.

MAJOR TRENDS IN RESEARCH

Social Aspects of Human Motivation

Assuming continuity between the realms of human nature and culture, psychological anthropologists have utilized psychoanalytic, behavioristic (learning theory), ethological, and other concepts, including temperament, in studying the role of motivation in cultural and social systems. Interest in motivation pervades much of culture-and-personality research, including socialization and cultural psychiatry. Among the motivating conditions most frequently studied are anxiety, hostility, and, frequently under the guidance of psychoanalytic thinking, sex. Anthropologists have written on how those motives are patterned in society and on how they are expressed or suppressed under cultural conditions. So they have asked about the cultural genesis of anxiety and cultural arrangements allowing anxiety to be discharged or reduced, for example through religion. Bernard Siegel (1955) has pointed out the role of a high anxiety level in sustaining tightly integrated social systems, such as the Hopi, ghetto Jews, and Hutterites. Like Freud in *Civilization and its discontents,* Siegel shows that people may pay a high price in the form of anxiety to maintain a way of life.

The role of hostility in social life has received almost as much attention as anxiety. Anthropologists have explored the cultural factors that generate high and low amounts of aggression and demonstrated how the drive may be displaced through sports and war (see, for example, Dollard, et al. 1939). How important societies may be in instigating aggression compared to the heritage of aggression retained by modern man since his days as a hunter is a question raised by Washburn's research. Washburn's thesis, which awaits critical examination, is that man's long career as a hunter, when humans learned to enjoy killing and to glorify conflict, deeply influenced his temperament and behavior. Hunting provided humans with a propensity to aggression at the same time that selection occurred for individuals able to control rage and therefore able to cooperate (Washburn and Yahraes 1969).

Under the influence of psychoanalytic theory, anthropologists began to pay considerable attention to the role of sex in social life and its frequently disguised expression in cultural behavior (for example, see Kardiner 1939, 1945; Holmberg 1950). This trend has become less conspicuous in recent work where, compared to anxiety and hostility, sex is not often referred to as an explanation of nonsexual behavior. Rather sexuality is more often treated as a dependent variable and, in the context of socialization, studied with regard to its control and patterning. Through the way the sex drive is culturally patterned it comes to possess motivating force, particularly with respect to interpersonal behavior of a sexual nature (for examples, see Honigmann 1947; Henry 1949; J. Whiting and Child 1953).

Another approach in anthropology and the other social sciences has dealt with the social significance of deficits in material gratification. This approach has been most conspicuous in research on deviant behavior. Thus in the ambitious study of Indians, Spanish-Americans, and Anglos in the western United States involving the anthropologist Graves, the theory successfully predicted that persons having the poorest access to the good things of life as defined in American culture would experience the greatest pressure toward deviance (Jessor, et al. 1968). More unusual has been the theoretical approach adopted by a psychologist, Aronoff (1967), employing Maslow's concept of a need hierarchy. His research in the Caribbean has shown the utility of the theory which asserts that as lower-level basic needs become satiated (note that the emphasis is not on deprivation), higher level needs of the personality are activated and motivate behavior.

PSYCHIATRIC DISORDER

Very prominent in psychological anthropology has been the trend to inquire into the sociocultural aspects of mental illness in Western and exotic cultures.

Patterning of Mental Illness

Early anthropological work concerning personality disorder emphasized the relationship between the pattern of aberrant behavior and cultural forms and personality traits shared by most people in the society. Interest in patterning has continued, for example, in Marvin Opler's work on the Midtown Study, examining the forms of schizophrenia that distinguish Italian-Americans from Irish-Americans (Opler and Singer 1956). Most of the extensive information available on so-called ethnic psychoses (pibloktoq, Arctic hysteria, etc.) belongs to this genre of research, though the question remains unanswered whether these are as culturally specific as has sometimes been thought (cf. Honigmann 1967: Chapter 13).

Etiology

Along with sociologists, anthropologists moved into the etiology of mental illness with the theory that culturally-produced stress affects mental health. Research has paid considerable attention to identifying potentially or actually stressful conditions in a culture — for example, in culture change, acculturation (Chance 1965; Chance and Foster 1962), and migration (Mangin and Cohen 1964). Naroll (1959) sought to measure stress, often using only indirect indicators rather than evidence provided from the phenomenological experience of the society's members (as in Langner and Michael 1963). Whereas stress promoting psychiatric strain has often been located in the community or culture generally, Bateson and Henry, working in American society, have sought it in the family context where it takes the form of disordered systems of communication between parents and children (Bateson, et al. 1963; Henry 1963).

One of the most extensive investigations of cultural factors in mental illness employing anthropologists is the Stirling County Study reported in three volumes (A. Leighton 1959; Hughes, et al., 1960; D. Leighton, et al., 1963). Working in a rural area of Nova Scotia, the researchers selected communities presumed to differ in the balance of benign and noxious conditions and successfully predicted that increasing stress would be regularly associated with increasing psychiatric disorder. Later the investigators replicated their research in Nigeria among the Yoruba and obtained results consistent with their Stirling County findings (A. Leighton, et al., 1963).

Cultural Factors in Diagnosis

When cultural relativism prevailed in American anthropology, anthropologists who interested themselves in the topic of mental illness took the position that whether an individual was mentally ill or not depended in large part on how the culture defined his behavior (Benedict 1934: Chapter 8). The American Historical Tradition flourishing in the 1920's and

1930's was strongly opposed to applying universalist criteria of normality across cultural boundaries.

The relativists' position is still valid. A person showing signs of what a Western psychiatrist diagnoses as behavior disorder, schizophrenia, or neurotic obsessiveness, for example, might indeed not be seen to need treatment or confinement in a social system with different standards of normality or wider limits of tolerance than Western psychiatrists endorse (see, for example, Cumming and Cumming 1957). That may well be true, but it does not preclude applying the universalist concepts of psychiatry to such behavior and that from there the behavior can simultaneously be categorized as psychiatrically abnormal (Honigmann 1968c).

Recently some anthropologists, including myself, have interested themselves in another problem involving cultural perceptions regarding mental illness. At issue are psychiatrists practicing in large-scale, culturally heterogeneous societies like our own. To what extent do class-bound cultural values operate when psychiatrists judge the seriousness of psychiatric symptoms? We may grant the validity of stress theory which maintains that the higher frequency of grave psychiatric disorder among North Americans of low social status is partly a product of noxious social conditions that wear people down until they show serious behavioral impairment. But when stress is carefully measured, as in the New York City Midtown Study, the difference between social classes is not proportionate to the frequency with which signs of grave impairment are found among patients of high and low socioeconomic status (Langner and Michael 1963). Something other than stress seems to be operating. There is a likelihood that middle- or upper-class psychiatrists from their cultural perspective evaluate even the normal style of behavior of persons in lower socioeconomic strata as less desirable than the style psychiatrists prefer and reinforce in their own families. In their diagnoses they are also likely to judge psychiatric disorder in individuals of that status as more distorted or more serious than similar disorders found in middle- and upper-class individuals. Such considerations affect the frequency with which mentally ill persons of low socioeconomic status are rated as more disturbed or worse off (Honigmann 1967: 413–421).

Therapeutic Milieus and NonWestern Psychiatry

Closely related to the study of mental illness as etiologically related to stress, has been the study of hospitals and other therapeutic milieus, in our own and other societies, and the forms of psychotherapy in non-

Western or non-literate societies. Anthropologists have pointed out how rituals, possession states, and other phenomena acting through symbols and their emotional properties serve to restore or maintain mental health, sometimes in ways closely resembling the treatment modes of Western psychotherapy (Kiev 1964; Opler 1959; Wallace 1959).

PERSONALITY VARIATION IN CROSS-CULTURAL PERSPECTIVE

Anthropology has made one of its most telling contributions in identifying differences in personality from one society or stratum of society to another. While the explanation of those differences has occasionally been innovatively adventurous, for example explaining them as the result of ecological demands (Barry, et al. 1959; Edgerton 1965, 1971), it is socialization that has been the explanatory factor most relied upon, ultimately also accounting for the action of ecological demands, or for the variation of personality from one period of history to another.

What Has Been Accomplished

Direct experience in a foreign culture using techniques of participant observation and psychological testing and, occasionally, indirect methods applied to foreign subjects observed away from their home communities ("the study of culture at a distance") have provided data on a number of national characters, including Russian, French, German, British, Japanese, and Chinese, and an even larger number of "basic," "social," or "modal" personalities in less complex societies (Honigmann 1968b). Closer to home, anthropologists looking at status personality (Linton 1945) have inquired into the psychological traits of the poor, blacks, and middle-class white Americans, though here their work has been outdistanced by that of sociologists and psychologists.

Studies of personality variation seen in cross-cultural perspective fall into two main types. One approach centers on grasping a personality SYSTEM and describing the organization of its discrete features. Theoretical points of departure vary greatly among ethnographers who have followed this orientation. The volume of such studies produced in the past twenty-five years appears to have declined very much from the previous quarter of a century. Instead, studies of personality variation between societies have increasingly concentrated on attending to a few specific psychological traits or features, chosen because the observer deemed them theoretically relevant, or because they were conspicuously revealed by the people being studied (for example need achievement, cognitive style, violence proneness, or a certain kind of psychological conflict). While the reduced focus has favored measurement and other techniques of objective observation, it has deprived the published results of the wide interest and readability of the earlier works by writers like Margaret Mead, Ruth Benedict, and Clyde Kluckhohn, qualities which recommended them to a diversified reading public.

A Model of Personality Formation

The model of personality formation devised by anthropologists, chiefly by J. Whiting and his associates (1966), begins the process "far" from the interpersonal nexus of parent and child. The causal chain starts with technological adaptation to the physical environment (the "maintenance system of culture") and extends to the structure of the household. Here ecology operates to shape parents' and other socializers' attitudes toward children and adults (see also B. Whiting 1963; Minturn and Lambert 1964).

The topics examined with the aid of the model and results obtained using the hologeistic method have been summarized (see Harrington and J. Whiting 1972). I would only add the evaluative note that, accepting the validity of the hologeistic method, the results have frequently been convincing and provide considerable support for psychoanalytically founded socialization theory, as it has developed in anthropology and other social sciences.

The long-term effects of child rearing on personality have, of course, long been controversial. Many such interpretations, as Orlansky (1949) and others pointed out, have been contradictory and poorly supported with empirical evidence. Concern aroused by those warnings may have contributed to hologeistic research designed to test hypotheses of early socialization. It also induced anthropologists to find alternative explanations for some of the simplistic psychoanalytic hypotheses that had attracted their interest. Thus Margaret Mead (1954) clarified the "swaddling hypothesis" applied to Great Russians by maintaining that rather than causing personality traits, swaddling furnishes clues to the nature of the constraints operating on the Great Russian child. Swaddling is but one of the channels through which the socializers communicate to the young person in the process of personality formation.

Assessment

One of the important values of comparative studies of social personality and national character has been humanistic. Documents of the wide range of human behavior in the world, the resourcefulness of human beings in meeting different social demands within a broad spectrum of social normality, and the potential for adaptation inherent in man, enhance our appreciation of man's endowments, particularly his flexibility. This attitude encourages tolerance at the same time that it reveals the nearly unlimited ability of society to define what is acceptable, meritorious, or bad in human conduct.

The decline of interest in studies of personality no doubt reflects several things, including a more scientific orientation taken by cultural anthropology. Perhaps the decline also indicates that the spate of such studies starting in the 1920's has been sufficient to make its contribution. The research has made its impact in showing enormous plasticity of nature. At present, led by the ethologists, social scientists appear more interested in the limits to that plasticity and in programmed behavioral tendencies that are independent of culture (see, for example, Tiger and Fox 1971).

That more books like *Sex and temperament, Culture and ethos of Kaska society*, or *And keep your powder dry* have not appeared, is doubtlessly related to the criticism that has been leveled against the genre (Lindesmith and Strauss 1950; Inkeles and Levinson 1954). Such criticism, directed by standards of scientific method followed in psychology and sociology, finds fault with anthropological studies of social personality on the ground that they can rarely be empirically assessed using measures of reliability, validity, or theoretical and methodological triangulation. Many anthropologists engaged in such research have said little to counter such criticism; yet they were deeply affected by it and, given the scientific climate pervading the social sciences from the 1950's, were persuaded to abandon personality study.

Others responded to the criticism by adopting methods as objective as possible in personality assessment (G. Spindler 1955; L. Spindler 1962). A few insisted that the conclusions of traditional culture-and-personality research should be judged by the rules of scholarship found in the humanities rather than in the more objective or positivistic social sciences. The acceptability of those conclusions, the latter argued, derives from qualities of plausibility and consistency contained in the written product, and the assessment of those qualities is primarily logical in nature, rather than, as in the assessment of reliability and validity, empirical (Honigmann 1963: 306–307; cf. Redfield 1953).

INTERPRETING CULTURE PSYCHOLOGICALLY

If studies of personality in different societies have been a major trend in psychological anthropology, so have studies that interpret group behavior and material culture traits in the light of psychological attributes.

Investigations that interpret culture psychologically, conform to no single methodological model but take several forms. The psychological state to which a cultural trait is referred may be a universal property of human nature, like the Oedipus complex from which Róheim (1973 [1943]) derives practically all of culture. Or, more commonly, culturally specific psychological states may be credited with motivating cultural behavior, as in the great bulk of culture-and-personality research (e.g. Yurok attitudes toward property in Erikson [1963: 116ff.]; Arapesh gentleness and Mundugumor aggressiveness in Mead [1935]; or the Manus children's lack of animism in Mead [1930]).

What Kardiner (1939, 1945) calls secondary institutions and what he views as derivatives of projective systems located in the basic personality, have been the cultural traits most often interpreted psychologically. Religion has also been approached as a defense mechanism (Spiro 1965) and, as I have already noted, many attempts have been made to interpret ceremonies and institutions like confession, magic, and shamanism in terms of their psychotherapeutic functions. Recently considerable attention has been paid to the psychological correlates of games (for several papers by John M. Roberts and others, see Sutton-Smith 1972).

Conformity to Reinforcement

Guided by reinforcement theory and following the functional viewpoint, some anthropologists have explained how individuals learn to conform even to onerous and painful social role demands (for a major work of this type, see Spiro 1961). Briefly, fulfilling roles which possess considerable utilitarian value for the society, enables individuals to simultaneously satisfy basic and learned personal needs. Roles continue to be carried out as long as they satisfy individuals' needs for health, prestige, protection, aggression-release, etc. While the theoretical aspects of this approach in psychological anthropology have been considerably developed, little empirical research has been carried out to test deductions drawn from the theory, which admittedly conforms to common sense and is congruent with the psychological theory from which it draws. Spiro, later a principal proponent of functionalism in psychological anthropology, once pointed out that learning theory based on reinforcement fails to account for cultural behavior. What reinforcement, he asks, does belief in malevolent ghosts provide for the people of Ifaluk? He answers that Ifaluk children accept a "punishing" (rather than reinforcing) belief in ghosts because it harkens back to compatible, early "punishing" experiences that taught them to accept ideas of the world as threatening (Spiro 1953). He calls attention to other paradigms of motivation that explain social conformity, such as the negative fixation theory employed by J. Whiting and Child in *Child training and personality* (1953).

Culture Change and Acculturation

The anthropological literature on the psychological consequences of acculturation and culture change is enormous and has never been extensively summarized. Nor is there a comprehensive reader in the subject, and available summaries are limited to particular learning psychologies (like Hallowell 1945) or they are forbiddingly formal (like Barnett 1964).

PERSISTENCE   How culture and social personality traits manage to persist despite the ubiquity of culture change is one of the most stimulating questions posed by research. How have some American Indian social personality traits managed to persist through several hundred years of acculturation (Hallowell 1946)? Or are those people right who claim that the resemblance between pre- and post-contact psychological features is superficial and the product of different conditions (James 1954, 1961)? Persistence of certain Great Russian personality traits from the Tsarist into the revolutionary period, reported by Inkeles (1955) has not, to my knowledge, been similarly challenged; hence the problem remains open. Psychological anthropology will not provide the whole answer to such questions, but it can probably throw more light on them than it has so far.

MODERNIZATION   Personality traits that motivate modernization and contribute to development have been the subject of considerable research in psychology and sociology. The achievement motive has also been diligently studied by anthropologists (e.g. LeVine 1966). Nevertheless a problem remains concerning the relative importance of personality variables compared to situational factors in guiding individual adaptation to change (Honigmann 1968a; Barger and Earl 1971). There is plenty of evidence that external situational factors may instigate modernization or restrict opportunities to adopt new forms of behavior, yet psychological limitations and incapacities are sometimes spoken of as if they were solely responsible.

PSYCHOLOGICAL CONSEQUENCES OF CHANGE   I have already referred to anthropologists' interest in the psychological consequences of culture change and exposure to acculturation. Among the results most often pinpointed have been those like anxiety and identity-confusion that are troublesome to the personality. Much resourcefulness has been displayed in empirically identifying such consequences through field research, but less attention has been paid to how social change enables people to achieve new values, find new gratifications, and experience growth. There are grounds for doubting that change, even in small-scale communities, is as universally traumatic as some anthropologists have suggested. A handful of research reports have revealed that new identities have been successfully assumed in change. In particular the work of Chance (1965) in North Alaska indicates that when new possibilities are readily available, change is not notably or generally traumatic; but when opportunities are restricted, as they were for the women Chance studied, adjustment problems ensue.

Consequences of change for personality are also touched on in studying how culture change has altered traditional processes of socialization (Wolfenstein 1951, 1955; Inkeles 1955). However, no work that I know explicitly shows how change in patterns of socialization resulted in altering personality. Reliance on the cross-sectional method in such research has been suggestive (see, for example, Miller and Swanson 1960) and will probably continue to be relied on, but one longs to see anthropologists adequately financed and sufficiently motivated to undertake long-term longitudinal studies on this and other problems.

An Evolutionary Perspective

Recently two suggestions have been made to orient psychological anthropology toward an evolutionary perspective. Barkow (1973) proposes that anthropology choose a particular type of motivation or social relationship, such as striving for prestige, courtship, or gregariousness, and study its role in the context of environmental adaptation. Let the anthropologist speculate concerning the selective advantage that the trait conferred on early man. LeVine (1973) offers a fuller conception of how a Darwinian view can be applied in culture and personality. He starts with three assumptions concerning personality (by definition limited to individual behavioral dispositions), the sociocultural system, and adaptation. First, he assumes that distributions of personality dispositions, like genetic and biological traits, are statistical characteristics of populations; second, a sociocultural system is a selective environment comprising institutional demands and opportunities that interact with individual behavior. Behaviors following from certain personality traits which are more compatible with the demands and opportunities of a sociocultural environment will be reinforced. Third, he assumes that individuals in a given population are not necessarily aware of the adaptations between personality and institutions. LeVine goes on to show how the cognitive activity of socializing agents preserves positively selected personality variants and through deliberate socialization duplicates them in the next generation. The socializers thereby mediate between selective pressures in the environment and the socialization process.

While there are no studies of culture-and-personality relationships that have been carried out with LeVine's theory, the literature (including works in cultural psychiatry) contains a number of works that illustrate the thesis (though they may not employ his concept of personality). LeVine refers to a few but does not fully exploit the available resources to show the fruitfulness of his theory.

Alcohol Use

Anthropologists have produced a large literature, not all of it psychologically oriented, concerned with the use and abuse of alcohol. From the standpoint of culture and personality, the aim has generally been to discover cultural conditions, or constraints, that regulate the use of alcohol or encourage excessive drinking and alcohol addiction. MacAndrew and Edgerton (1969) review a considerable amount of the work done and at the same time advance a social explanation of drunken comportment. A few researchers, notably Ferguson (1973) among the Navajo Indians, have looked for social and psychological factors that promote success in therapy for alcohol addiction. Like another study undertaken in the Mackenzie Delta (Honigmann and Honigmann 1970), her work demonstrates that deviant behavior associated with alcohol varies directly with the extent to which individuals possess a stake in society in the form of owning property and holding a steady job. Another recent approach in this area applies transactional theory to drinking, regarding drunken behavior as a means of enhancing status through interpersonal encounters akin to the status-climbing feasts found in some traditional cultures (Robbins 1973).

Social Movements

A social movement is a historical episode carried out by aggregates of individuals who adopt a common ideology and are governed by similar emotional attitudes. The most commonly studied social movements have been nativistic or culturally revitalistic, that is, designed to bring about a better form of social life (Aberle 1970; Wallace 1956). From the results of such research we have learned about the life-cycle of those movements, the social conditions under which they thrive, how they (or their leaders) adapt themselves to public opinion, how leaders and followers are recruited, and what their consequences are for morale and for social change. The studies have focused primarily on social conditions from which the researchers inferred compatible psychological states of alienation, anxiety, identity confusion, improved morale, etc. Anthropologists have not often undertaken to secure empirical psychological data on the individuals involved, except perhaps the leaders, for whom the psychological data have been extracted from ethnohistorical sources. As a result, the popular anthropological theories that purport to explain revitalistic and nativistic social movements in psychological terms must still be regarded as poorly supported. Procuring empirical psychological data demanded by the theories is a much-needed next step in research.

OTHER TOPICS

More briefly I will refer to other topics comprising the field of psychological anthropology.

Dreams and Altered States of Consciousness

Dorothy Eggan (1949, 1952), D'Andrade (1961), Bourguignon (1972), and others have accumulated considerable knowledge of dreams in exotic societies and have demonstrated relationships between dreams and socially patterned values, conflicts, and problems that are in turn connected with adaptation to given sociocultural environments.

Trance and possession were the earliest altered states of consciousness to be anthropologically examined, but recently a fair amount of interest has begun to be taken in cultural concomitants of drug experience (Dobkin de Rios 1974). The literature is reviewed and lines of research are delineated in Bourguignon's papers (1972, 1973).

Life Histories

The life-history approach is no longer much used in anthropology as a means of understanding personality in its cultural context, but early studies constitute evidence that biographical and autobiographical accounts when accompanied by annotations pointing to significant cultural contexts are vivid means of getting to know how the world is seen from the perspective of another culture. As a model of a good life history, I have in mind the one of Gregorio, Navajo hand-trembler (A. Leighton and D. Leighton 1949). The growing popularity of psychobiography among historians may move anthropologists once again to utilize this neglected device, following standards recently set forth by Langness (1965).

Ecology and Personality

Few social scientists have followed Thompson's (1951) pioneer attempt among American Indians to link psychological configurations with ecological configurations. Perhaps the recent example set by Edgerton (1971) and by research on perception (Segall, et al. 1963) will heighten anthropological interest in seeing what other relationships exist between personality patterns and cultural adaptation. I have pointed out that the socialization model followed by Whiting and his associates postulates a connection between maintenance systems, socialization, and personality. The model has proven successful when applied in hologeistic studies involving ecological variables. Such work has shown, for example, that the values strongly insisted upon in socialization vary between societies with and without food accumulations (Barry, et al. 1959) and that patterns of anxiety and defense mechanisms (in the form of dreams) vary between food-gatherers and food-producers (D'Andrade 1961).

Cognition

The "new ethnography," claimed by some proponents to provide a reliable means of discovering how people think, can be considered a new approach to investigating relationships between culture and personality. However, the published output of this interest — componential analyses of kinship or folk taxonomies of illness, for example — has rarely been concerned with individuals, and hence not strictly involved with psychological anthropology as conceived in this article. In his chapter on culture and cognition Wallace (1970) says little about cognizing individuals. Though he claims that the study of cognition in culture can help to solve the problem of how diversity is organized in a social system, he resolves the problem largely by eliminating it, as Frake also does when he dismisses a distinction between "psychologically real" and "structurally real" descriptions (D'Andrade and Romney 1964: 237).

Even if we grant that ethnographic semantics, with its approach to the categorization of experience by means of the words people use, is psychological, such research has so far shown very little promise of revealing much that is not already obvious about the relationship of forms of categorization to other aspects of the culture in which it occurs. The emphasis has been on categorization or cognition per se, with little attention being given to the way categorization is expressed in overt behavior. Marvin Opler, in a book review published in the *American Anthropologist* (1973), has criticized cognition studies from a related point of view. Anthropologically, he maintains, cognition and emotion cannot be studied separately from one another but only side-by-side as they manifest themselves in behavior, which I would add is what psychological anthropology has traditionally done.

More attention to cognition would be fruitful in culture-and-personality study. It would supplement the one-sided emphasis that has been devoted to emotional and motivational processes in social personality research by providing information about how, in cultural context, motives are cognitively balanced, how decisions are reached, how social rules constrain individual choice, and to what extent language influences thought. Ethnosemantics alone can contribute little to those problems which, like most work in psychological anthropology, require training in the concepts and methods of psychological research.

CONCLUSION

Psychological anthropology has produced considerable knowledge, but it has done so primarily by opening up a number of productive topics without pursuing many of them cumulatively over a long time. Many theories or hypotheses have been suggested regarding social personality, national character, and the relationship of personality to culture change, but comparatively few have been examined through sustained research that built on earlier discoveries. Methods, like the life-history method, have been dropped or, where used are not pushed to new levels of development.

Several researchers have wearied of psychological anthropology after working in the field for a time, turning instead to other research only faintly associated with the study of individuals in cultural context.

It is logical to conclude that anthropologists' failure to continue working cumulatively on promising topics of research, theories, and hypotheses has severely limited knowledge. Worthwhile and worthless hunches have without distinction been sloughed off into the repository of published papers where they languish, nobody knowing what insights are secure or promising and what could just as well be discarded. For this reason we should be grateful to the hologeistic researchers who have taken the trouble to test propositions comparatively. Failure to continue with lines of research after they are initiated has also prevented advice from critics being heeded or, perhaps, refuted.

My review has several times pointed out topics for further development or suggested problems that might be pressed to more satisfactory conclusions. Pulling these together and adding others, I suggest it would be worthwhile to:

1.   Do more appraising of rival theories to discover their potential for explaining behavior in cultural contexts.

2.   Study cognitive systems of culture as they are used or manipulated by individuals.

3.   Do research on the patterning and operation of "positive" motives to balance somewhat work that has been done on "deficiency" motives.

4.   Study the mental health of shamans while there is still time.

5.   Examine the efficacy of forms of psychotherapy in other cultures.

6.   Organize what we know about modal and social personality and personality in conditions of culture change.

7.   Research the psychological dynamics of role behavior.

8.   Find out how people in different cultures and on different status levels think.

9.   Examine the relative importance of psychocultural and situational factors in governing personal adaptation to change.

10.   Study behavior in modern society analogous to witchcraft accusations and look for a general theory to cover both systems of belief.

11.   Do more research on individuals involved in social movements.

12.   Apply rival theories of excessive drinking and other forms of alcohol use to appraise their usefulness or to define the conditions under which they apply.

13.   Follow up the significance of ecological factors in personality formation and socialization.

Many of my suggestions require fieldwork in single cultures, but only as the first step to generalization. Most call for a thoughtful systematization of available material, consulting also the relevant knowledge that has been obtained in psychology, sociology, and other disciplines, For many of the topics I suggest, measurement would be highly desirable. In studying exotic forms of psychotherapy, we do not need more examples of ritual and other cultural devices that are possibly therapeutic. We need to know how effective they are. Initially such information may be crude, perhaps only identifying the frequency with which people troubled in specific ways are drawn to particular therapies and how often they return still ailing. Such a problem calls for longitudinal research, and paid native assistants or local colleagues will be indispensable for keeping track of clients while the anthropologist is absent.

REFERENCES

ABERLE, DAVID
  1970   "Note on relative deprivation theory as applied to millenarian and other cult movements," in *Millenial dreams in action*. Edited by Sylvia L. Thrupp. New York: Schocken.
ARONOFF, JOEL
  1967   *Psychological needs and cultural systems*. Princeton: D. Van Nostrand.
AUGUSTINE OF HIPPO
  1972   [ca. 427] *Concerning the city of God against the pagans*. Translated by David Knowles. Harmondsworth: Penguin.
BACON, FRANCIS
  1937   [1625] "Of custom and education," in *Essays or counsels civil and moral*. London: Oxford University Press, World Classics.
BARGER, W. K., DAPHNE EARL
  1971   Differential adaptation to northern town life by the Eskimos and Indians of Great Whale River. *Human Organization* 30:25–30.
BARKOW, JEROME H.
  1973   Darwinian psychological anthropology: a biosocial approach. *Current Anthropology* 14:373–388.
BARNETT, H. G.
  1964   "The acceptance and rejection of change," in *Explorations in social change*. Edited by George K. Zollschan and Walter Hirsch. Boston: Houghton Mifflin.
BARRY, HERBERT, III, IRVIN L. CHILD, MARGARET K. BACON
  1959   Relation of child training to subsistence economy. *American Anthropologist* 61:51–63.
BATESON, GREGORY, DON D. JACKSON, JAY HALEY, JOHN H. WEAKLAND
  1963   A note on the double bind — 1962. *Family Process* 2:154–161.
BENEDICT, RUTH
  1934   *Patterns of culture*. Boston: Houghton Mifflin.

BENNETT, JOHN
1946 The interpretation of Pueblo culture: a question of values. *Southwestern Journal of Anthropology* 2:361–374.

BERLIN, ISAIAH
1965 "Herder and the Enlightenment," in *Aspects of the eighteenth century*. Edited by Earl R. Wasserman. Baltimore: Johns Hopkins Press.
1969 "One of the boldest innovators in the history of human thought." *The New York Times Magazine* (November 23): 76–77, 79–100.

BOURGUIGNON, ERIKA
1972 "Dreams and altered states of consciousness in anthropological research," in *Psychological anthropology* (new edition). Edited by Francis L. K. Hsu. Cambridge, Massachusetts: Schenkman.
1973 "Psychological anthropology," in *Handbook of social and cultural anthropology*. Edited by J. Honigmann. Chicago: Rand McNally.

BRINTON, DANIEL G.
1895 *The Aims of Anthropology*. Proceedings of the American Association for the Advancement of Science 44, 1–17.

CHANCE, NORMAN A.
1965 Acculturation, self-identification, and personality adjustment. *American Anthropologist* 67:372–393.

CHANCE, NORMAN A., DOROTHY A. FOSTER
1962 *Symptom formation and patterns of psychopathology in a rapidly changing Alaskan Eskimo society*. Anthropological Papers of the University of Alaska 11; 32–42.

COMTE, AUGUST
1911 [1854] *Early essays on social philosophy*. Translated by Henry Dix Hutton. London: George Routledge and Sons.

CUMMING, ELAINE, JOHN CUMMING
1957 *Closed ranks: an experiment in mental health education*. Cambridge, Massachusetts: Harvard University Press.

D'ANDRADE, ROY G.
1961 "Anthropological studies of dreams," in *Psychological anthropology*. Edited by Francis L. K. Hsu. Homewood, Illinois: Dorsey Press.

D'ANDRADE, ROY G., A. K. KIMBALL ROMNEY
1964 "Summary of participants' discussion," in *Transcultural studies in cognition*. Edited by A. Kimball Romney and Roy Goodwin D'Andrade. *American Anthropologist* (special publication) 66 (3): Part 2.

DESCARTES, RÉNÉ
1960 [1637] "Discourse on method," in *Discourse on method and other writings*. Translated by Arthur Wollaston. Harmondsworth: Penguin.

DOBKIN DE RIOS, MARLENE
1974 "Cultural persona in drug-induced altered states of consciousness," in *Social and cultural identity: persistence and change*. Edited by Thomas K. Fitzgerald. Southern Anthropological Society Proceedings 8.

DOLLARD, JOHN, NEAL E. MILLER, LEONARD W. DOOB, O. H. MOWRER, ROBERT R. SEARS
1939 *Frustration and aggression*. New Haven: Yale University Press.

DURKHEIM, ÉMILE
1964   [1895] *The rules of sociological method.* Translated by Sarah A. Solvay and John J. Mueller. New York: Free Press of Glencoe.

EDGERTON, ROBERT B.
1965   "Cultural" vs. "ecological" factors in the expression of values, attitudes, and personality characteristics. *American Anthropologist* 67:442–447.
1971   *The individual in cultural adaptation.* Berkeley: University of California Press.

EGGAN, DOROTHY
1949   The significance of dreams for anthropological research. *American Anthropologist* 51:177–198.
1952   The manifest content of dreams: a challenge to social science. *American Anthropologist* 54:469–485.

ERIKSON, ERIK H.
1963   *Childhood and society* (second edition). New York: W. W. Norton.

FERGUSON, FRANCES N.
1973   "A stake in society: its relevance to response by Navajo alcoholics in a treatment program." Unpublished doctoral dissertation, University of North Carolina at Chapel Hill.

FORSTER, GEORG
1968   [1777] "A voyage round the world," in *Georg Forster's Werke.* Adapted by Robert L. Kahn. Berlin: Die Deutsche Akademie der Wissenschaft.

FRAZER, JAMES G.
1910   [1899] "The origin of totemism," in *Totemism and exogamy,* four volumes. London: Macmillan.

GOGUET, ANTOINE YVES
1775   *The origins of laws, arts, and sciences, and their progress among the most ancient nations,* three volumes. Edinburgh: George Robinson and Alexander Donaldson.

HALLOWELL, A. I.
1945   "Sociopsychological aspects of acculturation," in *The science of man in the world crisis.* Edited by Ralph Linton. New York: Columbia University Press.
1946   "Some psychological characteristics of the northeastern Indians," in *Man in northeastern North America.* Edited by Frederick Johnson. Papers of the Robert S. Peabody Foundation of Archeology 3.
1955   *Culture and experience.* Philadelphia: University of Pennsylvania Press.

HARRINGTON, CHARLES, JOHN W. M. WHITING
1972   "Socialization process and personality," in *Psychological anthropology* (new edition). Edited by Francis L. K. Hsu. Cambridge, Massachusetts: Schenkman.

HENRY, JULES
1949   "The social function of child sexuality in Pilagá Indian culture," in *Psychosexual development in health and disease.* Edited by Paul H. Hoch and Joseph Zubin. New York: Grune and Stratton.

1963 *Culture against man.* New York: Random House.
HOLMBERG, ALLAN R.
1950 *Nomads of the long bow.* Smithsonian Institution, Institute of Social Anthropology Publication 10.
HOMANS, GEORGE C., DAVID M. SCHNEIDER
1955 *Marriage, authority, and final causes: a study of unilateral cross-cousin marriage.* Glencoe: Free Press.
HONIGMANN, JOHN J.
1947 Cultural dynamics of sex. *Psychiatry* 10:37–47.
1963 *Understanding culture.* New York: Harper and Row.
1967 *Personality in culture.* New York: Harper and Row.
1968a "Adaptation of Indians, Eskimo, and persons of partial indigenous background in a Canadian northern town." Paper prepared for the 67th annual meeting of the American Anthropological Association.
1968b "The study of personality in primitive societies," in *The study of personality.* Edited by Edward Norbeck, Douglass Price-Williams, and William M. McCord. New York: Holt, Rinehart and Winston.
1968c "Toward a distinction between psychiatric and non-psychiatric judgments of abnormality," in *Readings in the psychology of adjustment.* Edited by Leon Gorlow and Walter Katkovsky. New York: McGraw-Hill.
HONIGMANN, JOHN J., IRMA HONIGMANN
1970 *Arctic townsmen.* Ottawa: Canadian Research Centre for Anthropology.
HUGHES, CHARLES C., MARC-ADELARD TREMBLAY, ROBERT N. RAPOPORT, ALEXANDER H. LEIGHTON
1960 *People of Cove and Woodlot.* New York: Basic Books.
INKELES, ALEX
1955 Social change and social character: the role of parental mediation. *Journal of Social Issues* 21(2):12–23.
INKELES, ALEX, DANIEL J. LEVINSON
1954 "National character: the study of modal personality and sociocultural systems," in *Handbook of social psychology,* two volumes. Edited by Gardner Lindzey. Cambridge, Massachusetts: Addison-Wesley.
JAMES, BERNARD J.
1954 Some critical observations concerning analyses of Chippewa "atomism" and Chippewa personality. *American Anthropologist* 56:283–286.
1961 Social-psychological dimensions of Ojibwa acculturation. *American anthropologist* 63:721–746.
JESSOR, RICHARD, THEODORE D. GRAVES, ROBERT C. HANSON, SHIRLEY L. JESSOR
1968 *Society, personality, and deviant behavior.* New York: Holt, Rinehart and Winston.
KARDINER, ABRAM
1939 *The individual and his society.* New York: Columbia University Press.
1945 "The concept of basic personality structure as an operational tool in the social sciences," in *The science of man in the world crisis.* Edited by Ralph Linton. New York: Columbia University Press.
KIEV, ARI, *editor*
1964 *Magic, faith, and healing.* New York: Free Press of Glencoe.

LANGNER, THOMAS S., STANLEY T. MICHAEL
1963   *Life stress and mental health.* New York: Free Press of Glencoe.
LANGNESS, L. L.
1965   *The life history in anthropological science.* New York: Holt, Rinehart and Winston.
LEIGHTON, ALEXANDER
1959   *My name is legion.* New York: Basic Books.
LEIGHTON, ALEXANDER, ADEOYE T. LAMBO, CHARLES C. HUGHES, DOROTHEA C. LEIGHTON, JANE M. MURPHY, DAVID B. MACKLIN
1963   *Psychiatric disorder among the Yoruba.* Ithaca, New York: Cornell University Press.
LEIGHTON, ALEXANDER B., DOROTHEA C. LEIGHTON
1949   *Gregorio, the hand-trembler: a psychological study of a Navaho Indian.* Papers of the Peabody Museum of American Archaeology and Ethnology 40(1). Harvard University.
LEIGHTON, DOROTHEA C., JOHN S. HARDING, DAVID B. MACKLIN, ALLISTER M. MACMILLAN, ALEXANDER LEIGHTON
1963   *The character of danger.* New York: Basic Books.
LE VINE, ROBERT A.
1966   *Dreams and deeds: achievement motivation in Nigeria.* Chicago: University of Chicago Press.
1973   *Culture, behavior and personality.* Chicago: Aldine.
LINDESMITH, ALFRED R., ANSELM L. STRAUSS
1950   A critique of culture-personality writings. *American Sociological Review* 15:587–600.
LINTON, RALPH
1945   *The cultural background of personality.* New York: D. Appleton-Century.
MAC ANDREW, CRAIG, ROBERT B. EDGERTON
1969   *Drunken comportment.* Chicago: Aldine.
MANGIN, WILLIAM P., JEROME COHEN
1964   Cultural and psychological characteristics of mountain migrants to Lima, Peru. *Sociologus* 14:81–88.
MEAD, MARGARET
1930   *Growing up in New Guinea.* New York: William Morrow.
1935   *Sex and temperament in three primitive societies.* New York: Morrow.
1954   The swaddling hypothesis: its reception. *American Anthropologist* 56:395–409.
MILLER, DANIEL R., GUY E. SWANSON
1960   *Inner conflict and defense.* New York: Schocken.
MINTURN, LEIGH, WILLIAM W. LAMBERT
1964   *Mothers of six cultures: antecedents of child rearing.* New York: John Wiley and Sons.
MUEHLMANN, WILHELM E.
1968   *Geschichte der Anthropologie.* Frankfurt am Main: Athenaeum.
NAROLL, RAOUL
1959   A tentative index of culture-stress. *International Journal of Social Psychiatry* 5:107–116.

NEEDHAM, RODNEY
  1962   *Structure and sentiment.* Chicago: University of Chicago Press.
OPLER, MARVIN K.
  1959   "Dream analysis in Ute Indian therapy," in *Culture and mental health.*
         Edited by Marvin K. Opler. New York: Macmillan.
  1973   Book review. *American Anthropologist* (August).
OPLER, MARVIN K., JEROME L. SINGER
  1956   Ethnic differences in behavior and psychopathology: Italian and Irish.
         International Journal of Social Psychiatry 2:11–22.
ORLANSKY, HAROLD
  1949   Infant care and personality. *Psychological Bulletin* 46:1–48.
POWELL, J. W.
  1896   *Relation of primitive peoples to environment, illustrated by American
         examples.* Annual Report of the Board of Regents of the Smithsonian
         Institution to July, 1895.
RATZEL, FRIEDRICH
  1886   *Ueber die Staebchenpanzer und ihre Verbreitung im nordpazifischen
         Gebiet.* Sitzungsberichte der philosophisch-philologischen und histori-
         schen Classe der Königlichen Bayerischen Akademie der Wissenschaf-
         ten zu Muenchen, Heft II, 181–216.
REDFIELD, ROBERT
  1953   "Relations of anthropology to the social sciences and to the human-
         ities," in *Anthropology today.* Edited by A. L. Kroeber. Chicago:
         University of Chicago Press.
RIVERS, W. H. R.
  1924   *Social organization.* Edited by W. J. Perry. New York: Knopf.
ROBBINS, RICHARD H.
  1973   Alcohol and the identity struggle: some effects of economic change on
         interpersonal relations. *American Anthropologist* 75:99–122.
RÓHEIM, GÉZA
  1973   [1943] *The origin and function of culture.* Garden City: Doubleday,
         Anchor Books.
SEGALL, M. H., D. T. CAMPBELL, M. J. HERSKOVITS
  1963   Cultural differences in the perception of geometric illusions. *Science*
         139:769–771.
SIEGEL, BERNARD J.
  1955   High anxiety levels and cultural integration: notes on a psycho-
         cultural hypothesis. *Social Forces* 34:42–48.
SPINDLER, GEORGE D.
  1955   *Sociocultural and psychological processes in Menomini acculturation.*
         University of California Publications in Culture and Society 5.
SPINDLER, LOUISE S.
  1962   *Menomini women and culture change.* Memoirs of the American
         Anthropological Association 91.
SPIRO, MELFORD E.
  1953   Ghosts: an anthropological inquiry into learning and perception.
         Journal of Abnormal and Social Psychology 48:376–382.

1961   "Social systems, personality, and functional analysis," in *Studying personality cross-culturally*. Edited by Bert Kaplan. Evanston, Illinois: Row, Peterson.

1965   "Religious systems as culturally constituted defense mechanisms," in *Context and meaning in cultural anthropology*. Edited by Melford E. Spiro. New York: Free Press.

SUTTON-SMITH, BRIAN

1972   *The folkgames of children*. Austin: University of Texas Press.

THOMPSON, LAURA

1951   *Personality and government*. Mexico City: Ediciones del Instituto Indigenista Interamericano.

TIGER, LIONEL, ROBIN FOX

1971   *The imperial animal*. New York: Dell.

VAN VELSEN, J.

1967   "The extended-case method and situational analysis," in *The craft of social anthropology*. Edited by A. L. Epstein. London: Tavistock.

VIERKANDT, A.

1908   *Die Stetigkeit im Kulturwandel*. Leipzig: Duncker und Humbolt.

WALLACE, ANTHONY F. C.

1952   *The modal personality structure of the Tuscarora Indians*. Bureau of American Ethnology Bulletin 150.

1956   Revitalization movements. *American Anthropologist* 58:264–281.

1959   "The institutionalization of cathartic and control strategies in Iroquois religious psychotherapy," in *Culture and mental health*. Edited by Marvin K. Opler. New York: Macmillan.

1970   *Culture and personality* (second edition). New York: Random House.

WASHBURNE, SHERWOOD L., HERBERT YAHRAES

1969   "The origins of aggressive behavior," in *Mental health program reports* 3. Washington, D.C.: National Institute of Mental Health.

WHITING, B.

1963   "Introduction," in *Six cultures*. Edited by B. Whiting. New York: John Wiley and Sons.

WHITING, JOHN W. M., IRVIN L. CHILD

1953   *Child training and personality: a cross-cultural study*. New Haven: Yale University Press.

WHITING, JOHN W. M., IRVIN L. CHILD, WILLIAM W. LAMBERT

1966   *Field guide for a study of socialization*. New York: John Wiley and Sons.

WOLFENSTEIN, MARTHA

1951   The emergence of fun morality. *Journal of Social Issues* 7(4):15–25.

1955   "Fun morality: an analysis of recent American child-training literature," in *Childhood in contemporary cultures*. Edited by Margaret Mead and Martha Wolfenstein. Chicago: University of Chicago Press.

Biographical Notes

JEROME H. BARKOW (1944–) received his B.A. from Brooklyn College (CUNY) in 1964, his M.A. from the University of Chicago in 1967, and his Ph.D. from the same university in 1970. His fieldwork has involved the psycho-social study of Hausa-speaking groups in Nigeria and the Niger Republic; his present research interest is in the evolution of hominid biopsychological characteristics. He has been Assistant Professor in the Department of Sociology and Anthropology at Dalhousie University (Halifax, Nova Scotia) since 1971.

CHARLES A. BISHOP (1935–) was born in Kingston, Canada. He attended the University of Toronto where he obtained his B.A. (1961) and M.A. (1963) in anthropology before receiving his Ph.D. (1969) in anthropology from the State University of New York at Buffalo. He has taught at Florida State University (1967–1969), Eastern New Mexico University (1969–1970), and since 1970 at the State University of New York at Oswego. His special interests include ethnohistory, culture change, and Indians of the Subarctic. Dr. Bishop is married to the anthropologist, Dr. M. Estellie Smith.

JUDITH K. BROWN (1930–) received her Ed.D. from the Harvard Graduate School of Education in 1962 with a dissertation on the cross-cultural study of female initiation rites. She holds a Certificate in Child Development from the Institute of Education of the University of London (1955), where she studied on a Fulbright Grant. As a Fellow of the Radcliffe Institute (1967–1969), she engaged in research on the role of women in subsistence activities. Her publications deal with female initiation rites, the relationship of these rites to the economic role of women, the division of labor by sex, and the relationship of the economic role of women to socialization. Since 1969, she has been an Assistant Professor of Anthropology at Oakland University.

JOHN BUSHNELL (1922–   ) received both his baccalaureate and doctoral degrees in anthropology from the University of California, Berkeley. In addition to appointments as Research Associate and Staff Anthropologist, Mary Conover Mellon Foundation at Vassar College, and Director of Research, New York State Commission for Human Rights, he has taught at the University of California at Berkeley, Sacramento State College, Vassar College, New York University, and Brooklyn College of the City University of New York where he is Professor of Anthropology. He has conducted longitudinal field studies among the Hupa Indians of northwestern California and the Matlatzinca of San Juan Atzingo, Mexico. His investigations have also included an *in situ* study and analysis of campus culture at Vassar College. He has published on such varied topics as the cult of the Virgin of Guadalupe, psychocultural aspects of polygyny among the Matlatzinca, a psychoanalytic interpretation of social stereotopy in a Mexican village, the changing identity of the Hupa, supernatural belief systems evoked by floods on the Reservation, and biographical/psychological profiles of Indian men spanning two decades, as well as papers on the cultural dynamics of higher education. Currently he is collaborating with Donna Bushnell on a series of studies assessing culture, character, and cognitive orientation utilizing data from the Rorschach, Thematic Apperception Test, figure drawings, and group doll play administered to children and adolescents of San Juan Atzingo.

DONNA BUSHNELL (1922–   ) received her A.B. in anthropology from the University of California, Berkeley, her M.S. in psychology from Vassar College, and her Ph.D. in clinical psychology from New York University. She completed her analytic training in the Postdoctoral Program for Psychotherapy and Psychoanalysis at New York University and is currently a member of the staff in the Group Therapy Department of the Postgraduate Center for Mental Health. She was a Research Fellow at the Research Center for Mental Health, New York University, has taught at Bronx Community College of the City University of New York, and is engaged in the private practice of both individual and group analytic therapy in New York City. She has collaborated with John Bushnell in cross-cultural field studies and has co-authored with him a number of articles involving theoretical psychodynamic formulations and projective test data.

ROBERT L. CANFIELD (1930–) is Associate Professor of Anthropology at Washington University, St. Louis. He received the A.B. degree (in Clinical Psychology) from the University of Tulsa and the A.M. (in Linguistics) and the Ph.D. (in Anthropology) from the University of Michigan. He also studied at the School of Oriental Studies, University of London. He is author of *Faction and conversion: religious alignments in the Hindu Kush*. Presently he is doing research in the structure of leadership in traditional societies of the Muslim world.

JAY B. CRAIN (1941–) was born in Pasa Robles, California. He studied at U.C. Berkeley, Sacramento State College, the University of Washington, and Cornell University (Ph.D. in Social Anthropology, 1970). He is Associate Professor of Anthropology at California State University, Sacramento, and Assistant Professor of Medical Anthropology, U.C. Davis School of Medicine. His interests include Bornean ethnography, social and symbolic anthropology, and medical anthropology.

GORDON DARROW (1941–) received his B.A. in Anthropology from the University of Texas at Austin and is currently a graduate student of the University of Oregon. From 1972 to 1974 he taught at the Universidad del Valle in Guatemala and is now conducting fieldwork in that country.

ALFREDO MÉNDEZ DOMÍNGUEZ (1931–) was born in Guatemala. He received his M.A. from the University of Minnesota in 1956 and a Ph.D. in Anthropology from the University of Chicago in 1960. Author and co-author of over twenty scientific publications in English and Spanish on social stratification, nutrition, family structure, cognitive systems, and cultural change, he has done extensive fieldwork in Central America and Panama. From 1960 to 1966 he was head of the Anthropological Service of INCAP, Pan American Health Organization; in 1964 he taught at the University of Minnesota. He was subdirector of the Program Interamericano de Información Popular (PIIP) in Costa Rica from 1966 to 1968. Since 1971 he has been chairman of the Facultad de Ciencias Sociales at the Universidad del Valle in Guatemala.

MURRAY S. EDELMAN (1943–) received a Ph.D. in Human Development from the University of Chicago in 1973. He has worked as a statistician at the Census Bureau and has been a statistical consultant to CBS News since 1967. He is currently living in San Francisco and teaching classes through Lavender University — an open school for gay women and men.

IRENÄUS EIBL-EIBESFELDT (1928–) is a former student of Konrad Lorenz and is now head of the Max Planck Institute for Human Ethology in Percha, West Germany. Since 1963, he has been Professor at the University of Munich. He is the author of numerous scientific articles and books, including *Love and hate* and *Ethology: biology of behavior*.

MICHAEL W. EVERETT (1943–) received his doctorate in anthropology from the University of Arizona in 1970. He taught at the University of Kentucky before joining the faculty at Northern Arizona University. His past research among several Southwestern American Indian groups has been concerned with health and illness, suicide, homicide, alcoholism, and interpersonal conflict. He is currently active in American Indian health manpower training development.

JOHN L. FISCHER (1923–) is Professor of Anthropology and Chairman of the Department at Tulane University, New Orleans. He received the degrees of B.A. (1946), M.A. (1949), and Ph.D. in Social Anthropology (1955) from Harvard. He has conducted field research in Micronesia, a New England village, and a Japanese city, studying folklore, child rearing, and language. His most recent field research concerns the oral poetry of Ponape, Caroline Is.

JOHN J. HONIGMANN (1914–), Professor of Anthropology at the University of North Carolina, Chapel Hill, was born in New York City. Following undergraduate study at Brooklyn College (B.A., 1941) where his interest in culture and personality was awakened by association with Abraham Maslow, he attended Columbia University and studied with Ruth Benedict. He then enrolled at Yale University, where for the Ph.D. degree (1947) he undertook research among the Athapaskan Indians of Western Canada. His publications include works on general anthropology, culture and personality, and monographs based on fieldwork in the Subarctic, Arctic, Pakistan, and Austria.

JOHN M. JANZEN (1937–) was born in Newton, Kansas, studied at Bethel College, North Newton (B.A., 1961, social sciences and philosophy), University of Paris (the Sorbonne), and at the University of Chicago (M.A., 1964; Ph.D. 1967, anthropology). He has carried out fieldwork in Lower Zaire on social and economic organization and religion (1964–1965) and on comparative therapy systems (1969). He has taught at Bethel College (1968), McGill University, Montreal (1969–1971), and is presently at the University of Kansas in Lawrence. Publications include works on therapy in Zaire, social and economic organization, and a book, *An anthology of Kongo religion: primary texts from the Lower Zaire* (1974), with Wyatt MacGaffey.

DANIEL KRAKAUER (1915–) studied zoology at Cornell University and at Johns Hopkins, and dynamic psychology and psychoanalysis at Brooklyn College. Currently, he is the president of a manufacturing organization. His major professional interest is in the management and motivation of human beings, and he has also done work in the area of the evolution and nature of human nature.

VITTORIO LANTERNARI (1918–) has been Full Professor of Ethnology at the University of Rome since 1972. He was a student under the late Professor Raffaele Pettazone and has been concerned, since the beginning of his studies, with comparative religion and the religion of traditional societies. He was Professor of History of Religions and of Ethnology at the University of Bari from 1959 to 1972. Presently, he is primarily concerned with the study of traditional religions, culture contact, and socio-religious movements among non-Western societies. He did fieldwork in Ghana in 1971 and 1974, with an emphasis on the study of spiritual churches. His major publications include: *La grande festa: storia del Capodanno nelle civiltà primitive* (1959); *Movimenti religiosi di libertà e di salvezza dei popoli oppressi* (1960, second edition 1974) which has been translated into English (*The religions of the oppressed*), French, Spanish, German, and Hungarian; *Occidente e Terzo Mondo* (1967, Spanish translation 1974); and *Antropologia e imperialismo, e altri saggi* (1974).

ALEXANDER LOPASIC (1928–) was born in Belgrade. He received his Ph.D. in Anthropology at the University of Vienna in 1955. Between 1957–1959, he was Wenner-Gren Research Fellow in Anthropology at the University of London and, in 1960–1961, was Curator of the Nigerian Museum, Lagos. He taught at the University of Cologne (Department of Anthropology) between 1962–1965 and since 1965 has been Lecturer in Anthropology, University of Reading. His fieldwork was done in West and East Africa (Southern Nigeria, Coast of Kenya) as well as in the Mediterranean (Montenegro, Corsica, Malta, Sardinia). Dr. Lopasic's publications include articles on theoretical aspects of social anthropology; cults and traditional art in Southern Nigeria; social stratification in traditional Africa; feud, values and confraternities in the Mediterranean societies; and Negroes on the Montenegrin Coast as well as the book *Commissaire-General D. Lerman: a contribution to the history of Central Africa* (1971).

DAVID G. MANDELBAUM (1911–   ) has been Professor of Anthropology at the University of California, Berkeley, since 1948. He received the B.A. (1932) at Northwestern, and the Ph.D. (1936) at Yale. His first field research was among San Carlos Apache (1933), Plains Cree (1934, 1935), and in a small town in Connecticut (1935–1936). In 1937–1938, he began his fieldwork in South Asia and since then has often returned for more field research there, especially in South India. His interests include general theory (as in the paper in the present volume), psychological anthropology ("The study of life history: Gandhi," 1973), social organization (*Society in India*, two volumes, 1970), applied anthropology (*Human fertility in India: social components and policy perspectives*, 1974). His current work includes the writing of a book on the Todas of the Nilgiri Hills and a general work on religion.

LORNA MCLAUCHLAN MCDOUGALL (1942–   ) was born near Edinburgh and is presently a resident of the United States. She received her B.A. from the Honours School of Modern Languages, Trinity College, Dublin, and pursued the study of anthropology at the Institute of Social Anthropology, Oxford. Her special interests include several aspects of symbolization, classification, and cognition. She wrote her dissertation on "Comparative analysis of the symbolism of numbers" (B. Litt., 1969) and did subsequent field research in Ireland. Currently, she teaches at Pitzer College, The Claremont Colleges, Claremont, California.

WILLIAM E. MITCHELL (1927–   ) was born in Wichita, Kansas where he graduated from Wichita State University (B.A., 1950). At Columbia University he first studied philosophy (M.A., 1954) and then anthropology (Ph.D., 1969). His research and teaching positions include affiliations with Cornell Medical School (1955–1956), Jewish Family Service of New York (1956–1962), Cooper Union for the Advancement of Science and Art (1961), and the Hope Foundation (1962–1965). In 1965 he joined the University of Vermont to teach in the Department of Psychiatry and since 1973 has taught in the Department of Anthropology where he is an Associate Professor. He has published in the fields of kinship and the family, comparative therapeutic systems, and psychological anthropology and has done fieldwork among Jewish and Chinese Americans, hospitalized psychiatric patients, and the Iatmul, Lujere, and Wape tribes of Papua New Guinea.

RICHARD P. NIELSEN (U.S.A.). No biographical data available.

DONALD R. OMARK (1936–) studied electrical engineering at the Illinois Institute of Technology (B.S., 1959), worked with mentally handicapped children and counseling techniques at Chicago Teachers College (M.Ed., 1963), and obtained a Ph.D. in Human Development from the University of Chicago in 1972. He has studied the development of social interactions in young children in America, Switzerland, and Ethiopia and the evolutionary related development in juvenile Hamadryas baboons. He is currently at the Institute for Research on Exceptional Children at the University of Illinois-Urbana developing human ethological research techniques.

MONICA U. OMARK (1941–) was a teacher at the Laboratory School of the University of Chicago from 1963–1970 and 1972 after graduating from Illinois State University (B.S., 1963). She has participated in studies of the development of cooperative and competitive behaviors in school-age children in Switzerland, Ethiopia, and America, and has developed observational methods for the study of juvenile Hamadrayas baboons. She is currently engaged in an intensive study of human neonate development.

LOURDES R. QUISUMBING (1921–) of Cebu City, Philippines, received her B.Sc. in Education from St. Theresa's College, Manila in 1940, an M.A. from the University of San Carlos in 1956, and a Ph.D. in Education from the University of St. Tomas in 1963. She was recipient of a National Science Foundation of America scholarship to the 1968 Summer Institute of Anthropology, University of Colorado, Boulder, Colo., and speaker at the VIIIth ICAES, Tokyo and Kyoto, in 1968. At present she is Dean of College, St. Theresa's College, Cebu City, and Chairman of Graduate Education, University of San Carlos. Among her interests are culture-personality studies, the Filipino family, child-rearing patterns, national character, and Filipino sociocultural values and attitudes.

MANISHA ROY studied at the University of Calcutta (B.A., 1955; M.A., 1958), the University of Rochester, New York (A.M., 1964), and the University of California, San Diego (Ph.D. 1972). Currently, she is Assistant Professor at the University of Colorado, Denver. Her research and publications have been mainly in the areas of changing sex roles, interpersonal relationships, and role interaction within the family structure in both developing and modern societies; the changing meanings of value systems and behavior within the individual and cultural contexts; and psychological anthropology.

MICHAEL SALOVESH (1931–   ) studied anthropology at the University of Chicago (A.B. and Ph.B., 1956; A.M., 1959; Ph.D., 1971) and at the University of California, Berkeley. He has taught at the Chicago City Colleges, the Universtiy of Minnesota, and Purdue University; he is now a member of the Department of Anthropology of Northern Illinois University. His special interests include social and political organization, stratification, and interethnic relations; his continuing research in Chiapas, Mexico, began in 1958.

M. ESTELLIE SMITH (1935–   ) studied at the University of Buffalo (now SUNY-Buffalo) and is presently on the faculty of the SUNY-College at Brockport. She is also on the editorial board of *Urban Anthropology, Studies in European Society,* and *Journal of Political Anthropology.* She has edited the Festschrift *Studies in linguistics: in honor of Georg L. Trager* and is the author of *Governing at Taos Pueblo* as well as other short papers.

E. RICHARD SORENSON (1939–   ) studied at the Universities of Rochester and Stanford and then was at the National Institute of Health. While also a Research Associate at Stanford University, he developed a methodology for the study of passing phenomena using film archives. Presently, he is Director of the National Center for Anthropological Film, Washington, D.C. Dr. Sorenson is the author of several papers, books, and films dealing with behavior in New Guinea, Micronesia, New Hebrides, Solomon Islands, Borneo, Mexico, and Nepal.

LOUISE S. SPINDLER (1917–) was born in Oak Park, Illinois. She studied at the University of Wisconsin, the University of California at Los Angeles, and received her M.A. (1952) and Ph.D. (1956) from Stanford University in cultural anthropology. She is Lecturer and Research Associate in the Department of Anthropology, Stanford University, and serves as series editor, with George Spindler, for Anthropology (Holt, Rinehart and Winston, N.Y.). Her publications include an American Anthropological Association Memoir (*Menomini women and culture change*, 1962), "Menomini witchcraft" (in *North American Indian sorcery*, edited by D. Walker, 1972), and an article on the Menomini in the *BAE Handbook of North American Indians* (1975). She is co-author of *Culture in process* (1973), with G. Spindler and A. Beals, and has written numerous articles on American Indian culture change and psychological adaptation with George Spindler.

JOEL MATHLESS TEITELBAUM (1940–) studied Human Biology at Brown University (B.A., 1961) and at the University of Manchester (M.A., Economics, 1964) as a Fulbright Fellow. His Ph.D. (Manchester, 1969) in Social Anthropology was based on fieldwork in Tunisia. He taught and studied nutrition at the West Virgina University and Pennsylvania State University and did senior Fulbright research in North Africa. He is currently Associate Director of an African Universities Project in the Carolina Population Center and Research Assistant Professor in the School of Public Health of the University of North Carolina at Chapel Hill. His interests and publications include nutritional anthropology, land tenure, community structure, health beliefs, and work norms among rural Africans and Appalachians.

CHARLES F. URBANOWICZ (1942–) is a Visiting Assistant Professor of Anthropology and Social Science at California State University, Chico. He was awarded the B.A. in Sociology-Anthropology from Western Washington State College (1967) and the M.A. (1969) and Ph.D. (1972) in Anthropology from the University of Oregon. For 1972–1973 he was a Visiting Assistant Professor of Anthropology at the University of Minnesota, Minneapolis, and he has been at Chico since 1973. While interested in aboriginal Tongan society, he is also actively engaged in research on the impact of tourism in the Pacific, specifically for Tonga.

THOMAS R. WILLIAMS (1928–) was educated at the University of Arizona and Syracuse University and is now a Professor of Anthropology at Ohio State University. He has authored papers and books with a focus on North American Indian and Borneo ethnography and topics in psychological anthropology, including cultural transmission and the cultural structuring of personality, with particular attention to the process of socialization. He is the author of *The Dusun: a North Borneo society; Field methods in the study of culture; A Borneo childhood: enculturation in Dusun society;* and *Introduction to socialization: human culture transmitted.*

Index of Names

Index of Subjects

99